Democratic individuality

Democratic individuality

ALAN GILBERT

Graduate School of International Studies
University of Denver

CAMBRIDGE UNIVERSITY PRESS

CAMBRIDGE

NEW YORK   PORT CHESTER   MELBOURNE   SYDNEY

Published by the Press Syndicate of the University of Cambridge
The Pitt Building, Trumpington Street, Cambridge CB2 1RP
40 West 20th Street, New York, NY 10011, USA
10 Stamford Road, Oakleigh, Melbourne 3166, Australia

© Cambridge University Press 1990

First published 1990

Printed in the United States of America

Library of Congress Cataloging-in-Publication Data
Gilbert, Alan.
Democratic individuality / Alan Gilbert.
p. cm.
Includes bibliographical references.
ISBN 0-521-38271-8 – ISBN 0-521-38709-4 (pbk.)
1. Individualism.   2. Liberalism.   3. Radicalism.   4. Democracy.
I. Title.
JC571.G515   1990
320.5'12 – dc20   89-70844
                                                                      CIP

British Library Cataloguing in Publication Data
Gilbert, Alan *1944 Apr. 24 –*
Democratic individuality
1. Democracy. Ethical aspects
I. Title
172

ISBN 0-521-38271-8 hardback
ISBN 0-521-38709-4 paperback

For Lucy

He who enjoys the right of sharing in deliberative or judicial office attains thereby the status of citizen.

Aristotle, Politics, 1275a22–4

Although volume upon volume is written to prove slavery a very good thing, we never hear of the man who wishes to take the good of it *by being a slave himself*.

Abraham Lincoln, "Notes on Slavery"

According to our ancient faith [the Declaration of Independence], the just powers of governments are derived from the consent of the governed. Now the relation of masters and slaves is, protanto, a total violation of this principle. That master not only governs the slave without his consent, but he governs him by a set of rules altogether different from those which he prescribes for himself. Allow *ALL* the governed an equal voice in the government, and that, and that only, is self-government.

Abraham Lincoln, debate with Stephen Douglas,
October 16, 1854

In place of the old bourgeois society, with its classes and class antagonisms, we shall have an association in which the free development of each is the condition for the free development of all.

Karl Marx and Friedrich Engels,
Manifesto of the Communist Party

Contents

Contents

Contents

Contents

Contents

Preface

This book has taken some ten years to complete. It does not focus on a single debate in a particular field but weaves together, across personal and political change, themes in several. It is a conversational book. In 1985, at the twenty-fifth anniversary celebration of the founding of Social Studies (my undergraduate major) at Harvard, I realized that *Democratic Individuality* is my attempt, like that of others in the program, to come to terms with Marx's and Weber's politics. Here some of my debt to Stanley Hoffman, Barrington Moore, and Fritz Ringer is evident.

In April 1989, I attended the twentieth anniversary of the Harvard strike against university training of officers for the Vietnam War. Harvard ROTC is now charmingly a day-care center attended by the children of some of the strikers. This book's conception of democratic theory and institutions is a response to my experience with the promise of participatory democracy in Students for a Democratic Society and subsequently. It reaffirms the insight in SDS's founding Port Huron statement that "having one's way" is a distortion of a more human "having a way of one's own." Our disbelief and anger at the immense cruelty of the Vietnam War and the barbarism of American racism resonate in this book's arguments on just war and democratic internationalism. A comparatively depoliticized era has temporarily obscured a tradition of American dissident democracy that extends back to Shays' Rebellion, the abolitionists, anti-imperialist opposition to the U.S. seizure of the Philippines and Cuba, the IWW, and the CIO, among others. Downplaying the tenacity of movements and friendships, a recent Hollywood movie merges the exaggerated financial success of some former radicals with a public "big chill"; against that image, this book keeps faith with the resistant, creative spirit of democratic individuality.

My first book, *Marx's Politics: Communists and Citizens*, traced the political dynamic in a democratic movement that gave rise to communism. That portrait revealed unexpected political and moral facets of Marxian theory and suggested continuities with liberalism. But I found that today's political and social theory, liberal and radical, did not explain these dialectical connections. In this regard, postpositivist conceptions in philosophy – particularly the realism of Hilary Putnam and Richard Boyd and, later, the naturalism of Dudley Shapere – seemed promising. So did the democratic contractarianism of John Rawls and Michael Walzer's emphases on just war. *Democratic Individuality* moves deeply into contemporary philosophy to reinterpret political and social theory and vice versa, because, on my view, innovative theorists in each field have striking insights and yet neglect important related arguments or import confusions from the others.

By defending democratic individuality, this book means to radicalize liberalism and to deepen radicalism through the insights of liberalism. During the time I wrote it, my politics and life changed considerably. Those who know me will recognize – perhaps more than I do – the signature of my life in this argument. Some have thought that the connection between experience and politics must be ideological; for me, the integrity and awareness of that linkage are a part of individuality.

This book reflects dialogues with colleagues in several fields, some whom I know – as academics often do – only through their writings and others who are friends. Conversations over many years with Lucy Ware and Andreas Teuber played a central part in its creation. I have learned from readings of the manuscript by Will Kymlicka, David Levine, Richard Boyd, Richard Miller, Andrew Levine, Michael Smith, Andreas Teuber, Douglas Vaughan, and Manfred Halpern. In particular, Teuber and Kymlicka made helpful suggestions about organizing the argument. I am grateful to Richard Boyd for many enjoyable conversations about scientific realism, moral objectivity, and politics. Andrew Levine, Richard Miller, and Michael Smith provided valuable conventionalist criticisms. In the notes, I indicate responses to specific points. At a time when I was bogged down in technical concerns, Manfred Halpern conjured vivid images of the argument's significance and style.

In the last year of rewriting the manuscript, I benefited from discussions of democratic theory and moral objectivity with John Rawls and Michael Walzer. Among many colleagues, students, and friends who have offered criticisms and comments about related papers or parts of the argument along the way, I would like to acknowledge Bruce Ackerman, John Ackermann, Terence Ball, Benjamin Barber, Asma Barlas, Charles Beitz, Amy Benjamin, Paul Bennacerraf, David Blaney, Gardner Bovingdon, Mark Brandon, James Caporaso, John Charvet, G. A. Cohen, Josh Cohen, Joseph Desimone, George Downs, Michael Doyle, Jamie Drier, John Dunn, Robert Eden, James Farr, Michael Fry, Timothy Fuller, Alan Garfinkel, Robert George, Richard Gilbert, Walter Gilbert, Michael Goldfield, Robert Grafstein, Amy Gutmann, Nancy Hartsock,

Robert Hazan, Jeffrey Herf, Stanley Hoffmann, Steven Holmes, Syed Rifaat Hussain, George Kateb, Sudipta Kaviraj, Stanley Kelley, Haider Ali Khan, Friedrich Kratochwil, Gregg Kvistad, Percy Lehning, Steven Lukes, David Lyons, Steven Macedo, Sakah Mahmud, Harvey Mansfield, Jr., David Mapel, Horst Mewes, J. Donald Moon, James Moore, Michael Mosher, Bhikhu Parekh, Mustapha Pasha, Ellen Paul, Alan Ryan, Abdoulaye Saine, Tony Sebok, Dudley Shapere, George Sher, Judith Shklar, Henry Shue, Rogers Smith, Steven Smith, Patricia Springborg, Shannon Stimson, Tracy Strong, Nicholas Sturgeon, Andreas Teuber, Paul Thomas, Mark Van Roojen, Ritu Vij, Maurizio Viroli, Cheryl Welch, and Allen Wood. I would also like to thank Terence Moore, Mary Nevader, and Robert Racine of Cambridge University Press for their help.

I have learned how better to articulate this version of objectivity from questions raised by participants in my seminars at the Graduate School of International Studies of the University of Denver and the Politics Department at Princeton and during talks at Concordia, Colorado College, Princeton, Harvard, Yale, and several sessions of the American and International Political Science Association. I am grateful for an American Council of Learned Societies Grant to be a visiting scholar in the Philosophy Department at Cornell during 1979–80. This volume includes revised versions of a number of papers listed in the bibliography (Gilbert, 1981b, 1982, 1984a, 1984b, 1986a).

Finally, as each of our lives is woven across generations, I hope that my children and stepchildren, Brendan, Claire, Kathleen, Charles, and Nathan, will someday find something of interest here.

Introduction

1. Moral relativism and slavery

Many contemporary philosophers and social scientists consider values and conceptions of justice to be at base irrational. We may hope to explain these conceptions in their context or explore the internal consistency of a given choice of values, but such conceptions vary historically in a fashion beyond the reach of any objective assessment. Metaethical relativism seems to follow from these claims; values are simply relative to the conventions or experiences of the societies, groups, classes, or persons who hold them. At most, these views maintain, we may achieve a kind of sociological or anthropological – reductionist – objectivity about morals: We may show how particular values serve certain social or class interests. But no ethical conception – no idea about a good life for humans – may claim objectivity on its own terms.

Some judgments about justice and equality, however, seem more secure to most of us. Slavery, for example, and Nazi genocide are monstrous. They are abhorrent not merely as a matter of opinion – the Nazis still have many defenders and slavery once did – but because of their wanton murderousness and cruelty, their waste of lives, let alone of human potential for a good life. Such straightforward moral judgments clash irremediably with current metaethical preconceptions. It seems peculiar to maintain that slavery is just as defensible or "rational" as antislavery, Nazism as anti-Nazism. An ethical point of view has its own integrity and depth, features not to be explained (*explained away*) in sociological, anthropological, or semantic terms. Whatever the intricacies of moral argument, relativism cannot be right.

This book will defend a complex, nonrelativist account, some of whose distinctive components I will indicate at the outset. Slavery is an ancient institution, one of the most widespread in class-divided societies. Its proponents claimed that at least two distinct human natures

1

exist, that of masters, involving rationality and a capacity to command, and that of slaves, mere bodies, fitted only to obey. The modern ethical contention that given what humans are, it is wrong to enslave them is, on the face of it, an empirical claim that we have learned enough about human nature to rule out the ancient justification of slavery and to identify that institution as abusive and corrupt. This claim has two components. First, it registers the initial moral discovery that humans have an equally sufficient rationality, empathy, and sympathy to participate in political life (democracy) and to have rights and duties (the law). This empirical ethical discovery occurred, at least in broad outline, in ancient Athens. Second, the modern ruling out of slavery registers the dramatic empirical extension of this discovery about human potentials to those wrongly deemed deficiently human. Similar factual discoveries refute the classic defenses of the subjection of women and others. Taken together, these insights mark a great turning point in our understanding of human capacities for democracy.

Now, Marxian arguments extend and transform liberal claims about participation and community. But both liberals and radicals recognize the basic capacity for moral personality and defend equality, seen as the *mutual recognition* of persons or the nonexploitative social underpinning for the flourishing of diverse individualities. In modern terms, it may be helpful to think of capacity for moral personality as a capacity for individuality. The former involves a self capable of fair cooperation with others, a centrally ethical agent; the latter additional features relevant to living a life of one's own.[1] This dialectical combination of egalitarian social relationships and individuality is what Marx and Hegel might have called *social individuality*. As both liberal and radical theories insist, the human capacity for mutual recognition and individuality is inherently relational and has a political history; the original conditions of society were not congenial to human flourishing.

Yet the idea of a general capacity for moral personality is so embedded in modern political and ethical thinking that theorists often assume or overlook it. For instance, as we shall see later, many contemporary arguments overstress the significance of conflicts of other goods to deny any ethical objectivity. In the history of political thought, however, empirical debates over who counts as fully human, especially the rejection of Aristotle's defense of natural slavery, have played a central role in the emergence of modern notions of democracy and individuality. And a conception of a deliberative person, from, say, Aristotle to Hegel and

---

[1] Though he does not stress individuality, Rawls, 1980, 1988a, also distinguishes these two "moral powers."

2

Marx to John Rawls and Charles Taylor, underlies the idea of serious choices among other goods. Within diverse descriptions in moral theory, this core notion of individuality is the most important good.[2]

Straightforward conceptions of equality and individuality characterize at least the legal and political forms and the ethical aspirations of modern liberal and socialist societies. For the original liberal theorists, the abolition of slavery and serfdom alone created the socially transparent relations – relations not characterized by significant coercion – in which individuality could flourish. Contrary to common anticollectivist stereotypes, socialists and communists often claim that capitalism presents a similar coercive obstacle to the realization of individuality; many of today's liberals concur with radicals at least about earlier forms of capitalism. Both advocate (what they consider to be) democracy. An empirical analysis of the functioning of capitalist and socialist societies, in the light of these shared moral criteria, reveals that such regimes practice widespread repression and exploitation; that is, moral insight outleaps social practice. Yet unless these regimes achieve extremes of degradation, they still enjoy a common empirical justification against slaveholding societies and Nazism, whose very being denies democratic individuality. Thus, liberal and radical theories of social individuality may rightly claim an *ethical* superiority for these contemporary societies in virtue of the modern insight into the mutual recognition of persons or the general capacity for moral personality. These theories require claims about ethical progress – at least about the appearance of a free politics and the transition from slave to nonslave societies – and advance in moral knowledge.

Some nineteenth-century liberals deemed progress, including moral progress, a unilinear feature of human history. The example of Nazism and the nearly worldwide triumph of fascism, however, straightforwardly refutes that claim. From this instance of modern barbarism – one worse than that of any ancient regime – and a justified revulsion, rooted in contemporary anthropology, against ethnocentrism, some have inferred that no (ethical) advance exists. Relativists have denied moral objectivity as well. But the case of Nazism actually illustrates extreme moral decadence. It has enabled us to understand fully the possibilities and characteristics of genocide – of crimes against humanity, not simply war crimes – and instigated the United Nations genocide convention, which provides one important explication of this novel ethical cat-

---

[2] Theories of individuality are not just a quantitative extension of ancient conceptions of freedom but a qualitative transformation, one that an adequate moral epistemology and semantics needs to explain.

egory.[3] Contrary to relativists, the example of Nazism not merely fails to rule out objectivity; it highlights the objectivity of our moral judgments at least in extreme cases.

In addition, relativism is a problematic, puzzling doctrine. For instance, the anthropological relativist often wishes to defend an objective principle of tolerance: The diversity of cultures, the way their ethical standards fit their particular social conditions, and hence their putative ethical equality, so this anthropologist maintains, mandate toleration. Thus, he advances relativism to defend attractive features of liberalism. (A liberal theory claims broadly that the best social and political arrangements are those most favorable to the pursuit by each individual of a good life, just as she sees it, so long as she does not harm others.)[4] This anthropologist rejects bigotry; yet he insists metaethically that the advocates of tolerance cannot refute the judgments of the intolerant.[5] In response, however, an ethnocentrist may sarcastically note, "If your claims about relativism are right, then the view that intolerance is good is as justified as the notion that it is abhorrent." Thus, the anthropologist's practical moral conclusions contradict his metaethics and make this position self-refuting. A self-refuting argument – a view that by its assertion contradicts itself – is a special kind of philosophical error. As classic examples, consider the statement "I do not exist" made self-referentially by any speaker and the skeptical claim "I know that I know nothing."[6] This inconsistency between relativist metaethics and particular moral stands haunts many conventionalist arguments. (Call this the *self-refutingness of relativism objection.*)

Yet metaethical relativism is, for diverse reasons, widely influential among citizens, philosophers, and political theorists. Its acceptance stems from broad cultural changes: the decline of religious injunction, antipathy to ethnocentrism, and the like. Relativists rightly worry about absolutist, dogmatic moralisms that impose practices and beliefs on individuals to which they do not assent and to which they would not

---

[3] Even the international sphere exhibits practices, norms, and rules that influence conduct (Keohane, 1984; Kratochwil, 1989; Nardin, 1983). In fact, as the Universal Declaration of Human Rights as well as the genocide convention illustrate, it includes a quite articulate moral understanding.

[4] In this perspective, many radical arguments, including Marx's conception of social individuality, are varieties of liberalism.

[5] Richard Miller helped with this formulation of a relativist position. In fact, most conventionalists defend liberal or radical politics; the self-refutingness objection questions only whether they can do so coherently. Yet relativist metaethics often subtly affect social scientific and political argument – for instance, by suggesting the plausibility of self-contained paradigms and thus discouraging focused investigation of contending social and moral theories. See Chapter 13, note 12.

[6] Williams, 1972; Putnam, 1981, ch. 5.

assent under decent – noncoercive – conditions of reflection and choice. Given this impetus, philosophical conventionalism takes two dramatically different forms, a *substantive* and a *formal* antimoralism.

In the first case, even major contemporary innovators in democratic theory and ethics like John Rawls and Michael Walzer have defended a constructivism based on the values of "our" culture. Rawls, for example, seeks a public "overlapping consensus" on the idea of *political autonomy:* Each of us may imagine himself as a free and equal deliberator in a sovereign assembly, testing the justice of the principles that currently govern the basic social and political structure. This autonomy allows a plurality of reasonable (mutually regarding), comprehensive ideas of the good. Rawls hopes that appeal to public consensus can avoid deeper philosophical commitment. His constructivism aims to remove *superfluous* epistemological argument, fraught with dangers of intolerance, from ordinary political discourse. Yet his political critique of comprehensive perspectives can be misleading; for excess epistemological argument is not, on his account, all epistemological argument, just as the superfluity of comprehensive accounts of the good does not negate, on his view, the political *good* of mutual regard among persons embodied in political autonomy ("the right").[7] Substantively, Rawls shapes his constructivism to stress the integrity of "very great" ethical values.[8] Similarly, my account of moral objectivity defends democratic individuality; it retains many of Rawls's insights, yet attempts to remedy a metaethical weakness – a self-refuting feature – of his account.

In the second case, some philosophers of science like Gilbert Harman seek consistency at the expense of depth, articulating a formal relativism without moral commitment. But an internal ethical point of view, one that respects life and the capacity for moral personality and rules out slavery, Nazism, and ethnocentrism, is, prima facie, compelling on its own terms. Some very persuasive external considerations would be needed to justify metaethical conventionalism (call this the *integrity of*

---

[7] For instance, Rawls's conception of "free *public* reason" (my emphasis) involves common endorsement of scientific reasoning and suggests its objectivity. Contrary to his insistence on the philosophical noncomprehensiveness of overlapping consensus, this claim is a limited, but important *philosophical* commitment. Chapters 1 and 3 give a straightforward, naturalistic explanation of the reason internal to politics, stressing the role of inference to the best explanation in moral accounts of human capacities. As Rawls currently provides no epistemological interpretation of free public reason – he notes only the fact of agreement on scientific methods in noncontroversial cases – my account would strengthen his theory (Rawls, 1988b, c, 1980, 1985, 1987; Kymlicka, 1988).

[8] Rawls, 1988c, p. 1, insists that such values shape overlapping consensus. He seeks to allay "the misgiving that [this consensus] makes political philosophy political in the wrong way" by adjusting claims of justice to dominant, particular interests.

ethics, artificiality of relativism objection); for whatever the difficulties of claims about objectivity, it is hard to see how even a sophisticated conventionalism can be at once coherent and attractive.

A defender of objectivity might still conclude that the example of Nazism rules out moral progress. But though this case disqualifies simplistic claims about unilinear, irreversible ethical advance, it does not eliminate dialectical, Hegelian, or Marxian conceptions, according to which history proceeds through opposition and struggle. Refined versions of these arguments distinguish between empirically based moral claims about the best state of affairs for humans and the contention that because such a regime is best, humans will *necessarily* achieve it. Insights into the possibility of better regimes create at most a likelihood that women and men will choose to strive for them. But the limitations on social and political knowledge and the diversity and complexity of historical circumstances present continual obstacles to the realization of a good life. A potential for "common ruin," as Marx put it in the *Communist Manifesto*, shadows that of fully human regimes. On these accounts, the alternative of decline spurs a political defense of social individuality. So a liberal or radical condemnation of Nazism casts no doubt on – and in fact requires – an insistence on moral objectivity, ethical progress, and advance in moral knowledge.

This version of objectivity does not focus on overall moral theories such as contractarianism, utilitarianism, or eudaemonism. Instead, it arises from the enduring human project of attempting to envision and achieve a good life and respond to the question: "How am I to live?"[9] In this broad context, certain *facts* about humans distinguish respectably ethical judgments and theories from nefarious alternatives. Now a conventionalist might object that such facts are *moral* only in the light of this historical project of creating a good life. But that project is natural to humans. Every comparative theoretical reflection on political and ethical life invokes it, and even unreflective cultures provide – what we may see as – *some* response to it.

Within the ethical project, the existence of moral facts is not controversial. An equally sufficient human capacity for moral personality is one such fact. It justifies and is connected to core ethical standards about the good of life, respect for persons, and democratic individuality that underlie broader moral theories. Recognition of these standards does not,

---

[9] Aristotle, *Politics*, bk. 1; Williams, 1985, ch. 1. For the purposes of this argument, the question "How am I to live?" has important ethical aspects – for example, individuality is a central good – but it is not mainly moral, one that an ethical theory alone could decide. This view does not require – and in fact opposes – the notion that the "moralization" of individual choices would be desirable (Wollheim, 1984, chs. 6–7, esp. pp. 224–5).

6

just by itself, answer many complex questions or hard cases in ethics for which overall theories are needed.[10] Yet these standards set the parameters of the field and are part of an abstract specification of what *moral theory* is.

In this context, epistemological relativism and reductionism take on a significant argumentative burden. Denying the integrity of ethics, they make even condemnations of murder, rape, and savagely oppressive regimes mysterious. They can flourish only where philosophical argument has shifted our attention away from such examples – for instance, by suggesting fundamental contrasts between scientific and moral knowledge. (Some philosophers regard these contrasts as analogous to earlier dichotomies between science and religion.) Such comparisons are interesting and important, and Part I of this book will respond to them in detail. Nonetheless, their proponents' initial translation of ethics into society- or epoch-specific terms seems unmotivated; for prima facie, such contentions seem only artifacts of general considerations about knowledge or special philosophical accounts of science, not internal, critical explorations of moral practices and theories.

My argument – a version of moral realism – will alter the bearing even of subtle criticisms associated with alternate epistemologies.[11] Such claims show only that some important differences exist between the objectivity of scientific and ethical knowledge. They do not establish a glaring contrast between, say, "value-free science" and radically subjective morals. These objections relate to the character and degree of certainty we may have about (some) ethical judgments. Relativists and reductionists have exaggerated such differences to assert that all moral judgments are arbitrary or vague. In contrast, my argument will show that the distinction among true moral judgments, indeterminate ones, and moralistic, false, harmful ones is sound. Perhaps more surprisingly, it will also maintain that ethical objectivity is roughly in the same epistemological shape as objectivity in science and social science.

In politics in recent years, many features of liberalism have come under attack, especially commitments to tolerance, basic rights, and the extension of democracy. Curiously, even to its proponents, practical liberalism has lost its coherence. Increasingly, philosophers and political theorists – Rawls, Dworkin, Walzer, Kymlicka, Shklar, Holmes, Dahl, Gutmann, and Rosenblum among others – have sought to restore its central themes and varieties.[12] In this common project, my account will

[10] Sen, 1982, sec. 4. For Rawls, 1988c, pp. 3–5, such cases involve the "burdens of reason."
[11] Broadly, moral realism claims that ethical knowledge captures real properties of human well-being.
[12] As R. Dworkin's "Liberalism" (1985) suggests, this unclarity is far more pervasive than its obvious manifestation in the 1988 American presidential election.

emphasize a historically deepening insight into the political and social arrangements that further individuality.

Given widespread violations of rights, liberals stress physical security and freedom of conscience; yet their arguments are often legal rather than political. Shklar, for example, highlights protections against cruelty; so, in a less striking vein, do philosophical views that misguidedly characterize liberalism as itself a neutral conception. Rightly starting from equal regard under the law, these accounts exaggerate a derivative claim that the state should be *neutral* among (permissible) notions of the good and offer no positive vision of a noncoercive politics.[13] In contrast, moral realism emphasizes the institutions that sustain mutual regard and develops a theory of radical democracy. In today's controversies, it is closer to Rawls's and Walzer's accounts than to less political liberalisms.[14]

Part I of this book traces the great philosophical and historical debates and political transformations that mark the emergence of modern conceptions of democracy, individuality, and moral objectivity and progress. Against this background, Part II reinterprets the fundamental clashes between sophisticated radical (Marxian) and liberal (Weberian) theories as complex empirical controversies over the extent of human capacities for mutual recognition and individuality. *Democratic Individuality* weaves themes in ethics, moral epistemology, and social theory with central debates in political theory.

2. Cultural plurality, feminism, communitarianism, and a theory of individuality

This account of democracy stresses an idea of equality as an equally sufficient human capacity for moral personality. In opposition to ancient, hierarchical views, a defense of equality in this sense broadly characterizes the modern social sciences, human biology, and political theory as well as ethics.[15] The inference justifying egalitarian moral and empirical claims about this capacity is an *abstract* one. It focuses on the ethical agency that is exemplified in diverse cultural and political practices. This theoretical conception justifies what anthropologically informed philosophers like Walzer and Harman call "complex social constructions" and

---

[13] Shklar, 1984, ch. 1; R. Dworkin, 1985; Larmore, 1987; Nagel, 1986b; Ackerman, 1980. An emphasis on mutual regard among persons – on equality – is, once again, a positive account of a common good. See Gilbert, 1989.

[14] Rawls, 1988a. Josh Cohen, among philosophers, and Benjamin Barber, Amy Gutmann, and Carole Pateman, among political theorists, have all articulated a democratic – often a social or strong democratic – liberalism.

[15] Dworkin, 1977, p. 180.

inventions;[16] it emphasizes what theorists as varied as Mill, Hegel, Kant, Thoreau, Marx, and Whitman have invoked as individuality. A defense of moral personality rules out only predatory forms and pursuits that deny the agency of others. This version of limited objectivity undercuts the core ethical attraction of relativism: It maximally favors *individuality* and is *antimoralist*.[17]

In addition, relativists have sometimes favored democracy as a self-governing regime in which the consent of the people or their elected representatives determines the "rightness" of major decisions; they derivatively interpret nondemocratic institutions as a reflection of (ideal) local consensus.[18] My account of limited objectivity defends the *mutual regard among persons* that is a precondition of democracy and justified nondemocratic arrangements. Sustaining a diversity of regimes, it is antiethnocentric and *internationalist*.[19] Further, this ethical epistemology, sensitive to broad analogies with science and stressing moral discoveries about the basic capacities underpinning individuality, is *fallibilist*.[20] As the one-time prevalence of slaveholding and the continuing harms of, say, racism and sexism illustrate, humans are often mistaken about central moral beliefs and practices; any reasonable ethical epistemology has to account for this fact. But except for certain important kinds of cultural conventionalism that allow error relative to our social standards and complex philosophical characterizations of individual semantics, many versions of relativism implausibly rule out moral learning at all. Denying the integrity of ethics, they substitute for a dogmatism about particular beliefs a general dogmatism about error. Hence, as we will see in Chapter 4, only a few, fallibilist conventionalisms provide rivals to a sophisticated realism for inference to the best metaethical explanation.

Anthropologists rightly fear subtle forms of ethnocentrism. Perhaps any notion of equality and individuality, a critic of my argument might contend, rests on a distortedly Western approach to culture. Some contemporary theorists maintain that any notion of individuality must sup-

---

[16] Walzer, 1988a. Harman emphasizes "conventions" and, in a more skeptical vein, "moral fictions."

[17] It also has affinities with George Kateb's (1984) stress on democratic individuality.

[18] See Chapter 2, Section 10, on Walzer's *Spheres of Justice*.

[19] This book will stress "democratic internationalism." I use this term to include (a) recognition of the *universal* capacity for moral personality, (b) the justification, through that capacity, of a right to a culture of one's own and, as a stranger, to be treated decently, (c) a political insight, which Chapter 1 emphasizes, that conquest abroad undermines democracy at home, (d) the sanctioning of resistance by ordinary citizens to their own government's acts of aggression, and (e) some degree of empathy with democratic and radical movements in other countries.

[20] Nicholas Sturgeon (1986a) has emphasized this attraction of contemporary defenses of moral objectivity, Simon Blackburn (1981) of sophisticated quasi-realist alternatives.

pose isolated, utterly self-subsistent creatures, and thus conflict with the insights of feminism (that concern for the good of others can be part of one's own good), communitarianism, or even the simple truth that all social, political, and moral life is relational.

In Chapter 4, I consider several nuanced versions of the Western-relativity objection. But at first pass, this objection misunderstands the epistemological level of an argument that delineates an *abstract moral theory* of a decent political association and the (diversity of) human good(s). This theory does not maintain that all ideologically "individualist" societies realize democratic individuality; as Chapters 7 and 8 show, this argument, combined with uncontroversial empirical and social theory premises, becomes critical of many contemporary individualisms, and with additional, controversial premises it becomes radical.

In addition, as a form of eudaemonism, this theory includes a modified Aristotelian moral and psychological conception of the diversity of intrinsic human goods. It holds that varied insights into and practices realizing such goods can occur in *disparate* traditions; it does not require, for justification, self-consciousness about individuality. It might, for example, conclude that some Native American tribes had more livable practices of mourning than, say, much of today's American culture and *justify* such practices, even though they neither were seen as a way of enacting individuality nor could now be resurrected. Further, the human good is complex, and cultures and individuals are various. This theory expects that some important goods cannot be realized together and recognizes that human lives and history occasion many kinds of loss and regret.[21]

This eudaemonism also concurs with feminist critiques of isolated individualism (Carol Gilligan, Jean Baker Miller, Nancy Chodorow); as Chapter 7 shows, it seeks to endorse the best theoretical account of *relational* individuality, one that includes an androgynous view of the links among caring for others, friendship, and other activities.[22] With regard to today's communitarianism, it is a liberal theory of connectedness; it stresses forms of a common good that further individuality but excludes other specimens of republican virtue and nationalism.[23] In its full democratic version (Chapters 8 and 12), this notion of individuality is *constrained* by central egalitarian features of liberty. One might think of a

---

[21] Rawls, 1988c, p. 5; Berlin, 1988.

[22] Chodorow, 1986; Gilligan, 1986. The term "relational individuality" is adapted from Chodorow's equivalent "relational individualism."

[23] As Kymlicka, 1988, notes, both liberals and contemporary communitarian critics like Sandel adhere to a principle of equal respect for people's basic interests. Properly understood, this debate occurs *within* political liberalism, not outside it.

package of liberties, each growing out of and relying on others: the physical security of each, freedom of conscience, equal political liberty, democratic autonomy, and individuality. It will require a considerable argument to specify this version of moral objectivity and show that it provides a better epistemological account than any conventionalism. But whatever its internal difficulties, this theory opposes subtle, not just glaring, ethnocentrism; it sees individuality emerging as part of social and political relationships, not in some atomistic vein.

3. Individuality, diverse egalitarianisms, and objectivity

Once the abstract theory of equality as mutual recognition is in place, further arguments in democratic theory may drive a full-fledged conception in a more egalitarian direction. Thus, depending on empirical and social theoretical claims – for instance, a finding that capitalist inequalities relentlessly undermine the realization of equal liberty – investigators might endorse egalitarian conclusions about the distribution of income and wealth. That communist view, however, as well as less egalitarian versions of liberalism and socialism, rests on a common insight into the universal capacity for moral personality. Thus, as Chapters 7 and 8 contend, a theoretical stress on the primacy of democratic autonomy and individuality justifies economic egalitarianism, not a misguided insistence on absolute, across-the-board similarity of persons.

The recognition of human equality as the element of social likeness in individuality is, so I will maintain, part of our best overall picture of the world, of the total knowledge that, as Quine and Putnam rightly argue, shapes our particular beliefs and search for new knowledge.[24] That picture includes metaethical claims about objectivity and progress. The widespread influence of relativism has hindered our understanding of the dialectical emergence of liberal and socialist societies and of the modern theory of freedom and (social) individuality out of ancient society and philosophy, and has weakened the defense of democracy and individuality against their all too powerful opponents. Greater insight into the reasons for metaethical objectivity dovetails with a clearer recognition and advocacy of these goods.

To the ears of some readers, however, the very terms "equality" and "objectivity" have special, dogmatic connotations. Yet this book will justify the insights from which such criticisms are a mistaken inference. For instance, to such readers, any idea of equality seems associated with a narrow leveling tendency – what Marxians have sometimes stigmatized

---

[24] Quine, 1980, pp. 42–3; Putnam, 1975, 1:ch. 16; 1983, 3:ch. 5.

as "absolute egalitarianism" – which is hostile to individuality.[25] But as I noted earlier, the notions of mutual recognition, an equally sufficient capacity for moral personality, and self-respect defended here underpin individuality and democracy and support reasonable modern theories of the self.

Furthermore, this sense of likeness involves neither a reductionist equation of selfishness with individuality nor a related contention that individuals flourish only when they exert power over subordinate, "deficient" others and, hence, that "individuality" must be opposed. These ideas sanction relations of domination, expressing what Rousseau called the empire of opinion over those – including radical egalitarians – who advance them.[26] Even the individuals who prosper in such status hierarchies do so not for themselves but for the sake of external power and prestige. In contrast, given mutual respect for diverse persons and the truth of further empirical claims, even a radical regime would defend the individuality that this critic of equality desires, not enforce a constricting envy vested solely in regard for things at the expense of persons.

Like some critics of equality, two fine political philosophers to whom I explained this basic argument responded that objectivity is a "colorless," perhaps even a "chilling," notion, one devoid of the variety and interest of individuality in, say, Mill's eloquent depiction. This reaction stems from a mistaken contrast of an aspect of the objectivity of modern physics – which moves away, in its explanations, from the varied colors of sight to the postulation of nonvisible kinds – to the fullness of life.[27] The defenders of objectivity, so this criticism suggests, fail to discern that vibrancy or, worse yet, mistakenly seek to reduce it to some bare underlying reality. One who recognizes the intellectual fascinations of modern physics might facetiously respond that even quarks have color and charm. More seriously, physicalism, as defended by empiricists – but not by most realists – sometimes tends toward reductionism. An argument for objectivity, however, need not be – in my case, *is not* – physicalist.[28] Finally, the importation of reductionist misconceptions about the natural sciences into political science and ethics is reason for concern. But claims of ethical and political scientific objectivity may respect the relevant differences.

In general, it is difficult to see why continued openness to a (nonobjec-

---

[25] Hinton, 1966.   [26] Rousseau, 1964, 3:192–3.   [27] Quine, 1969, ch. 5.

[28] As Chapter 7 shows, among the sciences, this version of moral realism coheres with the contemporary psychoanalytic theory of the self; following the philosophical idiom of supervenience (nonreductionist identity of properties), I opt for a psychodynamic rather than an obviously materialist idiom. Moral realism is, nonetheless, consistent with Richard Boyd's nonreductionist physicalism.

tive) belief in phlogiston is colorful whereas recognition of oxygen and the rich profusion of modern chemistry is drab, Einstein's astronomy monochrome but the notion of a flat earth luxuriant. Bold scientific advances are unlikely to resuscitate *these* earlier, discarded theories. Analogously, in ethics, why are condemnations of the enemies of individuality – say Nazis or slaveholders – deathly examples of objectivity whereas neutrality toward them is lively? It is puzzling why theorists would prefer to be right about fine points in epistemology but not about glaring public issues. Here metaethical enthusiasm inverts political experience. Confronted with such examples, one might conclude that only an advocate of moral objectivity, not a relativist, can defend individuality. But as I have stressed, many relativists affirm liberal and radical values. My claim is only that the ultimate incoherence or moral superficiality of varied relativisms undercuts that defense.[29] Yet the influence of ideologies that run deep within prevailing academic paradigms is hard to shake. To avoid misconceptions, Part I will give plausible, widespread criticisms of objectivity their clearest statement and straightforward responses.

At the outset, I should note one widespread confusion about the term "objectivity." Recent philosophical usage has sometimes pitted relativism against absolutism, subjectivity against objectivity. That usage allows to "absolutists" no recognition of diverse, practical moral standards or complex cases; it forces them to deny the central ethical goods of deliberation and autonomy. Stressing a radical dichotomy between a priori notions of a human good or divine command on the one side and mere nonrational shifts in "values" on the other, it leaves no room for any version of limited objectivity and historical – a posteriori – moral discovery. In the ancient distinction between reason and revelation, it attempts to substitute relativism for reason.

But this contemporary opposition does not respond to the arguments about the self-refuting or arbitrarily reductionist character of many conventionalisms or about our comparative certainty in extreme cases. It fails to show that political philosophers like Aristotle and Hegel were wrong to think that although diverse mores exist, *some* moral judgments about human deliberation and freedom could be objective. Even from the standpoint of linguistic practice, the contemporary currency of a usage demonstrates neither that it draws on deep traditions in the history of moral practice or philosophy nor – what is more important – that the usage has a sound motivation. This book's specific claims about historic, ethical discoveries will, I hope, reveal the coherence of a notion of limited objectivity and advance – focused on the social and political

[29] Sturgeon, 1986a; Gilbert, 1986a.

equality that underpins individuality – compared with any version of relativism.

4. Outline of the argument

Chapter 1 provides the core argument for moral objectivity and progress, a novel account of the emergence of modern liberal and radical theory. It specifies the origins of distinctively *political* theory in ancient Greece and advances an internal critique of the historic debate among Aristotle, modern liberals like Montesquieu and Hegel, and Marxians over justice in war, slavery, individuality, and the nature of a common good. Recapitulating epochal struggles, this theoretical debate has centered on empirical claims about who counts as a participant in political life, as fully *human*, on the best characterization of such a participant (on the relationship of freedom to autonomy and individuality) and on the nature of cooperative (we would say, democratic) arrangements. This chapter's argument provides a specific alternative to relativist accounts in political theory and moral epistemology.

Chapter 2 sets the core argument as an internal critique of major contemporary views, such as those of Rawls, Walzer, Isaiah Berlin, Charles Taylor, Benjamin Barber, and David Wiggins, and responds to widespread criticisms of any version of moral objectivity. As I have emphasized, in philosophy, scientific epistemology has cast a long shadow over ethics. Chapter 3 sets a moral realist account in contemporary debates about scientific and moral knowledge. It contends that postpositivist insights have forged a new picture of science and undercut the putative dichotomy between science and ethics.

Chapter 4 responds to criticisms of any idea of moral progress. It entertains objections closely tied to the first chapter's argument; its rejoinders show why a version of limited objectivity is comparatively an inference to the best metaethical explanation. In addition, Hilary Putnam has rejected his own previous realism and proposed an unusual, across-the-board neo-Kantianism that recognizes mind-dependent ethical as well as scientific objectivity. If Putnam is right in other respects, his argument, unlike positivism and relativist neo-Kantianism, has many of realism's advantages; it endorses progress and the role of facts in the sciences, yet stresses the primacy of theories. Some readers may rightly surmise that Putnam's view could accommodate the notions of moral objectivity and advance defended here, making rival claims of coherence. They may wonder how overall epistemological arguments, distinguishing objective neo-Kantianism from realism, may (re)shape our views about moral objectivity. Surprisingly, however, Putnam fails to consider a sophisticated realist alternative, and so his argument does no damage to moral realism.

At first glance, modern liberal and radical agreement about the fact of an equally sufficient capacity for moral personality may seem a thin account of the good. But an argument on this central aspect of a good life coheres with broader claims about human well-being (eudaemonia) and individuality. Applying the insights of Part I, Part II shows that recognition of this capacity leads to unexpected results. It facilitates a reappraisal of the relationship of modern political and ethical arguments to ancient ones and highlights the impact of conflicting social theoretical and empirical claims on divergences between contemporary liberals and radicals. I take up Marxian moral conceptions before liberal ones because they will be less familiar to most readers, because the territory is, in general, less well charted than that of liberal argument, because insights into the objectivity of modern individuality suggest dramatic changes in the theory of radical egalitarianism, and because, having laid out a radical view, I can then critically reexamine liberal claims about equality and metaethical relativism.

Thus, the first four chapters of Part II recast Marx's theory internally in the light of concerns about democratic individuality and moral progress and extend these arguments, given subsequent historical experience, to create a theory of radical democracy. Chapter 5 remedies a fundamental ambiguity about objectivity in Marx's and Engels's accounts of justice and equality. Chapter 6 depicts the richness of Marx's ethical judgments and examines the interplay of social theory and moral argument in his claims about the transition from exploitative to nonexploitative societies. It also sets his view in relation to broader modern moral theories: Mill's utilitarianism and Rawls's contractarianism. Chapter 7 traces the relationship of Aristotelian and Marxian eudaemonism, suggesting that a modified Aristotelian ethical conception best coheres with radical historical theory. It deepens the analysis in Chapter 1 of the complex relationship between Marxian (and liberal) political theory and that of the ancients. Its defense of individuality, consonant with Marxian moral insights, transforms a radical account of the initial stage of communism. Finally, it answers Richard Miller's sophisticated objections to considering Marxism – or radicalism – an ethical viewpoint at all. Chapter 8 applies these political and moral arguments to criticize twentieth-century revolutionary regimes and to suggest the design of a radical democracy.

The last five chapters of Part II pit radical social theory against sophisticated liberalism, focusing on the relationship of social science to ethical and political judgment in the work of a great, nonradical theorist, Max

Weber, whose views and concomitant metaethical relativism have shaped today's political science and sociology. These chapters show that the main political and moral debates between radicals and Weberians are empirical in character. They suggest that claims about great-power rivalry – an international relations "realism" – govern Weber's domestic politics and sociology.[30] Thus, he opposed the internationalism that sustains liberal or radical democracy. This argument will use the framework of Part I to highlight ambiguities in Weberian theory, arising from a failure to recognize moral objectivity or coherently defend democratic individuality.

Chapter 9 contends that the main causal arguments in *The Protestant Ethic and the Spirit of Capitalism*, often supposed to answer materialism or economic determinism, cohere with a modestly dialectical Marxism. Furthermore, a radical could easily concur with that work's leading, though not spelled out, ethical conclusions. Part II then highlights the glaring differences between Weber and Marxians on the central issues of twentieth-century politics, particularly the conflict between imperialism and internationalism (Chapters 10 and 12), the interplay of class, status, and racism (Chapter 11), and the tension between bureaucracy and radical democracy (Chapter 12). As Weber's arguments are often doubtfully liberal, Part II will distinguish self-respectingly liberal claims from influential Weberian alternatives. In addition, Chapter 13 contrasts realist and relativist interpretations of the interplay of levels of moral argument: core ethical judgment, empirical and social theoretical claims, moral theory, and epistemology. Contrary to Weber's metaethics, it shows that his complex verdicts appeal to core ethical standards and that his account – though less dramatically than Marx's – could benefit from a sharp defense of individuality.

Part II claims only that a sophisticated radical theory is a contender for truth along with complex liberal ones and, thus, sets the terms of ethical debate among plausible accounts. By sophisticated, I mean theories that take into account obvious criticisms and evidence suggested by their leading opponent, as, for instance, Darwin's *Origin of Species* answered then-prevailing creationist views. Part II will not advance a sufficient argument to convince a reasonable, skeptical reader that, as I also believe, such a radical account is the most promising social theory.

Since the term "social theory" plays so large a role in this book, I should note, to begin with, two specific features of the way I use it. First, I mean to draw no distinction in kind between theory and fact. Instead,

---

[30] Great-power "realism" famously, though I will argue inconsistently, dismisses notions of ethical objectivity. As it differs so dramatically from moral *realism*, I refer, throughout the text, to statist "realism" in scare quotes.

I consider conflicting social theories and the relevant factual information as a whole. For reasons that I will elaborate in Chapter 3, relevant assessment of social theories encompasses theoretical evidence – the specification of causal mechanisms – contained in the most reasonable statement of a particular position, as well as observational evidence in the empiricist sense. In Dudley Shapere's useful idiom, both claims become *items* in a theoretical domain.[31]

Second, for purposes of this argument, I use the terms "historical theory" and "social theory" interchangeably with "political theory." Sociological accounts influenced by Weber and economic determinist versions of Marxism often regard social theory as distinctively antipolitical. On Weber's account of legitimacy, no objective notion of a common good is possible; political deliberation lacks integrity except insofar as it is absorbed in calculated violence; democracy is an instrumental, not an intrinsic good. Laissez-faire liberals, anarchists, and economic determinist Marxians regard politics as inherently despotic; they envision the dissolution of its locus, the "parasite state," and the disappearance of self-consciously common activity. In contrast, I regard the project of social theory as inescapably political and moral. Comparatively free forms of human association that elicit general political participation contrast with despotism, a politics that realizes or expresses individuality with one that denies it, a genuine political and moral explanation – one that respects nonpolitical activities and accounts for their specific relationship with a nonexploitative, nondomineering politics – with one that sanctions the domination of politics (or money) outside its sphere.

My use of the terms "political theory" and "social theory" broadly follows and transforms that of Aristotle, Hegel, and Marx. In Aristotle and Hegel, political philosophy depicts those communal arrangements most conducive to the full expression of humanity or, in Hegelian terms, individuality. For Aristotle, these arrangements involve an active public life, centering on debate among citizens over a common good. For Hegel, ethical universality is less democratic. Nonetheless, the modern idea of freedom is realized by individual pursuits within a complex of institutions and relationships: the family, civil society, the state, and world history. That freedom is ethically universal, realizing abstract mutual regard; even though Hegel's ideal modern state is not fully *political*,[32] it has moral justification. Criticizing Hegel's view, Marx's theory of revolutionary institutions, drawn from his study of the Paris Commune, and his contrast of communist human history to exploitative "prehis-

---

[31] Shapere, 1984, ch. 13; Quine, 1980, ch. 2; Putnam, 1975, 1:ch. 16; Sturgeon, 1984.

[32] Despite free public discussion, that regime does not achieve its legitimacy by democratic insight into a common good.

tory" lead to a conception of *democratic* individuality. For contextual reasons, however, he misguidedly pitted "social" against "merely political" association. Yet Marx's argument and, more sharply, my theory of radical democracy rest on broad Aristotelian and Hegelian claims about the political as well as social basis of individuality.

In summary, this book has several different, though related, purposes. It stresses the ancient and modern insight into the human capacity for moral personality and identifies those discoveries that have shown this capacity to be a universal one. Recognition of this common standard underpins empirical debates in social theory about the nature and appropriate extent of equality, democracy, and internationalism. Metaethically, this book argues for the objectivity of modern moral and political philosophy in order to further a self-aware defense of democratic individuality. It reassesses the connection between Marxian ethical judgments and historical theory and offers new contrasts of radical and liberal political theory. It illustrates these broad arguments with a variety of specific claims – for instance, concerning the lineage of the modern theory of individuality in Aristotle's conception of freedom, the roots of Marx's notion of alienation in ancient ideas of natural justice, the interplay of Rawlsian autonomy and eudaemonist individuality, the long-recognized (starting with Aristotle and Montesquieu) inconsistency of democracy and great-power domineering, the affinity of Weber's moral judgments in *The Protestant Ethic* with Marxian ones, the contribution of anticommunist ideology to legitimizing Weberian dismissal of democratic alternatives, a widespread ambiguity between relativist and objective arguments in contemporary liberal and radical theories, and the like. I hope the novelty and plausibility of these interpretations will commend the adoption of a moral realist point of view in studying the history of political thought. But the merit in these claims is, of course, for the reader to judge.

Part I

The theory of political freedom and individuality: slavery, mutual regard, and modern egalitarianism

Chapter 1

A common good and justice in war

This chapter advances the core argument of the book on the objectivity of a claim about the general human capacity for moral personality. In addition, it indicates the main characteristics of moral realism and a developed political theory. In today's philosophical debates, moral realism is an extension of scientific realism. Broadly speaking, the latter responds positively to the question "Does scientific inquiry give us knowledge of facts about unobservable entities?" As Chapter 3 will emphasize, it advances the claim that across theory changes, the basic terms of mature scientific theories refer to and capture more deeply features of the world. Moral realism responds positively to the question "Does our ethical inquiry give us knowledge of facts about human well-being?" This chapter concentrates on the basic ideas of a common good among free humans and ethical discovery. The first two sections sketch the main argument and suggest its significance; the last six offer a more worked-out version.

1. Some leading features of moral realism

In theoretical terms, Aristotle delineated the first, limited achievements of human freedom, manifested in the Greek city, and identified the justice of defensive wars. Yet he also legitimized that city's slaveholding; he contended that a large number of humans – so-called natural slaves – had no higher destiny than to furnish the material underpinnings of the citizens' good life. He even recommended slave hunting as a form of just war. In this context, the theory of war serves as a litmus test for differentiating potentially free humans and slaves. Based on the emergence of abolitionist movements and non-slave-based regimes, however, Montesquieu and Hegel rejected Aristotle's biological contention that slaves resembled other social animals rather than fully developed humans and his justification of slave hunting. They recognized a more universal capacity for cooperation, freedom, and individuality than Aristotle would have granted. Yet accompanying this important new insight, Montesquieu and Hegel retained many of Aristotle's arguments about the human capacity for freedom, the nature of a common good, and just war. We can therefore regard their version of social individuality and justice in war as a reformulation of Aristotle's theory, based on subsequent moral discoveries, *within* a single political scientific and ethical project. Their repudiation of slavery – though very important – is not a denial of Aristotle's general view.

By Aristotle's time, Greek cities had gone beyond kingship and recognized the *political* role of free citizens. The forging of the polis led to the practical and theoretical awareness of the qualitative diversity of regimes, the distinction between those that embodied a – however limited – common good and those that merely advanced particular interests. The emergence of this novel form also made possible the political distinction between wars of self-defense, undertaken to preserve free regimes, and predatory invasions. This diversity of regimes was the most elementary fact of, and justified the study of, comparative and international politics. For Aristotle, it inspired ethical reflection concerning which political arrangements enable humans to realize their capacities for a good life. Today, however, social scientists and philosophers often interpret such diversity as a mandate for relativism.

Metaethical relativism seems most plausible where there are stable domestic regimes and well-defined social orders and traditions. In such cases, we might hope to find disparate patterns of what is regarded as fitting conduct, all of which might be termed "moral." But war is the absence of such order. It brings the bare ethical issues of human life and freedom to the fore. So do regimes like slave hunting and Nazism – essentially internal wars. Historically, the assessment of war has been the least promising arena for relativism. As Walzer's *Just and Unjust Wars* shows, the basic judgments about aggression and minimally decent international arrangements have exhibited great constancy across diverse regimes, disparate epochs, and major theory changes. This stability contradicts relativist expectations and suggests the plausibility of moral objectivity.

Given the widespread influence of relativism, however, skepticism about metaethical objectivity marks even Walzer's argument. By isolating these conflicting strands in his account, I will clarify the case for moral realism.

Primarily, Walzer advances the view that common ethical judgments about war have objective roots in the massive waste of human life. War's carnage inevitably drives most women and men to evaluate its justice and condemn its initiators. Judgments about aggression and harm to innocents – noncombatants – stem, he suggests, from the elementary goods of life and ways of life. To recognize these goods is morally uncontroversial. Fierce debates and violent clashes about *what counts as just and unjust* stem from differences over matters of fact and antagonistic interests, not from incommensurable moral premises. Given core standards against aggression and cruelty to civilians, he maintains, we can, with sufficient evidence, decide the truth of contending claims.[1]

Yet Walzer's interpretation of the stability of underlying standards is ambiguous. He sometimes defends the objective position that the *real human consequences* of war require such moral judgments; he also asserts, however, in a relativist vein, that these ideas about just war may simply have arisen in the Western tradition. Perhaps *we* "have invented" them, and they can have no further justification.[2] But the latter claim contradicts the former. If human life is a good that cannot be wantonly destroyed, then judgments about aggression and defensive wars are not merely "Western" ones, on a par with, say, another "Occidental" judgment, the Nazi contention that a "master race" may properly exterminate "racial inferiors." They are also – and more importantly – true. Like other disciplines, ethics has a definite, potentially quite complex subject matter: knowledge about preservation of human life and the possibilities of a good life. We can use that knowledge to identify the relevant standards of previous societies (thus, we know what a *moral* order looks like), to recognize particular goods that they realized while successors do not, and to rule out criminal regimes. As Walzer rightly suggests in his international "legalist paradigm" of self-defense, the underlying norms about just war are no more controversial, from the standpoint of a good life, than similar, though simpler, standards about murder.[3]

The ambiguity in Walzer's conception partly stems from his recognition of the diversity of political communities that may legitimately defend themselves against aggression. In the theory of international politics since Aristotle, a claim about the possibility of forming free regimes has served as an important intermediate link between insights into individual well-being or rights and the justification of defensive wars. But this intermediate claim is not relativist. It sanctions cultural diversity based on freedom or its potential; it does not legitimize just *any* practices. Coherent modern conceptions require the egalitarian recognition that each has the ability to find her own way. Such views condemn all systemic practices that harm individuality.[4]

On a moral realist account, these theories distinguish a sphere of

---

[1] Walzer, 1977, pp. 11–12, 19–20.　　[2] Walzer, 1977, p. 54.　　[3] Walzer, 1977, pp. 58–63.

[4] What steps may be appropriate to change an unjust regime – ordinarily from within the society – depend on the degree of harm and feasible political alternatives. Harms to be expected from external intervention justify Walzer's notion of the – "as if" – legitimacy of most regimes in the international sphere.

straightforwardly objective judgments, concerned with the mutual recognition of persons, from a less determinate sphere in which the good of individuality plays the decisive role. The former is the medium through which, in Goldman's apt phrase, the *nonrelativist plurality* of the latter can be realized.[5] Though these spheres are distinct, the good of moral personality is closely related to and underlies that of individuality. Moreover, even the latter sphere, as we shall see in Chapter 7, requires a notion of objective need, determined by individual choice of ways of life, the nature of intrinsic goods, and the appropriate reasons for relationships and activities. That conception of need contrasts with the common relativist notion of preference. Ethical theory encompasses both spheres; it does not treat one as moral, the other conventional.

The complex structure of Walzer's basic argument about war is signaled by his justification of humanitarian intervention against genocidal regimes. Predatory nationalisms are outlawed. These cases highlight the objective limits beyond which no *liberal* or radical protection of national ways of life may extend.[6] In his occasional relativist claims, Walzer overstresses the variety of justifiable regimes at the expense of his objective defense of individual life and liberty. Yet comparable insights into the diversity of reasonable individual purposes do not rule out, and in fact presuppose, objective notions of individuality, autonomy, and self-respect.

Internally, Walzer's insistence on the stability of our standards for evaluating war needs a more coherent explanation and appraisal against likely counterexamples. In this context, Montesquieu's debate with Aristotle, and Marx's and Lenin's with modern liberals, illustrate the rare disagreements that *might* arise from epochal shifts in core moral standards. Prima facie, these cases seem likely to provide evidence for a conventionalist alternative, if anything about basic judgments concerning

---

[5] Goldman, 1986, pp. 69–71. Mill (1948, 1987) articulated this conception of social individuality in *On Liberty:* "The only purpose for which power can be rightfully exercised over any member of a civilized community against his will is to prevent harm to others. His own good, either physical or moral, is not a sufficient warrant. He cannot rightfully be compelled to do or forbear because it will be better for him to do so, because it will make him happier, because, in the opinions of others, to do so would be wise or even right." There are, however, hard cases in which paternalism may be justified, for example preventing the suicide of a person who is really "not in his right mind." Further, as David Lyons, 1984, pp. 173–5, astutely notes, an adequate defense of Mill's claims about liberty rests not on a notion that we know too little about others to make any decisions about a common good, but rather that we *know enough* to see that individuality and diversity are essential components of human flourishing (Wollheim, 1984, pp. 221–4).

[6] Walzer, 1977, pp. 101–8.

war does. I will contend, however, that these disagreements turn on empirical – biological and social theoretical – claims. For instance, Montesquieu's reformulation of the theory of just war – his recognition of slave hunting as a blatant form of aggression – focuses on who counts as human and the most reasonable forms of social cooperation. Ancient theorists had identified a human psychological and social organizational capacity for a free political life, based on an important aspect of likeness. That recognition highlighted the destructiveness of war. Later liberal insights broadened the theory of aggression to include types of belligerence – that is, slave hunting – previously seen as just. This chapter's historical and dialectical argument will show that the continuity in underlying standards about aggression between Aristotle and modern liberals neither stems from shared linguistic conventions nor depends on universal agreement, but rests instead on important, now obvious moral discoveries about the nature of a good life for humans. It will provide a consistent metaethical basis for Walzer's main argument about the stability of concepts of just and unjust war.

Modern political theory – liberal and radical – extends the possibility of freedom by denying Aristotle's defense of slavery. In this context, a moral realist account emphasizes several distinctive common features of any *political* theory. These claims do not elide the outstanding differences between liberals and radicals; instead, they isolate the level of argument – empirical and social theoretical – on which these clashes pivot. Eight main realist claims are, first, whichever refined social theory, liberal or Marxian, turns out to be true, both can concur with the ancient Greek insight into a human capacity for a free political life; second, either can *endorse* Montesquieu's refutation of Aristotle on natural slavery; third, both can adhere to a metaethical notion of objectivity, based on historical discoveries about human nature and capacities, and articulate at least a minimal conception of a good life; fourth, each insists on two interrelated ethical spheres, one of egalitarian mutual regard for persons in the design of basic institutions, the other of individuality; fifth, both recognize progress in morality at least in the emergence of freedom, the transition from slave to nonslave forms of social organization, and the development of international standards against slave hunting and aggression; sixth, each traces advance in ethical theory; seventh, both acknowledge that progress in moral theory depends heavily on advance in social, psychological, and biological theory and thus illustrates the unity of inquiry; and eighth, both can insist that the moral character of political struggles is an important, though hardly always decisive, feature in explaining their outcome. Historical explanations are, in part, moral explanations.

2. A common good and ethical discovery

This historical argument on free regimes and justice in war directly links these eight features, for moral realism emphasizes the *specific* kind of objectivity and advance characteristic of ethical and political knowledge. Two philosophical distinctions about political life characterize this objectivity. The first discerns the possibility of a common good among humans; the second envisions a succession of moral discoveries about such a good.

The first distinction emerged in the Athenian polis. There, appeals to the divinity of the monarch's will no longer settled claims to justice; instead, free citizens subjected such contentions to public debate. Their discussions illustrated – and self-consciously celebrated – the role of politics, an activity now recognized as, at least partially, autonomous from religion.[7] This politics was the initial appearance of human self-governance or democracy. Public contentions that clashing versions of justice each "served a common good," and Thrasymachus's notorious assertion that justice is merely "the advantage of the stronger" reflected increasingly self-aware claims about moral objectivity or the lack of it.

Plato's and Aristotle's theories separated genuine commonality from defective justifications of particular, oppressive interests. The possibility of a common good reflected the nature of man as a *political* animal, or was, from a human point of view, *natural*. A common good united other intrinsic goods and relevant political claims. Roughly, an intrinsically good activity or relationship reflects distinctive human capacities and needs, elicits participation for its own sake, and does not harm participants or others. In Aristotle's terms, the realization of disparate intrinsic goods gives rise to diverse kinds of eudaemonia. We might capture Aristotle's view of the basic political question as What form of political co-operation contributes to and facilitates the greatest realization of diverse personal happinesses? Note that this question features political community or an egalitarian conception of freedom – freedom among the like, the fully human – as itself an important intrinsic good, a component of the larger human good. In addition, it envisions that community as a mechanism or instrumental good in the realization of other intrinsic goods. Correspondingly, rule by a particular interest – say, (tyrannical) power or money outside its sphere – abridges the appropriate reasons for activities or the natural realization of diverse goods and substitutes oppressive domination.[8] Aristotle's idea on citizenship as ruling and

---

[7] Railton, 1986, pp. 197–8.
[8] Walzer, 1983, pp. 17–20, nicely captures this feature of Aristotelian argument. Chapter 6 stresses the distinction between intrinsic and instrumental goods in Marxian theory.

being ruled in turn identifies the appropriate form of political cooperation; it emphasizes a *self-governing* community as an agency of the common good at least in the modest sense that political activity has to bear a
discernable relationship to the good of citizens as each understands it,
and perhaps in the stronger sense that citizens should participate democratically in the forging of the *political* good. With regard to a diversity
of happinesses stemming from distinct activities, the above question is
eudaemonist and not utilitarian; with regard to a notion of persons (or
individuals), the question recapitulates an Aristotelian claim in modern
terminology.

Given the wars and class conflicts that played so central a role in ancient Greece, however, Aristotle acknowledged a grain of truth in Thrasymachus's view. Force shaped the sphere of international and internal
politics among the free, not just of household rule over slaves. This environment restricted the possibilities and nature of a common good; for
instance, it made military skill and the arming of citizens important components. For Aristotle, a theoretical investigation of justice derived from
and extended ordinary controversies. A distinction *within* Greek political life, involving a discovery of the potential for a common good, impelled philosophical reflection. Similar distinctions, embodied in additional political discoveries, have motivated subsequent philosophical
refinements.

On a realist account, the contingent adoption of an approximately
true theory or set of background beliefs contributes decisively to the
emergence of a mature scientific method.[9] Thus, Richard Boyd traces the
takeoff point of the modern natural sciences – due to adoption by leading investigators of mechanism and atomism – to the forging of Newtonian astronomy and atomic chemistry in the seventeenth and eighteenth
centuries. In Dudley Shapere's terms, such a point is the one at which a
branch of knowledge emerges as a domain – the object of coherent questioning, articulation of relationships and specification of relevant reasons, and increasing *internalization* as opposed to a disjointed patching
together of common sense, intuition, and appearance.[10] As a further
leading feature of moral realism, this chapter will contend controversially that Aristotle's theoretical contrast between a common good and
the tyrannies of particular interests was the takeoff point for mature reflection in ethics and political science.

On Aristotle's theory, a common good fuses diverse claims of justice –
for instance, those of the free, the wellborn, that is, gentlemen aristocrats, the virtuous, and so forth. Call common goods *c* and diverse

[9] McMullin, 1984, pp. 29–30; Boyd, 1980a, 1984.
[10] Shapere, 1984, chs. 13–14, esp. pp. 273–8.

claims of justice jf, jw, . . . , jv (where there are not a large number of such claims). Aristotle's theory adjusts such claims to the relevant particular features of a polis x: the number of the free citizens, the comparative weight of rich, poor, and small landholding middle classes, location in relation to other regimes, and the like. Thus, for any particular regime x, $cx = jfx + jrx + \cdots + jvx$.[11] This conception of a common good is social-need-centered. (It is broadly comparable, as we shall see in Chapter 7, to Marx's social- and individual-need-based conception of communism.) It looks to concordant realization of many goods, not simply, as in much contemporary liberal thought, to conflicts of goods. Furthermore, realization of each good for Aristotle displays a numerical aspect that he emphasized in the concept of a mean. A common good involves a series of concordant means in the actualization of diverse – in one important sense, incommensurable – goods; for the means are achieved in relation to each other, without, as Aristotle suggests in his subtle, ironic discussion of ostracism, exaggeration in any particular good.[12]

From a modern point of view, a peculiar feature of Aristotle's functional conception of politics is that intelligent rule by masters facilitates the greatest well-being of slaves. Any Aristotelian equation for c putatively includes js – justice for slaves. Confronted by the first, limited development of freedom in the Greek city, we might say, Aristotle got the notion of a common good right in one respect. He emphasized that good as a central feature of the theory of a self-governing community. Yet in another respect, as Hegel stressed, he got the claims of justice of slaves (js) and, we might add, women (jw) and artisans (ja) fundamentally wrong. Given the way humans are, one might even consider Aristotle's views about Greek realizations of a common good as universally wrong. Even so strong a conclusion, however, would still not justify Thrasymachus's claim that Aristotle meant by justice only the advantage of the stronger. Given the diversity among those recognized as human even in ancient Greece, Aristotle distinguished genuine commonality from spurious rationalizations that sanctified rule of the stronger (tyrannies). Abstracting from his particular claims, the structure of his characterization of a political association is, in important respects, right. Further, that theory rested on the greatest – though limited – *contemporary* achievement of a common good.

But the liberal criticism of Aristotle's contentions about slavery leads

---

[11] Of course, as Aristotle emphasizes, virtue is not simply relative to x (*Politics*, 1284b16–18, 23–34).

[12] Aristotle, *Politics*, 1284a17–b26. As we see in Chapter 3, Aristotle's idea of a common good is a paradigm example of what Richard Boyd calls a "homeostatic cluster property." Such complex properties like human health realize an array of features, but in particular, somewhat variable configurations.

naturally into a second *historical* distinction, emphasized by Hegel. Subsequent challenges may reveal as oppressive those arrangements that did not appear corrupt to earlier citizens – often a highly restricted group – or philosophers. Later investigators would supplement the original political and philosophical distinction between regimes that serve a common good and those that do not with a related one between arrangements that accord with human flourishing and those onerous ones that merely prevail at a particular time (even when that "time" may encompass several historical epochs). They saw that ordinary people have often created nonoppressive political and social relationships – genuine versions of a common good – only through lengthy struggles. They also recognized derivative, historic shifts in international association such as condemnation of slave hunting and the slave trade. Identifications of free arrangements count as objective moral *discoveries* about human nature. In today's philosophical idiom, they highlight the nonmoral human capacities on which ethical properties supervene.

On a moral realist account, though some of Aristotle's central components of a common good remain the same – for instance, the notion of a self-governing community, the search for knowledge, the importance of friendship, and the like – other aspects, concerning the claims of those who work with their hands and those who bear children, change dramatically. A modern conception exposes ancient freedom as the tyranny of free Greek males; yet in contrast to Thrasymachus's and reductionist claims about justice generally, this theory enables us to see the grain of truth in Aristotle's view. As this chapter will show, modern theories emphasize individuality. They refine the philosophical study of the basic problem of politics: the creation, within a difficult, often hostile international environment, of a self-governing association, organized around a common good of mutual recognition of persons, that rests on the insight and furthers the individuality of those who compose it.[13]

These two broad distinctions characteristic of moral and political philosophy mark a succession of important ethical discoveries whose character deserves emphasis. The original discovery or moral fact that needs explanation is the emergence, across diverse conventional realizations, of self-aware freedom, the innovation that was celebrated in Greek political life and Aristotle's theory. Aristotle's explanation of this fact is that man is a political animal or, as we might say, that these arrangements reveal distinctive *abstract* human capacities for freedom. Aristotle thought this explanation was complete; novel Greek freedom – which we may see as a moral discovery – contrasted with previous Greek kingship and barbarian servitude. As modern liberals and radicals would,

[13] In today's terms, self-governing means democratic.

however, rightly emphasize, the latter servitude is not a sign of lack of capacity but of unfavorable – comparatively oppressive – social conditions. In contrast to contemporary racist hypotheses, which alleged barbarian inferiority, modern complex historical accounts, including the injustice of despotism, are inferences to the better explanation(s).[14] In broad agreement with Aristotle's view, however, we might say that the human capacity for freedom – and despotism's injustice – *partly* explains the emergence of Greek freedom. For moderns, further discoveries need explanation, notably the defeat and disappearance of slave-based societies combined with a recognition of universal human capacities for moral personality and (ultimately) self-aware individuality. The explanation of these changes is also *partly* an ethical one: The moral fact that all humans have such capacities plays a causal role – along with other factors – in the emergence of free societies. On this view, the most salient *ethical* facts are just those facts about human well-being that contribute causally in important historical and political explanations.

Now, initially, claims about moral facts may sound quite bare, not part of a varied contender with conventionalism for inference to the best metaethical explanation. A critic might imagine that, apart from the *integrity of ethics* and *self-refutingness of relativism arguments*, the two epistemological theories were on a par. But recent innovative accounts by Peter Railton and Josh Cohen elucidate how moral *explanations* may work without inappropriately moralizing the historical evidence: Any of a family of characterizations of injustice – for example, violation of Railton's social rationality (impartiality in the design of social arrangements) or Rawlsian democratic autonomy or eudaemonist capacity for moral personality and individuality – allows investigators to explain and justify the specific grievances of the victimized as a (partial) result of an oppressive system, even when the oppressed *do not interpret their suffering in a general light*, let alone invoke the appropriate moral theories. Such moral explanations are better historical inductions on the evidence than, say, the contemporary ideological refrain that although slaveholding realized a common good, particular slave masters were brutal.[15] Railton's and Cohen's accounts widen the scope of moral explanation within historical explanation, suggesting that the multiple grievances and forms of resistance of slaves, as well as the need for concessions by owners, arose from slavery's injustice.[16] Marxian historical explanations, as I emphasize in Chapter 5, also include such ethical explanations. Since

---

[14] In Chapter 4, Section 1, I explore and reject the claim that conventionalist (nonmoral), nonracist explanations would do better still.

[15] Harman, 1965.   [16] Railton, 1986; J. Cohen, 1986a.

these causal accounts need not invoke moral agreements *within* particular coercive circumstances, they make any form of metaethical conventionalism unlikely.

On a moral realist conception, the emergence of *self-aware* freedom and *self-conscious* individuality are epochal moral and political discoveries about what a good life is for humans. The succession of such discoveries suggests an important analogy between ethical and scientific realism: In important respects, some older theories about abstract human capacities for moral personality and individuality are approximately true and are modified or abandoned because we develop theories that more closely approximate the truth.[17]

Since the idea of discovery, if overstressed, may be controversial, it is worth emphasizing the relationship of such abstract intrinsic goods and human capacities to unique social constructions and individual self-discoveries. Moral discoveries about, say, free agency are consistent with a diversity of realizations.[18] The sphere of discoveries about human likeness – Dworkin's egalitarian plateau – accords with and underpins that of plurality and individuality; in the latter sphere, given further discoveries about intrinsic goods of relationship and activity, each culture has a unique constructive aspect, each realization of individuality a creative component. In addition, as Chapter 7 shows, there is a distinctive kind of individual self-discovery in which a person comes to understand herself more clearly, changes her life in ways that further eudaemonia. Although Charles Taylor uses the term "self-interpretation," this experience is often seen as a self-*realization* or -*discovery*. Moreover, there is a risk, for each individual, of decline and deformation, not just an experience of self-articulation and growth. Here the term "self-discovery" captures more of a person's aim and the stakes involved, more of the abating, across personal growth, of something always partially opaque.

Further, as Will Kymlicka has stressed, this term captures a liberal conception of *fallibilism*, for in the changing stages of life, each of us discovers new possibilities of his identity, has the chance (partially) to shed conceptions borrowed from elders and to make a new start. Rawls's notion of the particularity and *rational* revisability of comprehensive conceptions of the good – given who each of us is – captures the psychological reality of fallibilism: We often know when such changes contribute to self-realization and when they fail to do so. As Kymlicka puts it:

---

[17] This formulation about discovery responds to questions raised by Michael Smith.

[18] Coinciding with the claims of this version of moral realism, Michael Walzer, 1988a, has recently insisted that longstanding social constructions, denying free agency, have gone fundamentally awry.

"Free persons conceive of themselves as beings who can revise and alter their final ends, and who give first priority to preserving their liberty in these matters" [Rawls]. The reason why we are not bound to any complex of interests, and why we give first priority to the freedom to revise our ends, is that we may come to question the value of our current ends. We recognize that our current judgments of the value of our activities could be mistaken. We wish to lead a life that is in fact good, not the life we currently believe to be good (a belief we recognize to be fallible). Hence our essential interest in living a life that is in fact good requires an ability to revise our ends, and to pursue those revised ends – to "track bestness" in Robert Nozick's phrase.

Conceptions of fallibilism and self-discovery are just as central to Mill's ideas of democratic experimentation and individuality. They make the idea of ethical discovery and even a historical succession of insights, more fully capturing what democracy or who an individual is, a central part of *political* theory. A focus on and ease of explaining self-discovery is a leading attraction of a moral realist interpretation of liberal and radical views compared with most conventionalisms; for the core modern political insight envisions the creation of cooperative arrangements that allow this experimentation to occur just in the way that seems most sensible to each individual.[19]

Yet the term "self-discovery" may suggest too easily a straightforward finding of something that is already there. Rawls's notion of *rational* revisability may invoke a solely mental process rather than a complex effort to *articulate* an integral emotional and intellectual – one might say, in another unconventional idiom, spiritual – identity. Chapter 7 emphasizes the contributions of modern psychoanalytic theory – its uniting of the unconscious and conscious, childhood experience and the painful emergence of a mature self – in explicating individuality. But even to oneself, individuality can only be fully articulated in its future unfolding.[20] Self-discovery is personal, diverse, ongoing, requiring particular imagination and deliberation, of a different level and kind than discoveries of general moral capacities; it gives the latter their point.[21]

---

[19] See Will Kymlicka's ingenious 1988 essay, pp. 186–7, 190.

[20] As Kierkegaard noted in his *Journal*, "It is perfectly true, as philosophers say, that life must be understood backwards. But they forget the other proposition, that it must be lived forwards" (Wollheim, 1984, p. 1).

[21] In conversations, Andreas Teuber has underlined some of the limitations of a notion of self-discovery.

Charles Taylor, 1977, advances a view of self-interpretation involving strong evaluations; the latter are qualitative contrasts about how an individual may choose to live that require deliberation. He opposes such interpretations to an overly constrictive "objective" utilitarianism that leaves little room for the diverse moral qualities of ways of life. Yet as he suggests, individuals come to recognize – in my sense discover – very impor-

The philosophies of history of modern liberals like Kant, Hegel, and Mill and of radicals like Marx and Lenin capture the second historical distinction about a common good realized in and transformed across a succession of moral innovations. In eloquently attacking the subjection of women, Mill argued:

> Some will object that a comparison cannot fairly be made between the government of the male sex and the forms of unjust power which I have adduced in illustration of it, since these are arbitrary, and the effect of mere usurpation, while it on the contrary is natural. But was there ever any domination which did not appear natural to those who possessed it? There was a time when the division of mankind into two classes, a small one of masters and a numerous one of slaves, appeared, even to the most cultivated minds, to be a natural, and the only natural, condition of the human race. No less an intellect, and one which contributed no less to the progress of human thought, than Aristotle, held this opinion without doubt or misgiving, and rested it on the same premises on which the same assertion in regard to the dominion of men over women is usually based, namely that there are different natures among mankind, free natures and slave natures. . . . But why need I got back to Aristotle? Did not the slave-owners of the Southern United States maintain the same doctrine, with all the fanaticism with which men cling to the theories that justify their passions and legitimate their personal interests? Did they not call heaven and earth to witness that the dominion of the white man over the black is natural . . . some even going so far as to say that the freedom of manual laborers is an unnatural order of things everywhere. . . . Nay, for that matter, the law of force itself, to those who could not plead any other, has always seemed the most natural of all grounds for the exercise of authority.[22]

In contrast, Mill defended, as the "peculiar character" of the modern world, the claim that "human beings are no longer born to their place in life, and chained down by an inexorable bond to the place they are born to, but are free to employ their faculties, and such favorable chances as offer, to achieve the lot which may appear to them most desirable." Against the oppressive background of slavery, serfdom, despotism, and the domination of women, Mill discerned the qualitatively new project of modern individuality. This historical distinction between justifications of oppression as "natural" and moral discoveries about human nature characterizes the greatest modern liberal and radical political theories. Failure to separate objective historical claims about human ca-

---

tant features of themselves in their successful strongly evaluative self-characterizations.

[22] Mill, 1987, pp. 138–9, 142–3. Section 3 of this chapter offers some reasons for thinking, contrary to Mill, that Aristotle entertained important doubts about contemporary justifications of enslavement.

pacities from mere conventionalist acceptance of changes has led such theorists as Strauss, MacIntyre, and Oakeshott to the mistaken conclusion that all modern thought is relativist.[23]

Thus, the recognition of the central role of the two broad distinctions in ethical and political knowledge – between a common good and the rule of particular interests, between initial theories of such a good and subsequent historical discoveries about it – is a leading feature of moral realism. Given this setting, we may turn to a deeper account of Aristotle's political theory and its modern reformulations.

3. Aristotle's two types of just war

On the basis of his political and biological theory, Aristotle deemed just two types of war, which, for clarity of analysis, I will separate: (a) those between free regimes, composed of human beings, which are an evil necessary to secure a just peace and (b) those of free regimes against barbarous ones, composed of incomplete humans, which are needed to acquire slaves. In analyzing wars of the first type, Aristotle defended the free political life of the rightly ordered polis, one that serves the common good and in which citizens rule and are ruled in turn. For the purposes of evaluating intra-Greek conflict, defectively ordered regimes such as oligarchy, democracy, or tyranny also counted as free since they were composed of Greek males and had the potential to accord with a common interest. On Aristotle's view, a rightly ordered polis expressed the nature of man as a *political* animal and diverged from Greek tyranny and even more strongly from Persian despotism. In book 1 of the *Politics*, he distinguished the four kinds of rule characteristic of such a polis: that of a statesman over citizens, of a monarch over subjects, of a manager over other members of a household, and of a master over slaves. He contrasted a multifaceted, free regime with the defective barbarian *single* form of rule. The latter identified the ruling of a city with the managing of a household; such regimes lacked a "natural ruler" (*to physei archon*).[24]

In examining the highest level of rule, that of a statesman over citizens, Aristotle celebrated what *naturally* marked off humans from gregarious animals such as bees. His conception fused ethics – the distinctive capacity to perceive, discourse about, and act upon issues of justice – with biology:

> Nature according to our theory makes nothing in vain; and man alone of the animals is furnished with the faculty of language . . . language serves

[23] Strauss, 1959; MacIntyre, 1981, pp. 1–5; Oakeshott, 1975.
[24] Aristotle, *Politics*, 1252a15–17, 1253a1–2, 1317a40–b3, 1257a7–13.

to declare what is advantageous and what is the reverse, and it therefore serves to declare what is just and what is unjust. It is the peculiarity of man, in comparison with the rest of the animal world, that he alone possesses a conception of good and evil, of just and unjust, . . . and it is association in these things which makes a family and a polis.[25]

In today's idiom, Aristotle's moral characterization supervenes on psychological and biological ones.

Given the improper or unnatural ordering of the souls of most citizens (a domination by the pleasure-seeking appetites of Sardanapalus), Aristotle maintained, the best-ordered cities would still need to defend themselves against foreign invaders and internal tyranny. Only a city that armed its male citizens could sustain a free political life. Aristotle stressed the connection between martial virtue, moderated by a temper of justice, and freedom.[26] He envisioned a just war as one of self-defense of such a city against conquest even by another free people.

In wars between free regimes, however, Aristotle sought two major reforms. First, in book 7, he used the example of the once great but newly fallen Sparta – whose legislator had designed its organization for war – as a warning to Athenians about the undermining of democracy through imperialist policies: "A polis should not be considered happy or a legislator praised, when its citizens are trained for victory in war and the subjugation of neighboring regimes. Such a policy . . . implies that any citizen who can do so, should make it his object to capture the government of his own city."[27] The licensing of external greed and tyranny would ultimately call forth greed and tyranny at home; citizens should check policies of conquest. In international political theory, as Chapters 7, 10, and 12 stress, Aristotle first articulated the centrality of *democratic internationalism*.

Second, Aristotle regarded slave hunting among Greeks as unnatural; it trapped humans capable of political participation and governing others: "Training for war should not be pursued with a view to enslaving those who do not deserve such a fate." Those wrongly seen as potential slaves were no longer foreigners but humans; he envisioned decent, international (though mainly inter-Greek) norms and posed three goals for a just war between free regimes: to prevent the enslavement of one's own citizens, to secure peace and leisure, and to acquire a limited empire for the good of the governed.[28] That political empire can be "for the good of the governed" is, of course, dubious. Nonetheless, among hu-

---

[25] Aristotle, *Politics*, 1252b5–9.
[26] Aristotle, *Nicomachean Ethics*, 1095b19–22; *Politics*, 1283a19–20.
[27] Aristotle, *Politics*, 1333b29–33.   [28] Aristotle, *Politics*, 1333a30–b3, 1333b40–4a2.

mans, Aristotle urged moderation in war. He aimed to avoid the extremes of lack of preparation – looked at anachronistically, pacifism – aggression, and enslavement.

Yet Aristotle also advocated the hunting of "natural" slaves as a second, hardly moderate type of just war:

> The art of war is in some sense a natural mode of acquisition. Hunting is a part of that art and hunting ought to be practiced . . . not only against wild animals but also against human beings who are intended by nature to be ruled by others and refuse to obey that intention . . . because war of this order is naturally just [*physei dikaion*].[29]

To legitimize slavery, Aristotle contended that substantial groups of deficient humans could concur with reason in others but could not govern themselves. They existed as less than political animals:

> We may thus conclude that all men who differ from others as much as the body differs from the soul or an animal from a man (and this is the case with all whose function is bodily service, and who produce best when they supply such service) – all such are by nature slaves. . . . A man is . . . by nature a slave . . . if he participates in reason to the extent of apprehending it in others, though destitute of it himself. Herein he differs from animals, which do not apprehend reason but simply obey their instincts. But the use which is made of the slave differs but little from the use made of tame animals; both he and they supply their owner with bodily help in meeting his daily requirements.[30]

Aristotle's contrast of citizen freedom with family and household domination flowed from an argument that barbarians and, to a lesser extent, Greek women resembled lower social animals more closely than humans. Given his teleological biology, he used the term "nature" (*physis*) in two opposed ways: The first differentiated the human from the animal in order to display the special potentials of humanity; the second projected certain features of animals onto large groups of humans in an attempt to justify slavery.

Aristotle's strictures against the political role of women also rest on biological arguments. Since women have the "faculty of deliberation" only "inconclusively," he maintained, they do not qualify for citizenship and must submit to rule by men. In the depiction of Plato's *Republic*, Socrates had suggested that women could become members of the ideal guardian class. With communal childrearing arrangements, no natural attribute could exclude the childbearer from political participation. Socrates also drew a general analogy between the deficient character even of guardians – who were not philosophers – and dogs: Regardless of

---

[29] Aristotle, *Politics*, 1256b23–6, 1255b37–90.   [30] Aristotle, *Politics*, 1245b16–24.

justice, both protect friends and attack strangers. Rejecting this proposal about guardian women on a functional basis, Aristotle sarcastically responded, "Unlike women, animals have no domestic duties."[31] Here Aristotle used a difference between humans and other animals – a type of argument he frequently employed to illustrate higher human capacities – to deprive women of full humanity. But Socrates did not mean to reduce men and women to animals; he contended that (some) women could potentially join men in politics, whether or not the best Greek cities provided the conditions for women to participate. Even though the rest of Platonic argument undercuts this claim, Socrates' account reveals the trivial political impact of actual biological – as opposed to socially created – differences.

Aristotle also cast suspicion on his own explicit argument. In book 1, he cited, with seeming approval, a commonplace from Sophocles' tragedy *Ajax:* "A modest silence is a woman's crown." The context of this comment, widely familiar to Athenians, is, however, ironic. Ajax was seized by madness and about to steal out alone at night to slaughter the oxen. His wife, Tecmessa, reports that he used this cliché to still her natural attempts to restrain him. But despite Aristotle's skepticism about many common views, his criticism of Socrates highlighted the limitation of his teleological biology to reinterpreting existing political arrangements as natural. Nonetheless, although Aristotle's dual use of the idea of *nature* sometimes legitimized servitude, it could also highlight original political accomplishments.

In fact, his higher conception of human nature represents the greatest defense of freedom compatible with the new political life of Greek cities. Aristotle's theory registers a Greek *discovery* about human political and moral capacities; nothing like freedom and mutual recognition existed before the emergence of the polis. Thus, he did not prefigure historicism or relativism when he contrasted these recently displayed *human* potentials with previous Greek and barbarian despotism: "The most natural form of the village appears to be that of the colony or offshoot from a family. . . . This, it may be noted, is the reason why each Greek polis was originally ruled – as the primitive peoples of the barbarian world still are – by kings." In averring that the polis arose by nature, Aristotle praised this novel Greek political organization – what we would call a historical achievement – as the full cooperative expression of the human

---

[31] Aristotle, *Politics*, 1260a12–14, 1226b4–6; Plato, *Republic*, 451d – 2a, 375a – 6a. Yet from an Aristotelian point of view, one might doubt that even guardians participate in *political* life; the legislator orders their lives in a way that resembles "natural slavery." Socrates' ideal city seems distinctively uniform, apolitical, and antidemocratic. See also Klosko, 1986, pp. 153–7.

capacity for a good life. He called the legislator who first *constructed* such a political association "the greatest of beneficiaries of mankind."[32]

As Vernant has emphasized, Greek citizens celebrated the polis as an original accomplishment, "une véritable invention."[33] Aristotle's theoretical description of this association laid the basis for an objective historical view about human nature, even though, given the contemporary uniqueness of this moral discovery, he did not interpret his argument in this way. His theory of the polis explicitly contrasted the "natural" – a common good – with the defective. It marked the first, central distinction in political reflection; yet we may also see his theory as an illustration of the second, historical distinction.

To explain the differences between free and servile regimes, Aristotle joined a climatic determinism to his social biology. Following his general philosophical principle of avoiding extremes, he suggested that Greece, geographically and climatically, represented a mean between the peoples of the North and those of Asia. Denizens of the cold North displayed the fiery temper or spirit necessary for freedom but lacked skill and ability; they "remain completely free but attain no political development and show no capacity for governing others." Inhabitants of the enervatingly warm East exhibited skill and intelligence but lacked spirit and fell into servitude. Only citizens of moderate Greece had the requisite skill and spirit to forge a free political life.[34] Thus, Aristotle's biological explanation of Greek freedom and barbarian servitude is overdetermined. If his climatic arguments are right, they sufficiently account for political differences; they require no additional claims about the inherent biological potentials of distinct human groups. Furthermore, despite his general justification of enslaving some strangers, Aristotle ironically praised a barbarian city, Carthage, as one of the three best existing regimes.[35] Yet he neither explicitly extended his arguments against Greek servitude to criticize slaveholding generally nor questioned whether a sufficiently large number of natural slaves existed to sustain the leisure of citizens.

4. The objectivity of Aristotle's political and moral theory

Major historical changes separate us from Aristotle. Despite the contemporary brilliance of his theories in nonhuman biology and astronomy, progress in those disciplines has, today, largely discredited his views. Why can we still see the point of his arguments about war among free

---

[32] Aristotle, *Politics*, 1252b16–23, 1253a30–1.   [33] Vernant, 1981, p. 44.
[34] Aristotle, *Politics*, 1372b23–33.
[35] Aristotle, *Politics*, 1272b24–3b26, 1316a39–b6, 1320b1–9.

humans, the nature of a self-governing community, or a common good? A relativist must see this continuity as a matter of common culture or shared linguistic conventions. But then, one might ask, why don't such linguistic conventions similarly preserve Aristotle's astronomy? In opposition to relativism, a moral realist needs to explain the continuing plausibility of Aristotle's political and ethical theory as part of a growing dialectical recognition of the human capacity for a free and cooperative political life; for this plausibility and comparative explanatory success contrasts with the decline, based on rival theories and subsequent discoveries, of his nonhuman biology and astronomy. The relativist wants to limit a priori every domain of knowledge to its cultural setting and, hence, to discern an even, culture-specific development. From this standpoint, the uneven development of different kinds of knowledge is troubling: If reality is really constructed by our knowledge, why are our insights and successes so varied diachronically in diverse theoretical domains? In a naturalistic vein, however, a realist seeks discipline-specific explanations for this uneven development.

Either of two realist arguments would suffice to explain the continuity of political and moral knowledge. The first, weaker claim would maintain that modern ethical terms as well as Aristotle's *refer* to some similar features of free regimes organized around a common good, of just war, and so forth. Such a view is consistent with the contention that advance in political science and ethics has rendered Aristotle's theories wholly obsolete; it could sustain later arguments in this chapter on moral objectivity and progress. The second, stronger realist claims would suggest that Aristotle not only theoretically described the first free association, but forged a general framework for the objective study of politics and ethics. Delineating the takeoff point for these disciplines in Greek political theory, that claim includes and strengthens the first. It vividly reveals subsequent theories – Montesquieu's, Hegel's and Marx's for example – as fundamental refinements in a common project, initiated by Aristotle. For this reason, I have chosen to defend the stronger claim.

Vernant has persuasively depicted the origins of Greek politics. When ancient Mycenean royalty declined and a class of commercial oligarchs emerged, he maintains, a strong egalitarian countermovement arose. Class struggle led to the discovery of the vital concept of political "likeness," the novel emphasis on speech and persuasion (*peitho*), and the alternation in office that characterized the citizenry of a polis. In addition, changing technology supplanted the heroes of single combat with hoplites, who fought shoulder to shoulder and depended on each other for protection. Military participation grew out of and reinforced political participation. Furthermore, this new political form, based on a (limited) recognition of human freedom, engendered novel kinds of social conflict and demands for justice.[36]

Aristotle's theory of politics elicited four broad conceptions from this experience: first, the notion that humans with partially conflicting interests – at least male Greeks – could share in a free political life based on a common good; second, an analysis of the political components of actual regimes coupled with a philosophical assessment of their clashing claims about justice; third, a theory of changes of regime arising from the interaction of these claimants in particular settings, combined with proposals to secure a just settlement – an adherence to a common good – among them; and fourth, a vision of ordinarily peaceful (nonaggressive) relations among regimes.

For Aristotle, practices of citizenship illustrated the general notion of human freedom, or what Hegel would later call the "freedom of some" as opposed to the "freedom of one," the Asiatic or Greek despot. Failed as well as successful attempts to balance the conflicting demands of free men – the rich and poor, those of military prowess, the virtuous – characterized this new political arena. Aristotle stressed the war of differing conceptions of justice between rich and poor – the role of class conflict – in altering political forms. He argued for the need to balance such ethical claims through the existence of a stable, small property holding middle class and policies to offset a predominant class's power. In the absence of moderating measures, the poor but formally free might extend their claims to expropriate the rich, the height of injustice as Aristotle conceived it. This trend toward extreme democracy could also instigate a revolution to restore the honor and wealth of the noble or rich.[37] Thus, Aristotle presented his theory of a common good as a philosophical *refinement* of the merits in ordinary opinions.

In the *broadest* comparison with more modern views, Aristotle's political theory lacked only a notion of fundamental change, embodying new and higher forms of equality and freedom and a full picture of individuality. In addition, his theory could not have foreseen eighteenth-century civil society or a corresponding political economy. Nonetheless, to this day, Aristotle's arguments on regime instability remain important contenders for truth, and his theory is strikingly superior to purportedly liberal, "value-neutral" reformulations.[38]

As we will see, one might also view major features of his eudaemonist

---

[36] Vernant, 1981, ch. 4. Even hoplites had to be able to afford weapons. George Klosko, 1986, p. 9, has suggested that Athenian naval power, requiring only the ability to row, was a further democratizing influence. It was also linked to Athenian imperialism.

[37] Aristotle, *Politics*, 1302a24–31.

[38] Cf., for example, Samuel P. Huntington, 1969, ch. 1; 1975, which combine Aristotle's thesis on extreme democracy with the ethics of Thrasymachus.

ethics – his emphasis on different kinds of happiness stemming from engagement in diverse activities and relationships – as components of a more plausible moral theory than utilitarianism or contractarianism. Modern conceptions of "happiness," as David Norton has maintained, often misinterpret the Greek idea of eudaemonia. The latter involves a fundamental integrity arising from listening to one's daimon. (Consider Socrates' rapt attention to his inner voice in the *Symposium* and *Crito*.)[39] Though ethical decisions are often complex, a deep understanding of individuals and circumstances reveals internal moral necessities, arising from the choice of an integral way of living. Thus, Aristotle emphasized the good of reflective character, not just the achievement of particular ends. In this respect, Greek ethical theories capture features of individuality more readily than prevalent modern moral arguments.

As Terence Irwin has argued, Aristotle did not envision a conflict between virtuous action and individual (so-called egotistical) interests.[40] He saw acting for the good of others – in citizenship and friendship, for example – not as an abnegation of self but as a choice to be a certain kind of person. He properly separated activities furthering integrity – ones embodying intrinsic goods and pursued for the relevant reasons – from merely selfish strivings for money or power (what we would call a distinction between individuality and mere individualism).

In its most general form, his theory of human goods lacks only a full conception of autonomy, individuality, and self-respect. His broad theory of the virtues suffers more sharply from gender and class stereotypes, a misunderstanding of the healthy interplay of reason and emotion, and a deprecation of manual as opposed to mental activity. Despite decisive corrections of some of his political and economic views, however, his successors have often overlooked outstanding features of Aristotle's ethics. For instance, Rousseau and Marx do not match his account of important goods, notably deliberation and friendship. In fact, as Chapter 7 shows, Aristotle's eudaemonism clarifies Marx's ethical judgments; in moral theory, I will contend, we can best understand Marx as implicitly – and often explicitly – a neo-Aristotelian. Mill's theory of friendship between women and men dramatically improved on Aristotle's[41] and initiated a lengthy process of theoretical reinterpretation. But a dialectical reassessment of the virtues and moral character – one informed by Marxian insights into exploitation, internationalism, and a

[39] Norton, 1976, pp. 5–6.
[40] Irwin, 1979, ch. 8; Brink, 1986, p. 34.
[41] Despite mistakenly emphasizing merger, Montaigne's sixteenth-century theory of friendship had already introduced the modern notion of individuality: "If you press me to say why I loved him [Etienne de la Bóetie], I feel that I can only express this by answering: because it was he, because it was I" (Montaigne, 1922, 1:242).

thoroughgoing rejection of sexism – could properly begin from a critique of Aristotle's theory. A complex, uneven development marks the socially charged disciplines of political science and ethics.

Since Aristotle's political and moral theory have survived while his physical theory has not, one might wonder what special features of political science made it possible to forge a relatively mature view in ancient Greece; for the maturing of the natural sciences occurred nearly two thousand years later, in the seventeenth century, with the adoption of approximately true theories (mechanism, atomism) and the introduction of relatively reliable instrumentation. Comparatively speaking, however, advance in political and ethical knowledge does not depend on instrumentation but upon the existence or emergence of the relevant phenomena. A broadly true political and moral theory, one that specified most of the main questions and relationships, could already appear once the first (however limited) free regimes arose in the Greek cities.

In the natural sciences outside of human biology, one can, to some significant extent, distinguish internal aspects of scientific advance – changes in theory and instrumentation – from external ones – shifts in historical setting. Furthermore, the latter domains include highly theoretical items like neutrinos; moral and political theory do not. In this respect, the natural sciences appear to be, in Shapere's idiom, more highly internalized. But novel political forms and moral discoveries – historical changes – are comparatively *internal* to the subject matter and advance of social science and ethics.[42] Thus, today's common notion of paradigm "revolutions" in the natural sciences refers to evidential and theoretical changes *within* disciplines; in ethics and political theory, however, often violent social and political revolutions, defending and demonstrating *relevant human capacities*, provide evidence for – or are partly instigated by – fundamental theoretical changes. As an important feature of moral discovery, investigators in the social sciences cannot neatly separate theory and historical practice.

The comparative integration of the latter disciplines has lent plausibility to the mistaken conventionalist view that all political and ethical theories are ideological (and false). But that conventionalism is, on its own account, an ideological thesis and, hence, false. Despite important differences with the natural sciences, ethics and political theory also achieve internalization;[43] for as Aristotle emphasized, early *nonpolitical* conceptions specified a common good affecting life and moderate prosperity, engendered from above by a monarchy, rather than the subsequent political good of a self-governing community of equals. In that

---

[42] Nagel, 1986a, p. 139.   [43] Shapere, 1984, ch. 13; 1988.

discipline-founding change, human equality and freedom – later democracy and individuality – were leading discoveries.

A brief contrast with a relatively advanced ancient physical science, astronomy, reveals some of the comparative advantages of Greek political science. Like the study of politics, that astronomy had a rich profusion of data. But though astronomical theory provided useful guidance for agriculture, navigation, and other practical purposes, investigators wrongly believed that the sun orbited the earth; they also lacked the crucial theoretical concept of gravitational force. Furthermore, Aristotelian terrestrial physics and cosmology reinforced what would come to be called Ptolemaic astronomical theory and provided deep *background theoretical obstacles* to forming a true conception.[44] Someone who wanted to draw a parallel for politics and ethics might contend that Aristotle's political theory lacked a concept of fundamental change, that his cosmology and biology created background obstacles to such a conception, and that the theory could not rely on a sufficiently rich and varied historical experience of class conflict. Further, subsequent insights into the political potentials of slaves, the colonized, workers, and women lead, in a liberal or Marxian theory, to revolutionary shifts in conception. In addition, a modern conception of democracy requires a full theory of individuality. Yet we may also see these dramatic changes as a reformulation of the concepts of equal freedom and a common good already elaborated by Aristotle. Compared with ancient astronomy, his delineation of class conflict, complex insights into political justice, and subtle eudaemonism adequately grasped the central theoretical features of politics.

Given the internal role of comparative observation in political and moral theory, Aristotle's acceptance of universally held opinion did not fundamentally damage his view. Despite this mistaken principle, his conception could begin to illustrate generally what human political life is "when its growth is completed" in contrast to any reflection possible in previous historical settings.[45] Thus, we might imagine counterfactually a philosopher who held an Aristotelian view before the emergence of the polis. That theorist would have had to acknowledge patriarchal forms of rule as the highest, or to conclude that *man is a patriarchal, despotic animal.* Aristotle's own characterization of the polis illustrates the historical distinction between forms taken to be just at a given time – divinely sanctified despotism – and subsequent moral discoveries. Further extensions of freedom would show that his conception of the "natural" range of political possibilities was defective.

Moses Finley has suggested that, for Aristotle, the notion of hierarchy embodied in "natural slavery" was an axiom, not a theorem. That pro-

---

[44] Kuhn, 1957, pp. 84–7. [45] Aristotle, *Politics*, 1252b32–43.

posal would be consistent with a conventionalist interpretation of *moral* theories, based on competing axioms, in which hierarchical accounts are one among many.[46] In contrast, my view suggests that *political* and *ethical* theories are ones that stress the human likeness involved in mutual regard among persons. Thus, the free city embodies the moral discovery central to Aristotle's and subsequent political theories. Aristotle's hierarchical cosmology and downgrading of slaves, artisans, farmers, women, and barbarians are, from the standpoint of political theory, secondary and mistaken. On a moral realist account, hierarchical conceptions – for instance, fascist ones – are normative, appealing to facsimiles of a common good, but neither political nor moral.

The application of general theories in political as well as natural science requires auxiliary statements or collateral information that includes widely accepted facts and related theories.[47] Though Aristotle opposed wrongful individual enslavement, his social biological theory of natural slavery recapitulated the uncontested economic basis of Greek life. From a realist point of view, the main theory concerns cities composed of free men. Interpreting what Finley calls "axioms" as auxiliary statements, we can see Aristotle's endorsement of slavery as mistaken background information. Given the fresh emergence of the central phenomena of freedom and cooperation, the first theoretical framework for the objective study of politics, the general existence of slaveholding, and the absence of any competing, approximately true, abolitionist theory, no methodological safeguard would have enabled Aristotle to see the error in this collateral information. For Aristotle, general slave rebelliousness had to appear, to use Thomas Kuhn's term, as an "anomaly." Thus, he interpreted the enmity of Spartan helots toward their masters as a consequence of defective household management, not as the result of a fundamentally corrupt political arrangement.[48] But slave revolts like the one led by Spartacus against Rome, the exodus of Jews from Egypt, the early Christian movement, the emergence of nonslave societies, and the forging of abolitionist theories would ultimately highlight these deficient background arguments.[49] They would spur a transformation in political science focused on a more general conception of individuality and the potential for social and moral progress.

5. Montesquieu's response to Aristotle on slavery and war

Aristotle's political theory strongly influenced Montesquieu's interpretation of the laws in the context the manners, climate, religion, geog-

---

[46] In correspondance, Richard Miller emphasized this point.
[47] Boyd, 1980a; Gilbert, 1981a, chs. 1, 14; Putnam, 1975, 1:ch. 16.
[48] Aristotle, *Politics*, 1269a36–b12.   [49] Walzer, 1985, pp. 22–5.

raphy, and commerce, or as he summarized it, the *spirit* of a people. Nonetheless, Montesquieu observed that men and women had increasingly made themselves free and proven the hunting of slaves unjust and unacceptable. A modern scientific argument about politics would have to explain this new fact about social life. In *Spirit of the Laws*, Montesquieu satirized ancient and contemporary arguments for the slave trade and the enslaving of prisoners of war.

Like Aristotle, Montesquieu used the term "natural" in two senses, an ethical one that identified the appropriate human arrangements in ideal circumstances and an explanatory one that delineated the climatic causes for the myriad abuses of humanity and natural justice. In book 15, he contended:

> As human beings are born equal, it is necessary to say that slavery is against nature [contre la nature] although in certain countries, it is founded on a natural cause [une raison naturelle]; and it is necessary to distinguish these countries from those where even natural causes reject it such as the European countries, where it has, so happily, been abolished.[50]

In this context, Montesquieu did not fully spell out the basis of natural equality; he apparently referred to a sufficient capacity to reason in every human in order to underpin moral agency and a rarer "virtue." At the outset of book 15, he spoke of the corruption of motive and practice involved in slavery, which is "bad in its own nature." The slave, he averred, "can do nothing through a motive of virtue"; the master unconsciously "accustoms himself to the want of every moral virtue." In exploring English freedom in book 19, Montesquieu stressed the capacity to reason that mandates legal and political recognition; he also ironically distinguished this claim from any egalitarian contention about the results of particular reasonings: "In a free nation, it is very often a matter of indifference whether individuals [les particuliers] reason well or ill; it is sufficient that they do reason: hence springs that liberty which is a security from the effects of these reasonings."[51]

Montesquieu's *ethical* argument about human *nature* contrasted with his *natural* or climatic *explanation* of the contemporary existence of slavery. Despite his admiration for Aristotle's political theory, he rejected Aristotle's social biological account of enslavement. In its place, he strengthened Aristotle's argument on climate as an underlying cause of the fundamental differences among regimes.

Some had advocated slavery in France. Montesquieu suggested that these gentlemen should draw lots with everyone else to determine who

---

[50] Montesquieu, *De l'esprit des lois*, hereafter *EL*, 1961, 1:260.
[51] Montesquieu, *EL*, 1:254, 342.

would be enslaved. Just as the most impoverished, but free men detested this institution, he argued, so the proponents of slavery for others would hold it "most in horror" for themselves. The ideal experiment of the lottery exposed this advocacy as an expression of "luxury and voluptuousness" (le cri du luxe et de la volupté) rather than of concern for the common good (félicité publique).[52] This sophisticated moral device helped to discern what is naturally just.

Montesquieu started from actual human potentials and desires, manifested in the new nonslave societies. Prefiguring Rawls's original position, he suggested, "In these matters, if you would know whether the desires of each are legitimate, examine the desires of all."[53]

Rousseau's *Social Contract* also advanced general arguments against slavery. One cannot justify an alleged right of the stronger, he contended, on grounds of security. Far from facilitating happiness, tranquillity, as in the case of the companions of Odysseus in Cyclops's cave, waiting to be devoured, can seal human misery ("Qu'y gagnent-ils si cette tranquillité même est une de leur misères?").[54] But, he insisted, slaves, like Cyclops's prisoners, are human; just societies must recognize the universal potential for freedom and happiness. Note that arguments for the preservation of bare existence also did not justify slavery on Aristotle's view. As opposed to Strauss's mistaken contention that Rousseau's notion of a general will could sanctify cannibalism or slavery, the recognition of the universal human capacity for moral personality underlies the general will and makes it a will to equality, citizenship, and freedom.[55]

Yet Montesquieu and Rousseau interpreted their antislavery arguments as examples of the first distinction in political philosophy. Both contrasted a common good, based on an ahistorical human nature, with domination by the powerful. If we disregard their claims about a fictitious state of nature composed of putatively isolated individuals, however, we can see that they still defended a general human potential for mutual recognition, freedom, and individuality. (Montesquieu, of course, sympathized with modern versions of individuality far more than Rousseau did.)[56] We can then interpret their arguments against slavery as the elucidation of a moral discovery, illustrating the second

---

[52] Montesquieu, *EL*, 1:262. Contractarian notions of impartiality are an important component of moral theory. But as Railton's notion of social rationality or impartial spectator utilitarianism shows, such devices need not be constructivist (Railton, 1986, pp. 189–97).

[53] Montesquieu, *EL*, 1:262.

[54] Rousseau, *Oeuvres complètes*, hereafter *OC*, 1964, 1:355–6; Locke, 1965, pp. 465–6.

[55] Rousseau, *OC*, 1:437, 440; Strauss, 1959, pp. 51–2.

[56] Gilbert, 1986a.

distinction in political and ethical argument. We can understand their theories as modified versions of Aristotle's account, and yet recognize that humans make their potentials for cooperation and individuality evident only in the course of an historical development.

Like Aristotle, Montesquieu attributed Eastern despotism and slavery to enervating climate. But his substitution of climate for social biology eliminated the notion that any humans, such as "barbarians" or women, are by nature inferior. In book 15, following out the logic of his moral and social theoretical argument, however, he questioned even a climatic extenuation of slavery, which chilled his "heart": "There is not perhaps any climate on earth where one could not engage free men to do the work. Because the laws were badly made, one found lazy men; because men were lazy, they were enslaved."[57]

If we look only at Aristotle's and Montesquieu's conception of political justice as a balance among divergent claims and powers, their theories nearly concur. But the minor, empirical premises, concerning who counts as human, have shifted dramatically. Given his climatic theory, Montesquieu dialectically took Aristotle's argument against enslaving Greek prisoners of war – that all Greeks were capable of freedom – and extended it to those Aristotle deemed barbarian. Just as Aristotle discerned in the polis an illustration of man's natural capacity for citizenship, Montesquieu interpreted the nonslave regimes of modern Europe as a further embodiment of freedom. A realist insists that new scientific arguments, nonslave forms of social organization, and increasingly powerful political movements for greater freedom proved Aristotle's theory mistaken. *These social and scientific changes* led to a metamorphosis in ethical conclusions: an objective defense of individuality and the general capacity for moral personality. Yet to a relativist, the qualitative shift between these ancient and modern moral conclusions *might wrongly appear*, neglecting the underlying social and scientific metamorphoses, simply as an ethical transformation.

Aristotle's social biology had provided the strongest defense of slave hunting as a form of just war. But some liberal theorists who rejected this biology retained weaker arguments in favor of enslaving prisoners of war. In Chapter 4 of the second treatise, for example, Locke contended that,

> having by his own fault, forfeited his own Life, by some Act that deserves Death; he to whom he has forfeited it, may (when he has him in his Power) delay to take it and make use of him to his own Service, and he does him no injury by it. For, whenever he finds the hardship of his Slavery out-

---

[57] Montesquieu, *EL*, 1:261.

weigh the value of his Life, 'tis in his own Power, by resisting the will of his Master, to draw on himself the Death he desires.

Locke justified slavery as punishment for aggression. But does soldiering, *outside* of battle, constitute an "Act that deserves death"? The theory of self-defense countenances killing soldiers and imprisoning captives for the war's duration. These practices do not deny the prisoners' capacity for freedom. Stripped of a social biological defense, however, the servitude of free men has no rational basis; thus, Aristotle opposed the subjugation of *Greek* prisoners of war. Locke acknowledged that making slaves of captured fathers could not legitimize their children's servitude. He oddly concluded, however, that the victor has a right to property in the soldier's person but no right to confiscate the soldier's (external) property; the latter rightfully belongs to the still free children.[58]

Locke's nonbiological defense of enslaving prisoners of war conflicted glaringly with his central theoretical claim about every individual's natural liberty. This contradiction may stem from his role as administrator of slaveholding colonies in America. By Locke's argument, however, the sanction given to the Royal Africa Company's forays did not extend to the servitude or sale of the children of the first generation. His conception did not justify American slavery.

Paradoxically, Locke's insistence on *enslavement as punishment* seems driven by his theory's revolutionary side, not by his emphasis on property. As in the state of nature, each may kill an aggressor like any "lyon or tyger," so a people may overthrow a tyrant in self-defense or may discipline unjust warriors by enslavement.[59] Thus, even though Locke's legitimation of slavery is a striking anomaly in his argument, it has a surprising theoretical, not ideological (colonial administrator) motivation.

Montesquieu rejected Locke's claims about prisoners of war as "senseless": "As soon as a man has made another a slave, he cannot say that he had been in any necessity to kill him since he did not do it." In book 15, Montesquieu also magisterially satirized slaveowner opinions and revealed their moral monstrousness. He showed how principles of natural justice, based on ordinary human capacities and recognized by Europeans *for Europeans*, identified the inhuman core of this commerce: "It is impossible for us to suppose these people [slaves] to be human, because

---

[58] Locke, 1965, pp. 435–8. Modern practices regarding prisoners of war recognize that soldiers are not responsible for the criminal policies of their governments, but rather for their own conduct; soldiers may be justly punished – though not enslaved – for crimes against civilians. Statesmen and officers, however, may be held responsible for major crimes of war, and especially rarer crimes against humanity.

[59] Locke, 1965, pp. 314–15.

if we suppose them to be human, one would begin to suspect that we ourselves are not Christians."[60]

Montesquieu's differences with Aristotle raise questions about every form of domination of human beings by group or category. For example, *Spirit's* climatic theory seemed to recognize a natural equality of women with men in capacity for reason. In hot regions, he maintained, women would reach puberty earlier, before their reason had fully matured, and men would predominate; in moderate climes, reaching puberty later and aging less rapidly, women would achieve "a sort of equality" with men; in cold regions, where men drink heavily and act intemperately, women, because of – an allegedly natural – reticence, would be "superior to men in the exercise of reason." Despite this somewhat egalitarian argument, Montesquieu still held, in a residual sexist vein, that the comparatively free institutions of the Roman republic and modern England should exclude women from political life.[61]

His satirical *Persian Letters*, however, pivoted on the unnatural cruelty of the despot Usbek to his harem. Usbek espouses a theory of republicanism and natural justice; he exhibits a spirit of adventure and scientific inquiry. These convictions, however, hold no sway over his personal relationships. He ultimately instructs his chief eunuch to punish those of his wives whom he believes to have been unfaithful. Unnatural relationships and physical distance pervert his judgment; he suspects loyal ones of treachery and trusts the one who most deceives him. When the eunuchs surprise and kill her lover, Roxanne poisons them and then herself. In her dying letter to Usbek, she demands recognition of her freedom and manifests her moral superiority:

> How could you think me so credulous as to imagine that I had no existence in the world except to adore your caprices? . . . No! I have lived in servitude but I have always been free: I have reformed your laws according to those of nature, and my spirit has always retained its independence. . . . Might it be possible that having crushed you with grief, I can yet force you to admire my courage?[62]

Her love expressed her individuality. She substituted "the laws of nature" for unjust ones. Although her revolt proved her independance, however, her circumstances sharply restricted that freedom; that revolt ended only in death. Yet Roxanne's noble individuality suggested a more thoroughgoing egalitarianism than Montesquieu allowed himself in *Spirit*. His conception of courage – and personality – differed from Aristotle's. Furthermore, the tale of Roxanne prefigured Hegel's philosophi-

---

[60] Montesquieu, *F.I.*, 1:255, 259.   [61] Montesquieu, *EL*, 1:272–3, 342; Gilbert, 1986a, sec. 4.
[62] Montesquieu, *Lettres persanes*, hereafter *LP*, 1960, p. 334.

cal analysis of master and servant, and Marx's conception that history proceeds by the "bad side" of oppression and resultant class conflict. These liberal and radical theorists defended social individuality through a factual rejection of ancient claims about the putative "natural" basis for major social inequalities.

In international politics, Montesquieu retained the ancient notion of just defensive war by free governments but repudiated slave hunting. As he foresaw, practices sanctioning (minimal) respect for persons and abolishing the slave trade would mark the creation of a new international regime.[63] Montesquieu also revived and transformed Aristotle's thesis on democratic internationalism. In *Considerations on the Grandeur of the Romans and Their Decline,* he celebrated that republic's egalitarianism and public spiritedness but condemned its brutality, exhibited in aggressive, imperial wars. Conquest abroad nurtured tyranny and decadence at home: "How many wars do we see undertaken in the history of Rome, how much blood shed, how many peoples destroyed, how many great actions. . . . But how did this project for invading all nations end – a project so well planned, carried out, and completed – except by satiating five or six monsters?"[64]

Montesquieu's insight into Roman destiny led to an Aristotelian conclusion – military republics would educate their people to public greatness and yet decline – and a non-Aristotelian one, in admiration for a new commercial society. That society's moderate laws and balance of governmental powers might ensure the security of each citizen in pursuing his private goals and create novel prospects for international peace; these changes might compensate for the absence of an ancient concern for the common good. (To some extent, Aristotle's admiration for commercial Carthage prefigured Montesquieu's views.)

Montesquieu contended that all individuals could contribute to a burgeoning trading republic. In describing natural justice, *The Persian Letters* envisioned the engagement of individuals in diverse activities for the appropriate reasons – for instance, in marriage for love rather than for compulsion, status, or money. The good Troglodytes of Usbek's imagination, Roman citizens, and Roxanne displayed such virtue. In contrast, monarchical honor and despotism's pervasive fear distorted the integrity of activities. Though a commercial republic did not elicit concern for the public good, it allowed greater individual choice of activity and required less personal dependence and compulsion than monarchy or

---

[63] Montesquieu, *EL,* 1:145. For the contribution of the "discourse" of individual rights to the emergence of liberal international norms, see Kratochwil, 1989. Colonialism and other forms of political, social, and economic domination would undercut that regime's liberalism.

[64] Montesquieu, *Oeuvres complètes,* 2:150.

despotism. Usbek contrasted Swiss and Dutch Protestantism as a spur to productivity and population with Catholic monasticism: "Commerce animates everything in the one society; monasticism spreads death everywhere in the other." [65]

The Persian Letters saw trade as a leavening force even in ancient Rome. Roman slaves could accumulate savings, purchase their liberty, and rejuvenate the republic: "All of this created an industrious people [un peuple laborieux] and animated industry and the arts." [66] A modern commercial republic would elicit the industry of all to a much greater degree.

Montesquieu's vision of commerce also transformed his theory of world politics. Trade, he thought, would facilitate an international practice of mutual recognition among peoples, gentle manners (*moeurs douces*) and peace. This commerce would supplant modern conquest, like Cortez's barbarous expedition in Mexico. He decried those Christian thieves "who would absolutely be brigands and Christians" and "were very devout." [67] Largely self-absorbed engagement in commercial activities rather than military virtue, Montesquieu argued, would become the "spring" or "principle" of a more civilized international order; he praised England at the expense of Spain.

This benign view of international commerce, however, coexisted uneasily with his critique of the slave trade. His celebration of England's peaceful commercial interests jarred with its conquests in America and India. Finally, Montesquieu's criticism of the luxurious rich for corrupting ancient, mainly noncommercial republics did not fit well with his confidence in a modern republic; the latter would tolerate the political impact of even greater inequalities of wealth than Aristotle's oligarchies had. [68] As a basic ethical contrast, Aristotle's theory of natural justice criticized the domination of money. Yet the commerce that Montesquieu celebrated, whatever its social vigor and diminution of some forms of coercion, distorted the relevant motivations for diverse activities:

> If the spirit of commerce unites nations, it does not similarly unite individuals [particuliers]. We see that in countries where one is only influenced by the commercial spirit, one traffics in every human action and every moral virtue: the smallest things, those that humanity demands, are there done . . . only for money. [69]

---

[65] Montesquieu, *LP*, pp. 138–48, 249. In contrast, *Spirit of the Laws* would emphasize these themes for Athens and especially England (*républiques commerçantes*), not warrior Rome or Sparta (*républiques militaires*) (Montesquieu, *EL*, 1:51–2, 336–7, 339–40).

[66] Montesquieu, *LP*, p. 243.   [67] Montesquieu, *EL*, 2:8, 1:258, 149.

[68] Montesquieu, *EL*, 1:49–50, 104–5, 120.

[69] Montesquieu, *EL*, 2:9. For a discussion of Montesquieu's multifaceted eudaemonist assessments of regimes, see Gilbert, 1986a, Pts. 3–4.

Given the limited historical experience of modern republics, he never explored these tensions deeply. But his hopes for peace relied on a controversial, embryonic economic and political theory of this new regime. Less sanguine empirical assessments of commerce could exacerbate the conflict between money seeking and integrity in Montesquieu's ethics.

6. Hegel's theory of freedom

From the point of view of moral realism, Hegel's interlocking philosophy of history and theory of the modern state strengthens Montesquieu's insights; his objective conception of historical advance makes the second distinction in moral and political knowledge explicit. Hegel affirmed the principle that "world history is progress in the consciousness of freedom" and that the "substantive aim of the world spirit [*Weltgeist*] is achieved through the freedom of each individual." Ancient societies, he contended, such as Eastern despotisms, permitted only the tyrant's freedom. In Greece, where the consciousness of freedom "first dawned," only some – male citizens – were free. As Hegel stressed, the defective ethical unity of these regimes offered little scope for individuality:

> The Greeks not only had slaves, on which their life and the continued existence of their beautiful freedom [der Bestand ihrer schönen Freiheit] depended, but their very freedom itself was in part only a contingent, undeveloped, transient and limited flowering, and in part, a hard servitude of all that is human and humane [eine harte Knechtschaft des Menschlichen, des Humanen].[70]

As exemplified in Sophocles' tragedy, figures like Creon and Antigone drew their duties and convictions from conflicting dimensions of Greek ethical life: the public law and the hidden, divine law of families. They did not engage in free, internal deliberation. They thus appeared as *characters*, lacking "particular individuality [*einzelne Individualität*]." In the polis, for Hegel, individuality could exist only as a negative, dissolving element. But a resilient politics must combine a universality of law and mutual recognition among particular individuals; it must acknowledge "that man is by nature free (dass der Mensch als Mensch frei ist)."[71]

Following Montesquieu, Hegel's *Philosophy of Right* viewed the spirit of modern Europe, influenced by Christianity and the overthrow of slavery, as superior to that of ancient Greece and the Orient: "[In the latter] the division of the whole into classes came about objectively of itself, because it is inherently rational, but the principle of subjective particularity was . . . denied its rights, in that for example, the allotment of

[70] Hegel, *Die Vernunft in der Geschichte*, hereafter *VG*, 1955a, p. 62.
[71] Hegel, *VG*, p. 62.

individuals to classes was left to the ruling class, as in Plato's *Republic* or to the accident of birth, as in the Indian caste-system." Like Montesquieu, Hegel saw commerce as a vehicle for enlivening individuality: "When subjective particularity is upheld by the objective order . . . then it becomes the animating principle of the entire civil society, of the development alike of mental activity, merit, and dignity."[72]

But Hegel's theory articulated the differentiated structure of this individuality more deeply than Montesquieu's. In the introduction to *Philosophy of Right*, Hegel distinguished the moments in the restless movement of the rational will: first, the will's ability to deny its immediate contents and attain the "negative infinity" of rejecting all specific pursuits; second, the will's sunkenness in particular desires; third, its capacity – based on reflection on the *idea* of freedom (the actualization of freedom in the structure of modern society) – to choose a common good or pursue self-consciously affirmed purposes of its own.[73] Hegel identified the discovery of the universalizing aspect of the will with Christianity. The Christian notion of "free infinite personality" incorporated the (internal) emancipation of slaves and rejected the false Greek division of human and deficiently human.

Aristotle saw the capacity for deliberation as natural to the free Greek gentleman. Though we can see this recognition as a moral discovery, Aristotle, as I have stressed, did not. For Hegel, however, human history began in physical and spiritual subjection to natural forces and social despots. On his account, the first religions that worshipped animal life represented human self-abasement. Before the Christian challenge, slaves often similarly submerged their wills, opposing, at most, the exactions of particularly onerous masters. They did not recognize themselves as free – as individuals – or resist slavery as a general denial of freedom. But practical and philosophical reflection, partly inspired by Christianity, negated these unjust determinations.[74] Compared to Aristotle's circumscribed concept of (free male) prudence, Hegel's dialectics of the will embodies further historical discoveries about human capacities. The abstract, theoretical specification of the will's moments and the universalization of freedom distinguish Hegel's conception from Aristotle's notion of deliberation.

A further juxtaposition of Aristotelian and Hegelian eudaemonism may clarify the continuity of the modern theoretical project with that of the ancients, for a conventionalist might suggest that Hegel's theory is (almost) incommensurable with Aristotle's. At least, the sections of *Phi-*

---

[72] Hegel, *Grundlinien der Philosophie des Rechts*, hereafter GPR, 1970, p. 347.

[73] Hegel, GPR, pp. 74–103.

[74] In dialectical contrast to Hegel's statism, these political arguments emphasized an international, often nongovernmental movement.

losophy of Right on the will, he might argue, do not make continuity obvious. As a grain of truth in this criticism, Hegel's discussion, unlike Aristotle's, does not arise out of reflection about the role of intrinsic goods and virtues in a good life. Yet if we consider *Philosophy of Right* and *Phenomenology of Spirit* in the context of earlier eudaemonism, we can see that Hegel affirmed a broadly Aristotelian account of intrinsic goods: knowledge (philosophy's absolute knowledge, natural and political science as moments within it), political community, personal affiliations (though Hegel's endorsement of sexism rivals Aristotle's, his insights into the *substantial*, emotional life of the family and love are a theoretical advance), and the like.[75] Hegel's account of the dialectical achievements of the rational will captures, as it generalizes, the eudaemonist virtue of integrity. Though his vision of providence at work in human history contrasts with Aristotle's view, Hegel saw piety as a good. In this respect, Aristotle's argument might seem to resemble a quietist, anti-historical-progress version of Christianity, such as Voegelin's, more than Hegel's. Ironically for this contention, however, Aristotle's *Politics* counsels rulers, including tyrants, on achieving a common good; *The Philosophy of Right* offers no such advice. Furthermore, contrary to the views of previous interpreters, the foregoing historical interpretation of Aristotle's theory of freedom might suggest, in a Hegelian vein, that the cosmos sustains human moral discoveries.

However, Hegel's conception of individuality or self-actualization – the dialectical infinite–finite, suprasensible–sensible, necessary–contingent, and universal–particular character of the will – contrasts with Aristotle's idea of deliberation. Yet we may also view Hegel's notion of self-actualization as a sophisticated gloss on deliberation, participation in intrinsic goods, and enactment of moral character, one refined by the modern recognition that "all [humans] are free."

In this context, the Aristotelian notion of participation in an intrinsic good – one that instantiates but does not exhaust the good – illustrates the Hegelian unity of universal and particular, infinite and finite. Hegel also opposed the inequities that he regarded as flowing from a misapprehension of the will's negative or infinite character; for that negativity – he speaks of Hindu fanaticism and French revolutionary terror – could

---

[75] His complex if ungainly formulations on friendship and love reveal his insight into individuality: "This freedom we already possess in the form of feeling, for instance in friendship and love. Here one is not one-sidedly in oneself [*in sich*] but in willingly limiting oneself in relating to another, one knows oneself in this limitation as oneself. In this determinacy, a man must not feel himself determined, but insofar as he treats the other as another, he first experiences his feeling of self [*Selbstgefühl*]" (Hegel, *GPR*, p. 84).

Like Aristotle, Hegel compares humans to other animals; his claims about the distinctiveness of human will supervene on biological ones (Hegel, *GPR*, pp. 85, 88).

be pitted destructively against differentiated political structures and complex individual deliberations.[76] Like Aristotle's, Hegel's political theory and ethics require a prudent appreciation of actual conditions and an even greater emphasis on the diversity of individuality. A conventionalist might point out that Aristotle is more sympathetic to democracy and the intrinsic good of free political discussion than Hegel. But a realist may grant this claim; for it suggests only that Aristotle's theory has more in common with modern liberalism and radicalism, in this important respect, than Hegel's – a point hardly comforting to relativism. Yet Hegel's notion of individuality also specifies the sense of self-awareness and mutual recognition that is vital to a common good in a self-governing community. His conception could justify liberal and radical theories of democracy where they are otherwise true; it is not tied to Hegel's defense of monarchy and prima facie conflicts with it.[77] I will thus speak, with I hope a permissible license, of Hegel's *political* theory.

Finally, Hegel's demarcation between theory and practice resembles Aristotle's, but is more restrictive in terms of advice to rulers. The owl of Minerva takes flight at dusk and does not determine policy. Yet philosophy strengthens a certain rationality – "the rose in the cross of the present" – within politics. Whereas Aristotle sometimes characterized ethics as knowledge of particulars, Hegel rightly focused on Aristotle's contribution to a general *theory of cooperation and freedom*. Hegel's identification of the meandering dialectical thread of freedom in history discerned a more universal character in Aristotelian ethics and political science than Aristotle's formulation recognized.

Thus, Hegel's theory of the modern state sought dialectically to revive an ancient understanding of the common good in the midst of a seeming chaos of individual pursuits, characteristic of civil society. His *History of Philosophy* recognized how completely this contemporary activity could extinguish awareness of a public good: "In modern times, the individual . . . enjoys citizen freedom alone – in the sense of that of a *bourgeois* and not a *citoyen* . . . . It is the perfect independence of the points, and the far greater independence of the whole which constitutes the higher organic life."[78] Hegel's theory of the state articulated the "invisible spirit" of the laws or the commonality of "abstract right" that might reconcile such individuals.

---

[76] Hegel, *GPR*, pp. 77–9.
[77] More deeply, Hegel's discussion of the principle of subjectivity and decision, vested in a monarch, has an appropriate, but overly restricted form; it denies individuality in others and substantively fails.
[78] Hegel, *VG*, 2:209–10.

7. Hegel's two kinds of just war

In *The Phenomenology of Spirit*, Hegel traced the historical dynamic that connected the ancient and modern conceptions of freedom; he strikingly reinterpreted the relationship between master and slave, arising from a "trial by death" in war. When, like Montesquieu's Usbek, the master conquered the servant and forced him to do his will, he seemed all-powerful, one of the few who were free. Yet in the completed relationship, for Hegel, genuine freedom shifted to the slave. The original warriors claimed to be free and equal. In their struggle, however, the quality of recognition, between unequals, based on servitude, degenerated. Acknowledgment by a slave demeaned and dissatisfied the now dependent master. But through dread of death, through labor for another to transform objects, and through restraint on his own desires, the slave became aware of his (or her) power in the world and achieved independent personality.[79]

A sequential analysis of stoicism, skepticism, and the unhappy consciousness follows *The Phenomenology*'s investigation of master and servant and delineates the inward side of the slave's reflections. Despite Christianity's alien, otherworldly solutions, Hegel revealed its liberating aspect, its recognition of the slave's humanity.[80] But insight into a universal capacity for moral personality conflicted with the restricted community of ancient republics. Yet both features, the emancipating dynamic of slave revolt and the remembrance of political participation, characterized Hegel's dialectical appreciation of the limits and virtues of Greek freedom.

Montesquieu's and Rousseau's arguments against enslaving prisoners of war had focused solely on the master's mistaken claims. Hegel, however, treated this pivotal issue as an example of a struggle for recognition. His theory highlighted the ultimately self-destroying deficiencies of slave-based societies. In the *Grundrisse*, Marx would concur with Hegel's argument. From the moment, he suggested, when slaves grasp their potential as humans, that they are not "the property of another," slavery has only an "artificial, vegetative existence."[81]

In contrast to slavery, Hegel celebrated the personal freedom that is recognized by impersonal laws. Modern individuality could only emerge against a background of free political institutions. Such social individuality requires not only the securing of universal experience (education) but also determinacy – negation or the choice of developing

---

[79] Hegel, *Phänomenologie des Geistes*, hereafter *PG*, 1952, p. 149.
[80] Hegel, *VG*, pp. 62–3; Montesquieu, *EL*, 1:280.   [81] Marx, 1973, p. 463.

some capacities at the expense of others – and mastery of a chosen activity. Both sides of this idea are reflected in his contention: "Genuine originality which produces the real thing requires genuine education." Hegel had studied the new capitalist civil society, depicted in the political economy of Smith and Ricardo. Given a framework of universal laws, he concluded, this civil society *might* provide the appropriate conditions for the pursuit of individuality.[82]

Hegel's philosophy of history represented a theoretical advance on Montesquieu and fleshed out Kant's sketch of historical progress. Hegel took over Montesquieu's views on climate and the complex structure of the spirit of a people.[83] *The Philosophy of Right*, then, gave Montesquieu's judgment of the modern world, his defense of liberty and commerce, an internal philosophical analysis as an ethical universality combined with the recognition of individuality. In contrast to Montesquieu, Hegel restored the higher aspect of Aristotle's teleological biology: The growth of modern social individuality further reveals the potential of man as a political animal.

Kant had projected an ideal, noumenal categorical imperative that considered humans as rational and autonomous agents and as ends in themselves. His sketch for a philosophy of history contended that humans would gradually, by a secret teleological plan of nature enacted in their own "unsocial sociability" (*ungesellige Geselligkeit*), create a society in accordance with this ideal. Originating the second distinction in political philosophy, he showed that modern liberalism – and radicalism – does not rest on fictions about a given, presocial human nature, but on historical discoveries that reveal human moral capacities. Hegel, however, offered a more realistic, integrated historical and philosophical account of the emergence of social individuality. He construed Kant's categorical imperative as an abstraction from the general laws of contemporary civil society; such laws dictate no particular outcomes and enable autonomous agents, ideally, to treat one another as ends. Domestically, Hegel might have contended of Kant what Montesquieu maintained of Harrington: He "built" an ideal "Chalcedon when he had a Byzantium before his eyes."[84]

With regard to international politics, Hegel's philosophy of history also deepened Montesquieu's theory. He not only envisioned a law of nations that justified the waging of defensive war by sovereign states, but acknowledged the rarer phenomenon of a war between newly emerged, higher civilizations – ones that extend freedom and coopera-

---

[82] Hegel, *GPR*, pp. 334, 377–8.   [83] Hegel, *VG*, pp. 189–91; *GPR*, p. 66.
[84] Montesquieu, *EL*, 1:174.

tion and transform international norms – and lower ones. In *Philosophy of Right*, he characterized wars of the latter kind as "struggles for recognition in connection with something of specific intrinsic worth." [85]

Victory for the more civilized power represented a fresh advance of the spirit. Hegel's second type of justice in war dialectically reformulated Aristotle's conception of a war between free and barbarous regimes. His view resembled Aristotle's in distinguishing clashes of like or free regimes from those between unlike ones. It conflicted with Aristotle's because, given the existence of nonslave societies and Montesquieu's social theory, he recognized a *fundamental change toward greater freedom and individuality* within and between civilized regimes and incorporated that possibility into the theory of war. More forcefully than Aristotle's, Hegel's theory focused on the internal organization of a free people as something valuable that required defense; he did not stress a spurious "right" of the more civilized to use, for its own advantage, a supposedly inferior subject people. Thus, the historical changes and transformation of social and biological theory that divide Aristotle and Hegel embody moral progress in the development of individuality and underpin advances in ethical theory.

Nonetheless, nineteenth-century liberals like Mill would employ Hegel's distinction to justify wars of colonial conquest, the domination by European powers over nonwhite peoples. Further, European colonial practices often recalled the worst aspects of ancient slavery. Yet for Mill, paternalist "tutelage" must prepare the subject people for eventual freedom; he regarded colonial regimes as inevitably defective. Though an officer of the East India Company, he offered only a qualified defense of its role in India. Thus, he criticized the English regime's reliance on an oppressive Indian elite for counsel about its policies. He also condemned the forcible introduction of a Christian education under the pretence of "tolerance of religion." Driving such conclusions further, one might note, if colonialism mainly exploited the subject people rather than tutoring it, then Mill's civilization–barbarism justification would collapse on factual grounds. [86] Given Hegel's chauvinism toward Africa and Asia, his argument also has colonialist overtones.

Yet the distinction between civilized and barbaric regimes also enabled liberals, such as Mill and Kant, and communists, such as Marx and Engels, to argue that democratic revolutions had extended freedom compared with preceding absolutisms. For example, countering an English historian who saw in the French Revolution only the acts of malicious individuals, Mill defended this great upheaval not as a Gallic event but as a "turbulent passage" in the moral progress of mankind. The fail-

[85] Hegel, *GPR*, p. 496.   [86] Mill, 1977, 19:510, 572.

ure of that revolution might have "arrest[ed] all improvement and bar-bariz[ed] down the people of France into the condition of Russian boors."[87] Kant's vision was explicitly internationalist. In "An Old Question Raised Again: Is the Human Race Constantly Progressing?" he contended that the "disinterested" sympathy of many Europeans for the French Revolution demonstrated the "moral tendency of the human race" and the possibility of ethical progress: "This revolution, I say . . . finds in the hearts of all spectators . . . a wishful participation that borders closely on enthusiasm, the very expression of which is fraught with danger; this sympathy, therefore, can have no other cause than a moral predisposition in the human race." With striking political insight, the first article of Kant's "Perpetual Peace" foresaw sources of the sometimes considerable resistance of modern citizenries to war:

> If the consent of the citizens is required in order to decide that war should be declared (and in this constitution it cannot but be the case), nothing is more natural than that they would be very cautious in commencing such a poor game [*schlimmes Spiel*], decreeing for themselves all the calamities of war. Among the latter would be: having to fight, having to pay the cost of war from their own resources, having painfully to repair the devestation war leaves behind, and, to fill up the measure of evils, load themselves with a heavy national debt that would embitter peace itself and that can never be liquidated on account of constant wars in the future. But, on the other hand, in a constitution which is not republican, and under which the subjects are not citizens, a declaration of war is the easiest thing in the world to decide upon, because war does not require of the ruler, who is the proprietor and not a member of the state, the least sacrifice of the pleasures of his table, the chase, his country houses, his court functions, and the like. He may, therefore, resolve on war as on a pleasure party [*Lustpartie*] for the most trivial reasons, and with perfect indifference leave the justification which decency requires to the diplomatic corps who are ever ready to provide it.[88]

---

[87] Mill, 1859, pp. 56, 59–60.

[88] Kant, 1963, p. 144; 1795, pp. 18–19. See also Jay, Hamilton, and Madison (1961), *The Federalist Papers*, No. 4. The abolition of slavery, slave hunting, and the slave trade is a great completed example of international moral progress. Full-scale "pacific union" and democratic internationalism are, comparatively, a promise. Nonetheless, as a contemporary Kantian, Michael Doyle (1983), has argued, an expanding number of liberal democracies, however colonialist and belligerent toward outsiders, have, with few, early exceptions, yet to go to war with each other. In addition, as Part II of this book emphasizes, internationalism from below has been especially effective in republican revolutions at the end of war (the February and October Russian revolutions, the German November revolution) and in resistance to (neo)colonial wars (to the French empire in Algeria and Indochina; to the Portuguese in Mozambique, Angola, and Guinée-Bissau; and to the United States in Vietnam). See Gilbert, 1978a.

Juxtaposing the integrity of a democratic internationalism for which war is a "poor game" with the proprietary authoritarianism for which the lives of others are delicacies in a "pleasure party," Kant identified possibilities of international moral advance. Since only three republics existed in the eighteenth century (the United States, the French republic, and the Swiss cantons), we can see his vision of "pacific union" as extending across novel liberal and radical democratic arrangements.

In contrast, Hegel meant to justify not only the French Revolution but, retreating from Kant's internationalism, the Napoleonic era. The emperor had left his mark on Europe, for instance in the impersonal laws – the Code Napoléon – imposed on the Rhineland. In his *Lectures on the Philosophy of World History*, Hegel stressed the role of "world historical individuals" – Alexander, Caesar, Napoleon – who had submerged their own happiness to pursue relentlessly a new stage of civilization. Such heroes, he suggested, became the instruments of a new unfolding of freedom, a "cunning of reason." This claim is at least as dubious, from the point of view of a higher conception of cooperation and individuality, as his endorsement of monarchy; for it celebrates a single, great individuality at the expense of individuals and transforms a general theory of a modern political community, based on mutual recognition, into a particular negation of that community. But how can a society defend individual rights, say the freedom of conscience that Hegel upheld, and yet not sustain political freedom? Denying democracy and internationalism, Hegel's theories of political change and ideal institutions become antipolitical. His arguments may be extenuated only in their recognition of the difficulties of moral advance and the need for political leadership.

Now, much historical progress, as Marx would emphasize, is instrumental. On Hegel's view, however, alien progress – the only kind – realizes some goods too easily at the expense of others: It "treats other intrinsically admirable interests and sacred rights in a carefree, cursory, hasty, and heedless manner. . . . A mighty figure must trample many an innocent flower underfoot and destroy much that lies in its path."[89] As Chapters 6 and 10 show, Marx's account of a fundamental, qualitative shift in the nature of political and moral advance dialectically criticizes Hegel's conception. Yet despite its deficiencies, Hegel's depiction of the unfolding of freedom from the whim of the ancient despot to the engaged participation of some in the polis and to reflective, universal modern citizenship is a profound defense of moral progress.

Further, as Hegel saw, liberal arguments about wars between civilization and barbarism rest on *factual* claims – such as Montesquieu's analy-

[89] Hegel, *VG*, pp. 89–93.

sis of slavery, Kant's vision of the French Revolution and a "pacific union" of republics, and Mill's contention about colonial benefits. Hegel's philosophy of history articulates the ethical implications of such empirical claims when they are true.

Though Hegel defended capitalist civil societies, he adopted a darker view of modern commerce than Montesquieu's. Following Ricardo, he saw dangerous necessities in capitalist production, among them, the creation of a large class of poor through external, systemic conditions, not through any fault of their own. Capitalist trends threatened to transform the poor into a "rabble" (*Pöbel*) who would rebel.[90] Though Hegel recommended state intervention to cure poverty, he doubted that it could. Here, his actual condemnation of revolt contradicted the implication of his argument; for if the poor were blameless and victimized and no remedy existed, their rebellion would be just. Systemically nurtured distinctions of rich and poor undermine the state's universality, its claim to incarnate a Kantian kingdom of ends. Even more strikingly than Aristotle's discounting of helot seditiousness, Hegel's analysis of the poor stood out as an anomaly in his theory of the modern state's ethical unity.

Like Montesquieu, Hegel identified enterprising peoples who bordered the sea as the relatively progressive forces of history. He linked the element of risk in commerce to the sea's "flux, danger and destruction." According to Hegel, capitalist civil society creates a glut that its own markets cannot soak up. Overproduction drives such regimes to "colonization." Furthermore, far from making peaceful commercial advance, the intertwined, clashing interests of modern states could frequently engender war. Against Montesquieu and Kant, Hegel invoked the image of ocean storms that disrupt civil society's stagnancy: "Just as the blowing winds preserve the sea from the foulness which would be the result of a prolonged calm, so also the corruption of nations would be the result of prolonged let alone 'perpetual' peace."[91] Thus, Hegel empirically challenged Montesquieu's theory of commerce's pacifying effects and undercut potentials for democratic internationalism. Given Montesquieu's and Kant's claims about individuality, he suggested, however, the necessity of war might ironically cure the stultification of modern civil life, its submergence of deliberative citizenship in the satisfaction of private needs. Yet the internal tensions and ferocious international clashes foreshadowed by Hegel's account of capitalist oppression, expansionism, and war would undercut the modern state's

---

[90] Hegel, *GPR*, pp. 377–8.
[91] Hegel, *GPR*, pp. 379–80, 181. Montesquieu's account of English politics allows a self-chosen patriotism that his initial presentation of ancient, self-consuming republicanism denies. Hegel's theory is consistent – and consistently modern – on this issue (Gilbert, 1986b, pt. 4).

ethical achievements. Capitalism might lead to the material denial for most citizens, oppressed at home or wasted in war, of freedom's promise. In that case, the ideal Hegelian unity of universality and individuality would conflict not only with the social arrangements of slavery but with those of capitalism – "wage-slavery" – as well. Given the subsequent history of capitalism and a new social theory, Marx and other radicals would drive Hegel's ethical arguments in the direction of communism or what I will call "radical democracy." Through internationalism from below, they would try to reclaim Montesquieu's and Kant's vision of the possibilities of peace.

8. Liberalism, Marxism, and democratic internationalism

Michael Walzer has subtly examined the role of judgments about aggression in Marx's and Lenin's theories, a moral continuity with liberalism. But liberals and Marxians have engaged in a further unresolved debate, comparable to the liberal denial of Aristotle's second kind of just war. Walzer's account obscures the influence of conflicting social theories in the complex moral and political verdicts that divide them.

Marx judged the Franco-Prussian War of 1870–1 in terms of aggression. In addresses prepared for the International Workingmen's Association, he condemned first Bonaparte's and then Bismarck's "policy of conquest." A letter of Marx's to Engels, Walzer notes, suggested that German victory would ultimately lead to the international preeminence of the German socialists, who leaned toward Marxian theory, over the French socialists who did not. On Walzer's view, Marx could not publicly have defended such a comment. Faced with European workers' moral judgments about the carnage and properly influenced himself by the same "inevitable" considerations, Marx's speeches stressed the crime of aggression and were external to his general historical theory.[92]

Yet one can discern a theoretical connection between Marx's account of socialism and internationalism, and his conception of just war. His theory depicted German and French capitalism as exploitative regimes that engendered class conflict. Patriotic ideology, Marx contended, would deflect emerging socialist movements in both countries. It would encourage the workers to unite with "their own" rulers, result in their needless slaughter for others' benefit, and strengthen antidemocratic institutions and policies. It would nurture reactionary national pride in the proletarians of the victorious power and national resentment among the vanquished. Marx recoiled at the massive waste of life, the generally recognized moral fact about war, but gave it a new causal interpretation.

[92] Walzer, 1977, pp. 64–6.

He claimed that German and French workers had a common, democratic internationalist interest in opposing war and combating, from below, each government's "national" – actually, the capitalists' – interest. Contrary to Walzer, in evaluating the Franco-Prussian War, internationalist considerations, based on Marx's general theory, coincided with judgments based on the theory of aggression and governed their application.

From this point of view, even Marx's letter to Engels has a comparatively inoffensive reading. During the first period of the war, the German socialist movement acted on democratic internationalist principles more forcefully than the French. (That changed only with the Paris Commune.) Radical parliamentary representatives, Bebel and Liebknecht, courageously refused to vote war credits for Bismarck; the Prussian government jailed them. In this context, Marx could have defended increased influence for German socialism on internationalist, not on *German* or egotistical grounds. Walzer's contrasting liberal account treats capitalist regimes as genuine national communities and assesses only interstate aggression. His misunderstanding of Marx's argument pivots on an empirical difference about the character of these regimes. The foregoing analysis, however, shows how core judgments about aggression are *internal* to a Marxian view, even though other theoretical considerations may override them. It thus reinterprets Walzer's basic conclusion: Marxian *social and political theory* incorporates the theory of justice in war.

Lenin's analysis of World War I, as Walzer suggests, illustrates the continuity of liberalism and Marxism even more strikingly. Interimperialist wars, Lenin maintained, are "just on neither side" because only oppressors take part. Walzer cites Lenin's historically resonant analogy: "Picture to yourselves a slaveowner who owned 100 slaves warring against a slaveowner who owned 200 slaves for a more 'just' distribution of slaves. Clearly, the application of the term 'defensive' war in such a case . . . would be a sheer deception."[93]

As Walzer contends, we can follow Lenin in penetrating the imperialists' ruse only because we understand the theory of aggression. To reinforce Walzer's claim, one might suggest that Lenin used one criterion – his historical and moral theory of imperialism – to override another – a justification of self-defense for rightly constituted powers. This war, Lenin argued, stemmed from intercapitalist rivalry to determine who would secure the benefits from the racist oppression of non-Europeans. Which power immediately initiated the war became less important.

But a specific Marxian feature of Lenin's analysis, going beyond Wal-

[93] Walzer, 1977, p. 60.

zer's discussion, contributed to his *overriding* of intra-European charges of aggression: (Wage) slaves are distributed not only in the colonies but within the imperialist powers. Internally as well as internationally, capitalist regimes failed to serve a common good. Even if we abstract from colonialism's depravity, this consideration shows why the initial theory of intra-European aggression did not determine Lenin's final evaluation.

For Lenin, European regimes forced workers, farmers, and intellectuals to waste their lives in imperialist wars, victimized them economically, divided them by racism (Germans and Polish immigrants, English and Irish workers) and sexism, repressed them by judicial harassment and restriction of voting (the Prussian three-class system, the denial of women's suffrage), and the like. Even the parliamentary democracies were not self-governing; as Chapters 7, 10, and 12 emphasize, politically difficult prospects for democratic internationalism stemmed from below. If Lenin's causal theory is accurate, however, these social, political, and moral *consequences of exploitation* make a formidable case against capitalism. Only revolution, Lenin maintained, could fundamentally alter such regimes. One could broadly contrast Leninist and liberal reasoning as in Table 1.1.

I should note two qualifications to this contrast. First, the harsher the stress placed on the economic and political basis and moral consequences of rivalry for colonies – or on neocolonial domination and dependency – within a liberal theory (social theory premise (a)), the more wars between great powers appear unjust on all sides and the more nearly a liberal explanation and the corresponding moral conclusions resemble Lenin's. Further, for a liberal, the military and police ("national security") apparatus needed to sustain external influence would also undercut domestic liberty and democracy. Thus, even if world wars were avoidable or accidental to a significant degree, the terrible consequences for most non-Europeans and Europeans of an economic system that created a strong dynamic toward belligerence would require drastic social and political change.[94] Social theory premise (a) is therefore the pivotal one.

Recently Charles Beitz, Gerald Doppelt, and David Luban have criticized Walzer's views on the ethical justifiability of foreign intervention in unjust states. This disagreement also highlights the role of overriding empirical claims about international domination in determining complex ethical conclusions. If internal injustice is sufficiently extreme – for example, the case of genocide against blacks in South Africa – both Wal-

[94] If the contemporary Soviet Union has become an imperialist power, then on a Marxian – and perhaps a sophisticated liberal – account, only the form, not the content, of a potential conflict has changed.

Table 1.1. *Conflicting social theories and the evaluation of World War I*

Liberal argument	Leninist argument
Moral premise Wars of aggression by free peoples against other free peoples are unjust	Same as liberal argument
Social theory premises (a) Capitalist monarchies and democracies in their colonialist phases are slaveholders or extreme oppressors externally but not internally	(a) Capitalist regimes in their imperialist phase defend freedom and a common interest neither externally nor internally
(b) Wars between such powers are avoidable or accidental (generated, e.g., simply by the choices of politicians, not by the long-term dynamics of competing capitalisms)	(b) Over considerable periods of time (decades), the conflict of such powers in Europe and elsewhere to redivide the world will lead to war
(c) Intra-European wars of aggression can be separated from efforts – colonial or neocolonial – to redivide the world	(c) Such separation is neither theoretically nor morally reasonable
(d) Whatever oppression exists internally is less severe than colonial oppression and is relatively easily remedied by reform	(d) Through war and internal oppression, these powers breed forms of class conflict that require a revolutionary solution
(e) With comparatively little pressure from below, at least parliamentary democracies will frequently adopt internationalist policies; in democracies, nationalism and internationalism often coincide	(e) Democratic internationalism, sometimes appealing to uncontroversial international norms, arises mainly through protracted pressure from below, sustained by antinationalist (antiprevailing government) views
Ethical conclusion Some wars among the European powers (and the United States) are just on one side but not on the other	Wars fought simply to serve the governing classes of imperialist powers – almost all wars in which they might engage – are unjust; only civil or anticolonial wars against such powers are likely to be just

zer and his critics consider humanitarian intervention as – at least potentially – appropriate. They differ, however, over whether most Third World dictatorships are similarly unjust. Unlike his critics, Walzer contends that other states must treat these regimes *as if* they were legitimate:

> Politics (as distinct from mere coercion and bureaucratic manipulation) . . . depends upon shared history, communal sentiment, accepted convention. . . . All this is problematic enough in the modern state; it is hardly conceivable on a global scale. Communal life and liberty require the existence of "relatively self-enclosed arenas of political development." Break into the enclosures and you destroy the communities. And that destruction is a loss to the individual members (unless it protects them from massacre, enslavement, or expulsion), a loss of something valuable, which they clearly value and to which they have a right, namely their participation in the "development" that goes on and can only go on within the enclosure.[95]

Walzer rightly questions just who will exercize a morally based right to intervene on behalf of oppressed people. He infers, however, that his critics' abstract philosophy conflicts with due respect for internal political processes. Instead, he might – philosophically – have emphasized the character and aims of intervening states, their likely resistance to democratic internationalism.

Walzer's opponents, however, see regimes in most less developed countries as servants of minority, exploiting classes and foreign powers. Adopting some version of dependency theory – a variant of Lenin's theory of imperialism – combined with evidence about the repressive impact of foreign investment and military aid, they would, Walzer notes, liken Latin American dictatorships – say, in Salvador, Guatemala, or Chile – to South Africa. As Beitz puts it:

> Particularly in the Third World, one finds today a relentless pattern of authoritarian rule, usually carried out by so-called modernizing elites, drawing support from industrial rather than traditional sectors of society and often sustained by infusions of foreign capital, technology and military aid. Walzer's conception of the roots of authoritarianism seems grievously unrealistic: "the history, culture, and religion of the community may be such that authoritarian regimes come as it were *naturally*, reflecting a widely shared view of life."[96]

Cruelty overrides any claims on behalf of these regimes to be rightly ordered political communities even in Walzer's very relaxed sense. Offering other moral grounds to sustain Walzer's opposition to interven-

---

[95] Walzer, 1980a, p. 228.
[96] Beitz, 1980, pp. 385–6; Luban, 1980, pp. 240–2; Chomsky and Herman, 1979.

tion, Beitz warns that such interventions often slaughter innocents. He insists that putative communal rights – as Walzer also recognizes – must derive from individual rights. So his moral view sustains Walzer's. Alternatively, someone who shared Walzer's empirical qualms might note that Beitz's political economy, emphasizing dependence on the military aid and economic domination of advanced capitalist democracies, does not make *their* intervention promising. Internally, the critics might more appropriately envision democratic internationalist movements from below to check harmful intervention rather than governmental humanitarianism. But the ethical differences between Walzer and his critics are not deep.[97] As in the case of South Africa if not Salvador, a sufficiently oppressive fact of the matter would compel Walzer to concur with them.

As a second qualification to the basic contrast, a Leninist could plausibly maintain that even imperialist democracies might, under special circumstances, act justly. Suppose, for example, that in World War II, the Soviet Union, a socialist power, waged a war of self-defense against Nazism. Suppose further that Nazi genocide transcended ordinary cases of aggression and was an overriding evil.[98] In that case, if other features of Lenin's historical theory were true, the capitalist democratic allies of the Soviet Union would participate – perhaps reluctantly – in a just war.[99]

In applying the theory of aggression, Walzer's differences with Lenin turn on empirical issues in social theory. Situating Lenin's claims in the context of earlier liberal arguments highlights their philosophical significance.

Lenin's theory of interimperialist rivalry contradicts Montesquieu's and Kant's views on the pacifying effects of commerce. Compared to Hegel, Lenin envisioned an exacerbated internal class conflict and severed the link between war and the "health of [capitalist] civil society." Where Hegel employed the theory of aggression to assess many wars between capitalist powers, the theory of imperialism, for Lenin, overrode claims of self-defense. Like Hegel, however, Lenin recognized a higher right of civilization. Given social theory changes, however, Lenin suggested that revolutionary civil wars, wars to defend socialist regimes, and anti-colonial revolts – reversing the nineteenth-century imperialist image of "civilized" and "barbarian" – extend the basis for cooperation, freedom, and individuality.[100] As a further contrast to Hegel, that theory suggests

---

[97] Walzer, 1977, pp. 53–4.

[98] Walzer, 1977, p. 253.

[99] Especially given the previous pact with Nazism and subsequent Soviet political development, it is unclear that the Soviet strategy of alliances with great powers was the most plausible Marxian approach to world war.

[100] Reflecting the weaknesses of a class theory drawn from classical political economy and the need to organize for a political war, Lenin, like Marx, insufficiently defended indi-

the importance of international democratic solidarity from below, not (mainly) unconstrained state policies.

Reformulating Hegel's philosophy of history, Lenin's notion of a second type of just war might capture the objective unfolding of freedom. But depending on which social theory is true, Hegel's argument can defend either a liberalism of Montesquieu's kind or communism. His theory places Walzer's static analysis of just war in the historical context of conflicts over the recognition of a general capacity for moral personality and the social conditions for its realization. Now Walzer sometimes appeals to broad considerations about unusual regimes – for instance, in justifying English bombing of civilian Germans, the calculated murder of noncombatants – as a defense of civilization against overriding Nazi evil. Since Walzer does not distinguish two kinds of just war, he provides no theory of how such overriding can occur. Instead he treats genocide as an isolated exception to a general legalist paradigm.[101] Unlike Hegel's, his argument misses the larger implications of empirical social theoretical and biological controversies for advance in the ethical analysis of war.

A conventionalist critic of my argument, however, might note that Hegel's or Kant's philosophy of historical and moral advance rests on its teleological biology. If, as Darwin showed, plants and animals have evolved without any predetermined goal, modern science would rule out any philosophical understanding of human history based on the putative existence of *Geist*. The critic might add, if contingency governs natural history, why should moral progress occur or perhaps, even granting the foregoing argument, *continue* among humans? Furthermore, since Marx repudiated teleological biology and admired Darwin's view, Marxian theory should be especially receptive to this objection.

As we have seen, however, Montesquieu's and Hegel's argument for the superiority of modern liberal society flowed from its recognition of freedom, the nonrepressive character of its laws, and an accompanying burgeoning of individuality. Given historical moral discoveries about *human* capacities, one can defend these liberal empirical claims without reference to an underlying "plan of nature."

Similarly, Marx and Lenin could adopt Darwinian theory and formulate a conception of historical development, in which humans, at first dominated by their natural and social circumstances, undergo epochs of oppression and conflict, but finally create social relationships in which

viduality. He did, however, follow Marx in emphasizing an "all-round development of the individual" in communism (Lenin, 1960, p. 378). See Chapter 7.

[101] Walzer, 1977, p. 90. Murderousness aside, that allied civilian bombing undercut support for Nazism is doubtful.

their individuality can flourish. The ethical merit in these claims would stem from the empirical accuracy of their appraisal of capitalism and not from an arcane invocation of *Geist*. But Marxians could still offer their own dual use of the term "nature." The moral irrationality or, in Montesquieu's terms, the *unnatural* character of much of history, explained as the result of the unfolding of modes of production and class conflict in a "*natural*-historical fashion" – one that substitutes these causes for Montesquieu's *natural*, climatic reasons – would ultimately give way, through political effort, to communist relations; the latter reveal the self-aware ethical potentials of *human nature*. This unfolding of human nature does not contradict Darwin, but illustrates an important natural difference between humans and other animals. Yet this modern radical claim retains Aristotle's insistence that humans reveal their natural characteristics historically in their democratic achievement of a good life.

Chapter 2

The capacity for moral personality and the ambiguities of liberalism

1. Six criticisms of moral objectivity

The preceding chapter's analysis of Aristotle, Montesquieu, Hegel, and Marx on a common good and just war stresses (limited) objectivity and progress in political theory and ethics. Several generations of liberal and radical political philosophers have, however, rejected even a minimal notion of objectivity, let alone moral realism. This chapter will explore how the adoption of epistemological relativism by major liberal theorists undermines their central claims about the general capacity for moral personality. Such conventionalist views rest on important misunderstandings about the scope of moral realism, which I will seek to clear up. They also suggest six criticisms of objectivity:

1. *The objectivity as absolutism argument:* a sweeping requirement that a moral philosophy, to be objective, must lead to clear decisions across the board. This critic claims that a notion of objectivity can countenance no areas of vagueness, borderline or hard cases, but requires bivalence (every moral question must have a true or false response).
2. *The diversity of moral meanings argument:* a related notion that any historical variation or contemporary transsocietal failure of uniformity in moral standards cancels objectivity.
3. *The conflict of goods argument:* the idea that frequent conflicts among major human goods rule out objectivity.
4. *The nonexistence of moral facts and moral explanations argument:* a denial that historical discovery in ethics – broadly comparable to discoveries in other branches of knowledge – can occur.
5. *The internalist constraint on an adequate moral epistemology:* a claim emphasizing the specially close connection between moral belief and practice. It maintains that to understand such a belief provides, just by itself, a reason for action.
6. *The coherence of relativism argument:* the notion that metaethical conventionalism does not contradict liberal or radical claims about individuality, equal freedom, and democracy or, alternatively, about what ethics is.

70

The first five claims provide the most common arguments for relativism. The last responds to an obvious question about conventionalism as a sound alternative to claims of objectivity. I will begin with examples from the anti-Hegelian liberalism of Isaiah Berlin and Karl Popper and the participatory democracy of Benjamin Barber. I will then explore ambiguities about metaethical relativism in contemporary philosophers – notably Rawls, Scanlon, Taylor, and Walzer – who have a sense of the depth and *integrity of ethics* and find an objective point of view attractive. Finally, the chapter will emphasize the plausibility, within liberal theories, of an inductive, historical account of ethics and examine some sophisticated versions of the conflict of goods objection.

2. Berlin on freedom

Berlin's famous lecture, "Two Concepts of Liberty," highlights an objective liberal conception of individual freedom, an area of "non-interference" and privacy in which the laws do not obstruct individuals in pursuing their own purposes. He regards this good as a great, modern achievement:

> There seems to be scarcely any discussion of individual liberty as a conscious political ideal . . . in the ancient world. . . . The sense of privacy itself, derives from a conception of freedom which, for all its religious roots, is scarcely older, in its developed state, than the Renaissance or the Reformation. Yet its decline would mark the death of a civilization, of an entire moral outlook.[1]

For Berlin, only major political struggles brought such freedom into the world, and its persistence is endangered. Now, a realist might see the general human capacity for freedom and privacy as a modern *moral discovery*, akin to earlier ones. Berlin, however, wants to emphasize an ineradicable plurality and conflict of goods. For example, he rightly insists that great inequalities of wealth may prevent the poor from exercising their liberties and realizing their capacities. In this sense, greater equality might extend liberty. Yet, he also stresses, we should not (simply) gloss the sacrifice of the liberty of the currently privileged to gain equality for others as a "higher achievement of freedom."[2] Given such conflicts, he contends, no moral objectivity exists.

But Berlin's account of this conflict does not impugn the objectivity of the notion of a general capacity for freedom and individuality. Granting some sacrifice to the rich, equality might lead, as he also suggests, to a more liberal society. To push his example in one direction, no decent

[1] Berlin, 1969, p. 129.   [2] Berlin, 1969, p. 125.

71

person thinks the overthrow of tyrants, say the Marcoses – a real loss to *them* – is an important moral consideration compared with relevant gains in Philippino liberty. Though Berlin means to distinguish kinds of liberty, his description is unclear. If the formerly wealthy have full legal and political rights in a democratic regime, they have lost something, but has their *liberty* been violated?[3] Alternatively, however, even if we suppose, as Berlin does, that a broad group of beneficiaries loses some liberty, the discovery of the general human capacity for moral personality still underlies his recognition of the liberties and potentials of the poor. Doctrines of natural slavery, inherent racial, sexual, and class hierarchies, and the like reject his acknowledgment of this moral fact and assert the existence of distinct human natures. Consistent modern liberal or radical views must repudiate such arguments as false and, if implemented, monstrous; they must defend an equally sufficient capacity for moral personality.

Berlin, however, does not. In concluding the essay, he assumes an ambiguous, relativist stance:

> It may be that the ideal of freedom to choose ends without claiming eternal validity for them, and the pluralism of values connected with this, is only the late fruit of our declining capitalist civilization: an ideal which remote ages and primitive societies have not recognized, and one which posterity will regard with curiosity, even sympathy, but little comprehension. This may be so; but no skeptical conclusions seem to me to follow. . . . Indeed the very desire for guarantees that our values are eternal and secure in some objective heaven is perhaps only a craving for the certainties of childhood or the absolute values of our primitive past. "To realize the relative validity of one's conviction," said an admirable writer of our time, "and yet stand for them unflinchingly, is what distinguishes a civilized man from a barbarian."[4]

His observation that the liberal ideal of freedom has enjoyed only a limited historical reign is not, however, an argument for metaethical relativism, the contention that one moral conception cannot be rationally compared with another. He fails to distinguish between *factual* claims about varying historical achievements in morality or limitations on ethical knowledge at a given time and *metaethical* claims about the lack of objectivity of all such knowledge. To take a parallel scientific case, Newton and Einstein arrived at their theories in modern times; yet few think this a sufficient reason to be an "unflinching relativist" about contem-

---

[3] On a liberal view, private property in the means of production is a derivative, not a primary, right comparable to life, capacity for moral personality, and personal property. If concentrated property conflicts with basic rights, there is no *moral* difficulty in sacrificing it.

[4] Berlin, 1969, p. 172.

porary physics. Conflating these factual and metaethical contentions flows from a peculiar, though widespread misconception of moral objectivity. For Berlin, the objectivity of a standard must reflect either recognition by all historical agents or divine sanction: the *objectivity as absolutism argument*. In that case, any historical variation – including the crosscultural diversity of putative divine commands – requires relativism. But why adopt such stringent criteria for objectivity? All branches of knowledge are critical enterprises, characterized not just by adoption of common theories but by disagreement even over important features or consequences of theory, subsequent discovery, and revision. Why should moral knowledge, unlike other kinds, require universal concurrence?

Other ambiguities mar Berlin's conception. We may separate an appropriate dichotomy of religiously based absolutism or dogmatism (often false and morally harmful) and (a limited) moral objectivity, based on rational conceptions of a good life, from the common liberal opposition between absolutism (any claim to objectivity) and relativism (tolerance of moral diversity). Berlin fails to see this distinction. Instead, in the latter contrast, he rhetorically scorns the "childlike" or "primitive" certainties of "absolutism." But contrary to Berlin, it could simply be a discovery about a good life that, as Aristotle thought, Greeks had the capacity to participate in free forms of political organization or that, as modern liberals contend, every individual has sufficient abilities to claim at least a narrow, legally equal, public and private sphere of freedom. Such claims cohere with Berlin's accounts of freedom and conflict of goods; his metaethical relativism does not.

Like the views of many other contemporary liberals, Berlin's *conflict of goods argument* also confuses the acknowledgment of a plurality of goods with the endorsement of a relativist pluralism. But this notion of plurality appropriately contrasts only with that of a single underlying standard to assess such goods, not with the moral objectivity of the goods themselves. In addition, his argument neglects the possibility that under some circumstances, human goods may flourish together. As noted above, for instance, Aristotle's concept of deliberation respects diversity and conflict of goods but recognizes the possibility of concord. With insights into human flourishing, hard moral choices, and debasement, his eudaemonism is superior to relativist liberal views. The Marxian justification of communism, as we will see in Chapter 6, also appeals to harmony of goods.

Berlin differentiates a notion of negative freedom from the idea of positive freedom – self-realization – advanced among others by Hegel. He sees Hegel's political philosophy as pitting an ideal of a true self against a false empirical self and asserts that politicians can use this distinction

73

to abuse or torture individuals. But he does not sufficiently follow out his conception of "negative" freedom; for he also recognizes that the ideal of noninterference contributes to the realization of diverse human purposes. A liberal – to *be* a liberal – must acknowledge some instances of a common good, say the abolition of slavery or the enactment of privacy-protecting laws, which nurture the flourishing of individuality. Given this acknowledgment, however, why should the observation of conflicting purposes within individuals or societies – dare one say a Berlinian "plurality" of purposes? – and a justification of some at the expense of others require a nefarious distinction between a true and false self?[5] Precisely because of our insistence on autonomy, we recognize that the lives of a drug addict or torturer are bad ones. Ironically, as Chapter 1 shows, Hegel's philosophy of freedom and individuality provides the coherent, objective defense of modern liberalism lacking in Berlin's account.

3. Popper on moral advance

Touching on central issues in philosophy of science, Karl Popper's denial of moral objectivity displays instructive, related ambiguities. In "The History of Our Time," he contends that the capitalist democracies of the Atlantic community, though still defective, have advanced ethically beyond the level attained by previous human societies: "The story of the successful fight against slavery has become the everlasting pride of the United Kingdom and the United States."[6] This dramatic claim about abolitionism underlines the need for a justification of ethical objectivity and progress as an important component of Popper's argument.

Yet he offers no such justification. As a critic of positivist notions of verification, Popper contends that investigators can only falsify theories, not confirm them. He opposes any Aristotelian – or Kripkean – notion that we can *discover* the essences, or primary properties, of things. He is also skeptical about ethical truths and hesitates even to acknowledge

---

[5] Berlin, 1969, p. 133. Berlin's terminology is not Hegel's. It may be borrowed from Bosanquet, though Bosanquet distinguishes a "real will" – not a true self – from actual wills. A real will may be either an ideally fully informed one – a relatively uncontroversial idea – or a will conforming to the objectivity of the prevailing state. If by the latter claim, Bosanquet meant – as he seems to – more than support for legal relationships that sustain mutual recognition, then the notion is defective and paternalist (Bosanquet, 1965, pp. 110–11, 142–3). Modern psychoanalytic theory, however, inverts what Berlin sees as the harmful use of these notions: Families often require children to cultivate an, as it were, "false self" to please parents; a process of self-discovery is needed to overcome inappropriate influence and become one's true self. Contrary to Berlin, a substantive conception of individuality sustains liberal social theory.

[6] Popper, 1968, p. 343.

74

that given historically demonstrated capacities for cooperation, rationality, and freedom, it is *wrong* to treat humans like (other) animals. Instead,
in *The Open Society and Its Enemies*, he adopts the standard *positivist*
metaethical distinction between facts and values – a version of the *nonexistence of moral facts and moral explanations claim* – and rejects objectivity:

> The decision to oppose slavery does not depend upon the fact that all men
> are born free and equal and that no man is born in chains. For even if we
> all were born free, some men might perhaps try to put others in chains,
> and they may even believe that they ought to put them in chains. And
> conversely even if men were born in chains, many of us might demand the
> removal of those chains. Or to put the matter more precisely, if we consider
> a fact as alterable – such as that many people are suffering from disease –
> then we can always adopt a number of different attitudes towards this
> fact. . . .
>   All moral decisions pertain in this way to some fact or other . . . and all
> (alterable) facts of social life can give rise to many different decisions.
> Which shows that such decisions can never be derived from the facts.[7]

Through this argument, Popper hopes to stress the notion of individual *responsibility* for action because moral decisions are so important,
"matters of life and death." He wants the moral agent, like the Popperian scientist, to take action on what are essential bold, risky conjectures.
He sometimes appears to think of the open society relativistically as the
political and moral *society of conjecture*. Unlike scientific boldness, however, Popper hopes for political moderation precisely because cases of
life and death are not entirely matters of conjecture.

In this passage, however, he looks at the facts of slavery – or preventable disease – in a peculiar way and asks the wrong question about
them. The issue is neither whether men and women can enslave one
another (evidently, they have) nor whether some have defended this
practice, but whether slavery – or letting the sick needlessly die – is a
morally appropriate way to treat humans. Popper would respond: It
isn't! Slavery and preventable illness are not ethically neutral facts about
human relationships or about a good life *for humans*. If he were right to
disconnect facts utterly from moral judgments, then opposition to slavery would become merely a matter of opinion. But ethical properties
supervene on other properties. The nonmoral *facts* about human nature
would have to be markedly different for the morality of slavery to be an
open question.[8]

More generally, Popper defends the open society against the closed

---

[7] Popper, 1963, 1:62–5.
[8] Harman, 1977, pp. 17–20; Lycan, 1986, pp. 79–81; Sturgeon, 1986b, pp. 74–5.

society – tribalism, totalitarianism – on the basis of its moral virtues, its critical search, characterized by humaneness and reasonableness, for institutions that facilitate liberty and equality. If he is empirically right, however, are these facts morally neutral? In that case, to *describe* the open society is to reveal its comparative admirableness. For Popper, the term "openness" indicates a lively scientific intelligence, not generalized vacuity; the term "closure" a stultifying bigotry, not particular discovery. If *mere denial*, however, is sufficient to discredit the objectivity of Popper's judgment, as he avers – to make inhumanity, irrationality, enslavement, and racist elitism as justifiable as their opposites – then Nazism, once again, is as good as the open society. But given that we are human, wouldn't our intelligence appear dialectically in our *closure* against this alternative? Contrary to Popper's intention to defend moral agency, his metaethical argument undercuts any notion of *moral* responsibility.

Like Berlin, Popper makes ethical objectivity rest on *consensus*, appealing to the *objectivity as absolutism* and *diversity of moral meanings criticisms*. For him, *moral* objectivity could exist only if wrong never occurred, that is, if ethical action were, in Popper's sense, an invariant, natural law.[9] In that peculiar case, the open society would be the same as the closed society. Thus, the consensus criterion eliminates the individual *choice, freedom, and responsibility* that Popper seeks to affirm; it is, for a moral *agent*, self-refuting.

Popper denounces Aristotle as an enemy of the open society and an apologist for slavery. Like Berlin, he dismisses Hegel as a sycophant of the Prussian monarchy. Yet ironically, as we have seen, these theorists contributed greatly to the theory of human freedom and provided arguments that could sustain Popper's admiration for democratic regimes *if* his social theoretical and empirical claims are true.

4. Barber on democracy, reasonable compromise, and truth

Benjamin Barber's *Strong Democracy* spiritedly defends political action and participation as intrinsic goods. As opposed to the alienation of most contemporary liberal democratic views, their sanctification of popular apathy and the alleged wisdom of "experts" and officials, Barber maintains, "In strong democracy, politics is something done by, not to citizens . . . the creation of public ends depends on the creation (through public action) of a community of citizens who regard themselves as comrades and who are endowed with an enlarging empathy."[10] Yet curiously enough, this telling critique of many features of liberal democratic theory and practice still endorses metaethical relativism.

[9] Popper, 1963, 1:58.   [10] Barber, 1984, pp. 24, 25.

Barber characterizes the broad political condition to which strong democracy is the best response as follows: We are faced with "a necessity for public action, and thus for reasonable public choice, in the presence of conflict and the absence of an independent ground for judgment." For Barber, this absence of an independent ground protects the autonomy of politics. Philosophers, he suggests, mistakenly look to "prepolitical" norms, based on claims to moral knowledge or the search for "natural" features of human existence. In contrast, however, we should regard political action, though sometimes reasonable, as self-generated and artificial:

> Among the several components of the political condition, the absence of an independent ground for judgment is probably the most novel and most central . . . to choose and act politically is to choose and act responsibly, reasonably, and publicly, yet without the guidance of independent consensual norms. Where there is certain knowledge, true science, or absolute right, there is no conflict that cannot be resolved by reference to the unity of truth, and thus no necessity for politics.
>
> Politics concerns itself only with those realms where there is not – or is not *yet* – truth. We do not vote for the best polio vaccine or conduct surveys on the ideal space shuttle. . . . Laetrile and genetic engineering, on the other hand, while they belong formally to the domain of science, have engendered sufficient conflict among scientists to throw them into the political domain – and rightly so. Where consensus stops, politics starts.[11]

Barber confuses action *within* his strong democracy – action sustained by the recognition of personality and the capacity to participate – with political action generally. But if we have no objective notion of individuality, as he maintains, how can we see that liberal democratic theory's attack on "mass participation" affronts human dignity? Within a functioning strong democracy, Barber envisions a *reasonable* compromise among individual interests. He characterizes such an agreement roughly as nondestructive, an accord that most citizens could *intelligently and voluntarily* accept. But that claim invokes underlying moral standards of informed, free individual action and a common good that limit the (plurality of) results of justified communitarianism; for no such compromise can occur in systems, including formally democratic ones, where large numbers of individuals are not recognized as such. In cases of slavery, Nazism, or the systematic racism of U.S. cities in the 1960s, rebellion, not strong democratic talk, is a reasonable response.

Barber identifies relativism – the absence of an "independent ground for judgment" – as "the most novel and most central" feature of the political condition. This claim, however, undercuts a central substantive

[11] Barber, 1984, p. 23.

feature of strong democracy – its defense of political agency – and also fails to separate this theory from that of his chief polemical opponents, contemporary liberal democratic theorists – Popper, Berlin, Rawls, Walzer, Dewey – who almost universally endorse it. To justify relativism, Barber adopts a consensus theory of truth – a version, once again, of the *diversity of moral meanings objection* – and avers that where there is truth, no politics occurs. But truth does not require agreement, and without struggle, true knowledge often does not gain acceptance.

Since scientific method is theory dependent and complex, consensus among researchers is not necessary for truth. Einstein reasonably disagreed with quantum mechanics; he turned out, however, to be wrong. More importantly, cases where scientists concur, that is, on Darwinian theory, have not prevented findings threatening to particular religious claims or social interests from becoming political issues. Contrary to Barber's account, even authoritarian public enforcement of fundamentalism would not affect the truth of Darwinian theory. Furthermore, although Nazi race theories were known to be false, no reference to "the unity of truth" defeated them.

To reformulate Barber's view, one might recognize moral truths – including basic notions of individuality – but see them as external to politics. Yet following out that claim, we see that previous struggles for mutual recognition generate the particular *political* condition, to which if Barber is right, strong democracy – but also liberal democracy, Marx's communism, and what I call radical democracy – respond. Mutual regard is an inescapable precondition for democracy. Thus, the justification of democratic regimes requires a distinction of a sphere of moral *and political* truth – insights into the human capacity for public action – and a sphere of less determinate conflicts and results – reasonable "compromises" that do not threaten but, hopefully, facilitate individuality. Even this latter sphere has some determinacy. For instance, Athenian accomplishments in theater and science required the use of specific skills and resources. Given deliberated political choices, their distributions of goods (among citizens, in these respects) illustrated a good life. Even in the realm of plurality, there are independent standards concerning the intrinsic goods about which individuals and societies deliberate. The dialectic of comparative determinacy and indeterminacy in these two spheres of political and ethical argument captures the grain of truth in Barber's claim about "an absence of an independent ground" in some political judgments.

5. Rawls on slavery and democratic autonomy

Theorists of liberal as well as strong democracy – Berlin, Popper, and Barber – seem in the grip of widespread misconceptions about moral objectivity. But the arguments of other contemporary philosophers, who are tempted by realist views, display similar ambiguities; some have even moved recently in a strikingly relativist direction. For example, in *A Theory of Justice*, John Rawls vacillates between the objective claim that equality – an "equally sufficient capacity" for moral personality to participate fully in political life – is a fact about humans and the relativist argument that *this* sense of equality is merely "our" modern intuition. In his subsequent lectures on Kantian "constructivism," Rawls adopted Dewey's relativist account – a striving for equality and freedom characterize *American* public life since "let's say, the Declaration of Independence," but have no further, objective basis.[12]

He still acknowledges that facts about human nature limit possible moral claims.[13] If Aristotle's contention that large numbers of natural slaves exist were true, one might think it would rule out an egalitarian moral and political philosophy as a plausible view of a good life. In *A Theory of Justice*, Rawls appealed to specific psychological theories, and to a lesser extent sociological and economic ones, to suggest the stability of a just society. In a gesture toward objectivity, his Dewey lectures stress the exceptional character of changes in the theory of human nature and social organization that could affect our conception of a basic moral capacity:

> It is hard to imagine realistically any new knowledge that should convince us that these ideals are not feasible, given what we know about the general nature of the world, as opposed to our particular social and historical circumstances. In fact, the relevant information on these matters must go back a long time and is available to the common sense of any thoughtful and reflective person.[14]

The struggle against slavery – decisive to Rawls in his original contrast of a contractarian theory to utilitarianism – and other historical recognitions about the capacity for personality provide such epochal, ethically relevant information, accessible to "reflective people" and "going back a long time." Yet he does not consider these examples.

Instead, he inconsistently suggests that we can interpret such facts about human nature solely through a neo-Kantian prism: Ethical facts exist *only relative* to particular public conventions about justice. Through offering a sophisticated *denial of moral facts argument*, Rawls hopes to pre-

---

[12] Rawls, 1971, pp. 19–20, 46, 50, 508, 510; 1980, p. 578; 1985.
[13] Rawls, 1980, p. 534; Gilbert, 1978a. [14] Rawls, 1980, p. 566.

serve the integrity of ethics, avoiding an inappropriate reduction of moral concepts to others.[15] Further, he cautiously restricts such constructivism to ethics and politics, noting that his view may be consistent with realism about scientific knowledge. Perhaps because philosophers are still working out a thoroughgoing naturalistic theory and only beginning to draw analogies between scientific and moral realism, he does not see how to fit an argument envisioning discoveries about human capacities with a nonreductionist account of moral personality.

But a realist may turn Rawls's empirical claim against his metaethics: The historical *facts* about moral personality – manifested in a series of ethical discoveries – discredit Aristotle's thesis about the duality of human natures. In contrast to empiricist reductionism, as Chapter 3 shows, today's arguments on contingent identities of properties permit Rawlsian moral autonomy and naturalism; for the moral capacity to govern oneself and cooperate with others supervenes on psychological and biological properties: rationality, empathy and sympathy, life, health, and the like.[16]

Some contemporary theorists have claimed that no human nature exists. But as G. A. Cohen has rightly pointed out, radical and liberal proponents of a notion of human nature can deny the specific attributes alleged by reactionaries – the putative innate irrationality of slaves, workers, or women, for example.[17] In this regard, the appropriate liberal or Marxian metaethical responses appeal to the second historical distinction concerning the common good. Further, as a general position about human psychology, moral realism maintains that humans are intelligent, flexible social animals – they create and partially adjust to a diversity of regimes – but are not infinitely malleable. Realism is thus an antihistoricist, antirelativist view.

Within Rawls's argument, an objective claim about general capacity for moral personality underpins broader ethical potentials – for instance, those of the autonomous individuals envisioned in the "model-conception" of the original position. But contrary to Rawls's or Scanlon's version of constructivism, the core ethical discovery does not require a particular, worked-out theory of individuality. Instead, this underlying standard provides the basis for such theories. Thus, Rawls offers one elaboration: a potential to form, act, and reflect on a conception of justice with regard to others (the right), to create and revise an overall,

---

[15] For a recent defense of democratic convention-relative objectivity in political theory, see Rawls, 1988d.

[16] Railton, 1986; Brink, 1986, pp. 30–1. These moral properties are, once again, relative to *human* nature. As Hilary Putnam, 1981, p. 168, suggests, our ethical concepts would not fit easily cloned robots who could not experience pain.

[17] G. A. Cohen, 1978, pp. 150–1.

individual plan of life (the good), and to adopt a suitable – derivative – understanding of the relevant virtues.[18] An Aristotelian account has different emphases: the capacity to develop a particular character able to deliberate about diverse intrinsic goods in specific circumstances. (Note that the good of cooperative political activity overlaps with what Rawls means by the right.) On John Finnis's complex image, this capacity – called "practical reasonableness" – includes the ability to form a life plan with a harmony of purposes, to recognize intrinsic goods, to avoid arbitrariness in the treatment of persons, to detach oneself from particular realizations of intrinsic goods, to be faithful to commitments, to be efficient technically (in those aspects for which efficiency is an important consideration), to respect goods in which one chooses not to participate, and to follow one's own reason authentically.[19] Unlike Aristotle, Rawls and other moderns rightly describe this capacity as a range property possessed by all – or all but a very few – humans. In addition, recognition of this common potential requires no doctrine downplaying differences of moral and political achievement.

Scanlon partially recognizes the difficulties that moral facts pose for contentions about the *unique* role of a constructivist theory; he suggests that constructivism is indispensable in explaining such facts:

> There are also right- and wrong-making properties which are themselves independent of the contractualist notion of agreement. I take the property of being an act of killing for the pleasure of doing so to be a wrong-making property of this kind. Such properties are wrong-making because it would be reasonable to reject any set of principles which permitted the acts they characterize. Thus, while there are morally relevant properties "in the world" which are independent of the contractualist notion of agreement . . . their moral relevance – their force in justifications as well as their link with motivation – is to be explained on contractualist grounds.[20]

But Scanlon's account of the wrong of murder – "it would be reasonable to reject any set of principles" that denied it – though plausible, is not unique. A eudaemonist theory also explains this fact – the good of life creates the possibility of a good life. So do utilitarian theories that place great weight on the pain caused by death (except, perhaps, caricatures that would count the pleasure of the sadist). The deep weakness in utilitarian theory is, instead, comparatively subtle. In dire circumstances,

---

[18] Rawls, 1980, 1988a.
[19] For a parallel epistemological conception of a core notion of justifiedness underlying particular versions, see Goldman, 1986, pp. 58–9; see also Sturgeon, 1985, p. 28; and Finnis, 1980, ch. 6, esp. pp. 126–7. For a more detailed account of core standards, see Chapter 13. As I argue in Chapter 7, contemporary psychoanalytic theories of the self provide another important explication of deliberation.
[20] Scanlon, 1982, p. 118.

any reasonable *political* and *moral* theory will allow some sacrifice of individual liberty to preserve or extend central goods like life and liberty. In such cases, however, utilitarianism tends to sacrifice the fundamental moral goods – life, liberty, capacity for moral personality – of some to advance the nonmoral (or at best subsidiary) goods – for instance, pleasure – of others.[21] Thus, it misses basic features of morality and exaggerates derivative ones. Furthermore, Scanlon's central explanatory notion of a *reasonable* rejection is neither unique nor, more importantly, independent: It requires some core appeal to moral facts about noncoerciveness and the human capacity for individuality and rational agency.

Constructivist moral theory offers a skeptical response to skepticism, one that grants the skeptic's starting point of doubt about every ethical claim and then seeks to undercut that view through appeals to intricate theoretical argument based on a comparatively noncontroversial starting point. Particularly given Rawls's insistence on the integrity of ethics and the importance of democracy, however, this stance seems paradoxical; for such "coherence" theories – when they fail to acknowledge moral facts independent of particular arguments – are incoherent.[22] But a conjunction of two broad kinds of ethical claims – realist insistence on the objectivity of the basic capacity for moral personality and the forging of a contractarian theory to resolve clashes or specify the plurality of equally justified alternatives – would render such theories metaethically consistent.[23] To recognize ethical facts, as Scanlon and Rawls sometimes do, however, deprives contractarianism of one of its initial attractions: the claim that this kind of agreement *uniquely* overcomes skepticism. That acknowledgment makes moral insight and the reliability of ethical learning less dependent on any particular, abstract theory. Yet a defense of objectivity sustains the interest of constructivism. On a careful comparison with other views, that argument might still provide the best overall interpretation of the conflicts of goods and controversies about just social structure that spur moral theorizing. Rawls has recently interpreted his theory as a distinctively ethical and political pragmatism; yet Chapter 5 suggests that his constructivist notion of reflective equilibrium captures important features of scientific as well as ethical reasoning.[24]

Further, in a recent series of articles, Rawls has integrated *A Theory of Justice* into democratic argument. We may now think of the original position as embodying not only mutual regard among persons, but Rous-

---

[21] I am grateful to Will Kymlicka for discussions of this issue.
[22] R. Dworkin, 1975, pp. 49–50; Rawls, 1988c, p. 1.   [23] Rawls, 1980, pp. 565, 571–2.
[24] Rawls, 1980. This argument will not contrast overall eudaemonist and contractarian theories in detail. Though I favor the former, this book will only indicate some important insights of both.

seauan *political autonomy* – the capacity of each, as a free and equal member of an ideal sovereign, to deliberate on principles to govern social structure. These essays infer autonomy from a pretheoretical *overlapping consensus* among comprehensive moral, religious, and metaphysical theories. Rawls contrasts deficient Hobbesian views of rights-mediated competition among narrowly self-interested individuals with self-aware democratic ones, focusing on each person's political capacity and sanctioning the pursuit of plural visions of the good that do not harm others. Rawls's theory thus establishes a sphere of *permissible* conceptions of the good, excluding despotism, slaveholding, racism, and so forth. His political insight, concentrating on democratic autonomy, overlaps with a modern eudaemonist theory of individuality; for a *distinctively political* contractarianism best explains the central role of capacity for moral personality in democratic theory.

Yet precisely because autonomy is so important, its justification is more controversial than Rawls suggests. Suppose, for instance, that capitalist inequalities undermine equal liberty.[25] Then realized *democratic autonomy* cannot rest on an existing American consensus; rather, an ideal feature of that consensus – its commitment to equal liberty – requires a dismantling of capitalist institutions and greater egalitarianism. (Call this the *democratic-autonomy-driven* justification of economic equality.) In various contemporary liberal versions, Rawls's difference principle, Dworkin's equality of resources, Sen's promotion of basic capabilities, and as Chapter 7 shows, an argument for equal incomes all follow from this basic democratic – in today's context, *radical* democratic – critique. Just as Rawlsian political autonomy uncontroversially rules out slaveholding, so such autonomy may also exclude capitalism.

But then, our ideal, seemingly consensual notion of autonomy might justify sharp social divisions, pointing toward more democratic arrangements. In that case, Rawls's appeal to consensus about a purified political intuition is insufficient; for proponents of capitalism might say that given the comparatively weak justification of underlying agreement and *these* very threatening results, why should we not abandon our commitment to equal liberty rather than our admiration for entrepreneurship? They might invoke a *philosophical* skepticism to justify secession from democratic consensus. Although interests may motivate (some of) them, a democratic response must counter this rejoinder with reasons; it seeks to deepen agreement. Thus, moral realism stresses the *ethical- or political-autonomy-driven character of overlapping consensus*, one that shifts historically with important moral discoveries. In Rawls's terms, these discoveries must be accessible *within* the domain of "free public reason."

---

[25] Rawls, 1971, p. 226.

A democratic public can treat the main ethical inferences – for instance, about slavery as an oppressive institution – as part of ordinary common-sense and scientific reasoning rather than relegate them to potentially sectarian philosophical debates. In fact, these inferences provide independent standards determining when democratic agreements embody "very great ethical values" and prevent what Rawls calls the wrong kind of political convention (one that licenses the tyranny of particular interests). Now he supposes that many citizens require no fully developed political view to support democratic autonomy; they need only conceive themselves as self-respecting, equally free persons. That insight is a great attraction of *political* contractarianism.[26] *Epistemologically,* however, an inductive, realist account of autonomy explains its driving role in democratic theory and major political clashes better than Rawlsian constructivism.

6. Taylor on history and moral personality

Charles Taylor's "The Diversity of Goods" touches on a central feature of my argument for moral realism. He maintains that the modern recognition of the universal capacity for moral personality is "valid" and an important, though not the sole, feature of an objective ethical position. He also remarks that philosophers often assume this insight rather than integrate it into their argument. To explain this common omission, I suggest that the recognition of this capacity highlights a *negative* feature of a good life, or is, as Walzer contends, "abolitionist."[27] It rules out subordination of allegedly defective groups of humans and defends a social framework that facilitates the flourishing of individuality. Insight into this capacity is a deep feature of a moral view because, as noted above, its vitiation in slaveholding or Nazism is monstrous. Yet this central aspect of moral objectivity only provides a setting for individuality. Aside from the good of participation, important features of the politics of mutual recognition vanish in its realization.

As Taylor eloquently points out:

> Behind these Kant-derived formulae stands one of the fundamental insights of modern Western civilization, the universal attribution of moral personality: in fundamental ethical matters, everyone ought to count, and all ought to count in the same way. . . .
>
> In a sense, this principle is historically parochial. This is not the way the average Greek, in ancient times, for instance, looked on his Thracian slave.

---

[26] Rawls, 1988a. I am grateful to John Rawls for helpful discussions of how my view intersects with his political conception.

[27] Walzer, 1983, p. xiv.

But in a sense, it also corresponds to something very deep in human moral reasoning. All moral reasoning is carried on within a community; and it is essential to the very existence of this community that each accord the other interlocutors this status as moral agents. . . .

What modern civilization has done . . . has been to lift all the parochial restrictions that surrounded this recognition of moral personality in earlier civilization. The modern insight, therefore, flows very naturally from one of the basic preconditions of moral thinking itself, along with the view – overwhelmingly plausible, to us moderns – that there is no defensible distinction to be made in this regard between different classes of human beings. . . . But clear reasoning ought to demand that we counteract this tendency to slip over our deepest moral convictions unexamined. They look like formal principles only because they are so foundational to the moral thinking of our civilization. We should strive to formulate the underlying moral insights just as clearly and expressly as we do all others.[28]

He rightly calls for a clear historical account of this recognition but does not provide it. Instead, he vacillates between the qualified, though repeated, relativist assertion that the claim of universal moral capacity is "historically parochial . . . overwhelmingly plausible, *to us moderns,*" and "foundational to the moral thinking of *our* civilization" and a primary, objective contention that such a view is a "fundamental insight . . . very deep in *human* moral reasoning," and "valid." The moral realist argument of this book sustains an objective view of the latter modern contentions.

7. Fishkin and metaethical consensus

James Fishkin's *Beyond Subjective Morality* defends an objective metaethical argument. He draws an important distinction, similar to my own, between a requirement of morally absolute or inviolable judgments – the *objectivity as absolutism claim* – on the one side and a limited objectivity on the other. For Fishkin, absolute judgments have an unrevisable, apodictic character of the sort that Berlin and Popper envisage. Such judgments, whatever their source, are ones that it would never be right to override. Objective ones, in contrast, have a common prima facie rationale – for example, acknowledgment in *all* moral theories; yet given conflicts of important goods, the ethical agent may sometimes override them. Though Fishkin does not offer examples, one might think here of the prohibition against the taking of human life and self-defense against aggression. He rightly seeks to counter the self-undermining relativism often associated with modern liberalism.

---

[28] Taylor, 1982, pp. 130–2.

Fishkin usefully portrays the diversity of metaethical positions; yet he makes objectivity *relative* to the devices of abstract moral theories – for instance, Rawls's original position or the impersonal spectator of utilitarianism. He maintains that judgments are objective when "their consistent application to everyone is supported by considerations that anyone should accept *were he to view the problem from what is contended to be the appropriate moral perspective.*" [29]

For Fishkin, what counts as moral is the *consensus* or point of intersection of what *we* take to be ethical points of view. But what, a critic might still ask, is the basis for this alleged objectivity? Why should one prefer the endorsement of any of the particular devices of contemporary moral theories to a rejection of all of them? And why couldn't that rejection still count as moral? In fact, this critic's practical stance need not be obviously nihilist. He might uphold the prevailing morality with whatever elements of bias and oppressiveness as well as objectivity and reliability it contains. Though the critic cannot draw the needed distinction between these opposed aspects of ethical practice, neither can Fishkin's formal, theoretical-consensus definition of objectivity.

We might try to recast his argument more substantively. He appears to endorse a step toward universalization, or away from considerations reflecting an individual's particular circumstances, as the common component of moral viewpoints. Such abstraction is certainly an important feature of morality. If it is made central, however, the critic can still ask why. An appropriate answer would require reference to the oppressiveness of most social arrangements and the existence of harmful ideologies, such as racism and sexism, which, if unchecked by universalization, would lead to choices of principles that harm others. Stepping back from and questioning one's particular claims is *often* an important part of challenging unjust practices.

This principle is limited, however, in two ways. First, given the absence of an approximately true theory that highlights an injustice, merely stepping back, as Chapters 1, 7, and 11 indicate, is often not enough. For example, in ancient Greece, no theory justified the abolition of slavery. Despite his profound philosophical insights – certainly as much ability to "universalize" as Fishkin might require – Aristotle criticized only particular kinds of wrongful enslavement but failed to see the *general* wrong. Second, sometimes victims of oppression – for instance, the Spartan helots, whom Aristotle describes as "lying in ambush" for their masters – rightly detest particular practices without adopting a universal point of view. Universalization and a better social theory may deepen our understanding of helot discontent, but their re-

[29] Fishkin, 1984, p. 12 (my emphasis).

sponse was right, even though it lacked these features. In contrast to this refinement of Fishkin's argument, the basic substantive point about ethics still has to be a claim about general human capacities, which reveal past and contemporary forms of oppression and ideology as harmful. That claim is an inference to the best explanation among competing theories about such capacities. It is, in moral practice, a core standard, one invoked in all ethical theories but not a *formalization* common to such theories alone; for larger moral theories are about human well-being, not about themselves. Stepping away from one's particular circumstances is, as Fishkin suggests, an important critical principle of morality; it is not, however, an independent, self-sustaining standard. My version of moral realism provides an historical defense of what Fishkin properly calls "limited ethical objectivity."

As illustrated by the persistent ambiguities even in theorists like Walzer, Rawls, Taylor, and Fishkin, sympathetic to an objective view, metaethical relativism has enormous, diverse influence in contemporary Anglo-American university life. To list only some of its main tributaries, relativism appears in sociology, political science, and history, in Weber's conception of a "legitimacy" that brackets the question of whether any regime is in fact just or unjust, in historicist versions of Marxism, and in Foucault, structuralism, and poststructuralism; in philosophy, in empiricist claims about the fact–value distinction, emotivism, relativist neo-Kantianisms, Oakeshott's notion that theories of modern political association solely reflect *European* self-understanding, and Nietzsche's and Heidegger's interpretation of moralities as masks for a will to power; in literary theory, in deconstruction; and in anthropology, in common affirmations of the equality of cultures to combat ethnocentrism. A critic of realism might ask, Why aren't such relativist views simply right?

In response, the realist again insists that all these conventionalist assertions and ambiguities are self-refuting. Most recommend some political and social arrangements as superior to others on specific grounds. Yet they maintain metaethically that one moral view is ultimately as good as, or cannot be assessed rationally in relation to, any other. But if that is the case, then, varying the examples, why is a tolerant society preferable to a closed society, democracy to Nazism, just to unjust war, communism to capitalism or vice versa, human excellence to mediocrity, and so forth? If, more rarely, they endorse no practical conclusion, they still need to offer an independent characterization of what counts as moral.[30] The metaethical gloss is inconsistent with the underlying ethical and political argument. In fact, even the bare assertion of relativism provides, on its own behalf, no reason for its opponents to abandon their

---

[30] See Chapter 4, Section 1.

preference for antirelativism; moreover, given the integrity of ethics, this option is superficial.

Democratic Individuality defends a specific version of moral objectivity, one based on a modified Aristotelian eudaemonism. It maintains that participation in a diversity of intrinsic human goods – life, deliberation, friendship, political community, knowledge, play, aesthetic achievement, and the like – gives rise to disparate forms of happiness. It rejects utilitarian reductionism, which maintains that a *moral* fact of the matter exists, describable in a putative common quantifiable mental and emotional entity such as pleasure, about every individual deliberation or collective choice. Williams and Putnam have mistakenly contended that a realist view can leave no room for vagueness or unresolvable cases, translating the *objectivity as absolutism* into a *realism as absolutism criticism*. But this moral realism centrally distinguishes between cases affecting the capacity for moral personality and democracy and those in the broad, less determinate sphere of individuality. The latter sphere includes unresolvable dilemmas arising from conflicts of goods. (In such instances, either ethically compelling course of action, however strong its merits, has important, negative consequences in virtue of neglecting the alternative.)[31]

This moral realism is also eudaemonist in that it recognizes goods of character – integrity, respect for others, courage, commitment, and the like – and looks toward a modified Aristotelian theory of virtue. On this account, ethical conduct reflects a conception of and commitment to self – a desire to be a certain kind of person. It is an achievement of individuality, not an unreflective adherence to tradition or authority.[32] But a eudaemonist theory of individuality justifies actions whose motivations are not themselves moral: many kinds of participation in intrinsic goods, that is, science, play, and so forth. It thus differs from a Kantian view that makes morality a special motivation, set against all others, and moralizes too large a part of political life and individual choice. Dissatisfaction with utilitarian and rights-based arguments has led to a recent, diverse revival of neo-Aristotelian accounts of practical deliberation.

Yet these accounts are inadequate in two ways that this argument will seek to rectify. First, even when they accept modern moral achievements, they are insufficiently historical and fail to justify a liberal or radical position. Second, they provide interesting variations on Berlin's mis-

---

[31] Williams, 1973, pp. 204–5; 1982, ch. 2; Taylor, 1977, pp. 118–23.

[32] Wollheim, 1984, pp. 224–5. Wollheim spiritedly rejects the view that morality is "ultimate or overruling": "No one would dispute the total commitment to his art of a painter just because he occasionally took time off to get drunk or to go to a smart dinner-party, and did so without claiming that it would make his art either more profound or truer to life. I see no reason why morality should ask more."

taken theme that conflicts of intrinsic goods render any objective conception of human flourishing impossible.

8. Eudaemonism without history: Finnis, Hampshire, and Putnam

John Finnis's *Natural Law and Natural Rights* offers a sophisticated account of practical reasonableness. In a Thomistic vein, however, he sees intrinsic human goods as "self-evident." To justify this claim, he argues that it would be self-refuting for a reflective individual to deny the good of knowledge; in that sense, he infers, knowledge is a good for which we can and need offer no further justification.[33] But that negative argument does not require his positive conclusion about "self-evidence." We can also see the good of seeking knowledge as a general ethical *induction* from the intrinsic fascination of a variety of scientific, aesthetic, and philosophical projects and from its usefulness in ordinary life. In addition, although he emphasizes the basis of "self-evidence" in experience, his conception suggests too narrowly that any reflective individual – without historical limitation – could appreciate the diverse forms of human good. Contrary to Aristotle, however, Finnis opposes slavery and the subjection of women. But then, on his own neo-Aristotelian account, we cannot regard basic facts about moral personality and political community as "self-evident" to the reflective individual. Often, only lengthy historical conflicts make such facts plain. In examining political and ethical life as a whole, we require a notion of moral discovery that conflicts with that of self-evidence. More generally, today's arguments against a priori knowledge rule out an appeal to self-evident truths.

Stuart Hampshire's *Morality and Conflict* also defends Aristotelian ethics as the most plausible moral theory. He distinguishes between universal principles of moral argument – the natural features of ethics – and varying, customary ways of life – conventional features. Hampshire characterizes the former aspect as a "stripped down" view, an abstract notion of human nature common to a range of political philosophies. Only the latter aspect, however, guarantees flesh-and-blood individuality. His interpretation makes conventional features primary in ethics and stresses the conflict of ways of life, not moral objectivity. Yet his characterization of such clashes differs from other accounts; for he does not explain why diversity, just by itself, involves conflict – as opposed to, say, innocent differences – in the ways persons choose among intrinsic goods and express their individuality. Furthermore, his chief example of a conflict – that of Aristotelian hierarchical and Rawlsian egalitarian con-

[33] Finnis, 1980, ch. 3.

ceptions of justice – treats the issue of human equality and moral advance in a strikingly relativist way:

> In spite of this abstract and formal identity (an equal distribution of good things to equals), ideals of justice obviously differ greatly in different places and at different times in their specific content, that is, in what actions they specifically prescribe. Aristotle's ideal of justice is not difficult to understand, and his defense of it is intelligible as part of the whole way of life he is advocating, and also as a defence specifically of justice. This way of life, and this moral ideal, have as their centre the development of superior character and superior intelligence, and a superior political organization as the supreme priorities. Other virtues must be sacrificed to these ends, and a particular ideal of justice is required if these ends are to be obtained; unequal advantages to persons of unequal quality. In the modern liberal philosopher, Rawls, the same formal notion of justice, with its constant relation to equality, is employed to a contrary end: to prescribe that discrimination in access to primary goods should be reduced to a minimum rather than maintained, and this reduction is to be prescribed in the name of justice. The choice and pursuit of either one of these two conceptions of justice entails a cost in the loss of the values realized by the choice of the other.[34]

Hampshire recognizes that a modern liberal might deny "that any substantial human good is lost when the Aristotelian conception of a just society is abandoned. . . . On this second-order question Aristotle would be in agreement: not an irresoluble conflict, but a rationally justified choice between that which is finally shown to be the correct conception and the incorrect one." Hampshire disagrees with this objective metaethical account, because he doubts that one could embed an egalitarian conception in other ways of life without damage to correlative, deeply rooted virtues. But he makes this case too easily. First, he offers no argument to show that the abolition of slavery compromises important goods or virtues – does the ideal philosopher or citizen really have to be a parasite on slaves and women? Second, suppose we grant his claim about the loss of, say, tightly knit political community. Though such an account would undermine the initial liberal claim, it would not defeat a modified version. The liberal might simply insist that although some important goods disappear, gains in abolitionism and individuality far outweigh them. As Hampshire pointedly rejects slavery, his quarrel with such a neo-Aristotelian liberal is unclear.

Hampshire's comparison focuses on the wrong issue. Not singular ways of life but the possibilities of human cooperation, freedom, and

---

[34] Hampshire, 1983, pp. 147–8. Richard Miller, 1985, pp. 535, offers a sophisticated post-positivist, relativist interpretation of Aristotle's views. His localized, static account of moral learning avoids the issue of whether ethical discovery and progress are possible.

individuality demarcate the realm of morality. The Nazis had "a way of life" but not one, as he emphasizes, that features in the variety of plausible moral practices. A colloquial emphasis on "the mores" elides the fundamental political and philosophical issue of *which mores* are justified.[35] It frames the argument in a conventionalist idiom. But without a more general specification of what ethical knowledge is about, how could we even detect and compare diverse practices alleged (by us) to be moral?

Further, Hampshire's acknowledgment of a stripped-down core of human nature, common to many moral theories, conflicts with relativism. Yet it does little work in his argument. As he insists in comparing Aristotle and Rawls, the former did not recognize the good of individuality. Thus, a common conception of humanity from Plato to the moderns does not defend the central feature of Hampshire's view: a recommendation of diverse national and individual ways of life. Like relativist anthropologists, he thinks the fact of diverse cultures can do this. Aristotle, however, recognized diversity but rightly did not infer Hampshire's conception of individuality. Instead, though Aristotle sanctioned a range of justifiable regimes, he identified the deficiencies in nonpolitical conceptions of justice and despotisms. As a neo-Aristotelian liberal might suggest, whatever the range of just forms, many *unique* communities deny the individuality of their members and see no virtue in human diversity.

Like Walzer's defense of nationalism, Hampshire's account improperly conflates national ways of life and the individuality that sometimes justifies them. As a defense of individuality, a liberal theory requires a *historical* account of moral discovery and advance that reveals the cruelty of denials of human political and moral capacities and the error of theories of disparate human natures. To be consistent, Hampshire's neo-Aristotelian view needs to stress the continuities of Aristotle's and liberal theories – given modern moral discoveries – not their radical disjunction.[36] Acknowledgment of the general capacity for moral personality underdetermines specific choices. But no other good overrides this one. (He does not nominate an alternative.)

This recognition makes the natural features of ethics primary over their particular realizations; for the latter are not, from the standpoint of an ethical theory of individuality, merely conventional. That theory is an abstract account of social individuality and political association, embodied in a historical variety of complex illustrations. It is not, as Hampshire suggests, a rendition of bare universal claims contrasted with the (extramoral) richness of life.

In *Reason, Truth and History*, Hilary Putnam defends a version of moral

---

[35] Hampshire, 1983, pp. 154–6.　　[36] Hampshire, 1983, pp. 1–2, ch. 2.

objectivity close to my own. He recognizes the existence of ethical facts and explanations and exposes the incoherence of relativism. Yet he touches on the possibility of moral advance only at the conclusion of his book. His contrast of aesthetics, in which, he claims, no progress exists, with science, in which advance is evident, fails to situate ethics. Like Finnis and Hampshire, however, Putnam defends modern individuality as a modification of Aristotelian eudaemonism. His argument thus requires an explicit account of moral progress, which he does not provide. Though brilliant, his defense of objectivity also fails to emphasize the deliberation and individuality that are at the center of modern ethical theory. Consequently, he does not consider the role of empirical clashes in social or biological theory not only in the moral conflicts between ancients and moderns, but also in contemporary ethical and political debates between liberals and Marxians.[37]

Other adherents of an Aristotelian view have tended to dismiss modern moral and political life as relativist. In "What is Political Philosophy" Leo Strauss contends that later theorists lower their expectations about ethical conduct in glaring contrast to the lofty philosophical conception of the ancients. What he interprets as earlier versions of historicism, centering on mere life (Hobbes), property (Locke), and an allegedly unspelled-out, contentless freedom (Rousseau), once flowed like a great river toward modernity but have since exhausted themselves in the stagnant pools of contemporary relativism. Strauss makes this claim much too easy for himself by omitting modern achievements, like the abolition of slavery, cessation of the legal subjection of women, and the extension of democracy. (He leaves it unclear whether he favors these achievements.) As a Platonist, he says nothing direct about modern individuality. Considering the discoveries about the human capacity for moral personality embodied in such changes, contemporary liberalism and radicalism, though historical, have a strong, eudaemonist defense.

A similar condemnation of all postmedieval political thought as relativist, though coupled with an acknowledgment of specific modern advances, mars Alasdair MacIntyre's witty *After Virtue*. In a historicist vein, MacIntyre sees contemporary relativist moral philosophies – characterized as forms of emotivism – as emanations of the decadence of modern life. In their stead, he commends the revival of an Aristotelian conception of practical reasonableness and virtue, exemplified in such lives as those of Trotsky and Saint Benedict. Given his (extreme) relativism, however, he does not suggest that this older theory is a better elucida-

---

[37] Putnam, 1981, p. 176. His account of the Nazis' antimoral view also underestimates the role of conflicting biological theories, given common abstract moral premises. See Chapters 4, 11, and 13 below.

tion of moral features still existent in modern life (though what, then, would the virtues of Engels and Eleanor Aveling be?). This eccentric account fails to make clear what purchase Aristotelian notions – or, more accurately, neo-Aristotelian ones – could have on ethical and political practice.

9. Conflicts of goods: Wiggins on deliberation

As a second weakness, contemporary relativist versions of neo-Aristotelianism stress diverse features of the conflict of goods argument against objectivity. Such theorists recognize a plurality of goods and the virtues of deliberation; to deny objectivity, they must depict clashes as (almost) universal. But in their very recognitions, it is clear that such conflicts are not universal; they recommend deliberation, individuality, and the realizations of particular goods and deprecate their opposites. Hence their relativism fails. Nonetheless, the argument from conflict provides the most serious, distinctively moral basis for metaethical relativism and is worth examining in some detail.

For instance, David Wiggins skillfully portrays the complexity of practical reason and defends Aristotle against common utilitarian and neo-Kantian misinterpretations. He emphasizes the particular, ultimate character of individual moral choices and stresses the diversity – for him, almost an infinity – of goods that an individual must shape into a coherent ideal in a specific situation. Such deliberation requires neither means –ends calculations nor the uniform application of a rule but rather, as Wiggins rightly insists, an imaginative *specification* of a good life or of what those activities that generate happiness (eudaemonia) consist in:

> It is the mark of the man (or woman) of practical wisdom on this account to be able to select from the infinite number of features of a situation those features that bear upon the notion or ideal of existence which it is his standing aim to make real. . . . In no case will there be a rule to which a man can simply appeal to tell him what to do (except in the special case where an absolute prohibition operates).[38]

He fails, however, to demarcate the "special cases" of objectivity – where something like a general rule or "absolute prohibition" holds sway – from other cases in which the diversity of goods and situations promote highly individual "ideals of existence." Once again, denials of the general capacity for moral personality fall under the former heading. Unfortunately, Wiggins considers general features of deliberation but not specific instances of conflicts of goods. Nonetheless, his sophisti-

---

[38] Wiggins, 1980, pp. 236–7, 234.

cated Aristotelian account does not require metaethical relativism, and in fact, his admiration for deliberation contradicts it.

10. Walzer on relativism and democracy

Michael Walzer's important defense of contemporary democratic equality, *Spheres of Justice*, sees deliberation among an irreducible plurality of goods and conflicts between goods as central features of moral life. Yet he views these seemingly Aristotelian considerations as motivations for metaethical relativism. His account of conflicts is more finely drawn than Berlin's. For instance, Walzer contrasts the choice of ancient Greek communities to bestow their surplus on theater and of medieval Jews on education with possible investments by either community in shelter, health care, or provision for the aged. Who could say, Walzer emphasizes, that these choices, either internally or comparatively, were wrong? To specify their character, he summons an Aristotelian idiom:

> So democratic citizens argue among themselves and opt for many different sorts of security and welfare, extending far beyond my "easy" examples of public health and old-age pensions. The category of socially recognized needs is open-ended. For the people's sense of what they need encompasses not only life itself but also the good life, and the appropriate balance between these two is itself a matter of dispute. The Athenian drama and the Jewish academies were both financed with money that could have been spent on housing, say, or on medicine. But drama and education were taken by Greeks and Jews to be not merely enhancement of the common life but vital aspects of communal welfare. I want to stress again that these are not judgments that can easily be called incorrect.[39]

Walzer's relativist metaethical gloss, however, does not follow from these recognitions. His examples show only an indeterminacy or justified plurality in *some* major choices affecting a good life. No general rule exists for resolving the specific kinds of conflicts Walzer outlines; yet an objective distinction remains between extreme threats to life – his condemnation of Nazism is stark[40] – and enhancements of the quality of life at the modest expense of other goods. He invokes Aristotle's *broad* non-relativist conception of a good life. Given preservation of existence, that conception facilitates the description of many comparatively fine distinctions concerning the diversity and complexity of goods. Walzer's examples work because they involve serious ethical dilemmas. But he does not present acquiring more wealth to fund public performances through aggressive war as an appropriate Athenian *moral* alternative. More generally, his defense of democratic egalitarianism rests on straightforward

---

[39] Walzer, 1983, pp. 83, 67; Hampshire, 1983, pp. 41–2.   [40] Walzer, 1977, p. 253.

Aristotelian criticisms of the domination of money and the power of political leaders outside their spheres. Further, as opposed to today's sociological or group-based ("countervailing powers") versions of pluralism, Walzer's account is an innovative *eudaemonist and political version of plurality.*

Ordinary pluralism reduces politics to a fortuitous offshoot of interest rivalry. In contrast, Walzer's theory envisions the reasoned choices of individuals arising through conversation. If we supplement his argument with an objective justification of individuality, Walzer's account contrasts individual imagination with merely socially based "self"-interest, the nonreductionist rationality of individuality with an external, spuriously individualized "rationality" of social interests. His argument might suggest a further innovation in democratic theory; for the diverse cultures and histories of democratic peoples, insofar as they are noncoercive, affect otherwise hard moral choices. Even a genuinely free – nonslaveholding – Athens could still have affirmed the theater as an expression of who Athenians were. Similarly, as Chapter 7 shows, a better theory of the self can justify particular *individuality-based resolutions* of otherwise indeterminate choices. A sound justification of majority rule cannot be procedural – for substantive reasons must sanction a decision for one procedure against another – but arises from the importance, so far as the public arena allows, of furthering mutual regard and individuality. In complex, morally difficult cases, *democratic justifications* grow out of individuality-based justifications. Walzer's recent account of social criticism – of the way, for instance, Jewish prophets spoke a rich particular idiom – highlights the attractiveness of this insight into the thickness of popular traditions and their role in democratic theory.[41]

A eudaemonist account might also make Walzer's important notion of the "open-endedness" of social goods more explicit. In contrast to Wiggins, Walzer stresses the realization of only eight or nine quite general ones such as self-respect, community, and the like. The idea of open-endedness suggests that in different societies, diverse realizations of ethical goods may occur. It might also envision historical additions or deletions of categories of good. Thus, a modern view might question the existence of "divine grace" and reject earlier Aristotelian and Christian injunctions of piety; yet descrying moral continuity even in this case, it might still experience – as an important good – awe at the reach of the

---

[41] Walzer, 1987, ch. 3. Similarly, Rawls's account of the pride of a democratic people and his explication of increasingly resilient, persuasive, still not fully realized American traditions of free speech captures such traditions (Rawls, 1988a; 1981, sec. 12). A contractarian view inclines to emphasize central political traditions, Walzer's to capture common pride in other intrinsic goods. This difference reveals a merit in a eudaemonist theory of democracy as opposed to a solely contractarian one.

95

universe and the plenitude of life joined with the reality of suffering. A liberal or radical might emphasize the novel modern recognition of the goods of individuality and self-respect. Moreover, on a modified Aristotelian view of open-endedness, if the human good is a complex property, whose features occur in varied concordant configurations, a reasonable ethical theory might suggest that disparate societies would realize diverse features of that good. If we imagine a sharper distinction of Athenian theater and Jewish education – neglecting Greek scientific and philosophical education – we might take those traditions as an example; perhaps as David Wong suggests, virtue-centered moralities nurture quite different goods of character than more impersonal rights-centered ones. Following Hampshire and Berlin, one might insist on a diversity of configurations of the good; some historical changes or different social structures might entail balanced, but irreversible trade-offs. Insight into these features of the open-endedness and complexity of human goods mandates the empathy and tolerance that anthropologically oriented relativists rightly recommend.[42]

But in fact, neither past changes nor the potential for additional ones – for instance, the likely transformation of notions of moral character in a more androgynous direction – nor realizations of disparate configurations of goods in particular traditions cast doubt on the existence of a substantial set of intrinsic goods that humans have discovered. Instead, such claims underline the historical nature of these moral discoveries and open the question of the benefits and losses attendant upon modern possibilities of (some greater degree of) concordant realization and ethical progress.[43]

In this context, Finnis's account of a limited number of broad, objective human goods is superior to Walzer's or Wiggins's. Finnis speaks of such goods as *basic values* in which humans can participate; choices among them become self-consciously moral only when individuals or societies engage in practical deliberation. More pointedly than Walzer's, Finnis's account distinguishes practical reasonableness as a unique, cen-

---

[42] Boyd, 1986a, sec. 7; Wong, 1984, chs. 10–12. This argument also challenges Richard Miller's relativist account of diverse ways of moral learning about (roughly the same) social properties; for once again, if the properties are sufficiently complex, then different cultures might achieve insight into – harmlessly – different features of them. Miller also invokes some aspects of reliable moral learning within an isolated culture that are, nonetheless, no part of the human good – Yanomamo male fierceness toward women. But an adequate account of moral progress might leave other cases intact (Miller, 1985, pp. 532, 541).

[43] In bk. 19 of *Spirit of the Laws*, Montesquieu is particularly sensitive to this issue. The English realize goods of freedom, toleration, commerce, and patriotism based on a common good; yet their social life is abysmal. The French have a much more status-oriented society; yet their liveliness and gaiety are attractive. See Gilbert, 1986b, sec. 4.

trally important good.[44] Adopting that insight, this version of moral realism, focused on democratic advance, the complexity of the good, and individuality, modifies and strengthens a eudaemonist argument.

This reinterpretation of Walzer's contributions to democratic theory and eudaemonism points up a fundamental weakness in his moral theory and metaethical account, for ethics focuses on the concepts of a deliberative person and a democratic practice that facilitates individuality. Though Walzer's insights require a clear argument on these points, he touches on them only in discussing membership. Yet even his seemingly relativist reinterpretation of tyranny – political impositions that violate a "society's" sense of shared meanings – relies on an underlying appeal to a *nonrelativist* concept of individual integrity: "We are (all of us) culture-producing creatures; we make and inhabit meaningful worlds. Since there is no way to rank and order these worlds with regard to their understanding of social goods, we do justice to actual men and women by respecting their particular creations."[45] Not relativism about social meanings but respect for individuals as the – putative – creators of such meanings underpins Walzer's opposition to tyranny.

In this section, he extenuates even the ancient Indian caste system on misguided, seemingly democratic grounds. That regime, he contends, *may* have reflected the self-determination of each member; for it stigmatized landlord violations of "shared meanings," – for instance, their appropriation of too much grain at village distributions – as injustices. *If* outcastes accepted those meanings, some of which acknowledged their particular demands, and measured out their ritual distance from brahmans and kshatriyas, Walzer maintains, *we* must justify that caste system on grounds of self-determination. It is doubtful, however, that an articulation and defense of individuality – the basis of his argument – is consistent with the claim that, in a borderline case, the integrity of outcastes was sustained by preservation of caste regulations. He is critical of capitalism and defends equality; yet his social theory – both of ancient India and modern pluralism – underestimates the impact of great differences of wealth and power in maintaining a prevailing culture.

Here we can see a subtle linking of social scientific and moral relativism. As a democratic critic of capitalist hierarchy, Walzer underlines the moral, but fails to sort out the social theoretical, implications of these inequalities. As a metaethical relativist, he traces the internal radical logic of a single moral and political tradition – a democratic one, the conventions of "our" culture – but does not assess (in addition) conflict-

---

[44] Finnis, 1980, ch. 5.
[45] Walzer, 1983, pp. 312–14. Chapter 10 considers a variant of this argument in Max Weber.

ing worked-out social theories – say, Marxian and pluralist ones – of how serious the likely curtailing of democratic change by capitalist inequalities, suggested by his own argument, might be. Further, the justification of democracy depends on general recognitions about equally sufficient human capacities, not on imputations of popular support to (idealized, unusual) inhuman regimes. But a theoretical emphasis on free agency and individuality sanctions the plethora of unique social constructions and democratic diversity that Walzer wants to commend.[46]

Walzer's affirmations of human dignity and democracy internally undermine his relativism in other ways. For instance, he contrasts the rights not to be robbed of life or property, which have universal force, with "shared meanings" about other goods, which are "local and particular in character." He distinguishes an objective, though limited, theory of just war from a relativist account of distributive justice. Following Hegel, he even analyzes intrasocietal conflict between masters and slaves as mortal, implacable combat, not a set of pushes and pulls generated by diverse interpretations of "shared meanings."[47] The demands of slaves, Hegel emphasized, arise from their capacity (in themselves) for moral personality. In that conflict, the slaves manifest this capacity (for themselves). (Unlike Walzer's, Hegel's argument is explicitly neo-Aristotelian.) Now, empirically, the ancient caste system, as most liberals surmise, and capitalism, as Marxians maintain, may also be social wars. In fact, given Walzer's underlying moral criteria and different social theory claims, a Marxian eudaemonist might contend that a sphere of indeterminate, plural moral choices – those of Walzer's theory of distributive justice – would become less exceptional only in various forms of communism. But that empirical variant of his basic claim about war is hardly promising terrain for any version of metaethical relativism.

Walzer rigidly divides justice into two spheres, international and distributive, governed by different metaethics. But in cases of internal conflict like slavery, murder, or theft, the former, centrally moral understandings limit the latter. Walzer's relativist gloss and arbitrary demarcation obscure this interrelationship. An appropriate moral and metaethical recasting of his view – similar to that of Barber's, Rawls's and Hampshire's conceptions – would depict two internally linked spheres: one subject to universal claims about human political capacities and intrinsic goods, the other – sanctioned by underlying individuality – that flows from particular historical understandings, choices, and ways of life.

[46] Walzer 1983, pp. 302–3, 1988a, now recognizes the central importance of moral agency.
[47] Walzer, 1983, pp. xv, 250 n. 1.

11. Harman's inadvertent moral explanation

Gilbert Harman has offered a variety of important, mainly epistemological criticisms of any conception of moral objectivity. His arguments are, however, less substantive in political and moral theory than, say, those of Rawls and Walzer. Harman's "Human Flourishing, Ethics and Liberty" starts from the claim that conflicts of basic goods mandate metaethical relativism. His variant of the general argument makes the idea of human flourishing framework-relative, or perhaps even person-relative; one might dub his view the *vacuity of flourishing criticism* of objectivity. As a naturalist about scientific knowledge, however, Harman wants to restrict person relativity to ethics. He provides a sophisticated version of the *nonexistence of moral facts and moral explanations objection*. He also has an a priori view of what a moral point of view must be like. Yet as we shall see, his account of the struggle for liberty is inadvertently subject to a plausible, naturalistic (Humean), a posteriori explanation; it undermines his epistemological contrast of science and ethics. The next section will examine Harman's interpretation of the "internalist constraint on adequate epistemology" – the idea that ethical beliefs automatically provide reasons for action. After setting an argument for moral realism in the context of contending scientific epistemologies in Chapter 3, Chapter 4 responds to a telling conventionalist alternative, based on Harman, that grants many features of my account, but challenges its starting point.

Harman opposes any eudaemonist notion of flourishing:

> Of course, the mere fact of disagreement over values and therefore over what constitutes flourishing is not sufficient to show that there is no absolute flourishing, as opposed to flourishing in relation to one rather than another set of values. But it is difficult to see how one rather than another conception of flourishing is to be validated simply in "the nature of things" or in "the nature" of persons – except in the sense in which different sets of values yield different conceptions of nature or of the nature of a person.[48]

He contrasts, for instance, a vegetarian with a fancier of meat. To give this conflict of goods maximum force, let us grant that no fact of the matter exists, from a moral point of view, about the (objective) value of animal life that would either rule out meat eating or convince vegetarians to become carnivores. The good of full respect for animals, recognized by some and denied by others, is, to invoke a common relativist description, *essentially contested*. One might still ask whether such an unresolvable conflict would compromise the value of human life. Would it

---

[48] Harman, 1983, pp. 312–13.

make a debate about cannibalism – even of the already dead – no different from a dispute about consumption of other meat?[49] In fact, the good of preserving human life defines the idiom of the debate over animals, that is, the vegetarian contends that animals feel pain as humans do, the nonvegetarian that animals lack relevant capacities, and the like. Furthermore, the uncontroversial standard about human life shows the conflict in this example to be far less pervasive and ethically significant than Harman's argument requires. The appropriate conclusion from hard cases, even ones involving rare, essentially contested goods – that there is no moral fact of the matter within *some* important choices – differs dramatically from his unargued claim that we cannot discern goods from evils and, hence, that no conception of human flourishing escapes person relativity. (I will consider Richard Miller's powerful version of the conflict of goods argument against Marxian claims to objectivity at the end of Chapter 7.)

Harman's claim that moral conventions are simply a result of struggle suggests a poignant observation: Animals cannot comparably fight back. But the genetic fact that comparatively free societies emerge naturalistically as a result of struggles and not just because the powerful voluntarily adopt an abstract ethical viewpoint does not show that democratic regimes are not *decent* compared to alternatives. Their justification is independent of their genealogy.

As we will see, the same point undermines Harman's seemingly Humean account of the origin of basic rights. On his view, any claim to objectivity would lead to the imposition of "my values" on others – a form of "moral absolutism" (the *objectivity as absolutism objection*). He characterizes the basic rights we acknowledge as those to life, (personal) property, and religious and political liberty:

> Sometimes we recognize certain things as basic rights because they are immediately important to all (or almost all) people, as in the right not to be injured by others. But there are other basic rights which we recognize for different reasons, among them the right to liberty, including freedom of speech and religious and political freedom. These rights are not of immediate importance to everyone in the same way in which the right to life and noninjury is immediately important. They may be indirectly important to

[49] Even that great skeptic of prevailing moralities, satirist, and admirer of republican cannibals, Montaigne, did not defend that claim (Montaigne, 1922, 1:ch. 31). W. B. Gallie, 1962, and William Connolly have proposed the concept of "essentially contested goods." Though Connolly explores some important examples, this metaethical term exaggerates standard neo-Kantian claims about – sometimes slight – shifts in meaning, fails to show how any solely linguistic contest, just by itself, could be "essential," and rests uncritically on the older positivist and neo-Kantian semantics that Chapter 3, Section 7 will discuss (Connolly, 1983, pp. 10, 213–14, 225–7).

everyone for the sorts of reasons Mill stresses, but that does not seem to be why we recognize these rights as basic. What seems to be the crucial factor here is that often, when these rights have been denied, there have been *many* people who found the resulting situation intolerable and some of these people have been willing to fight the issue out. The basic rights of liberty have come to be recognized only as the result of these bitter conflicts.[50]

In this account, Harman appears to have some preconception of ethical knowledge as a priori; for any attempt to describe this struggle naturalistically – in terms of what we have learned about the way humans are – undercuts his claim about the "vacuity of flourishing." Now, Harman offers a tacit conventionalist, quasi-naturalistic explanation, based partly on Hume, of why the historic fight for these liberties occurred. He maintains that the preservation of life and property – insofar as the latter universally, though differentially, wards off harm rather than serves as an instrument of it – issues from the common needs of rich and poor. The other liberties, so he contends, at least do not harm the interests of either group. Yet only the poor would benefit from stronger duties of mutual aid and egalitarianism.[51] Hence, in the United States, common support exists for liberties of property and opinion but not for equality.

For Harman, this tacit conventionalist theory, because the motives it postulates are closer to our interests, provides a more promising practical account than the abstract Rawlsian original position. (Ideal contracting occurs behind a veil of ignorance about the particular social circumstances of the participants, though Rawls takes them to know, in detail, what human interests and social settings are like.)

But a critic might advance two internal objections to Harman's account. First, Hume, as Harman recognizes, thought that we could step aside from *genetic* explanations about interests and morally justify some bargains through sympathy. We might call the latter standpoint *Humean naturalistic justification,* one closely tied to the way humans are. Unlike Harman, Hume calls conventional arrangements that serve a common good "natural" (expressive of human nature), a shared feature of his "conventionalism" and Aristotelian "flourishing." Harman's anthropologically and psychoanalytically inspired reductionist reinterpretation fails to answer Hume's straightforward claims in ethical theory.

[50] Harman, 1983, p. 322.
[51] Contrary to Harman, Peter Railton, 1986, pp. 198–200, plausibly contends that this *pattern of variation*, notably the widespread recognition of security – protection from murder and assault – before political liberty and that liberty before social equality, suggests an inference to *some* common human goods as the best explanation. That claim counts as evidence for moral realism, not against it.

Second, a critic might object, Why doesn't Harman's account turn out to be an apology for what is rather than a moral theory that separates the good aspects of contemporary democracy from – perhaps minor – oppressive ones? Now, Harman could plausibly distinguish what is really a common good – glossed roughly as what many victimized people have been willing to fight for – from what is not. A Humean justification of these liberties rather than equality might then rest on a difference in the putative level of opposition by the privileged and the spiritedness of rebellion. Yet religious and political authorities tortured the defenders of liberty, even when they were many. But the temporary successes of inquisition, a Humean might say, did not justify spiritual oppression. Similarly, if deep inequalities harm most humans, the opposition of the rich could not sanction contemporary arrangements. And as the persecutions of modern socialist and communist movements in the United States and elsewhere show, equality, like liberty, has found courageous defenders.[52]

To separate liberals from more radical egalitarians, such a Humean would have to demonstrate that the claims of the latter, unlike those of earlier proponents of liberty, would, if enacted, harm most humans, not just the privileged (in their role as oppressors); for as a Rawlsian might insist, actual, though tacit, conventions are often exploitative rather than reflective of common interests. But again, sympathy might reveal that fact. A *Humean* tacit conventionalism may have resources, which Harman denies, to reach an evaluative stance comparable to Rawls's. Either account of a common good as a condition for realizing diverse individualities could defend liberty and justify or criticize – depending on empirical claims – economic equality. Both can see the struggle for equal basic liberties and some degree of social equality as central features of the historic movement for democracy. Thus, without some further argument, Humean justification, not Harman's genetic debunking, provides the better account of liberty's emergence.[53] Further, in democratic theory, Rawls's argument is superior to either. Ideal political autonomy is realized in explicit overlapping consensus on a common good ("the right"). Invoking a less democratic view of a common good, Humean views provide a weaker test of the lack of coerciveness.

Harman tries to find such an overriding claim. In the opening chapter of *The Nature of Morality*, he maintains that ethical, unlike scientific, observation is not subject to empirical challenge and plays no role in explanation – the *nonexistence of moral facts and moral explanations argument*. Contrary to his own epistemology, however, he sets up this critique in a residual positivist or falsificationist idiom; for in historically important

---

[52] Caute, 1979; Duberman, 1988.   [53] Harman, 1965.

cases, moral claims might contribute to the best explanations. In fact, I will suggest, on *his* initial account of morality, conceptions of the good life influence historical outcomes: "Many people have found the [suppression of liberty] intolerable and some of these people have been willing to fight the issue out." More deeply, as Humean naturalistic justification shows, these liberal conceptions appear to supervene on important psychological and sociological observations – that humans generally have sufficient rationality and desire to govern themselves, not be enslaved, and the like. *These moral facts* contribute to the historical explanation of why humans sometimes strive, against considerable odds, to achieve comparatively egalitarian, democratic societies. If we imagine counterfactually that humans lacked just the relevant psychological capacities, neither liberal regimes nor the struggle to achieve them would occur. Further, as Chapters 1 and 4 indicate, absence of these liberties – tyranny, injustice – may help to explain particular frustrations and resistances, even before movements for freedom of conscience and toleration became articulate and strong. The role of these moral observations is broadly comparable to that of natural scientific ones.

Contrary to Harman's positivist suggestion that such beliefs are not testable, their role in the best explanations is the relevant test.[54] His argument also leaves open the striking question, Why do people hold some of these beliefs so strongly? Harman's appeal to Freud – moral conventions are inculcated by a superego – is no help here. Not every claim associated with such socialization has like motivating force; we might well want to attack some (say, Nazi eugenics), debunk others (those of American Prohibition), and affirm still others (those sustaining religious toleration). As Sturgeon points out, to make good on Harman's epistemological claim, we would have to think that other nonmoral capacities and historical circumstances do *all* the explanatory work and that approximately true – Humean naturalistic – claims about a good life do none. But supervenience in the sciences does not work this way: Though the element oxygen supervenes on a complex microphysical structure, it has causal properties irreducibly relevant for combustion that Harman – as a naturalist about science – would recognize.[55] He

---

[54] Ironically, Harman also does not apply his own epistemological approach to specifying the difference between his conventionalism and metaethical realism.

[55] Sturgeon, 1984, pp. 58–63, 73. Harman's response, 1986a, pp. 63–4, comes close to acknowledging moral facts, yet denies them any role in explanation. See also Lycan, 1986, pp. 86, 88–9; Sturgeon, 1986b, p. 75. Richard Miller, 1985, pp. 526–9, points out that in neglecting the role of moral claims in historical explanations – say, of abolitionism in the American Civil War – Harman appeals to an a priori, quasi-positivist criterion: "From [Harman's] standpoint, when the question is what entities exist, the rule, in the final analysis, is to choose the sparsest vocabulary permitting appropriate derivations of data."

needs some argument to show that this peculiar nonexplanatory status of moral properties – as against other supervenient ones – is not just logically possible, but plausible.

12. Why internalism fails

Harman also reinterprets the *internalist constraint on adequate moral episte-mology objection* to realism. Many relativists think that ethical claims, just by themselves, have persuasive – emotive – force. To affirm one is immediately to have a reason for action. Their position captures the point that morality is practical. A view that separated moral beliefs utterly from motivating force, given the way human beings are – as an exaggerated objective view *might* do – would lose all interest. Harman's characterization of Nazism highlights the force of internalist considerations. It may seem odd to say that Hitler "ought" not to have committed genocide even though he was – given our conventions – evil; for, he notes, our moral judgment has no internal purchase on Hitler's motives.[56]

"In Externalist Moral Realism," David Brink has partially countered a common version of the internalist constraint. He maintains that noncognitivists cannot explain the quite plausible position of an amoral skeptic who understands ethical arguments but simply doesn't experience their persuasiveness. As Brink suggests, normal psychological capacities for sympathy are sufficient to make moral judgments motivationally effective for many people in ordinary circumstances.[57] Further, in contrast to a Humean alternative, though the emotivist view rightly stresses the practical character of ethics, it is a mere description and provides no explanation of morals' "emotive force." Thus, given emotivism's artificial reduction of ethics to desire, that view cannot sustain the claim that moral judgments are *importantly* action guiding, differing, say, from a yen for brussels sprouts, other things being equal. This substantive defect is too high a price to pay for definitional internalism.[58] On Brink's reinterpretation, moral judgments are action inspiring only to people of normal psychological disposition and, one might add, in favorable circumstances, where clashing, nonmoral or ethically overriding considerations are absent.

The idea of favorable circumstances highlights a difficulty in the idioms of "externalism" and "internalism," for any eudaemonist theory points to activities and relationships to which humans will be drawn for

[56] Harman, 1977, pp. 107–9.   [57] Brink, 1986, pp. 35–6.
[58] Lewis, 1983a, 1:8–9. Cognitivist Kantian versions, appealing to the substance of moral reasons, are more profound *internalist* views. Yet they rest on a characterization of who we are – rational beings – and are thus, from a bare emotivist standpoint, "externalist."

their own sakes. On that view, moral beliefs are often likely to motivate. Any eudaemonist externalism is, *in that sense*, not strong; it may also be seen, given human psychology, as an activity- and relationship-specific internalism. In another sense, however, contrary to emotivist reductionism, a eudaemonist realism emphasizes the complexity of *moral* argument and circumstance. Its proponents are, thus, unsurprised at how little political effectiveness the decency of most people often has.

Contrary to Brink's view, however, a follower of Harman might contend that Hitler was not a skeptic; he believed in the survival and flourishing of Aryans. Further, he may have had a – distorted – sympathy for "nondefective" Aryans.

But a sophisticated realism can powerfully counter this reinterpretation, for ethical noncognitivists mistakenly identify ideologies of a moral form with sound moral reasons; no reasonable ethical distinction, they suggest, can be drawn between these alleged types of judgments as reasons for action, since statements following conventions about, say, a common good or the moral thing to do, are just motivated expressions of approval or disapproval.[59] A Harman-like view, however, allows a reconstructed distinction. Ideologies are deviations from current bargains; convention-based claims may be sociologically, but not morally, true. In contrast, a realist view separates ideologies about a common good from true claims. Ideologies are partly parasitic for their activating force on the straightforward claims and normal motivations that provide moral reasons for action – advertising injustice, in the idiom of Chapter 5, as justice.[60] Thus, the Nazis did not deny core moral standards, the preservation of life and – a facsimile of – moral personality, for *humans*. Instead, based on a pseudoscientific theory (eugenics), they restricted humanity to (healthy) Aryans and overrode decency toward millions of others.[61] Discredit eugenic theory, and by underlying moral standards shared by the Nazis, they were monstrous.

Nazism also distorted genuine grievances – the Versailles treaty, the ravages of inflation and depression – through the lens of racist ideology. The perversion of these moral concerns, the projection of pain and anger onto racial scapegoats, enabled Nazism to lead a mass movement to gain power, to encourage, not just force, millions to fight in World War II, and to recruit perpetrators of genocide. It is no explanation, the realist might note, to interpret their deformed ethical appeal as definitionally a matter

---

[59] In a naturalist, externalist vein, once again, Harman, 1977, pp. 60–3, maintains that the motivating beliefs are charged by the superego.
[60] See Chapter 5, Section 7.
[61] Chorover, 1975, pp. 98 102. For a more complete analysis of the Nazi example, see Chapter 4, Section 6; Chapter 10, Sections 2–3; and Chapter 13, Section 7.

of preferences or to observe that a considerable number of Germans – far from all – came to share Nazi "conventions." Harman cannot show why *just this ideology* should have had so dramatic an effect, unless his Freudian account is joined to a sophisticated historical and ethical theory.[62]

But a realist can also invoke a complex psychological theory to distinguish the deformation of normal motivations in cases of evil from the – comparatively transparent – dynamics of morally justified actions. Such a genetic psychological theory would be part of a full-fledged, "externalist" moral realism. Further, a range of sophisticated theories is already available.[63] In the context of historical and psychological explanations of Nazism, a realist distinction between moral insight and a complex counterfeit ideology is far more illuminating than thin emotivist alternatives.

In this chapter, we have seen that widespread criticisms of moral objectivity, which influence or create ambiguities in the theories of many liberal and radical philosophers – contractarians, utilitarians, and eudaemonists – are not compelling. All these views, I have claimed, require a historical argument that the capacity for moral personality is an ethical fact about humans. I have also stressed several additional features of a moral realist view: an emphasis on distinct ethical spheres of democratic equality and individuality, the basic features of eudaemonism, the interplay of a reinterpreted Rawlsian democratic autonomy with a eudaemonist theory of individuality, a recognition of broad, comparatively noncontroversial (nonmoral) characteristics of human nature needed for moral argument, the explanatory usefulness of an externalist account of moral motivation including a complex psychological theory, and the like. These aspects supplement the epistemological characterization in Chapter 1 of the emergence of mature political and ethical theory and the objectivity specific to these disciplines, its analogy and distinction between historic moral discoveries and individual self-discovery, and its account of the underlying commonalities of modern liberalism and radicalism concerning the initial free regimes, the abolition of slavery, a common good, just war, and individuality. These characteristics set this version of moral realism apart, as a full-fledged account of *political* as well as moral philosophy, from recent, largely epistemological proposals, undermining empiricist distinctions between science and ethics, advanced by Boyd, Sturgeon, Brink, and Railton.[64] Chapter 3 also explores

---

[62] Nazism is a common, telling example in ethics. Yet a zeal for philosophical parsimony is no excuse for lack of relevant explanation. That parsimony – in Harman's and many other cases – is merely apparent, not well founded in historical theory.

[63] See Chapter 4, Section 1, and Chapter 7, Section 2.

[64] Boyd, 1986b; Sturgeon, 1984, 1986a; Brink, 1986; Railton, 1986. Aside from technical dif-

the impact of mistaken pictures of scientific epistemology in undercutting moral objectivity. There remain, however, important conventionalist criticisms tailored to my account of ethical progress, as well as Putnam's alternative, neo-Kantian interpretation of objectivity. Chapter 4 responds to these objections.

ferences, although some of these papers broadly emphasize social movements for equality, none specifies a *theory* of individuality, traces the relation of ancient to modern political theory, or accounts for the interplay of liberal and radical conceptions of democracy.

Chapter 3

Empiricism, neo-Kantianism, and realism in science and ethics

In political and social science as well as philosophy, affirmations of metaethical conventionalism often stem from broad philosophical arguments about what exists and the nature of our knowledge. Political theorists frequently marshal sweeping skeptical arguments that have no special bearing on ethics as if they licensed a restricted *moral* relativism. Worse yet, these broad arguments are often taken for granted or not fully stated; for lack of investigation and articulation, they haunt particular, implausible claims. A specification of these ontological and epistemological debates will help us to separate general skeptical contentions from specific criticisms of moral objectivity. It will also enable the reader to see that the case for ethical objectivity fits in with powerful recent epistemological arguments, ones not easy to dismiss. If successful, the example of a worked-out moral realism will contribute to the broader case for epistemological realism. Furthermore, it will allow us to assess the clash between radical and liberal claims about democratic individuality in a new context. For these reasons, this book defends a highly articulated version of moral realism.

Given the dismal current state of these debates in ethics and political theory, however, this project will require some fleshing out of neglected patterns of philosophical argument. Unfortunately, many contemporary philosophers have regarded ethics as a less interesting, secondary discipline. (As one of its main contributions, Rawls's *A Theory of Justice* galvanized deeper moral and metaethical debates.) They have failed to investigate the impact of today's postpositivist, especially realist, arguments in ontology, epistemology, and semantics on moral epistemology. More strikingly in the social sciences, the echoes of positivism, justifying various forms of behaviorism and game theory, and of Kuhn as a lone neo-Kantian alternative, predominate. Thus, many readers may not be familiar with a realist alternative or, however hotly realism has been debated elsewhere in philosophy, with even the main outlines of a *moral* realism. To set this argument's context, I will summarize the fundamental ideas of realism and ethical realism and then broadly contrast realist contentions with the corresponding features of positivism and neo-Kantianism. Since a depiction of the nuanced epistemological controversy about the natural sciences would require a separate book, I will outline important debates, citing more worked-out arguments elsewhere. This book provides a fully developed account for only the important case of moral realism.

1. A realist alternative

In ontology, realism is the claim that common sense entities and (many) nonvisible entities postulated by mature science exist, independently of our beliefs about them.[1] In epistemology, realism contends that in ordinary life and scientific research, over time, we achieve a complex, theory-saturated knowledge of a mind-independent world (universe) composed of such entities. In our interactions with the world, we learn from feedback: realism is a strongly fallibilist view. In semantics, realism is the thesis that our understanding of natural-kind terms is not mainly definitional and conceptual, but ostensive. Our ordinary inductions and scientific theories accommodate our terms to causal features of the world, give rise to more focused, intelligent definitions, and lead to more coherent practice. In mature branches of knowledge, a term can often retain a common reference to a particular kind of entity across theory changes, involving significant shifts in meaning.

Scientific epistemology – and inductions to ontology based on it – has been the focus of controversy about realism; for as empiricists emphasize, many of the kinds characteristically postulated by the natural sciences – subatomic particles, genes, and the like – are not simply observable with the eye. To be more precise, they are not "observable" except in their effects, though sometimes manipulable and observable with the help of instruments – for instance, microscopes and accelerators.

Furthermore, the inferences of a general scientific theory go beyond any humanly possible set of observations; its laws require a context of collateral information or auxiliary statements – including facts about instruments, laws, and predictions from other well-confirmed theories, relevant abstractions from particular circumstances, and the like – to be applied. In these senses, theories are radically *underdetermined* by evi-

---

[1] The notion of independence here is focused only on the objectivity of our beliefs: Mistaken views about the world or society can survive for epochs, and yet we can discover some of these errors. In another more trivial sense, however, almost all knowledge – true and false – is *our* knowledge, and thus not "independent" of human beliefs. I say *almost* all because animals know things also.

dence. On an empiricist account, the evidence for any particular theory, postulating nonvisible entities, can be explained by alternative theories, positing contradictory ones – the *evidential indistinguishability thesis*. The only way to choose between theories, positivists suggest, is to assess the theories' relevance to the manipulation of observations, together with additional extraexperimental criteria such as simplicity of modification (given the body of current theory).[2]

Realists, for instance the earlier Hilary Putnam and Richard Boyd, however, look at the evidential progress of science in a more dynamic, internal way. Thus, both ordinary life and science are characterized by important inductive successes. Empiricists, neo-Kantians, and realists alike recognize the enormous instrumental reliability of scientific theory and its experimental achievements in the prediction of observations and, hence, in technology and our interactions with the world.[3] But realist theories claim that the best and, in fact, the only coherent explanation of this success is that we acquire a deepening knowledge of the world. We have good reasons, the realist maintains, to think that the nonvisible entities that modern science posits exist and that contemporary total scientific theory, though we anticipate its future revision and refinement for particular, internal reasons, is preferable to arbitrary, abstract alternatives. As Shapere has emphasized, the latter alternatives provide no specific, compelling reasons to doubt current scientific practice, while that practice produces legion, plausible questions about such candidate theories.[4] Only imagined alternatives quite similar to current total science, ones resting on particular internal modifications, would even seem worthy – to scientists – of consideration. But then eligible alternatives – precisely because their attractiveness depends on their maintenance of most background knowledge, including a vast web of theoretical posits – do not help *generalized* antirealism. The standard, most straightforward empiricist critique of realism fails. The plausibility of novel realist accounts – a complex still-controversial matter – has to be assessed against that of sophisticated, overall empiricist and neo-Kantian views.

Now, other strategies for defending realism are available. For instance, Michael Devitt, in a spirited recent book, *Realism and Truth*, suggests that we settle the ontological issue of realism prior to any epistemological or semantic debate. Given the plausibility of commonsense realism, this view has some appeal. It rests on the success of everyday practice – of

---

[2] Even Quine's pathbreaking critique "Two Dogmas of Empiricism" retained these positivist conceptions (Quine, 1980, pp. 44–5; Putnam, 1975, 1:ch. 16; Gilbert, 1981a, intro., chs. 9–14).

[3] Taylor, 1982, pp. 105–6.   [4] Shapere, 1984, pp. xxxix – xl.

ordinary inferences "to the best explanation" – and the extension of this principle into science: If such inference works for observables, why not for unobservables and for more philosophical, that is, epistemological and ontological, claims? Yet in contrast to the version of realism sketched above, Devitt is quite skeptical about truth. He maintains that a reasonable alternative might combine ontological realism – the view that the world exists independently of our knowing of it – with epistemological skepticism – a doubt that we could ever know it.[5] Although Devitt ultimately finds this thin realism, which he attributes to Quine and Stephen Leeds, self-refuting, his interpretation concedes a great deal to realism's opponents.[6] If the case for epistemological skepticism is strong enough to be in the field after sophisticated, fair examination, realism appears much less compelling. It is one thing for a realist to acknowledge that some aspects of reality may be too complex to be accessible to our knowing, quite another to surmise that most, let alone all, are. The Boyd–Putnam strategy for justifying ontological realism, based on an intricate explanation of scientific and ordinary epistemological success, is a far more powerful account of the process of our knowing and its relation to the world. Similarly, my argument for moral realism is sustained by broad inductions from the history of human cooperation, freedom, and individuality and a complex account of theorizing about it.

On the realist view, theories in mature sciences are successive approximations to the truth. In this sense, realists – along with some others – hold a kind of correspondence theory of truth: We gradually accommodate our natural-kind terms – and to an increasing extent, our total knowledge – to the structure of the world.[7] Empiricists attempt to sort beliefs a priori into neat categories of knowledge and nonknowledge. In contrast, realists emphasize a historical process of reliable regulation of belief, characteristic of mature scientific enterprises. They maintain that our knowledge and method, because they are dependent on the contingent emergence of approximately true background theories about the world, dialectically become more reliable over time.[8]

Readers familiar with empiricism might expect that a defense of objectivity must arise from a contention that theory-independent observations are the primary feature of our knowledge and that the knower is a

---

[5] Harman, 1965; Devitt, 1984, pp. vii – viii, 3–4, 67–9, 73–5. In ch. 7, Devitt justifies realist inferences about unobservables. His worries about truth – ch. 6, esp. p. 102 – seem exaggerated.

[6] Leeds, 1978; Devitt, 1984, p. 98.

[7] Michael Devitt, 1984, p. 36, points out that positivists think that ideas – meanings – correspond to sense-data. That view is idealist; sense-data, on this account, are subjective and provide no evidence for the existence of an external world.

[8] Boyd, 1980a, 1984; Goldman, 1986, ch. 5; McMullin, 1984.

passive observer, drained of otherwise contaminating subjectivity. On the contrary, however, for the realist, perceptual knowledge is caused by active interaction with external objects. This conception stresses the role of theory and the dependence of the observational successes of science on theoretical knowledge.

More generally, as Quine, Shapere, Boyd, and Devitt have stressed, contemporary realism rejects all foundational approaches to the study of epistemology, whether drawn from metaphysics or philosophy of language. It seeks to study how modern science and ethics learn about the world and simultaneously learn how to learn. Its philosophical inferences about the knowledge-seeking enterprise, metaphysics, and semantics are thus strongly *naturalized to,* not restrictive of, the process of our knowing. Humans start out from some successful, relevant beliefs in particular areas of knowledge and, through a complex, historical, "bootstrapping" process, arrive at others. Over time, the nature of particular branches or domains, the sophistication of theories, and the notion of what counts as a sound argument all change dramatically. Through the process of theoretical investigation, new domains, exploring different, more explicit questions and relationships, emerge – say, the forging of a sophisticated economic theory in the eighteenth century or a unified theory of electricity and magnetism in the eighteenth and nineteenth or psychoanalysis in the twentieth. The progress of our knowledge is uneven.[9]

Empiricist and neo-Kantian philosophers often claim to establish general, regulative standards in epistemology – for example, about guidance by naked-eye observation or about the paradigm-based conventionalism of facts (the contention that all facts are theory relative, "produced" by our intellectual categories) – before they study actual scientific investigation. But it is doubtful that such contentions are significantly a priori; they are more like misguided examinations of complex experiences, such as the dramatic changes in twentieth-century physics, which lead to one-sided specifications of scientific method.[10] In contrast, realists maintain that our standards of method and knowledge are heavily shaped by our practical successes and are multidimensional; hence, our criteria of rationality unfold historically. Epistemological and ontological realism are, once again, inductions – or as explanatory theses, abductions – based on the actual explanatory successes of science. They do not seek to be regulative except in the nontrivial sense of oppos-

---

[9] Quine, 1969, ch. 3; Boyd, 1980; Shapere, 1982; 1984, pp. 273–6, 350–1; Devitt, 1984, pp. 51–2, 63–9; Sturgeon, 1985, pp. 26–33.

[10] McMullin, 1984, p. 210. Particular empiricists and neo-Kantians are sometimes sympathetic to naturalism, but their a priori isolation of features of scientific investigation – evidence, theoretical presupposition – gets in the way.

ing the distortion of research by a priori epistemological strictures. Yet anyone familiar with the history of behaviorism in the social sciences and its often curious pronouncements on what counts as "meaningful" investigation will understand the practical importance of adopting a realist epistemology; for as Part II of this book shows, in failing to grasp the theoretical clashes relevant in the current state of social science, such methodologies have obstructed promising lines of research.

In fact, the naturalism or internal, dialectical emphasis of modern realism emerges most clearly in the claim that the existence of successful scientific method depends on the logically, epistemologically, and historically *contingent* discovery of approximately true theories and background beliefs about the way the world is. Thus, contemporary realism, contrary to earlier versions – that of J. J. C. Smart, for example – does not accept the empiricist account of scientific method and evidence and merely countenance more entities (nonvisible ones) than positivists do.[11] Instead, it insists that the discovery and refinement of approximately true theories in turn shapes our methods.

Against empiricism, neo-Kantians also emphasize the theory saturation of those methods. But in contrast to realists, they then ask, How can we construe such theory-dependent methods in any way other than as constructions? How could these methods not *simply* be conventional artifacts of our theories? This epistemology, however, fails to explain the instrumental reliability that neo-Kantians otherwise recognize. To paraphrase an example of Boyd's, Do scientists sometimes successfully send rockets to the moon because the paradigm of a rocket is moon homing and crash resistant? An alternative induction about a theory-saturated method is possible: one that emphasizes the discovery of approximately true theories about the structure of the world that enable us to interact with it in new ways. Yet much debate in philosophy and social science between empiricists and neo-Kantians has unfortunately ignored this plausible alternative.

To head off a common, antiempiricist misunderstanding of realism, I should note that a misguided "copy theory of ideas" is sometimes taken to infect the notion of a "fact" – facts are then supposed to be isolated entities (or sense impressions) that our ideas passively reproduce. But on the realist account, an active, long-standing theoretical project is needed, say, to identify oxygen and explain its role in combustion or to discover the general human capacity for moral personality and differentiate a range of decent societies from intolerable ones. Claims about oxygen and moral capacity rest on a web of theoretical claims; we do not learn about them as isolated entities. Yet the respective phenomena ex-

---

[11] Smart, 1963; Boyd, 1984, p. 42.

ist; they are facts about the world that contribute to important scientific, historical, and ethical explanations and practices. On a realist view, the terms "oxygen" and "moral personality" refer to independent entities or properties, whereas such terms as "phlogiston" and "natural slave" do not. More generally, the modern semantic theory of *reference,* due to Putnam, Kripke, and Boyd, replaces an implausible, quasi-empiricist "copy theory" with a notion of the *epistemic access* provided by our terms to particular aspects of the world.[12]

The theories in which these facts or discoveries are embedded are complete in regard to certain questions, incomplete in regard to others. The respects in which theories are complete – for instance, the ethical claim that humans generally have the capacity for moral personality – are comparatively unlikely to be fundamentally revised. Now, the history of modern science has shown the need to alter many views previously taken as basic. But as Shapere suggests, the appropriate induction from this fact – the notion that doubt may arise in relation to any of our views – is not a specific source of concern about any well-founded conclusion and does not alter the central distinction, internal to science and ethics, between such conclusions and hypothetical or difficult cases. Nonetheless, a realist argument need not see any mature scientific discovery, theory, or definition of a domain of inquiry as final and exhaustive, but merely as one that specifies and answers some – perhaps many – important questions.

2. The justification and decline of positivism

A brief rehearsal of the recent history of debates in philosophy of science, with specific examples, will help to clarify the polemical point of realist conceptions (Table 3.1). In the 1930s, logical positivists tried to explain the instrumental success of science by emphasizing the role of theory-neutral observations and public agreement both about them and about the meaning of concepts. Their philosophical theory attractively highlighted the long-standing empiricist emphasis (Bacon, Boyle) on experiment in the modern scientific revolution. They also hoped to rule out, as metaphysical, ideas or branches of study that – they claimed – investigators could not subject to observational testing. Thus, they proposed the verificationist criterion of meaning, captured in the slogan "the meaning of a statement is its method of verification," as a *metaphysics filter* to sort meaningful from meaningless statements. Put differently, positivists contended that ordinary language, including moral and even scientific language, was too vague. That language required "rational re-

[12] Putnam, 1975, 2:chs. 11–13; Kripke, 1980; Boyd, 1979, 1984, 1986a.

Table 3.1. *Leading epistemological differences*

Contemporary representatives in science[a]

Empiricism	Carnap, Feigl, Hempel, Fine,[b] Van Fraasen
Neo-Kantianism	Kuhn, Feyerabend, L. Laudan
Realism	Boyd, earlier Putnam, Goldman, Shapere (except in semantics), Miller, Hacking, Lewis, McMullin

Contemporary representatives in ethics

Empiricism	Moore, Brandt, Stevenson, Mackie
Neo-Kantianism	Rorty; solely in ethics: Walzer, Rawls, Harman[c]
Realism	Boyd, Sturgeon, Railton, Brink

Characterization of driving force of scientific method

Empiricism	Puts an a priori stress on naked-eye observation; occasional naturalism about discovery Chief induction: from success of scientific experiment to primacy of observation over theory
Neo-Kantianism	Places a priori emphasis on paradigm relativism; facts and observations are radically governed by scientific theories; some naturalism about the role of theory conflict in the history of science Chief induction: based on an internal critique of empiricist epistemology, a neo-Kantian inference moves from the importance of theoretical assumptions to paradigm relativism[d]
Realism	Offers an a posteriori, naturalistic, multidimensional characterization of theory-saturated insight into a theory-independent world; stresses inductive inference to the best explanation in both the sciences and epistemology Chief induction: *from* the instrumental success *and* theory governance of science *and* the use of once hypothesized items in the investigation of now hypothetical ones *to* the existence of some theoretical entities

View of theory

Empiricism	Structures theory through an a priori model of scientific explanation, putatively valid in each branch; denies the theory saturation of the observations relevant to scientific progress, views theoretical terms as *instruments* in the manipulation of observations, and suggests that alternative theoretical entities could as plausibly explain the observational data (the *evidential indistinguishability thesis*)
Neo-Kantianism	Emphasizes conflict of theories and the role of background information in the design of crucial experiments and scientific change; stresses the politics of theory adoption and can acknowledge the diversity of theoretical knowledge

Table 3.1. *(cont.)*

Realism	Also insists on the role of theoretical criticism, background information, and the evidentiality of entrenched theoretical considerations in research design; contra positivism, notes the frequently successful conjunction of theories tested against *disparate* evidence; accounts for the role of extraexperimental criteria (familiarity, simplicity), the ordinary restriction of relevant theories in a field to a few, often two, and the small number of striking predictions or explanations that justify adoption of a new theory as features of the best explanation of scientific success (instrumental success *and* success in identifying theoretical entities); sees the multidimensionality of scientific method and the contingency of discovery as an internal explanation of sometimes lengthy disputes about novel theories and of the politics of science (in astronomy, biology, political theory, and ethics, external religious, social and political factors often exacerbate these clashes); stresses the domain-specific diversity of theories

Broad view of truth

Empiricism	Confines verification to (possible) naked-eye observation; in semantics, some versions suggest a correspondance of natural-kind terms to sense-data
Neo-Kantianism	Allows *intra*paradigmatic "truth," which involves *coherence* of different levels of argument; provides a paradigm-relativist, constructivist account of truth
Realism	Maintains that science captures important – approximate – truths about theoretical as well as observational items; relevant terms refer to (extratheoretical) features of reality

Basic conception of ethics

Empiricism	Insists that ethics has no independent subject matter, hence, no objectivity; ethical terms are vague and (often) need reconstruction in some other idiom
Neo-Kantianism	Allows no *moral* objectivity except relative to prevailing basic conventions; ethics are linked to group interests and/or social and historical meanings; elides the distinction between a justified moral claim and an ideology
Realism	Emphasizes the integrity and objectivity of ethics as the study of a good life for humans; in stressing individuality, an adequate moral theory allows more plurality than any scientific one, yet like science, through exploration of contending theories and relevant evidence, ethics discovers

	(some) approximate truths; attends to historical context but distinguishes between truth and ideology

View of progress

Empiricism	Allows advance in manipulation of observables, but not about theoretical entities (except as better instruments to predict the former)
Neo-Kantianism	Sees no transtheoretical progress; acknowledges the improved instrumental reliability of scientific theories[e]
Realism	Insists on theoretical progress as the explanation of instrumental progress

View of ethical advance

Empiricism	Envisions no *moral* progress or fallibility
Neo-Kantianism	Allows intraparadigm *conventional* progress based on empirical controversy; can thus envision a *convention-based* "moral" fallibilism
Realism	Stresses *moral* fallibilism: Moral discoveries about human capacities and learning are possible; so is ethical decline

Semantics

Empiricism	Seeks a priori to compile the characteristics associated with a term or specify the law cluster in which it is embedded; stresses primacy of meaning over reference
Neo-Kantianism	Notes that the primacy of meaning over reference *within empiricist semantics* undercuts the continuity of theoretical terms across theory (meaning, law cluster) changes; makes an induction from the occurrence and semantics of theory change (phlogiston to oxygen, diverse meanings of electron) to the epistemological and semantic view that theoretical terms cannot refer to *transtheoretical* items; localizes reference to paradigm (a *weak-reference* view)
Realism	Suggests internally that a complex notion of reference is primary in science, ethics, and epistemology over meaning (a *strong-reference* view); theory changes can provide continuity of *epistemic access*; on Shapere's alternative, chain-of-reasoning connections replace reference, allowing theoretical advance; overemphasis on semantics, Shapere insists, hinders naturalistic accounts of scientific transformation

Ontology

Empiricism	Suggests that what exists is what can be discerned with the naked eye; sets up a verificationist metaphysics filter that delegitimizes theoretical as well as ethical terms and entities

Table 3.1. *(cont.)*

Neo-Kantianism	Maintains that existence is relativized to paradigm; moral properties, however, exist in broadly the same sense as scientific ones
Realism	Envisions an open-ended ontology: the novel items scientists discover often exist as well as those identified by ordinary perception; in line with the *integrity of ethics argument*, moral properties exist

a Each of these views has, of course, diverse predecessors and other current representatives.
b In some respects, however, Fine's pragmatism also has commonalities with Rorty's and might be classified as neo-Kantian.
c Rawls, 1985, 1988d, says that constructivism is the right approach in political philosophy but leaves open the possibility that realism might be (part of) the appropriate moral epistemology. In contrast to *Spheres of Justice*, Walzer, 1988a, no longer holds a conventionalist view.
d Given the centrality of this induction, I have grouped some pragmatists like Rorty as neo-Kantians, even though pragmatists in a non-neo-Kantian vein equate truth and practical success.
e In *The Essential Tension*, Kuhn, however, inconsistently allows progress along such transtheoretical dimensions as *fruitfulness* in puzzle solving. In general, as McMullin, 1984, and Miller, 1987, suggest, Kuhn's transtheoretical criteria for scientific advance – elegance, fruitfulness, coherence, and the like – fit a realist account well.

construction," a reduction to other terms – for instance, to an idiom of sense-data.

Originally, positivists designed this filter to combat revealed religion. On the face of it, however, investigation of the best life for humans – of concepts of justice, a common good, and well-being – are natural to humans in a way that faith is not; a belief in fairness is not the same as a belief in miracles. Swept up in a *general* concern to exclude nonobservable entities, positivism attacked moral objectivity and sought to pit science against ethics. Even today, this empiricist view survives in the purported political science distinction between "empirical" and "normative" theory. Carnap and others also sought to sidestep metaphysical and epistemological debate. They maintained that only particular knowledge claims, rendered in a sense-datum idiom, could be scientifically meaningful and that the controversy between realism and (subjective) idealism – the ontological claim that external reality exists and the denial of the claim – is a "pseudoproblem."[13] They never considered the prima facie attractive possibility that the increasing instrumental knowledge of modern science can be explained as the result of successful inferences, based on human interaction with an external world.

In fact, however, this sense-datum version of empiricism casts doubt on any general concepts. Its metaphysics filter sifted out not only the claims of religion and ethics but even theoretical concepts about non-visible entities in the well-confirmed sciences that positivists took as the paradigm of knowledge. They maintained that electrons do not exist; the term "electron" serves merely as an instrumental convenience in the manipulation of observations. Still more embarrassingly, empiricists ruled out claims about the psychological states of others. In a famous example, Carnap suggested that we could not know that "John is joyful" but only that "John's face exhibits such and such expressions."[14] Yet we often infer joy – and sometimes know how to recognize the feigning of joy – in a way that this attempted translation botches. Further, even the terms "face" and "expression" are universals. An eviscerating translation into a putative language of "sense-data" fails to characterize this observation report – and the knowledge it contains – accurately. In the name of precision, it ironically exhibits the very flaw – obscurity – that positivists allege of ordinary language and adds *artificiality*. Finally, positivists promised but failed to discover a language of sense-data into which translators could reduce statements about medium-sized physical objects. Even scientific talk about such objects could not be "conclusively verified." If, as David Lewis has stressed, philosophy measures the price of trading common sense for (purportedly) rigorous, but arcane reformulation, this view is too dear.[15]

Hilary Putnam has pointed to a deep initial error in the positivist project; for empiricists recognized the validity of only two kinds of statements: analytic truths – the truths of mathematics and logic – and empirical ones – those that can be registered in the sense-datum language. But what then, a critic might ask, is the status of the positivists' own criterion of verification: "The meaning of a statement is its method of verification"? That statement is neither analytically true nor observationally verifiable. On the logical positivist account, it is "scientifically meaningless." At its inception, this project was self-refuting.[16]

As the empiricist program failed, historians and philosophers increas-

---

[13] Carnap, 1969, pp. 332–4.   [14] Carnap, 1969, pp. 334–9.   [15] Lewis, 1983a, pp. 8–9.
[16] Putnam, 1981, pp. 105–6, 112; Shapere, 1984, ch. 6. By 1956, Carnap had changed his semantic view, suggesting that the meaning of theoretical terms is determined by the overall theory in which they are embedded. This conception is near to Kuhn's.

ingly recognized the central importance of theory and conflicts of theory in scientific discovery. I will first point out how these insights contribute to scientific and ontological realism, show how they undermine influential positivist attempts at "rational reconstruction" of moral judgments, and then explain and criticize neo-Kantian interpretations in philosophy of science and ethics.

Following an earlier insight of Duhem, Quine and Putnam showed that evidential challenges to prevailing theories call into question not basic principles so much as *auxiliary statements*, the background or collateral information that enables investigators to test a general theory. In Quine's phrase, our theoretical knowledge as a whole "faces the tribunal of experience." Confirmation or refutation (Popper) through particular instances does not work.[17] Instead, through sophisticated contrasts of leading theories against the evidence, scientists make inductive inferences to the best explanation.

As Boyd has argued, theoretical criticisms or "hunches" about plausible alternative causal mechanisms to accepted ones play a central role in experimental design to confirm a prevailing conception (normal science) and to elaborate a new one (revolutionary science). Within an accepted total science or theoretical domain, investigators confidently conjoin theories that they have tested only against different bodies of observation or that, together, suggest novel measurement techniques. In most cases, this nonpositivist practice, reflecting the unity of science, succeeds. The likely explanation for its reliability is that different bodies of theory make discoveries about nonobservable entities; (theory-governed) observations play an important role in science, as positivists rightly emphasize, but are not, by themselves, the arbiters of theory. Further, following an empiricist account, scientists should consider a large number of theories, even highly esoteric ones, plausible until experimentally falsified. Yet innovative scientific practice conflicts with this expectation at every turn. At any given time, scientists entertain only a small number of theories, perhaps only two, as serious contend-

---

[17] As Quine elegantly put it in "Two Dogmas," "The totality of our so-called knowledge or beliefs, from the most casual matters of geography and history to the profoundest laws of atomic physics or even of pure mathematics and logic, is a man-made fabric which impinges on experience only along the edges. Or, to change the figure, total science is like a field of force whose boundary conditions are experience. A conflict with experience at the periphery occasions readjustments in the interior of the field. . . . But the total field is so underdetermined by its boundary conditions, experience, that there is much latitude of choice as to what statements to reevaluate in the light of any single contrary experience. No particular experiences are linked with any particular statements in the interior of the field, except indirectly through considerations of equilibrium affecting the field as a whole" (Quine, 1969, pp. 42–3). Imre Lakatos's refined falsificationism (1970) recognizes the complexity of scientific investigation.

ers for truth. Telling contests and new theories usually arise in particular domains only when an old theory has given rise to glaring anomalies.[18] In addition, only a comparatively small number of crucial experiments and observations, or striking explanatory or predictive successes, figure centrally in the adoption of a new theory.[19] Such successes focus on just those cases where background information suggests that a new proposal is most likely to go wrong.[20] The most plausible explanation of these practices, as Boyd argues, is the central role of theory. In fact, given the configuration of theory clashes, the need for auxiliary statements, the phenomenon of entrenchment, and instrumental success, theoretical considerations, not just relevant observations, count as *evidence* in designs for the assessment of novel proposals.

Thus, the entrenchment of theoretical terms – the prima facie criterion of simplicity for changed accounts of such terms – arises from their approximate truth. As realists have emphasized, even revolutionary successor theories preserve not just the accurate observation statements, but the true causal mechanisms and laws postulated by earlier theories. Thus, the central role of theory helps to integrate what positivists see as external "*extra*experimental" criteria into our direct understanding of scientific advance. A realist account also explains how reasonable disagreement can persist even after a new theory has achieved some important successes – say, Priestley's with the oxygen theory, Einstein's with quantum mechanics. As a result of increasingly reliable, multifaceted scientific procedures, novel views often have difficulty gaining a hearing and, despite anomalies for the received theory, require a considerable period of formulation and assessment to gain the upper hand.

Scientific progress is therefore theory saturated in two senses: the foregoing long-term, dynamic one, emphasized by Boyd, in which theoretical criticism is evidential in considering new proposals and the one commonly recognized by neo-Kantians and realists – that the observational evidence sought in crucial experiments is shaped by theoretical interests. Against empiricism, the first contention is far more devastating than the second; for the realist, like the positivist, notes that factual knowledge must be grounded in experience and that there is no a priori factual knowledge. To counter the difficulties for the theory–observation distinction raised by the second claim, a sophisticated empiricist can re-

---

[18] Kuhn's notion of anomaly also undermines neo-Kantian conventionalism; if the world were really as our theories made it, how could there be anomalies?

[19] Positivism and falsificationism praise prediction and deprecate the role of explanation in science. They implausibly question a Darwinian account of the origin of species, one that is not directly predictive, but that has led to a vast number of corollary explanations and discoveries (Monod, 1975; Putnam, 1981, pp. 109, 198).

[20] Boyd, 1985, pp. 4–6, 10.

draw the line between theory and evidence – including some entities detected by complex instruments to whose soundness ordinary observation testifies – concede that this distinction is a rough one independent of attempts to create a "sense-datum" language, and assess the "empirical adequacy of models" rather than the meaning of terms and statements. These positivist moves, though they lend some plausibility to realism, might still permit an *evidential indistinguishability thesis about theoretical entities*. But the role of theoretical knowledge in explaining the historical success of science and rightly shaping the judgments of scientists about alternative (bodies of) theory disqualifies even this positivism. That argument makes the questions raised for empiricism by the common claim that observation is theory saturated fully effective.[21]

To set a realist argument as a response to neo-Kantian insights, I should also note that my use of the terms "moral fact" and "moral objectivity" incorporates all of the foregoing points about the complexity of theoretical – scientific and ethical – projects.

On this new theory-governed view of science, moral judgments, which appeal strongly to facts about human nature and well-being and suggest inductions to general principles, look much more like a species of objective – potentially true or false – *knowledge*; for these insights undermine the impact of G. E. Moore's influential *open question argument*. On his view, ethical properties are "nonnatural" because it is always a question whether any specific factual – naturalistic – description requires a particular ethical verdict. To obtain such a judgment, he suggests, we need an "undefinable" – though on his view "simple" – nonempirical premise. Given this starting point, however, a positivist interpretation, maintaining that ordinary ethical judgments, at least in their factual component, are vague and that moral intuitions require some occult faculty different from normal human capacities, seems justified; so does a neo-Kantian claim that we impose nonjustifiable ethical categories on an otherwise recalcitrant world. But consider the factual statement: Hitler murdered some millions of noncombatant Jews, Slavs, and gypsies. Any recognizably ethical theory, one that appeals to the value of human life, let alone to rights or some more elaborate conception of happiness, combined with an account of how these facts arose – auxiliary statements that disqualify any notion of self-defense – reveals Hitler as a monster. The most minimal discoveries and inductions about human capacities underpin that moral claim. As Nicholas Sturgeon has

---

21 Boyd, 1984, pp. 43, 54–5, 60–1; 1985, pp. 20–1, 28–30. For such a spirited, sophisticated empiricism, see Van Fraasen, 1980, esp. pp. 13–19, 64–9; 1984, 1985. On Van Fraasen's reinterpretation, the moons of Jupiter are observable (by astronauts), subatomic particles are not (Churchland, 1985a, pp. 44–5; Musgrave, 1985, pp. 204–9, 221).

suggested, although this judgment is theory dependent, so are objective scientific verdicts; in fact, this ethical claim appears much less subject to dispute than most well-founded scientific ones.[22] Moore's diagnosis of a distinctive naturalistic fallacy in moral argument fails.

David Lyons has skillfully undercut the longstanding positivist depreciation of ethics:

> So part of the simple contrast between scientific and moral beliefs is untenable, since scientific beliefs typically go beyond observable facts. On the other side, moral judgments are not completely independent of empirical facts or observation. Consider my judgment that John's breaking his promise to Mary was reprehensible. This can be discredited by reference to the facts – if, say, there was no John or no Mary, John never made a promise to Mary, Mary tricked John into making it, or John never broke the promise.
>
> Someone might try to preserve the idea that moral judgments go beyond the facts by claiming that my judgment does not merely describe what happened but pronounces a verdict on it. It may be said, for example, that my judgment presupposes a general principle of some sort, such as the principle that breaking a promise is reprehensible. And this, it may be claimed, cannot be established by appeal to observation. This reply assumes, however, that moral principles cannot be established on the basis of facts (not even facts about the human condition). But while that is an important philosophic theory about morality, it is not an observable fact about it. And there are competing theories on the other side, which seek to show how moral principles can be decided by reference to facts about the human condition. The question that we face, once more, is whether this is possible. The simple contrast initially suggested between science and ethics fails to answer that question.[23]

3. The eccentricities of ethical empiricism

Three positivist proposals reveal the odd implications of rational reconstruction in ethics. First, emotivism tried to translate moral statements or injunctions into the language of ordinary, natural desire (preference) without residue.[24] This view equates the statements "Murder is bad and should be enjoined," or "Slavery is wrong for humans and should be abolished" with "I dislike pistachio ice cream; do so as well" ("I dislike murder; do so as well"). These translations invite the general suspicion of empiricism that, in the name of "clarification," its reductionism trivializes important concerns.

Second, in *Ethics: Inventing Right and Wrong*, J. L. Mackie updates

---

[22] G. E. Moore, 1951, pp. 1–18, maintains that the notion of the good must serve as "an axiom" in moral argument (Sturgeon, 1984, pp. 67–71).

[23] Lyons, 1984, pp. 13–14.   [24] Stevenson, 1963, pp. 16–17, 26–30.

Moore's "nonnaturalism." He maintains that ethical properties of "to be doneness" are "ontologically queer." Such properties do not seem to be part of "the basic furniture of the world" as envisioned by modern physics. Yet for the sciences, he insists, an empiricist reduction to the terms of physics is possible; for ethics, in contrast, entities and properties are merely "invented."[25] But contrary to Mackie's empiricism, humans are as much a part of the "furniture" of the world as anything else – other medium-size physical objects, electrons – is. His view is sensible only given a reductionist physicalism and a failure to examine moral argument internally. We say, "Murder is wrong (for humans)"; no one would say, "Murder lacks the moral property 'to be doneness.'" The undoubted "queerness" of the latter locution is a rhetorical artifact of Mackie's general perspective. By focusing his analysis on moral injunctions, he begs the question of whether some arrangements – for instance, comparatively nonmurderous ones – are good for humans. Nothing in Mackie's account blocks the expectation that the disciplines concerned with human health and well-being – physical, psychological, and social – may hope to achieve objectivity in broadly the same sense as other branches of study.

Third, in his sophisticated, recent *Theory of the Right and the Good*, Richard Brandt maintains that moral language and intuitions are unclear. In their stead, he offers a naturalistic reduction in terms of behaviorist psychology (notions of pleasure and pain, want and aversion). For him, a justified moral notion is one that survives criticism in the light of the best available contemporary knowledge: A rational action is the best criticized action, and an acceptable moral code for a society is one that a rational being would choose in the light of such knowledge. Brandt suggests a range of utilitarian codes. He emphasizes the role of a specific version of scientific psychology in providing the "best available knowledge." As a seemingly obvious point – one that he almost neglects to state – he includes *no ordinary moral standards* in such knowledge. Like much contemporary moral philosophy, Brandt seeks an independent theory that will settle every ethical question. Thus, he treats all such claims according to a method that, on his account, would be especially appropriate in solving the most difficult cases. Brandt's is the most interesting, important attempt at an empiricist reconstruction of ethics.[26]

Now, Brandt argues that every ordinary moral standard is vague. For this claim to be plausible, however, he would have had to show that the

---

[25] Mackie, 1977, pp. 38–40. Contrary to Mackie, as I noted above, a modern materialism does not entail reductionism.

[26] Brandt, 1979, chs. 1–2, 5–6. Though for quite different reasons, Brandt's striking utilitarian arguments (1979, pp. 311–26) sustain the same conclusion – equal monetary incomes – as Chapters 7 and 8 below.

notion of nonextinguishable elementary desires – ones that do not disappear in "cognitive psychotherapy" – is clearer than the moral judgments cited above. But on the level of ethical theory, one might ask, Why is the psychological notion of a stable, "fully criticized" pleasure or course of action good compared to its opposite? Lacking any argument for the internalization of empirical claims in ethics, Brandt has no answer. On a metaethical level, he needed to justify a choice of a behaviorist version of rational reconstruction rather than one based on, say, some version of psychoanalysis or a Marxian theory of ideology. For instance, psychoanalytic theories often claim that (temporarily) successful behavioral adjustments preserve neurosis; they fail to deal with continuing archaic feelings of inadequacy of self. Though he has thoroughly explored contemporary behavioral psychology, Brandt fails to compare his view with leading rival psychological and social theories. Furthermore, he would have to justify his particular explanatory choice through notions of (approximate) truth, fruitfulness, coherence, and elegance, that is, our values in theory selection. Denying the clarity of ordinary normative judgments, he could not justify these methodological decisions. But even if he successfully argued for scientific values, he would still have to show that *this* normative justification was clearer than that of the ordinary moral standards he deprecates.

4. Theory saturatedness, revolutionary change, and neo-Kantianism

Given the broad recognition of the importance of theory clashes in science and the inadequacies of ethical reductionism, some philosophers, notably Kuhn, Feyerabend, and Rorty, have advanced neo-Kantian alternatives to logical positivism. Their view emphasizes the tenaciousness of leading scientific theories that have had some instrumental successes. Such theories become paradigms for normal research in which investigators acquire much informal, not just explicit, formalizable knowledge about how to proceed. (In realist terms, this point stresses the importance of background knowledge.) As Feyerabend contends, academic politics and the aura of expert status bolster the prevalence of particular paradigms. Scientific progress occurs not as a steady accumulation of facts – the accretions of judicious magpies, to borrow a witticism of Alasdair MacIntyre – but through the emergence of glaring anomalies, rival theories, and fundamental shifts of paradigm. Such periods of revolutionary science, this view insists, differ dramatically from normal scientific "puzzle solving." In its emphasis on paradigm entrenchment, the theory dependence of factual knowledge, the paramountcy of theory clashes in scientific change, the role of informal knowledge, and the politics of science, this view has made important contributions to the philosophy of science.

Neo-Kantian views undermine the positivist distinction between scientific and ethical knowledge, for political and moral conceptions also dramatically shift historically (undergo "revolutions"). On this view, both science and ethics have at least local integrity; empiricist efforts at reconstruction are misguided. Curiously, however, most versions of neo-Kantianism *share with positivism* the claim that all moral standards are arbitrary. Where empiricists have always insisted that ethics, in contrast to science, was merely conventional, neo-Kantians have remade science in the positivists' image of ethics. They subjectivize both kinds of knowledge.

These neo-Kantian perspectives mistakenly reject the role of evidence and progress in scientific research. They oppose the claim that successor theories in mature sciences approximate the truth about reality more nearly than their predecessors. Where realists stress the role of contingently discovered, approximately true theories in establishing and refining scientific method, neo-Kantians insist on a radically conventionalism-determined process of investigation. But that convention relativism makes the transtheoretic, instrumental success of science, which neo-Kantians recognize, hard to explain. Though Kuhn qualifies an extreme denial of objectivity, his arresting, thematic phrase, "When paradigms change, the world itself changes with them," illustrates this exaggerated relativization of factual discoveries to particular theories.[27]

But striking examples of neo-Kantian historical research undercut their own argument. For instance, Paul Feyerabend's *Against Method* contends that observational evidence originally discredited Galileo's defense of Copernicus. Early celestial telescopic observations were recognized – by today's as well as contemporary criteria – to be problematic. To make fair comparisons between Copernican and Ptolemaic theories – ones acceptable to both sides – astronomers could use the telescope only for terrestrial observation. On falsificationist (or empiricist) grounds, Feyerabend insists, scientists should have rejected Copernican theory. Yet Galileo made that argument plausible rhetorically – Feyerabend colorfully refers to "propagandistic machinations" – by misinterpreting a new highly theoretical account of the earth's motion as a natural approach to observation.[28]

In contrast to empiricism, Feyerabend describes a complicated theoretical and observational rivalry, concludes that scientists must give a novel theory time to prove out, and praises anarchic diversity for its own sake. As he rightly maintains, investigators sometimes revive old, ap-

[27] Kuhn, 1970, p. 110.   [28] Feyerabend, 1975, pp. 64–8, 89, chs. 6–7, 10–12.

parently surpassed insights in new form; thus, Pythagoras had claimed that the earth moves around the sun. Though he does not directly consider realist arguments, Feyerabend contends that his argument refutes any version of scientific progress.

Part of this story – about the complexity of scientific rivalry – is well argued. Yet Feyerabend's central epistemological point fits his history badly; for he shows only that on a first fair comparison of telescopic results, the fledgling theory might have lost – it provided poorer explanations – but with a chance for proponents to develop fuller arguments and improve telescopic observations, it won – it provided superior ones. That argument does not license anarchy; it establishes only that a contrast of developed theories, checked against sophisticated objections, is a requirement of *fair comparison*. The latter claim supports a standard realist contention about the possibility of pairwise, theory-neutral comparison of contending views: that, for any two plausible rival theories, there are experimental tests based on a method *legitimized by both theories*.[29] As Hacking's studies emphasize, even Feyerabend's point about the initial problems in telescopic optics supposes the kind of optical progress in which artisan-scientists can accurately distinguish "bugs" – artifacts of the equipment – from what is seen. We know the problems with those telescopes because modern ones are so much more complex, powerful, diverse.[30] Further, if the theories are radically incommensurable, as Feyerabend suggests, how can we fairly compare them? How could we even recognize that the first contrasts were unfavorable to Galileo's Copernicanism? Finally, the fact that some theories have been resuscitated in new form does not show that *every* discredited theory has that potential.

Feyerabend's stress on the role of scientific politics – rhetoric, the later stultifying role of "professionalism" – is important. But that argument suggests a quite unanarchic conclusion. Hitting upon an approximately true theory may be central to progress in any branch of science, even when contemporary or subsequent methodological strictures appear initially to rule it out. The powers that be may persecute such a theory – the Catholic church's harassment of Galileo and burning of other scientists. Politics – favorable external conditions, including

---

[29] Boyd, 1984, p. 46; Miller, 1987, ch. 4. Theory neutral here means only neutral between particular scientific theories. Except for nondecisive logical points, say internal consistency, no nonnaturalist, a priori criteria exist for the general assessment of such theories.

This realist account of theory contrast suggests why successor theories are so closely linked to earlier ones: Each involves the *internal critique* of a rival theory used on *mutually specified* relevant evidence. The more successful theory is thus bound by a chain-of-reasoning connection (Shapere) to its predecessor.

[30] Hacking, 1984; 1985, p. 152.

social movements – may be needed to give the novel theory a chance to develop.

To take an important social scientific and moral example, the Jewish and Christian traditions advanced the profound antislaveholding claim that humans generally have souls.[31] These slave-based, originally persecuted religious movements contributed to the emergence of (comparatively) free societies and the theoretical discrediting of the doctrine of natural slavery. Contra anarchism, not just any theoretical and political alternative provides an equally rational substitute. Chapters 7 and 11 offer further examples of the role of social theory discoveries and political movements in generating progress in moral theory. In contrast to Feyerabend's conception, which legitimizes *any* kind of struggle and is, in this respect, vague as well as misguided, these chapters will underline the impetus – for modern liberals and radicals – provided by the struggles of the oppressed in creating conditions in which approximately true political theory can flourish.

Against this criticism, Feyerabend maintains, fair comparison is possible for Galileo's proposals because both theories are part of the same tradition. That tradition, however, is merely a construction, no more justified than any other. Except for polemics against empiricist believers, however, that claim removes the interest in Feyerabend's description of this case. It also fails to explain the foregoing examples of complex epistemological progress – growing insight into the solar system's workings or the abuses of slavery – and thus provides an implausible alternative to the realist account of the increasing reliability of scientific and (important features of) moral knowledge.[32]

Unlike Feyerabend, Rorty's *Philosophy and the Mirror of Nature*, defends neo-Kantianism directly against realism as well as empiricism.[33] If we take a long enough perspective, he suggests, our views contrast with those of our ancestors across the board. Our future galactic successors, he imagines, will regard our scientific and ethical notions with a mixture of incomprehension and odd resonance, much as we view those of animists. We may legitimately tell stories about the succession of points of view that achieve greater approximations to reality, but this approach simply writes the history of particular disciplines "Whiggishly." As a

---

[31] Walzer, 1985, ch. 1. That Feyerabend (1975) means to defend liberal and Marxian movements can be seen at pp. 17–21, 146–7, and 153–4.

[32] Feyerabend, however, affirms a core idea of progress – cutting across "any one of the senses one cares to choose" – that conflicts with his relativism (Feyerabend, 1975, pp. 26–27, 30, 32–3, 156).

[33] Against Kant, R. Rorty styles himself a pragmatist; despite his attacks on any attempt at *philosophical* mirroring, however, his views on the status of knowledge and the role of theory are straightforwardly neo-Kantian.

pragmatist, he maintains, no second-order philosophy is needed to justify these disciplinary contentions. No argument could sustain scientific or moral objectivity, but, he contends, none is needed.

On the face of it, however, these claims are hard to fit together. Within a particular science or ethics, on his account, we maintain that objectivity and progress exist. But the natural induction from these intradisciplinary histories is epistemological realism: a conclusion that over time investigators make discoveries about different aspects of reality. In fact, to deny "first-order" relativism, Rorty affirms this feature: "Except for the occasional cooperative freshman, one cannot find anybody who says that two incompatible opinions on an important topic are equally good."[34] Externally, however, he maintains, we see, by the *galactic successor* argument, that objectivity and advance cannot exist and that, within disciplines, investigators have merely made a particular stylistic decision about how to write history. But his argument is inconsistent first in its claims about levels of analysis and second in its contrast between local disciplinary and general epistemology. First, it requires some second-order philosophy to see that we have merely made a stylistic decision among varied hermeneutic possibilities (and why "we"? – after all, we don't all make it); yet he denies that we need *any* second-order view. Second, contrary to his first-order denial of relativism, his version of that philosophy is relativist. But the obvious induction from *his* account of disciplinary histories is realist.

In arguing for epistemological relativism, Rorty takes on a feature of realism directly. He denies Boyd's claim that currently reliable theory and procedure reasonably serve as a check on novel theoretical proposals:

> Boyd here confuses the sense in which a procedure is reliable in respect of an independent test (as thermometers are reliable indicators of how uncomfortable it is outside) with the sense in which a procedure is reliable because we cannot imagine an alternative. To check new theories by old ones is not an optional procedure. How else would we check them? The fact that new theories often go wrong just where old ones say they might is not something which requires explanation. It would require explanation if they went wrong somewhere else.[35]

But Rorty ignores some important features of a realist argument. An infinite number of theories – chemical reactions occur only if God wills them and only if she did not sneeze today – might explain a particular reality. Yet at a given time, scientists consider only a few theories as plausible contenders for truth not because, as Rorty mistakenly suggests, they lack imagination, but because the instrumental success of

---

[34] R. Rorty, 1982, p. 166.   [35] R. Rorty, 1979, pp. 283–4, 273–99.

science demonstrates the (broad) *reliability* of theory and method in contrast to the results of other theory-saturated investigations, theological and astrological ones for example. Contra Rorty, an explanation of that comparative success is needed, and realism provides it.

Rorty's galactic successor view also requires the *equal lack of objectivity of all theories*. But even though a quantum mechanical understanding of microphysical processes transforms our understanding of chemistry, it does not deny the role of oxygen in combustion or revive phlogiston. Although modern psychoanalytic theory is more plausible than preceding ones, it sustains the earlier discovery that slavery is bad for humans. No subtle theory of distortions of the self within families is necessary to answer the question Is there a duality of human natures such that a large group of humans is closer to cattle than to full humanity? Contemporary nonreductionist arguments about the supervenience of some properties (moral, psychological, biological) on others (physical, chemical) strikingly capture this point.[36]

To make the galactic successor argument plausible, Rorty notes that we cannot agree on "a set of rules which will tell us how rational agreement can be reached on what would settle the issue *on every point* where statements seem to conflict."[37] But this conception of commensurability goes far beyond the claim that *agreement* determines truth. (As I will argue below, it doesn't.) Even more stringently, he demands the potential resolution of *every question* – an *across-the-board determinacy of theories* as an alternative to incommensurability. But Rorty's argument disregards the internal scientific distinction between discoveries – oxygen, capacity for moral personality – and the perhaps many areas open to specific doubt, some of which, given limitations of human capacities, may prove unresolvable. Furthermore, if no notion of truth that goes beyond acceptability to the best contemporary investigators were justified, then why, in ethics, should one prefer liberty and the continuation of conversation, as Rorty does, to tyranny?[38] Merely because it is "our view"? How would we even identify the best investigators?

5. Realism as theory-dependent insight into the world

In contrast to empiricism and conventionalism, we need an epistemological alternative that stresses the central role of theory in science but recognizes the importance of evidence and progress. We also need a metaethical conception that explains the broadly comparable role of facts in ethics, focusing on empirical theories of human nature and the

---

[36] Lycan, 1986, pp. 80–1.   [37] R. Rorty, 1979, p. 316.
[38] R. Rorty, 1979, pp. 280–1; 1982, pp. 166–7.

possibilities of social cooperation. Such facts and theories lead to inductions to broader moral theories of *human* happiness, needs and capacities, rights, and individuality. Now, some of these conceptions, notably (democratic) individuality, suggest a far greater limit to relevant discoveries in ethics than in science, a broader moral role for invention, plurality, diversity. Nonetheless, an appropriate philosophical view must account for the analogies, not just the differences, between ethics and other kinds of knowledge. In contemporary debates, sophisticated realists have defended the main, though not the sole, version of that alternative.

Realism explains the grains of truth in empiricism and neo-Kantianism. As strongly as the former, it stresses the role of factual knowledge, observations, experiments, and progress; it also insists on additional facts – for instance, the existence of electrons – and takes theoretical considerations as evidence in considering a hypothesis. Like the latter, it emphasizes the theory dependence of scientific advance and the importance of dramatic theory changes; it interprets these transformations not as shifts in convention but as the contingent discovery of approximately true theories that establish the reliability of scientific method. Realism does justice to the central merits in these other views; yet its explanation of the instrumental successes of science avoids implausible positivist reductionism and neo-Kantian relativism.[39]

Opponents of sophisticated realism sometimes fear a naïve materialism that fails to do justice to the complexity of scientific and moral investigation. They insist on the peculiarity of achieving such a *theory-saturated* knowledge of a theory-independent world. Realism responds to that complexity but focuses, unlike neo-Kantianism, on the appropriate further inferences from our ordinary and scientific epistemological successes. Nonetheless, in Chapter 4, I explore Putnam's subtle version of this objection and his attempt to work out an *objective* neo-Kantian alternative.

But Arthur Fine has proposed a telling empiricist argument against this broad strategy of justifying realism. He grants that realism might provide the best explanation for the instrumental success of science. He then asks, however, Why, philosophically, should we accept the principle of inference to the best explanation, with regard to theoretical entities or to empirical epistemological hypotheses such as realism? He rightly points out that the realist induction, just by itself, does not re-

---

[39] Realism recognizes the revisability of particular scientific conclusions and theoretical descriptions, hence its insistence on *approximate* truth. The notion of a final truth plays little role in this conception, although, once again, insights into, say, the universal human capacity for moral personality are comparatively unlikely to be revised.

spond to the verificationist claim that all factual knowledge is *observational* knowledge.

This challenge, however, is difficult to sustain internally. First, as an empiricist, Fine recognizes that inference to the best explanation is a feature of many ordinary inductions about observations. He gives no reason why we should not extend this normally reliable principle to theoretical entities. Second, much recent, powerful research – neo-Kantian and realist – in the history of science demonstrates the theory saturatedness or total science dependence of empirical research. If Fine is correct about the principle of inductive inference and those historical and philosophical arguments are right, his skeptical argument would discredit scientific inductions about observables as well. To justify his position, he would need an equally powerful, positivist account of scientific change. Third, though the realist argument depends on inference to the best explanation about unobservables, that principle is not controversial in contrast, say, to reliance on horoscopes for predicting the future. In fact, if such inductive inference is illegitimate, it is unclear what tools would be left to the evolutionary biologist, physicist, historian, or psychologist.[40] If realism is, as Fine acknowledges, the best inductive account of scientific progress, then it is doubtful that skepticism about an uncontroversial principle of induction – endorsed for observables by Fine himself – can undermine it.

Like empiricism, realism insists on the reliability of ordinary observational knowledge. Over the past decade, however, philosophers have offered a new account of that reliability. A broad realist account invokes the naturalist psychological claim that the best explanation for the reliability of many perceptions is that normal human senses are good detectors of medium-sized external objects; it recommends that such reliable methods feature in an unabashed – nonreductionist – *causal* theory of knowledge, one that recognizes the causal powers of objects.[41] Such claims contrast with the positivist contention that we perceive only sense-data and the skeptical bracketing of objects; they clash with a Humean interpretation of causality as contingent regularity. These controversial claims gain in plausibility from the overall persuasiveness of realism, given the difficulties of empiricism and neo-Kantianism.

Fine adapts his position to capture some realist claims. He speaks of a pragmatist "natural ontological attitude" according to which we assume that commonsense terms and theoretical posits at any particular time refer to real entities: "NOA [the natural ontological attitude] sanctions ordinary referential semantics and commits us, via truth, to the exis-

---

[40] Fine, 1984; Boyd, 1984, pp. 65–74.   [41] Goldman, 1986, ch. 5.

tence of the individuals, properties, relations, processes and so forth referred to by the scientific statements we accept as true." But this view elides the issues raised by dramatic theoretical changes; after such transformations, it maintains, we simply accept the new posits seemingly for whatever reasons scientists do. Yet Fine also insists:

> In taking this referential stance, NOA is not committed to the progressivism that seems inherent in realism. For the realist, as an article of faith sees scientific success, over the long run, as bringing us closer to the truth. His whole explanatory enterprise, using approximate truth, forces his hand in this way. But a "noaer" is not so committed.[42]

Fine's epistemological contention about nonprogressivism, however, undercuts his claim about adhering to the views of scientists, who often consider later theoretical posits or versions of posits nearer approximations to truth. Furthermore, in the original debate between empiricists and realists that centered over whether "today's" electrons are like tables and hearts, he is, like Rorty, a *quasi-realist*. But he then needs to show some gain in epistemological explanation from this apparently arbitrary, static argument. In contrast, a realist inference about advance in developed sciences does not require a rigid preconception that every discipline is mature or rule out particular examples of decline. A Marxian realist will think that important features of prevalent, non-Marxian social science illustrate such a decline; whatever she learns from it, she will try to provide a sociological explanation of what she takes to be its contradictions. Further, if, as Fine wants, we are to be open to the possibility of decay, surely we should be able to detect it; yet the NOAer is not. The grain of truth in Fine's position is that we need an alternative theory, possibly a sophisticated version of an allegedly discredited one – say, Marxian accounts in many contemporary social science debates – to identify such decline. That detection occurs *within science*, but, contrary to Fine, the defense of its validity is an empirically based *philosophical* induction.

Fine also insists on a special *stringency requirement* for philosophical theories. They must supposedly be better grounded than other empirical hypotheses.[43] But as we have seen, given the theory dependence of observation and diachronic instrumental reliability, Fine's putatively restricted use of inductive inference about observables requires scientific realism; his attempt to pare away such inductions about broad philosophical positions as well as theoretical entities is a failure. But a further objection to this stringency claim is possible. Ian Hacking's recent experimentalist realism suggests a far stronger basis for the existence of many

[42] Fine, 1984, p. 98.   [43] Fine, 1984, p. 86.

theoretical entities than inference to the best explanation, just by itself; that account also strengthens the epistemological induction.

Hacking focuses on contemporary work with electrons – the paradigm theoretical entity in much philosophical discussion. He points to an important dialectical change in their epistemological status, distinguishing Stoney's initial 1879 inference about their existence – about which many scientists (and philosophers) were rightly skeptical – and their subsequent employment to probe, at the frontiers of science, for evidence about further, hypothesized theoretical entities. As Hacking and Shapere stress, scientists now maintain that they "see" many subatomic particles – those which they can manipulate – in contrast to "hypothesized" ones, which they hope to "see":

> Antirealism about atoms was very sensible when Bain wrote a century ago. Antirealism about *any* submicroscopic entities was a sound doctine in those days. Things are different now. The "direct" proof of electrons and the like is our ability to manipulate them using well-understood low-level causal properties. Of course, I do not claim that reality is constituted by human manipulability. Millikan's ability to determine the charge of the electron did something of great importance for the idea of electrons, more, I think, than the Lorentz theory of the electron. Determining the charge of something makes one believe in it far more than postulating it to explain something else.
>
> Millikan got the charge on the electron; but better still, Uhlenbeck and Goudsmit in 1925 assigned angular momentum to electrons, brilliantly solving a lot of problems. Electrons have spin, ever after. The clincher is when we can put a spin on the electrons and thereby get them to scatter in slightly different proportions. . . . The best kinds of evidence for the reality of a postulated or inferred entity is that we can begin to measure it or otherwise understand its causal powers. The best evidence, in turn, that we have this kind of understanding is that we can set out, from scratch, to build machines that will work fairly reliably, taking advantage of this or that causal nexus.[44]

Shapere has recently traced a similar use of neutrinos – "hypothetical" as of the end of World War II though now "seen" – in investigation of the "hot core" of the sun. This argument neatly illustrates the trend in philosophy of naturalizing our knowledge, adapting philosophical in-

---

[44] Hacking, 1984, pp. 169–70, 155; 1985. He likens his view of scientific practice to Marx's: "Engineering not theorizing is the best proof of scientific realism about entities. My attack on scientific antirealism is analogous to Marx's onslaught on the idealism of this day. Both say that the point is not to understand the world but to change it." Hacking, however, too easily separates realism about entities from realism about theories. If claims for entities are strong, then further explanatory inferences about the theories in which they figure are appropriate and important. See also R. Miller, 1987, ch. 10.

ductions a posteriori to the best insights of the relevant science rather than seeking a priori epistemological "foundations."[45]

Hacking contrasts real theoretical entities – ones with which we interact – to others – even very long-lived ones such as the ether or black holes – that have a more problematic status; for ether, postulated by a number of well-confirmed theories, turned out not to exist.[46]

He also remarks that much of what we see through instruments is, though invisible to the naked eye, not theoretical. Microscopists, for example, produce grids with lettering and reduce them photographically. They can see whether observations of the grid – and consequently other microscopic objects – are accurate because they know what it was before they shrank it. Modern microscopes employ a dozen different physical processes, even acoustic ones, and produce the same image of a specimen. A common realist argument about theoretical entities, originated by Smart, notes that it would be a miracle if observations constantly worked out so nearly the way our best theories tell us, and yet nothing like the nonvisible entities, postulated by those theories, exists. Given our ability to study such nontheoretical entities, Hacking makes the same point about coincidence and properly criticizes Fine's and Van Fraasen's "religion of the naked eye."[47] Though Hacking's considerations are not conclusive in themselves, they are explained and reinforced by the overall realist induction about the advance of science.

As another stringency objection, Larry Laudan has asked what new discoveries or explanations realists have advanced on the basis of their overall philosophical hypothesis.[48] To give a few examples, Hacking's argument on electrons or Shapere's on "seeing" neutrinos provide one kind of illustration; as I indicate below, Field's argument on partial denotation and Boyd's more inclusive theory of epistemic access as accounts of reference and scientific advance are a second; Boyd's subtle assessment of the contributions of corpuscularism to the rise of modern atomic theory – a borderline case of knowledge – which I describe in Chapter 4, and his general account of complex cluster properties, are a third; the argument of this book, offering a reinterpretation of a controversial field, ethics, is a candidate for a fourth. In fact, given widespread preconceptions about the rigid distinction between science and ethics, the interpretations that I offer of the historical debates concerning slavery or of the nuanced relationship, in Marxian and liberal conceptions, between justice and individuality are interestingly *independent* arguments for realism. And in turn, claims about moral realism are strengthened by arguments for overall epistemological realism.

---

[45] Shapere, 1982; 1984, ch. 16.   [46] Hacking, 1984, p. 170.
[47] Hacking, 1985, pp. 145, 146–8, 151–2; Smart, 1968, p. 150.   [48] L. Laudan, 1984, p. 243.

Even where they did not previously notice these important examples, other epistemologies could offer alternative accounts. The differences between realism and well-stated alternatives are, as Sturgeon rightly puts it, a complex matter of "argumentative coherence and advantage" in science, social science, political theory, and ethics, not simply, as some philosophers might imagine, a matter of logic.[49] Yet these differences are real enough. In this context, today's realism is a promising program for empirical research on the structure and history of our knowledge and the complex relationship of its branches.[50]

6. Scientific epistemology as a guide to semantics

As Shapere and Devitt have rightly insisted, in contemporary discussion, semantics has often played a central role, not just as a locus for working out epistemological and ontological theses, but as the source of inductions to other branches of philosophy.[51] Yet semantics is an especially difficult, controversial field; the justification for using it as the source of such inductions is not obvious. Moreover, the difficulties of empiricism and neo-Kantianism in accounting for scientific change are underscored in the philosophy of language typically associated with them.

Both positivist and neo-Kantian semantics tend to regard the meaning of a term, for example a cluster of characteristics associated with it, as vested primarily in an individual speaker. Meaning involves a "disguised definite description" or, in the case of scientific theories, a "law cluster." Such definitions might be viewed as analytic and – less plausibly for science – a priori. Further, meanings conceptually set the reference of a term. Even where proponents substitute public agreement on criteria for individual understanding, this semantics is static; for given this general conception, *any* change of meaning, across historical epochs, severs continuity and obscures scientific and moral progress.

Quine's famous "Two Dogmas of Empiricism" successfully challenged this view. The philosophical implications of that challenge, one might suggest, are still being worked out, for "meanings" are not analytic; they depend on a web of belief that has a complex, changing relationship with the world.[52] Subsequently, as Putnam contended in "The 'Meaning' of Meaning," extension – the reference of terms to features of the world within social and historical projects of gathering knowledge – is primary

---

[49] Sturgeon, 1986a, pp. 135–6.   [50] Boyd, 1984, pp. 85–6.
[51] Devitt, 1984, pp. 4–5, 40–1, 118–19, 196–7.
[52] Putnam, 1988, ch. 1, argues for a resultant "meaning holism."

over their "meaning" to individual speakers. For instance, over time, scientists discovered the internal structure of gold; that structure could not have been exhibited in the original definitions, which focused on secondary qualities, that is, a durable, yellow metal, soluble in aqua regia, and the like.[53] Although a description of qualities is important in understanding and using a term, reference is established as a causal relationship between a term and an aspect of the world, not a conceptual truth. Further, as Putnam notes, ordinary users of the term "gold," seeking to guard against counterfeits, know how to find and expect to defer to experts. Complex discoveries about the world require specific *sociolinguistic divisions of labor*.[54] In addition, across their physical theories, ancient Greek and contemporary chemists both *referred* to gold. Sometimes, we may need a cautiously formulated epistemological principle of the "benefit of the doubt" or charity to specify the relevant continuities. We then give the best statement of an ancient scientific usage from a modern standpoint and critically assess it. Such interpretations are frequently multifaceted and microstructural.[55] But as a result of discoveries and scientific advance, the modern chemist can identify as nongold specimens that would have deceived the ancients. A theory of reference

---

[53] Quine, 1980, pp. 20–37; Putnam, 1975, 2:223–9, 235–8; Kripke, 1980.

David Lewis, 1983a, 1:chs. 6, 7, has followed Quine in abandoning the theory–observation dichotomy, yet provided a complex surrogate notion of the analyticity of theoretical terms and psychological states. His argument is, however, a version of scientific realism.

[54] As Putnam, 1975, 2:227, 229, puts it more precisely, "We could hardly use such words as 'elm' and 'aluminum' if no one possessed a way of recognizing elm tree and aluminum metal; but not everyone to whom the distinction is important has to be able to make the distinction." Boyd, 1979, pp. 388–91, points out that a social division of mental or cognitive labor underlies this linguistic division.

[55] Putnam, 1975, 2:274–81; 1988, ch. 1. R. Miller, 1985, pp. 514–18, gives one useful characterization of this microstructural assessment: "In ascribing meanings, we adopt a charitable attitude toward our subjects' actual failings. So far as possible, we make their actual epistemically flawed conduct reliable, reasonable, coherent and intelligible, and attribute meanings and corresponding beliefs and desires that would directly and simply account for this idealized practice. In particular, if their practice in applying a term was flawed, we associate with that term the extension that would have resulted from unflawed labelling. Then, in assessing the validity of the statements we have attributed to them, we abandon charity. Thus, although the Greeks classed nonfire and fire together, and occasionally took gold and fool's gold to be the same, we ignore this in the translating phase. If they regarded the stuff in rivers as having essential features that it lacks, we ignore this, too. Then, having preserved Aristotle from inability to talk about water, we account for much of what he said as a result of errors." For useful criticisms of overemphasis on "benefit of the doubt", see Devitt, 1981, pp. 200–202. Boyd's theory of epistemic access rightly qualifies this principle, suggesting that alternative traditions, with partially different classifications, could get particular disciplines mainly right (Boyd, 1979, pp. 396–7, 400–401).

derived from scientific research counters the artificial epistemological relativism generated by a misguided semantics.

7. Semantics-generated moral relativisms

The driving force of empiricist and neo-Kantian philosophy of language in licensing moral relativism appears vividly in contemporary egalitarian arguments, Walzer's *Spheres of Justice* and Amy Gutmann's *Liberal Equality*. In *Spheres of Justice,* Walzer claims that philosophy is a convention-based radicalism. By pursuing the internal logic of shared meanings about a plurality of social goods and using the consequent understanding to oppose unjustified domination of particular goods outside their spheres, he contends, citizens can arrive at a radical critique of prevailing practices: "Another way of doing philosophy is to interpret to one's fellow citizens the meanings we share. . . . If a [just and egalitarian] society isn't already here – hidden, as it were, in our concepts and categories – we will never know it concretely or realize it in fact." [56] This semantics clashes with Walzer's ethical theory; for he offers a substantive eudaemonist indictment, derived from Pascal, Marx, and ultimately Aristotle, of the corrupting power of wealth in such diverse spheres as love and political community. Aristotle, for example, distinguished friendships based on mutual concern from defective versions stemming from flattery or hopes of gain. Overall distributions of social goods need to cohere with the integrity of particular practices and relationships (intrinsic human goods) or, one might add, with the needs and purposes of individuals. Inequalities of power and money, however, often distort those distributions. To justify egalitarianism, Walzer's argument stresses the *relevant reasons* for relationships and activities. Yet as a result of his philosophy of language, he paradoxically interprets this ancient view as a relativist, "Western" one. This misinterpretation is comparable to his self-refuting metaethical claims about justice in war.

Similarly, given an overall semantic conception, Amy Gutmann has criticized Bernard Williams's – and Walzer's earlier – quasi-objective formulation of this relevant-reasons argument. In the absence of a priori, "conceptual truths" or a fixed "social logic" of ethical terms, she maintains, all moral meanings become context relative. For instance, Williams asserts that illness is a necessary condition for the proper distribution of medical care. In a class-divided society, such a criterion, he notes, is egalitarian; it distributes care according to need, not wealth. But Gutmann cites a contrasting Greek view: Socrates admired those artisans who lived only to fulfill their function and, when ill, scorned treatment

---

[56] Walzer, 1983, p. xiv.

that would preserve mere life without activity. The ancients, she suggests, had a different understanding of the relevant reasons for medical care; hence Williams's claim – and the egalitarianism that flows from it – cannot be true simply as a result of the analysis of moral terms. It applies at most – here she affirms his ethical conclusion – in the contemporary West, where the connotation is shared. Taking reflection on meanings as her standard, she rejects objectivity as analytically false and opts for metaethical relativism.

Like Walzer, however, her example does not fit an epoch-relative "shared meanings" view very well, for Socrates opposed the followers of Herodicus. The latter defended the "modern" notion that life is a sufficiently important good to deserve preservation. That overriding purpose must guide medicine in a more life-sustaining direction than Socrates, for functional reasons, recommended. A substantive dispute about the core features of the "modern" conception already existed in Athens; ancient Greeks did not simply distribute care according to the "meaning" putatively elicited by Socrates. Furthermore, Socrates recognized life as a good when combined with useful activity. In his judgment, if the two conflict, the latter consideration would override the former. His view is more a health-sustaining than a life-sustaining one. Although Herodicus stressed life, both sides saw life and health as important human goods. Contrary to Gutmann's semantics, this controversy ironically illustrates an uncontroversial "shared meaning" between ancient and modern medical practice and ethics. It suggests not that moral conflicts are mainly internal to language but that semantics follows a real conflict of goods. The example also reveals a general, not merely ancient, complexity of deliberation about such clashes; for today's discussions of the justification of maintaining existence where mental activity has ceased also appeal to standards of a fully *human* life.[57]

Williams avers that sickness is the relevant, in fact "necessary," condition for medical care. As Gutmann perceptively stresses, he does not explain his conception of necessity. His argument thus appears to be conceptual, meaning oriented, and open to her critique; as we will see in Chapter 4, he has recently defended a subtle form of relativism.[58] But we need not regard his intuition as analytic; in a realist vein, his claim might report an ancient discovery about the intrinsic goods – for humans – of life and health. Scientifically speaking, that discovery initiated a domain of research into the causes of disease and their cures. Ethically, it provided an uncontroversial, core standard about a good and relevant

---

[57] Gutmann, 1980, pp. 96–105. Socrates caricatures Herodicus's view at *Republic*, 406a – c. For a discussion of a parallel example in Weber, see Chapter 13.

[58] Williams, 1973, pp. 240–1; Walzer, 1973, 1983, p. 9. Walzer's *Spheres of Justice* moved in a more relativist direction, partly as a response to Gutmann's criticism.

needs and motivations in its distribution. That standard rules out, for instance, treatment for counterfeit illnesses or attending the rich to the neglect of the poor.

Socrates' functionalism, we might say, mistakenly invoked too strict a tie of the concept of a person to a particular vocation and an overly unified common good, too indistinct a notion of individuality. He also relied on claims about diverse human natures, widespread in ancient Greece, which subsequent history and theoretical discoveries have shown to be false. As against empiricist and neo-Kantian views, a realist semantics stresses a posteriori discoveries within long-standing practical and theoretical medical and moral projects.

Gutmann also refers to needs without linguistic or epochal qualification: "Historically, needs [i.e., for medical care] have not been universally recognized as a sufficient basis of rights to their fulfillment." One might add caveats to her argument: Such needs vary somewhat with historical discoveries about the nature of disease and, hence, exhibit historically tensed limitations on identification and treatment – the supplanting of ghost with germ theories, for example. Even so, common needs – in terms of symptoms – and even some genuine treatments have existed transepochally. In this context, Gutmann's concern is practical and political as well as moral; public responsibility for health care must precede the general satisfaction of such needs. Ideologies that stigmatize large groups as subhuman or insist on private contract as the primary means of allocation block a decent response. But the moral recognition of the goods of life and health provides standards to criticize such rationalizations, past and present.

Pragmatically, however, Gutmann also insists, "The *usefulness* of the relevant-reasons argument as an *independent* standard will therefore depend upon how closely the language of relevant reasons reflects the universal needs of citizens *within the society* one is addressing."[59] But this claim confuses political concerns about the way citizens regard needs – "usefulness" – with ontological, epistemological, and moral questions of whether the needs exist. It mistakes social effectiveness for truth. Yet it also stems from a justified moral concern about democracy and individuality. The relevant individuals must ultimately articulate their own needs, and democracy is the best form to register that identification. Given what we know of humans, however, a moral realist conception, appealing to a eudaemonist or a Rawlsian moral theory, would specify the ideal, noncoercive circumstances in which such identifications could occur. At least for needs as basic as health, such theories, combined with

---

[59] Gutmann, 1980, p. 103 (my emphasis). Conversations with Amy Gutmann clarified this interplay of pragmatic and ethical concerns.

suitable historically tensed empirical information about the nature and cures of diseases, can quite easily identify the inadequacies of previous social conventions. If the need for adequate universal health care eventually overrides capitalist modes of distribution, that democratic victory will not reflect a common insight into a feature of English grammar but a political fight to make an ethical conception based on genuine needs – an "independent standard" – triumph over a putative good, the "sanctity of contract" – in this case, the exaltation of money making at the expense of life.[60]

To highlight the clash between realist and alternative semantics, consider a typical example of the insufficient determinacy of reference: Though seventeenth-century scientists identified whales as fishes, Darwinians recognize that whales are mammals. A conventionalist treatment dissipates theoretical progress; for, by seventeenth-century criteria, conventionalists assert, whales *were* fish; the classifications of modern biologists differ wholly from those of the earlier view. (At most, in a reductionist vein, scientific progress may have taken place in the manipulation of putatively nontheoretically influenced observations.)

In contrast, on the realist conception, the seventeenth-century scientific notion "fish" included more than one natural kind – fish and whales; yet investigators still referred to fish. A Darwinian theory not only provides epistemic access to the same kind as the earlier view, but enables us – by excluding whales – to understand it better. Such theory change exemplifies scientific progress.

Similarly, in ethics, despite shifts in meaning between the Greek *dikaiosune* and modern senses of "justice," when we use the latter term, we participate with Aristotle in a common project of gathering and refining moral knowledge about freedom, a common good, equality, and the like. With regard to slavery and the subjection of women, however, contemporary moral views dramatically improve upon Aristotle's. In analogy to the scientific distinction between fish and whales, we have now discovered that just wars and slave hunting are morally opposed kinds of conflict.

For the conventionalist, shifts in moral terminology are just linguistic changes; he stresses the meaning of terms "in the head," their intension. For the realist, however, such transformations sometimes reflect a rational discovery about human political and psychological potentials and needs; she stresses the reference of terms "in the world," their extension. Those changes reflect an ethical discovery just in case they are part

---

[60] The keeping of promises and contracts, in decent societies, is an uncontroversial prima facie component of mutual recognition. But contractual arrangements that violate individuality have no such justification.

of a process of investigation, involving new evidence about social and political organization, which initiates or is based upon an approximately true theory of human capacities for mutual recognition and individuality. For the conventionalist, one set of "preferences" – Athenian ones for slavery, for instance – gives way to another – liberal, antislavery "preferences." For the realist, humans have over time made clear their capacity to participate in a (comparatively) free political association.

8. Theoretical progress and semantic complexity

A standard criticism, internal to science, of realist semantics invokes terms that have an ambiguous reference – say, mass in Newtonian and Einsteinian physics – or lack any referent at all – phlogiston, ether. Given these problems, the critic asks, how is transtheoretical reference possible?[61] Hartry Field has persuasively described what he calls the partial denotation of some natural-kind terms; Newton's term "mass" referred to what scientists now identify, using Einstein's theory, as two distinct types of mass with differing properties (proper mass, relativistic mass). Further, some physicists use the term to capture the continuity of Newton's mass with one type of mass, some with the other. As Field argues, the term "mass" in Newton's theory did not neatly denote either entity; yet, it *partially denoted* both of them. Though Field's case is more promising for antirealists than most – it is genuinely indeterminate between true, conflicting references – it is unusual.[62] In most cases of ambiguity of reference, investigators learn that, for instance, bats are not – as eighteenth-century biologists thought – birds. As science progresses, encompassing major theoretical and factual changes, particular denotations are unraveled, ambiguities overcome, without "the world changing."

Yet as neo-Kantian arguments suggest, the semantic "fit" of theories to the world is often quite complex. Alvin Goldman has, however, supplied a useful sartorial metaphor: Different styles of clothes fit human bodies for diverse social purposes and according to varied cultures and tastes; nonetheless, fit is determined by the shape of the body, not just the tailor's versions.[63] In this context, despite its setting in scientific epistemology, the Putnam–Kripke version is too focused on the piecemeal, particular reference of individual terms. As a refinement, Boyd has advanced an *epistemic access* account of reference, one more attuned to the theory saturatedness of scientific advance. The first scientific theories, even fundamentally mistaken ones like corpuscular or phlogiston chem-

---

[61] L. Laudan, 1984, p. 231.   [62] Field, 1973.
[63] Goldman, 1986, pp. 153–4; Goodman, 1978, p. 138.

istry, make possible investigation in particular areas. As investigators, by a process of bootstrapping and inductive inference, contingently hit on approximately true background theories, the production of scientific knowledge within a discipline becomes comparatively reliable and mature. The terms of the original, approximately true theories, or perhaps of their immediate predecessors, provide "access" to the relevant phenomena that subsequent research refines, disconfirming certain laws, causal relationships, and terms while upholding and reinterpreting others.[64] Thus, the term "phlogiston" did not refer to an actual substance; yet given its role in an atomic theory of combustion, it provided a degree of epistemic access vital to the discovery of oxygen.

In initiating this process, theoretical metaphors – by suggesting not yet precisely understood causal relationships in the world – sometimes play an important role. Boyd's view captures the insight of McMullin's notion of "metaphorical extension" of theories and Harré's of iconic models. In geology, for example, Wegener's original conception of continental drift was suggestive but, in important respects, wrong – continents do not themselves shift relative to the ocean floor; yet the metaphor of continental drift and subsequent empirical investigation led to the theory of plate tectonics. That theory suggests that underlying plates, rather than continents or the ocean floor, are the dynamic elements.[65]

Boyd's account of epistemic access is complex. It explains many of the features that nonrealist arguments stress with regard to meaning. With some elision of the distinction between the use and mention of a term, Boyd lists important relations that might obtain between a term t and a kind k:

(1) Certain of the circumstances or procedures which are understood to be apt for the perception, detection or measurement of $t(s)$ are in fact typically apt for the perception, detection, or measurement of $k(s)$ (operationalism).
(2) Some of the circumstances which are taken to be indicative of certain features or properties of manifestations of $t(s)$ are in fact typically indicative of those features or properties of manifestations of $k(s)$ (operationalism).

---

[64] Boyd, 1979, pp. 377–401. In Dudley Shapere's apt expression, we can discern the chain-of-reasoning connections that, in the course of scientific interaction with the world, give rise, internally or dialectically, to a deeper understanding of its configuration. Shapere goes further than Boyd in rejecting the notion of reference and term-localized charity; nonetheless, the "chain of reasoning" and "epistemic access" accounts are sophisticated, less restrictively semantic, epistemological explications of the phenomenon of scientific continuity (Shapere, 1984, pp. xxxiv–xxxv). Either of these accounts accords with the argument about justice, equality, and individuality of Chapter 1.
[65] Boyd, 1979; McMullin, 1984, pp. 32–3; R. Laudan, 1980; Frankel, 1979.

(3) Certain significant effects attributed to $t(s)$ by experts are in fact typically produced by $k(s)$ (Putnam's example of theoretical term introduction by citation of typical effects).

(4) Some of the central laws involving the term t are approximately true if they are understood to be about $k(s)$ (the law cluster theory of meaning).

(5) There is some generally accepted putative definite description of t which is in fact true of $k(s)$ and of no other kind, property or magnitude ("disguised definite description" theories of meaning).

(6) The socially recognized t-experts form an organized community whose t-beliefs are so regulated that they tend to be true when they are understood to be about $k(s)$ (Putnam's "division of linguistic labor").

    (1)–(6) are related in that, when many or all of them obtain to a significant extent with respect to a term t and a kind k, they will tend to bring it about that:

(7) The sorts of considerations which rationally lead to modifications of, or additions to, existing theories involving the term t are, typically and over time, indicative of respects in which these theories can be modified so as to provide more nearly accurate descriptions, when the term t is understood as referring to $k(s)$.

This argument will emphasize two further refinements of the theory of reference. First, to account for such complex terms as "health" or those that identify biological species, Boyd has introduced the term "homeostatic cluster property." A cluster property is a family of mutually occurrent traits that are causally mutually reinforcing and/or have an underlying natural causal unity.[66] An appropriate notion of "scientific method" or a philosophical account of "epistemic access" illustrates homeostasis. With careful attention to the specifics of nonbiological theories, I suggest, in Chapters 5, 8, and 9, that such important moral, social scientific, and political theoretical terms as a "good life," a "common good," "individuality," "radical democracy," and (the rise of a) "capitalist social system" exemplify comparable cluster properties. In particular instances, homeostasis may break down; specific traits may be lacking or distorted. Thus, this account expects and explains a plethora of borderline cases.

Second, many important philosophical properties and terms are dialectical: Our particular understanding, and its conformity to the world, arises in the course of a historically contingent investigation and discussion and is partly shaped by those contingencies. Nicholas Sturgeon has strikingly formulated this point for the notion of rationality:

> This last circular looking thesis – that thinking something rational consists partly in being in a state responsive to what others think is rational – seems to me one a cognitivist about rationality ought to accept; not because of

---

[66] Boyd, 1986a; Sturgeon, 1985, pp. 28–9, 31.

anything special in beliefs about rationality but because what one's thoughts are about (and what one's terms refer to) is partly constituted by complex relations to other language-users as well as to the rest of the world.[67]

This emphasis on the particularities of conversation reinterprets an important neo-Kantian insight. But in contrast to empiricist and neo-Kantian semantics, a complex theory of reference (see Table 3.2) can cohere with an adequate scientific and moral epistemology.

The realist account of reference leads to a deeper critique of G. E. Moore's and Mackie's claims about a putative "naturalistic fallacy" in ethics. As noted above, Moore rightly maintains that moral characteristics are not simply identical with natural ones and that ethical terms lack naturalistic analytic definitions. But scientific terms, not just moral ones, lack analytic definitions. In science also, to follow out Moore's argument, it would be an "open question" whether particular claims are right and it would take a posteriori theoretical and empirical arguments to establish them. For instance, one might ask whether the colorless liquid we identify as water is in fact H_2O, though that question would hardly lead to a telling objection. Not the analytic synonymy of terms but what Putnam has called "synthetic identity of properties" is a crucial aspect of scientific progress.[68]

Similarly, in ethics, psychology, and political science, investigators might discover, contrary to early definitions of humanity, that slaves, women, artisans, and barbarians had fully human capacities for moral personality. Initial accounts deprecated emotional life and physical activity, and mistakenly celebrated the parasitism, not just the politics, of the leisured citizen. Subsequent theories showed that an appropriate notion of political association included these previously proscribed groups and suggested a greater unity and different relationship of human characteristics and virtues. Through a process of historical change, theorists discovered ethical properties in the social world of a sort that Moore and Mackie denied. Such discoveries require ordinary capacities,

[67] Sturgeon, 1985, pp. 29, 32–3, subtly interprets competing theories of rationality as attempts to specify a cluster property: "Rationality looks to be a disposition of humans in arriving at and maintaining beliefs and plans, one that plays a crucial role in accounting for their cognitive and practical success. A key component is surely respect for consistency; what other features are essential to it, if any, I take to be the empirical question of which other features contribute to the distinctive causal role of rationality by clustering with this one in the appropriate way. Leading competing theories of rationality can then be taken to suggest candidate features for such a cluster; the question of the extent to which each is right will then be difficult but presumably not impossible." Supplementing this account, Boyd, 1989, offers a realist interpretation of the role of convention in scientific research.

[68] Putnam, 1981, pp. 205–8; Harman, 1977, pp. 17–20; Lycan, 1986, pp. 79–81.

Table 3.2. *Some important features of a sophisticated realist epistemology and semantics*

Standard objections	Realist responses
Any realist view must be governed and constrained by semantics	Realism is governed by epistemological, not semantic considerations; it is a naturalistic view, starting from an *internal* examination of our knowledge and theories in any domain and giving rise to a complex, specific account in each;[a] it continually reshapes semantics to fit *theoretical* insights and concerns[b]
Realism supposes an a priori essential relationship of a term to a feature of the world	Realism is an account of *contingent* epistemic access of scientific terminology to features of the world; it also emphasizes complex chains of reasons connecting old views and the relevant evidence to new ones
Realist semantics requires the direct reference of terms to simple, clear-cut properties	Realism can stress complex cluster properties, borderline or hard cases, and synthetic identities of properties, not just the *meaning-determined* reference of each term to a unique property; it can account for the role of metaphor in providing epistemic access both in the origins and progress of scientific theories
Realism focuses solely on understanding of terms by (isolated) individual speakers	Realism views individual understanding as arising from a long-standing social process: a sociolinguistic and epistemic division of labor in different branches of knowledge; yet individuals can acquire relevant learning in any field, e.g., democratic politics
Realism is a univocal, self-contained account, supposing the existence of "one true theory" in each domain and perhaps the whole of knowledge	Realism is a *conversational* view, emphasizing a dialogue about the best explanation(s) of scientific progress; it can stress Hegelian internal (chain-of-reasoning) critiques of alternate theories, given the relevant evidence; depending on the

Table 3.2. *(cont.)*

Standard objections	Realist responses
	domain, it can foresee a *plurality* of approximately true descriptions, claims, or theories; for instance, moral realism emphasizes the common abstract theoretical framework for ethics and politics through which such a theoretical plurality (in ethics, eudaemonism, ideal contractarianism, Mill's utilitarianism) might pass
Realism is reductionist, emphasizing physics – physicalism – as the deepest level of knowledge	Realism sees the unity of human knowledge as a complex web (Quine); it stresses topic- or domain-specific diversity in the levels of internalization and abstraction in particular theories; it envisions nonreductionist *supervenience* of properties from one domain on others

a In political theory, realist accounts of moral learning and semantics are tailored to the goods of *democracy* and *individuality* (see Chapters 7 and 8).
b Contemporary notion of reference, the sociolinguistic division of labor, epistemic access, cluster properties, and chain-of-reasoning connections illustrate this *epistemology-driven* reshaping of semantics.

the same ones involved in daily life and the sciences, not some alleged special "moral faculty" or "intuition."

This book contends that the project of acquiring moral knowledge achieves objectivity; ethical terms, such as "good life" or "just regime" or "(relational) autonomy," refer to real forms or possibilities of social and political organization and individual ways of being. Further, as Chapter 1 shows, just as scientific investigation advances over time, so moral investigation dialectically progresses, especially in the light of certain epochal changes like the abolition of slavery and the emergence of self-aware individuality. In addition, though we cannot reduce moral claims to factual ones, empirical discoveries in history, political science, biology, and psychology underpin central ethical conceptions.[69] Paralleling Quine's influential slogan of epistemology naturalized, one might

[69] Railton, 1986, pp. 204–7; Sturgeon, 1986b, pp. 74–5; Baier, 1985, pp. 230–1, 241–4.

say that this realist view of ethics is – in a specific, nonreductionist sense – ethics naturalized.[70] Moreover, the *supervenience* of moral on other empirical claims illustrates a general realist argument on behalf of the unity of inquiry, or what is sometimes called, more narrowly, the "unity of science." On that principle, scientists expect that the causal mechanisms discovered in different branches of theoretical investigation – in empiricist terms, confirmed by different bodies of evidence – will turn out to be mutually consistent. Realism contends that this scientific principle is reliable because different branches of investigation reach out to features of a common reality. Emphasizing the unity of inquiry, this version of moral objectivity and discovery controversially casts the great debates between liberal and radical political and ethical theories as primarily complex empirical ones, dependent upon historical changes and possibilities, not as clashes of underlying moral premises.

[70] Quine, 1969, ch. 3.

Chapter 4

Neo-Kantianism and moral realism

In Chapter 2, I responded to widespread contemporary criticisms of any notion of moral objectivity; Chapter 3 highlighted the promise of new arguments in philosophy of science in capturing the integrity of ethics. But many influential relativist criticisms of moral realism focus on the issue of progress. In addition, those naturalists who wish to downgrade ethics compared with the exact sciences share some of these objections. This chapter counters versions of these conventionalist objections tailored to my historical argument and then explores an alternative, overall view that resembles realism: Putnam's neo-Kantian "mind dependent objectivity." By examining nuanced ontological, epistemological, and semantic differences, I hope to show that moral realism is more plausible than Putnam's neo-Kantianism. Nonetheless, this book's basic depiction of ethical objectivity and progress and its separation of clear issues, affecting the capacity for moral personality and democracy, from difficult cases of deliberation can cohere with the best general view.

I will outline nine further objections to the idea of moral progress and answer them one by one. The first – a *conventionalist mimicking of realism* – reinterprets the historical argument for ethical advance philosophically. It suggests that what I call moral discoveries are simply new conventions; the ethical discovery-based empirical disagreements that drive complex political and moral clashes are convention-based empirical disputes. The second – the *uneven development of branches of knowledge objection* – maintains that ethics, unlike the natural sciences, lacks the relevant agreement among practitioners (or fails, as a naturalist might put it, to make the requisite discoveries about the world and, consequently, to achieve consensus) to be characterized as objective. There is no moral analogue, so this critic maintains, to scientific advance. This criticism is the broadest, most interesting attempt to undermine the objectivity of ethics on behalf of science.

The third objection is the *arbitrary historical continuities argument*. It acknowledges some survivals in ethical claims across epochal changes, perhaps even those about just war. But why, its proponents ask, should we see these continuities as progress? The realist view, they insist, arbitrarily identifies survivals as advances. The fourth criticism – the *dissolution of theory in practice objection* – emphasizes a discontinuity in the epistemological views of Aristotle, Hegel, and Marx to undercut claims about progress in moral theory. The fifth objection insists on a *Western relativity of the idea of progress*. It stresses the difficulty of identifying ethical judgments, comparable to Western ones, in isolated, non-European settings. If we consider the incommensurability of such cultures with ancient Greece, we can recognize the moral progress, alleged by the realist, as a parochial Occidental phenomenon.

The sixth criticism, due to Bernard Williams, stresses the *nonreplicability of ways of life*. He contrasts real moral conflicts with notional ones; the latter concern ways of living whose social preconditions have faded. For current cases, Williams acknowledges the necessity of judgments of right and wrong, based on claims about truth. But although we may envision past agents as being true to a certain way of life, he contends, our judgments here are merely notional: We can make no other evaluative judgments fairly. His view endorses a kind of contemporary objectivity, yet denies moral progress.

The seventh and eighth criticisms – *individual moral view quasi-realism* and *pure quasi-realism* – largely rely on Simon Blackburn's conception, suggesting that alleged ethical facts and moral progress may be equivalently explained as individual-view relative or as, across possible worlds, conventional. The ninth – the *slenderness of realism objection* – maintains that this account of *abstract* human likeness and democratic individuality leaves too much moral indeterminacy; we need a thicker, though perhaps related, view.

1. The best conventionalist challenge: a mimicking of realism

If right, the first objection is especially damaging because it uses the claims that seem to justify my version of moral realism to undercut it; for a critic might ask whether an alternative, nonrealist explanation of continuities, tailored to this specific argument, is possible. Given the underlying standards of most Western society, we (or the relevant agents) can reach empirical agreement about complex moral questions. Nonetheless, as Gilbert Harman suggests, these standards are simply conventions that arise from bargaining and struggle. Thus, the critic reinterprets my argument's moral discoveries as the emergence of conventions; when this book claims that moral discovery-based empirical disagreements in social theory drive complex ethical and political clashes, the critic insists on the central role of *convention-based empirical disputes* in complex normative clashes. An alternative explanation, he suggests, will then do all the work of epistemological realism, not only with regard to the disputes traced in Chapter 1, but to the complex political and social theoretical conflicts between radical and liberal accounts explored in Part II; it seeks only to shift the starting point.[1] My version of realism (see Table 4.1) seeks to capture an interplay between human likeness and individuality. So unlike Harman's *general cultural bargain, anthropological* version, a close conventionalist account is a *special, moral overlap of diverse individualities* variant. (Given this qualification, we may still call this conventionalist "Harman.")

This criticism separates a strong (epistemological and practical/empirical) and weak (practical/empirical) version of my argument. Granting the latter, it seeks to undermine the former. Further, this conflict of metaethical explanations involves two versions of limited (conventional/moral) objectivity, carefully molded to the particular moral and political claims and social theoretical and factual disputes to be explained. Both suggest that we could be mistaken about important moral issues; these *fallibilist* versions contrast favorably with absolutism and emotivism.[2] Both also emphasize a sphere for individuality, as opposed to, say, absolutist claims that there is a general moral theory that will yield yes or no responses in every case and an emotivism that treats individuality as but a matter of (just as easily rejected) preference. In fact, in contrast to emotivism, this conventionalist version of individuality is what Harman calls a "relativistic realism," or Putnam an "internal realism."[3] As opposed to self-refuting relativisms, this version, once again, self-consciously *makes no commitment to any practical moral claim*. In Harman's version, it insists that no grounds – aside from appeal to underlying societal conventions – can be given for such claims.

This insightful conventionalist criticism allows an assessment of which comparatively plausible competing theory of the core moral and political standards in Chapter 1 is an inference to the best metaethical explanation. It arises in the course of a naturalistic investigation that takes ethics and moral theory from the ground up, arrives at a characterization of the two spheres of political and ethical argument, and then structures a debate about their epistemological significance. It permits external considerations – say, contrasts of science with ethics or semantic controversies – only at this point, but does not, as empiricists and con-

---

[1] I am indebted to Michael Smith, Gilbert Harman, and James Moore for help in formulating this criticism.

[2] Nicholas Sturgeon, 1986a, and Simon Blackburn, 1981, pp. 174–7, have stressed this attraction of these accounts. See also Kymlicka, 1988.

[3] Harman suggested this apt phrase in conversation.

Table 4.1. *Some broad features of a moral realist conception of the two spheres of ethics and political life*

I. In the sphere of *abstract equality* or a *common good*, realism
   (a) Stresses mutual regard for persons in the design of basic political and social institutions, accompanying the abolition of despotism, slavery, sexism, and the like
   (b) Highlights the importance of democratic autonomy; with further empirical claims (Chapters 7–8, 12), suggests the need for a socially egalitarian, participatory democracy and views the search for a full-fledged democratic theory as an ongoing project
   (c) Emphasizes broad criteria for justice in international politics, based on an equally sufficient capacity for moral personality; envisions democratic internationalist cooperation among liberal and/or radical movements and regimes, each of which internally realizes a common good (Chapters 7–8, 10)
   (d) Stresses moral learning and discovery about the nature and extent of human capacities underpinning mutual recognition and democracy
   (e) Also recognizes that *abstract* mutual regard can be embodied in a diversity of justified political and social institutions
II. In the sphere of *relational individuality*, realism
   (a) Emphasizes the discovery of a plurality of intrinsically good activities, relationships, and traits of character; stresses self-respect and the capacity to deliberate as the most important goods
   (b) Expects diverse individual deliberations and self-discoveries or self-enactments
   (c) Maintains that the full characterization of individuality is a continuing project, relying on empirical claims that include the best psychological, cultural, and feminist theories (Chapter 7)
   (d) Provides an externalist account of the motivational effectiveness of moral beliefs; that effectiveness is supported by ordinary capacities for sympathy and empathy, hindered by oppressive social structures and ideologies as well as by motivational and circumstantial complexity
   (e) Also expects a plurality of intricate social constructions
   (f) Looks for moral discoveries about particular goods in diverse traditions (is antiethnocentric)
   (g) Justifies *an abstract theory of individuality*, critical of some "individualisms"
   (h) Sees concordance(s) as well as conflict(s) of intrinsic goods: concordances occur in specific, often nonreplicable configurations; conflicts reveal the loss and regret that are an important part of moral experience

A justified ethical or democratic theory is one that delineates both spheres. Beyond this commonality, diverse moral theories – for instance, ideal contractarianism and eudaemonism – highlight different aspects – say, autonomy as distinct from individuality – and may differ in overall characterizations of the second sphere.

ventionalists sometimes do, previously attempt to *reconstruct* (one might even say, re-found) moral argument.

Yet dialectically, the realist response also rests on an internal challenge, based on Harman's account of induction. Both sides concur that common conventions or moral standards underlie complex, broadly empirically driven ethical and political disputes (Harman's relativistic realism). Harman denies that a further moral explanation of these conventions is ever appropriate. The realist, however, wonders whether some of these conventions are to be *morally* explained (and some others morally criticized). Following Harman's naturalistic epistemology, he defends discoveries about human capacities for moral personality and individuality as *inferences to the best metaethical explanation*.

The realist response proceeds in three parts, two of which I have already emphasized. The first insists on the *integrity of ethics*, the plausibility of an *internal* moral viewpoint concerning at least some claims about a good life for humans. On central issues, such as the initial appearance of freedom against tyranny or the discovery that slaves are fully human, it looks as if we do learn something important about *human* well-being. Harman would need an unusually compelling external argument to suggest that a social convention-based relativism best explains *these* judgments. The *burden of proof* lies with the conventionalist.[4]

Second and worse yet for Harman's alternative, moral explanations contribute to good historical explanations. Thus, Aristotle explains slave anger as a result of defective household management. We see the fact of helots waiting in ambush for their masters, grievances ("shirking," unarticulated expressions of discontent),[5] and slaveholder concessions as so many signs that this ruthless system violated the universal capacity for moral personality (autonomy, social rationality); for the causal role of this moral fact does not depend upon agreement – we may suppose that rebellious slaves concurred with their owners on the broad conventions and putative facts about slaveholding. They imagined only that they had mean spirited masters or that they were unjustly enslaved though others were not. Yet either slave interpretation would be (partially) mistaken; the *injustice of the institution* still produced – and, thus, would be appropriately invoked to account for – their discontent.[6] Reasonable overall

---

[4] Failing to articulate a plausible competing realist alternative, Blackburn, 1981, p. 164, misplaces the burden of proof.

[5] In the modern American case, consider the vision and passion of spirituals.

[6] Joshua Cohen's (1986a) Rawlsian ideal consensus version nicely captures this feature of moral explanation.

Starting from a conventionalist view close to Harman's in its emphasis on cultural agreements, Walzer, 1988a, has recently emphasized the special importance of moral agency. He imagines a *hard case* of women who might agree to become objects of ex-

explanations include this moral feature and rule out Aristotle's. The existence of such *moral explanations*, however, makes a conventionalist account utterly unlikely.

Third, in addition to the *integrity of ethics, burden of proof,* and *ethical explanation claims,* although Harman's bare conventionalism is not obviously self-refuting, it is nonetheless self-refuting. Though he takes no particular stands, Harman makes an important practical – nonmetaethical – claim about the nature of morality. His epistemological argument is plausible only if we can figure out what counts transsocietally as the *moral* conventions. Against Harman's relativism, the realist may ask, Isn't there a hidden, nonrelative standard about what ethics is that makes it at all promising for us to suggest that some claims in quite different, non-self-consciously moral societies are in fact *moral* ones? Harman's view allows three possible rejoinders, a relativist and two reductionist ones.

First, on an iterated relativist account, it suggests that *we* may judge what counts as moral by the conventions of our society (appraiser relativism). Then we will see continuities about freedom between ancient Athenians and ourselves. But the realist counters, What happens if, following an iterated relativism, we take pre-Athenian Greek societies as the appropriate measure (agent relativism)? They may not have had self-aware moral standards; they certainly had no practice or idea of political freedom. Yet on a relativist view, their nonmoral, nonfree conventions are just as appropriate in their community as ours are in modern ones (Harman's seemingly consistent first-order relativism); this comparison requires some common basis for saying that their conventions, which in some ways conflict with, but in many ways are simply different from, ours, are *ethical* standards. This refinement of Harman's account identifies no perspective within distant societies for making such comparisons. It fails to justify its – independent – standard of what to count as moral. As a second-order *moral* epistemology, this account is self-refuting.

change. But he notes, they can never become such objects; to make this a difficult *moral* case as distinct from a (near) straightforward instance of oppression, the description pivots on *their* agency. Thus, the women's rejection of this institution, he says, would just by itself morally discredit it. Further, *we* might know that they were discontented – for instance, by inarticulate expressions of suffering and malaise, as well as more overt instances of frustration and resistance. Walzer's critique of sexism would be explained and justified, against a conventionalist prosexist alternative, by my account of moral explanation. Further, this book's theory of moral agency and individuality justifies the "complex cultural constructions" that he sanctions – all except those that deny the capacity for moral agency in oneself and others. (The women-who-choose-to-be-objects example fails because a theory of moral *agency* cannot consistently justify the canceling of that agency – Rousseau, 1964, 3:355–6.) A moral realist theory might underpin Walzer's new position.

At this juncture, Harman could propose an independent criterion: Ethics concerns whatever standards characterize a minimally decent life for humans – for example, to achieve physical security and freedom of conscience and/or restrict harms and realize important goods, and/or to recognize major features of human likeness and individuality, and/or to resolve explosive communal fights, and/or to settle pressing conflicts within individuals arising from the inseparable questions How am I to live? and How am I to live as one among many others? and the like.[7] But if Harman chooses this path, based on an identification of ethics as some cluster property, then his standard of what counts as moral is not convention based. Instead, he needs a reductionist interpretation of morals; his account suggests two.

On one version, he regards ethics as the study of bargaining to resolve disputes arising from conflicting interests. That view, however, implausibly reduces this complex branch of knowledge to a single, controversial facet, tailored to a conventionalist account, at the expense of obvious moral claims, say, about some human goods and harms or likeness and individuality.[8] Further, an examination of the interests that enter into bargains – particularly the struggles for freedom that Harman sometimes stresses – seems likely to yield a full characterization of ethics against his reductionism. Take the case of slaveholding: Not negotiation between slaveowners and slaves but political and social *transformation* is needed to create more fully *ethical* circumstances – ones that accord with the universal capacity for moral personality. In contrast to Harman's univocal account, this broader interpretation, highlighting moral explanation, plausibly invokes the second, historical distinction about a common good.

In addition, this *reduction of ethics to bargaining* still begs the question that it was designed to answer: *Which* disputes, interests, and customs – especially which important ones – in distant *non-self-consciously bargaining* societies are the *moral* ones? Thus, an adoption by Harman of a plausible, multiple property account of ethics is clearly self-refuting, but so is an implausible attempt to reduce it to interest negotiation.

Harman's account suggests another reductionist approach: a *genetic, psychoanalytic* one. To capture the motivating force of ethical beliefs, he maintains that *moral* standards are conventions specially emotionally

---

[7] In seeking a "speaker relativism" – a view more concerned than Harman's with individuality – Jamie Drier, 1987, has rightly treated the transtheoretical notion of moral as a cluster property to explain very significant overlaps in ethical practices across speakers and societies. Unfortunately, he opts for an iterated relativist account of this use of moral.

[8] Simon Blackburn, 1981, in contrast to standard conventionalist accounts, emphasizes how little social, how much concerned with individuality ethics is. His moral view recognizes the integrity of ethics that his metaethics denies.

charged by the superego.[9] Thus, he explains why ethical standards are hard to abandon, even for those of us who understand their "fictive" basis, because they are connected to a human need to be loved by parents. This explanation invokes a common psychology underlying otherwise diverse moral practices. That commonality, however, undercuts his reductionism.

The realist might ask, Isn't wanting to be loved by parents an obvious part of a human wish for a good – happy – life? Why isn't such a wish simply morally justified, even if, given the empirical realities of family life, many particular forms are filled with distortion and illusion? Isn't there a clear ethical distinction *within psychoanalytic theory* between a good life for humans – one in which adult practices nurture children or at least restrict harm in child rearing and sustain abstract mutual regard in social and political life – and distorted ones, connected to harmful moralisms or destructive features of morality? In fact, the realist might suggest, that distinction explains the comparative stability of some conventions – ones supporting at least some attention to and responsibility for children – as opposed to others. Thus, the reasons justifying this ethical distinction are not only clearer than those underpinning Harman's reductionism (the *artificiality* of conventionalism), but also the very psychological theory Harman invokes – contrary to his interpretation – requires it.

Finally, as Chapter 2 argues, Harman appeals to an everyday *moral* psychology, a Humean justification of some practices based on sympathy.[10] This view also sanctions parental nurturing. Thus, internal examination of Harman's accounts of contemporary psychoanalytic theory and of Humean psychology gives rise to an *ethical* critique of some moralities or moralisms. Those critiques make Harman's relativism self-refuting. A moral psychology, based on sympathy and the capacity for deep self-examination and individuality, provides a more attractive, powerful explanation of ethical practices. That psychology is a component of moral realism.

2. The uneven development of branches of knowledge objection

The *uneven development of branches of knowledge objection* also raises comparatively deep problems for the moral realist; for as a relativist might insist, fundamental debates still characterize political science and ethics. How then could Aristotle have forged a true paradigm in these fields

[9] Harman, 1977, p. 62.   [10] Harman, 1977, p. 104.

many centuries before an agreed-upon – an ethically skeptical naturalist would say, approximately true – theory became dominant in chemistry or physics? Further, the critic might add, once mature scientific theories emerged, scientists concurred about them. After subsequent major conceptual changes, most researchers establish a new consensus. Among political scientists, no similar agreement about social theory or moral conclusions has ever existed. The most plausible inference from this comparison, the skeptic suggests, is that ethics – and perhaps political science – lack a subject matter.

Aristotle's theory, a realist might respond, explains the absence of moral and political scientific consensus. Antagonistic class interests and different conceptions of justice generate persisting clashes. Extending his argument, one might suggest that such interests and ethical opinions subsequently coincide with conflicting social theories specifying opposed causal mechanisms and allocations of blame – for instance, biological justifications for slavery and the subordinate status of women in contrast to historical theories of these arrangements' injustice. Even given a high level of original agreement on core moral standards, such clashing interests, opinions about a common good, and social theories might lead to widely divergent political conclusions and practices. Thus, on a sufficiently abstract level, Aristotle, Spartacus, and Montesquieu could have concurred about the injustice of enslaving *humans*. Sustained by new forms of class conflict, inimical interests and empirical claims prevent consensus in modern ethics and political science. This Aristotelian and Marxian *social conflict* argument specifies an object for political and moral theories (the good life for humans), yet explains the unusually severe dissensus among these investigators compared with natural scientists.

3. The arbitrary historical continuities criticism

The third objection – a variant of Harman's – contends that the realist makes arbitrary historical continuities out as progress. Certainly, the conventionalist acknowledges, the argument of Chapter 1 illustrates some similarities between Aristotle, Hegel, and Lenin and exposes social theory differences that look, given subsequent history, like advance. But as a result of cultural similarities between these thinkers, wouldn't some major continuities exist, whatever the historical eventualities? Couldn't we make any increase in a continuous feature look like "progress"?

Both modern liberal and Marxian arguments claim that objective human capacities and needs, registered in historical demands and achievements, underlie a complex, dialectical moral progress. Given enormous oppression existing to the present day, such progress is evidently not unilinear. Thus, not just any examples of historical development illustrate it. For instance, consider Europe between England and Russia in 1941 when fascism had temporarily triumphed. If one examined Aristotle's theory from the standpoint of the victors, Nazi race theory, a modern pseudobiological version of Aristotle's justification of slavery, would have emerged as the most striking similarity.[11] (In addition to the campaign of extermination against Jews, Slavs, and gypsies, Nazi slave hunters forcibly deported to Germany millions of French, Belgian, and Russian workers.)

In the light of post-Greek historical experience and the preceding argument, however, this feature of Nazism represents not moral progress but glaring degeneration. The Nazi view denies Aristotle's great achievements in political science and ethics and appropriates only his most inadequate contention. The assessment of that regime requires no fine discrimination among worked-out ethical theories. Given the facts about Nazism, even the weakest identification of a *human* capacity for moral personality condemns it. The continuity between ancient and modern liberal and radical theories, emphasized by moral realism, is not arbitrary.

4. The dissolution of theory in practice objection

Chapter 1 stressed the sharp demarcation of theory from practice in Aristotle and Hegel. Marx's conception of theory is, however, practice oriented. As a fourth objection to moral progress, a conventionalist might subtly challenge the notion of a dialectically continuous *theory* of human cooperation and freedom, marked by successive ethical discoveries. Marx's rejection of philosophy, the antirealist might note, is not just a qualitative change, like that between the ancient notion of freedom and modern ones of autonomy and individuality. It is, instead, a radical shift (*coupure*) of epistemological domain that cannot be explicated as a Shaperean chain-of-reasoning connection.

To fix the argument, the critic notes that for Aristotle, theory focuses on the universe's invariable aspects. Philosophers contemplate changeless divinity of which the stars are only the most visible manifestation. Practical knowledge concerns things that change. Thus, moral deliberation does not invoke general laws, but reaches particular decisions. Contrary to *Theses on Feuerbach* and Marx's extensive political activity, hu-

---

[11] Chorover, 1975, chs. 3–5; Proctor, 1988. See Chapters 11 and 13 below.

mans cannot apply theoretical knowledge in practice; attempts to do so will probably issue in grave injustices. Further, the critic adds, epistemologically, Aristotle could envision nothing like Marx's economic theory.

The realist might counter, however, that this objection rests on an uncritical reading of book 6 of *The Nicomachean Ethics;* for if, in an Hegelian vein, we focus on Aristotle's theory of human likeness and political freedom, we can reinterpret the relationship between theory and practice. Political and moral knowledge derive from discoveries about human capacities for a good life, manifested in the polis. Aristotle maintained that the term "good" is species relative: What is "wholesome" (medically) and good (morally) for humans differs from what is appropriate for fish. Nonetheless, medical knowledge and political science aim at "what is advantageous for the good life [for humans] in general." The prudent man has such general knowledge or knows how to listen to those who do. Contrary to this objection, Aristotle's prudence does not consist in "knowledge of general principles *only*"; it also requires recognition of "particular facts." [12] That claim hardly denies general knowledge. It maintains that particular ethical decisions appeal to diverse, sometimes conflicting general principles.

On Aristotle's view, practical knowledge suffers only in the contrast with "lofty" knowledge – knowledge of the divine. In that highly technical, philosophical comparison, even his political science putatively lacks "theory." But his overly sharp demarcation of theoretical and practical wisdom stems from particular – today untenable – features of *this* contrast. Modern scientific discoveries – for example, Kepler's recognition of a comet that would have crashed through heavenly spheres – and better astronomical theories have ruled out Aristotle's claims about the changeless divinity of celestial beings. [13] Even someone who endorsed a fully Platonic realism – a realism focused on contemplation of the (putatively) unchanging, on being as opposed to becoming – could still consistently recognize that ethical theory exhibits the specific, historical kind of objectivity depicted in Chapter 1. [14]

Hegel's view proposes a dichotomy comparable to Aristotle's: The philosophical owl, in its living with death and achievement of absolute knowledge, flies at dusk. The dialectical search for wisdom, on Hegel's view, contrasts with the unreflective vigor – and passing away – of enti-

---

[12] Aristotle, *Nicomachean Ethics*, 1141a21–30, 1140a25–8, 1141b14–16, (my emphasis).

[13] Aristotle, *Nicomachean Ethics*, 1139a2–16, 1141a32–b2. Darwinian theory has overturned related arguments from the appearance of design in nature to the existence of a designer.

[14] I owe this point to Timothy Fuller.

ties within the realm of practice. But this distinction neither undermines his discoveries about human freedom nor the justification, contained in his theory of the modern state, for defending that freedom. Furthermore, his contrast of class conflict in England with German maintenance of corporations has practical implications. He recommended an ideal modification of the German regime to curtail the harsh impact of capitalism.[15] Instead of a dichotomy of wisdom and practice, Hegel might, more appropriately, have contrasted a general philosophical theory of politics and history – one that sustains free regimes and relates reflective individuality to a common good – with practical advice to rulers in particular situations.

In contrast to Aristotle and Hegel, Marx's eleventh thesis on Feuerbach appears to dissolve philosophy into scientific theory-based practice: revolutionary counsel to workers and their allies stemming from Marx's theory of history. But Marx drew general ethical insights about, say, the relation of internationalism to justice in war from his critique of Aristotle, Montesquieu, and Hegel. If the latter's conception of theory is more practical than the conventionalist suggests, Marx's notion of practice is more theoretical. Despite important differences, Aristotelian, Hegelian, and Marxian theories are far more continuous as objective, even scientific, conceptions of a self-governing regime organized around a common good that facilitates freedom and individuality than standard views on the chasm between philosophy and practice can allow.

5. The Western relativity of progress objection

A conventionalist might advance a fifth, related, transsocietal rather than transhistorical objection: Even if the argument of Chapter 1 holds for Western Europe, it is unlikely to be true of more distant cultures – for instance, that of (an imagined) ancient Samoa. The conventions of this society, the critic maintains, did not reflect a putative human capacity for freedom in anything like the ancient Greek or modern European sense. Imagine that they learned to value completely different kinds of conduct, ones as near to incommensurable with ours as possible.

Though plausible on the surface, however, the criticism in this form defeats neither realism generally nor ethical realism. Its notion of convention is neither a verificationist stipulative definition of terms nor a result of a bargain; instead, the term "convention" signifies custom adapted to diverse psychological and environmental needs. But the realist might respond, parallel to the case of Harman's reductionism, an-

---

[15] Hegel, 1966, pp. 320–1.

thropological and psychological researchers could identify transsocietal underlying features to explain diverse conventions. Granting the conventionalist's ethical objection, *scientific* realism could be true for these disciplines. In that case, however, their findings might contribute to a *theoretical* account of a good life and mandate moral realism. For instance, across cultural differences, an environmental explanation of Eskimo hospitality to strangers, based on the harshness of arctic survival, justifies this moral practice. A eudaemonist theory whose ultimate good was individuality might learn from this (and other) Eskimo practices. To provide a successful nonrealist account, the conventionalist would have to propose a better – more explanatory – anthropological theory, envisioning a radical noncomparability of even the categories with which we seek to analyze different cultures. That anthropological theory would undercut the plausibility of any abstract moral theory of *human* well-being. But it remains to be shown that the conventionalist could specify the case of ancient Samoa well and yet uncover relevant, across-the-board explanatory and ethical differences from other cases.

A genuinely incommensurable example would have to preserve enough of our *moral* understanding to be unobjectionable; it could not involve extreme attitudes toward life or even toward individuality. Yet it must diverge in some fundamental way, difficult to explain, from ours. Since the notion of total incommensurability is incoherent, sophisticated proponents of relativity move toward a divided moral conception. Two well-stated postpositivist arguments – David Wong's and Richard Miller's – grant at least the good of life and point only to a further sphere of ethical indeterminacy.

Wong's *Moral Relativity* contrasts traditional virtue-centered – Confucian, Greek, Zuni – and modern rights-oriented cultures. Yet he acknowledges a broad basis for moral objectivity, recognizing that moral facts exist, that moral statements can be true, that nonmoral facts are relevant to the assessment of the truth of ethical statements, and that moral positions can be sound. Good or bad arguments can be offered for them. Facts about human nature, he insists, condemn racial segregation. Beyond these quite sweeping objective claims, however, he rightly maintains that significant cases of indeterminacy exist. Ideals of moral character in a society accustomed to defending rights might differ dramatically from those cultivated in virtue-oriented cultures. Since such conflicts rule out objectivity across the board for "adequate moral systems" – the *objectivity of absolutism objection* that I considered in Chapter 2 – he calls his view a relativist one.[16]

---

[16] Wong, 1984, chs. 9–10.

Yet Wong does not explain the existence of the moral facts or core ethical claims that he recognizes. He does not rule out a naturalistic historical investigation of the human capacity for cooperation and freedom, which underlies his core standards. As Chapter 1 showed, however, that account ironically links the theory of his leading virtue-oriented philosopher (Aristotle) with those of modern rights-oriented liberals. Further, he presents no argument for his claim that the sphere of relativity outweighs that of objectivity.[17]

Richard Miller's account of moral learning skillfully answers many standard conventionalist criticisms of moral realism.[18] He rightly maintains that disparate processes of ethical learning about human harms and goods occur in diverse societies and that each might be an important, self-sufficient kind. Within a normal context-specific framework of such learning – that which prevails in industrial societies – we can decide questions of right and wrong objectively – an element of moral realism. Confronted with a stranger's clashing stands, acquired by a different, equally reliable educational process, however, neither can convince the other: a truth in relativity.

Miller contrasts moral with scientific reliability. But his examples do not reach to the multifacetedness of human goods, the diversity of realizations in particular cases.[19] Instead, he focuses on doubtful cases, arrived at by a reliable method. As part of exploring warrior virtue, Yanomamo males treat their wives ferociously; to preserve social ties, Tiv legal proceedings accept paid witnesses and – what we would see as partisan – testimony from relatives. Yet, Miller acknowledges, human goods and harms provide the basis for distinctively reliable *moral* learning. But in that case, why shouldn't such processes, within a particular society, broadly resemble scientific ones? They might be generally reliable, but *mistaken* in important instances. Given what we know about human capacities, why shouldn't we say that Yanomamo treatment of women – like Victorian marriage laws – fails to respect persons or that Tiv justice is insufficiently concerned with truth and the fate of individuals?[20] *Moral* plurality and complexity probably do not license such strik-

---

[17] Boyd, 1986a. Wong, 1984, p. 208, maintains that we learn about "equal worth" and "respect for persons" from Taoism. These claims are not good candidates for incommensurability.

[18] R. Miller, 1985, pp. 507–31.

[19] Even if they did, taking on a feature of my proposed eudaemonist version of moral realism, Miller's argument would still require an important sphere of objectivity to identify patterns of *moral* learning (R. Miller, 1985, pp. 531–5, 541–4, 548–56).

[20] R. Miller, pp. 537–40.

ing differences about the nature of particular goods. Ways of learning may be *reliable,* but *invalid* in important cases; progress in ethical practice and theory are possible.

To counter a moral realist view, a conventionalist must insist that human psychology is remarkably malleable. For instance, she might maintain that the ethical practices, appropriate to a given environment, mold human psychology, needs, and desires to accord with them: a *moral convention or environmental determinism.* In varied settings, human psychology and needs would become sufficiently disparate to rule out *any* unambiguous reference for a term like "good life." This fact about humans would produce the necessary division between social science and ethics. Realism could explain the results of anthropological and psychological investigation, but nothing like moral realism would be true.

Contrary to this malleability argument, the psychic costs of prevailing systems of morality – the chafing and rebellion they occasion – are a prominent fact of human history; in a Marxian idiom, "the history of all hitherto existing societies is the history of class struggles." That fact counts against the contention that prevailing moralities forge the human natures they need. Now a relativist, strongly economic determinist Marxian might claim that conflicts and metamorphoses arise strictly from changes in the productive forces that reshape moral practices and psychology – *a productive forces determinism about changing human natures.* But wisely, no historicist Marxian has attempted to describe, for instance, the transformation of joyous serfs, before the emergence of commercial agriculture, into rebellious peasants afterwards. In contrast, across varying forms of production, Marxian theory emphasizes the transepochal *exploitation* of man by man – or in a less sexist vein, person by person.

To undercut relativist intuitions empirically, a realist might also extend the argument of Chapter 1 to many non-Western societies. For instance, Hindu political theory of the Sutra and Epic period – 500 B.C. to 300 A.D. – differentiates royal rule that facilitates prosperity and peace from that which does not. As Manu colorfully put it, "If the king did not, without tiring, inflict punishment on those worthy to be punished, the stronger would roast the weaker, like fish on a spit." This basic distinction of justice from "the advantage of the stronger" is the one drawn by Socrates against Thrasymachus. It seems deeply rooted in attempts to justify early kingship, not just in subsequent, comparatively elaborate arguments on developed *political* forms. The former invoked common interests in life and prosperity; the latter focus on the human agency and freedom characteristic of a good life. Manu's international ethics sanctioned resistance to aggression by foreign princes; it included a familiar chivalric code, barring murder of foes with concealed weapons, while they slept or while disarmed.[21]

Today's students of international affairs might look to the Iran–Iraq conflict for an example of incommensurable "holy war." Many criticize Iranian sacrifice of children as martyrs. The United Nations' Human Rights Convention commits parties "to take all feasible measures in order that children who have not attained the age of 15 years do not take a direct part in hostilities." Morally speaking, this restriction derives from the goods of life and sufficiently mature reason to act responsibly in combat (or in a democratic vein, to assess responsibly the cause one is obliged to defend).

But Iranian claims are not incommensurable. The *Koran* also recognizes the value of life and views just – including holy – war as a response to aggression. Sura XXII maintains, "To those against whom War is made, permission is given [to fight] because they are wronged."[22] Divine guidance arises here from ordinary standards of just war.

On the Iranian government's account, Allah inspires "volunteers" with these moral insights. Even the term "volunteer," for recruits younger than fifteen, betrays a certain embarrassment; the government would not like to be seen as coercing children to fight. Trying to speak "incommensurably," an official maintained, "Their [the volunteers'] heroism and enthusiasm were based on the notion of martyrdom, which materialists were unable to understand. Every Muslim has a religious duty to defend *human honor and dignity against aggression.* The children were helping their parents to fight to liberate their soil, to defend the values in which they believed and to protect the revolution."[23]

This argument, however, appeals to the common notion of aggression and routinely contrasts political obligation to serve a just cause with selfish preservation of one's life ("materialism"). Even the claim about heroism invokes generally recognized virtues. In this considerable common context, the Iranian spokesman still controversially stresses an unusual religious good, martyrdom, to *override* those of life and individuality – to some extent – for minors.[24] Yet the religious good plays only a limited empirical role in extenuating a lowered age of maturation. Though the Iranian government recruits younger "martyrs," the United Nations con-

---

[21] Crawford, 1982, pp. 56–8. For a related analysis of Taoism, see Wong, 1984, p. 213.

[22] Sura II adds restrictions on the conduct of war: "Fight in the Cause of Allah those who fight you, But do not transgress limits. . . . If they cease, Let there be no hostility except to those who practice oppression" (Ali, 1983, Sura II, 190–3; Sura XXII, 39–41).

[23] *Rocky Mountain News,* March 12, 1984 (my emphasis).

[24] This claim is not distinctively non-Western. Medieval Christians legitimized crusades – we now think wrongly – by conjuring putative goods of faith and holy war.

vention's recommended age – fifteen – is hardly ancient. Thus, for hypothetical and actual "primitive" contexts, for that of more differentiated cultures that lack a concept of freedom, and for a leading contemporary instance of "holy war," the influential conventionalist challenge to realism about transsocietal incommensurability is difficult to sustain.

6. The nonreplicability of ways of life argument

Bernard Williams's essay "The Truth in Relativism" suggests a sixth objection to any conception of moral progress. He notes that vulgar relativism – metaethical relativism combined with advocacy of toleration – is self-refuting. Nonetheless, he asks, aren't there many historical circumstances on which our moral standards have no purchase? If so, we might regard ethical judgments about the past as *true to ways of life* but *not true about anything.* Across distinct ways, no advance could occur.

Williams separates real moral confrontations from notional ones. In notional choices, he contends, we can imagine ourselves in the world of, say, a samurai or a Bronze Age Greek chief, but cannot reenact their character. Given historical shifts in consciousness, notably the emergence of modern individuality, contemporary efforts to revive the past can only – often disastrously – counterfeit older realities. Capturing a strain in the rise of Nazism, Williams conjures the example of attempting to lead the life of a Teutonic knight in 1930s Nuremburg.[25] At best, he maintains, in understanding notional alternatives, we can have empathy. In contrast, for real options, we can assess the truth of opposed moral visions. Williams's notion of a real confrontation about "ways of life" resembles Hampshire's "stripped down objectivity" argument and Miller's notion of objective contemporary moral learning. It seeks to capture a truth in relativity but exclude an implausible deprecation of current conflicts. As Williams puts it:

> What vulgar relativism tries to do is to treat real confrontations like notional confrontations, with the result that it either denies there are any real confrontations at all, or else brings to bear on them a principle which is inadequate to solve them, and is so because while it looks like a principle for deciding between real options, it is really an expression of the impossibility or pointlessness of choosing between unreal options.[26]

---

[25] An important liberal interpretation of Nazism insists on the survival of the feudal past, a Marxian one on Nazism as a response to a class conflict characteristic of capitalism (Gerschenkron, 1943; Moore, 1965; Mosse, 1964). See also Chapter 11 below, and Gilbert, 1984a, sec. 5.

[26] Williams, 1982, p. 143.

For Williams, relativism arises from a distinctive problem about ethics *in contrast to* science. Ethical terms ("beliefs"), he suggests, do not refer to features of the world; no moral progress exists. Yet he contradicts this central claim: Not all judgments about the past are notional. In that case, ethics must have a specific, common object over time:

> With those types of *S* [moral beliefs] for which relativism is not true, it is not true that there is no distinction between real and notional confrontations, but that questions of appraisal genuinely arise even for *S*s in notional confrontation. But if that is so, then the status of those *S*s will reveal itself also in the relevant criteria for distinguishing real and notional confrontations, the considerations that go into determining that a given *S* is or is not a real option for a given group at a given time. This is important for the case of scientific theories. Phlogiston theory is, I take it, not now a real option, but I doubt that this just means that to try to live the life of a convinced phlogiston theorist in the contemporary Royal Society is as incoherent an enterprise as to try to live the life of a Teutonic knight in 1930s Nuremberg. One reason that phlogiston theory is not a real option is that it cannot be squared with a lot that we know to be true.[27]

Williams provides no "relevant criteria" to identify the commonality of those notional and real options that require moral appraisal; instead, he, rather vaguely, relativizes those notional to particular "real options." In contrast, a realist claim about moral personality suggests cases of slavery, cannibalism, tyranny, *suttee* – the Hindu practice of immolating widows on their husbands' funeral pyres – and so forth. Like phlogiston chemistry, Aristotelian claims about slavery and the subordination of women "cannot be squared with a lot that we know to be true."

Williams captures the issue for science:

> These considerations [about the wrongness of phlogiston theory], if pursued, would lead us to the subject of realism. One necessary (but not sufficient) condition of there being the kind of truth I have tried to explain in relativism as applied to ethics, is that ethical realism is false, and there is nothing for ethical *S*s to be true of – though there are things for them to be true to, which is why many options are unreal. But scientific realism could be true, and if it is, relativism for scientific theories must be false.[28]

Even the notion of ways of life, however, is about humans and human capacities; it is as odd to affirm that "there is nothing for ethical *S*s to be true of" as it would be to maintain that the social sciences and psychology lack an object.

Like Walzer's and Hampshire's, William's argument draws its persuasiveness from a vision of morality as a whole way of life. Such ways are likely candidates for uniqueness and unrepeatability. This focus also

---

[27] Williams, 1982, p. 143.   [28] Williams, 1982, p. 143.

captures that central aspect of ethics which asks, How am I to live? But the rhetorical force of Williams's examples rests solely on asking about the life of a samurai rather than those of a serf or concubine. Despite Williams's concern about real issues, his account loses its grip on what *ethical* commonality is.[29] In contrast, moral realism stresses a different though related question: What can we learn from past and contemporary practice about human cooperation, freedom, and individuality? That question focuses only on particular features of past ways of life, not the whole. Yet as Williams wants, a realist can oppose moralism and affirm empathy and toleration without relativism. Further, realism bars attacks on moral personality and, thus, marks out a range of choices and regimes in which humans may enact their individuality.

7. Individual moral view quasi-realism

If the differences among overall moral views do not arise from clashing underlying cultural standards, perhaps they stem from conflicting individual ones. As a seventh objection, let us consider a Simon Blackburn-like quasi-realist relativism starting from the claim that the moral *view* of each person is fundamentally different from that of any other, although such views may accidentally overlap. In terms of ethical attractions, this conception seeks to capture individuality and resist moralism. Nonetheless, it aims to redescribe moral views semantically, in an empiricist vein, as *projections*, not to think about ethics from the inside.[30] Like Harman's, its challenge to naturalistic views is an *equivalence argument*; it can shape itself to anything a realist contends we have learned in ethics without any implication of moral discovery. But the quasi-realist view is superior to realism because it makes no unreasonable ontological claims and includes itself.

---

[29] Thomas Nagel, 1986a, pp. 140–1.

[30] Simon Blackburn, 1981, pp. 163–4, 174–8. Blackburn emphasizes moral learning and subtle individual disagreement; unlike Harman's, his view is not convention oriented. It draws much of its quasi-realist flavor, however, from a contrast with a bare, nonhuman, physicalism; for it grants a core conception of the good *for humans*, exiling Nazism "beyond the moral pale." Yet shifting metaphors, it fails to describe fully, let alone explain this "trunk" from which the "branches" of diverse individual moralities extend. Further, he undercuts his insights into the good, offering a thin behaviorist reduction: "To moralize at all involves commitment to some way of using an input of information to determine an output of reaction" (p. 175). He does not explain how he can emphasize just these *morally sensitive* "projections" – hardly just "some way" of translating inputs – as opposed to others. Now, Blackburn's broad view of ethics, stressing individuality, concurs with moral realism. Since he fails to motivate his account against a plausible realist alternative, his view – given my earlier arguments on the integrity of ethics and moral explanation – is better explained by realism.

In contrast to Harman's account, this projectivist notes that any particular, empirical person has a diverse, perhaps internally contradictory set of moral *beliefs*. He then says, Let us imagine the ideal purification of these beliefs into a coherent *moral view* by a process of reflection that removes inconsistencies, based on a historically tensed acquaintance with all relevant facts. This process results in myriad, complete individual moral views, as myriad as there are individuals. Many of these views, however, overlap on some important issues, say the wrong of murder. Call that overlap the *conventional* moral standards.[31] Furthermore, to the characterization of *moral* belief, let us add the emotivist claim that such beliefs are just those that are charged by strong approval or disapproval – call these *commitments* – and that provide reasons for action. This view is a developed inside-out version (from individuality to convention) of Harman's "commonality across diverse individualities" objection.[32]

Like moral realism, this individual ethical view quasi-realism can have a general conception of progress and decline. From the standpoint of a later speaker, any significant change in his moral practice will usually appear to be progress. From that of any earlier speaker (or the same speaker taken at an earlier time), the same shift will ordinarily appear as a decline. This conception thus allows for more complex cases, say, of speakers who have changed their moral views and yet experience decline and regret; they can no longer, for instance, take up bold projects that seemed available in youth and now seem utopian. In addition, the account allows, in special cases, a Harman-like, empirical discovery-based progress: A speaker may argue that he changed his moral view when apprised of relevant facts. He insists that he would have kept the old ethical view *if* the facts had turned out otherwise; the later purified position rests on the same underlying moral standards as the earlier one but alters the empirical content of some complex ethical conclusions. In

---

[31] As Michael Smith has stressed, such a theory might, following David Lewis's explication of theoretical terms and mental states, analytically specify moral terms as ideally purified functions of the content of all the commonsense claims – ethical truisms – in which the term appears. Think of this function as a Ramsey sentence that substitutes for such terms as "freedom" and "common good" an existentially quantified bound variable.

Lewis's account of meaning rests on ordinary and scientific practice; following Quine, he denies any special observational compartment in our language. This analytic interpretation can cohere, as he emphasizes, with scientific or moral realism, although it may not semantically be best suited to it (Lewis, 1983a, 1: chs. 6–7; Peacocke, 1979, pp. 142–3). But this sophisticated account of meaning – or a near modified version – is an interesting way of interpreting realist ideas of common reference across theory change.

[32] This formulation of quasi-realism emerged in discussions with Michael Smith and Tony Sebok.

such cases, the earlier and later speakers have a *continuous* moral view; they arguably make discoveries through internal critique or conversation with others, based on shared core standards. These empirical discoveries contrast with the ethical discontinuities – bordering on solipsism – that this quasi-realist reconstruction easily captures.[33]

Yet this quasi-realist redescription of progress is, as the realist might insist, a *mechanical artifact* of a general skeptical view; for the fact that one might give such a redescription of any realist claim does not mean that it is compelling to do so. In fact, this projectivist view appears parasitic on any particular version of realism, shifting with arguments *internal* to morality. Worse yet, the quasi-realist picture is strikingly counterintuitive about evils Blackburn decries. Compared with previous positions, the Nazis saw their own views as progress; others deemed Nazism a barbarous decline. Do we want a metaethics that, as in more standard relativisms, makes a genocidal view right for them and past views right for others? To avoid this consequence, we might probe the informational criterion for forming a moral view. Is it to include relevant *ethical* facts – for example, an equally sufficient capacity for moral personality as opposed to racist claims? If so, then projectivism is defeated: Realism is required to explain justified ethical overlap.[34] But if quasi-realist purification does not include such facts, then it collapses into ordinary relativism, which must implausibly describe the Nazi judgments as if they were moral ones.

Perhaps a projectivist might try to explain Nazism as a common ethical standard-based, empirical controversy *decline;* erroneous Nazi eugenic theories overrode ordinary moral standards otherwise applying to all people. But why, the realist might ask, should *some* important empirical differences, given common underlying standards, lead not to progress but to decadence? And why should there be such barbarous decline, defining crimes against humanity? This *formal* account can implausibly invoke no internal ethical reasons to explain either the nature of this change or its magnitude.

---

[33] In describing hard cases, Simon Blackburn, 1981, p. 177, stresses moral learning: "It is not inevitable that I immediately classify the man who diverges from me as victim of an inferior sensibility. For I may doubt my own, and I may be impressed by other evidence that his is as good as mine; experience may teach me that his is better, since as I improve I may find my judgment tending towards the ones he made all along. Such occasions give us opportunities for learning." Unfortunately, his epistemology and semantics do not support this attractive account.

[34] Blackburn, 1981, p. 177, adopts this alternative.

8. Pure quasi-realism

As an eighth objection, a critic could advance an even more abstract version of Harman's criticism and the ancient Samoa example: "pure quasi-realism." This conventionalist grants the case for moral objectivity for all practical human affairs; major moral disputes are driven by complex empirical and social theoretical differences. This critic could even entertain a stronger version of moral realism – a less historical and political one – than my argument. Standard relativism about values does not work, this critic insists, because we all concur about the relevant underlying conventions; as we have seen, even Harman's favorite "nonmoral" example, Hitler, accepted such standards for (healthy) Aryans.[35]

On this objection, "insofar as relativism is an interesting thesis, its interest doesn't require that there are *actually* creatures with a different moral system than our own any more than the interest of conventionalist accounts of necessity requires that there are *actually* creatures with different conventions concerning necessity from our own."[36] There is still an *epistemological* issue, radically separated from human practice, about whether facts about goodness are moral facts – whether ethical claims have a common object – or whether they are conventional. Let us recognize, the critic continues, that putative facts about goodness are always relative to some standard – they are *relational* facts. Then we need merely imagine an ideal dissenter from human morality who assesses goodness according to a different standard. On this abstract, possible-world view, moral relativism immediately follows. Further, the conventionalist suggests, this account is attractive because it appeals to the common intuitions that (a) no single true moral theory exists and (b) moral knowledge (discovery) is not like scientific knowledge (discovery).

But the realist has several rejoinders to this challenge. First, the abstract objection gives up so much empirical territory to moral realism – all actual ethical judgments – that an inference to realism looks like the better explanation. We just do learn some things about a decent life for humans that make disagreements about goodness sufficiently unusual as to be – as the critic indicates – *practically* uninteresting.[37]

---

[35] Harman, 1977.   [36] This formulation is Michael Smith's.

[37] Blackburn makes his quasi-realism depend on the overall attractiveness of a Humean projectivism. But as I argue later in this chapter, alternative accounts of causal powers are now available to counter Hume's contingent regularity interpretation. General quasi-realism is probably felled by objections similar to those that undercut ethical quasi-realism. For instance, Crispin Wright's elegant, positive review of *Spreading the Word* stresses the tension between Blackburn's epistemology and projectivism: "the blade cuts in both directions: the more success the quasi-realist program enjoys, the harder it be-

Second, if this version of quasi-realism is right, it makes moral episte-mology an arcane subject, radically disconnected from practical con-cerns. But here the critic forgets the important distinctions between sci-ence and ethics that he otherwise emphasizes. Morals are much closer to us than the issue of epistemological necessity – they are about a good life for *humans*. If metaethical relativism is to be an interesting thesis, doesn't it require that there be the relevant kinds of moral differences among us?

In fact, we can easily think of creatures – say, chickens – for whom a good life is different from ours (and different from the one forced on them by the conditions of mass production of meat); of course, it would be our, not *their* understanding of such a life.[38] We can imagine ideal creatures – rational, self-clonable robots – for whom life, pain, social re-lationships, and individuality play no comparable role to their centrality in our ethics. Perhaps their view would be an external consequentialism based on the achievements but on neither the self-preservation nor the moral integrity of the agents. These examples, however, are not telling.[39] The interest in questions of moral epistemology is not nearly so deter-mined by abstract considerations. A coherentist, moral realist account – clarifying the interplay of modern (liberal and radical) democratic theory, ethical theory, social theory, and moral epistemology – is a much more attractive, powerful interpretation of moral argument than a view only of interest in specialist – not even ethical theory – possible-world epistemology and semantics.

comes for the projectivist to maintain the nonfactual stance. If it really can be explained – and Blackburn takes imaginative strides towards doing so – how the moral projectivist can acknowledge the susceptibility of moral judgments to conditional and other forms of embedding, and even how we can have a worthwhile truth predicate for them, then, so far from vindicating a form of moral anti-realism, why has it not been explained how the moral realist, can, in effect, cut past the epistemological difficulties which beset non-naturalism without incurring any obligation to furnish reductions? . . . Once the quasi-realist has earned himself the right to a truth predicate, must not the projectivist sulk in silence unless he can somehow distinguish that predicate from the one which is charac-teristic of genuinely factual statements?" (Wright, 1985, 317–19). As an antirealist, Wright's argument has a special philosophical virtue, showing that considerations that superficially undercut an alternative view in fact support it.

[38] Singer, 1975, pp. 96–113. We cannot know their inner experience. Nonetheless, we can find evidence in their diverse responses to a range of conditions for the claim that *our* judgment about a good life for them conforms, to a considerable extent, with that expe-rience. And we, at least, are moral agents.

[39] Blackburn, 1981, rightly eschews them.
   Michael Walzer's example of an isolated ancient Indian caste system – and his new case of women who consent to be objects of exchange – are among the few attempts in current literature to work out such a relativism (Walzer, 1988a). The pure quasi-realism argument attempts to generalize these cases and eliminate the doubtful assumptions about *human* psychology and well-being that they require.

A distinction due to David Lewis highlights this objection's implausibility. The critic employs the term "moral" not as a rigid designator, identifying in a possible world the properties it indicates for humans, but as a nonrigid, *diagonalized* one, specifying the good for that world's occupants. The criticism is thus part of a modal realist view, based on scientific (and moral) realism for each possible world.[40] That view is interestingly relativist only if Aristotle was a moral relativist.

Finally, the attractions of quasi-realist "relativism" are ordinary moral and epistemological intuitions about plurality and the contrast of science and ethics.[41] But the foregoing realist argument has explained the grain of truth in each intuition; this "quasi"-realist has granted those explanations for human epistemology. Thus, the appeal of this possible-world criticism is deliberately cut off by the constraints on its formulation.

9. The slenderness of realism objection

The ninth objection, concerning the *abstractness of realism*, suggests that, internally, the argument about moral progress, centered on the example of slavery, a common good, justice in war, and individuality, is too thin a basis for an overall realist verdict.[42] Perhaps a relativism, characterized by intersubjective agreement, better explains this continuity. Or perhaps, granting the power of my previous objections to conventionalism, the critic suggests that this realism is pitched at too abstract a level; we should still search for a more fleshed-out account.

The realist can, however, offer two responses. First, the case of the emergence of Greek freedom and the decline of slavery is, just by itself, central to the justification of modern liberal and radical democratic theory. It sets the framework of a political association in which appeals to diversity, plurality, and individuality can fairly be made.[43] The relevant theoretical *abstraction* with regard to human capacities is an inference from – and justifies a diversity of – (comparatively free) realizations or complex social constructions.

Second, moral realism is richer than this initial account. It can offer

---

[40] Lewis, 1983a, 1:xi, 87.

[41] To divide ethics from science, Blackburn has claimed that the supervenience of moral on psychological or social scientific discoveries is a "brute mystery" (Blackburn, 1971, p. 2; 1981, p. 186). But he fails to entertain the relevant examples. The notion of supervenience is part of a successful inference to the best explanation of the role of moral explanation in historical explanation.

[42] This objection is due to Andrew Levine and Benjamin Barber.

[43] Based on individuality, this argument could justify the account of collective rights in a culture of one's own advanced by Joseph Raz, 1986, ch. 8, and Will Kymlicka, "Liberalism and Native Rights," 1987.

similar arguments for many abstract political framework-sustaining claims – for instance, concerning the subjection of women, those exemplified in Montesquieu's *Lettres persanes*, the works of John Stuart Mill, Mary Wollstonecraft Shelley, and Harriet Taylor, the international movement for universal suffrage, and contemporary feminism. Parallel indictments cut against restrictions on voting based on lack of property, status as a manual worker, and putative racial and national inferiority. More controversially, a realist can stress arguments for democratic internationalism, beginning with Aristotle and extending, for example, to contemporary anticolonialism. In addition, moral realism does not just focus on a quantitative extension of freedom, but emphasizes a distinctively modern political theory, democratic autonomy, and a new self-understanding, individuality.

Chapters 7 and 8 explore the implications of these qualitative changes. Chapter 8 studies the institutions of a radical democracy seen as a regime most conducive to the formation of a deliberated public will. That account will draw on Aristotle, Rousseau, Marx, Rawls, Thoreau, Dewey, Gutmann, Walzer, Kateb, Barber, and many others. If the theory I advance is empirically misguided, the core notion of democracy – and many of the institutional insights of these theorists – will play a role in a better view.

Chapter 7 maintains that just as Hegel advanced a novel theory of individual self-determination in modern political and economic life, so also Charles Taylor, David Levine, and the modern psychology of the self offer further insights. A realist can seek a richly elaborated theory of individuality, drawing on the best arguments among contending psychoanalytic paradigms, anthropological explanations of varied realizations of human goods, and feminist accounts. She can provide a full-fledged *eudaemonist* argument about a diversity of intrinsically good relationships and activities.[44] Given a core underlying moral framework linking democracy and individuality, we can figure out – as Part II suggests – what kinds of evidence would settle important contemporary debates about liberal – capitalist or market socialist – and radical democratic regimes. Contrary to the slenderness criticism, this realist view moves from a substantial starting point to a rich account of current political and social theoretical controversies.

10. Putnam's criticisms of realism and moral realism

While Boyd, Kripke, Quine, Goldman, Devitt, Hacking, Shapere, Miller, McMullin, Field, and Lewis have all contributed to the forging of con-

---

[44] I have benefited from conversations about the possibilities of a thicker eudaemonist conception of individuality with Michael Walzer, George Sher, and Robert George.

temporary sophisticated realism, Hilary Putnam played a particularly important role. Yet he has now proposed an objective neo-Kantian alternative. When a major philosopher abandons a view, he often testifies internally to its unclarities and lends opponents a significant voice. Yet he also offers proponents of the rejected view the chance to match the brilliance of his former arguments against that of his current ones, to pit Putnam 1 against Putnam 2. It is, just by itself, a major achievement to have refined our view of the two major, currently contending philosophical positions. Although I disagree with his neo-Kantianism, nothing in the subsequent account diminishes my debt to his work.

Ordinary neo-Kantianisms, like those of Kuhn and Feyerabend, succumb to relativism. So do related pragmatist arguments like those of Rorty and Fine – views that allow intradisciplinary realism about objects but bar philosophical claims about objectivity and progress. In contrast, Putnam has strengthened neo-Kantianism by incorporating realist insights into scientific and moral objectivity and – at least – scientific advance. He also endorses realism as an explanatory theory of the contribution of linguistic behavior to the success of overall behavior and sometimes characterizes his current view as an "internal realism." Thus, Putnam could accept the preceding empirical argument on ethical objectivity and progress, characterizing it as an internal moral realism analogous to the best explanation of scientific progress.[45]

Putnam does not radically distinguish ethical knowledge – and objectivity – from other forms of knowledge. Instead, he criticizes realism on far-reaching grounds that affect every branch of philosophy. Nonetheless, his general objections may seem to many readers powerful against *moral* realism. Even though he could consistently endorse the foregoing argument, the ethical bearing of his neo-Kantian criticisms of realism deserves independent consideration.

In characterizing his new position, however, Putnam uses the term "realism" tendentiously. He explores only one version, what he calls "metaphysical realism" (realism 1). That doctrine, he maintains, has two leading features. Ontologically, this view affirms that a world of mind-independent entities exists. Epistemologically and semantically, it insists that our (true) terms and predicates (come to) correspond on a one-to-one basis with physical features of the world. Though Putnam stresses these aspects, he sometimes advances a further epistemological claim. Metaphysical realism contends that we have *direct* access to the

---

[45] In "Language and Reality," the earlier Putnam stressed the possibility of moral realism: "I do not believe that the account of reference presented here is limited to the institution of science. I would apply a generally causal account of reference also to moral terms and terms from many other areas of life" (Putnam, 1975, 2:290; 1:xiii – xiv).

world, one not mediated by our theories or human perceptual structure. In effect, he assimilates realism to empiricism, a doctrine that focuses on putatively theory-neutral observations.

But this definition is a highly controversial *characterization of realism.* No major contemporary realist, including the earlier Putnam, defends metaphysical realism.[46] Instead, as I argued in Chapter 3, sophisticated realism (realism 2) endorses Putnam's first, ontological thesis as an inference to the best explanation from the success of everyday practice and the sciences. Epistemologically, that inference (roughly) suggests a correspondence theory of truth. Yet this realism stresses that such truth is theory dependent, only approximate, and subject to revision. Further, it recognizes that major scientific discoveries – for instance, the emergence of oxygen chemistry – arise only in lengthy theoretical projects and are hardly "given by nature." Contrary to Putnam's characterization, sophisticated realism rejects a direct access view. It makes the theory saturatedness of our knowledge an *epistemological* problem, not, as in Putnam and neo-Kantianism more generally, an *ontological* one.[47] Finally, as part of the overall epistemological induction to realism, a philosopher may espouse realism about reference: The reference of – epistemic access through – terms to features of the world may be part of the reality that that notion of reference helps to explain.[48]

Given his retention of (internal) realist semantics, however, Putnam's antirealism is problematic. On his account, meaning does not determine reference. Instead, a causal chain, involving the common intentions of scientists and ordinary speakers to identify features of the world, connects current uses of natural-kind terms and previous ones. He suggests that scientists, artists, philosophers, and ordinary language users participate in distinct, collective projects, securing diverse kinds of knowledge. Though we engage in these pursuits – for instance, the artistic widening of our perceptual and imaginative horizons – for their own sakes, these activities also sometimes have instrumental use in practice (applied natural sciences, inductions – including ethical ones – in every-

---

[46] Boyd, 1980a, 1984. For instance, in "Language and Reality," Putnam cautiously maintained that "as language develops, the causal and noncausal links between bits of language and aspects of the world become more complex and more various. To look for any one uniform link between word or thought and object of word or thought is to look for the occult; but to see our evolving and expanding notion of reference as just a proliferating family is to miss the essence of the relation between language and reality. The essence of the relation is that language and thought do asymptotically correspond to reality, to some extent at least. A theory of reference is a theory of the correspondence in question" (Putnam, 1975, 2:290).

[47] I owe this formulation to Lucy Ware.

[48] Devitt, 1984, pp. 188–91; Lewis, 1984, pp. 224–6.

day life, and the like).[49] The best explanations of our practical successes, he suggests, are (internal) realist ones. Unlike Fine, Putnam accepts the general pattern of intradisciplinary abduction. So the sophisticated realist might well ask, If inference to the best explanation is justified throughout our other practices (versions), why isn't it legitimate in philosophy as well?[50]

Moreover, Putnam himself makes abductive philosophical inferences from the theory saturatedness of knowledge to epistemology and ontology, sometimes quite obscure ones about the utter structurelessness of a world in itself.[51] But he does not show that sophisticated realist abductions are weaker than his own. Contrary to Putnam, an induction from the empirical realism that explains our successes in science (that nonobservable or theoretical terms refer to features of the world) to ontological realism (the thesis that common sense and scientific entities exist, independently of our conceptualization) differs from the claim that we can know such theory-independent objects directly.

Putnam's imputation of a "magical theory of reference" to realists obscures the comparatively finely grained differences between the two positions; for both views oppose relativism and recognize epistemological progress, yet insist on the importance of theory and reject reductionism. To undermine sophisticated realism, he would have to show that our diverse (internally objective) versions posit so many conflicting features that we can no longer speak of a single reality. Here a schematic clarification of Putnam's argument may be helpful. The *theory saturatedness of reference* claim (reference 1) responds effectively only to metaphysical realism (realism 1). A compelling neo-Kantian objection to inductions from empirical realism to an overarching epistemological and metaphysical realism (realism 2) arises not from theory saturatedness, which is a component of a realist view, but from a putative *general indeterminacy of reference* (reference 2).

Most of Putnam's arguments, however, do not try to establish general indeterminacy. For instance, he rightly contends that our terms refer only as part of definite theories, which undergo revision and refinement. Reference, to this extent, differs with the context of inquiry; the reference of the term "jade" for commercial purposes diverges from its reference for geological ones: jadite and nephrite. The Kripke–Putnam

[49] Putnam, 1983a, 3:165–9.
[50] As David Lewis, 1984, p. 231, puts it, the internal realist speaks just like a realist outside the "philosophy room." If an epistemologist accepts inference to the best explanation, as Putnam does, it seems odd to regard the "philosophy room" as so segregated a facility.
[51] Putnam, 1981, pp. 62–4. Putnam has repeatedly endorsed Quine's induction from the history of the natural sciences to the general epistemological principle that there are no important a priori truths (Putnam, 1975, 1:ch. 15; 1983a, 3:98–9, 90–1).

causal account of reference requires human intentions to refer.[52] But we might still achieve definite knowledge of features of the world. The human interest dependence of reference (reference 1) defeats any claim about unmediated correspondence, but does no harm to realism 2.

11. Is reference indeterminate?

Against the metaphysical realist, Putnam claims, following Kant, we must see the world as a noumenal whole – a thing in itself or, really, a world in itself – which influences our theoretical descriptions (hence, we can have objectivity *within* versions) but which our versions, even after lengthy historical processes of interaction, inquiry, and refinement, fail to capture. He rightly emphasizes the theoretical complexity and bootstrapping quality of our knowing. Further, as he points out in a realist vein, to say that what is true is what is currently rationally acceptable rules out the possibility of error and learning. He proposes a conception of ideal rational acceptability, which permits us to learn, yet insists that, under the best circumstances – ones in which our knowledge claims obeyed all reasonable theoretical and operational constraints – we could not know that we were mistaken. Like the relativist who can never get beyond the social, the sophisticated neo-Kantian can never *ideally* get beyond the theoretical.[53] Putnam's argument, however, suggests a number of rejoinders. First, his characterization of ideal acceptability misreads the issue. Like the relativist, the realist may grant that all knowledge claims are social; nonetheless, some are false. Analogously, a contention about the reference of our theories to the world, the realist may insist, is a bit of theory, but it may be a *true bit*, a philosophical induction to be included in a comprehensive view.

Second, the practice of science and Putnam's justification of *ideal* rationality insist on the ordinary possibility of error and revision: The world may outstrip our knowing. For an ideal philosophical conception,

---

[52] Putnam, 1981, pp. 46–7, 207–8.

[53] Most neo-Kantians and Rortians never *ordinarily* get beyond the (currently) theoretical (Putnam, 1978, pp. 107–9, 130, 132, 133, 137–8; 1981, pp. 54–6, 104, 133–4, 216; 1983a, 3:18). In *Reason, Truth and History*, Putnam explains the continuity with realism that undermines his ideal conception: "Truth cannot simply *be* rational acceptability for one fundamental reason; truth is supposed to be a property of a statement that cannot be lost, whereas justification can be lost. The statement 'the earth is flat' was, very likely, rationally acceptable 3,000 years ago; but it is not rationally acceptable today. Yet it would be wrong to say that 'the earth is flat' was *true* 3,000 years ago; for that would mean that the earth has changed its shape. . . . What this shows, in my opinion, is not that the externalist view is right after all, but that truth is an *idealization* of rational acceptability. We speak as if there were such things as epistemically ideal conditions, and we call a statement 'true' if it would be justified under such conditions" (Putnam, 1981, p. 55).

why isn't the appropriate abduction the realist claim that, under the best circumstances, our knowledge may still be subject to error and revision? Given our capacities, we may never be able to know some features of the world. Ironically, this realist view seems more robustly Kantian than Putnam's neo-Kantianism. Imagine a species of intelligent creatures, which, because of inadequate senses, could not acquire knowledge of some aspects of the world, say, dolphins and subatomic particles. Why not then imagine that with regard to some important areas of possible knowledge, we are such creatures?

Further, as David Lewis has remarked, Putnam's notion of ideal rational acceptability is paradoxical: We get objectivity – of a sort – because our "ideal" subjectivity cannot fail to do so. Moreover, this view appears to be antirealist only in stipulation, not in substance; for the usual antirealist contends that we achieve no objective knowledge, a *poverty* of objectivity. Yet realism ironically founders, according to Putnam, because we achieve too much knowledge, a *plethora* of objectivity.[54]

Third, his ideal conception of rationality is torn in conflicting directions. On the one hand, his argument suggests *commonality* neither in the world (the conjoint, objective results of our investigations) nor in the characterization of rationality itself. Explorations in different versions should yield autonomous – in a cross-disciplinary context, clashing – results. On the other hand, he endorses the unity of science as a principle of "empirical methodology," stressing such cases as the contribution of discoveries in geology and chemistry to the triumph of Darwin's theory over creationism.[55] He could thus adopt the foregoing argument about the supervenience of the human capacity for moral personality on other psychological and sociological properties. Moreover, against disintegrative notions of reason, he wants to allow rightness in ethics, aesthetics, and the arts along with scientific rightness. Once again, the obvious inductive explanation of his claims about unity is a realist one: Entities posited in different mature domains refer to features of a common world. Instead, in striking conflict with his ordinary recognitions about science and his emphasis on the unity of inquiry, Putnam ideally denies any naturalistic characterization of rationality.[56]

Fourth, he insists on ideal acceptability because he wants to maintain

[54] Devitt, 1984, pp. 188–95; Lewis, 1984, pp. 231–2; Shapere, 1984, pp. xli – xlv.

[55] Putnam, 1981, p. 109 n. 2; 1978, pp. 20–2, 36–7; Monod, 1975.

[56] As Nelson Goodman, 1978, pp. 109–10, puts it for ethics in the same neo-Kantian vein, the "relativity of rightness and the admissibility of conflicting-right renderings in no way precludes rigorous standards for distinguishing right from wrong."

    The multiple features of rationality that Putnam emphasizes – a notion of truth that goes beyond justification, social conversation about what is true, consistency, and the like – are just those that a sophisticated realist would endorse (Sturgeon, 1985, pp. 28–9).

an independent notion of truth as a guide to justification. But a sufficiently generalized indeterminacy of reference to discredit sophisticated realism would also eliminate Putnam's claims about truth and be self-refuting. (Is a claim about universal indeterminacy of reference itself indeterminate?) Thus, a clarification of his argument against contemporary realism does not seem likely to justify objective neo-Kantianism. Nonetheless, I will explore three further criticisms to see if they provide resources for a consistent antirealist position.

Putnam maintains, first, that the theory of learning is primary over other aspects of semantics and philosophy and that this theory, taken in isolation, must be verificationist, not realist. Second, based on the theory of models in logic, he shows that it is possible to scramble utterly the reference of terms within sentences, yet preserve truth value and consistency. Reference can be just as we make it. Third, he reconsiders the standard positivist notion of equivalence between scientific theories that postulate conflicting underlying entities – the *evidential indistinguishability thesis*. As examples, he offers Heisenberg's matrix mechanics and Schrodinger's wave mechanics as well as Maxwell's electromagnetic fields and Newtonian particles acting at a distance. In both cases, though the theories postulate conflicting entities, they achieve mathematical equivalence. Putnam suggests – what he calls – a realist account of such equivalence by arguing that such theories *explain* the same phenomena. Nonetheless, he observes, we have no way to decide which of two conflicting entities actually refers to underlying reality. Instead, scientists legislate this point, deciding to use one or another ontology for particular purposes; they achieve objective knowledge *within* theories but do not map their concepts onto a theory-independent world.[57]

Putnam defends the first objection in *Meaning and the Moral Sciences*. There he proposes a version of verificationism, assimilating the theory of understanding to that of use and isolating it from the rest of semantics. We can know how to flip on a light switch (use), he suggests, even if we fail to grasp the theory of electricity (reference).[58] Nonetheless, he emphasizes, we can still maintain an "internal realism" about the latter.

Unlike the old positivist verificationism, the theory of use, on Putnam's account, does not govern epistemology. But in contradictory fashion, he also contends:

> Whatever language I use, a primitive sentence – say, "I see a cow" – will be assertible if and only if *verified*. And we say it is verified *by saying the sen-*

---

[57] Putnam, 1981, p. 73. Putnam, 1983a, 3:ch. 2 brilliantly explicates and criticizes Reichenbach's analysis of equivalence, revealing the dependence of our knowledge on theories as a whole, not on particular observations.

[58] Putnam, 1978, pp. 99–100.

tence itself, "I see a cow." To use a term of Roderick Firth's, "I see a cow" is self-warranting in this kind of epistemology – not in the sense of being *incorrigible*, not even necessarily in the sense of being fully determinate (i.e. obeying strong bivalence – being determinately true or false). (Facts are "soft all the way down" on this picture, Dummett says.) The important point is that *the realist concepts of truth and falsity are not used in this semantics at all.*[59]

Like positivists, Putnam here makes a lethal induction about truth from theory of use to semantics and epistemology as a whole. But it would be hard to maintain – for instance, his claims about linguistic division of labor and the role of experts – if semantics gave up *all* notions of true and false. Though, as the realist insists, we learn the idioms of many "language games," germ theories of disease work; ghost theories do not. Furthermore, it is implausible to take *local conclusions* within a difficult area – a theory of understanding or even semantics as a whole – as a basis for abductions to epistemology when we can instead – naturalistically – explore comparatively secure ordinary and scientific knowledge as a source of philosophical inferences. In any case, Putnam counters his own antirealist claims:

> One can still be a *realist* even though one accepts this "verificationist" model. For the realist claim that there is a correspondance between words and things is not *incompatible* with a "verificationist" or "use" account of understanding. Such a correspondence, in my view, is part of an *explanatory theory* of the speakers' interaction with their environment.[60]

As a second objection, Putnam uses model logic to show that the reference of terms within sentences can be systematically interchanged without loss of consistency. Reference, he concludes, cannot arise from unique physical features of the world. Yet we are not troubled in our reference to cats on mats – as alternatives to "cats*" on "mats*," which refer to cherries on trees – because reference is fixed within human perceptual knowledge and use of language. This elaborate model-theoretic criticism, however, once again undermines only the direct access materialism of a metaphysical realist.[61]

The sophisticated realist can internally marshal Putnam's own account of reference against this view. His *Reason, Truth and History* still distinguishes natural properties of our world sharply from possible-world properties or miscellaneous ones. Thus, he invokes his famous example of two communities, one on earth and the other on twin earth, which use the term "water" to refer to apparently alike, chemically different

---

[59] Putnam, 1978, p. 128 (my emphasis); 1983, 3:19.   [60] Putnam, 1978, p. 129.
[61] Putnam, 1981, ch. 2, appendix; 1983a, 3:ch. 1.

substances. They ultimately discover – from our point of view, that of earth – that what both communities originally took to be water is, on twin earth, another molecule:

> Suppose, now, that the rivers and lakes on Twin Earth are filled with a liquid that superficially resembles water, but which is *not* H_2O. Then the word "water" as used on Twin Earth refers *not* to water but to this other liquid (say, XYZ). Yet there is no relevant difference in the mental state of Twin Earth speakers and speakers on Earth (in, say, 1750) which could account for this difference. The reference is different because the *stuff* is different.[62]

In our interaction with the world, we gradually and unevenly achieve knowledge separating natural or eligible properties – say, the set of green emeralds – from ineligible ones – the set of grue emeralds, mauve hotdogs, and plastic candy wrappers. As we may see by abduction, David Lewis and G. H. Merrill have suggested, this distinction is built into the world and not merely a property of our world making.[63] Following Putnam's own argument, that claim removes the force, against sophisticated realism, of his model-theoretic criticism.

Many independently weighty objections overdetermine Putnam's argument against metaphysical realism. In comparison, however, he has only one striking objection to sophisticated realism. Ironically for a neo-Kantian, that argument, based on equivalent predictions or explanations by theories that posit contradictory entities, is the standard positivist *evidential indistinguishability thesis.* Though this claim appears to Putnam and may appear to some readers to be less sophisticated and original than the model-theoretic critique, it is, from the standpoint of establishing indeterminacy of reference, more plausible. Within some of our best theories – those of physics or mathematics – investigators posit contradictory theoretical entities. Appeals to diverse entities, however, still achieve mathematical equivalence (in positivist language, common

---

[62] Putnam, 1975, 2:223–35; 1981, p. 23. In "Possibility and Necessity," Putnam has qualified his and Kripke's earlier account of the rigid designation of natural-kind terms by suggesting that we might consider the "essence" that the sciences discover – say, that temperature is mean molecular kinetic energy – as "a sort of *paradigm* that other applications of the concept must *resemble* rather than as a necessary and sufficient condition, good in all possible worlds" (Putnam, 1983, 3:63–4).

[63] Putnam, 1981, pp. 193–4; Lewis, 1984, pp. 227–9; 1983a, pp. 370–7. G. H. Merrill, 1980, suggests that realists advance this distinction to answer the model-theoretic argument but is not himself a realist (Quine, 1969, pp. 115–17, 120–1). In a famous 1953 criticism of positivism, Nelson Goodman offered the riddle of "grue emeralds" – emeralds that are green if examined before future time *t* but blue if examined afterward – to point out that no formal empiricist principle can distinguish projectible from nonprojectible predicates (Goodman, 1973, pp. 72–75).

observational results). Given such conflicting claims, Putnam suggests, we must give up the idea of a theory-independent world.

Yet standing by itself, this thesis has never seemed to legitimize Putnam's epistemological conclusion; for, as empiricists have long said, this line of argument is comparatively certain about the objectivity of theory-independent observations and skeptical only about *theoretical* entities.[64]

Along with empiricists, most neo-Kantians deny the *atheoretical* existence of the scientific posits acknowledged by realism. Yet Putnam's "internal realism" meant – within versions – to oppose exactly these empiricist and neo-Kantian doubts. In the context of today's philosophy of science debates, it is thus especially ironic that Putnam's most powerful objection to sophisticated realism turns out to be the elegant, long-standing core thesis of *positivism*.

Within his account, however, one can marshal several broad considerations that undercut any inference from these examples to general indeterminacy of reference. An argument for *radical* indeterminancy cannot allow equivalent explanations *in the same stuff;* yet Putnam's explanation of specific cases does. Moreover, many specimens of ordinary perceptual knowledge and science do not display anything like the indeterminacy of those special cases.[65] Why should we emphasize instances of seeming ontological conflict – even if they were many – to guide our epistemological and ontological understanding rather than the other examples? How could we then explain the success of many accepted theories that posit a single entity? Finally, for physics, Putnam produces only two cases. An appropriate induction from scientific practice as a whole does not suggest generalized indeterminacy of reference.

The best current arguments about the role of background knowledge in scientific progress reinforce these considerations. Even in instances of conflict between two local theories, couldn't we find aspects of theoretical commonality – positing of similar entities and auxiliary statements – between them? Furthermore, one might ask how complete, with regard to equivalent explanation, the two theories are. Perhaps in these areas, subsequent inquiry will yield a more comprehensive, nonconflicting theory as it has in others.

In addition, the new realist arguments against positivism also work against Putnam's view; for Putnam needs to insist that examples of on-

---

[64] Sense-data empiricism, as I have noted, can be a form of idealism; yet in comparison to Putnam's, even that version comparatively casts special doubt on theoretical posits.

[65] McMullin, 1984, pp. 26–9. Note that this response is not positivist; I suppose that we achieve objective knowledge, including theoretical knowledge, in many other cases and regard the cases of ontological difficulty as either exceptional or, at least, not decisive (Putnam, 1983a, ch. 2).

tological conflict lead to indeterminacy among total sciences. But even if current total science is locally indeterminate, its general theory dependence, particularly the evidential character of theoretical considerations in research design, would rule out alternative sciences with the same empirical consequences.

Putnam also draws examples from mathematics. But realism about science, social science, political theory, ethics, and experience – all forms of inductive knowledge – differs dramatically from realism about the more abstract entities of mathematics, a deductive discipline.[66] The appropriate characterization of mathematics might be constructivist, whereas the former epistemologies were not. In effect, Putnam tries to make the issue of realism in mathematics primary over the (internal) realism about inductive knowledge, which he otherwise espouses.[67] This decision needs an appropriate motivation, but Putnam offers none. His ideal conception of rationality is implausible on its own terms and is not sustained by strong objections to sophisticated realism.

12. Causality and borderline cases

Putnam advances two other arguments that have figured widely, in less sophisticated form, in neo-Kantian and verificationist criticisms of realism: first, that the notion of causality is a human construction, dependent on our interests, and therefore no more a feature of the world than reference; and second, that realism requires the bivalence of statements (for any statement p, it must be the case that $p \vee -p$) and does not allow for borderline cases or vagueness. These claims do not raise the issue of generalized indeterminacy of reference and, thus, do not independently affect the overall debate between Putnam's objective neo-Kantianism and sophisticated realism. Given their influence, however, they deserve separate consideration.

The first criticism centers on the *practice or interest relativity of causality* The term "cause" serves mainly explanatory purposes: Causality does not exist, as it were, "in nature" but varies with human interests and the context of inquiry. Attributions of causality are, if anything is, a *construction*. To support this account, Putnam notes that our explanations never depict the "total cause" of phenomena – a full description of the sufficient conditions of an event – but depend on what we take as background conditions. For instance, we can investigate the origins of a forest fire from diverse perspectives; a ranger might mundanely stress

---

[66] Putnam, 1983a, 3:19–21; Harman, 1973, 1986a.
[67] Even for mathematics and logic, Putnam has made very interesting, realist-tending points about the natural origins of our concepts (Putnam, 1975, 1:ch. 10; 1983a, 3:5).

some individual's failure to snuff out a campfire and omit the dryness of the leaves and the weather, let alone the chemistry of combustion. Counterfactually, Putnam imagines a conversation between extraterrestrials, one of whom says, "I know what caused that fire. The darn planet's atmosphere is saturated with oxygen." [68] This interest relativity of explanation might seem to apply even more strongly in ethics, which concerns good *human* arrangements, than in other disciplines.

Yet a sophisticated realist may respond: Of course, our explanations – and the extraterrestrial's – exhibit elements of salience. But realism 2 insists that our knowledge is theory saturated, and explanations are (often) practice oriented. Why should this interest relativity compromise the objectivity of our explanation of combustion, one that includes oxygen chemistry and specific causes? As Putnam's nonrealist *Meaning and the Moral Sciences* acknowledges, "The fact that explanations may be interest-relative doesn't mean that they can't be *correct*, however – which is all that is needed for the argument I am advancing for (internal) realism." [69] That insight also sustains sophisticated realism against his objection.

Putnam uses this claim against an actual feature of contemporary realism, the account of non-Humean causation advanced by Goldman, Boyd, Shoemaker, and others. As I note in Chapter 3, on a naturalist view, the best overall explanation of our daily successes is that our senses are adequate detectors of external objects and of our scientific accomplishments, that our successful interactions with the world license inferences about the causal powers of theoretical entities. These non-Humean arguments view causation as a fact about the world that requires no independent justification. They reject the skepticism about regularities in nature, widely influential since Hume's classic empiricist account. As Putnam notes, these philosophers are physicalists or materialists. He ironically pits their epistemological claims against their ontology:

> Boyd would probably reply that the "causal structure" of reality *explains* the success of "the knowledge institution" (the inherited tradition which defines for us what is a background condition and what a salient variable parameter): our successful explanations simply copy the built-in causal structure. *Be that as it may*, salience and relevance are attributes of thought and reasoning, not of nature. [70]

Putnam does not show that sophisticated realists are wrong about the non-Humean character of causation ("Be that as it may"). Instead, he characterizes their view as a form of objective idealism: If causality is

[68] Putnam, 1983a, 3:212–14; Garfinkel, 1981, ch. 1.   [69] Putnam, 1978, p. 107.
[70] Putnam, 1983a, 3:215; Boyd, 1980a; Goldman, 1986, pp. 35–6, 42–4; Lewis, 1984, p. 229.

primitive, nature must resemble a mind. But he is too absorbed in contemporary arguments; Plato, Aristotle and Hegel, after all, were plausible realists – and moral realists – who defended versions of objective idealism. Putnam says, rather flippantly, that today's claim is incorrect in view of resembling "medieval Aristotelianism." But the truth of arguments is hardly determined by who first proposed them.[71] Causal powers could inhere in the world without the world resembling a mind, just as, on Darwinian theory, design occurs in nature without a designer. In addition, Putnam was a creator of functionalism in psychology and ethics – the notion that mental states or ethical properties supervene on (perhaps diverse) others. That account makes it possible to be, in Boyd's phrase, a physicalist without reductionism.[72] So reductionism is also not at issue in claims about non-Humean causation.

Now one might opt for Putnam's characterization of causality if human legislation played a much greater role in it – for instance, if radical indeterminacy of reference turned out to be true. But the question of whether sophisticated realism or objective neo-Kantianism is right turns on broad epistemological and ontological issues, not on local concerns about causality.

Putnam's second further criticism contends that realists view every statement as exhibiting bivalence – the statement is true or false for the particular state of affairs or property to which it refers – and rule out borderline cases. He rightly resists the conventionalist equation of *moral* objectivity with absolutism. Sophisticated realism, however, recognizes the complexity of our knowledge. Thus, Boyd stresses the homeostatic configuration of factors that regulate the sustained production of (approximately true) scientific beliefs:

> Approximate truth of background theories, soundness of experimental design, emphasis on observational/experimental method, appropriateness of metaphysical "hunches" (like the anti-"animistic" hunches of 17th century mechanists), freedom from prejudicial political interference, reliability of the indoctrination of graduate students with respect to the more "intuitive" and as yet unarticulated features of the "paradigm," etc. Although

[71] Putnam, 1981, pp. 148–9; 1983a, 3:74–5. In other contexts, Putnam likes to be unfashionable; in moral theory, he emphasizes his debt to ancient and medieval Aristotelian eudaemonism.

David Wiggins and Putnam distinguish natural kinds – natural substances and physical magnitude terms, which "play a role in determining the extensions of the terms that refer to them" and are studied by theories of objective law – from human artifacts (where the causation is more obviously ours). As Putnam notes, this distinction is Aristotelian. Wiggins neatly contrasts moral accounts of a "person" that treat the terms as a natural kind and those that treat it as conventional (Putnam, 1983a, 3:74–5; Wiggins, 1980, pp. 87–99, 221–3).

[72] Boyd, 1980a, p. 24.

these features are all related – logically and epistemologically and causally – they do not represent anything like a single dimension along which the reliability of belief regulation can be assessed.[73]

In every domain including epistemology, important borderline cases will exist. For instance, to assess the role of corpuscular theory in the origins of mature chemistry, Boyd suggests that we need a multifaceted, historical (tensed) account. As a background atomic theory, corpuscularism was approximately true and contributed to accurate modern beliefs. Yet corpuscles do not exist; it was the wrong atomic theory. Further, scientific method reliably regulated belief production over time. But we could not characterize the first generation of true beliefs, based on atomic chemistry, as itself reliably produced because the previous generation was not. The appropriate epistemological judgment about this borderline case is a dialectical, microstructural one.

Similarly, Aristotle's overall theory of freedom, enslavement, and a common good is – as we saw in Chapter 1 – a complex and, in important respects, borderline case of moral knowledge. Given contingent discovery of an approximately true background theory in science (or ethics), the other dimensions, emphasized by Boyd, play an important concomitant role. Science has a bootstrapping methodology in which theory suggests more reliable methods, and these methods lead to theoretical refinements: "The problem of classifying beliefs as knowledge or nonknowledge is not merely that there are borderline cases. The problem, instead, is that the reliable regulation of belief has too many important dimensions, interacting in too complex a way."[74] In view of the intricacy of the items studied, a scientific realist – or a eudaemonist in ethics – would expect many indeterminate, borderline cases.

Ironically, Shapere has challenged the Kripke–Putnam theory of reference on roughly the grounds that Putnam now criticizes realism. That theory, Shapere suggests, defends a nonnaturalist claim about linguistic essentialism that distorts the process of scientific reasoning and ignores

---

[73] Boyd, 1980a, p. 24; Sturgeon, 1984. As Alvin Goldman, 1986, p. 120, puts it, "The main sort of bootstrapping scenario runs as follows. We start with a set of available [epistemic] processes with varying degrees of reliability. We use the more reliable processes to identify good methods. We then use the more reliable processes together with some of the good methods, to identify the various processes and their respective degrees of reliability. The superior specimens are so identified, and their use is said to be justification-conferring. The inferior specimens are so identified, and their use is said to be non-justification-conferring. If the faulty processes are subject to direct or indirect control, we try to avoid those processes. Or we try to devise methods to minimize their impact. In this manner, epistemic melioration is possible." This conception, as we will see in Chapter 5, resembles Rawlsian "reflective equilibrium"; it also captures some of Putnam's complex empirical account of rational acceptability.

[74] Boyd, 1980a, p. 24.

multidimensionality. On his reconstruction, the claim that water rigidly designates H_2O, justified by Putnam's twin-earth example, exaggerates one feature. He imagines an alternative universe in which the relation of fields and internal atomic forces is such that entities like water have the same "secondary" properties we find on earth but lack the relevant chemical structure. Given their theory, our scientists could explain this difference; they would still, Shapere contends, refer to water in that environment. Like empiricists and neo-Kantians, he suggests, the Kripke–Putnam account of reference misguidedly appeals to a priori semantic considerations to constrict scientific reasoning.

Shapere's criticism is mistaken. The essentialism of the Kripke–Putnam theory is a posteriori, following scientific practice. Thus, as a realist in "Explanation and Reference," Putnam discussed Engels's example of lungfish as a borderline case, insisting naturalistically that "the concept [fish] is continually changing as a result of the impact of scientific discoveries." He could simply acknowledge Shapere's counterexample as a correction and suggest that what science identifies as the essence of an element in our environment is, functionally speaking, a range of relationships of internal forces through which a particular configuration of properties may be realized. A realist response could draw on Putnam's claims about psychological functionalism (ones he has recently rejected) and paradigm of reference.[75]

Similarly, for social scientific terms like "civilization" or moral ones like "common good" and "democratic individuality," the relevant features of reality are multidimensional cluster properties. For example, in specifying the reference of the ethical terms, mutual recognition plays a decisive – perhaps, given historical experience, one should say *essential* – role, but the concomitant notion of individuality is diverse, multifaceted, and not – even in dire situations – "less essential."[76] Thus, a naturalistic borderline case or complexity objection undermines neither realist semantics in general nor Putnam's version.

As an additional irony, Putnam's criticism casts doubt on ordinary neo-Kantian objections to sophisticated realism; for if the only knowledge of the world we can have is that which *we* put there, why should any borderline cases exist? Why shouldn't our scientific and moral knowledge exhibit only a single dimension rather than their actual com-

---

[75] Putnam, 1983a, 3:63–4; 1988; Shapere, 1984, pp. 388–92. Putnam's original account elucidated Shapere's concept of transtheoretical terms like "electron" (Putnam, 1975, 2:197). As I noted above, Boyd's account of epistemic access and of homeostatic cluster properties is an even more persuasive response to Shapere's "chain-of-reasoning connections." See also Gilbert, 1981a, ch. 12.

[76] The capacity for individuality is what is mutually recognized; individuality is reflected in political insights into and action about direness.

plexity? In contrast, a realist who imagines that given the intricacy of the world and our knowing, investigators may not arrive at mature theories in many domains for long periods of time and not at all in some can explain borderline cases with comparative ease.[77]

13. Value presuppositions versus moral objectivity

As we have seen, Putnam's failure to distinguish two versions of realism and his persistent focus on the less plausible one undercut the force of his criticism. Furthermore, his objective neo-Kantianism has a deep internal flaw – a dependence on an ambiguous theory of value and human flourishing:[78]

> The notion of truth itself depends for its content on our standards of rational acceptability, and these in turn rest on and presuppose our values. Put schematically and too briefly, I am saying that theory of truth presupposes theory of rationality which in turn presupposes our theory of the good.
> "Theory of the good," however, is not only programmatic, but is itself dependent upon assumptions about human nature, about society, about the universe (including theological and metaphysical assumptions). We have had to revise our theory of the good (such as it is) again and again as *our knowledge has increased* and our worldview has changed.[79]

An ordinary neo-Kantian might suggest, however, that although Putnam's talk of objectivity is interesting, truth and rationality on his account depend strongly on values that he himself describes as "presuppositions" and even "assumptions." His objective neo-Kantianism threatens to collapse into ordinary – as he points out, self-refuting – relativism.

This argument about values is central to Putnam's critique of positivism and his account of rationality. His chapter entitled "Fact and Value" elegantly shows how values of coherence and simplicity influence our choice of scientific theories. Given the underdetermination of theory by observational evidence, empiricists also note the role of these "extraexperimental criteria." But they metaethically affirm the "value neutrality" of scientific method. Those claims are inconsistent.

In contrast, Putnam suggests, so-called extraexperimental values are part of our scheme of rational acceptability. They identify properties of theories as much as any of our other – factual – judgments do. In this

---

[77] Shapere's discussions of the "readiness" of scientific domains to consider specific problems – their degree of internalization as it were – elucidates this important feature of realism. Shapere, 1984, pp. 276–9, 284–6, 307–8.
[78] I have benefited on this point from an unpublished paper by Lucy Ware.
[79] Putnam, 1981, p. 215.

respect, they resemble many ordinary descriptive claims about ethical properties; he stresses the moral charge contained in a *description* of someone "who would do anything for money." Putnam rightly concludes that cognitive virtues are part of our conception of human flourishing, of the good of knowledge as a component of eudaemonia.[80]

Other values underpin his vision. Thus, he claims that a conception of "respect for persons as autonomous moral agents" is an unavoidable regulative ideal. Such norms are part of a coherent, transcendental understanding of ourselves as persons and rational beings. He invokes mutual respect and autonomy to counter a misguided charge of authoritarianism – that any moral claim is an imposition – from an ethically skeptical, would-be defender of individuality: "If there were no such thing as moral wrong, then it would not be *wrong* for the government to impose moral choices."[81]

But how do we decide what counts as human flourishing? Though Putnam briefly endorses a modified Aristotelianism, he does not defend it. Within his account, however, one might attempt two possible lines of justification.

The first maintains that these values are "presuppositions of our conceptual scheme." But that claim, as we have seen, leads to relativism. His concluding formulation is inadequate to his argument. The second contends that the recognition of the human capacity for moral personality and self-reflection are moral discoveries. Such insights are based on straightforward *empirical* claims about what humans are like. Unfortunately, Putnam's possible-world examples tend in the former, relativist direction.

For instance, he considers the case of a "rational Nazi," who tries to justify his monstrous activities. As Putnam points out, arguments for Nazi sociobiological theory as an empirical justification – "capitalism and socialism are Jewish conspiracies," eugenic claims about Aryan superiority, and the like – are "rubbish." But, based on his social theory, such a Nazi might claim – "as Nazis in fact, if not in philosophers' examples, generally did" – that Hitler's regime would further human ("Aryan") happiness.[82] Following out this argument, the Nazi's political clash with liberals and radicals looks like an empirical dispute, involving inductive inferences and evidence about putative racial differences and reasonable terms of social cooperation. At a certain level of abstraction, such a Nazi acknowledges core ethical standards in common with us. For instance, he seeks to preserve healthy children; yet he then uses eugenic theory to claim that "defective" Aryan as well as Jewish and Slavic children need to be exterminated "for the good of [racial] humanity."

---

[80] Putnam, 1981, p. 134.   [81] Putnam, 1981, p. 149.   [82] Putnam, 1981, p. 212.

Such Nazi contentions about happiness are wrong – they combine core moral standards with false biological theories – and their consequent practices monstrous. This analysis, however, points strongly toward realism.

Despite his recognition of what Nazis ordinarily claimed, Putnam then makes his example, in a derogatory sense, a "philosopher's one." He suggests that this Nazi may repudiate "ordinary moral notions altogether." But he fails to distinguish between *rejecting* core standards outright – is murder and oppression of Aryans, for Nazis, usually good? – and *overriding* them, on the basis of a false social theory, in many – in this example, systemically many – cases. In fact, his examples are really ones of overriding, not rejecting, core standards.

Thus, he offers no account of Nazi rejection but refers instead to his analogous example of super-Benthamites who might torture children for small increments of net "hedonic tone." Putnam claims that their scheme of rational acceptability repudiates moral standards, but on the face of it, in this case, too, an *empirical theory of human flourishing* – a crude utilitarian one, hence the unfair invocation of Bentham – overrides shared, ordinary judgments and reshapes the relevant vocabulary.

Now, Putnam maintains that super-Benthamites would develop unique terms for specific hedonic tones; they would fail to describe instances of torture negatively.[83] It is central to his case that these torturers invoke the same facts as we do – none of their statements would be descriptively false. Though not obviously in error, he avers, *we* would say that their view was not "adequate and perspicuous."[84]

But Putnam's defense of moral objectivity falters here; for the ordinary neo-Kantian might point out, super-Benthamites are crazy and murderous from our standpoint, and their views lack perspicuity, but, following Putnam's account, we are "softheaded, superstitious and prisoners of irrational tradition" from theirs. Who is to say which overall perspective is right?

The answer to this neo-Kantian objection requires an insistence on overriding, not the rejection that Putnam confuses with it; for his super-Benthamites share some underlying moral standards with us – an opposition to suffering, for example:

> I will assume that the superBenthamites are extremely sophisticated, aware of all the difficulties of predicting the future and exactly estimating the consequences of actions and so forth. I will also assume that they are extremely ruthless and that while they would not cause someone suffering for the sake of the greatest happiness of the greatest number if there were

[83] Putnam, 1981, p. 212. Bentham worked to reform cruel practices (Shklar, 1984, ch. 1).
[84] Putnam, 1981, pp. 140–1.

reasonable doubt that *in fact* the consequence of their action would *be* to bring about the greatest happiness of the greatest number, that in cases where one knows with certainty what the consequences of the actions would be, they would be willing to perform the most horrible actions . . . if the result of these actions would be to increase the general satisfaction level in the long run (after due allowance for the suffering of the innocent victim in each case) by any positive *e*, however small.[85]

They recognize the underlying standard of human life as we do – they even count the suffering of their innocent victims. They also make straightforward *empirical* claims; there are commensurable pleasures and pains about which we may make fine, sometimes "certain," calculations. Their dispute with us turns on advanced points in the argument – whether such calculations are available and, if so, whether they justify extreme, cruel measures.

But Putnam fails to recognize the internalization of ethics as a branch of knowledge, for the super-Benthamite account is wrong; it does not adequately explain the shared standards about the centrality of life and health in the example of abuse of children. Psychologically and ethically speaking, there is no common, quantitative indicator that sums up and trades lives and other goods. In ordinary circumstances, the augmented pleasure of some does not justify torture of others; recognizably ethical arguments, including utilitarian ones, begin from this point. Further, a moral psychologist might question Putnam's claim that these super-Benthamites recognized differences, let alone fine distinctions, in suffering; for sufficient empathy and imagination to discern subtle forms of pain are probably not characteristic of people as ruthless as those whom he describes.[86]

Furthermore, his notion of ideal rational acceptability misleadingly substitutes corollary cognitive virtues for truth. But such virtues of true theories as perspicuousness and elegance follow from their explanatory power – one can imagine simpler, more elegant theories than those of modern physics, say, that three physical magnitude properties govern the world and their relationships explain every event as being either a root or power of three. This mystical conception is misguided neither

---

[85] Putnam, 1981, p. 140.
[86] Lawrence Blum persuasively argues for the cognitive role of an emotion – compassion – in friendship and ethics more generally (Blum, 1980, pp. 129–39). If moral action is contingent on human motivation, then sympathy is likely to create the imaginative basis for such action (David O. Brink, 1986, pp. 30–31). Such claims are consistent with Thomas Nagel's account of the independent contribution to sympathy and altruism of reasoned insight into the reality of other persons, or awareness of being one among others (Nagel, 1978, pp. vii–viii). A plausible psychological view traces the interaction of reason and emotion in moral insight.

just because it is vague – a proponent could identify some properties and try to "sophisticate" the example – nor because it lies "outside our conceptual scheme." It is wrong because it has no explanatory fruitfulness. Putnam is right that diverse conceptual schemes have disparate, associated normative properties; he is mistaken to suggest that a consideration of normative properties, isolated from substantive claims about truth, can defeat relativism.[87]

What gives the super-Benthamite case a semblance of ethical plausibility is an unstated distinction between normal and extreme situations. That contrast is reasonably at work in ordinary liberal and radical justifications of war and revolution. As we saw in Chapter 1, extreme threats of aggression sanction acts of self-defense that would otherwise themselves be murder. Such dire circumstances might sometimes even extenuate horrible practices toward innocents. Yet only a very unusual complex of conditions would even be a candidate – perhaps it might be justified to brutalize a captured officer whom one reasonably suspects possesses surprise attack plans of a genocidal enemy. Since, as Walzer and Shklar have suggested, such practices involve plain cruelty to the helpless, however, it is doubtful that they can be extenuated.[88] In any case, most circumstances are not dire. On Putnam's account, super-Benthamites implausibly extend practices, not even justifiable in extreme cases, into ordinary ones where only a monster would consider them. Their argument has no merit.

But resistance in dire cases – self-defense against aggression, slavery, genocide, and, if Marxians are right, capitalism – plays an important ethical role in political theory. Liberal and radical justifications of such policies make common core claims with their opponents about the fundamental goods of life and capacity for moral personality but then try to show that particular regimes massively violate – and will continue to violate – them. Complex modern views combine claims about promotion of intrinsic goods and better consequences. *Unlike the Nazi's invocation of eugenic theory, some of these liberal and radical arguments are, when they are true, examples of successful overriding.* Yet they still involve recognizable conflicts of goods. They extenuate practices – even the killing of combatants – which, under normal circumstances, in societies whose laws and basic social practices incorporate mutual respect, could not be justified. The super-Benthamite case implausibly trades on an ethical distinction

---

[87] Putnam, 1981, pp. 212–13. The same argument counters his claim that a Nazi who refused to offer a justification would be acting arbitrarily. Not mere arbitrariness but as he rightly suggests, unparalleled, systematic, murderous lack of respect for persons is what is wrong with Nazi conceptions.

[88] Shklar, 1984, ch. 1; Walzer, 1977.

about overriding in dire cases, which, carefully delineated, can some-times have merit from either a liberal or radical point of view.[89]

A clear defense of Putnam's claim about human flourishing and its interplay with notions of rationality, history, and truth is thus a realist one. As I noted earlier, he was one of the first philosophers to advance a functionalist account of our mental life, one that is neither reductionist nor transcendental. An objective justification could include a function-alist account of respect for persons. In that case, a realist would say, moral properties supervene on other historically manifested capacities for social and political organization and the like. Where Kant's transcen-dental reasoning about regard for rational beings coexisted uneasily with his historical account of the difficult emergence of mutual respect, a functionalist reformulation, acknowledging moral discoveries, would make his defense of autonomy coherent. Similarly, a modern, integral account of human flourishing – one that emphasizes the interplay of em-pathy, sympathy, and other emotions with reason – would depend on discoveries in related disciplines. Further, Putnam does not justify his dramatic isolation of mental versions, particularly concerning mutual re-spect or capacity to be a self, from naturalistic ones.[90] In fact, his failure to consider moral discoveries – and related psychological and political discoveries – makes his invocation of history in the title surprising, for he offers no specific, historical account in ethics.[91]

Thus, the realist argument on the mutual recognition and individual-ity of Chapter 1 highlights a deep flaw – the source of important ambi-guities – in the structure of Putnam's argument: His account depends on a worked-out version of moral (normative) objectivity and progress that he does not supply. It also requires an articulate account of ethical and political theory as largely self-subsistent, internalized branches of

---

[89] If we can't invoke true biological, psychological, sociological, and ethical claims about human nature and distinctions of extreme from ordinary situations, then what is the point of Putnam's criticism of John Dewey's "objective relativism" or his own notion of an *idealized* rational acceptability? If "idealized" acceptability is merely an extension of our tradition and does not permit rational comparison with idealizations of others – if we can see our own past errors, but make no objective assessment of others' views, even to learn from them – then Putnam's conception collapses into relativism.

[90] Putnam, 1981, pp. 78–82; 1975, 2: chs. 14–22.

[91] Briefly advocating eudaemonism, Putnam, 1981, p. 148, offers a glimpse of differences with Aristotle over individuality, but no account of their origin and development.

In conversation, Putnam suggested that there might be no analogy in ethics to the semantic shift in biology from the mistaken notion that whales are fish to the insight that they are mammals. But the example in Chapter 1 of Aristotle's error about slave hunting as a kind of just war is a parallel, one that fits, in moral semantics, either with Putnam's "internal moral realism" or with moral realism.

knowledge. But moral realism is the obvious epistemological inference from the foregoing account of advance in ethics and political theory, just as scientific realism is the best inference from theory-governed technological progress.

Since Putnam advances the most attractive, subtle version of neo-Kantian epistemology – one that is not prima facie relativist and self-refuting – the strength of realist counterarguments suggests that moral *realism* is a worthwhile project. But let us suppose that an overall realist response to Putnam – or some closely related, reformulated version of mind-dependent objectivism – is ultimately unsuccessful. As I have stressed, Putnam's neo-Kantianism still recognizes objectivity and – often – progress within versions and defends ethical knowledge. In fact, his overall argument on rationality and truth depends on the objectivity of the theory of human flourishing. If that neo-Kantian alternative turned out to be right, its proponents could still endorse the claims about *moral* objectivity and progress, the role of empirical and social theoretical clashes in determining complex moral and political conflicts, the distinctive spheres of ethical judgment, and even the *particular* examples of the unity of inquiry advanced in this argument. That "mind-dependent objectivism" could thus sustain and be reinforced by the complex account of Marxian moral judgments and the debates between liberal and radical democrats in Part II of this book.

Part II

Democracy and individuality in modern social theory

Chapter 5

Historical materialism and justice

1. Marx, Weber, and moral objectivity

Part I showed that liberals and radicals, to be consistent, must affirm some version of moral realism and that both are committed to recognizing significant ethical progress. In fact, they have similar – often identical – reasons for endorsing realism and insisting on the historical advance of human freedom, notably the abolition of slavery. As one major theme, Part II contends that given these underlying moral similarities, the major social theoretical and political disagreements between the leading competing democratic and social theories – radical and liberal, Marxian and Weberian – are empirical; they do not arise from opposed underlying moral premises. Relativists have insisted on the comparative intractability of moral disputes; this part, however, suggests how important contemporary debates can be objectively resolved.[1]

As a second central theme, Part II contends that the underlying ethical unity of liberal and radical theory requires a reworking of each. Marx defended social individuality – a society in which "the free development of each is the condition for the free development of all." Yet he neither elaborated a theory of communist individuality nor explored the implications of clashing views of individuality – for instance, eudaemonist conceptions versus reductionist class accounts – for the political theory of a revolutionary regime. Further, Marx started his career as a revolutionary democrat; in 1848, like many other democrats, he merged a strategy for political equality with social equality, republicanism with red republicanism, democracy with communism. Contextually, however, Marx opposed those "plain" republicans who sought to redesign political institutions but left capitalist inequalities untouched. Moving away

---

[1] In political theory, conventionalism has mainly derived its legitimacy from affirmation by Marxian and Weberian social theorists rather than technical epistemological argument. I am indebted to Richard Boyd for emphasizing this point.

197

from his theory's dialectical starting point, he pitted the "social," which he affirmed, against the "political," communism against republicanism, social association against an alien state that would "wither away."[2] Even so, in 1871, he would celebrate the radical democracy of the Paris Commune. Yet in the broadest theoretical perspective, he seemed to suggest that if class-based politics dissolved, so would any politics of dealing with common problems, any conversation of diverse voices, any democratic individuality.

That gloss seems equally inappropriate to this defense of the Commune and his commitment to the "freedom of each," for Marx's communism actualizes rather than dissolves democratic individuality. Chapters 5 to 8 of Part II recast his social theory, based on the insights into moral objectivity of Part I. This part aims to capture neglected themes in Marx's theory and to transform that view through a full-fledged account of radical democracy. Chapter 5 sketches the debate on moral realism within Marxian theory and proposes a coherent metaethical explanation of Marx's views on justice and equality. Chapter 6 explores the richness and complexity of his evaluations, especially the fundamental distinction between "prehistory" – that of exploitative societies – and communist, human history. Chapter 7 begins reworking radical theory, tracing the dialectical inheritance of Aristotle's ethics and political theory in Marx's moral judgments and sketching a conception of the self that fills out his claims about social individuality. It also counters Richard Miller's doubts about the moral objectivity of Marxian argument. Chapter 8 employs this transformed theory to criticize twentieth-century socialist status hierarchies and to work out the institutions of a radical democracy.

The latter section of Part II – Chapters 9 to 13 – explores the consequences of a moral realist framework for a contrast of liberal and radical theories. Weber's inspiration of modern social science and his epistemological neo-Kantianism make his argument a creative test case for the philosophical accounts of Kuhn, Feyerabend, Rorty, Fine, Putnam, and others. But his political and ethical stands – his strident nationalism and racism, his aim, above all, to advance the German *"Machtstaat"* – are often antiliberal. Further, as Chapter 9 shows, *The Protestant Ethic*, famed for its disagreements with Marxians, displays no moral enthusiasm for capitalism and little for liberalism. Ironically, its verdicts are far closer to radical than liberal ones. Given the contemporary importance of modified Weberian theories, the critique of Weber in Part II seeks to restore a self-aware liberal dimension to political science and sociology: a defense

---

[2] Thus, pt. 2 of the *Manifesto* identifies *political* power as the "oppressive power of a ruling class," and conflates "winning the battle of democracy" with the emergence of a free, *social* association. Reinforced by later economic determinist conceptions of communism, this terminological decision has done theoretical and political damage.

of individuality and a common good. If successful, it will dramatically alter the substance and formulation of important tenets of Weber's theory: his idea of a legitimation that needs no moral, let alone democratic, commonality, his dialectic of class and status incorporating racism, his affirmation of imperialism at the expense of democratic internationalism, his ethic of responsibility that checks murderousness only in "means" but not in "goals," his reductionist critique of socialism that – paradoxically, given his account of the rise of capitalism – denies any impact to radical ideas, and the like. My argument has three aspects: an insistence on the ethical objectivity of liberalism, its affirmation of the capacity for moral personality found, in Weber's words, in medieval "city air"; an internal recasting of Weberian theory as democratic and liberal; and a reinterpretation of what is causally at issue between sophisticated liberal and radical theories. Part II further extends into political, social, and moral theory the philosophy of science arguments – neo-Kantian and realist – that feature in the contemporary critique of empiricism.

2. Three interpretations of moral epistemology

A central observation of Marxian historical theory can help frame the issues dividing clashing metaethical interpretations. Moral ideas have often inspired political commitment in great social movements, revolutions, and wars. In contrast, mercenary or coerced armies are usually enervated. The defense of a free way of life – emphasized in Pericles' funeral oration to the Athenians – early Christian, egalitarian opposition to slavery, Münzer's communism in the German peasant war, and the political and social egalitarianism of the French Revolution unleashed enormous political energies. In Marxian experience, the International Workingmen's Association and the socialist and communist internationals in their more radical phases envisioned transnational proletarian solidarity to oppose capitalism and forge nonexploitative political communities. These movements involved millions of workers, peasants, and intellectuals. Despite the vast initial material advantages of hierarchical regimes, radical movements have often grown strong against and overcome them; they have, in seemingly utopian fashion, defied the "material" odds. Such experiences provide the main political illustration of the *Communist Manifesto*'s thesis that "the history of all hitherto existing society is the history of class struggles."

As a critical and practical revolutionary theory, Marxism rejects important aspects of prevailing moralities. For instance, Marx insisted that dominant religious visions and moral duties reflected alienation: an imagined vesting of special powers in alien creations – divinity, the state

– by believers who could not visualize their human source. Some commands – laws against murder – were, morally speaking, rational. But even where predominant views did not sanctify slavery, serfdom, and other forms of oppression, they stifled deliberation and diminished movements toward practicable possibilities for a good life. In contrast, from an Aristotelian point of view, the Marxian vision of communism straightforwardly defends such a good.

Yet Marxians have strongly disagreed over whether and how the preceding account of class struggle does their historical theory justice. For instance, some versions of economic determinism claim that advance of the productive forces governs political and intellectual life and deny any significant, dialectical role for ideas, even conceptions of equality and human flourishing, in social change. As a result, however, these conceptions have little explanatory power. For instance, they implausibly ignore the historical vigor of the radical egalitarian movements, including Marxian ones, mentioned above. But more sophisticated Marxian theories can recognize that ideas – or ideologies – play a decisive role in class struggle.

Yet in response to the query "Why do political and ethical ideas exert such influence?" Marxians have still given conflicting answers. Some have seen them merely as a mask for exploitative interests; so, one might contend, the novel Athenian conception of politics sanctioned slaveholding, and revolutionary French republicanism capitalist exploitation. Such Marxians defend only the *Manifesto*'s debunking claim that "the selfish conception that induces you [the bourgeois] to transform into eternal laws of nature and reason the social forms springing from your present mode of production and property – historical relations that rise and disappear in the process of production – this misconception you share with every ruling class that preceded you."[3] Prima facie, however, this citation says only that the ruling class irrationally projects as "eternal" the forms that serve its interests; it does not deny that some social forms may be reasonable, ethically justifiable.

To sustain their denial of moral objectivity, such Marxians stress the successes of science, including their own historical theory, at the expense of ethics. In the natural sciences, as Engels sometimes maintained, investigators pursue genuine knowledge and achieve agreement; by contrast, moral disputes, lacking objectivity, result in ceaseless wrangling: the *uneven development of science and ethics criticism*. He also sometimes insisted that epochal historical shifts in ethical judgments render rational standards impossible: the *diversity of moral meanings objec-*

[3] Marx and Engels, 1974, p. 49.

tion. Some theorists have been elaborated Marxian cousins of the anti-realist scientific and ethical epistemologies that I explored in Part I.

In a relativist vein, Leon Trotsky and Milton Fisk maintain, moral standards serve specific class interests and are incommensurable. Their interpretation debunks the morality of slaveholders and capitalists and adheres to that of the proletariat; yet, they insist, no rational, ethical arguments can be offered for this partisanship. They advance what David Lyons has called an "agent's group relativism": A moral judgment is right if and only if it is consistent with the standards of the agent's group.[4] These theorists treat the clashing moral ideas of different epochs or classes as equally valid; they then affirm a class-based stand of their own time. To explain these shifts, Fisk claims that circumstances radically shape human needs; class structures get the human natures – at least in elites – that they require.

Like other relativisms, this Marxian version is self-refuting.[5] It makes the peculiar epistemological suggestion that rational comparison of, say, Aristotle's advocacy of natural slavery and Marxian opposition to exploitation is futile. It affirms a communism whose rationality it metaethically refuses to defend.

Thus, in "Their Morals and Ours," Trotsky insists that bourgeois and proletarian morality are incommensurable, a "supraclass" ethics impossible. Yet he concludes with the contrasting plausible claim that Lenin's critique of erroneous political theories leads to an approximately true understanding of the social preconditions for *human well-being* and that Lenin was morally committed to this view:

> The "amoralism" of Lenin, that is, his rejection of supraclass morals, did not hinder him from remaining faithful to one and the same ideal throughout his whole life; from devoting his whole being to the cause of the oppressed; from displaying the highest conscientiousness in the sphere of ideas and the highest fearlessness in the sphere of action, from maintaining an attitude untainted by the least superiority to an "ordinary" worker, to a defenseless woman, to a child. Does it not seem that "amoralism" in the given case is only a pseudonym for *higher human morality?*[6]

The sense of fidelity, conscientiousness about knowledge, fearlessness, humility, compassion toward innocents, and egalitarianism that this de-

---

[4] Trotsky, 1963; Fisk, 1975; Lyons, 1976.
[5] An economic determinist account maintains that the level of development of productive forces *narrowly* circumscribes political, moral, and intellectual possibilities. For a developed account of what the term "narrowly" entails on various versions of economic determinism, see Gilbert, 1981a; Miller, 1984.
[6] Trotsky, 1963, p. 395.

scription invokes needs no special "proletarian" interpretation; these are perfectly ordinary virtues from a transsocial viewpoint. This "higher human morality" provides standards to assess capitalist – and communist – practice; it cancels Trotsky's claim about incommensurable, narrowly circumscribed class ethics.

Marxian relativists rightly insist that political and moral clashes between rulers and the oppressed can be settled only by revolt, not by rational persuasion. But they ignore the internal Aristotelian and Marxian critique of their view, advanced in Chapter 4: Conflicting class interests generate persisting disagreements, even though some moral claims – for instance, that revolt by the *oppressed* often furthers ethical progress – are true.

Fisk advances a group-based ethical naturalism, claiming that the radical class dependence of human nature rules out common standards. For Fisk, the question "What is a good life for humans?" has no transclass, let alone transepochal, response. Analogous to the less class-struggle-oriented Marxian version of human nature relativism, which I considered in Chapter 4, this class determination of psychological needs and personality structures might make a local incommensurability true. Athenian citizens, one might say, through their parasitism upon slaves, became vampires. Yet being subjugated, slaves developed a different personality structure; among themselves, they displayed greater needs and habits of cooperation. But this static incommensurability would not justify Fisk's denial that *some* successive moral views are progressive; for the needs and morals of serfs and workers – say, for full recognition as persons, self-respect, political participation – might repeat important features of those of slaves. If we imagine, counterfactually, that a liberal could have explained a non-slave-based economy – or a Marxian communism – to a rebellious slave, then that conception would have revealed novel aspects of the slave's oppression or depicted, in his own terms, the possibility of a comparatively good life.[7] Why should we not take slave standards – or perhaps common standards appropriate to these groups – as a more fully *human* standpoint than that of slaveholders? Further, if no moral "commensurability" exists, why did proponents of servitude talk of common interests, trying to limit the possibilities of slave *eudaemonia* on a biological basis?

Even if it were empirically plausible, Fisk's human nature relativism would justify incommensurability only *within a class structure*, not on a transepochal basis. Alternatively, a relativist might defend a radical mode of production determination of character, diversely shaping oppressed personalities to be servile, not just conditioning elite ones. That

[7] Putnam, 1975, 2:235–8.

claim would be a plausible candidate for generalized, *dynamic* incommensurability. But the history of slave, serf, and worker hostility and revolt empirically rules out this *radical malleability argument.* Neo-Kantianism in ethics, joined to economic determinism, is not a tenable view.

Like the emotivists Mackie and Brandt, some Marxians claim that ordinary moral standards are hopelessly vague and must be translated into an alternative theoretical language: Objective "moral" standards are those that advance productivity. Allen Wood has defended the most sophisticated version of this sociological reductionism.[8] On his account, Marxian observers can acknowledge the existence of contending moral notions in a society but subject them to no internal, dialectical assessment. Instead, they designate one as objectively just *for a given period* because it coincides with prevailing *relations of production.* That conception, they say, is true, but its objectivity is *sociological*, not ethical. For Marxians, Wood recommends an impoverished moral conception: Contrary to ordinary radical intuitions, justice is a law-bound, conservative, unimportant idea, not a critical one. Wood dismisses radical claims that prevailing juridical arrangements sanctify exploitative forms of association and that those victimized by ruling moralities might ask – as communists have – whether more genuinely cooperative arrangements – ones more expressive of *human* nature – are possible.

Yet he affirms the role of ethical goods like freedom, political community, and self-realization in Marx's theory. Given his strictures about justice, he calls these goods "non-moral."[9] But that odd choice rests on a quasi-Kantian, noumenal understanding of justice as emerging from reflection on the free will of rational beings, not in thinking about the human capacity for a good life that arises from natural characteristics. His division of "moral" and "non-moral" goods implausibly places Aristotle's and Mill's arguments outside morality. When fleshed out, however, Woods' account is contradictory; for by his own argument, a Marxian could assess prevailing conceptions of justice from the point of view of human goods – community, freedom, and self-realization – and recognize their ethical deficiencies. Beyond this, if a free will is the center of a *moral* point of view, then Wood's affirmation of Marx's claims about freedom undermines his contrast. A Marxian could simply affirm a Kantian starting point – capacity for rationality and possession of a free will – as an empirical, moral fact about humans. But it is then unclear, on *Wood's* argument, why Marx could not have adopted a fully Kantian ethical theory. In that case, he could have translated Kant's notion of an initial "asocial sociability" or Hegel's "cunning of reason" into his anal-

---

[8] Wood, 1980a, b.   [9] Wood, 1980b, pp. 124–6.

ogous claim that (pre)history proceeds by the "bad side" of oppression and class struggle; Kant's ultimate view of mutual recognition – treatment of each human as an end in herself – into communism.

Alternatively, let us suppose, however, that Wood denied these other ethical goods and insisted on a bare production relations reductionism. This reductionism does not explain Marx's own moral conclusions. For instance, on Wood's view, the Marxian observer can bizarrely concur with a slaveholder that slavery is – temporarily – just but deny the slaveholder's reasons: that "barbarians" are mere bodies, requiring command, and that slavery is a common good. But the modern theoretical and empirical recognition that slaves have the full range of human capacities shows that this institution is *unjust* and that no such common good is possible. Thus, Marx celebrated Spartacus, leader of the great Roman slave revolt, as one of his "two favorite heroes." He admired slave rebellion even where it promised no immediate success. Not Marx's judgment, but rather Wood's empiricist claim that moral condemnations of slavery are "vague" and that sociological reductionism is perspicuous, needs justification.

In addition, Wood's type of reductionism is not an obvious choice within an economic determinist Marxism. He claims that a production relations reductionism explains Marx's opposition to Proudhon's "eternal justice" because it stigmatizes radical appeals to any concept of equality and fairness. But a more typical reductionist Marxism would stress the unfolding of productive forces. In that case, where a conflict existed between the relations and forces of production, revolutionary demands would advance productivity and deserve to be warranted as sociologically objective claims of justice.

On a productive forces reductionism, Marx might have sympathized with Proudhon's and Lassalle's claims about injustice and recommended popular working-class conceptions – those involved in unionization, strikes, demands for shorter hours – as well. Like Wood's, this version refuses to recognize internal distinctions about the empirical objectivity of moral conceptions – it *externally* sanctions different ones than Wood's in eras of productive fettering. But consider the *internal*, dialectical distinction suggested by Marx's critique of working-class demands for "a fair day's pay for a fair day's work." This slogan may temporarily palliate, but cannot remedy, proletarian grievances because it does not attack capitalist exploitation. Marx thus affirms the workers' claims, but not their full interpretation of justice or embryonic social theory. Instead, he commended the revolutionary – moral – slogan "abolition of the wage system" in place of defective ones, and supported a movement for higher wages and shorter hours, under the aegis of this communist conception, until workers and their allies had sufficient political momentum to overthrow capitalism.[10]

Neither reductionist account can explain Marx's critique. Wood's interpretation denies demands for both fairness and the abolition of classes as appropriate *moral* claims under capitalism; they do not conform to predominant production relations. In contrast, the productive forces account indiscriminately affirms ideas of fairness and abolition of classes, for each conforms with burgeoning productive powers. On these views, existing moral standards are neither critical of prevailing practices nor are they (potentially) internally connected to more thoroughgoing social theoretical critiques.

Now, one might try to square productive forces reductionism with Marx's account by saying that this view sustains only revolutionary, not reformist, conceptions. Demands for "fairness," though they tax capitalist relations, do not sufficiently advance productivity. This reductionism would then sanction radical claims against exploitation but not demands for higher wages. That argument, however, extenuates Proudhon's and Lassalle's views – they defended mutualism and cooperatives – but opposes the ideas of ordinary strikers. Yet Marx condemned the former and supported the latter. To make economic determinism yield even an approximation of Marx's judgments, one needs to affirm an autonomous conception of moral objectivity.

On a realist alternative, however, a Marxian can contend that egalitarian claims have played an enormous historical role because they support human capacities for a good life that exploitative societies systematically deny. The initial conceptions, which instigate and justify radical movements, provide epistemic access to the possibilities of egalitarian cooperation; later theories sometimes offer deeper, more complex insights into these possibilities. If Marxian social theory is right, such movements dialectically mirror and transcend the moral discoveries about human cooperation and individuality traced in the theory of freedom from Aristotle to Hegel. On a realist account, they draw *some* of their force from the approximate truth of their ethical vision. Along with analyses of configurations of social forces, historical materialist explanations – and strategies – would be, in part, moral explanations. As Engels contended in *Anti-Dühring*, Marxian theory would trace "progress in morality as in all other branches of knowledge" and detect in communism "an actual human morality [wirklich menschliche Moral] which transcends class antagonisms and their legacies in thought."[11]

---

[10] Marx and Engels, *Selected Works*, hereafter *SW*, 1:446.
[11] Engels, 1966a, p. 105; Marx and Engels, 1959, 20:87.

Marx's practical moral judgments accord with this point of view. From the *Manifesto* on, he condemned slavery, serfdom, and capitalism as, factually, systems of "exploitations of one part of society by the other," harmful to most individuals, whatever the prevailing legal "rights" or claims of "justice." He advanced the slogan "Workers of the world, unite!" neither as a matter of opinion nor as an eccentric call to increase production. This vibrant internationalism reflected his social theoretical and factual claim that capitalism provides an inhuman setting for the unfolding of human potentials. Contrary to reductionist debunking, Marx's sociological argument, if true, justifies his moral conclusion: the need for a communist society in which "the free development of each is the condition for the free development of all." [12] Ironically, a conception of individuality as strong as that of any liberal view – an insistence on the free development of *each* – leads to the *Manifesto*'s recommendation of a cooperative society. Claims about ethical objectivity and advance are deeply rooted in Marx's own moral judgments.

The next section of this chapter examines a typical ethical debate between contemporary liberals and radicals to highlight the interplay between Marxian social theoretical, moral, and metaethical claims. The fourth section explores the political and scientific considerations that made relativist or reductionist inferences attractive to Marx and Engels. The fifth section probes Marx's paradigmatic rejection of Proudhon's "eternal justice" to see if his argument suggests a consistent *nonmoral* alternative. The sixth traces the radicalizing impact of Marxian social theoretical claims on contemporary rights-oriented and utilitarian ethical theories. The seventh assesses the relationship between Marx's and Engels's scientific and moral realism. The remaining two sections discuss the relationship between structural and ethical explanation and the ambiguous reference of Marx's use of the term "exploitation."

3. What can Marxists fairly say about injustices?

In his 1973 *One Hundred Countries, Two Billion People*, Robert S. Mc-Namara, then president of the World Bank, passionately called for international redistribution. Pointing to the glaring injustice of poverty in India, he insisted:

> It is the poorest 40% who despite their country's gross economic growth remain in conditions of deprivation that fall below any rational definition of human decency. . . . When we reflect that of the more than half a billion persons living on the Indian subcontinent, some 200 million subsist on

[12] Marx and Engels, *SW*, 1:54.

incomes that average less than $40 a year, how are we to comprehend what that really implies?[13]

One might add that if the bottom 40 percent are so poor, the circumstances of the vast majority are only slightly less oppressive and uncertain. By any conception of meeting minimal human needs, ones that include food, shelter, jobs, health care, and schooling, let alone broader conceptions of individuality, these vast inequalities, characteristic of particular countries and more strikingly of international society, seem unjust, perverse, outrageous. Furthermore, McNamara notes, inequality of income shares is increasing in India, as in many other poor nations.[14]

On McNamara's account, the causes of this impoverishment seem unclear. They may reside in some absence of dynamism among entrepreneurs or the masses of people, or perhaps in some putative cultural or psychological deficiency. They do not stem mainly from the heritage of colonialism or contemporary foreign intervention. Yet once a common concern, spurred by McNamara's book, becomes widespread among policy-making elites, he expects that the conditions of the least advantaged will improve.

How might a Marxist respond to this appeal for justice? In a classic strategy suggested by Engels's 1873 *The Housing Question*, a Marxian might stress certain facts about the international situation, pertaining to the *interaction* of rich and poor, that make McNamara's appeal, ineffective.[15] In the poor nations, he might note, the new elites – bourgeoisie – benefit from skewed income distribution.[16] Furthermore, the advanced capitalist elites have a common interest with the new elites in maintaining impoverishment; they benefit from cheap labor, for example. Hence, they supply economic and military aid to sustain repressive regimes and social structures. The austerity policies of international monetary institutions flow from these common elite interests, creating further impoverishment. For the Marxist, a political version of Lenin's theory of imperialism or today's dependency theory would appear to explain the increase in inequality in poor countries. Such a theory stresses the gap between at best skewed and unequal economic growth and elite rhetoric about redistribution.[17] Correspondingly, only mutual support among nonelite social forces – workers, peasants, and students in the poor na-

---

[13] McNamara, 1973, pp. 104–5. See also Beitz, 1975; Gilbert, 1978b; O'Neill, 1985; and Singer, 1972.

[14] Since little has changed in the past decade and a half, I treat McNamara's conclusions in the present tense.

[15] *The Housing Question* responds to Mülberger, a German Proudhonist.

[16] Tucker, 1977, pp. 154–5.

[17] Myrdal, 1970, pp. 60–1; Chomsky and Hermann, 1979; McCamant, 1984.

tions and workers, students, and intellectuals in more industrial ones – offers any hope of securing redistribution to the less advantaged.[18]

McNamara's view suggests that the World Bank, having recognized international injustice, would welcome attempts at redistribution. On a Marxian conception, the bank, tied to certain class interests and rhetoric notwithstanding, would oppose serious reform alternatives. For example, consider the World Bank's reaction to the 1970 Chilean election of the democratic socialist Allende regime. Far from encouraging even this nonrevolutionary attempt at redistribution, the bank slashed its aid from over twenty million dollars per year to zero. After the 1973 coup, it nurtured the Pinochet dictatorship.[19] Thus, the Marxist might conclude, the facts and an accurate social theory show that major redistribution cannot occur within a capitalist international economic order.

Yet something seems peculiar about this Marxian response. Mc-Namara agonizes over the arbitrariness of mass impoverishment joined with superfluous riches for the few; the Marxist, however, says nothing about it. Perhaps he holds a relativist interpretation according to which McNamara has a "bourgeois" conception of justice and such conceptions are simply a muddle; perhaps he holds the reductionist view that McNamara rightly sees this distribution as unjust – capitalism as a productive system has passed its historical zenith – but is wrong about the reasons. If true, however, a Marxian social analysis *undermines* only McNamara's contention that the World Bank can serve as an instrument for redistribution; it leaves his claim about the glaring injustice of international distribution – in Engels's phrase, the "crying contrasts" of rich and poor – perfectly intact.[20] Furthermore, Marxian social theory shows who benefits from these injustices and suggests a defect of character in McNamara, who at least deceives himself. Though this Marxist might contend that a condemnation of injustice can occur only on McNamara's ethical premise, it is hard to see why a Marxian wouldn't share this standard. Marxians do, after all, object to enormous disparities of wealth and poverty and their social consequences; an indictment of these consequences provides central motivations for communism. Actually, a common moral concern lends urgency to this Marxian criticism of McNamara's solution. Nothing in the empirical critique of the latter's remedy – calling on conscientious elites to rectify impoverishment – requires a rejection of all concepts of justice.

Furthermore, this Marxist's refusal to address McNamara's moral assessment seems ironic, for, if anything, a Marxian has stronger reasons for calling this international situation *unjust*. Given McNamara's hazy

[18] Gilbert, 1978b.   [19] Cusack, 1977, p. 144; Payer, 1975.
[20] Taylor, 1973; Engels, 1966a, pp. 173–4.

views on the causes of such inequalities, he may blame the victim – the national character trait explanations – or historical accident. But suppose the citizens of poor nations, through internal environmental causes, lack initiative, or suppose international inequalities have come about through no one's fault. We might call the former situation – where these citizens, due to their own inadequacies, end up impoverished – sad, perhaps tragic, but not an *injustice*. Even in the latter case, though Rawls has forcefully defended rectifying social and natural arbitrariness as a matter of fairness, no one is to blame. However much it may require remedy, this situation resembles, say, a catastrophic flood and is not *obviously* unjust.[21] But a Marxian analysis, if true, shows how victimization has occurred and fixes appropriate responsibility on the beneficiaries. More plausibly than McNamara, a Marxian can view contemporary international distribution as an *injustice*.

In this context, a realist argument, revealing the grain of truth in McNamara's moral conception, seems a far more appropriate metaethical characterization of these Marxian historical claims than relativism or reductionism. This example highlights the inaccuracy of Marx's and Engels's occasional interpretation of their scientific views as simply a historical critique of prevailing conceptions of justice. Since, paradoxically, their theory leads more decisively than McNamara's to moral condemnation, this analysis invites a deeper inquiry into the reasons why Marx and Engels found relativist and reductionist formulations attractive.

4. Marx's and Engels's metaethical ambiguities

Marx's and Engels's metaethical argument vacillates between relativist or reductionist conceptions of justice and a realist one. Their conception of revolutionary strategy undercuts a moralistic view. Thus, on their historical argument, prevailing notions of justice derive from a system of law that suits the needs of a predominant mode of production. Pointing to the epoch relativism or functional validity of such ethical concepts, this historical theory deflates the grandiose claims of theorists who seek to transform society morally; for ironically, Marx and Engels maintained, radical claims about injustice frequently share in prevailing conceptions and offer no adequate analysis of social structure and political alternatives. Instead, they sometimes argued, communists require only a clear understanding of capitalism's internal conflicts and definite political strategies to overthrow it. On Marx's account, the cultural prevalence of procapitalist ideas and, hence, the lack of well-articulated political alternative except in (some) situations of widespread social conflict, as well

[21] Gilbert, 1978b, pp. 109–10, 117.

as ruling-class control of arms, make revolution difficult. Moral fuss not only cannot substitute for relevant theoretical analysis, but points in the wrong direction by obscuring the need for a patient, realistic perspective.[22] Moreover, indignation encourages an elitist radicalism that scorns actual struggles: "Can't you see that capitalism is wrong?" the elitist avers; "Workers must be stupid not to have overthrown it long ago." Or perhaps, more modestly, he might insist, "As workers *should* know, it's counterproductive to strike for higher wages; they should form cooperatives, instead."

Thus, Proudhon sought fair exchanges among small propertyholders through mutualist banking arrangements. He opposed unions on the grounds that they violated individual liberty and even defended the French government when it shot down striking miners at Rive-de-Gier.[23] Alleging racial inferiority, he commended American slavery and czarist domination of Poland. Similarly, the German tailor Wilhelm Weitling, sometimes celebrated as a Christian, humanist alternative to the "heartless," atheist Marx, dismissed the industrial working class as unready for immediate revolt; he advocated communist uprising by the "thieving proletariat."[24] Both these influential radical opponents of Marx relied on moral concepts as the central feature of their social theory and scorned the actual working-class movement. Ideal-typically, moralistic radicalism encourages a dialectic between intense, isolated action and ultimate discouragement, blamed on the apathy of the victims of capitalism.

In contrast, Marx suggested, as strikes and other protests show, workers respond to various features of their oppression. Respect for such responses – union movements, peasant uprisings, democratic revolutions – is a starting point for the difficult project of reorganizing society. Such struggles can serve as an arena in which participants might discover the validity of a revolutionary perspective.[25]

From this critique of moralism, Marx and Engels inferred an extreme conclusion. They sought to demarcate neatly communist politics – designed to make socialism and internationalism issues within class conflict – and moralistic radicalism. In quasi-positivist fashion, they contrasted their scientific arguments with their opponents' ethical, ideological ones. They interpreted mistaken moral arguments on a relativist or reductionist basis. Given their own account, a critic may properly ask, Is Marx's and Engels's quarrel with all moralities or only with the use of ethical concepts by ruling-class spokespersons and radicals who hold erroneous theories of capitalism?

[22] Marx, 1961, 1:84–5; Marx and Engels, 2:25, 30.
[23] Marx, 1963, pp. 125–6; Proudhon, 1924, pp. 377–80, 384–5.
[24] Förder et al., 1970, pp. 220–1; Wittke, 1950, p. 110; Gilbert, 1981a, chs. 3–4.
[25] Gilbert, 1981a, ch. 2; 1979.

In a democratic vein, Marx's and Engels's critique honored the use of moral standards by ordinary workers, artisans, and peasants to articulate grievances against a nefarious social order. As Engels remarked in *Anti-Dühring*, the demand for social equality became the battle cry of the sixteenth-century German peasant war and expressed "the revolutionary instincts of the peasantry," their "spontaneous reaction against crying social inequalities, against the contrast of rich and poor, feudal lords and their serfs, surfeit and starvation." He also praised French communist workers' egalitarian demands and called for "the abolition of classes" as the "real content" of equality.[26]

But such indignation over great divisions between rich and poor is a central component of the idea of justice. Thus, practically and theoretically, Engels and Marx did not oppose all moral concepts. Furthermore, in the actual development of inegalitarian economies, crises – famine, increased elite revenues for war, conscription, and the like – fall with especial severity on the poor. But class societies, even feudal ones, legitimize customary expectations of subsistence. Extreme consequences of such social divisions in increased exploitation, suffering, and death often appear as an abridgment of nonproducer obligations (in modern times, as a violation of individual rights). Since the lives of ordinary people depend on the reliable fulfillment of these expectations, their violation – a seeming breach of promise – provokes a vivid sense of outrage.[27] Historically, hatred for class divisions has played an important causal role in popular revolts. But that hatred arises not just because of a particular "legitimacy" or "social construction." Instead, the legitimacy of exploitative orders stems in part from their ability to guarantee, or at least not to savagely damage, the goods of life and dignity for most people.[28] Whether or not Marxians concur with a particular customary interpretation, they can justify such revolts, based on shared underlying ethical standards. If true, a Marxian social theory strengthens the moral case. Recalling an Aristotelian notion of democracy in modern settings, such a theory may also enter into deliberative conversation about a movement's pursuit of a common good.

Any adequate moral conception must assess the effects of given social arrangements on the needs and capacities of individuals. Minimally, it

[26] Engels, 1966a, pp. 117–18.
[27] Thompson, 1971; Scott, 1976; B. Moore, 1965.
[28] Concurring with the spirit of Walzer's account of social criticism, a Marxian may see how reactionary, alienated, and pro-ruling class some traditional religious and social conceptions are – say, ideas of the organic order of feudal society and the like – and yet recognize that such ideas capture an element of moral truth, betrayed by prevailing practice. Unlike Walzer's, however, this Marxian view is a complex microstructural one based on (explicit) eudaemonism and a novel social theory.

would condemn those systems of distribution that provided superfluity for the few combined with starvation for and waste of talent in the many; it would justify popular indignation. Maximally, as we shall see in Chapter 7, such a view could attend to the needs of diverse individuals. This standard for condemning divisions of rich and poor invokes an ancient conception of natural justice and the appropriate reasons for activities. It follows Aristotle's suggestion that the best flute player rather than the handsomest or wealthiest should receive the best supply of flutes. Yet it incorporates the role of historical achievements and discoveries in creating novel potentials for individuality.[29] Thus, Engels and Marx did not reject the *proletarian* demand for equality as ideological but justified it with an argument about need. Furthermore, they reformulated this demand in their own vision of the abolition of classes.

Marx's 1865 address entitled "Value, Price and Profit" to the General Council of the International Workingmen's Association advocated strikes and unions as vehicles to drive up workers' wages at least temporarily.[30] In the long run, however, he contended that capitalism would undercut these gains and drive workers to revolt. Through radical participation in this "real movement," he advocated the substitution of the "revolutionary watchword," abolition of classes, for the "conservative motto, 'a fair day's pay for a fair day's work.'"[31] The ordinary conception of a "fair day's pay" is conservative because that demand does not question the validity of capitalism and seeks only a "better rate of exploitation" (*Exploitationsgrad*) from a proletarian point of view. Yet Marx defended the workers' anger. He supported their demands for higher wages and a shorter working day with this particular moral gloss removed. Furthermore, his own social theory dramatically *extended* the workers' claims to end all capitalist control of surplus value and create a classless society. Since his analysis illuminates and reinforces proletarian indignation, it seems peculiar to view this change of demands, in positivist fashion, as the utter replacement of an ideological moral notion, devoid of scientific content, with a social theoretical one, devoid of ethical content. On a more plausible, dialectical interpretation, science does not neatly replace evaluation. The revolutionary demand morally grows out of the original grievance and, in a Hegelian sense, recalls it. Like Boyd's account of corpuscular chemistry, Marxian theory provided a multifaceted, mircostructural assessment of proletarian claims about justice and equality.

[29] Aristotle, *Politics*, 1282b30–3a4; Brecht, 1966, p. 128.
[30] Marx drew a new distinction between a relatively invariant, physical element of subsistence and a much more elastic moral or social element.
[31] Marx and Engels, *SW*, 1:446.

In today's philosophical idiom, on Marx's naturalistic conception, indictments by workers, artisans, and peasants arise from their understanding of a given social system's oppressiveness and indicate some steps needed to combat it; their moral terminology provides epistemic access for further investigation and refinement. Internally, a complex ethical argument accompanies Marxian social theory, enabling Marxists to join in expressions of outrage at exploitative systems and engage in conversation about what is adequate and inadequate in popular views. Given the approximate truth of this theory, a Marxian could suppose that she could undermine some of the factual and ethical ideas surrounding another worker's conception of fairness and convince that person about exploitation.[32] A naturalist argument about continuity of reference across theory changes displays the dialectical thread in these conversations; in contrast, on a relativist or reductionist interpretation, all that a Marxist can fairly say about concepts of justice is to debunk them.

5. Engels's and Marx's critiques of Proudhon's "eternal justice"

In *The Housing Question*, Engels dismissed Proudhon's conception of "eternal justice" as a fantasy. As one strategy for defending this claim, he criticized all conceptions of justice as relative to a mode of production: "The justice of the Greeks and Romans held slavery to be just; the justice of the bourgeoisie of 1789 demanded the abolition of feudalism on the ground that it was unjust. For the Prussian Junker even the miserable District Ordinance is a violation of eternal justice."[33] Engels extended this relativism to the ideas of individuals: The concept of eternal justice "belongs among those things of which Mülberger correctly says 'everyone understands something different.'"[34] In adopting either mode of production or person relativism, he seemed to endorse a positivist stand toward moral concepts: Unlike scientific investigation in which researchers can ultimately resolve disagreements, humans can never resolve disputes about justice.

Earlier in this essay, Engels criticized Mülberger's wish that contemporary rent agreements could be "pervaded by a conception of right . . . carried out everywhere according to the strict demands of justice." This "justice" guarantees to each artisan or peasant ownership of a dwelling. Engels counterposed the facts of capitalist production to Mülberger's dream. That system concentrates wealth. It persistently uproots small

[32] Putnam, 1975, 2:237–8; Marx, 1961, 1:539–40; Marx and Engels, *SW* 1:429–30.
[33] Marx and Engels, *SW*, 1:624. [34] Marx and Engels, *SW*, 1:624.

propertyholders, forces them into large cities, and replaces independent homeownership with capitalist landlordship:

> What does this rigamarole mean? Nothing more than that the practical effects of the economic laws which govern present-day society run contrary to the author's sense of justice and that he cherishes the pious wish that the matter might be so arranged as to remedy the situation. Yes, if toads had tails they would not longer be toads! And is then the capitalist mode of production not "pervaded by a conception of right," namely, that of *its own right to exploit the workers?* And if the author tells us that is not *his* conception of right, are we one step further?[35]

In Engels's argument, the thesis about the person relativism of justice – "the author's sense of right" – does not follow from the Marxian claim about mode of production relativism. In fact, he used one class sense – a bourgeois conception of right – to debunk another – the smallholder's notion, advanced by Mülberger but rendered anachronistic by capitalist expansion. From a Marxian point of view, one could drop the person-relativist argument and stick with the mode of production-relativist one. Yet given this Marxian account, Engels's interpretation still seems peculiar; for he characterized capitalism's "justice" as "its own right to exploit the workers" – a communist description that a capitalist would hardly endorse. Yet Engels did not phrase this indictment skeptically in quotes – as his own opinion or a merely proletarian class sense – on a putatively equal ethical footing with a capitalist one. His acerbic factual comment on exploitation does not follow from his occasional metaethical relativism or reductionism but rather from an embryonic realist conception.

In this work, Engels also condemned miserable housing conditions and merchant cheating as examples of the "countless small, secondary abuses" (*Ubelstände*) of capitalism and stigmatized exploitation (*Ausbeutung*) in production as the "fundamental evil" (*Grudübel*). Recalling *The Communist Manifesto*, he criticized the Proudhonists in a realist vein: "It is the essence of bourgeois socialism to want to maintain the basis of all the evils of present-day society and at the same time to want to abolish the evils themselves."[36] On this conception, a revolutionary strategy, based on an accurate social theory, would strike at the basic evil in the mode of production.

Engels pointed to the facts against Proudhon's appeal to eternal justice and analyzed them in the light of Marx's historical theory; his empirical claims depend upon the approximate truth of that theory and include specific explanations of capitalist exploitation, of the fundamental conflicts that grow out of it such as the fight over the working day's dura-

---

[35] Marx and Engels, *SW*, 1:562–3.   [36] Marx and Engels, 1959, 18:214–15; *SW*, 1:558–81.

tion, of capitalism's increasingly concentrated control of industry and creation of a large, propertyless proletariat, of the tendency of the rate of profit to fall and engender crises, and the like. Through exploitation and its social consequences, capitalism inspires workers and their allies with the motivation – given the appropriate political organizing – to overthrow it. Scientifically speaking, workers could not overturn capitalism by establishing a Proudhonian "sincerity of exchanges" among revivified, smallholders any more than according to Darwin's account of amphibian descent, toads could have tails.[37]

In *Capital*, Marx gave an ironic twist to this critique. Proudhon identified justice among peasants and artisans with the regulation of production and exchange by the equal labor times embodied in commodities. On his view, the violation of such exchanges by large capitalists could occur only through "swindling" or usury – taking more than their due. In contrast, Marx showed that capitalists could regularly extract surplus value – and its concrete forms of profit, interest, and rent – without willful stealing; such stealing took place, as Engels would suggest, over and above *normal* exploitation. Marx contended that one commodity in use – labor power – creates a greater value (surplus value) than its own value in exchange (subsistence). But, he insisted, the capitalist acquires surplus value without violating the laws of circulation, that is, the prevailing juridical standards; in this sense only, capitalist exploitation is not robbery.[38] Satirizing Proudhon's thesis, he showed that the generalization of commodity production, characteristic of capitalism, led to the gradual expropriation of smallholders rather than their salvation: "So long as the laws of exchange are observed in every specific act of exchange, the mode of appropriation can be completely revolutionized without in any way affecting the property rights which correspond to commodity production."[39] He likened Proudhon to an incompetent chemist:

> Proudhon begins by taking his ideal of justice [*Gerechtigkeit*], of "justice eternelle" from the juridical relations that correspond to the production of commodities; thereby it may be noted he proves to the consolation of all good citizens, that the production of commodities is a form of production as everlasting as justice. Then he turns round and seeks to reform the actual production of commodities, and the actual legal system corresponding thereto, in accordance with this ideal. What opinion should we have of a chemist who, instead of studying the actual laws of the molecular changes in the composition and decomposition of matter, and on that foundation solving definite problems, claimed to regulate the composition

---

[37] Proudhon, 1924, 1:258.
[38] Marx, 1961, 1:193–4; Marx and Engels, 1959, 19:382, 359–60.   [39] Marx, 1961, 1:587.

and decomposition of matter by the "eternal ideas" of "naturalité" and "affinité"?[40]

Based on his scientific criticism of Proudhon's theory, Marx made seven claims: (1) He identified Proudhon's specific conception of justice as an ideological reflection of capitalist juridical relations, (2) he argued that conceptions of justice are transitory – limited to one or several historical epochs – rather than eternally valid, (3) contrary to the Ricardian socialists and Proudhon, he showed that capitalist exploitation occurs without robbery in the process of commodity circulation, (4) he argued that strategically, workers could not overcome capitalist oppression by reforming the juridical system to accord with its corresponding ideal of justice, but rather by making political revolution and transforming the mode of production, (5) he contended that given the nature of capitalism, appeals to the moral sense of capitalists would do no good,[41] (6) he opposed Proudhon's overrating of conceptions of justice in historical explanation, and (7) he criticized all ideas of justice in the name of science. If Marx's scientific argument is right, however, it establishes only claims one through six. It does not show that all claims of injustice and exploitation are relative to specific modes of production but just that Proudhon's is, nor does it show that every claim of justice must serve as the foundation of or be based upon an inadequate social theory and political strategy. Marx's argument does not rule out, for example, a scientific and moral theory – say, one of exploitation – that could evaluate class systems over several epochs and contribute politically to the forging of communism. Claims one through six are consistent with any of the three main metaethical interpretations of justice. Only claim seven – an implausible one given Marx's specific critique of Proudhon – would sustain a relativist or reductionist account against a realist one.

Furthermore, Marx and Engels undermined that claim because their argument shares a common moral standard with Proudhon's. In criticizing Dühring's appeals to justice, for example, Engels maintained:

> If for the imminent overthrow of the present mode of distribution with its crying contrasts of want and luxury, starvation and debauchery [schreienden Gegensätzen von Elend und Uppigkeit, Hungersnot und Schwelgerei], we had no better guarantee than the consciousness that the mode of production is unjust [*ungerecht*] . . . we should be in a pretty bad way. The mystics of the Middle Ages who dreamed of the coming millenium were already conscious of the injustice [*Ungerechtigkeit*] of class contrasts.[42]

---

[40] Marx, 1961, 1:587, n. 1; 84–5; Marx and Engels, 1959, 23:99–100.
[41] Marx and Engels, *SW*, 1:62, 582.
[42] Engels, 1966a, p. 173; Marx and Engels, 1959, 20:146.

He plainly recognized the "crying contrasts" of rich and poor, the *injustice* of class society. Yet he also commented that "to economic science, moral indignation, however *justifiable*, cannot serve as an argument, but only as a symptom."[43] Though Engels's point is obscurely phrased – symptoms are real signs of disease and provide evidence for a diagnosis – he justified egalitarian anger:

> The indignation [*Zorn*] which creates the poet is absolutely in place in describing these terrible conditions, and also in attacking those apostles of harmony in the service of the ruling class who either deny or palliate these abuses, but how little it can *prove* anything for the particular case is evident from the fact that in *each* epoch of all past history, there has been no lack of material for such indignation.[44]

Ethically speaking, he viewed such inequalities as a reprehensible feature of all previous epochs, except early communal society. Although a sense of injustice alone, without the appropriate historical circumstances, movements, and theory, could not do away with class divisions, moral criticisms of "illusions of harmony" had contributed to a political atmosphere in which a more thoroughgoing radicalism could unfold. Furthermore, he suggested that the proletarian demand for equality had a "double meaning." One sense dialectically grew out of the bourgeois insistence on political equality and had a certain validity or "real content." Engels also stressed a second meaning: a "spontaneous reaction" against divisions of rich and poor, a "simple expression of the revolutionary instinct" of workers and peasants that "finds it justification in that and only in that."[45] He saw both meanings of equality as morally appropriate. Once again, Marx's theory of the extraction of "gratuitous or unpaid labor" reinterpreted the source of these inequalities.

On a first reading, some might think that when Engels appealed to facts to overcome ethical disagreement, he described a necessary course of social development and was morally neutral between capitalism and communism. Yet he always condemned capitalist exploitation and praised communism. For instance, the Proudhonists saw the dispossession of individual homeowners as a retrogression "below the savages." In contrast, Engels insisted that "the English proletarian of 1872 is on an *infinitely higher level* than the rural weaver of 1772 with his 'hearth and home.' And will the troglodyte with his cave . . . ever accomplish a June insurrection or a Paris Commune?"[46]

For Engels, the latter workers' movements exemplified a specifically admirable ethical achievement. Marx also spoke of the Communards' heroic "heaven storming"; he celebrated the political action of proletar-

---

[43] Engels, 1966a, pp. 173–4.   [44] Engels, 1966a, p. 166; Marx and Engels, 1959, 20:139.
[45] Engels, 1966, p. 117.   [46] Marx and Engels, *SW*, 1, p. 564.

ian officials who discharged their tasks at a skilled worker's wage, not to make money or gain prestige but to forge a cooperative society.[47] Engels's praise for the Commune cannot be reconciled with his mode of production relativism, for this political community not only accorded with socialist relations of production but, on his account, was intrinsically admirable, an example of moral progress. In fact, given French underdevelopment and the Commune's mainly noneconomic program, the forging of a political community largely preceded the inauguration of socialist economic relationships; mode of production determinism isn't a plausible explanation of Engels's judgment. Instead, he stressed the Commune's distinctive political character. His theory of the facts and tendencies of capitalism coincided with the ethical need to create a classless society in which the "richest" flourishing of human individuality could occur.[48]

Like Engels, Marx justified the moral outrage that underlay, in his view, inadequate demands for social equality. Thus, in 1865, he praised the fire of Proudhon's "epoch-making" *What Is Property?*, its "provocative defiance, laying hands on the economic 'holy of holies' [large-scale private property in the means of production], superb paradox which makes a mock of bourgeois common sense . . . *a deep and genuine feeling of indignation* at the infamy of what exists [and] revolutionary earnestness." He also noted that, although characterizing property as theft, Proudhon had entangled himself in obscure speculations about "true," that is, small, bourgeois property. Marx distinguished Proudhon's achievement from a pretension to science, a caricature of Hegel's dialectics, and a lack of anger in his *Philosophy of Poverty*.[49]

Thus, Marx and Engels shared with Proudhon a factual recognition of the division of rich and poor and indignation at its consequences. Their judgments rested on core moral standards about the minimum physical preconditions for human well-being. We can state their agreement as in steps 1–3 of Table 5.1 and highlight the social theoretical sources of conflict at steps 4 and 5.

In summarizing this disagreement, Marx and Engels mistakenly saw a drastic conflict between ethical judgment and scientific theory. They surmised that their argument made contact with Proudhon's only on the level of social theory and not that of moral verdict. But since they, like Proudhon, condemned "crying contrasts" of luxury and need, their scientific argument had an inextricable ethical component.

Once we discern Marx's, Engels's and Proudhon's common underly-

---

[47] Marx and Engels, 1971, p. 153.
[48] Marx, 1973, pp. 325, 487–8; Marx and Engels, *SW*, 2:24.
[49] Marx and Engels, *SW*, 1: 391–2 (my emphasis).

Table 5.1. *Shared moral standards and empirical clashes*

	Proudhon	Marx and Engels
(1) Moral standard	Social systems should prevent the starvation or extinction of their members – and ultimately give individuals their due	Social systems should prevent the starvation or extinction of their members – and ultimately give individuals their due
(2) Factual premise	Divisions of rich and poor exist that give some abundance while many others at worst starve and certainly do not receive their due	Divisions of rich and poor exist that give some abundance while many others at worst starve, and certainly do not receive their due
(3) Conclusion	Divisions of rich and poor are infamous and unjust	Divisions of rich and poor are infamous and unjust
(4) Factual premise	In the capitalist form of this division, capitalists regularly violate the laws of commodity exchange by monopoly, swindling, and usury	In the capitalist form of this division, capitalists regularly extract surplus value from workers in ways consistent with the laws of commodity exchange, depriving small-holders of the means of production, pitting a majority of proletarians against a small number of property owners and creating increasingly harsh conditions for the propertyless; as Chartism, the June insurrection, and the Paris Commune demonstrate, working-class solidarity and political community are possible
(5) Conclusion	Reestablish a society of small, equal property-holders, regulating their economy through a mutualist banking system in accordance with the exchange of equal labor times or the principles of eternal justice	Abolish exploitation by revolution and work to establish a classless society in which social individuality can flourish

ing moral standard, we can also see the grain of truth in Marx's comparison of Proudhon to an incompetent chemist. Marx disagreed with Proudhon not over the desirability of opposing capitalism, but over the inadequacy of mutualism as a vehicle to transform it. In other words, the dispute turned not over the need for indignation, but over the issue, in today's philosophical jargon, of "ought implies can." Contrary to Engels's and Marx's occasional relativist or reductionist remarks, they appealed to facts, social theory, and actual political movements to show how complex moral disputes might at last be successfully resolved.

6. Utilitarianism, contractarianism, and glaring social inequalities

The foregoing analysis has broad implications for a comparison of a Marxian view with other arguments about justice. Marx shares his ethical premise – opposition to vast divisions of rich and poor and their consequences – with much of today's moral theory; he would disagree empirically with contemporary theorists over the nature of modern society and the means needed to change it. For instance, a Rawlsian would object to divisions of income that fail to benefit the least advantaged or that corrupt political equality and undermine mutual respect. As Rawls puts the appropriate social theoretical issue, "Of course, Marx would question the stability of a well-ordered society in the absence of some form of socialism, but . . . the principles of justice do not exclude certain forms of socialism and would in fact require them if the stability of a well-ordered society could be achieved in no other way." For utilitarians, deprivation of the poor would undercut overall or average happiness.[50] If Marx's social theory is true, then on either of these moral arguments, a justification for socialism or communism follows. As Wood has rightly maintained, *any recognizably moral* principles would lead to the condemnation of capitalism and its consequences as Marx understood them; a

---

[50] Rawls, 1975, p. 546. John Stuart Mill powerfully linked the case for socialism to previous liberal and democratic arguments against oppression: "No longer enslaved or made dependent by force of law, the great majority are so by force of poverty; they are chained to a place, to an occupation, and to conformity with the will of an employer, and debarred by the accident of birth both from the enjoyments and from the mental and moral advantages which others inherit without exertion and independently of desert. That this is an evil equal to almost any of those against which mankind have hitherto struggled, the poor are not wrong in believing. . . . The working classes are entitled to claim that the whole field of social institutions should be re-examined, and every question considered as if it now arose for the first time; with the idea constantly in view that the persons who are to be convinced are not those who owe their ease and importance to the present system, but persons who have no other interest in the matter than abstract justice and the general good of the community" (Mill, 1977, 5:710–11).

theory that could condone these consequences would not be an ethical view at all.[51] Contrary to Wood's general reductionist interpretation, this claim suggests a greater objectivity in core standards and even in larger moral theories than has often been supposed.

A Rawlsian might deny this degree of moral objectivity by arguing that Marx's – and Rawls's – criticism of divisions of wealth and poverty rests merely on a relatively purified intuition. However altered by social theory and ethical principles to achieve a reflective equilibrium, such a condemnation remains ultimately "our" historically limited judgment. But one might look at such intuitions as embryonic moral generalizations and analyze the notion of human nature and needs and capacities on which this indictment rests. If one interprets intuitions in this way, one can argue about whether they are empirically right or wrong. In this context, Aristotle's *Politics* offers intuitive arguments about the "naturalness" of slavery. Given subsequent historical practice – slave revolts, the existence of nonslaveholding societies, and the like – Montesquieu, Hegel, and others showed that this intuition – or more precisely, collateral information – rested on a mistaken theory about other humans. Marx would similarly criticize the "naturalness" of wage slavery, engaging liberals in further conversation about the terms of political and economic cooperation, characterized by a common good, that could serve as a setting for individuality.

On a moral realist account, clashing intuitions become targets for rational criticism. This view considers such intuitions as moral observations, which might play a role in ethical theory more nearly akin to theory-loaded scientific observations than Rawls envisions.[52] Furthermore, as Kuhn and others have emphasized, "tacit" – intuitive – knowledge figures importantly in *scientific* research, contributing to advance within a paradigm and theory shifts. For a realist, the emergence of approximately true theories and background conceptions helps to establish sufficiently reliable methods and initiate a process of refinement; mature scientific projects constrain the range of appropriate theoretical alternatives and differentiate important "hunches" or intuitions from myriad implausible possibilities.[53] Analogously, previous moral theory and observation have elicited some truths and become a mature domain; sophisticated ethical intuitions are broadly comparable to scientific ones. Thus, the neo-Kantian contrast between method in ethics – "reflective equilibrium" – and an empiricist account of science fails because

---

[51] Wood, 1972, pp. 281–2.
[52] Railton, 1986; J. Cohen, 1986a; Sturgeon, 1986a. The last section of this chapter will explore more fully how moral explanations contribute to social scientific ones.
[53] As corpuscularism shows, an original, nearly scientific theory need not be very close to the truth.

scientific method, properly understood, is also one of reflective equilibrium.[54] A naturalist view captures the complexity, which is the grain of truth, in a constructivist account, but discards its unjustified appeal to – "our" – special moral intuitions; it stresses the analogy of multifaceted ethical to multidimensional scientific reasoning.

7. Scientific realism and moral realism

In debating with Mülberger, Engels unfavorably contrasted the idea of moral progress with that of scientific advance. Here, too, however, his argument is more ambiguous than it seems at first glance. Engels likened justice to a sort of "social phlogiston":

> While in everyday life, in view of the simplicity of the relations discussed, expressions like right, wrong, justice and sense of right are accepted without misunderstanding even with reference to social matters, they create, as we have seen, the same hopeless confusion in any scientific investigation of economic relations as would be created, for instance, if the terminology of the phlogiston theory were to be retained. The confusion becomes still worse if one like Proudhon believes in the social phlogiston, "justice," or if one like Mülberger avers that the phlogiston theory is as correct as the oxygen one.[55]

Once again, in a positivist vein, he contrasted scientific investigation that achieves agreement with historically varying, unresolvably conflicting moral standards. He mistakenly praised Mülberger's person-relativist conception of justice but refused to commend Mülberger's peculiar view of oxygen-based and phlogiston-based chemistry as, scientifically speaking, equally valid. In this context, Engels's analogy of justice with phlogiston seems to interpret the former as part of an inadequate ethical theory that a purely scientific one has replaced. His mode of production-relativist claims reinforce this impression. On this view, Proudhon's notion of eternal justice, reflecting commodity production, seems just so much erroneous, ideological mist that will dissipate in the sunlight of a communist mode of production.

Yet Engels's analogy has an alternative, realist interpretation. In a footnote to this passage he contended that phlogiston theory focused on a *single element* that triggered combustion even though it got most of that element's properties backward. It contributed importantly to the discovery of oxygen:

> Before the discovery of oxygen, chemists explained the burning of substances in atmospheric air by assuming the existence of a special igneous

[54] Boyd, 1986a. Rawls, 1971, pp. 49–50; 1980, p. 565, is of course not committed to an empiricist view of scientific progress.
[55] Marx and Engels, *SW*, 1:625.

substance, phlogiston, which escaped during the process of combustion. Since they found that simple substances on combustion weighed more after having been burned than they did before, they declared that phlogiston had a negative weight so that a substance without its phlogiston weighed more than one with it. In this way, all the main properties of oxygen were gradually ascribed in phlogiston, but all in an *inverted* form.[56]

The phlogiston theory was not even approximately true. Yet it helped to frame the causation of combustion in such a way that a novel (mature) theory could explain it. In this sense, Lavoisier's discovery of oxygen, which combined with other elements upon burning, grew out of and solved the central problem of phlogiston chemistry. Introducing volume 2 of *Capital*, Engels remarked that "this [phlogiston] theory sufficed for the explanation of most of the chemical phenomena then known [until the later eighteenth century] although not without forcing in many cases."[57] Compared with his relativist description of justice as mere shifting ideology, this argument seems strikingly favorable to the scientific accomplishments of phlogiston theory. For Engels, modern chemistry explained anomalies in a previously mistaken, but not wholly inadequate chemistry. He gave a microstructural, realist description of the latter's role.

Thus, the analogy of justice with phlogiston reflects a realistic inkling on Engels's part about moral questions. A realist interpretation also explains his objective claim that everyday matters of right and wrong are not confusing. If this major feature of ethics presents no important difficulties, it is hard to see why investigators could not ultimately achieve similar objectivity in theories about the basic structure of society.[58] Self-interest and rationalizations certainly affect everyday judgments in one's own case. Comparable legitimations, based on class interests, might render progress in moral theory and practice more difficult, though not insurmountably so, than advance in daily life and the sciences.[59]

We can gauge the strength of his realist inkling by examining his most important use of the phlogiston analogy: his exploration of the significance of Marx's discovery of surplus value for political economy and

---

[56] Marx and Engels, *SW*, 1:625. As we have seen, an exaggerated emphasis on the nonexistence of phlogiston – one that mistakenly conflates later, less striking theory changes with the unusual transformation that creates a branch of mature scientific investigation – provides a basis for antirealism.

[57] Marx and Engels, *SW*, 1:470.

[58] In his comment about "social matters," Engels may even have recognized the ordinary stability of political judgments about just war. Weber advanced a similar claim about everyday judgments concerning "scoundrels." These classic social scientific proponents of metaethical relativism both strikingly undercut their own arguments with regard to core moral standards.

[59] Marx and Engels, *SW*, 1:582.

moral argument. On Engels's account, the first scientific exponents of a labor theory of value had seen that capitalists extracted a surplus from the workers. In *The Principles of Political Economy and Taxation*, Ricardo maintained that Adam Smith had confused the value of the labor time incorporated in the actual production of commodities and the value of the labor time that workers' wages could command on the market. Ricardo isolated the amount paid for the use of the worker's labor – what Marx would call "labor power" – in contrast to the extra value created by the worker in production – what Marx would call "surplus value." Yet he never identified this surplus as a central theoretical concept nor used this insight to reexamine previous political economy.[60]

Engels likened Ricardo's identification of surplus and Priestley's and Scheele's discovery of "dephlogisticated air" or "fire air." As he suggested, these chemists, though close to discovering oxygen, remained entangled in the "phlogistic categories as they found them," just as Ricardo remained enmeshed within the older political economy. But the Ricardian socialists and Proudhon abandoned Ricardo's distinction. They asked, "What is the value of labor?" and decided that it was the full value of the product. They then condemned capitalist appropriation of any portion of the output as stealing. Here we can see a different, particularly strong motivation for Marx's and Engels's dismissal of eternal justice. Instead of solving the pivotal theoretical problem concerning the value of labor, Proudhon offered moral rhetoric. Thus, a scientific disagreement with other economists fused with Marx's and Engels's general antipathy to Proudhon's moralism – his substitution of inadequate ethical categories for clear social theorizing. The Marxian scientific and political critique, focused on the moralists' economic analysis, seemed to go hand in hand. Engels's phlogiston analogy reveals the full force of Marx's characterization of the Proudhonists, who derived political remedies from erroneous social theory, as bad chemists.[61]

According to Engels, Marx, like Lavoisier, approached the main anomaly in previous theory with fresh eyes: Where others "had seen a solution, he saw only a problem." He solved this problem – "placed previous political economy on its feet" – with his remarkably fruitful discovery of surplus value.[62] Marx could now offer novel, coherent explanations of crucial issues in classical political economy – such as the relation of commodities and money, the character of class conflict under capitalism, and the nature of rent, profit, and interest. Older theories had seen a falling rate of profit monocausally as an inevitable result of increasing population (Malthus) or rising rent (Ricardo). Marx now persuasively interpreted it as a complex, qualified tendency resulting from a rapid

[60] Marx, 1961, 1:515–16, 537–8.   [61] Althusser, 1965, 2:118–26.   [62] McMullin, 1976.

introduction of machinery or shift in the organic composition of capital.[63] Engels marked this broad theoretical recasting of a discipline: "With this fact [surplus value] as his starting point, [Marx] examined all the categories he found at hand, just as Lavoisier, with oxygen as his starting-point, had examined the categories of phlogiston chemistry he had found at hand."[64]

Marx's manuscripts for a projected fourth volume of *Capital, Theories of Surplus Value,* dialectically examine the discoveries in earlier economic arguments and show how the concept of surplus value could resolve their internal conflicts. Both Marx and Engels considered preceding political economy – the study of the real relations of capitalist production – a mature scientific theory.[65] On their view, the changes wrought by Marx's insight into surplus value might seem to mirror, say, the subsequent relation of Einsteinian and Newtonian physics, rather than the paradigm, near at hand, of the shift between oxygen and phlogiston chemistry. Emphasizing shifts in theory, their epistemological views foreshadow scientific realism, not empiricism. In this context, one might also note, surplus value is unobservable with the naked eye; it is an explanatory "theoretical entity" just as much as oxygen or electrons. Yet Marx and Engels exhibited no positivist qualms about the alleged "metaphysical," merely conventional nature of scientific posits. Marx's epistemology was far more influenced by scientific practice and Hegel than by classical empiricism.[66] In today's idiom, he assessed the history of political economy from a naturalistic perspective, demonstrating its progress in achieving successive approximations to the truth.

In historical theory, Engels's phlogiston analogy suggested that Marx had developed a mature science; in ethics, he maintained, that theory had abandoned inadequate categories. The former founds, the latter destroys, a (seeming) branch of investigation. Both conclusions are questionable. Morally speaking, in contrast to classical political economy, Marxian theory is a communist critique of prevailing practice and theory. It not only explains and justifies reform within an existing sys-

---

[63] Dobb, 1973, p. 157. The former explanations stress causes external to the operation of industrial capital; Marx depicted internal ones.

[64] Marx and Engels, *SW*, 1:471–2.   [65] Marx, 1961, 1:80 n. 2.

[66] Marx, 1961, pp. 19–20. Struck by the relationship of Hegelian critique and *Capital*, Lenin also metaphorically insisted on the complexity of theoretical argument and advance: "Dialectics as *living*, many-sided knowledge (with the number of sides eternally increasing), with an infinite number of shades of every approach and approximation to reality (with a philosophical system growing into a whole out of each shade) – here we have an immeasurably rich content as compared with "metaphysical" materialism, the fundamental *misfortune* of which is its inability to apply dialectics . . . to the process and development of knowledge" (Lenin, *Collected Works,* hereafter *CW*, 1974, 38:318–19, 360–63).

tem, as Ricardo's legitimized repeal of the Corn Laws; it envisions revolutionary transformation. Where Engels deemphasized any dialectical *moral* shift, the ethical and political changes wrought by Marx's theory seem comparatively dramatic. In economic theory, in contrast, the distinction, embodied in the notion of a *"critique* of political economy," seems less striking than the dichotomy of modern and phlogiston chemistry; yet Engels's analogy implies something stronger.

In fact, one might argue, the spell wrought by the problems of classical political economy subtly holds Marxian economic theory in thrall. Thus, *Capital* captures the dynamics of a self-undermining market rather than, as in classical economy, the possible coherence of a self-ordering one. That theory does not fully articulate the political emphasis in Marx's historical explanations and radical activity – for instance, his insistence that in Britain, the division of English and Irish workers, sustained by colonialism, not the domestic level of productivity, was the chief obstacle to proletarian revolution. If that revolution is even more difficult politically than Marx surmised and if, as seems clear from his theory, capitalist economic contradictions, though very oppressive, do not simply lead to catastrophic decline, then the theoretical project of *Capital* may be deficient with regard to the central issue of creating communism.[67]

Given the inadequacies in Marx's most general formulation of the theory, a more articulated conception of individuality and a greater acknowledgment of the role of ethical judgment in politics, particularly in the forging of a classless society, might be part of a (fully) mature radical argument, one responsive, as Marx's evolving theory was, to the lessons

---

[67] Gilbert, 1978a, 1979, 1981a, 1984b. For example, the *tendency* of the rate of profit to fall is contingent on the increase of the value of machinery – the organic composition of capital

$$\left(\frac{\text{constant labor-time}}{\text{variable labor-time}} = \frac{c}{v}\right)$$

– exceeding the increase of the rate of exploitation

$$\left(\frac{\text{surplus labor-time}}{\text{variable labor-time}} = \frac{s}{v}\right)$$

Where exploitation rises more quickly, and it can rise as a consequence of increased productivity, the rate of profit

$$\left(\frac{s}{c+v} = \frac{\text{surplus labor-time}}{\text{constant plus variable labor-time}}\right)$$

need not fall. Capitalism need not experience utter breakdown, and no argument in *Capital* shows that economic breakdown would, just by itself, lead to revolution. In fact, Marx's whole strategy requires the creation of a visible, clearly articulated political and economic alternative. In addition, in an 1852 letter to Weydemeyer, Marx characterized the reasoning about a dictatorship of the proletariat that leads to a classless society as his distinctive theoretical contribution (R. Miller, 1986).

of ongoing political experience, or so I argue in Chapters 7 and 8. If this claim is right, then both parts of Engels's creative phlogiston analogy prove important but exaggerated. A better version of that analogy would undercut the claim that Marx's mature theory is mainly an economic criticism of classical political economy. Correspondingly, it might highlight the moral and political impact of Marxian social theory. Developed conceptions of democratic individuality would turn out to be central to a Marxian account.

Even without this reinterpretation of Marxian theory, however, Engels's comparison of justice with phlogiston chemistry seems favorable to the former. At least popular conceptions of justice, one might surmise, would exhibit a grain of truth – they would serve as a first approximation; Marx's theory appropriately reinterpreted this grain. Engels was prevented from seeing the force of his analogy in sustaining moral realism by his criticism of Proudhon's labor theory as a mistaken solution to the leading difficulty in Ricardo's political economy, by his opposition to Proudhon's focus on the putative "eternality" of justice, and by his rejection of moralism in contemporary radical debates. But although Engels's metaethical account wobbled between a relativist (or reductionist) and a realist formulation – he generally gave more weight to a relativist gloss – his specific arguments and particular uses of moral concepts were strongly realistic.

For instance, as I have noted, he contended that proletarian activists in the Puritan and French revolutions drew "more or less correct and far reaching demands" for social equality from the demand for political equality. Yet he reformulated their conception: "The real content of the proletarian demand for equality is the abolition of classes. Any demand for equality which goes beyond that, of necessity passes into absurdity." [68] He partially criticized this radical slogan – he suggested that a notion of across-the-board human equality denies individuality – but called for the realization of a fundamental aspect of equality, the abolition of exploitation, as a prerequisite for [social] individuality. Contrary to Wood's reductionist repudiation of equality, Engels contended, in "On Marx's *Capital*," that capitalism "develop[ed] the productive forces of society to a level which will make possible *an equal development worthy of human beings* for all members of society." [69]

On a realist social theoretical and moral view, earlier radical theories – those of Münzer, Fourier, Blanqui, and Bray – provided approximately true descriptions of exploitation and the corruption of bourgeois society.

[68] Engels, 1966a, pp. 117, 24–5.
[69] Marx and Engels, *SW*, 1:468–9; A. Wood, 1986, pp. 286–8, 301. Wood's otherwise thoughtful discussion suffers form a lack of attention to contemporary realist semantic theory.

Marx's theory improves on them and exemplifies moral progress, just as proletarian socialist movements represent an ethical advance over the egalitarians of the Puritan Revolution, the Levellers. Or if one wants to put it less strongly, these mainly inadequate moral conceptions, analogous to phlogiston chemistry, posed problems that a better theory could solve. The Marxian historical theory of exploitation, class conflict, and the abolition of classes captures the grain of truth in previous claims of injustice. Even this weaker claim for predecessor theories recognizes moral advance.

Metaethically, Engels's *Anti-Dühring* defends progress in ethics and likens it to natural scientific advance:

> As society has hitherto moved in class antagonisms, morality was always class morality; it has either justified the domination and the interests of the ruling class, or, as soon as the oppressed class has become powerful enough, it has represented the revolt against this domination and the future interests of the oppressed. That in this process there has on the whole been progress [*Fortschritt*] in morality, as in all other branches of human knowledge [*Erkenntnis*], cannot really be doubted. But we have not yet passed beyond class morality. An actual human morality [*wirklich menschliche Moral*] which transcends class antagonisms and their legacies in thought becomes possible only at a stage of society which has not only overcome class contradictions but has even forgotten them in practical life.[70]

In exploitative societies, all moral judgments – true as well as false – serve class interests; such political oppositions and the ideologies they engender cloud ethical argument and prohibit the clarity that exists, according to Engels, in everyday morality. But the removal of such class divisions and ideologies makes communist social relations as ethically transparent as personal relationships. It permits a genuinely "human morality" in an Aristotelian sense: the *actualization* of multifaceted human potentials.[71]

Wood has properly recognized a conflict between his reductionist interpretation of Marx on justice and Engels's claim about an "actual," nonrelativist, human morality. He suggests, however, that in the foregoing citation, "Engels denies that the 'proletarian morality of the future' is 'true' as contrasted with its predecessors."[72] To concur with this judgment, one would have to ascribe to Engels the notion that neither truth nor progress exists in chemistry and political economy, a view that he plainly rejects. Furthermore, the chapter in *Anti-Dühring* that refers

---

[70] Engels, 1966a, p. 105; Marx and Engels, 1959, 20:87.
[71] In Chapter 7, I explore another way in which Marx's scientific realist critique of Aristotle's political economy requires a corresponding moral realism.
[72] Wood, 1979, p. 291.

to moral advance also dismisses the "eternality" of chemical and biological theory; for the latter disciplines, like ethics, achieve approximate
truth only eventually, after major conceptual changes.[73] Engels's critique
of putative scientific "eternality" affirms the possibility of true biological
knowledge. This analogy between biological and moral argument is far
more accurate as an epistemological description of Marxian theory than
his occasional pitting of science against ethics. In modern naturalistic
terms, Engels articulated the likeness of these complex, a posteriori, empirical disciplines.

Marx's and Engels's opposition to prevailing, exploitative moralities
can mistakenly be interpreted as denying any autonomy to moral argument and reflection. On that historicist view, a Marxian would see all
moral judgments, including her own, as inextricably context or origin
dependent. The relativist or reductionist fails to distinguish this sense
in which moral judgments might serve social classes – a sense that Marx
did not endorse – from a political impact or consequence dependence,
which he did. Marx and Engels believed that (true) moral judgments
tend to benefit a certain class (or classes) at the expense of others; therefore opposed classes tend to adopt clashing (complex) ethics. In this
sense, until communism, all morality is class morality. Yet ethical argument – for example, about the harms of great social inequalities – retains
an internal integrity. Criticisms of such inequalities have some – often a
large – element of truth; defenses of them are false and ideological.
Wood's failure to see Engels's scientific realism leads him to overlook the
strong element of moral realism in the latter's account of justice.

8. Structural and ethical explanation: why injustice needs to advertise

A reductionist might still try to refine Wood's argument. In today's philosophical idiom, she might suggest, perhaps Engels wished to claim
that such moral judgments, though true, always supervene on other,
nonmoral causes. As a Marxian theorist, he might stress economic ones.
The latter would then be substitutable for – one might say causally prior
to – the former. In that case, there would be ethical facts and even progress but no moral explanations. In response, however, a Marxian might
loosen the connection between economic structure, class struggle, and
alternative political strategies open to radical movements such that no
neat generation of political ideas by structure exists. Then competing
complex ethical views are likely to have independent causal conse-

---

[73] Engels, 1966a, pp. 98–9.

quences. Marx's own explanations and strategies require such loosening and stress the role of politics; they incorporate moral claims.[74]

Further, as Miller has suggested, ethical arguments frequently contribute to the causal depth of good historical explanations. We can see the importance of moral explanation as an irreducible part of comprehensive accounts by examining how shifting the basic questions posed in social theory may lead to sharply differing conclusions. For instance, in investigating the recurrence of radical movements in the history of capitalism, a methodological individualist might ask, Why do just these individuals join? For each movement, the researcher would seek out sets of individuals and obtain some correlations of characteristics – perhaps young people are disproportionately represented. In contrast, a Marxian or structuralist liberal might ask, What features of the prevailing social system – notably its morally objectionable ones, those that conflict with interests in life and autonomy – make themselves tellingly present to diverse individuals? The former is a question about individuals, the latter about the impact of the structure as a whole.

In response to the former question, individualists claim – perhaps inadvertently – that radical movements persist or reemerge under capitalism, despite heavy persecution, because of particular psychological and political histories. Subtract just those histories, and the movements, along with their social and moral causes, vanish. Note, however, that this reductionist line of argument begs the question of recurrence; it is hyperspecific, dissolving patterns of victimization into overly detailed accounts of individual circumstance. It ascertains the agents' beliefs, yet fails to ask the obvious question – What explains those beliefs? – and is thus superficial.[75]

A sophisticated individualist might acknowledge that these biographies involve insights into capitalist injustice, making moral facts, to some degree, causally effective. Yet given supervenience and the complex causation of historical events, he would still rate nonmoral aspects

---

[74] Gilbert, 1981a; Miller, 1984. Even if a tight economic determinist account were right, however, moral facts about structural injustice and psychological capacities for sympathy and solidarity would play some role in showing why – in terms of human motivation – a more cooperative society would replace capitalism. But ethical claims would have less sociological and political importance; the underlying economic explanation would be the more complex, interesting argument.

[75] On causal priority see R. Miller, 1987, ch. 2. On structuralist and individualist explanations, see Gilbert, 1978a, and Garfinkel, 1981, chs. 3–5.

Slaveholding societies persisted for a long time. Nonetheless, they have been overturned and, as I note in Chapter 4, however limited the liberation, no movement has transpired among former slaves for their restoration. Given these facts, Josh Cohen, 1986a, has emphasized, attempts to confine an explanation to "beliefs about slavery" are remarkably superficial.

as decisive. Perhaps failures of nurturance in privileged families lead some members (intellectuals) to take up (nonetheless true) radical ideas; perhaps historically created gender ideologies have sometimes discouraged proportionate participation of women, and countervailing factors are needed to account for their presence, and the like.[76] Further, many participants have grievances, but their perceived interests are not in abolishing the unjust structure itself. How, this individualist might ask, can systemic injustice play a large explanatory role?

In this nonreductionist individualism, however, a critic might note, particular causes coexist uneasily with general social and moral ones. The ethical claims, acknowledged to be objective, point to structural, not solely personal, causes. The latter look overdetermining, not the former; for we may widen the scope of moral explanation. As Peter Railton and Josh Cohen have suggested, the fact that a system is unjust may generate many kinds of discontent against it. Further, one might expect especially vigorous elite dissemination of claims that the structure is (potentially) just precisely to maintain systems like slavery that are fundamentally unjust; justice, as it were, has less need to advertise. In the absence of an alternative radical conception, however, beliefs about the potential justice of a harmful basic structure may temporarily become widespread even among the victims.[77] Over time, however, patterns of fissure, reinforced in Locke's words, by "a long train of Abuses, Prevarications, and Artifices, all tending the same way," produce many forces seeking change.[78] Even if participants still did not recognize systemic injustice, the structure's multifaceted damage to morally legitimate interests would explain these countermovements. Eventually, through political action and discussion, many would probably come to recognize structural injustice.[79]

The sophisticated individualist might still respond, What distinguishes a "legitimate" interest from those of, say, capitalists or slaveholders? Can't moral claims about "the oppressed" be debunked as ideologies in roughly the sense that Marxians criticize "oppressive" interests? This individualist neglects his previous recognition of struc-

---

[76] Miller explores David Donald's claims that younger members of the declining New England mercantile aristocracy became abolitionists. Reductionist attempts to substitute putative family or psychological causes of student protest against the Vietnam War for consideration of that war's injustice are similarly superficial.

[77] In these cases, individualist approaches are especially misguided.

[78] Locke, 1965, p. 463 and ch. 19, offers a striking account of the distinction between injustices breeding widespread movements and more limited discontents.

[79] If injustice must advertise, a radical account needs to specify some psychological mechanisms to explain the adoption by victims of self-destructive views. Some arguments are canvassed in Chapter 7, Section 2. Chapter 9 explores the way in which this problem – the psychological and ethical conflict between human well-being and social reality –

tural injustice. (Legitimate) interests in life and selfhood are not morally on a par with interests in, say, murder and domination.

In addition, class conflict accounts, especially Marxian ones, speak of the *universality* of the interests of the oppressed. Both Peter Railton and Josh Cohen refine this idea.[80] Railton suggests a viewpoint of "social rationality" – an *impartial* one that takes account of the interests of all those potentially affected by a policy or system – as a way to detect cases of subjugation. For slavery, serfdom, various forms of discrimination, and – at least early – capitalism, it is not difficult to find empirical evidence about social irrationality. Emphasizing moral facts, Railton means to capture a *transmoral-theory perspective*, fitting with either a utilitarian or rights-oriented characterization of the interests of all.[81]

Alternatively, Cohen proposes a Rawlsian ideal consensus view; for we may think of the *legitimate interests* of the victimized as those that informed individuals would choose to advance in designing a cooperative social structure under ideal, noncoercive conditions. As he tellingly shows for American slavery, the variety of actual grievances, sometimes visible in modest concessions by oppressors to head off discontent, captures features of slave interests in autonomy, dignity, and material well-being. Railton's and Cohen's arguments help to track legitimate interests in particular claims of unfairness and thus widen the scope of ethical explanation.[82]

Such conflict accounts are especially suited to defend moral realism, for as Railton stresses, realists claim that moral terms refer to moral facts independent of our initial understanding; yet we may interact with these facts and gain "feedback." The constraints of objective social structures on human well-being, regardless of contemporary legitimations, are a paradigm of such facts. To clarify these constraints, he describes an individual and oppressed group "wants/interests" mechanism. The desires one has, so the argument runs, are modified by attempts to realize

makes Weber's explanation of the emergence of a Protestant work force sociologically, because morally, interesting.

[80] As Railton, 1986, p. 193, and Cohen, 1986a, indicate, many modern historical arguments – those of Moore, Tilly, Thompson, Patterson, and the like – make claims about subjugated interests and structural injustice. Their arguments are consistent with either a sophisticated liberal or Marxian theory of previous forms of exploitation, early capitalism, and contemporary forms of discrimination.

[81] Railton claims it will fit an emotivist account as well, presumably because emotivists may describe moral judgments as those that express "universal" preferences. Since the theory debunks that "universality" – it is merely someone's expression of preference – this contention is inconsistent with an argument that seeks to separate the *legitimate* interests of the oppressed from the ideological claims of oppressors (Railton, 1986, pp. 189–94).

[82] Railton, 1986, pp. 191–2.

them. Given improved knowledge, wants may come, to some degree, to accord with interests, or, alternatively, perceived interests with objective interests. On a Marxian view, through practice, participants sometimes learn more of the truth about either how to remedy their grievances or what desires they may reasonably aim to satisfy; they also learn what the social structure is like.[83] For instance, Marx's account of the emergence of socialist and communist movements out of those for a "fair day's pay" neatly fits Railton's model. Similarly, on a modern eudaemonist theory, given oppressive social structures, a full understanding of the many-faceted character of the human good and individuality requires a lengthy process of practice and theorizing. Hence, it emphasizes the historical distinction between inadequate, initial claims about a common good and subsequent moral discoveries.

The individualist might still ask, How much apparatus in ethical theory is needed to clarify the role of moral explanation? In one respect, a realist might respond, not much; for as my earlier critique of Rawls and Scanlon on moral facts shows, the notion of capacity for individuality underlying a conception of ideal, noncoercive consensus is objective; it constrains the result of such deliberations.[84] Further, a eudaemonist might also claim that multiple abuses of human goods instigate such movements, employing counterfactuals about unforced, informed *deliberation* comparable to those offered by a contractarian. In another respect, however, the realist might respond, some; for the ideal consensus or democratic autonomy view seems a fine tool for capturing this important point about social explanation.[85] In fact, standard questions – "Who benefits (who loses) from this practice?" or "Is this practice consistent with an ideal consensus (or social rationality)?" – justified by ethical theory, are initial background tests for the *reliability* of moral intuitions and social scientific hunches and hypotheses.

---

[83] As Railton, 1986, pp. 172, 174–81, notes, a traveler, sick abroad, may have an objective interest in drinking clear liquids, not milk. Politically, in the America of the 1960s, a radical pluralist or a Marxian might suggest, those who opposed racism toward blacks may have had an interest in organizing sit-ins, other nonviolent demonstrations, and even "riots" (rebellions), not mainly, as one might have hoped, in writing letters to powerful political figures (Piven and Cloward, 1977; Miller, 1984, chs. 3–4). Thomas Nagel, 1986a, pp. 138–9, poses the problem to which Railton's argument is a striking response.

[84] Cohen and Rogers, 1983, p. 160, stress this point. Failure to recognize an underlying capacity for moral personality and mutual regard weakens Habermas's attempts to justify his alternative, ideal view of communication (Habermas, 1979, ch. 1; 1984). Factual insights into human capacities, not analysis of presuppositions of "speech acts" just by themselves, underlie coherent moral theories of reasonable conversations among individuals.

[85] No wonder Montesquieu appealed to an ideal lottery as a simple, yet telling vehicle to discredit advocacy of the slave trade.

The recurrence of radical movements in diverse classes against the odds – say, of mass union, socialist, and communist movements in many countries – strongly suggests that a capitalist system has structural tendencies that would, counterfactually, have ultimately provoked others to take similar steps if these individuals had not. In contrast to any individualist view, a structural account addresses the relevant question about common causes and legitimate interests; it explains recurrent radicalism. With suitable use of auxiliary statements to capture specific international and historical circumstances, it can answer many questions about these movements' comparative success or failure.[86] As this contrast has shown, structuralism is more responsive to such questions. Note that a liberal can also emphasize structural oppression and a resulting indignation, yet hope for democratic reform; for structural claims make radicalism reasonable in many situations on the same underlying *moral* grounds that liberalism is.[87] A liberal might maintain, for example, that Marxian attempts to reach communism will always end in despotism, a claim that I consider in Chapter 8.

Critics sometimes suggest that structural explanations must underemphasize the motivations of individuals. Though a structural argument initially abstracts from diverse psychological and political histories, nothing prevents a reasonable proponent from offering a full historical account. Structuralists can answer the individualist question, describing the mechanisms and experiences by which particular people decide to join a radical movement in contrast to others, of like background, who do not.[88] In fact, as we shall see in Chapters 7 and 8, for

---

[86] Gilbert, 1981a, chs. 1, 9–10, 12, 14, on the role of specific historical settings and auxiliary statements in Marxian explanations.

[87] Though it endorses some important Marxian structural claims and moral standards, Cohen and Rogers's account of democracy (1983) *may* be a sophisticated liberal alternative. What differentiates a serious liberal view from even a reasonably close Marxian cousin is an insistence on the ultimate independence of the democratic state and a claim that ultimately responsive, to pressure from below, it can serve as an instrument of radical reform. Their argument does not fully treat these issues. But a really thoroughgoing, effective conception of democracy, which they seek to articulate, is also what Marxians have always hoped for. See Gilbert, 1981a, 1986c, and Chapter 8 below.

In today's political idiom, answers to structural questions *may* also be conservative; for if certain controversial theoretical and empirical claims were true, radical movements might be generated by the consequences of concentrated, non-laissez faire capitalism; the free working of the market *might* promote a common good.

[88] Such structural explanations satisfy the "rock bottom" descriptive criterion of methodological individualism: that good explanations cite causal mechanisms consistent with the wants and reasons of individual actors. But methodological individualism was originally proposed as an *a priori empiricist constraint* on social explanations, designed to rule out particularly Marxian and functional, if not all sociological ones. On this account, the descriptive criterion turns out to be true but trivial, excluding no major school of contem-

decisive ethical and political reasons, a *Marxian* structuralism must insist on individual agency. On a structural view, however, aspects of overdetermination no longer clash with perceptions of structure as they do on individualist ones – perhaps participants are more open, given particular psychological dynamics, to seeing structural injustice. As moral realism insists, ethical progress stems from the recognition of equally sufficient human capacities for moral personality. Historically, structural obstacles are just what inhibit equality and individuality. In an ironic reversal of the received view, a sophisticated structuralist account places greater weight on *ethical facts, ethical explanation, and individuality* than methodological individualist ones do.[89]

9. The indeterminate reference of Marxian exploitation

Marx's analysis of the abuses of capitalism highlights his alternative vision of a good society. His account explains multifaceted, *systemic* injustice. As we saw in Chapter 1, this historical theory not only condemned exploitation in production, but identified a further gamut of negative social, political, and moral consequences that flow from this structure. Yet within political economy, Marx largely restricted his use of the term "exploitation" – s/v – to comparatively narrow, technical concerns. The preceding clarification of Marxian metaethics permits a broader characterization of exploitation and of the *interests* that might politically lead to communism.

We may recall, on Marx's account, some broad consequences of an exploitative class structure for most people. Any racist animosity of the white American worker toward the slave, he insisted, served as a politi-

porary explanation without further empirical argument. The harmful misconception that it does rule out some *important*, otherwise not fantastic explanations – a way of misguidedly discrediting contending theories – is, however, visible in some recent Marxian individualists, notably Jon Elster. Elster's most inappropriate instance is his a priori attempt to exclude Marxian theories of racism (Elster, 1985, pp. 21–2); see Chapter 11 below. The bad explanations that he rightly criticizes can be shown to be mistaken by a simpler, a posteriori principle; given the relevant contest of theories in a field, place a low-research priority on badly stated, empirically implausible, theoretically uninteresting hypotheses.

[89] Some influential attempts at structural explanation – relativist ones like Althusser's or Foucault's – depict a history without a subject, without selves. Nothing in the interest in Foucault's innovative democratic studies of power in, for example, prisons requires this claim (Foucault, 1975). Further, one might wonder what the point of radical movements, and of individual experiences of commitment, love, and pain are, if we aren't really there. But a reasonable structural argument shows only how historical conditions, arising outside the control of individuals, affect their deliberations. On this view, communism is the creation of self-aware social individualities, not the working – behind the back of individuals – of settings that move merely apparent, nonexistent selves.

cal tool to perpetuate capitalist domination: "Labor cannot be free in the white skin wherein the black it is branded."[90] Given subsequent theoretical insights, analogous arguments apply to sexism or, more generally, to ideologies of competitive individualism in contrast to an appropriate theory of the self. For Marx, exploitation led to the crippling of formal democracy, government protection of basic capitalist interests, and the use of force in suppressing worker, peasant, and artisan revolt. Furthermore, regimes that defend exploitative social structures instigate wars to foster patriotism and blunt the spread of democratic or socialist consciousness – Prussia in 1848, the Franco-Prussian War.[91] These claims highlight wide *political* and personal interests among the victims. Furthermore, in production, an exploitative structure means domination by a will alien to each worker's purposes. Taking these social, political, and moral consequences in tandem, capitalism turns out to be a worse bargain for workers – and many others – than Marx's technical theory of exploitation suggests. His qualitative use of this concept – as in "the exploitation of man by man" – is a richer ethical indictment of capitalism than the narrowly quantitative notion of swindling characteristic of preceding individual rights-oriented definitions.

Marx's broad notion of exploitation grows out of Hegel's classic argument on the dynamics of master and servant. It shows how capitalist social structure fundamentally conflicts with the mutual recognition of persons. In this respect also, Engels's striking phlogiston analogy paradoxically misses the moral impact of Marxian theory, its internal recasting of the most sophisticated, philosophical defenses of liberalism; for its ethical aspect is detachable from Marx's particular theory of value. Not robbery of the product but subjugation of the person is the heart of his moral critique. In today's semantics, the reference of the term "exploitation" is not simply an economic one (*s/v*). Instead, Marx adapted a broader concept, whose connotations are ethical, and yet, out of misguided epistemological reluctance, failed to spell them out. Even in *Capital*, many of his characterizations – for instance, capitalism's "vampire" or "werewolf-hunger," when unchecked by class struggle, for every last instant of the workers' time – go far beyond swindling in exchange.[92]

Thus, within Marx's theory, the term "exploitation" has some indeterminacy of reference. His broad characterization traces the systemic interconnection of an underlying capitalist structure and its consequences; yet his circumscribed, technical use of "rate of exploitation" deflects at-

---

[90] Marx, 1961, 1:301. This Marxian social theoretical conception of the *consequences of exploitation* fits Railton's and Cohen's accounts of moral explanation. My subsequent argument is an alternative, eudaemonist version of their views.

[91] Marx and Engels, 1971, p. 96.   [92] Marx, 1961, 1: ch. 10; Gilbert, 1979.

tention from this central social theoretical, moral, and political point. His broad account, however, provides epistemic access to a multifaceted view of victimization. A full theory of the self – of social individuality – and of democracy would go further in delineating harms to persons than even this interpretation does. Thus, one might be inclined to say, just as the term "justice" is at best only partly adequate to capture the notion of abolition of classes, so the term "exploitation" does not fully convey Marx's moral argument, let alone suitable refinements. As the formulation "exploitation *and its consequences*" suggests, the term might become too charged with multifaceted, diverse implications, say, those shown by a eudaemonist theory. But the foregoing account seeks to capture what is ethically true in Marx's use of the term and explicate its role in his social theory. It need not recommend the continued central employment of this notion as opposed to say a moral – and social – theory of individuality. Nonetheless, as Marx surmised in using the term and as contemporary realist semantics might note, the ethical reference of "exploitation" is partly retained across these changes of social and psychological theory from liberal critiques of slavery to Ricardian socialist indictments to Marx's broad characterization of the consequences of capitalism to a modern theory of individuality. Hence I provisionally use the term to characterize the difference between exploitative prehistory and communist history, even though it at best approximates an aspect – the social aspect – of social individuality.

An explicit eudaemonist conception, however, specifies the multidimensional structural consequences, captured by Marxian social theory, for human well-being. It highlights the diverse motivations and *moral justifications* of a communist movement. It reveals the overdetermined victimization of workers; it explains a concordant harming of others. Eudaemonism articulates the *social interests* that go into a political alliance against capitalism.[93] To take only one example, the notion of a cooperative search for truth, contrasted with money or status seeking, coheres with a broad Marxian conception of the radical interests of intellec-

---

[93] Adam Przeworski's interesting account of the nonradicalism of electoral social democracy insists on a restricted notion of "material interest" which capitalism may often satisfy. He rightly combats an economic determinist Marxism which argues that proletarians have a simple economic interest in socialism, but then, given the absence of socialism in advanced capitalist countries, makes the bizarre elitist inference that workers must be irrational or display "false consciousness." But Przeworski's argument is harmed by methodological individualism. He fails to consider any alternative based on the widespread historical development of diverse, serious radical movements and the political possibility, sometimes captured in features of such movements, of a more multifaceted conception of *social interests*. This failure is probably an artefact of his positivist epistemology, since he, like Elster, is sympathetic to broader moral critiques of capitalism (Przeworski, 1980, 1985).

tuals.[94] A modern eudaemonist theory may give diverse class- or activity-specific features of oppression, as well as individual interest in being a self, full political weight.

Some modern economic theorists, seeking to modify the tradition of classical political economy, have criticized the labor theory of value; philosophers, notably G. A. Cohen, have separated Marx's ethical critique from that theory and defended its core. Cohen suggests that labor creates not value but "what has value."[95] The foregoing account shows how Marx's basic moral criticism of capitalism, like the liberal indictment of serfdom, focuses on the ideas of mutual recognition and individuality and does not depend on the correctness of his theory of value. The claim that he provided an Aristotelian, eudaemonist, rather than a rights-based, critique of capitalist exploitation is consistent with what is true in these economic and ethical criticisms of his technical theory.

[94] Unlike Socrates, Thrasymachus demanded external rewards for speaking about justice; other interlocutors insisted, "For the money's sake, speak." Hopes of domination and fame also prompted him (Plato, *Republic,* 336b–337a, 337d–338c). "I welcome every scientific criticism. Toward prejudices . . . to which I have never made concessions, the saying of the great Florentine [Dante] is mine: 'Follow your own course and let people talk!'" Marx, 1972a, p. 17.

[95] G. A. Cohen, 1980, pp. 154–7; Levine, 1986; Roemer, 1982, 1985.

Chapter 6

Two kinds of historical progress

1. The defectiveness of utilitarianism

Even though Marx and Engels offered a realist reinterpretation of justice, they were hesitant about making overall ethical assessments of exploitative societies. Difficulties arising from the harshness of human progress might provide an independent argument against Marxian use of ordinary moral standards. As Engels's praise of the Paris Commune indicates, however, he and Marx evaluated communist progress differently from preceding alien advance. This chapter will explain this shift. It will counter a Marxian version of the "conflict of goods" objection: the claim that Marx reached no overall moral verdicts on many historical systems because intrinsic goods inevitably clash and no objective judgment is possible.

As a first approximation to Marx's argument, let us divide many past cases where the working class was neither large enough nor sufficiently politically sophisticated to contend for power from instances where communism is possible. For the earlier contexts, we might then say, Marx frequently made utilitarian-like judgments about the expansion of productive forces. He invoked a broad positive criterion of ultimately enlarging human capacities for self-realization and happiness. He might also have appealed to a negative, roughly quantitative standard of *ultimately* diminishing suffering. Yet we should proceed cautiously in calling Marx a utilitarian. In an Aristotelian vein, he distinguished two kinds of good – activities and relationships that were *intrinsically good*, for example, scientific discovery, and *instrumental goods*, which contributed to limited present and broader, ultimate individual self-realizations only at the expense of the contemporary producing classes. As a secondary feature, intrinsic goods may also be instrumentally valuable; in such cases, progress is no longer alienated.[1] For Marx, capitalist and pre-capitalist

[1] Plato, *Republic*, 357b–d.

productivity exemplified the negative aspects of his dictum "men make their own history but . . . not under circumstances chosen by themselves."[2] He recognized the atrocious human consequences of such development, the maiming of generations of individuals so that individuality might eventually flourish. Unlike utilitarians, Marx refused simply to count these "costs" against greater benefits in future happiness. Instead, he characteristically indicted the cruelty of exploitative systems and rarely embroidered his utilitarian-like judgments with favorable moral rhetoric.

Further, though Marx made few comments on ethical theory, he rejected utilitarianism. He decried Bentham's circumscription of human nature within the crippled vision of an English shopkeeper:

> To know what is useful for a dog, one must study dog-nature. This nature itself is not to be deduced from the principle of utility. Applying this to man, he that would criticize all human acts, movements, relations, etc., by the principle of utility, must first deal with human nature in general, and then with human nature as modified in each historical epoch [*menschlische Natur;* in jeder Epoch modifizierte Menschennatur]. Bentham makes short work of it. With the driest naivete he takes the modern shopkeeper . . . as the normal man. Whatever is useful to this queer normal man [*Normalmensch*], and to his world, is absolutely useful. . . . The Christian religion, e.g., is "useful," "because it forbids in the name of religion the same faults that the penal code condemns in the name of the law." Artistic criticism is "harmful" because is disturbs worthy people in their enjoyment of Martin Tupper [an English poet], etc.[3]

In criticizing Bentham, Marx invoked a conception of human nature that, though modified by successive historical achievements, provides a basis for nonhistoricist, nonrelativist ethical judgments. For instance, he envisioned a *human* intelligence and imagination that could transform its environment and itself and ultimately understand and control social development.[4] Such a view might plausibly include capacities for sympathy and empathy involved in moral and political activity, solidarity, and friendship. A Marxian might also stress a capacity to deliberate on one's purposes, character, and the nature of intrinsic goods and to choose or affirm a way of life.[5] To say that humans are reflective, empathetic social animals, capable of individuating themselves, is sufficiently definite to distinguish *human* characteristics from those of other animals;

---

[2] Marx and Engels, *SW,* 1:246.   [3] Marx, 1961, 1:609–10.

[4] G. A. Cohen, 1978, pp. 151–2. As Marx, 1961, 1:178, put it, "A bee puts to shame many an architect in the construction of her cells. But what distinguishes the worst architect from the best of bees is this, that the architect raises his structure in imagination before he erects it in reality."

[5] Taylor, 1977.

yet this description is sufficiently broad to allow for flexibility and creativity, to avoid biological reductionism.[6] Marx rejected Fisk's radical class relativism about human needs and mode of production relativism.

He also opposed Bentham's reductionist notion of uniform human pleasure seeking. That utilitarianism denied any internal, dialectical consideration of the grain of truth in religion, even as Feuerbach and Marx saw it, as the alienated expression of human capacities and dreams. It derided aesthetic standards in the name of mere marketability. It sought to recast diverse intrinsic goods according to a Procrustean standard. Marx here shared the critique of pleasure of Aristotle's *Nicomachean Ethics*: A Benthamite cannot distinguish a friendship of convenience among flatterers from a friendship involving mutual caring if the two yield a like amount of pleasure. More deeply, a contemporary Marxian might maintain, this utilitarianism – in contrast to Mill's sophisticated version – conceives of individuals as bundles of pleasures; it has no theory of the self or individuality.

In *The German Ideology*, Marx and Engels emphasized the social features of this critique. They characterized utilitarianism as an ideology of "mutual exploitation" that substituted *external* relations of "usefulness" and manipulation for the relevant reasons for activities. Such "cost-benefit" analysis neatly suits the bourgeoisie. But their critique was excessive. Given the facts of capitalism as Marx understood them, even a rough utilitarian notion of suffering and pleasure would justify a communist alternative. In an Aristotelian vein, however, Marx aptly stressed the relationships and activities needed "for the full development of individuals," as opposed to the "narrowness of exploitative forms of enjoyment which were outside the actual content of the life of people and in contradiction to it."[7] To borrow Rousseau's image, utilitarianism encouraged individuals to orbit only in the expectations of others, not to become absorbed in activities for their own sakes, to be internally at peace, and to unfold to and for themselves.[8] Marx's critique stigmatizes all merely instrumental justifications of alien social progress.

His comments are decisive against act-utilitarianisms as well as those rational actor models that suppose agents who do cost–benefit analyses of every relationship and activity.[9] I will examine below, however,

---

[6] Such reductionism involves the attribution of deficient conduct, especially alleged political incapacities, to putative racial or sexual characteristics. Though Marx was mainly an internationalist and fought against political restrictions, his correspondence sometimes casually employed racial stereotypes. That use was wrong and inconsistent with the rest of his view (Gilbert, 1981, p. 113).

[7] Marx and Engels, 1964, p. 460.

[8] Rousseau, 1964, 3:192–3. The idea "for themselves" is of course more Hegelian.

[9] Some game theorists try to incorporate broader psychological characterizations into their model (Keohane, 1984, pp. 74–5, 122–3). But this framework is often constrain-

whether some sophisticated rule-utilitarianism – one that justifies non-calculating activities by their contribution to overall human happiness, measured by some unique standard – could account for his claims about nonalienated social advance.

A broad eudaemonist conception, however, provided the underpinning for Marx's multifaceted, quasi-utilitarian judgments. Thus, for exploitative societies, he sometimes offered qualified arguments of the following utilitarian form: In particular historical circumstances, the end, expansion of man's productive capacities, *extenuates* the means, widespread human suffering. In *The Communist Manifesto*, for instance, he celebrated the bourgeoisie's revelation of human powers: "It [the bourgeoisie] has been the first to show what *man's activity* can bring about. It has accomplished wonders far surpassing Egyptian pyramids, Roman aqueducts and gothic cathedrals; it has conducted expeditions that put in the shade all former exoduses of nations and crusades."

Yet along with these achievements, Marx stressed that the bourgeoisie uprooted all traditional relationships, reducing them to a "cold cash nexus." It dissolved the livelihood of peasant and artisan smallholders and exploited workers.[10] Combined with his praise for "man's activity," he condemned capitalism's inhuman costs: It contributes to future flourishing mainly through grotesque contemporary suffering.

Further, Marx restricted even this consequentialist *extenuation* of capitalism through an unfavorable comparison with Greek slavery. Ancients like Aristotle "excused" (*entschuldigten*) the slavery of one only as a means to the "full development of another" – for instance, citizenship. In contrast, despite capitalism's massively increased productivity, it stretched out the working day. This modern status hierarchy victimized the producers to elevate creatures of social position, "eminent sausage-makers" and "influential shoeblack dealers," slight in humanity, accomplishment, and individuality.[11]

Marx offset this extenuation of slavery, based on the ideal and, to a limited extent, the realization of human nobility, with a fierce condemnation of its oppressiveness. He detected in slave and worker revolt the harbingers of a novel political alternative to alienated social and political development; he saw proletarians not only as a suffering, but as a subversive, creative class. After meeting with German communist artisans

---

ing. Caught within it, for example, Jon Elster, 1985, p. 9, insists that "altruism" is parasitic on "selfishness." But is finding one's own good in the good of one's friend "selfish"? Yet such friendship, even when it involves sacrifice, is an individual's own good, not *self*-sacrifice. Being a self is not the same as selfishness.

[10] Marx and Engels, *SW*, 1:37, 44–5.

[11] Marx, 1961, 1:408, 431. I use the term "extenuation" – Marx sometimes used "excuse" – because his judgment does not amount to anything like a full *justification*.

in Paris in 1844, Marx enthusiastically, perhaps onesidedly, stressed the "nobility of man" (*Adel der Menschheit*) that "shines . . . from these toil hardened visages" and celebrated their need for association, for a (modified) Aristotelian friendship.[12] Nonexclusive political community underpins Marx's vision of a flowering of individuality. In a eudaemonist vein, he recognized the multifacetedness and potential conflict of goods for individuals and social structures. Like Boyd's interpretation of corpuscular chemistry, his nuanced portraits of alien advance arrive at no overall assessment.

For early capitalism, Marx came closest to a narrowly instrumental idiom. In the 1840s, for example, he and Engels redefined Hegel's second criterion for just wars of advancing "civilization" as opposed to "barbarism." Given a different political theory, they saw "civilization" as the institution of democratic and capitalist arrangements, counterposed to the "barbaric" survival of feudalism.

On this criterion, in the *Neue Rheinische Zeitung*, Engels, with the tacit consent of his editor Marx, defended the U.S. wresting of Texas from Mexico in the war of 1846–8. Victorious American capitalism, he argued, would open up new cities and railroads in California and inaugurate a "world-historical" epoch of commerce with the Pacific. He crassly extolled the worth of capitalist institutions, embodied in rights of some at the expense of misery for others: "The 'independence' of a few Spanish Californians and Texans may suffer because of it, in some places 'justice' and other moral principles may be violated; but what does that matter compared to such facts of world-historical significance?"[13]

Rawls has criticized this tenor in utilitarianism and offered a competing rights-oriented view: "Each person possesses an inviolability founded on justice that even the welfare of society as a whole cannot override. For this reason, justice denies that the loss of freedom for some is made right by a greater good shared by others."[14] Yet the crudeness with which Engels rejected an individual-rights-based argument accentuates the more nuanced appraisal that he and Marx usually gave of the suffering of those ground under the "progressive" capitalist juggernaut.

[12] Bottomore, 1964, p. 176; Easton and Guddat, 1967, pp. 206, 200; Marx and Engels, 1959, 5:140–2.

[13] Marx and Engels, 1959, 6:273–4. Linking abolitionism and democratic internationalism in his essay entitled "Civil Disobedience," Thoreau prefigured the subsequent Marxian critique of the American oligarchy's conquest of Mexico: "The objections which have been brought against a standing army, and they are many and weighty and deserve to prevail, may also at last be brought against a standing government. The standing army is only an arm of the standing government. . . . Witness the present Mexican war, the work of comparatively a few individuals using the standing government as their tool; for, in the outset, the people would not have consented to this measure" (Thoreau, 1981, p. 416).

[14] Rawls, 1971, pp. 3–4.

2. The historical dialectic of conflicting moral standards

Marx's *Poverty of Philosophy* suggests that history has proceeded not by the good side of noble intentions and peaceful progress but through exploitation and struggle.[15] His microstructural account of instrumental progress distinguishes capitalist advance from the increasingly less alienated efforts of the oppressed to emancipate themselves. In the latter case, suffering and exploitation – abridgement of rights in Rawls's terms – dialectically engender popular outrage and rebellion.

We may set Marx's complex judgments in the contemporary debate between utilitarian and contractarian theory. Within his – quasi-utilitarian – exenuation of alienated progress, he retained a second standard, delineating oppression and prefiguring an eventual emancipatory movement from below. He seems to have held two contradictory ethical intuitions about many exploitative societies, a utilitarian one and a rights-oriented one. In eudaemonist terms, these intuitions capture *basic clashes of goods* – say, the advance of science at the expense of exploitation. Though Marx never invoked fundamental rights, he insisted on the goods of life and personality that underlie such claims. In this respect, his judgments resemble contractarian ones. He extenuated exploitative progress *only* for those past cases that created the possibility of a fundamentally different association, only for those in which, counterfactually, it was hard, given natural and social circumstances, to imagine a nonexploitative alternative.

We can see Marx's underlying eudaemonist indictment of suffering at work even in his appraisal of early capitalism and colonialism. He condemned the bourgeoisie's victimization of slaves seized and deported from Africa and of peasants forced off the land in English "primitive accumulation." Since capitalism wrote its history "in letters of blood and fire," he already foresaw the proletariat's future "expropriation of the expropriators."[16] Differing from Engels's morally fatuous appraisal of the U.S.–Mexican War, Marx dialectically transformed a partial utilitarian extenuation for the sordid "dawn" of bourgeois domination into a justification of a movement to overthrow it.

Similarly, he regarded British colonialism as a positive force insofar as it broke down "the stagnant Indian village," introducing railways and a measure of capitalism. He evaluated this village's "barbaric" stagnancy not by its customary moral standards as Walzer does, but by the potentials for human achievement revealed, mainly in alienated form, in some bourgeois regimes. Yet Marx also rightly stressed the villagers' innocence. He indicted colonialism's tearing apart of their lives, its "sordid

[15] Marx, 1973, pp. 120–1.   [16] Marx, 1961, 1:715, 734, 751, 760–3.

passion" for gain. In his scathing phrase, "Has [the bourgeoisie] ever effected a progress without dragging individuals and peoples through blood and dirt, through misery and degradation?" Though foreign capitalism would "lay down the natural premises" to "mend" the oppression of the "mass of people," only an Indian independence movement or the granting of independence by an English communist regime could turn these "premises" to their benefit.[17]

Given these tensions in Marx's moral standards, changes in historical theory have an enormous ethical and political impact. Between the 1840s and 1860s, he revised his theoretical estimate of the importance of anticolonial revolt. Marx had initially argued that English proletarian revolution would emancipate Ireland; in the 1860s, however, he concluded that the survival of advanced capitalism depended upon the division of English citizens and Irish immigrants and the successful propagation of an ideology of "Irish inferiority." Anticolonial liberation, supported by a unified British working class, must precede the victory of socialism in England. Marx's historical analysis and moral argument shifted from a temporary extenuation to an advocacy of rebellion against colonialism at home and abroad.[18]

Given this political theory transformation, he stressed the second criterion, the ferocity of capitalist exploitation, and revolt. Marx did not fully extend his argument about the harmful impact of colonialism on the English working class from the case of Ireland to that of India.[19] Nonetheless, the international arena for further instrumental progress had, in his view, contracted dramatically. Moreover, his moral evaluation exhibited a new structure: In modern circumstances, nationalist and/or democratic revolt against oppression overrides utilitarian claims deriving from further alienated productive advances in colonial or capitalist form. As in Hegel, the structure of Marx's ethical argument was dialectical – the old forms nurture and give way to conflicting new ones.

Marx deemed any narrowly utilitarian argument morally defective. He extenuated social systems instrumentally only insofar as they contained the seeds of their own ethical critique and political overthrow. As a complex, eudaemonist view would suggest, he employed a rhetoric of indictment even in such cases. Further, extenuations apply mainly to the past. Where Marx could exert political influence, notably in the German democratic revolution of 1848, he aimed to organize workers to over-

---

[17] Avineri, 1968, pp. 137, 206.

[18] Marx and Engels, 1965, pp. 230, 232, 235–7. Elster, 1985, p. 17, oddly discounts Marx's views on international politics as "largely devoid of theoretical interest."

[19] During the Sepoy mutiny, however, he had stressed that English workers were forced to pay for colonialism with their lives and taxes and saw the Sepoys and English proletarians as potential allies (Gilbert, 1978b).

throw their exploiters.[20] On his account, advances requiring mainly utilitarian justification exemplify at best human achievement in inhuman circumstances. Interpretations that highlight Marx's extenuation of colonialism or early capitalism miss this basic dialectical insight.[21]

Despite these changes, however, he still extenuated democratic and anticolonial revolutions, unless they were followed immediately by communist ones. Noncommunist revolutions would facilitate capitalist expansion and subsequently heighten class conflict, not inaugurate an epoch of mainly admirable progress. Thus, the new element in his ethical argument has a weaker and stronger version, the former focusing on the role of a democratic movement in creating conditions for further instrumental advance, the latter on proletarian self-emancipation and the cessation of alienated social development.

Economic determinist arguments, mirroring Engels's justification of the U.S. conquest of Mexico, have sometimes sanctioned socialist allegiance to modernizing colonialism or communist support for procapitalist revolutions. Since the productive powers – and by implication, the producers – are not yet ripe for a cooperative society, these views suggest, radicals must defend (or worse yet, become) the exploiters who will advance them. They may criticize such oppressors for vacillation in fulfilling this historic mission. Only at some later stage could communists advocate their full viewpoint or initiate a revolutionary movement. As a variant, today's Soviet and Chinese leaders often encourage parties with the goal of economic development rather than political and social egalitarianism, seeking a "noncapitalist" or "new democratic" alternative, not communism.

Many Marxians, however, contend that such economic determinist arguments cruelly extend the period of alien progress by restricting political possibilities. Radical regimes, for example, have temporarily flourished even in largely peasant settings. Given modern conditions and evidence, they maintain, a sophisticated Marxian political theory should
· rid itself of economic determinist survivals. In this regard, Marx's theory and strategy provide some help. For example, in 1848, he already pointed to the potential of a worker–peasant alliance to achieve proletarian revolution in mainly rural Germany. His theoretical and strategic willingness to envision novel political alternatives, based on particular radical movements – in this case, the French Revolution, Chartism, and in the 1844 Silesian weavers' revolt – clashes sharply with economic determinist views. His stress on learning from political practice captured the role of what Richard Boyd has termed "naturally occurring social

---

[20] Marx and Engels, *SW*, 1:65; Gilbert, 1981a.   [21] Tucker, 1977, p. 142.

and moral experiments."[22] As Aristotle theorized the polis and Hegel modern liberal society, so Marx recognized the political and ethical discoveries and possibilities in further egalitarian movements. An economic determinist view highlights the dominant side of the conflict of goods characteristic of exploitative regimes, the productive and other *instrumental* achievements, and downplays oppression. In contrast, a Marxian political theory dialectically explains alien development and yet stresses suffering and egalitarian revolt.[23]

Now, the Soviet and Chinese revolutions partly resuscitated Marx's conclusions about the interplay of democracy and communism, political and social equality. Their strategies focused on the complexities of Marx's account of communism, which the next section will explore; they concentrated on the moral tension between instrumental and nonalienated advance and sought to quicken the latter. But the failure of Marx or his successors to provide an adequate political and economic theory of communism undercut these attempts. Offering criticisms of socialism based on democratic individuality, Chapters 7 and 8 pursue this tension in the structure of Marxian theory.[24] The political and moral stakes involved in different empirical versions of that argument are high.[25]

3. Proletarian self-emancipation and political community: a different kind of moral progress

Given exploitation, capitalism – and previous regimes – could exhibit no genuine common good; proponents recommend the form of a justified political life without the substance. In contrast, Marx contended, a revolutionary movement can embody the common interests of all working people and elicit a special quality of participation. In his 1845 *Theses on*

---

[22] Gilbert, 1981a, 1979; Boyd, 1986a.

[23] Walter Benjamin's insistence on remembrance for the victims, in contrast to fixation on the "grand course" of history, captures an important feature of creative Marxian historiography. As Benjamin put it, "there is no document of civilization which is not at the same time a document of barbarism"; a Marxian does not "move with the current" but "regards it as his task to brush history against the grain," to "fight for the oppressed past . . . to save the dead from oblivion." Compared with complacent, sociological alternatives, this interpretation is true to historical experience and individuality. Ronald Beiner's eloquent tribute to Benjamin mistakenly suggests an inconsistency between remembrance and a dialectical notion of moral progress (Beiner, 1984, pp. 428, 431).

[24] Pleading "economic backwardness," socialist regimes have often justified limited participation of workers and peasants in the actual running of society, as well as quite dramatic wage differentials and status stratification. As Chapter 8 maintains, these arguments recapitulate older economic determinist and liberal ones.

[25] Miller, 1984, chs. 5–6.

Feuerbach, he stressed the educational role of political action, its impact on the integrity of the self: "the coincidence of the change of circumstances and of human activity or self-change." For instance, he insisted that the German revolutionary movement of 1848 must first overthrow the monarchy, that "lightning rod" for popular discontent, so that capital would sit "glaringly" on the throne. The armed masses of workers and peasants could then see capitalism as their main enemy and proceed to communist revolution. Similarly, universal suffrage in the French Second Republic, coupled with crushing mortgages, usury, and the new wine tax, would radicalize the peasants. In this *political* sense, Marx argued, "revolutions are the locomotives of history."[26]

For Kant and Hegel, passionate individuals, driven by narrow self-interest, spur historical changes that occur "behind the backs" of the agents. The "invisible hand" of Adam Smith's market notoriously illustrates unintended, socially useful results of selfish agency. In contrast, from the outset of his career, Marx maintained that capitalist class conflict could provide an arena for self-change – a revolutionary movement would make substantive mutual recognition and individuality characteristic of a new political association. His delineation of the noble character of participants clashed with the characterizations of self and motivation offered in classical political economy. Thus, he dedicated *Capital* to his friend and comrade Wilhelm Wolff, "faithful, noble, intrepid protagonist of the proletariat." Class struggle, as described for instance in the famous chapter of the working day, can nurture a more cooperative, resolute, and reflective – a non-money- and non-status-hungry – self. In the light of Marx's political activity and historical explanations, a modern reader may criticize the theoretical project of *Capital* as overly economic and inadequate to his political and moral insights.[27]

Some have supposed that, on a revolutionary view, workers can learn only through the rejection of reform and greater suffering – roughly, Bakunin's and Nechaev's cynical strategy of "the worse the better." Contrary to this manipulative view, however, Marx thought that the political experience of winning reforms could reveal the character of the workers' enemies and accentuate the need for proletarian revolution. On his theory, even reforms could only come from mass struggle from below and would be fought, yielded grudgingly, and ultimately undermined by the powers that be.[28] These movements would illustrate important possibilities of cooperation and deliberative political action, in contrast to Bakuninesque deceit.

Given such experiences, vigorous advocacy of a revolutionary view

---

[26] Marx and Engels, *SW*, 1:217.   [27] Gilbert, 1984b.
[28] Miller, 1984, chs. 3–4; Piven and Cloward, 1977.

would find adherents. Marx's *Capital* justified union organizing in opposition to those forces in the International Workingmen's Association who thought reforms could accomplish nothing. Yet he also showed how long-term capitalist trends would undermine reforms and make communist revolution the only appropriate vehicle to realize proletarian aspirations.[29] Throughout his political career, Marx defended the *Manifesto's* conception that communists must be the most "resolute" present fighters for reform – strikes, democratic revolutions – and yet unceasingly project the movement's "future" by advocating internationalism, abolition of private property in the means of production, and after the Paris Commune, a new kind of state.[30] They must be reflective, self-possessed, loyal, and bold, and encourage that character in others.

In the first stage of communism, Marx expected comparable political experiences to fuel revolutionary advance. He even saw the Paris Commune as "the political form *at last discovered* in which to work out the economic emancipation of labor." According to Marx, the Commune's "greatest measure was its own organization . . . proving by its life, its vitality, confirming its thesis by its action," the creation of a political arena in which those previously oppressed could deliberate, act, and transform society.

In the Commune, the private, social sphere of suffering and oppression quickened into political life. Parisian working women, "heroic, noble and devoted like the women of antiquity," participated on an unheard-of scale. In praising their citizenship, Marx's argument incorporated an important element of antisexism; he thus touched upon an area – the analysis of the baneful consequences of the oppression of women for both sexes – in which Marxian psychological and moral theory requires major refinement.[31] Further, in the midst of war, Parisian workers defiantly asserted democratic internationalism; they elected a Pole and a German to high communal offices. (As Marx's role in the multinational Communist League and International Workingmen's Association shows, internationalism was the hallmark of his radical activity.)[32] Proletarian officials discharged their new political tasks to achieve a cooperative society:

> The whole sham of state-mysteries and state pretensions was done away
> [with] by a Commune, mostly consisting of simple working men, organiz-
> ing the defense of Paris . . . doing their work publicly, simply, under the

[29] Gilbert, 1984b, secs. 1–3; 1979. [30] Marx and Engels, *SW*, 1:46, 64–5, 22.
[31] Nonetheless, in theorists like Montesquieu and Rousseau, ancient republican women played a notoriously secondary, dominated role. Montesquieu records that the Roman republic forbade women to shed tears at the battle of Cannes (Montesquieu, *OC*, 2:150). Gilbert, 1986a, sec. 4.
[32] Gilbert, 1978b; 1981a; chs. 2–10.

most difficult and complicated circumstances, and doing it, as Milton did his *Paradise Lost*, for a few pounds.[33]

For Marx, these proletarians had converted public offices into "real workmen's functions." Given their political awareness, they needed neither special incentives nor any aura of "infallibility." Some of Marx's famous examples of individuality – for instance, Milton, Dante, Ricardo, Darwin, and Aristotle – focus on artistic and scientific creation. Their activities, though done in a social and historical context, are distinctively individual, not collective. Fascinated by these images, some interpreters have downplayed the role of politics in Marx's conception of individuality. His analogy of worker leaders and Milton discredits that claim. Moreover, any study of his historical explanations and strategies highlights political deliberation and action as central features of individuality.[34]

Along with its antistatus orientation, the Commune relied on a citizen, rather than a standing, army. From that experience, Marx described the democratic institutions, including political participation, electoral recall of leaders, official salaries no higher than those of skilled workers, and citizen bearing of arms, that would characterize a communist regime. That association would unite peasants and other nonexploiters with workers. In the initial postrevolutionary stage, the intrinsic good of cooperative political activity carried at least equal weight with the ultimate goal of a full flourishing of individuality. Marx regarded this political activity as a component of the final good and not merely a means to it. In this context, any mainly instrumental argument, stressing achievements undercut by an alien form, seems particularly out of place. For the phases of communism, the structure of Marx's moral judgments shifts from extenuation fused with dialectical indictment to – a primary – praise.

Yet his ethical assessment of the initial stage is complex. Surveying the brief life of the Commune in the *Civil War in France*, he foresaw a long series of clashes in socialism through which workers would learn the necessity for advances from adverse political experience:

> The commune does not do away with the class struggle . . . but it affords the rational medium in which that class struggle can run through its different phases in the most rational and humane way. It could start violent reactions and as violent revolutions . . . the catastrophes it might still have to undergo would be sporadic slaveholders' insurrections, which, while for a moment interrupting the work of peaceful progress, would only accelerate the movement by putting the sword into the hand of the Social

[33] Draper, 1971, p. 153; Thomas, 1966.
[34] Elster, 1986, pp. 116–19; Gilbert, 1981a, ch. 1; 1978b.

Revolution. . . . The [workers] know that this work of regeneration [the lengthy transition to communism] will be again relented and impeded by the resistance of vested interests and class egotisms.[35]

Far from defending an economic determinist conception of socialism as state ownership combined with laissez-faire for wage and status differentials, Marx looked to continuing class conflict, within a setting of deepening democracy, to sustain workers' power.

In this context, Marx's *Critique of the Gotha Program* has striking egalitarian implications. There he maintained that socialism would direct the surplus toward social needs: health, education, and the like. As the new system unfolded, the social basis for an individual to realize her potentials would consistently improve, and the amount directed toward this common objective would increase. Furthermore, these shifts would contribute to unifying mental and manual work and prefigure communism. Capturing an important subsequent modification of Marx on socially stereotyped gender differences, Hilary Rose has suggested that communism should embody the unity of brain, hand, and heart.[36]

Yet for Marx, communism would emerge with the spell of capitalism heavily upon it. Those workers, peasants, and technicians, unconvinced by revolutionary politics or unmoved by a need to participate in activities for their own sakes, would seek extra monetary rewards. Thus, he concluded, a socialist system must permit pay differentials and limited inequalities according to work contribution. In this sense, socialism would come closer to realizing the vision of an individual-rights-based labor theory than capitalism. Yet Marx regarded this application of "bourgeois right" as an instigator of inequality and a "defect" from the standpoint of genuine community. In direct payments to workers, socialism would take account neither of need minimally considered – a person with a family has different necessities for physical provision than a single worker – nor of need fully considered in a communist sense – the requirements of diverse individualities. Even more tellingly, those specially oppressed by capitalism – women, ethnic minorities, the unskilled – would tend, in the absence of public, compensatory measures, to lose out under socialism also. More Horatio Algers might emerge, but Horatia Algers would remain a comparative rarity. The role of wage differentials was not for Marx a competing *good* to be balanced off against political community. Given the likely historical conditions, however, the result – the greater productivity of a socialism – still seemed to justify alien, but subordinate means – material incentives and some distributive inequalities.

[35] Draper, 1971, pp. 154–5.
[36] Rose, 1983, pp. 80–4; Marx and Engels, *SW*, 2:21–4; Fox-Keller, 1985, chs. 5–6.

But Marx also kept his eye on the political future of the movement. General provision for health, education, and the like would rectify distributive injustices arising from wage differentials. Furthermore, a deliberative, antistatus political community would propel the society in the direction of self-aware egalitarian reciprocity. As opposed to reliance on material incentives, these policies would nurture, in the political sphere, selves capable of individuality.

This communist association would also defend the interests of workers in other countries; predatory policies would undermine this regime even more than in the case of the democratic movements of 1848.[37] Thus, the initial revolutionary phase, as Marx conceived it, would exhibit conflicting practical features and moral justifications.[38] Adherents of capitalism – technicians, former entrepreneurs, proletarians influenced by the old ideas – perhaps given maneuvering room through concessions justified by narrowly utilitarian arguments, might press toward the reversal of communism. A radical party would have to stress the social needs, democratic community, and individuality, legitimized by Marx's deeper ethical argument, if the initial stage were to become full communism.

Marx's 1847 *Poverty of Philosophy* emphasized the role of political insight as a spur to productivity: "The greatest productive power is the revolutionary class itself." Given the absence of practical communist experience, however, he could never fully explore this possibility. Furthermore, in *Capital*, he envisioned an ultimate "realm of freedom" of self-chosen activities as superior to even this socialist "realm of necessity": "Just as the savage must wrestle with nature to satisfy his wants, to maintain and reproduce life, so must civilized man, and he must do so in all social formations under all possible modes of production." Yet Marx still saw an important sphere of political freedom in cooperative communist work:

> Freedom in this field can only consist in socialized man, the associated producers, rationally regulating their interchange with nature, bringing it under their common control, instead of being ruled by it as a blind power; and achieving this with the least expenditure of energy and under conditions most favorable to, and worthy of, their human nature.[39]

---

[37] Gilbert, 1978b, pp. 350–1. Marx would have opposed Robert W. Tucker's claim (1977, pp. 163–8) that a rich socialist state would inevitably dominate poor ones. As Chapter 12 shows for Weber's similar view, this claim is an artifact of his great-power "realist" theory of international politics rather than a specific account of the dynamics of socialism.

[38] I am using Marx's term – the "initial stage of communism" – in part to refer to socialism. But as Chapters 7 and 8 show, I also mean to recapture emancipatory possibilities in that idea, undercut by today's socialism.

[39] Marx, 1961, 3:799–800.

His argument may be construed in divergent ways. Either political, activity- and individuality-oriented motivations play a major role in the first stage of communism, or the realm of necessity requires mainly monetary incentives to stimulate a still burdensome production. The former interpretation reinforces Marx's celebration of the insights of a revolutionary class, the role of the Commune's leadership, and the flourishing of productive powers; it is "worthy of [the workers'] human nature." The latter undermines his conception of political community and the fusing of mental and manual work; it undercuts the transformation to full communism. Thus, the first interpretation seems nearer to Marx's intent; subsequent revolutionary experience, as we will see, provides important evidence for these claims.

4. Mill, Rawls, and Marxian communism

Given Marx's depiction of a conflict-ridden socialism, two new objections – one empirical, one theoretical – emerge to even a sophisticated utilitarianism. In *On Representative Government*, Mill proposed a special, unequal role for the educated through plural voting. For Marx, empirically, such an approach, distrusting workers and neglecting the class character of capitalist education, would have undercut the democracy embodied, for instance, in the Commune. A sophisticated utilitarian could abandon Mill's prejudice toward the intelligentsia and stress the special contribution to well-being of proletarian political activity.[40]

At this point, however, combining social and ethical theory, a Marxian might criticize even this utilitarianism. The attempt to quantify happiness according to a uniform standard blurs the conflict between the regime's decisive features that sustain communism – radical democracy, cooperative forms of work, facilitation of individuality – and secondary expedients such as wage differentials. A putative underlying calculus of pleasure misreads the multidimensionality of human goods, ignores the central importance of equal freedom, and obscures the distinction between individuality and individualism.[41] In contrast, radical historical and moral theory captures the ethical complexity of this regime's internal conflicts.

Yet a sophisticated utilitarian might acknowledge this point. A special role for intense sentiments fostering political community would resemble Mill's defense of those surrounding the principles of justice as "social utilities which are vastly more important and therefore more ab-

---

[40] Mill, 1948, pp. 281–90.   [41] Mill, 1961, p. 248.

solutely imperative than any others as a class."[42] In fact, in a eudaemonist vein resembling Marx's, Mill saw democratic activity as an intrinsic good:

> The passive type of character is favored by the government of one or a few, and the active self-helping type by that of the many. Irresponsible rulers need the quiescence of the ruled. . . . Notwithstanding the defects of the social system and moral ideas of antiquity, the practice of the dicastery and the ecclesia raised the intellectual standard of an average Athenian citizen far beyond anything of which there is yet an example in any other mass of men, ancient or modern . . . the public education which every citizen of Athens obtained from her democratic institutions must make them . . . very different beings, in range of ideas and development of faculties, from those who have done nothing in their lives but drive a quill or sell goods over a counter.[43]

Where there is no "school of public spirit," he insisted, "there is no unselfish spirit of identification with the public." As David Lyons has shown, Mill's analysis of rights and justice can be wholly disengaged from his ultimate utilitarian justification; so can his argument on democracy.[44] Further undercutting pleasure-based theory, as Chapter 1 showed, Mill emphasized the forging of equal liberty to justify the French Revolution. He articulated a central point of democratic theory: In dire circumstances, the liberty of some may be sacrificed to extend liberty to many others. Such justifications count the consequences involving basic rights in evaluating overall states of affairs; they assess what Amartya Sen has properly called "goal" or "capability rights."[45] In addition, radicals might learn from *On Liberty*'s spirited defense of individuality. At this point in Mill's theorizing, however, the notion of a com-

---

[42] Mill, 1977, 19:410–12. Mill advocated representative government rather than direct democracy (Teuber, 1986).

[43] Lyons, 1978, pp. 4–12.

[44] For an internal recasting of Mill's utilitarianism in terms of individuality, see Wollheim, 1984, pp. 222–5. He argues that a preliminary utilitarianism – one in which individuals work out their own conceptions of happiness – governs utilitarianism proper (the summing of pleasures now viewed as the summing of these diverse conceptions of happiness). Though a sound interpretation of Mill, this view of individuality, as Wollheim recognizes, undercuts what philosophers have ordinarily understood as utilitarian justification.

Similarly, Mill's arguments against the subjection of women stress individuality against utilitarianism proper. (He discounts putative pleasures arising from subordination of others). Yet he may have regarded admirable friendships among men and women – notably his marriage to Harriet Taylor – more as a merger than a relationship of distinct individualities (Zerilli, 1986). A modern theory of the self, as I show in Chapters 7 and 8, strengthens liberal – democratic socialist – as well as Marxian accounts.

[45] Sen, 1982.

mon, pleasure-based standard has become obscure. The best statement of his position, a radical might insist, is not utilitarian, but a eudaemonism incorporating political autonomy.

Marx's argument also empirically conflicts with a feature of Rawls's democratic contractarianism. Like Mill, Rawls surprisingly regards equal working-class participation as a secondary, easily sacrificed liberty.[46] If Marx's social theory of class domination were true, Rawls would adopt a form of socialism.[47] He contends, however, that a planned economy unnecessarily limits liberty. His principles of justice allow only a market socialism, which would generate substantial inequalities.[48] Yet if such inequalities enable the wealthy to dominate government and corrupt political liberty or if they fail to benefit the least advantaged and thus violate the difference principle, Rawls's principles proscribe them.[49] He would expect substantial political intervention to uphold the principles of justice even in a market socialism.

But Marx would have regarded this form of socialism, ruled mainly by material incentives, as overly utilitarian. On his view, a substantial component of cooperatively motivated productivity, political participation, and individuality would be necessary to sustain communism. Motivations consistent with a eudaemonist conception of personality – ones that include the good of others in one's own good – would play a substantial political role.[50] Without a state resembling the Commune, government intervention would forestall neither major inequalities of income nor their corrosive effects on equal political influence and self-respect; it would not prevent a reversal of social and political power.

Yet a radical can bring this Rawlsian theory close to a Marxian one; for, first, an informed Rawlsian deliberator in the original position, aware of all true social theories, might adopt a Marxian account of political power and a psychological view consistent with eudaemonism. Those changes would rule out any proposal to limit worker participation. Second, within the framework of equal liberty, the difference principle aims to secure genuine economic cooperation: Rawls calls it a "democratic principle."[51] Inside his theory, a radical might also question whether the difference principle – in contrast to equality of resources or equal incomes – was the appropriate distributional policy to further individuality. In either case, however, *if* Marxian social theory is true, only communism could realize Rawlsian principles. Conversely, as Chapter 8 shows, Rawls's theoretical conception of an overlapping consensus on demo-

---

[46] Rawls, 1971, pp. 232–3.   [47] Rawls, 1975, p. 546.   [48] Rawls, 1971, pp. 271–3, 280–2.
[49] Rawls, 1971, p. 226. That, given a more realistic social theory, the priority of equal liberty sharply limits inequalities permissible under the difference principle has been shown in Daniels, 1975; Gilbert, 1978a; and Garfinkel, 1981, pp. 100–104. See also R. Miller, 1975.
[50] Brink, 1984, p. 122.   [51] Rawls, 1971, p. 75; J. Cohen, in press b.

cratic autonomy, across diverse individualities, explains the fundamental insight in Marx's endorsement of the Commune.

5. Liberal and radical accounts of moral progress

Eudaemonist insights into the clash of goods help to clarify the tension in Marx's theory of past societies and explain his reticence about moral verdicts. A eudaemonist view also straightforwardly contrasts two stages of history, that of exploitative regimes, for which no overall ethical assessment is possible, and that of communist ones, characterized by concordance of goods and human flourishing. The moral structure of Marx's argument recalls the historical dimension in self-aware liberal theories of individuality. As Kant put it, "Only the later generations will in fact have the good fortune to inhabit the building on which a whole series of their forefathers (admittedly without any conscious intention) had worked without themselves being able to share in the happiness they were preparing."[52] As Kant's, Hegel's, and Mill's arguments show, sophisticated liberals discern two stages, the first characterized by conflicts of goods, the successor by mutual recognition and individuality.

In addition, Marx's account mirrored a basic psychological theme of classical political economy. Adam Smith, for example, suggested a "chain connection" between capitalist accumulation and worker well-being. Yet that accumulation required two classes with distinct life chances. It thus tended to reduce personality to what was suited, in calculating, utilitarian terms, to the appropriate class activities. Classical theory, however, envisioned a "historical mission" of capitalist accumulation – to create a society of opulence and a common good. In Hegel's interpretation, this economy might permit novel leeway for individuality.[53]

Such liberal theories implied or depicted two distinct types of self, the first ruled by self-interest in the sense of an overriding search for gain at the expense of others, the second characterized by a greater capacity for mutual recognition, engagement in relationships and activities for their own sakes, and concern for individuality – a genuine interest in the self. The former was a utilitarian calculator, responding to status hierarchy

---

[52] Kant, 1963, pp. 43–4.
[53] Smith, 1979, ch. 8. Though concerned with opulence, a common good, and market freedom, Smith did not articulate a modern conception of individuality in *Wealth of Nations*. John Rawls, 1971, pp. 80–3, uses the term "chain connection"; as we shall see, he offers an explicit historical account of the shift. Hegel, 1970, pp. 334–5. As Chapter 1 emphasizes, Hegel worried about whether capitalism was consistent with a political framework that could facilitate individuality. I have benefited from conversations with David Levine and Lucy Ware on this point.

and money, the latter a self-possessed individual. For Kant and, to a lesser extent, Hegel, deficient selves had inhabited – preliberal – history; only in the modern era is mutual recognition and the flourishing of individuality possible.[54] Marx, as we will see in Chapter 7, detected a wider presence of (features of) individuality during exploitative "prehistory." Nonetheless, on Marxian and self-aware liberal theories, humans *discover* their freedom historically and, in Hegel's description of the rational will, individually.

Yet even socialist accumulation, on Marx's conception, would partially feature the same kind of deficient self, motivated by status and income inequality, that, on the classical account, had fueled capitalist accumulation. The initial phase of communism would be less oppressive than capitalism because of its curtailment of private control of the means of production and great inequalities of wealth. Political and individuality-oriented motivations would play an important role. Yet as capitalist accumulation was dialectically needed in liberal theory to achieve a generalized civilization, so, on Marx's view, a process of partly instrumental socialist accumulation would be required to achieve an ethically distinct, communist destination. His socialism has a partially alien historical mission. Subsequent revolutionary experience would suggest, however, that Marx's account was too pessimistic.

Classical political economy traced a self-ordering market and sought to limit politics; Hegelian liberalism internally emphasized the role of ethical universality and politics in that economy. But Marx focused his critique in *Capital* on that expressly apolitical, classical framework; his own view of communism strikingly reveals that account's counterinfluence. As Marx thought capitalist society would "stamp" communism with its "birthmarks," so this earlier theory ironically marks his own.[55] That inheritance, linked to Marx's complex moral characterization of deficient historical advance, creates important tensions in his theory of communism, not just in his account of anticapitalist revolutionary possibilities; for the underlying character of Marxian theory is more sharply moral and political than Hegel's. His theoretical project brought the liberal insight into mutual respect to bear on the consequences of exploitation, yielding a communist version of democratic participation and social individuality. A Marxian conception of the good life would in-

---

[54] As if history had ceased, Kant presents his moral reasoning in isolation from his analysis of previous advance.

[55] Marx's claim referred to economic birthmarks, notably wage incentives. But a Marxian theory might appropriately stress other aspects. For instance, the survival of racist, sexist, anti-working-class, and competitive, egotistical images among the victims might contribute to feelings of self-hatred and inhibit participation.

corporate egalitarian recognition, at least in broad political terms, in the lives of individuals.

6. Two ethical models of Marxian historical theory

A critic of this argument might still wonder whether there is any special relationship between Marx's diverse moral standards – his utilitarian extenuation of capitalism, his indictment of its exploitativeness, his concept of social individuality and distribution according to need – or whether they are simply independent. Marx himself, he could stress, never sought to justify his ethical judgments by appeal to a general philosophical principle. As a matter of historical scholarship, it might seem fair to leave Marx's judgments as they stand and not form them into a more general pattern.[56]

Yet Marx saw his social theory and moral argument as an important competitor for truth. In refining this argument, I follow the spirit of his proposals. Similarly, Darwin's original formulation of evolution was important. Yet a reasonable contemporary statement – for instance, one that combines his argument with Mendelian genetics – captures and transcends it. Marx's social theory is more politically charged and controversial than Darwin's; it is often less clearly understood than alternatives. In this respect, as the criticism emphasizes, scholarly care is especially needed to do the theory justice.[57] Nonetheless, interest in its truth motivates what are otherwise narrow concerns. Furthermore, Marx was confused about metaethics. Yet as I have argued, a sophisticated Marxian historical theory requires moral argument. Moreover, an articulation of the interplay of that social theory and his ethical claims about individuality leads to surprising changes in the original version. In the present context, two moral theories – one more extensive than the other – might explain the interplay of Marx's two types of historical advance.

First, at a certain historical point, he replaced an extenuation of capitalism as a contributor to instrumental progress with a conception of the moral importance of a proletarian movement – and political association – which becomes the main vehicle for communist advance. The structural relationship between these verdicts seems formally analogous to the one between Rawls's general and special conceptions of justice.

---

[56] Allen Wood offered this criticism.
[57] Some of the misunderstanding is due to Marx's failure to work out a full political theory. He chose to criticize an explicitly less political theory in "political economy" and left many of his political insights in his historical explanations, strategic writings, and journalism. His choice of theoretical project, however, only partly explains the remarkable neglect of elaborated democratic argument, especially about postrevolutionary regimes, which is an important problem in the sociology of Marxian movements.

Rawls's general conception mandates those advances in the primary social goods – liberty and opportunity, income, and the bases of self-respect – that benefit the least advantaged. His special conception emphasizes the priority of equal liberty. In evaluating developing societies, he contends that one should always keep the special conception in mind, noting the sacrifice of liberty while extenuating it. Like Marx, that view emphasizes conflicts of goods. At a certain historical moment, however, movement toward equal liberty – the special conception – must override increased income to the least advantaged where the two conflict.[58] Interestingly enough, Rawls's historical division recapitulates the classical picture of accumulation and transformation of self.

One might suggest a Marxian general conception including both Rawlsian primary goods and specially valuable activities and relationships.[59] The first expansion of productivity and other human achievements would be morally acceptable, on this conception, primarily because they would benefit future generations. At a certain point, however, that of the shift from "prehistory" to human "history," a *special conception* becomes appropriate: The emancipation by their own efforts of those oppressed by feudalism or colonialism has *priority* over expansion of productivity and the realization of other goods in the previous form, and worker political emancipation ultimately has priority over any further, primarily alienated advance.[60] In Marx's general list of goods, political community and individuality now take precedence. Note that this characterization of the historical shift, derived from a broad ethical conception, differs dramatically from a mistaken relativist picture in which moral change echoes alteration in mode of production.

We might also, even more aptly, look at Marx's defense of communism

---

[58] Rawls, 1971, pp. 202–3, 542–8. His "chain connection" between the incomes of the main beneficiaries of economic progress and those of the least advantaged follows Adam Smith.

[59] Rawls's conception of primary goods is contractarian, specifying those *moral personality-based goods* needed to realize the freedom and equality of each (Rawls, 1982, 1988a). In his recent idiom, one might speak on an overlapping consensus on these preconditions for the *comprehensive* aims of diverse individuals or eudaemonist intrinsic goods. Rawls suggests that we expand the list of primary goods to include leisure and, responding to Sen, basic capabilities – for instance, compensation for handicap. Within a theory of democratic autonomy, these changes open the way toward a eudaemonist view. An *individuality-based conception of primary goods* overlaps with and perhaps amends Rawls's *moral personality-based conception*.

[60] "Opulence" is Smith's term for a higher stage. But Marx, 1973, pp. 487–8, offered a non-alienated interpretation: "When the limited bourgeois form is stripped away, what is wealth other than the universality of human needs, capacities, pleasures, productive forces, etc., created through universal exchange? . . . . The absolute working out of [humanity's] creative potentials with no presupposition other than the previous historical development." Marx, 1977, p. 183.

as a form of eudaemonism: a theory that evaluates relationships, activities, and character traits by asking how they advance individual happiness and affect the quality of human lives.[61] In communism, many intrinsic goods would flourish jointly; yet different features of those goods would be exemplified in diverse societies at earlier historical stages. Where alienated progress still had to occur, the concept of – a merely – instrumental good would enable a Marxian to extentuate it. But even in exploitative regimes, some intrinsic goods may have instrumental usefulness; for instance, goods of political activity – Greek community or Roman slave revolt – served as examples to future generations. Thus, Marx could approve of some aspects, both instrumentally and occasionally intrinsically good, of precommunist societies. He could also condemn each form of exploitation and its consequences as denials of human potentials. Given their undoing of so many lives, he withheld overall moral approval. Once proletarian revolution became a real possibility, however, Marx envisioned a fusing of intrinsic and instrumental goods, first in the radical movement, later in radical democratic association, and ultimately in the flourishing of social individuality. From an ethical point of view, he approved of the two stages of communism, the first in a qualified way, the second unequivocally. We can now redescribe the historical shift in Marx's judgments as one occurring at that point at which a *uniting of intrinsic and instrumental goods* characterizes further social development.

Contemporary moral theorists, as we have seen, often exaggerate particular conflicts of goods to infer metaethical relativism. Yet intrinsic goods frequently cluster and, as Aristotle suggested, are realized in interrelated means. So, a Marxian might argue, an individual might achieve a concordance of goods by reflection, a political movement by democratic deliberation. To stress clashes in disregard of harmony, a eudaemonist would emphasize, is misguided.[62]

In the special realm of evaluating societies, Marx's judgments capture this homeostasis. For example, Hegel and Marx argued that the emergence of science, philosophy, and political community in ancient Athens could be purchased only at the expense of slavery. If so, Marx could conditionally approve these aspects of slaveholding society, even though he recognized its exploitativeness and truncation of achievements. (Ancient political philosophy, for instance, had no worked-out view of individuality.) He could admire slave revolt. Yet no one class of people in

---

[61] Irwin, 1979, ch. 8, esp. pp. 249–51.

[62] Richard Boyd's excellent article, 1986a, captures the semantics of complex biological, medical, social scientific, and moral terms. Yet it does not – I think mistakenly – stress the role of individuality as the primary human good, without which the others cannot be coherently realized.

that society could fuse radical political association and scientific discovery. The flourishing of goods was distorted.

Given capitalism's instrumental accomplishments, he contended, a communist movement could bridge the division between mental and manual work. Revolutionary proletarians and their allies could fuse noble character and individuality, the forging of political community, and scientific achievement. On a Marxian view, moral progress and a corresponding advance in ethical theory can occur historically.

This eudaemonist conception avoids two errors of some common accounts of progress. First, Marx looked to dialectical advance through struggle and transformation, not unilinear development. Capitalism's alien political structure – though in liberal forms, it came to recognize the capacity of each person to vote – retained few of the positive, participatory aspects of the polis. But the Paris Commune could realize the potential prefigured in Greek politics.

Second, concordance of goods does not require one-sided, let alone infinite, realization of any good.[63] Instead, a Marxian could suggest a relationship between a good life for an individual – implied in modifications of *everyday* experience – and removal, through communism, of important social obstacles nurtured by capitalism – for instance, ideologies of self-hatred (denial of self-respect). This radical view is *individuality, not duty centered; it* supposes *ordinary psychological growth, not utter transformation.*[64] In general, a Marxian argument sees a dialectical promise of communism in the accomplishments of liberalism. For example, in the seventeenth century, an exhilarating coincidence occurred – at least for certain members of the English middle classes – between the intrinsic goods of discovery and their instrumental consequences. Drawing on these experiences, great liberal theorists like Montesquieu hoped for a concomitance of religious toleration, abolition of slavery, free political

---

[63] It also does not license Trotsky's exaggerated vision of "everyone an Aristotle or Goethe."

[64] Thomas Nagel, 1986a, pp. 206–7, articulates this project: "The world that . . . would emerge from a process of political reconstruction would not contain 'new men' unrecognizably different from ourselves in being dominated by impersonal values, so that their individual happiness consists in serving humanity. That might be better than the world we have now, but quite apart from the problem of whether such a thing is possible, it would be a poorer world than one in which the great bulk of impersonal claims were met by institutions that left individuals – including those that supported and operated those institutions – free to devote considerable attention and energy to their own lives and to values that could not be impersonally acknowledged." More than Nagel suggests, a theory of individuality includes both kinds of motivation, realizing oneself in relationships and in personal unfolding; the good of individuality can be objectively – in his idiom, impersonally – acknowledged.

Steven Massey, 1983, defends self-respect; Rawls, 1971, pp. 440–6 treats it as the most important primary good.

association, the supplanting of war by commerce, individuality, opulence, and dissemination of the arts, sciences, and gentle manners.[65] On Marx's critique, given exploitation, concordant flourishing was not yet possible; in communism, however, a wide fusion of goods could occur.

A eudaemonist theory best explains the moral judgments embodied in Marx's complex social theory; Chapter 7 traces his often explicit affinities for Aristotle's original version. Nonetheless, a modern radical theory must not merely sketch a conception of individuality. Starting from Marx's embryonic insights, Chapters 7 and 8 suggest a more worked-out account. They apply that conception, internally, to criticize previous radical views of the initial phase of communism.

[65] Gilbert, 1986a. Richard Boyd and Richard Miller have both suggested the simple analogy of choosing an automobile – each person looks for some conjoint realization of safety, handling, beauty, speed, economy, and the like. Each realization involves trade-offs and limits on any particular good.

Chapter 7

The Aristotelian lineage of Marx's eudaemonism

This book has advanced a moral realist view, based on a transepochal study of leading ethical and political theorists. Although contemporary Anglo-American moral theory has mainly divided between contractarians and utilitarians, my argument appeals to an Aristotelian and Marxian eudaemonism. Yet, a critic might suggest, my conception overemphasizes the interplay, across massive social and theoretical changes, of ancient and modern ethics. Seeing the foregoing argument as too enthusiastic about an ostensible Marxian eudaemonism, even a scientific realist might make this criticism.

Marx himself, however, characterized Aristotle as that "giant thinker" who "first analyzed so many forms of thought, society and nature."[1] As the critic might insist, Marx's *particular* views about such issues as justice, slavery, women, and property differ dramatically from Aristotle's. Recalling the argument of Chapter 1, however, if we were to remain at the level of particular disagreements, we would miss profound general similarities of ethical framework that qualify both thinkers as eudaemonists and moral realists.

First, this chapter shows that Aristotelian conceptions underlie three central features of Marx's concept of alienation. Second, it contends that the Aristotelian psychology of self-love and friendship explains important Marxian claims about individuality and foreshadows modern refinements in the theory of the self. We can characterize a eudaemonist ethical theory as one of *social* or *democratic* individuality, even though Aristotle did not use these terms. Third, both theorists stress political association and action as especially important goods. Moreover, in studying politics, they adopted a common framework that included five broad notions: (1) the importance of a cooperative, free political life, based on a common good, (2) the role of politics as an arena for the display and development of moral character, (3) the need to criticize inter-

---

[1] Marx, 1961, 1:59.

263

nally and refine existing opinions about justice and other intrinsic goods, (4) the dialectical dynamic of a democratic regime that threatens the rich, and (5) the importance of practical – or in modern terms, democratic – deliberation in serving a common good. Fourth, the chapter explores striking epistemological similarities between Marx's scientific realist critique of Aristotle's political economy and an accompanying, previously unexamined moral realism. Fifth, Richard Miller also traces affinities of Marx's normative stance and Aristotle's; this section will counter two subtle objections by Miller to claims that Marx held an ethical point of view and that moral appraisal of social structures can be, in important respects, objective.

1. Eudaemonism and alienation

As we have seen, Marx's critique of utilitarianism stems from a vision of the diversity of intrinsic goods and individuality. In *The German Ideology*, for instance, he insisted on the "peculiarity" of activities and relationships, such as speech or love, that are "definite manifestations of definite qualities of individuals," done on their own account, not as part of some alien, monetary "third relationship."[2] He contrasted the integrity of activities that express human nature and their corruption.

Aristotle's critique of pleasure in book 10 of *The Nicomachean Ethics* explains Marx's arguments. Aristotle maintained that mature happiness differs from that of a child, and an adult would never confine himself to childlike pleasures, whatever their intensity. Only malign pleasures, such as those of a sick man or woman, he insisted, accompany depraved activities. To be a good, pleasure must arise from the intrinsic merit and quality of an activity or relationship. In this vein, as we have seen, Aristotle contrasted true friendships characterized by mutual concern from defective ones.[3] Such distinctions make Marx's point about the "definite" qualities of relationships and activities in *The German Ideology* more exact. Furthermore, the happiness and wonder that arise from the search for knowledge differ from those of friendship, sight, or political action. A good life includes disparate kinds of well-being. In addition, diverse, justified needs stem from particular activities. Olympic prizes should reward the swiftest, not the wealthiest.[4] For Aristotle, distortions arose from status and power seeking, and especially grasping after money. His careful differentiation of appropriate and corrupt motivations for activities and relationships is consistent with Marx's indictment of utilitarianism.

[2] Marx and Engels, 1964, p. 449.   [3] Aristotle, *Nichomachean Ethics*, 1173b21–4a13.
[4] Aristotle, *Politics*, 1282b38–3a24.

But a critic might ask, Did Marx regularly draw such a distinction? In fact, this contrast clarifies a number of the central themes of *Capital* and highlights the varied political impact of different features of Marx's theory of alienation. For instance, in the chapter entitled "The Results of the Immediate Process of Production," he compared productive activity in general with labor under capitalism in a precisely Aristotelian way. Milton, Marx contended, created *Paradise Lost* as an "expression of his own nature," not for monetary gain. Marx likened his artistry to a silkworm's spinning of silk. This genuine, natural activity – unproductive from a capitalist point of view – contrasts with the "productive" work of a hack who grinds out a political economy text on a publisher's commission. As we have seen, Marx recurred to Milton, a favorite example, in commending the nonmercenary political activity of the Communards. Milton also supported the Puritan Revolution; Marx's affection for his achievement was, in part, political. Furthermore, in *Capital*, Marx counterposed someone who "sings like a bird" – again, the image of a natural activity – and a person who sings for hire, a teacher and a time server at a "knowledge-mongering institution."[5] Capitalism fuses material and social – value-producing – activities; it is partly natural – expressive of human nature – as well as historical. Thus, Marx need not maintain that capitalist productivity corrupts all activities; individuals may find aspects of their work consonant with their own nature – "sing like birds" – even though it also realizes profit for an employer. In fact, the existence of noncorrupt relationships and activities foreshadows the good of communism. But occasional consonance highlights its general absence; the capitalist system as a whole, he maintained, undermines such integrity.

A first, important feature of Marx's theory of alienation focuses on the impact of capitalism on motivations for work.[6] Productive activity here serves only as a means of life, not its expression.[7] As Marx put it in "Wage-Labor and Capital," "What he [the worker] produces for himself is not the silk that he weaves, not the gold that he draws from the mine, not the palace that he builds." Invoking an Aristotelian sense of natural justice, he characterized wage labor as "unnatural." He compared this activity to the production of his favorite animal, the silkworm, but, this time, to a hypothetical, perverse one that spun not to become a butterfly but to "maintain its existence as a caterpillar."[8]

A second, closely related feature of alienation, which also relies on eudaemonist arguments, highlights the corrupting impact of great differences of wealth and poverty on human qualities and relationships.[9] Marx frequently recalled a speech of Shakespeare's Timon of Athens:

[5] Marx, 1977, 1:1044.   [6] Marx, 1967, pp. 281, 290.   [7] Marx and Engels, *SW*, 2:24.
[8] Marx and Engels, *SW*, 1:82–3.   [9] Marx, 1967, pp. 270–1.

Gold, yellow, glittering, precious gold!
Thus much of this will make black white; foul fair;
Wrong right; base noble; old young; coward valiant;
. . . This yellow slave
Will knit and break religions, bless the accurs'd
. . . place thieves
and give them title, knee and approbation.[10]

Money, that bewitching "equation of incompatibles," enabled the rich to counterfeit the human qualities they lacked; its absence and oppressive labor to survive deprived the poor of the chance to discover and exercise their gifts and capacities. Marx admired Shakespeare's Aristotelian indictment of the trafficking of friendship, love, and office.

More subtly, he saw the real wealth of society as the Hegelian social education of the senses, embodied in the historical flourishing of diverse activities: "The *development* of the five senses is a labor of the whole previous history of the world." Hegel contrasted objective rationality as an aspect of such achievements with mere arbitrariness:

> The rational is the high road where everyone travels, where no one is conspicuous. When great artists complete a masterpiece, we may speak of its inevitability, which means that the artist's idiosyncrasy has completely disappeared and no mannerism is detectable in it. Pheidias has no mannerisms; his figures live and declare themselves. But the worse the artist is, the more we see in his work the artist, his singularity, his arbitrariness.[11]

Within the practice of intrinsically good activities, a historical conversation exists: New achievements and styles, through their complex relationships to previous ones, achieve an often self-aware, dialectical interplay, visible in the work of the artists and to a sophisticated audience. For instance, if we judge dramatic twentieth-century innovations in the style and content of painting and poetry solely by the criteria of paradigmatic earlier artists, we might find it difficult to identify them as variants of a common art form. Yet as we can also see, they are internally connected to predecessors by a series of innovations that explore those forms' possibilities. This interplay distinguishes the "rational" in Hegel's sense from the arbitrary, individuality from idiosyncrasy.[12] In the 1844 *Economic and Philosophical Manuscripts*, Marx gave an Aristotelian interpretation of this theme, one that he would stress throughout his writing:

[10] Marx, 1961, 1:132.
[11] Hegel, 1970, pp. 92–3.
[12] Miller, 1986, ch. 2. Hegel's claim is an artistic analogue to Shapere's scientific chain-of-reasoning connections.

As music alone awakens man's musical sense and the most beautiful music has *no* meaning for the unmusical ear – is no object for it, because my object can only be the confirmation of one of my essential capacities and can therefore only be so for me insofar as my essential capacity exists explicitly as a subjective capacity . . . – for this reason, the *senses* of social man *differ* from those of the unsocial.[13]

This characterization, Marx insisted, applies not only to the historical sophistication of the ear or aesthetic sensibility but to "the so-called spiritual and moral senses (will, love, etc.), in a word *human* sense." Objective ethical insights are, for Marx, as much a component of historically forged human capacities as any other achievement – informed by intelligence – of the senses. He proposed a eudaemonist and realist understanding of what Goodman calls aesthetic "rightness."[14] Furthermore, his ethical judgments rest on a definite, comparatively developed eudaemonist conception, one that incorporates his merely adumbrated interpretation of other kinds of sensory rightness. Thus, he contrasted diverse social, *unnatural* frustrations with "nature *humanized*," the starving man who wolfs sustenance with leisurely enjoyment of good food, the mineral dealer who sees only exchange value – "he has no minerological sensitivity" – with someone open to natural beauty, a sycophant with a citizen, and the like. He offered a rich, Aristotelian portrait of intrinsic goods and human senses realized in the history of their embodiments.

A third feature of alienation is the isolation of individuals from one another and from their "species-being" (*Gattungswesen*).[15] Aristotle stressed the political association of citizens, who rule and are ruled in turn, as a defining human characteristic. Despite an inversion of the ancient scorn for manual work, Marx insisted, the Commune was a "*republic of labor*," the Communard a *political* animal.

On first reading, the idea of species-being has a somewhat illusory quality. How can humans alienate, one might ask, a species-being that they have, so far, been unable to realize? But as Aristotle recognized, Greek politics provided an important example. For a Marxian, as I suggested above, subsequent egalitarian movements – the Roman slave revolt led by Spartacus, the German Peasant War, the Levellers in the Puritan Revolution, and the sans-culottes in the French Revolution – pointed to further human possibilities. In the early 1840s, to satirize the alien character or "zoology" of German feudal and bourgeois life, Marx

---

[13] Marx, 1967, pp. 309–11.
[14] Or as Wittgenstein, 1958, p. 230, allusively put it: "Compare a concept with a style of painting. For is even our style of painting arbitrary? Can we choose one at pleasure? (The Egyptian, for instance.) Is it a mere question of pleasing and ugly?"
[15] Marx, 1967, pp. 294–5.

found the Aristotelian conception of human nature an apt benchmark: "A German Aristotle, who would derive his politics from our conditions would begin by saying: man is a social but wholly apolitical animal." [16] The social republican movement of the nineteenth century, especially the Commune, gave a more precise, institutional, and political picture of what species-being might look like. To explicate this concept, Marx utilized the best features of already realized political experience. Similarly, he discerned lineaments of other communist possibilities in less central sensibilities, relationships, and activities.

Marx's theory of alienation has two additional, more familiar features. First, the worker in capitalism sells her labor power and carries out her productive activity under the rule of another. Second, that alien power, capital, the creation of accumulated labor, dominates the worker. [17] Although these aspects of alienation interfere with choice, they are not distinctively Aristotelian. Their centrality at least partially accounts for the failure of many scholars to see the striking affiliation of Marxian and Aristotelian conceptions. [18]

Marx's mature economic theory in *Capital* traces the source, combination, and differential bearing of these aspects of alienation. On that view, capitalism fuses the material, physical labor process of humans using land, raw materials, and machines (*Arbeitsprozess*) and the social process of extraction of value and surplus value (*Verwertungsprozess*). [19] This distinction is originally nonmoral. In looking at these two features of the production of a commodity, Marx differentiated concrete labor, which produces particular useful things from the abstract average – socially necessary – labor time, which produces values. But his further explanation of capitalism reveals the *moral* cutting edge of this distinction. In the production of value, the achievements of science and effort – in the form of accumulated capital – dominate workers. [20] The value process perverts the physical labor process and harms the producers:

> If we consider the process of production from the point of view of the simple labor-process, the labourer stands in relation to the means of production, not in their quality as capital, but as the mere means and materials of his own intelligent productive activity. In tanning, e.g., he deals with the skins as his simple objects of labor. It is not the capitalist whose skin he tans. But it is different as soon as we deal with the process of production from the point of view of the process of creation of surplus-value. The means of production are at once changed into means for the absorption of the labor of others. It is now no longer the laborer that employs the means of production, but the means of production that employ the laborer. *In-*

[16] Marx, 1967, p. 206.   [17] Marx, 1967, pp. 289–93.
[18] Ollman, 1975; Avineri, 1970; Kolakowski, 1978.
[19] G. A. Cohen, 1978, ch. 4.   [20] Marx, 1961, 1:607–8.

stead of being consumed by him as material elements of his productive activity, they consume him as ferment necessary to their own life-process, and the life-process of capital consists only in its movement as value constantly expanding, constantly multiplying itself [als sich selbst verwertender Wert].[21]

In Marx's metaphor, "death" – the creation of past labor – devours "life." This description of the alien "life-process" (*Lebensprozess*) of capitalist value accumulation that uses up workers is mirrored in the image of the "vampire" or "werewolf hunger" of capital for the laborer's time in the chapter on the working day and in Marx's discussion of the monstrous social, political, and moral consequences of capitalism – war, unemployment, racism, the ransacking of agricultural districts, and the like – in the chapter on the general law of capitalist accumulation.[22] These arguments render the two commonly emphasized features of Marx's theory of alienation specific and vivid.

The vampire-like features of alien domination in *Capital*, however, mainly, though not exclusively, affect the goods of life and dignity; they are as easily condemned by a rights-oriented theorist, or perhaps a utilitarian, as by a eudaemonist. But the robust material, natural relationships and qualities of individuals highlight the dwarfing, impoverishing impact of the capitalist value process and point beyond it. The distinctive, eudaemonist arguments on alienation that Marx inherited from Aristotle – work only as a means of life, not as its varied expression; money as the forger of simulacra of human senses and qualities; alien politics as a profound negation of human flourishing – pick out central features of his vision of communist individuality.[23]

Eudaemonist arguments cast new light on two other important themes in *Capital*, namely, the distinction between science and vulgar economics, and the contrast between the gigantic productivity of capitalism and its sustained denial of leisure for workers. First, Marx repeatedly juxtaposes reality and appearance, and science and "vulgar economy." On his theory, capitalism manufactures such strange characters as "Madame La Terre" and "Monsieur Le Capital," who seem to accrue an income out of their particular, physical characteristics rather than out of any common social trait.[24] Vulgar economy sticks to such appearances or "illusions"; Marx's theory treats such incomes as manifestations of an underlying social phenomenon: the production of surplus value. The latter explains appearance and concomitant vulgar economy as alien features of the process of value creation. Science, for Marx, grasps the inner connections or reality that render otherwise irrational appearances comprehensible. In this sense, vulgar economy, a *mistaken* theory, is a social

---

[21] Marx, 1961, 1:310, my emphasis.   [22] Marx, 1961, 1:243, 302; Gilbert, 1984a.
[23] G. A. Cohen, 1978, pp. 129–33; Marx, 1973, p. 325.   [24] Marx, 1961, p. 3, ch. 48.

product, a creature of alienation and appearance. But a scientific theory of capitalism is not a social product *in the same sense*. It is a refinement of a more general, natural, human quest for knowledge; the collective contribution to it is important but nonnefarious. Like *Paradise Lost*, a scientific accomplishment is an expression of human nature, a natural activity of the individual theorist. This eudaemonist argument strikingly demonstrates Marx's antirelativism. A scientific theory may learn from history and benefit the workers, but there is no such thing as a "proletarian" or "bourgeois" science.

Second, for Aristotle, humans conduct the highest activities – nonproductive ones – not under the pressure of necessity but by choice.[25] For Marx likewise, work for subsistence is least chosen; it is *necessary* labor. As Marxian theory emphasizes, capitalism's expansion of productivity enormously increases potential free time, which could serve as an arena of individuality and choice. This expansion and potential, however, lead to a moral paradox; for capitalism, unless checked by radical movements, also fights to stretch out the working day and restrict leisure; it impoverishes the worker as a social individual.[26] To drive home the *inhuman* character of capitalist production, Marx recalled Aristotle's dream of looms that would move of themselves, like Haphaestos's sacred tripods, and release weaving women from slavery (even with this imagined automation of production, Aristotle still thought domestic slavery would underpin the leisure of citizens). "Oh, those heathens!" Marx remarked ironically,

> they understood, as the learned Bastiat and before him the still wiser MacCulloch have discovered nothing of Political Economy and Christianity. They did not comprehend that machinery is the surest method of lengthening the working-day. They perhaps excused the slavery of one on the ground that it was a means to the full development of another. But to preach slavery of the masses in order that a few crude and half-educated parvenus might become "eminent spinners," "extensive sausage-makers" and "influential shoe-black dealers," to do this, they lacked the bump of Christianity.[27]

Marx thought Aristotle's general priorities clear enough. The latter mistakenly justified slavery only because it served a grander "full [human] development." In contrast, despite its abolitionist merits, Protestant abnegation of self was imposed on believing workers, but also, though less fiercely, on entrepreneurs, whose striving for social status

---

[25] Aristotle, *Nicomachean Ethics*, 1105a30–b4.

[26] Even today, overtime for some, unemployment for others is a normal feature of capitalism.

[27] Marx, 1961, 1:408–9.

and money glorified the spiritual wealth of the divine other.[28] Vulgar political economy incorporated this alienation; Marx satirically contrasted Aristotle's eudaemonist vision to its crass myopia. For Marx, communism meant worker control over labor time, the forging of a non-exploitative social nexus, and the flourishing of human capacities. His notion of communist individuality adapts Aristotle's notion of deliberation. Some of Marx's most original, deepest arguments against capitalism are eudaemonist in inspiration.[29]

2. A theory of the self

G. A. Cohen has strikingly claimed that Marx, in contrast to Hegel, had no reasonable conception of the self. Instead, he contends that Marx's anthropology – his notion of social individuality – is one-sided in emphasizing the realization of productive talents at the expense of ways of life. Cohen is right that Marx failed to spell out the view underlying his varied remarks about human well-being and sometimes exaggerated a – seemingly superhuman – display of multiple capacities. For example, the *Grundrisse*'s claim about "the *absolute working out* of [humanity's] creative potentials with no presupposition other than the previous historical development" suggests this problematic standpoint.[30] It also appears to substitute collective human creativity for the accomplishments and perspectives of different individuals. Focusing on the latter in *The German Ideology*, however, Marx conjured up an overly pastoral image of the communist person engaged in diverse activities: hunting, fishing, writing an occasional critique. Yet this person still seems a geyser of talents and whims. His independence borders on isolation and conflicts with a putative communism, for this catalogue of activities peculiarly omits any relationship except criticism.

Cohen's objection is, however, overstated. The *Grundrisse* also notes a self-discipline and concentration needed for genuine achievement. Communist work in no way "becomes mere fun, mere amusement, as Fourier . . . conceives it. Really free work, e.g. composing, is at the same time the most damned seriousness, the most intense exertion."[31] A self-disciplined individual might become competent in a variety of activities.

---

[28] As Montesquieu emphasized, Protestantism became the outlook of industrious, ascetic capitalists. Classical economic justifications for accumulation, mirroring religious alienation, paradoxically required a "self-seeking" that was also, even for capitalists, a denial of self. Chapter 9 stresses the similarity in Weberian and Marxian criticisms of this feature of the rise of capitalism.

[29] G. A. Cohen, 1978, ch. 11; Gilbert, 1984a.

[30] Marx, 1973, pp. 487–8.   [31] Marx, 1973, pp. 541, 611–12, 325.

Yet even here, for Marx, a relentless exercise of capacities, almost suggesting drivenness, overshadows ways of being and relationships.

Cohen rightly maintains that Marxian theory requires a developed conception of the self. But he overlooks Marx's admiration for the solidarity involved in political community and internationalism, the collective element in social individuality. Solidarity is a political relationship and a self-chosen way of being; it is not the realization of a productive talent. He also misses Marx's celebration of deliberative, revolutionary character. Marx's anthropology and ethics evoke a more robustly democratic, well-rounded, definite conception of individuality and suggest a more adequate theory of the self than Cohen allows.

That conception also points to a deeper insight into moral character and individuality than game-theoretic explications of solidarity as an instrumental, "conditional altruism" envision;[32] for an individual chooses such actions not just to further other ends but to realize an intrinsic good – a kind of human cooperation – and to be a certain kind of person, even a person who could sacrifice herself for great political commitments.[33] Marx's barely sketched moral psychology sustains his affirmations of the stability of egalitarian communism, a social form that eliminates status hierarchies and egotistic competition. To capture his notion, one needs a complex political and ethical conception, one not based on altruism, but cognizant of friendship, citizenship, and virtue, one not based on egotism, but insistent on reflective agency and individual integrity. Marx took as his starting point for such a view the moral psychology of Aristotle.

Like Aristotle and more clearly than Hegel, Marx emphasized the *participatory political setting* for individuality. As I argued in Chapter 1, we may interpret Hegel's discussion of the will as a refinement of Aristotle's account of deliberation. Hegel's argument reveals important features of modern individuality. Nonetheless, two of the deepest aspects of a contemporary theory that develop or transform Marxian – and previous liberal – insights also have their roots in Aristotle, first, the notion of the integrity of self and, second, the idea of an objectivity of need that characterizes genuine individuality.

[32] G. A. Cohen, 1984. Cohen neglects Marx's Aristotelian conception of *human* nature and mistakenly infers from these remarks a mechanical materialist, narrowly biological view of human personality as a collection of capacities and talents. As Chapter 1 emphasizes, after his adoption of Darwin's theory for other social animals, Marx retained a eudaemonist conception for humans (Elster, 1979, pp. 21, 105–6).

[33] As Richard Wollheim, 1984, p. 224, puts it, "Whatever may be the content of obligation, obligation itself is primarily self-directed. It is self-directed, though it may be other-regarding. For it expresses itself in a thought that a person has about what *he* ought to do: though he may well, and appropriately, think that he ought to do is something for the benefit of others."

In book 9 of *The Nicomachean Ethics*, Aristotle's nuanced depiction of friendship (*philia*) draws its strength from a theory of the well-ordered self. The good man – or as moderns would rightly emphasize, woman – is a lover of self in an important sense, a person who has a certain integrity and self-sufficiency. Such a self contrasts with alien selves defined by power, money, or prestige. For Aristotle, the former, healthy person has a soul ruled by intelligence and can form genuine friendships. The latter, however, have souls dominated by the corrupt appetites of Sardanapalus, exhibit an ostensible, but deficient love of self, and establish defective friendships. Psychologically, Aristotle saw self-love as a necessary concomitant to love for others. Each friend, on his account, achieves insight into and is concerned for the other's good. Further, that good is one's own good (friendship and solidarity have similar roots in self-love); for a friend can recognize the personalities of others and distinguish their needs, based on his own sense of self. His concern involves genuine recognition. Such a friend – we might say – displays individuality. He is capable of a life of his own and has a sense of purpose, self-command, difference.

In Aristotle's subtle portrayal, a friend need not hide from himself, as the evil person does, in the company of others. Because bad people despise themselves, they recall, when alone, only "unpleasant memories." Lacking integrity, they need blind approval or money in an ever-failing attempt to reassure themselves.[34] Others exist for them merely as means to sustain their illusions, not as independent persons to whose needs they might attend. Driven by appetites, yet haunted by reason, such people are always at war with themselves. Their self-hatred rules out genuine friendship. For Aristotle, in friendship, the dialectic of self-love and concern for others is at its most intense. Across important differences, this "social individuality" is also displayed in weaker forms of affiliation, such as citizenship.[35]

Despite major theoretical changes, one can detect Aristotelian resonances in the modern psychoanalytic conception of the self offered by Heinz Kohut, Harry Guntrip, and Alice Miller. To indicate these striking dialectical relationships, I will briefly describe this view. In contrast to the misguided instinctual determinist strain in Freud's view, Kohut focuses on the *social* formation of the self in the context of its early relationships. He contrasts a notion of integrity of self, illustrated in particular examples of flourishing, with that of a fragmented self. The healthy self

[34] In a modern idiom, one might suggest, such people fabricate an external persona, largely a pretence, to hide their inner sense of inadequacy. On such illusions, see also Plato, *Republic*, 337e–8c, 361a–e, 516c–17c, 619b–d.

[35] Aristotle, *Nicomachean Ethics*, 1166a1–b29. Political life evidently involves a much more abstract, formally egalitarian kind of recognition.

often overcomes early failures of nurturance through participation in intrinsic goods – painting, music, friendship, nurturing, and the like. Perhaps deliberately recalling Aristotle, Kohut refers to creative activities of these kinds as diverse illustrations and aspects of a good life. What previous psychoanalysis takes as basic and natural – oedipal anxiety or aggression – he sees as derivative from deficiently human, empathic mirroring.[36]

On this account, parents have typically trained their children in the "appropriate" feelings and encouraged them to suppress many of their emotions and needs. Such rearing seeks to mold or even "live through" the child; it presses her to take care of the parent and fails to respect her individuality. The child's suppression of needs in favor of an imposed image leads to an inability to recognize and work through her own emotions, to be fully her own person, and engenders self-hatred or, in Aristotle's terms, psychic "civil war." Outward idealization of parents compensates for underlying anger.[37] In contrast, in contemporary psychoanalytic theory, respect for children – roughly the parent's capacity to draw boundaries and acknowledge the child's feelings – stems from respect for – in Aristotle's terms, love of – self. Broadly analogous dialectics of an integrated self and respect for others apply to friendship and political cooperation.

Alice Miller has captured the moral impact of this psychodynamic argument; for though Freudian theory blames the child for *natural* – instinctual – aggressiveness toward the parents, a better theory studies the way in which a handed-down pattern of *social* and familial victimization damages the child.[38] The modern theory of the self shatters a pattern of blaming the victim and misguided natural determinism, which has had deep roots in psychoanalytic theory; it defends mutual recognition and individuality.[39]

This theory supports the Marxian claim that current gender stereotypes of the "good" man or woman – for men, achievement in the status-ridden alienated public world, "mastering" and suppressing one's emotions, coupled with treating family relationships, except for external

---

[36] Instinctual determinism is only one – inadequate – side of Freud's argument. Oedipal interaction is easily susceptible to an "object relations" interpretation (Guntrip, 1973; Kohut, 1977, pp. 119–21; 1984, pp. 26–8; A. Miller, 1981; Taylor, 1977, pp. 133–5).

[37] It imprisons the individual who, in the eloquent phrase of Robert Frost's "Mending Wall," "will not go behind his father's saying."

[38] The older theory focused on broad natural determinations of personality; this theory casts much more light on a particular social determination. Neither appears to elucidate – what seem to be – natural personality differences, relevant to individuality, in children.

[39] If this theory is right, traditional ethical notions of family piety are deeply misguided. In such relationships as elsewhere, gratitude arises from a recognition that has the potential for becoming mutual recognition.

relations of power, as the province of women; for women, a greater sense of connectedness but also submergence, loss of self and emotional dominion in family relationships combined with an uncertain sense of self in public life – *harm* both. Ethically, as Carol Gilligan has suggested, men are bound over to the "heartless" world of abstract right and – at least partly – artificial selves; women are, without deliberation, plunged into a quasi-Aristotelian and Hegelian world of connectedness, need, and ethical life. To the extent that they are psychologically influenced by such stereotypes, both lack social individuality. These sexist stereotypes often dovetail with other socially created sources of self-deprecation and self-hatred – for instance, the internalization by their victims of anti-working-class and racist ideologies.[40] Despite greater contemporary criticism by ordinary people of such harmful, imposed self-images, a Marxian theory maintains, capitalism still furthers such divisions; communist egalitarianism transforms and defeats them. If true, the psychoanalytic theory of the self, coupled with recent social theories of gender, racist, and anti-working-class stereotypes, deepens Marxian and previous liberal conceptions of individuality, friendship, and respect for self and others. These insights might become part of a modern eudaemonist account of personal and social interest in being a self.

Further, one can use this Aristotelian and modern theory of integrity of self to undermine relativist conceptions of the individual. A eudaemonist theory of human goods already rules out the relativist calculation of "preferences" characteristic of Bentham's utilitarianism, neoclassical economics, and emotivism; for these views contend that we have no real – objective – needs, not even the need to be recognized as a person. They adopt the corrupt notion of self-seeking that humans aim for infinite power or wealth. In contrast, modern psychoanalytic theory suggests that an individual needs to shape a life of self-chosen purpose and coherence. As David Levine has rightly argued, individuals do not need an infinite supply of resources for such a life – What would one do with an infinity of ever bigger and better yachts? A scholar needs certain books, a woodworker certain tools, friends the availability of common activities in which to enjoy and reveal their personalities. Over a lifetime, as Marx maintains, an individual might pursue a variety of relationships and activities, with differing requirements; given conflicts of needs, she would have to choose or change which ones to regard as central. Moral fallibilism, as the Introduction emphasized, characterizes those deliberations. These projects would involve considerable, varying resources; a notion of the coherence and integrity of self, however, objectively limits each individual's needs.

[40] Gilligan, 1982; J. B. Miller, 1966; Rubin, 1976; Sennett and Cobb, 1972.

On a Marxian version of this conception, politics and friendly regard are part of individuality. Yet in an important sense, relationships and accomplishments concern the individual alone.[41] They are done for their own sakes, for reasons suited to the activity or affiliation itself. Participants are not motivated by the *social* hierarchy of prestige and money characteristic of capitalism and other exploitative societies. As opposed to egotistical competition in which one's eye is always on others, a person can temporarily "lose" himself, concentrate all his attention and energy, in such vocations.[42] In Aristotelian terms, these relationships and activities are natural accomplishments, and the needs connected with them express individuality. They reveal what is humanly (socially) natural as opposed to what is (also socially) corrupt.

In contrast, a common, misguided kind of liberal social theory imagines "natural" characteristics of isolated individuals – preferences that are instinctually or genetically driven – which, then, as unexplained, exogenous causes, determine *social* interaction. That view mistakenly reduces social individuality to a spurious natural one and does not acknowledge the Aristotelian insight that human activities – rightly ordered and not, natural and unnatural – are all social.[43] An alternative view stresses particular *social* structural interactions. The contemporary theory of the self emphasizes the social and family dynamics that serve as a starting point for individuality; its claim that each individual then shapes a life of integrity by choosing among diverse, intrinsic goods deepens a eudaemonist conception of natural activities and relationships. This theory stresses that although we can easily identify extreme examples of evil and insufficiency of self (murder, rape, drug addiction), diverse enactments of self have no common measure. It elaborates the emphasis on individuality of modern liberal and radical political theory.

Both political conceptions have a distinctively social component. Against antecedent slavery or serfdom, liberalism recognizes the equal worth of persons with regard to the law and democracy or, more exactly, an equally sufficient capacity for agency. Yet capitalism produces constant inequalities of worth, hierarchies of status. Private enterprise, like utilitarian theories, tries to encompass the diverse enactments of indi-

---

[41] Again, following Marx's example of someone who sings beautifully, an individual can sometimes realize himself in what are, externally, exploitatively organized activities.

[42] As Chapter 13 shows, the Weberian resonance of "vocation" is deliberate (David P. Levine, 1986, ch. 1).

Jon Elster, 1984, pp. 288–9 worries that many individuals might have preferences for resource-expensive goods; their demands might conflict with communist equality. Either Aristotle's or Levine's theory of objective human goods undercuts the notion that such needs would be a frequent, let alone overwhelming component of individuality.

[43] That view is a methodological individualist one (Garfinkel, 1981, chs. 2, 4).

viduality in a single currency. It induces constant striving for relative social position and undermines equality. Capitalism is thus inconsistent with the basic moral insight into the mutual regard among persons and the social individuality characteristic of modern liberalism, not just contemporary radicalism.

Levine's argument attaches objective needs to self-enactment and, hence, grounds a right to work or a right to income not just in "preferences" but in the recognition of individuality. Yet he articulates no definite, Aristotelian conception of a broad list of intrinsic goods or values in which individuals might participate. Though the Aristotelian view is, in this respect, more sophisticated and would strengthen Levine's economic theory, even Levine's account, which makes *almost* all human goods relative to individual choices, stresses a single central good, that of individuality, the capacity to be a self. His argument shows that an objective defense of equal regard and individuality is at the core of every coherent, non-self-refuting modern political theory.

But the criticism of capitalism for abridging these goods can be extended to modern socialism. Except in contrast to feudalism, the reward structure of private enterprise bears remarkably little relation to the individual "merit" or hard work that is its putative moral justification. But socialism is sometimes deemed to reward desert, to realize the meritocratic status hierarchy promised by liberalism. Thus, socialist justice actualizes the previously utopian currency of capitalism; economic inequality, social status, and differential estimates of persons are based on merit. Yet that measure remains distorted. It flows from and reinforces a deficient self – one that will work only for fear of starvation or to gain a place in a hierarchy at the expense of others – rather than a healthy self that seeks to shape a particular life of integrity, aware of the appropriate reasons for activities. Under socialism, the specific virtues often claimed for capitalism, for instance, ingenuity or initiative, are also – often – elicited in the service of deficient selves. Further, the sense of self cultivated by private enterprise and market socialism contradicts the individual well-being and self-respect needed to deliberate on great political issues and, thus, to encourage democratic participation. A status- and wealth-bound theory of justice coheres neatly with influential contemporary elitist sanctioning of apathy and is thus strikingly antidemocratic.[44]

Given an appropriate theory of individuality and need, as Levine contends, liberal arguments that stress the importance of self-respect and mutual recognition, like those of Rawls and Dworkin, probably require the elimination of capitalist and socialist hierarchies of status and

---

[44] Gilbert, 1986c; Huntington, 1975.

wealth. Instead, the best method for distributing resources, short of full communist distribution according to need, would be the allocation of equal individual incomes. Such incomes would include a *social* minimum necessary for decent medical care, education, housing, and transportation, for this sphere has important standard features and is comparatively easily susceptible to planning. (Even here, however, citizens might want to encourage individual decisions about provision.) Beyond this sphere, given equal incomes, individuals would have sufficient discretionary funds to realize their other main needs without the inegalitarian distortions and "self"-seeking at the expense of others characteristic of capitalist, Soviet and Chinese status hierarchies.[45] A partial market, driven by individual demand, would remain for the distribution of those goods not already dispensed according to social need; one might call the commodities available on this market *individuality-related goods*. That market, however, would neither govern the sale of labor power nor lead to differential wages and status hierarchy.

This view parries Hayek's interesting criticism of socialist planning. In a modern economy with shifting needs, he suggests, only a market can respond adequately to the judgments of individuals. Planners cannot know beforehand the outcome of complex individual deliberations and will generally get them wrong.[46] An egalitarian communism acknowledges the grain of truth in Hayek's argument. Yet it insists that democratic planning can overcome the harms of unemployment and degradation, impelled by an absence of resources, characteristic of capitalism, and secure other important collective goods.

An individuality-governed economic theory expands the definition of work. For instance, nurturers of children would also receive equal incomes, and at least sufficient incomes would be provided to support children. Every person would thus have a claim to a share of social wealth. In an important sense, the first stage of communism would move to abolish wages or at least reduce their dominion. In the latter case, citizens might require, for example, that nondisabled adults work in order to obtain a share. In such a society, an egalitarian economic and social order, sustaining a healthier sense of self, would dialectically reinforce thoroughgoing democracy and vice versa. The communist actuality of self and mutual respect would supersede hierarchies of status.

A liberal critic might object that this communism would still restrict individual choice of occupation. Granting the rest of the argument, such

---

[45] David Levine, 1986, conclusion; R. Dworkin, 1981; Elster, 1984, pp. 298–99. I leave aside the forging and repair of basic means of production of social wealth that, in a planned economy, are also not governed mainly by a market.

[46] Hayek, 1945.

a person might say, that constraint points to a persisting clash of goods, pitting egalitarianism against individuality. Given this conflict's seriousness, certain types of liberalized capitalism or market socialism could better realize eudaemonist aims than communism. A Marxian might respond, however, that this stage of communism would still further individuality much more than capitalism, yet also achieve egalitarianism. Within this economy, individuals would be able to choose jobs according to their interest in the work itself, not for pay. Further, lack of resources would not drive them to seek undesirable forms of employment. These and other changes – if Marxian social theory is right, the overturning of racist and sexist discrimination and the like – would further greater, more widespread self-expression in work.

Yet given the level of social need, relevant criteria would competitively restrict access to some desirable jobs. Other, comparatively undesirable ones might be shared or perhaps externally rewarded in ways that would not lead to status differentiation. For instance, routine work could either be done cooperatively (household chores, street cleaning by neighborhood associations) or be differentially remunerated (perhaps by a shortened work day). Some aspects of necessary labor, however, further individuality: The order and decoration in housework, for example, is aesthetically important; participation is integral to the sharing of lives, responsibility, self-reliance. Given the decline of status hierarchy and gender stigmatization, individuals would appreciate these aspects more keenly.

The impact of remaining limitations on individuality might also diminish with the subsequent flourishing of communist productivity and general diminishing of the work day. Nonetheless, a critic could still invoke Marx's qualms about necessary labor: The self-realization characteristic of artisans who controlled their own production process – and routine endangers the interest in even that work – is rare in industrial circumstances. So are jobs that nurture self-enactment and self-disclosure. Even in communism, many would realize their individuality more directly outside work than within it.

A theory of the self focused on leisure and politics reinterprets Marx's claim in *Critique of the Gotha Program* that nonnecessary "work becomes life's prime want": Relationships and activities that realize individuality become "life's prime want." [47] Necessary work within a communist economy is one aspect of *personal differentiation* and individuality, but neither the only, nor even the central, facet. But political insights into mutual regard and integrity of self require that the sphere of necessary work should not be an arena for inegalitarian pay and *status differentiation*.

---

[47] Marx and Engels, *SW*, 2:24.

We can now separate different features of Hayek's epistemological defense of the market. A theory of the self recommends individual deliberations about ways of life. The choice óf books, musical instruments, recreation equipment and leisure activities, kinds of education, items for a home, and the like cannot be left to the homogenizing guesses of planners: hence, the need for an individuality-related market. Given the preceding distribution of income – an egalitarian one – this market will, epistemologically speaking, secure the relevant information. But a comparable Hayekian argument in favor of an inegalitarian labor market fails because of the need to curtail status hierarchy and further individuality. A neoclassical theory, with its impoverished conception of self as a bundle of homogenized preferences, cannot draw this distinction. Hayek confuses two justifications for the market, one a matter of the efficiency that arises from "special knowledge of the fleeting moment not known to others," the other arising from "the freedom of individuals."[48] Ethically speaking, however, the latter underlies the former. If planning turned out to be more "efficient" in furthering a war economy but radically abridged individuality, it would not be justified. Further, alleged particular knowledge on the part of enterprise managers, compared to planners, in the use of individuals does not sanction a *labor* market; for the individuals themselves, not managers, have the relevant knowledge about their own capacities and interests; Hayek's epistemological argument does not license a capitalist (labor) market.[49] Thus, a coherent theory of the self clarifies Hayek's view by separating individuality from individualist misconceptions.

This discussion of individuality, labor markets, and status differentials also suggests a distinctively communist feature of Marx's nonetheless exaggerated reservations about justice. Many notions of distributive justice, including ones based on socially necessary labor time, propose a distorted, uniform standard to measure merit and allocate resources. Such conceptions give rise to status hierarchies that violate individuality and any sense of a common good. In contrast, a dialectical Marxian theory of justice envisions the abolition of classes and statuses as a social precondition for the flourishing of individuality. It is uniform – egalitarian – only in its abolitionism. A communist association realizes the Marxian sense of a common good. But his vision of justice assesses need and "merit" based on diverse deliberations about and enactments of individuality. For a radical account, only a theory of the self that stresses a

---

[48] Friedrich Hayek, 1945, overemphasizes ephemeral economic efficiencies rather than the complex, comparatively stable, though revisable concerns of individuality.
[49] It might legitimize an artisan and small-farm economy.

range of intrinsic goods and the integrity of individual choices of *disparate* ways of life is appropriate.

As Charles Taylor has suggested, particular, qualitative contrasts mark realizations of discrete goods – one may be a defender of truth or a merchant of words, a friend or an obtuse sycophant, politically motivated or a mercenary. This point applies centrally to the concept of an individual. Contrary to quantitative, zero-sum principles of status hierarchy, one cannot, in relation to others, be more or less a person, though in qualitative terms, one can become a murderer, a tyrant, a moral monster. Individuality can vary in a different, very important sense: An artist or a person can realize a style or self more fully, become an individual. The notion of democratic individuality incorporates these two aspects or perspectives. Thus, a radical conception of communism criticizes previous uniform, rights-oriented or utilitarian conceptions of "justice" (non-Aristotelian ones) and might seem, given the abolition of previous, corrupt social determinations, not to be a theory of justice at all. This subtle indictment of prevalent moral theories perhaps contributes to Marx's mistaken metaethical deemphasis on justice in his overall historical theory.[50]

A standard liberal and economic determinist Marxian objection to this egalitarian argument focuses on the need for material incentives to spur productivity. Given human deficiencies and the need to accumulate, this criticism insists, communism cannot outproduce its socialist and capitalist competitors. This peculiar contention makes productivity the sole criterion of human well-being. In response, Elster and Cohen have recently suggested that only arduous – that is, other than self-imposed – work, under circumstances of scarcity, requires material incentives.[51] These circumstances hinder the expression of human nature. The development of productivity and civilization increasingly engender a healthy sense of self-confidence and release the (humanly) natural creativity and skill

---

[50] Steven Lukes, 1982, rightly sees full communist "justice" as beyond rules concerning distribution but misses the dialectical retention of fundamental rules preserving life and the mutual recognition of persons. These extensions of previous social and political achievements partly explain what Lenin referred to as the long-familiar "elementary social rules" that would be more easily observed in communism (Lenin, 1960, 2:373). Contrary to Lukes, the ends of communism and the standards justifying revolutionary action are not rigidly separated. On a dialectical view, how could definite aims concerning the human good license their utter violation in "prehistory"? Lukes's explanation of the putatively "beyond morality" character of a Marxian theory of the good – its beneficent transcendence of the conflicts of scarcity coupled with an alleged moral agnosticism toward such conflicts – mirrors the self-refuting aspects of relativist Marxian metaethics that he otherwise astutely criticizes.

[51] G. A. Cohen, 1984, p. 246.

that Marx identified with communism. As another way of interpreting the epochal change to communism, the foregoing account suggests, self-generated choices ultimately supplant scarcity and money as instigators of productivity.

Elster and Cohen's important thesis, however, understates the role of connectedness and relationship – politics, friendship, nurturing – in communist creativity, the decisive social element in the realization of individuality. In his 1958 "Critique of Soviet Economy," Mao pointedly distinguished the mistaken Soviet emphasis on material incentives – wage differentials and individual bonuses – as the driving force of socialism from the Marxian stress on political insight as an intrinsic good, inspiring action and production for their own sakes and instigating cooperative, revolutionary development:

> Page 485 [of the Soviet political economy textbook] says "In the socialist stage labor has not yet become the primary necessity in the lives of all members of society, and therefore material incentives to labor have the greatest significance." Here "all members" is too general. Lenin was a member of the society. Had *his* labor not become a "primary necessity" of his life?[52]

The instance of Lenin here stands for the Communards and, as we shall see, millions of subsequent communists. A Marxian theory of the integrated self, objective need, and political community, based on Aristotle, Kohut, Levine, and diverse political achievements – the polis, modern nonslave societies, the Commune and subsequent revolutionary movements, and the like – provides a stronger, more coherent psychological and economic account of how the fundamental historical changes, emphasized both in Elster and Cohen and in more political versions of Marxism, might occur.

Revolutionaries have sometimes inappropriately referred to the democratic element in individuality as a "moral incentive." The notion of ethical *incentives* is in fact an alienated, economic determinist one – once again, as if the way to understand all human relationships and activities were in the common currency of "economic development" or "modernization." This curious antidemocratic view treats the income and status hierarchy, enshrined by Teng Hsiao-p'ing or the contemporary Soviet regime, and mass revolutionary efforts to forge an egalitarian, cooperative society as more or less equal "instruments" in "socialist" industrialization. As in the classical account of capitalist accumulation, the well-being and integrity of individuals in work and politics is at best an incidental accompaniment to some larger, alien social purpose. In con-

---

[52] Mao, 1977, p. 83.

trast, on a Marxian conception, integrity is a vital, commonly acknowledged component of democratic cooperation. In these conflicting visions of socialism and communism, we thus have two sharply opposed theories of social life and individuality.

Levine interprets his argument about the self and mutual recognition as a modification of the claims of classical political economy, including Marx's, about an objectively defined level of subsistence. He elaborates a flexible notion of objective need, suited to capitalism's promises about individuality and the wealth of civilization rather than some bare, physical standard. This theory, as Chapter 8 shows, conflicts with the role of the "law of value" and consequent wage and status differentials in Marx's notion of socialism. In the context of an Aristotelian and Marxian theory of democratic *individuality* and the self, however, Levine's conception of the objective needs of individuals explains a central aspect of the radical vision of communism.

3. Deliberation and democratic internationalism

Political participation was central to Marx's conception of the revolutionary movement and the initial stage of communism. He adapted five other specific features of an Aristotelian view of political life. First, Marx concurred with Aristotle's distinction between regimes that incorporate a common good and those that do not. For Marx, all stable regimes in exploitative societies, whatever their forms, serve particular, ruling-class interests. Thus, he saw Greek democracy as a tyranny over slaves and modern liberal democracy as a social despotism over workers. To dominate the producers, such regimes require an *alien* repressive apparatus, revealed most sharply in the "parasite state" of mid-nineteenth-century Europe.[53] They debilitate political life. But proletarian revolution ushers in a new kind of historical progress; for a communist association institutionalizes a common good, based on mutual recognition, for the vast majority of members. On Marx's view, that regime would be a dictatorship toward former exploiters but a radical democracy for workers and their allies. Either a politics of a common good or a community beyond a need for – certain types of – politics contrasts with previous exploitative hierarchies.

Second, Aristotle envisioned politics as an arena for noble action. Marx likewise thought that revolutionaries would develop a specific character, involving sympathy and friendship for the oppressed, hatred for oppressors, dedication, enthusiasm, and reflective willingness to learn from errors, given fresh political experience. Though he rejected

[53] Gilbert, 1981a, ch. 12.

the haughtiness of Aristotle's "great-souled man," Marx admired the refusal by this unusual character of all truckling to opinion. Marx's democratic internationalism followed this example: In 1848, his support for the June insurrection's fallen rebels cost him half the subscribers of his newspaper, the *Neue Rheinische Zeitung;* in 1871, the English press denounced the defense of the Commune by the "red doctor." Marx held that a capacity to grasp and act on great issues distinguished women and men of real political ability – Spartacus, Babeuf, Wilhelm Wolff, the Commune's "heavenstormers" – from others. Moreover, his vision of revolutionary character stresses, in specific situations, the need for heroism and self-sacrifice. He opposed any merely egotistic, selfish model of human motivation. Once again, a theory of individuality explains both mundane and courageous features of radical political action, arising from considered decision to be a certain kind of self.[54]

Third, for Aristotle, an understanding of the common good arose from an internal philosophical assessment of diverse claims about justice.[55] His ethics has a democratic, *conversational* quality; it is complex but not arcane. As Chapter 5 shows, Marx also refined existing moral opinions; for instance, he criticized formally fair transactions, involving the private ownership of capital, on the consequentialist grounds that such contracts harm workers and, thus, undermine possibilities of a good life. Though Marx and Engels hesitated to characterize the "abolition of classes" as a reinterpretation of justice, this revolutionary demand incorporates a broad Aristotelian conception of a common good.

Fourth, Aristotle's political theory features the clashing claims of justice of democrats and oligarchs. He organized much of the *Politics* around such issues as the impact of population growth and impoverishment on class conflict in small cities (book 2), the relation of violent changes of regime to a common good and warring conceptions of justice (book 3), causes of revolution – transformation from oligarchy to democracy or vice versa – and class-conscious measures to secure regime sta-

---

[54] In *The German Ideology,* Marx contended: "The communists do not put egoism against self-sacrifice or self-sacrifice against egoism, nor do they express this contradiction theoretically either in its sentimental or its highflown ideological form . . . the communists do not preach *morality* at all, such as Stirner preaches so extensively. They do not put to people the moral demand to love one another, do not be egoists, etc.; on the contrary they are very well aware that egoism, just as much as self-sacrifice, is in definite circumstances a necessary form of the self-assertion of individuals" (Marx and Engels, 1964, p. 104). Marx opposed moralism – in this case, an appeal to general moral principles – as a special kind of motivation abstracted from and opposed to what Hegel called "ethical life." But as the dialectical relationship of Marx's view of social individuality to Hegel's and Aristotle's shows, to resist moralism is neither to reject ethics nor to deny the possibility of admirable moral character.

[55] Aristotle, *Politics,* 1282b14–3a23.

bility (books 4–6). Marx could easily have read this work as an illustration of his thesis that class struggle (among citizens) is the decisive characteristic of history. Contrary to Aristotle, however, a Marxian or modern liberal would see the helots "waiting in ambush" for their masters as a fundamental form of such conflict.

As book 3 stresses, the claims of democrats can extend to expropriating the rich. Given Aristotle's view of the justifiable origins and role of property, he stigmatized such communist demands.[56] But Marx also emphasized this dialectic of social and political equality in explaining the emergence of communism in the French Revolution and in organizing to transform the German democratic into a proletarian revolution.[57] Though Aristotle and Marx shared an account of the importance of freedom and the fundamental political and social clashes that characterize (precommunist) democracy, Marx's social and moral theory identifies the rich, including slaveholders, as exploiters. He not only concurred with Aristotle about the harms of oligarchic rule, but advanced a further critique of exploitation against Aristotelian polity. Although these theorists disagree about the nature of a common good, their ethical conflict is, as moral realism suggests, a straightforwardly objective one.

Fifth, Aristotle emphasized practical deliberation about courses of action. Given the diversity of goods, he recognized that moral choice often involves conflicts. One way of reading his complex argument in book 6 and 7 of *The Nicomachean Ethics* is to interpret failures of deliberation as the superimposition of pursuit of one good – usually a lesser one – on another. Thus, in one of his examples, Niobe placed love for her children above piety; life is a good, but cowardice in defense of a decent city is not.[58] Prudence plays a decisive role in political action.

But deliberation is also central to Marx's conception. He extended the Aristotelian idea of a common good to include democratic internationalism; communists would make the "common interests of the proletariat independently of all nationality" a linchpin of their political strategy and conception of justice. This internationalism is democratic because it envisions widespread pressure from below to check the predatory policies of one's own (even a parliamentary) government. It is also internationalist in the stronger sense that citizens of one nationality empathize with resistance to oppression by those of another. They put common moral interests above the policies and "interests" of the nation's elite. Opposing major governmental initiatives, often military ones, internationalism requires hard choices.

Thus, Marx's inaugural address of the International Workingmen's As-

---

[56] Aristotle, *Politics*, 1289a37–39, 1281a15–18.   [57] Marx and Engels, *SW*, 1:65.
[58] Aristotle, *Nicomachean Ethics*, 1142a23–3b3.

sociation praises the "heroism" of English workers who vehemently supported abolitionism in the American Civil War and opposed the "criminal folly" of their rulers.[59] The elites had campaigned for breaking the Northern blockade. They advertised the acquisition of Southern cotton as a cure for widespread unemployment. Though British workers needed jobs to stave off starvation – a very important good – they were keenly aware that slavery was evil and that they themselves would be asked to fight and pay for a proslavery war. Moreover, they saw that the victory of a slaveholding republic in North America would push international politics in a reactionary direction and ultimately harm them. Their meetings and demonstrations thwarted an "infamous" crusade by the ruling classes on behalf of slavery. Marx cited a resolution passed by the London workers:

> Therefore this meeting considers it the particular duty of the workers since they are not represented in the senate of the nation, to declare their sympathy with the United States in its gigantic struggle for maintenance of the Union, to denounce the base dishonesty and advocacy of slaveholding indulged in by the *Times* and kindred aristocratic journals, to express themselves most emphatically in favor of a policy of strictest nonintervention in the affairs of the United States . . . and to manifest the warmest sympathy with the endeavours of the Abolitionists to bring about a final solution to the question of slavery.[60]

Sheffield demonstrators shouted at Roebuck, a prowar union leader who wanted to recognize the South: "Never! We should have a Civil War in England [first]." Given the longstanding democratic tradition of opposition to slavery stemming from the French Revolution, English proletarians chose a great international public good – one affecting the quality of their existence – over some short-run gains contributing to survival.[61] Their insights recall Aristotle's internationalist thesis, stressed in Chapter 1, that support for oppression abroad undermines democracy at home.

These five broad similarities, along with a common emphasis on pub-

---

[59] Marx and Engels, *SW*, 1:384.
[60] Marx, 1972a, pp. 112–13, 157–60, 266, 152–6, 161–3; Harrison, 1965, pp. 66, 64, 76–7. Marx stressed the antidemocratic impact of a successful Southern secession even in the North: "In the northern states, where Negro slavery is unworkable in practice, the white working class would be gradually depressed to the level of helotry. This would be in accord with the loudly proclaimed principle that only certain races are capable of freedom and that as in the South real labor is the lot of the Negro, so in the North it is the lot of the German and the Irishman or their direct descendants." An analogous argument applies to English workers.
[61] Gilbert, 1978b; 1981a, ch. 1.

lic action as an intrinsic good, reveal the affinities of an Aristotelian and Marxian conception of politics. Plato theorized an apolitical warrior republic, whose subjects were radically subordinated to the legislator's will. In contrast, Aristotle was friendlier to democracy and democratic internationalism.[62] He advanced a distinctively *political* theory of the achievement of a common good through conversation among the free; though he lacked a full notion of individuality, he emphasized citizen deliberation. Modern liberal and Marxian arguments have independent democratic roots in antislavery and revolutionary movements. Yet Aristotle's theory of the dynamic of citizen and communist equality and democratic resistance to foreign expansion prefigures the internal connection of liberal and radical views. Against economic misinterpretations, an Aristotelian perspective reasserts central political themes within Marxian theory: Modern communist movements seek to realize democracy – and internationalism – as a framework for the flourishing of individuality.[63] Given this restored vision, Chapter 8 criticizes some important features of twentieth-century revolutionary experience and recasts the image of a radical democracy.

A critic might object, however, that Marx foresaw the state's dissolution in the higher phase of communism. As opposed to Aristotle's, his ultimate conception seems postpolitical. But a proletarian revolution overthrows only the "parasite state" and its alien politics. Following the Commune, as Chapter 6 stressed, workers and their allies take up all the functions of political life. For Marx, such a regime, though strongly democratic, gradually abolishes any remnants of the parasite state. An Aristotelian conception of the intrinsic good of political activity underscores this form's nonalien character and strengthens a Marxian view. In the later stage of communism, so Marx thought, the need for proletarian preparedness for war against external and internal counterrevolutionaries would cease. Following his argument internally, however, features of democratic association would persist in internal cooperation in the production of necessities, regulation of clashes between humans and even a partially "humanized" natural environment, international coordination, creation of a varied pattern of social relationships, and the provision of mechanisms to resolve severe conflicts among individuals. Marx's suggestion that communism abolishes the *politics* of deliberation on common problems as opposed to that of war and class war has furthered an economic determinist misinterpretation of socialism and di-

---

[62] Gilbert, 1986b; Plato, *Republic*, 414b–15c, 462b–d; Aristotle, *Politics*, 1261a20–5.

[63] As the *Manifesto* argued, "The first step in the revolution by the working class is to raise the proletariat to the position of ruling class, to win the battle of democracy" (Marx and Engels, *SW*, 1:53). Gilbert, 1981a, chs. 1, 9–10.

minished radical emphasis on democracy and internationalism. It is one of Marx's most serious theoretical mistakes.[64]

4. Scientific and ethical realism in Aristotle's and Marx's economics

In committing himself to a transformed eudaemonism, Marx affirmed Aristotle's judgment that objectivity exists in morals as well as in science. His complex realist interpretation of Aristotle's theory of exchange underlines the role of discoveries in political economy and ethics; it illuminates the particular character of communism.

Aristotle recognized the difficulties in defending moral objectivity. In book 5 of *The Nicomachean Ethics*, he acknowledged contemporary conventionalist arguments that distinguished invariant nature from mutable political and moral practices. Contrary to metaethical relativists, the *uneven development of science and ethics criticism* of moral objectivity is neither novel nor distinctively modern. As Aristotle noted, the laws of each regime combine natural and conventional justice, and vary; in contrast, "fire burns here and in Persia." He sarcastically compared conventional justice to wine and grain measures that merchants adjust one way in wholesale and another in retail markets; at best, he maintained, specific rules of conventional justice – for instance, a particular punishment for a crime or character of a religious sacrifice – are, before they are legally set, indifferent.[65]

Yet Aristotle viewed response to a type of crime – for instance, punishment for the taking of innocent life – and piety as matters of natural justice. Further, novel Greek political arrangements set a standard for the general distinction between regimes oriented toward a common good and corrupt ones. We might interpret his account of the emergence of the polis as a striking illustration of his claims that *even* standards of natural justice vary.[66]

Marx's scientific and ethical distinction between the – humanly – natural and the – distortedly – social aspects of activities and arrangements recaptures this Aristotelian view. Furthermore, in assessing previous theories in mature political economy, Marx began from Aristotle. An internal examination of his critique reveals its moral, not just its scientific, force.

In *Capital*, Marx avowed that the "brilliance" of that "giant thinker's"

---

[64] Marx's early comments on the dissolution of the – alien – political in the social are, at best, an overly context-specific gloss on his argument (Gilbert, 1981a, pp. 36–40).
[65] Aristotle, *Nicomachean Ethics*, 1134b18–5a5.
[66] Aristotle, *Nicomachean Ethics*, 1134b28–32.

political economics "shines" (*glänzt*) in three ways – first, in his discovery of the distinction between use and exchange value; second, in his insight that money – what Marx called the "money form" – further developed the value form of commodities; and third, in his recognition that equality between two physically disparate commodities, subject to radically different uses, must embody some underlying, common characteristic. Aristotle's three observations, Marx maintained, had founded scientific political economy.[67]

Yet Aristotle provided no explanation for the equality between disparate commodities identified in his third discovery. According to Marx, he considered it "a makeshift for practical purposes" (Notbehelf für das praktische Bedürfnis). From the standpoint of economic explanation, Marx's criticism was well taken. Aristotle's analysis in book 5 of *The Nicomachean Ethics*, however, contained a deeper *moral* insight than Marx's gloss recognized. Aristotle viewed money, the medium of commensurability, as a political tool to knit together the complementary functions and activities necessary for any form of justice to work. He related money (*nomisma*) to law or custom (*nomos*), not to nature (*physis*). His play on words prefigures the central distinction between conventional and natural justice in this same book. But although the use of money can corrupt, it can also unite diverse activities and needs (*chreia*).[68] In the latter case, it furthers *eudaemonia*, strengthens the life of the polis, and is, to that extent, natural.

On Marx's account, Aristotle's question about commensurability was scientific and profound, his solution mistaken. Marx saw abstract human labor time as the source of this equality. This modern conception, he noted, featured centrally in the elaboration of mature political economy. But since the Greek polis rested on a radical division of labor among humans – free males in politics, slaves in production – Aristotle could hardly have arrived at a solution that presupposed the comparability of *human* labor. The discussion of reciprocity and equality in book 5 underscores the theoretical and moral impact of this division: "The existence of the polis depends on proportionate reciprocity; for men demand that they shall be able to requite evil with evil – *if they cannot, they feel that they are in the position of slaves* – and to repay good with good."[69] Aristotle discerned no commonality in the activity of slaves and citizens or, among citizens, between that of makers and doers.[70] As Marx contended, investigators could unravel the "secret" (Geheimnis) of commensurability only in a historical context in which the idea of equality "pos-

[67] Marx, 1961, 1:60–1, 85. [68] Aristotle, *Nicomachean Ethics*, 1133a26–b10.
[69] Aristotle, *Nicomachean Ethics*, 1132a32–3a2 (my emphasis).
[70] Aristotle, *Nicomachean Ethics*, 1140a1–7.

sessed the fixity of a popular prejudice" (die Festigkeit eines Volksvorurteils besitzt).[71] Though his choice of the term "popular prejudice" seems tinged with relativism, the underlying claim about the human capacities that determine the "fixity" of this view is an objective one. (Marx's account displays the same metaethical ambiguity that we saw in Rawls and Walzer.)

For Marx, *major social transformations,* such as the emergence of non-slave-based social organization, the Puritan and French revolutions, and Chartism, as well as better biological and social theories, had subsequently revealed Aristotle's error. Those changes provided a setting that made possible the adoption of an approximately true economic theory: the labor theory of value. Only on the basis of such a theory could political economists at last answer Aristotle's clearly posed question.

Morally speaking, the modern labor theory presupposes the distinctive liberal recognition, emphasized in Chapter 1, that humans generally have a sufficient capacity to participate in political life. No society based on legalized human bondage can be justified. Thus, massive historical changes played a decisive role in both economic *and* ethical theorizing. But Marx's political economy accords even more deeply with a moral realist view of Aristotle than this argument about slavery would suggest, for his labor theory stresses not only the equality of alienated productivity (that of abstract labor, which yields exchange value); it also emphasizes production for use and capitalist perversion of the appropriate motivations for work. Following Aristotle, Marx suggested that humans must engage in activities for their own sakes if they are to further happiness. If they cannot, the world of action is turned upside down. Marx aimed to set the world aright, to make the social accord with the (*humanly*) natural. This eudaemonist view underlies his communist conception of social individuality that measures out resources: "from each according to ability, to each according to *need.*" Here Marx's view dialectically transforms Aristotle's insight into the relationships that permit the appropriate functioning of money. In communism, use and need, consonant with natural justice – not money and abstract equality – rule production and distribution.

As Chapter 1 stressed, transformations in social and political organization often play an *internal* role in social science and moral theory. For instance, in Marx's critique of Aristotle's economics, the rise of egalitarian movements and abolition of slavery provided important background conditions for a theoretical revolution. But ethics, being concerned with democratic individuality, pivots even more fundamentally on historical

[71] Marx, 1961, 1:61, 81.

discoveries about the relevant capacities. Such capacities are often exemplified in radical movements and new social and political forms that serve as *evidence* for advances in moral theory.

Furthermore, given the fusion of the natural and social aspects of human activity, there is a sense for Marx in which, following Hegel, history just *is* the complex, nonrelativist story of cooperation, freedom, and individuality. History is the dialectical unfolding of material, natural human capacities, though in a setting of socially created distortion. The latter makes advance heavily dependent on class struggle. Marx's theory of the production of value is so striking – as an economic and ethical explanation – because capitalism is the most complicated, extreme form of that social distortion, namely "enchantment" or "fetishism." Thus, Marx's theory of history unites scientific and moral discovery.

Hegel's philosophy of history had adopted Aristotle's categories of the potential and the actual. It displayed the unfolding of the idea of human freedom, as it was implicitly (*an sich*), into the complex structure of explicit, self-conscious individuality (*für sich*) and mutual recognition in the modern state. Hegel set Aristotle's conception of the capacities and actualization of human nature in historical motion. For Marx as for Hegel, history pivots on this Aristotelian distinction. As the 1844 manuscripts have it, "Nature developing in human history – the creation of human society – is the *actual* nature of man."[72]

On a realist account, both Marx's theory of political economy and implicit moral theory have an Aristotelian lineage. Yet his recognition of and advances over Aristotle in the former contrast with his comparative silence about the latter. Marx's hesitancy about clarifying this relationship stems from misplaced, metaethical caution, which, as we have seen, results in occasional contrasts of his science with other radicals' moralizing. But Marx's new historical theory identified capitalism's manifold harms to human well-being; that theory justified his opposed, communist vision of social individuality. In the marked divergences of Aristotle's and Marx's particular ethical judgments, disputes about facts, including claims in social and biological theory – *not* clashes of underlying moral premises – play the pivotal role. These essentially empirical disputes in social theory led to Marx's achievements and stature as a moral theorist. The dynamic character and profound ethical impact of these differences help to explain, though they do not justify, his failure to spell out the relationship of his conclusions to Aristotle's. But Marx's eudaemonism and moral realism dialectically transform an Aristotelian inheritance.

---

[72] Marx, 1967, p. 311.

5. Miller's criticisms of moral objectivity

A Marxian eudaemonism and moral realism appear to be an impressive, (potentially) fullfledged moral point of view and to clarify central issues in Marx's social theory. But not all Marxians will be convinced. Indeed, Richard Miller has advanced two important, subtle criticisms of any such interpretation. The first, which I will call the *two-components objection*, contends that this social theory lacks the distinctive general structure of a moral viewpoint. Marx's normative judgments depend too heavily on his theory of history and are too empirical or contingent to count as ethical ones. The second – the most sophisticated version of the *clash of goods criticism* – maintains that extreme conflicts pervade not only exploitative societies but even the first stage of communism. According to Miller, such clashes prevent unanimity of moral choice and consequent political action even among eudaemonists.

Yet refinements of two eudaemonist arguments I offered earlier respond to Miller's objections. The first emphasizes, once again, the role of discoveries – such as the emergence of the polis and of nonslave societies – in ethical theorizing, the other stresses the expectation of Aristotelian practical deliberation that choices involving limited conflicts of goods do not undermine moral objectivity.

Miller has defended general views about the central role of politics in Marxian historical theory, the importance of internationalism, and (ironically) the relation of Marx's to Aristotle's eudaemonism close to my own. His recent *Fact and Method* presents a sophisticated scientific realism. After responding to Miller's particular critique of morality, I will dialectically use his general argument for realism to sustain an account of ethical objectivity and advance.

In *Analyzing Marx* and "Marx and Morality," Miller envisions a distinctive structure of moral argument that, he suggests, conflicts with Marxian social theory and political strategy. Here his view is a variant of a more common philosophical position. Philosophers have often thought that ethics must be a kind of a priori knowledge. Hence, moral theories involve two components. First, they discern the most general ethical principles without regard to empirical circumstances and institutional practices. Second, the latter become relevant – as a subordinate, almost external component – only in applying the theory. Miller makes a similar division:

> The validity of those [moral] norms is not subject to direct empirical controversy. . . . Thus, whatever maximizes the general welfare is best, for the utilitarian. But he or she may claim to know little about what would actually maximize welfare. Factual questions about institutions and strate-

gies largely, if not entirely, *belong somewhere outside moral theory*, in politics, social theory, or social engineering.[73]

He identifies three broad features of morality as a basis for political decision: equality, an appeal to general norms, and universality. He contends that Marx's communism, like Nietzsche's aestheticism and Weber's nationalism, lacks just those aspects. Thus, for Weber, the triumph of Germany in the struggle of the great powers in the early twentieth century overrode all three. Similarly, Nietzsche celebrated aesthetic achievement, which he saw as at odds with equality, and debunked *moral* norms as masks for a nonmoral "will to power."[74]

Even if we grant Miller's problematic conception of nonmorality, however, Marx does not easily fit it. At least full communism, as Miller recognizes, is a much more egalitarian, internationalist society than the preceding ones. Prima facie, Marx's position resembles an ethical one.

[73] The citations are from R. Miller's conference paper entitled "Marx and Morality," 1981a. His sophisticated postpositivist account of moral learning (1985) and realism (1987) has deepened, but, I will suggest, also undercut his position.

In correspondance, Miller says that he does not – or at least since his *Analyzing Marx*, 1984, no longer – hold(s) the two-components view. It seems to me, however, that he still does. Miller, 1984, p. 42, slightly alters his basic view of morality, suggesting that "the validity of moral norms *does not depend on highly controversial empirical claims*" rather than that such norms "are not subject to direct empirical controversy" (my emphasis). Yet at p. 43, he contrasts multidimensional Marxian political arguments, which like scientific ones, are subject to postpositivist analysis, and moral views, which are a priori: "Traditional moral theories are like traditional logics of induction, which try to justify, on general and a priori grounds, norms that assign at least a rough degree of confirmation to every hypothesis, given any body of data." This claim fits mistaken traditional ethical epistemologies rather than moral theories.

Further, Miller's *generalized axiomatic hierarchy criticism*, which I discuss in Chapter 1, permits a great diversity of quasi-analytic starting points in ethics for what becomes an instrumental rationality. Ironically, the undeveloped permissiveness of this thought conflicts with his restrictive official characterization of a moral standpoint. In contrast, realism sees particular, sharply defined moral claims, involving a diversity of goods, as emerging a posteriori. Ethics and politics are about likeness; hierarchical views are normative, but neither moral nor political.

[74] Nietzsche characterized his view as beyond morality, but we need not accept this description. In Aristotelian terms, his conception looks like a distortion of the good of artistic creativity -- in the broad sense of shaping cultural values – at the expense of more central goods. His view is beyond conventional morality, not beyond an ethical theory of the good life. One might even suggest that such creativity resembles that of Aristotelian legislation, but without the latter's concern for the common good. Further, if artistic and cultural creativity merely express a will to power, why are they preferable to other versions of that will? Nietzsche appears metaethically to deny his claim that a blossoming, playful will to power is superior to the cramped envy of prevailing conceptions of "good and evil." To recognize that Nietzsche is not a moralist is not to affirm that his argument transcends ethical considerations.

Thus, compared to Weber and Nietzsche, Miller speaks of Marx as holding a *decent*, though nonmoral, point of view. This concession about humaneness, however, makes it unclear that Marx's conception is, even by his standards, nonmoral. Miller also identifies many common features of an Aristotelian and Marxian eudaemonism, ones that make his claim to distinguish Marx's nonmoral from Aristotle's ethical argument even more implausible.[75]

Yet his two-components objection raises important questions about the structure of Marx's normative vision; for we cannot readily resolve this theory into a general definition of goodness and subordinate empirical claims. In addition, as we have seen, Marx's judgments about the fundamental conflicts of goods in exploitative societies rest on contingent features of human history. Though he condemned suffering, he concluded that for past epochs, no social alternative to instrumental progress existed: The exploiters' propagation of reactionary ideas was too intense, the scale of production too narrow, revolutionary experience too limited. Given these historical contingencies, he restricted his moral judgments to microstructural specification of conflicts of goods. Moreover, Marx advanced empirical arguments on the contemporary possibility of a more cooperative society. Those claims – not general ethical distinctions – separated the present epoch from past ones and spurred revolutionary activity. Thus, the fusing of diverse intrinsic goods in communism is also a contingent factual claim.

Miller rightly maintains that Marx's historical theory strongly governs his moral judgments. What Miller considers the secondary, external component of an ethical theory becomes primary; the distinctively analytic component drops out altogether.

This two-components view, however, is far too sweeping. It rules out paradigmatic liberal moral theories, not just Marxian ones. Thus, it cannot do the work of discrimination that Miller wants it to do. For instance,

---

[75] R. Miller, 1981a, 1984. A defender of Miller's position might claim that Aristotle, among others, does not have a moral point of view; Miller himself, 1984, pp. 6, 18, notes that Aristotle's account lacks one basic feature, the premise of equality. Since Rawls and Dewey start metaethically from the norms of American democracy, he suggests, their theories depart from universality. These hypothetical exclusions reveal how overly restrictive an a priori conception of an ethical standpoint can be.

In contrast to his 1981a account, Miller, 1984, maintains that a moral view needs two or perhaps only one of the three dimensions. The 1981a argument views ethics as a cluster property, one potentially subject to a postpositivist reinterpretation. The 1984 change envisions a less homeostatic, more narrow a priori conception. Still Marx appears to meet all three criteria; they have to be very restrictively interpreted, as Miller admits, to make his claim attractive (pp. 17–18). Since Marx's account is even more likely to meet one criterion than three, Miller's 1984 shift makes his insistence on Marxian nonmoralism less plausible.

on the surface, Rawls's theory of justice seems a likely candidate for a two-components distinction. He offers a general definition of the original position. Those principles are just, he contends, which individuals would adopt after negotiation in that ideal situation. A Rawlsian can apply these principles, however, only with the addition of specific empirical statements pertaining to particular social configurations and moral dilemmas. Yet a two-components description inadequately characterizes Rawls's contractarianism; for even deliberation in the original position depends on facts in three important ways. First, as Ronald Dworkin has shown, Rawls's characterization of the original position rests on a deep commitment to claims about the general capacity for moral personality and mutual respect – ones that the foregoing argument has highlighted as moral *discoveries* about human nature. Second, no moral principles follow from the general definition of the original position alone. To adopt such principles, Rawls acknowledges, the individuals would have to know how human beings are constituted *psychologically* and have at their disposal *all true social theories*.[76] Third, to be plausible as a device for moral reasoning, the original position requires empirical claims about the centrality and specific character of contract, consent, and bargaining in our conception of justice.[77] Thus, Rawls's methodological devices and general principles depend on sometimes controversial empirical claims.

Similarly, utilitarianism appeals to facts about what constitutes human happiness or welfare; so does Aristotle's eudaemonism. Now, Marx's ethical viewpoint does not look like that of Rawls or of utilitarianism; it is much more embedded in and dependent upon the validity of particular empirical claims. But Miller's two-components criterion still rules out leading ethical theories rather than contrasting them with merely normative Marxian ones.[78]

---

[76] Rawls, 1971, pp. 137–8.

[77] In Rawls's democratic contractarianism, the relevant empirical claims are, as I have emphasized, facts about the general human capacity for moral personality. Particularly with regard to constitutional essentials (basic rights), the contract has a specific character, for these rights are guaranteed by the political autonomy of deliberators; they are not the result of a bargain, but secure conditions in which bargaining may fairly occur.

[78] Miller also claims that a Marxian view, unlike moral conceptions, violates the standard of treatment of others as equals, for a revolutionary movement will act against some capitalists and police who have personally committed no wrong. But this *harm to innocents objection* excludes obviously moral arguments about other large-scale political conflicts. For instance, it rules out those of Kant and Mill in justification of the French Revolution or the North in the U.S. Civil War – comparably innocent aristocrats and slaveholders would be affected – and even standard liberal defenses of the bombing of military targets in which some civilians will be killed. Miller's objection would pose a special problem for Marxians only if they were barred from taking the same steps as other justified political actors to limit such harms. But they aren't.

In addition, a two-components interpretation has sometimes been part of a neo-Kantian view, which looks for analytic definitions in science and ethics. Alternatively, a reductionist or (metaethical) relativist might hold the two-components interpretation in ethics alone, contrasting that argument with a naturalist view of scientific definitions, which are dependent upon empirical investigation. Miller's version is closer to the latter; for, as he acknowledges, it is routine in science for definitions to rest on contingent discoveries about the way the world is. Moral realism maintains, however, that the search for the definition of the term "good" can be similarly (theoretically and empirically) grounded.

A comparison between one of Putnam's leading examples of scientific change and Miller's account of Aristotle on slavery highlights this similarity. As Putnam notes, a modern chemist can identify as fool's gold glittering specimens that would have deceived Archimedes. If we suppose a conversation between the two in a possible world, the former could point out features of the sample that differed from those of gold even *without* persuading the latter of the truth of modern chemical theory. As Miller recognizes, we can see continuities of reference even if the modern chemist has a more profound theory of gold's microstructure and even if the ancient chemist mistook iron pyrites for the genuine item.[79]

Miller, however, denies comparable progress in moral theory. For instance, he asserts, "That Aristotle would have changed his mind about slavery if he had appreciated some fact or argument does not fit with what we know of Aristotle and his contemporaries."[80] On Miller's view, we cannot hold both that Aristotle is rational and that progress has occurred since the ancient polis; so much the worse, he concludes, for moral advance. But his contention about Aristotle seems wrong on the face of it; for, as I noted earlier, given the facts of his day, Aristotle already challenged slavery for Greek males and many barbarians as well. Despite contemporary stereotypes, he insisted, these men were not incapable of self-government. Furthermore, his ideas of citizenship and the contribution of political action to a good life depended upon an *empirical moral discovery*: the emergence of the polis. His account reveals the existence of progress. Confronted (hypothetically) with a possible world characterized by non-slave-based societies, Aristotle could, *by his own argument*, have concluded that man is *not* a despotic – that is, slaveholding – animal. As I noted in Chapter 3 Miller has subsequently made exactly this point about Aristotle's use of the term *"hudor."* Alternatively, as

[79] Putnam, 1975, 2:235–8.
[80] R. Miller, 1985, pp. 513–18, presents a realist account of the reference of moral terms within advanced industrial societies.

we will see below, even if Archimedes or Aristotle had failed to draw the relevant conclusions, scientific and moral rationality do not require consensus.

Sometimes Miller also appeals to a specialized, controversial notion of "rationality" to underpin his rejection of moral progress: People must reason the same way – instrumentally – from the axioms given by morality. On this amended view, Aristotle's hierarchical axioms – purportedly the central part of his ethics – eliminate slaves and artisans from politics. Supposedly, no empirical claim could affect the axioms themselves. In contrast, as I have argued, given Aristotle's egalitarian political and ethical claims about Greeks, evidence that slaves could participate fully in political life *empirically* discredits the doctrine of natural slavery. More deeply, he rightly suggested that we can *reason* about the nature and aims of moral theory and politics, about a good life for humans. Aristotle invokes a *substantive rationality,* not an instrumental rationality; for ethics involves an element of likeness or equality, a common good. Since Miller insists on equality as a leading feature of ethics, it is hard to see how, on his view, arguments that are normative but *nonmoral* can play so central a role in assessing *moral* rationality.[81]

Miller's other broad objection to the objectivity of a Marxian account – what I call the *universality of the conflict of goods argument* – strikingly extends fundamental clashes from exploitative societies to the first phase of communism. It pits a proponent of free speech, who agrees with a Marxian account of the facts, against an advocate of the dictatorship of the proletariat. Both acknowledge that in the immediate postrevolutionary era, capitalists have important political advantages. For instance, they can rely on the continuing influence of some older, reactionary ideas and practices among the masses and on differential organizational skills, arising from the network and experience of the comparatively small number of exploiters who seek to *disorganize* the much larger number of workers and their allies. To counter residual bourgeois power, a dictatorship of the proletariat would have to curtail freedom of speech and association for its enemies. As Miller emphasizes, a Marxian would justify these restrictions "to reduce the level of violence and increase access to politics and culture," goods that a liberal would also endorse.[82]

Depending on the severity and extent of such restrictions, however, a

---

[81] As we will see below, Miller sometimes conflates difficult but subtle cases of conflict, based on the integrity of ethics and the diversity of human goods, with seemingly glaring "ethical" contrasts, which arise from axiomatic, normative hierarchy, and are not, *morally speaking,* hard cases.

[82] R. Miller, 1986, pp. 69–71, provides a notably clear account. To elucidate undemocratic measures that on balance further democracy, he cites Lincoln's suspension of habeas corpus for Confederate sympathizers in the border states and suggests some not very

dispute could arise between a radical and a liberal who affirm a common list of intrinsic goods and view of the facts. For instance, as part of the good of acquiring knowledge, both recognize the intrinsic value of being able to speak one's mind without (coercive) restraint. Yet the liberal ranks freedom of speech so highly that he opposes the dictatorship of the proletariat.[83] Thus, Miller contends, on quite reasonable assumptions, a clash of fundamental values in communism prevents any *determinate* moral judgment or course of political action to which every *eudaemonist,* let alone every rational person, must assent. As I have noted, for Miller, a distinctively *moral* point of view requires universal rationality: that each rational person, capable of the normal range of emotions and fully informed of the facts, must reach the same conclusion. The example suggests that Marxian "morality" fails such a test even when it makes judgments about the nearly ideal conditions of early communism.

Miller envisions a liberal and a Marxian who agree about the facts. But this condition has a dramatic effect on the persuasiveness of the example as a putative conflict over basic values. In order to highlight this point, we need to examine three ways in which a dispute between a Marxian and a liberal might arise: First, those adhering to a roughly similar view about intrinsic goods could disagree empirically; second, eudaemonists, who could even hold a similar ranking of goods, could clash given the novelty of and uncertainty about a future communism; third, proponents of a common view of the facts could clash about evaluation. Miller contends that the third kind of disagreement has great moral weight.

But suppose that the basic dispute over the comparative goodness of liberal capitalism and early communism arises from empirical clashes of the first kind. That debate contrasts a good society with a very bad one. If Miller did not recognize *how decisive* such factual disagreements are, he might conflate the two kinds of examples and exaggerate the difference over ranking of goods. For instance, *if* Marxian theory is right, communist revolution emerges as the only way to avoid increasingly destructive world wars and recurrent fascism; liberal objections would vanish. Similarly, suppose Sidney Hook's description of a barracks communism and the virtues of liberal capitalism were true.[84] That evidence would compel a formerly Marxian eudaemonist to recognize the merits of liberalism. The sharp conflict between these positions derives from empirical disputes in social theory, not from clashing ethical premises.

---

controversial steps that a hypothetical liberal dictatorship might have taken to sustain multiracial Reconstruction regimes as an alternative to the Hays–Tilden sanctioning of Ku Klux Klan violence.
[83] Miller, 1984, pp. 10–11, 14–15.   [84] Hook, 1965.

This first kind of disagreement therefore casts no doubt on moral objectivity.

A clash between a liberal and Marxian could arise in a second way; for a liberal might suggest that the future course of any Marxian experiment is unclear. Even if communism secures some important goods, it might endanger others, such as freedom of speech. But liberal objections on the grounds that communism is new or that the first attempts to create a nonexploitative society have foundered do not involve conflicts over the ranking of intrinsic goods. Instead, they are a species of social theoretical and factual disagreement and might well, on further empirical examination or in the light of subsequent historical developments, turn out to be wrong.

For Miller, such disagreements challenge the notion of universal rationality that he sees as basic to a moral point of view. Thus, even if the social theoretical and factual case for communism turned out to be substantial, the remaining disagreement of *some* liberal critics would rule out moral objectivity. But again in this example, Miller's argument is too *sweeping;* his criterion for a moral view would impugn scientific as well as ethical rationality; for given the complexities of a theory-saturated method, science is unlikely to be characterized by consensus during periods of discovery and dramatic theoretical change. Thus, Priestley opposed the oxygen theory and Einstein quantum mechanics. No one considers their positions irrational at the time; yet their disagreement with what turned out to be the true theory does not throw scientific rationality into doubt.[85] As I argue in Chapter 3, these disputes suggest only that scientific rationality is more multidimensional than positivists imagined. Similarly, the complexity of intrinsic goods, given uncertain results, can lead – rationally – to different ethical choices. Yet even in such cases there would eventually turn out to be a fact of the matter as to which alternative was better. Reverting to my earlier hypothetical examples, even if Archimedes and Aristotle – lacking a full modern theory – had persisted in their original views, fool's gold would still be iron pyrites and slavery an inhuman institution. Contrary to Miller, the absence of consensus no more undermines ethical objectivity than lack of agreement on novel scientific theories undercuts scientific rationality.

Yet, one might insist, surely there must be some circumstances in which examples of the sort Miller stresses can arise. Such cases, however, would have to emerge from a *far less acute* conflict between the two societies than those characteristic of the first kind of factual dispute. To

---

[85] For instance, in *Fact and Method,* ch. 10, R. Miller (1987) provides a telling example of reasonable disagreement among nineteenth-century chemists about the existence of molecules.

arrive at the empirical agreement he requires, we would have to split the difference between liberal and Marxian social theory. Thus, imagine a non-barracks communism that facilitates substantial worker participation and solidarity, including the activity of formerly specially oppressed groups, such as women and the victims of racism. Nonetheless, in checking counterrevolution, some intimidation of speech occurs for intellectuals and harms the progress of knowledge. Imagine, further, a capitalist democracy that allows more erosion of racism and sexism than Marxian theory suggests. Yet that regime still discourages worker political participation and promotes ideas sanctioning "apathy" and the like. In addition, suppose that the two societies are roughly alike on other major moral dimensions; for instance, neither is prone to dominate others or to wage war. Finally, imagine that no transition is possible from one society to the other without harm to solidarity or speech. The Marxian chooses the former society; the liberal the latter. Their disagreement results from a difference over values. Would this hypothetical dilemma require the denial of moral objectivity?

The *indeterminacy* of this case arises precisely because it rules out so many of the things we commonly reject. This liberal and Marxian both condemn slavery, the servitude of women, colonialism, Nazism, aggressive war, and the like on grounds of their harm to life and the realization of individuality and happiness. Indeterminacy in this choice coexists with and dialectically presupposes moral discoveries about the nature and concordance of intrinsic goods and about who counts as human. As described, both regimes would be *comparatively good ones*. Thus, the example proves to be an unusual, large-scale instance of a common moral phenomenon. Individuals often confront choices between goods in which no extreme exists. For such cases, an ethical theory that leaves wide scope for individuality need offer no specific advice.

This argument against the *clash of goods objection* appeals to a distinctively Aristotelian conception of practical deliberation. Aristotle recognized a diversity of goods; he suggested that individual choices among them, even when there is a limited conflict or sacrifice of one, do not involve important wrongs. Such cases fall short of the *excessive* pursuit of one good at the expense of another. To be objective, an ethical theory need not rule out ties or near ties between such alternatives, including those between broadly morally similar types of society. A eudaemonist theory envisions, in Goldman's apt phrase, a "nonrelativist pluralism."

These choices might be described as matters of individual, societal, or political preference. They would be differences of *preference* precisely because they do not involve severe moral conflicts. More deeply, however, following Kohut's and Levine's theories of the self, such clashes might affect the self-determination of persons, not just their preferences. Specific decisions would then reflect a person's integrity, given real needs. Seemingly unresolvable conflicts of goods, when placed in the context of the deliberations of particular selves, might no longer be indeterminate. (Call this *individuality-based resolution of hard cases*.) A Marxian social theory emphatically leaves such choices to particular persons. But even if that theory is wrong, any reasonable liberal account should retain this defense of individuality.

This insight underpins an important distinction in democratic theory. Thus, as Walzer suggests, the specific history of a people may resolve otherwise morally indeterminate cases, explaining, say, the Athenian affection for theater rather than additional education. Involving the historically evolved self-determinations of citizens, we might speak here of *democratic individuality-based justifications* of difficult choices. In contrast, about many issues – how many performances to sustain through taxes, for example – preferences, elicited by voting, play a role. Call the latter *majority-rule- or preference-based justifications.*[86] Only the former, democratic individuality-based choices, not the latter, resolve hard cases. Thus, contrary to bivalence objections, plural cases play a significant role in a moral realist theory of the self and democracy.

Miller's criticism focused on the major *clashes of goods* in exploitative "prehistory" and sought to project them into a Marxian account of the first phase of communism. For Marx, however, communism overcomes fundamental conflicts. In order to construct a case that makes a choice of goods between a liberal and radical central, Miller has unintentionally conflated examples of the third kind – ones of value – with instances of the first kind – ones of fact and social theory. But the participants in this debate are no longer, say, Lenin and Sidney Hook; this disagreement among eudaemonists is far more benign.

Miller's realist *Fact and Method* further undercuts his account of moral knowledge. That argument stresses the role of conflicting causal attributions, based on a comparison of contending theories, in scientific confirmation. He resourcefully criticizes a priori positivist expectations that the appropriate form of explanation combines general laws or hypotheses and statements of particular conditions without preceding contrast to alternative theoretical accounts.[87] In a discipline-specific justification

---

[86] As Chapter 2 argues, a theory of individuality underpins democratic justifications of majority rule.
[87] Though the development of general, predictive laws is a striking achievement of some scientific theories, it is doubtful that "the best explanations" in particular disciplines need have such a form. Along with other naturalists, Miller argues that a priori strictures often legitimize bad social scientific explanations: A high observable correlation between skin color and technological achievement at the turn of the twentieth century once

of realism about theoretical entities, he shows how long after the acceptance of Dalton's theory of chemical combination, many practicing chemists and physicists still thought atoms an instrumental convenience. But when, based on molecular theory, Einstein and Perrin provided an unexpected explanation of Brownian motion (the sustained dancing of nonorganic particles in liquids), secured experimental confirmation, and excluded competing causes in the contemporary theoretical repertoire, leading skeptical scientists were convinced. As Henri Poincaré exclaimed, "Atoms are no longer a useful fiction . . . the atom of the chemist is now a reality." On Miller's reading of this change, striking success was not sufficient to justify the inference. As neo-Kantian claims about incommensurability rightly insist, skeptical chemists lacked, in many respects, common ground with realists; what linked them, as a last resort of comparison, was joint acceptance of ordinary perceptual knowledge. Miller thus stresses the noncontroversial – he says "truistic" – perceptual basis of the explanandum: If nonorganic particles in solution move, then lacking some internal cause of motion, they must be moved by something.[88]

The foregoing criticisms of Miller's rejection of Marx's moral realism, however, broadly mirror his sophisticated critique of positivism. In contrast to a priori empiricist views about the centrality of observation in science, Miller naturalistically investigates the contending theories about causation and inferences to unobservables researchers actually defend. Yet his characterization of a moral viewpoint offers no similar, naturalistic account of the emergence of democracy and concomitant changes in political and ethical theorizing.

Analogous to Miller's emphasis on the scientific role of perceptual truisms, however, moral realism stresses core standards about humans that underlie complex judgments about a good life. In his terminology, these standards are *moral truisms*. In natural scientific epistemology, one might even consider his concentration on perceptual truisms something of a weakness, for realism seeks to explain inferences to unobservables; a leading sense of physicists' claims to "see" neutrinos is, as Shapere has suggested, straightforward but not obviously perceptual. Other versions of realism capture more easily the theory-governed character of a method that achieves striking instrumental successes. In modern ethical theory, however, claims about unobservable entities play hardly any role. (Perhaps Marxian claims about surplus value would be a candi-

seemed to license Western ethnocentrism toward nonwhite peoples. Alternative, antiracist intuitions stimulated the painstaking field work and language acquisition, leading to new conceptions of culture, of Franz Boas and his followers. The latter turned out to be true; the former illustrates how seriously positivism can go wrong.

[88] R. Miller, 1987, chs. 4, 10.

date.) An epistemological thesis, parallel to Miller's, about the role of moral "truisms" seems even more plausible.

Miller's account of confirmation permits a more sophisticated version of his earlier objection to moral progress, emphasizing the discontinuity of Aristotle's and modern accounts of slavery. He stresses another level between checklists of contemporary theoretical and causal claims and perceptual truisms. That level focuses on particular kinds of background information that help to determine the plausibility of hypotheses. He depicts fair causal comparison as the willingness of a theorist not to appeal to any argument that is absent from the framework of one's opponents. Instead, she must allow shared background claims about plausibility to discredit particular arguments. For instance, Copernicans could not fairly use telescopic claims against Aristotelians, Miller contends, because the latter had a specific background belief about the difference between terrestrial and celestial optics. Nonetheless, Copernicans could win the argument on other grounds.[89]

Now a refined critique of ethical advance could insist that Marxians and modern liberals failed to share *relevant* background beliefs with Aristotle: Even a moral realist argument about slavery captures an accidental continuity. Modern theories, for example, deny the central, divinely sanctioned role of humans in the universe. Yet this criticism is implausible; for as Chapter 1 argued, across important differences, Aristotle, Montesquieu, and Hegel held many common background assumptions about social and political theory. In addition, on Miller's view, at the level of abstract information about intrinsic goods, Aristotle's and Marx's eudaemonism nearly coincide. Insisting, as he does not, on modern insights into individuality, moral realism shows that the remaining continuities between subsequent conceptions and Aristotelian deliberation are striking.

Finally, Miller maintains that some moral facts – for instance, that Caligula or Hitler were evil – have the same soundness as objective scientific judgments. More importantly, he traces the role that ethical claims sometimes play in reasonable social science explanations – for instance, violations of dignity in Edward Thompson's account of Chartism or the harmful impact of the cotton gin on slaves in the rise of abolitionism. These moral causes contribute to the explanation of particular class struggles. As he rightly insists, these inclusive, morally objective accounts are *causally deeper* than reductionist ones. He concludes that ethical facts contribute importantly to *some* social science explanations but perhaps not to others and suggests that researchers investigate their role on a case-by-case basis with fair attention to competing interpreta-

---

[89] R. Miller, 1987, ch. 4.

tions.[90] His argument thus sustains a central claim of realism about the contribution of moral facts to ethical and historical explanation. Internally following his philosophy of social science, we should look for an objective characterization of a moral viewpoint.

Miller's is easily the most nuanced, important attempt to exclude a straightforward ethical aspect from Marxian theory based on postpositivist epistemology and semantics. He appropriately stresses the role of facts, including social theory, in Marxian normative judgments and opposes overrating the role of moral injunction in radical strategy and ethical considerations in historical explanation. Yet conceptions of human dignity and a good society play an important role in class conflict and revolutionary movements; Marx's own vision provides an impressive example. Miller's claim that Marxian theory is decent but nonmoral is mistaken. His criticisms discredit the objectivity neither of Marxian moral judgments nor of Aristotelian or Marxian eudaemonism.

[90] R. Miller, 1987, ch. 2.

Chapter 8

Radical democracy and individuality

1. Twentieth-century revolutions: is Marx's first stage of communism viable?

The influence of Marxian theory on the Russian and Chinese revolutions is substantial and highly controversial. According to their self-understanding, these regimes originally sought to act on many Marxian ideas, but as we have seen, the theory itself exhibits tensions, and the regimes confronted novel, specific problems. Today both societies are status ridden and authoritarian and, as the Chinese (and the East European) case shows, provoke democratic protest. Far from moving to full communism, they "converge" with many objectionable features of capitalist regimes. From a radical viewpoint, they could be – at most – unprepossessing candidates for lesser evil by contrast to the continuing cruelties of the latter, and probably fail even in this comparison. Yet Marxian theory stresses the abolition of classes as an accompaniment to the flourishing of individuality; the relationship of socialism to communism is at its heart. Particularly given subsequent political history, the Marxian account of communism requires elaboration. A useful exploration of the theory's ethical tensions should contribute to that analysis.

As a result of the reversals of revolutionary socialism, liberal criticisms have become an especially forceful challenge to Marxism. In addition, on contemporary epistemological accounts, contests of theories are vital to scientific advance. I would therefore like to set this investigation in the context of a discussion between sophisticated liberal and radical theorists, ones who acknowledge common underlying moral claims and seek to specify the leading arguments for and objections to such regimes. Some of what I say about the Soviet Union and China will be sketchy; yet I hope that this account will bring out the structure of the debate between liberals and radicals over the nature of democracy and show how a more articulated view of Marxian ethical argument casts new light on it. Particularly in the final section, this discussion will weave together features of radical political experience with possible measures to strengthen democracy.

As I have suggested, Marx presented a powerful, telling critique of capitalist democracy as a regime that requires substantial apathy and major divisions among workers to sustain itself.[1] That critique could justify a more cooperative and free regime *if* one is possible. Further, as we have seen, even market socialist versions of liberal theory are hesitant about widespread political participation. In contrast, Marxian movements have broadly and successfully involved workers and peasants in attempts to forge a new society. Compared to the limited involvement – restricted to occasional voting – of capitalist democracies, vibrant radical movements have been *socially* democratic: They have facilitated political deliberation and action among ordinary, formerly "apathetic" people. This fact underpins Marx's and Lenin's claim that, in comparison to truncated liberal regimes, such movements are not only *more*, but even *qualitatively*, democratic. A common concern of both radical and liberal theorists, highlighted by this contention, is the extent to which genuine democracy can be made workable and durable.

Against this argument, advanced by revolutionary Marxians and in a different way by Hannah Arendt, a liberal may object that such democracy is, unfortunately, a limited enthusiasm, admirable but shortlived.[2] We must set far lower objectives, he continues, for enduring institutions in a large, complex society. Yet as a Marxian might respond, revolutionary participation has often been sustained for considerable periods against the odds. Further, radical Marxian alternatives have important achievements to their credit: peasant political initiatives in the lengthy social transformation of agrarian China, worker participation in the Russian Revolution, the Soviet defeat of the massive Nazi onslaught in World War II, mobilization of workers in antifascist and antiracist movements, and the like. In addition, abolishing exploitation and the parasite state, that is, creating a genuine democratic regime, are more complex, difficult aims than those of the older liberal democratic revolutions. In this respect, Marx's broad claim in *Capital* – that proletarian revolutions would be less lengthy, conflict ridden, and violence prone than their pro-capitalist predecessors – overemphasizes the abstract force of economic trends and underestimates the political difficulties of forging communism.[3] Yet the accomplishments of radical movements and the continuing oppressiveness of capitalist regimes make a Marxian alternative promising.

Still, the liberal has a further, powerful rejoinder: The most successful

---

[1] Gilbert, 1986c, 1990a. See also Chapter 11 below.
[2] Arendt, 1977.   [3] Marx, 1961, 1:764; Gilbert, 1981b, sec. 5.

revolutionary movements have over time – by sophisticated Marxian criteria – given rise to dictatorships. Such regimes seem hostile to many Marxian political and moral ideas, favorable to more economic determinist ones that justify "modernization"; for the former emphasize participation, deliberation, and the importance of individuality in the creation of communism, the latter the role of putatively neutral experts – planners – who grasp the "laws" of state development of productive forces.

Further, the liberal might continue, whereas socialism once undercut hierarchies of status – Bolshevik propelling of large numbers of communist workers into positions of political leadership, Chinese Communist attempts to break down divisions between mental and manual work, internationalist policies directed against unequal treatment of nationalities, antisexist policies, and so forth – today's socialist regimes strongly exhibit such hierarchy. Even if status inequalities arose from reward for individual effort, such divisions reflect a competitiveness that undermines self-respect and mutual respect – the public elevation of some *at the expense* of others – and coincide with hierarchies of power, privilege – shopping in special stores, vacations at elite spas, and the like – and wealth. If a class – for instance, one composed largely of leading members of the Communist Party – controls the economic "surplus" and state power and uses both to its advantage, then the notion that these exploitative systems resemble capitalist ones more nearly than communist ones becomes a plausible Marxian contention. Though differences of form and economic dynamic are important, this contrast reveals the aptness of the often used Marxian term "state capitalism" to refer to such regimes.

Having concurred with a largely Marxian analysis of the facts, however, this liberal can turn these arguments against communist political and moral conclusions. A more reasonable inference, he maintains, is that sustained democracy – though admirable on shared moral grounds – is simply not possible. This liberal might even concede a central point in the theory of the democratic state. Criticism of the harmful class bias of the capitalist democracies is sound, but the failure of a revolutionary alternative parries the force of that true Marxian insight in undermining reformist conclusions.[4] No regime can escape the conflicts that marked ancient Athens and capitalist advance; democracy must be fused with very substantial victimization. Such regimes may lack a *common* good. For a committed liberal, this alternative is not very palatable; it defends what is evidently a lesser *evil*. Yet it is a fair position – one that grants many reasonable Marxian criticisms of capitalist democracy, given common moral insights; it then dialectically applies those insights to con-

[4] Duncan, 1982, pp. 138–9; Lukes, 1982, p. 204.

temporary socialist regimes and asks whether Marxian theory can plausibly envision a communist realization of social individuality.

In the context of this debate, I will not offer a more worked-out argument about state capitalism or respond empirically to those who might want to defend current "socialist" regimes. Instead, I want to explore whether a Marxian theory has the resources to articulate an alternative path of communist development, one that would strengthen these regimes' earlier, revolutionary features, those admired by radicals whatever they think of contemporary socialism. Unlike a lesser-evil defense, such an argument would justify the basic contrast of communist and capitalist democracy. To make good on their dialectical critique of liberalism, I will contend, Marxian regimes would have to eschew capitalist and "socialist" practices, justified by economic determinist arguments, and become more directly communist. They would also have to adopt and maintain democratic and ordinary constitutional innovations. Interestingly enough, this argument develops the moral and political claims that jointly underlie liberal and Marxian theory.

On a Marxian account, as I have noted, contemporary socialist regimes are dictatorial. The term "dictatorship," however, plays a large, partially obscuring role in the controversy between radicals and liberals over the character of a revolutionary state. Unsophisticated liberal arguments often extend an appropriate, ancient moral contrast between regimes into a rigid social theory dichotomy between democratic "societies" and dictatorial ones. Neoclassical and even pluralist theories make the fundamental coerciveness of modern democracy – its character as a regime that *rules* somebody – almost invisible. Such theories, however, do not adequately account for apathy or the glaring social inequalities and coerciveness of capitalist institutions.[5] Marxians also despise tyranny. But they more easily extend this political critique from the Prussian monarch to the time-study expert whose rule is also a petty, exploitative "despotism."[6] Thus, they view democratic regimes dialectically as a democracy for slaveholders, a dictatorship for slaves; a democracy for capitalists, a dictatorship for immigrants, workers, and most of the middle classes; a democracy for workers and their allies, a dictatorship for the capitalists. But in a setting of counterrevolutionary war and violent civil dissension, this conception has been used to justify abrogation

---

[5] Factory, military, and even much educational experience in capitalist society is authoritarian. If there is a plausible justification for such institutions, it must be a moderated version of Aristotle's claims about natural slavery. But that justification is false and antiliberal. Socialization in these institutions is *congruent* with an oligarchical, formally democratic regime; that it is consonant with genuine democracy is doubtful (Eckstein, 1968; Foucault, 1977, pp. 209–14; Walzer, 1980b, pp. 276–9).

[6] Marx and Engels, 1974, pp. 41–2.

of many initially democratic practices. If some version of the Marxian account has merit, it must affirm and strengthen the democratic aspect of a "dictatorship of the proletariat."

Marx envisioned a regime in which the centralization and separation of the exploitative, "parasitic" state apparatus and its accompanying ideological aura – control of weapons but also status divisions – dissolved into an armed, politically active populace of equals. The democratic vigor of the Paris Commune – contrasted with the deathly dominion of capitalism – inspired Marx's and Lenin's theory of a proletarian regime. Yet that theory was rough – barely sketched by Marx.

As we have seen, his conception of the first stage of communism fused dominant revolutionary features – democracy, egalitarian pay for officials, social distribution of many resources according to need, and vigorous advocacy of abolition of classes and the wage system – with secondary concessions to procapitalist practices and motivations. The famous image of communist life emerging stained by capitalism's "bloody birthmarks" suggests this regime's dialectical tensions.

To explain why the revolutionary democratic aspects of socialism have ultimately dissolved into dictatorship, those sympathetic to a Marxian viewpoint may specify the noncommunist features that this regime ultimately exaggerates. Except for the brief rule of the Commune, Marx could not base his theory on postrevolutionary experience. Features of radical twentieth-century regimes are thus important to this inquiry. A plausible Marxian argument must combine deeper theoretical insights into communism with at least some evidence for their practicality.

2. Socialist concessions to class, status, and political hierarchy

Socialist regimes have employed three kinds of concessions, all of which require evaluation: (1) particular ones arising from noncapitalist or insufficiently capitalist economic backwardness, (2) ordinary market concessions, universally characteristic of socialism, and (3) political and economic ones spurred by aggressive wars waged on revolutions by external capitalist powers and/or by internal class dissensions. Socialists have legitimatized the first type of concession by emphasizing the low level of productivity of the initial revolutionary settings. Such justifications insist on *special* features of the Russian and Chinese revolutions; we might call them *economic-determinism-justified concessions to backwardness*. (An economic determinist version of Marxism, we might recall, insists that the development of productive forces drastically shapes successive social forms and *narrowly* circumscribes possibilities for democracy.) The second type has been sustained by economic determinist and liberal arguments about scarcity, fear- and pay-based motivation, and desert-oriented justice, which apply to all *socialist* regimes. On these accounts, even following a revolution, a regime must rely heavily on monetary rewards to elicit economic participation. We might call these policies *individual desert-based market concessions*. They have sometimes been taken to further a decentralization that might undermine dictatorial, planned regimes. Seeking to unite Western democracy and market socialism, liberal theorists then invoke them as desirable mechanisms.[7]

Both the fierce internal repression of social uprisings and international ruling-class intervention against successful ones – the Spartacus revolt; the German peasant war; European aggression against the French Revolution; the June insurrection; the Paris Commune; foreign intervention in the Russian Civil War and the subsequent Nazi invasion; the twenty-year Chinese military struggle; the responses to mass egalitarian movements in Vichy France, Austria, Italy, Spain, Germany, and Chile; French and Portuguese colonial wars in Algeria, Angola, Mozambique, and Guinée-Bissau; the U.S. interventions in Vietnam and against the Sandinistas in Nicaragua, to name only the most glaring – have justifiably oriented radical movements toward war. In self-defense against violent counterrevolution, revolutionary regimes have sometimes adopted highly centralized forms of military organization, recruited officers from the old standing army, and the like. We might call these *crisis or war-based political concessions*. Such concessions have two forms: They may take over older hierarchies (Bolshevik military organization) and/or they may internally limit democratic practices. The menace of intervention has also licensed the first two kinds of concession. Unfortunately, if liberal social theory theses that capitalist democracies are comparatively plastic, easily reformed regimes are mistaken, as they well may be, then even those radical regimes that reject many particular concessions of previous movements will still need to prepare for war.[8]

---

[7] These concessions lead to the perpetuation of what John Roemer has called "status exploitation." He attempts to justify some of this inequality with a game-theoretic argument as "necessary socialist exploitation." Since, on his account, there are no *direct* beneficiaries of this "exploitation," that moral characterization is puzzling. More importantly, Roemer ignores the impact of such inequalities on the fundamental issue of who controls the state and possible systemic *political* harms to workers. He criticizes the law of value to clear away misconceptions that hinder the development of current socialist regimes. See the useful discussion in Roemer, 1982, pp. 248–9; 1985, p. 64. In contrast, my argument questions the putative necessity of socialist "exploitation" and challenges the law of value, based on an explicit conception of communism as democratic individuality.

[8] To achieve this plasticity, a liberal theory may endorse large-scale, sometimes violent, extraparliamentary reform activities often stressed by radicals. But as Marxians note, once the mass movements that force concessions decline, the reforms themselves are commonly eroded. This fact is the basis for the Marxian inference that these limited de-

War-based concessions, in particular, exerted an enormous, antidemocratic influence on the Bolsheviks. For instance, the attack by numerous foreign-sponsored armies and assassination or wounding of leaders – Volodarsky, Uritsky, Lenin – led that regime to reverse its original ban on capital punishment, abandon its attempt to work with other parties, and erode formal democratic practices. Further, the need to defend itself legitimized recruitment of former czarist officers and officials. Appeals to ward off external threats reinforced arguments for economic-determinism-based concessions to backwardness: installation of former capitalists to manage plants, reliance on previously privileged professionals to organize university and cultural life, and the like. This argument also sustained individual desert-based concessions, the use of material incentives among noncommunists, and finally, in the mid-1930s, to prepare to combat Nazism, a decisive anti-Commune-like concession – the introduction of wage differentials among Bolsheviks. These and other measures reinforced an older capitalist-like state structure and economic regime. They eroded revolutionary democracy. Such concessions suggest, a liberal might note, further formally democratic and market modifications of the Soviet "parasite state" as at least a "lesser evil" alternative.

Yet dialectically, given the justice of their cause, radical regimes have had important successes. They have initiated popular levées-en-masse and fostered worker and peasant participation in political leadership. Such policies contributed to the regimes' élan, their democratic and voluntary aspects. That élan surfaced in the Russian Revolution and flourished in China. Thus, the Soviet government relied heavily on radical workers in winning the Civil War and in subsequent industrial construction. The Bolsheviks became a predominantly working-class party by 1914; they overwhelmingly recruited proletarians through the mid-1920s and insisted on a maximum wage for party members equivalent to a skilled worker's. Later, they utilized egalitarian distributive policies in the massive effort to defeat Nazism.[9]

mocracies will not evolve into a decent society (Dutt, 1974, chs. 5–7; Miliband, 1969, ch. 6; Piven and Cloward, 1977).

[9] Contrary to a scholarly stereotype that the Bolsheviks were composed of isolated intellectuals, Lenin and his colleagues created a mainly proletarian party, focused on revolutionary organizations in industry and the military. *What Is to be Done?* is often misread as opposing union activity; yet it defended bold advocacy of communist politics – internationalism, the need for democratic or socialist revolution, and the adoption of a commune-like political form – within the real workers' movement as against self-restriction of radicals to bread-and-butter unionism. Even before the 1905 revolution, Lenin opposed the resistance of Social Democratic intellectuals to recruiting workers on such spurious grounds as that they "did not know enough" about Marxism: "The workers have a class instinct, and even with a little political experience, they quite quickly

Going further in a democratic direction than the Soviets, the Chinese communists mobilized a multimillion-member peasant army. In addition, they emphasized an egalitarian supply system – distribution of scarce goods according to need – and the abolition of signs of rank. Further, they applied these policies in the large regions of China liberated before 1949. Though they appealed to nationalism and sought to ally with the "national bourgeoisie," their original military and social organization relied neither on former Kuomintang officers nor on wage incentives. Yet this political strategy dramatically succeeded. In his "Critique of Soviet Economics," written during the Great Leap Forward, Mao utilized the political heroism of Chinese and previous democratic revolutionary experience to criticize Bolshevik stress on material incentives:

> Our party has waged war for over twenty years without letup. For a long time we made a nonmarket supply system work. Of course at that time, the entire society of the base areas was not practicing the system. But those who made the system work in the civil war period reached a high of several hundred thousand, and at the lowest still numbered in the tens of thousands. *In the War of Resistance Against Japan the number shot up from over a million to several millions. Right up to the first stage of Liberation our people lived an egalitarian life, working hard and fighting bravely, without the least dependence on material incentives, only the inspiration of revolutionary spirit.* At the end of the second period of the civil war we suffered a defeat, although we had nothing but victories before and after. This course of events had nothing at all to do with whether we have material incentives or not. It had to do with whether or not our political line and our military line were correct. These historical experiences have the greatest significance for solving our problems of socialist construction.[10]

Historic successors, however, often critically modify rather than transform earlier patterns that they admire. In 1949, the Chinese Communists adopted many components of the Soviet model. These features included backwardness concessions – recruitment of former capitalist managers, reliance on educators of elite background – and extensive market concessions – salary differentials for noncommunists and even *inequalities within the communist party*. Thus, Mao's 1958 critique articulated the role of egalitarianism in inspiring millions of people and yet sought to blunt the contemporary radicalism of many cadre and peasants – what he called "the ultracommunist wind." By Marxian standards, however, the

become steadfast Social Democrats. I would like very much to see eight workers on our committees for every two intellectuals." After that revolution, the Bolsheviks became predominantly proletarian in composition (cited in Krupskaya, 1930, 1:139–40). Haimson, 1964; Badayev, n.d.; Rabinowitch, 1976, pp. xvi-xviii, xxi, xxviii, xxxi; Basseches, 1952, pp. 188–206; Adelman, 1978; Gilbert, 1976b.
[10] Mao, 1977, p. 85 (my emphasis).

Chinese experience highlights democratic possibilities, providing striking counterexamples to Bolshevik *economic determinist backwardness, individual desert-based market,* and *war-based political concessions.* Still, Soviet and postliberation Chinese practice pitted one important sector of society, those spurred by pay and status differentials, against another: worker and peasant revolutionaries motivated by the need to associate and forge communism. Bolshevik egalitarianism until the mid-1930s, as well as the later Chinese supply system and opposition to military rank, strengthened the revolutionary side of this dialectic. Abandonment of the principles of the Commune and facilitation of status divisions, one might think, decisively reinforced the reactionary side. In general, policies elevating members of the former elite to positions of power, reliance on market incentives, lack of political trust in workers and peasants, and failure to ensure deliberation about the movement's future all foster dictatorship.

To explain the consolidation of dictatorship, a liberal emphasizes the regime's political practices; a Marxian attempts to tie such practices into a broader theory of the (re)emergence of an oppressive class structure. A genuine democracy is difficult to sustain; given past political structures and styles, dictatorship is comparatively easy. Insofar as a centralized state is isolated from society, as the previous chapter noted, former exploiters and would-be new ones have advantages in expertise, experience, and organizational skills. Such forces draw strength from the weight of nonradical traditions and (neurotic) psychology – for instance, those underpinning the prevalence of material incentives, ethnic oppression, sexism, and the like. Given the novelty of communist politics, a qualitative shift in character from a – somewhat – revolutionary to exploitative state apparatus can happen through peaceful corruption, signaled by the emergence and consequences of substantial status differentials. Focusing on Soviet experience, one might conclude that this transformation is likely to occur without substantial overt class war from below.[11] The outburst of the Chinese Cultural Revolution or left wing Polish worker revolts, however, indicate the depth of social conflict. The crushing on the Chinese "ultraleft" may even be a counterexample to a general thesis about the peaceful evolution of revolutionary socialist into exploitative regimes.

Specific political experiences and diverse strategies, a Marxian might insist, dramatically affect outcomes. The enormous effort to ward off unparalleled Nazi brutality exhilarated the millions who fought; yet it was also exhausting. That exhaustion, coupled with the prevalence of a pro-status outlook and authoritarian style, sustained a reactionary Soviet

[11] Sweezy and Bettelheim, 1971, p. 74.

leadership. In contrast, in China, greater respect for peasant radicalism and dissemination of communist ideas, initially during a lengthy civil war and then during World War II, instigated a leftist countermovement to check socialist status hierarchy – for instance, in the Great Leap Forward and the Cultural Revolution.

In a liberal perspective, socialist market concessions create polyarchic centers of power; workers' self-management is more participatory than Soviet "one man management." Yet, a Marxian might respond, given the market advantages of well-positioned firms, uneven success, and differential wages, a self-managing system could exacerbate status differentials and bend the state apparatus to serve a privileged group. As the Yugoslav case illustrates, this practice, just by itself, does not inspire political participation, prevent mass unemployment, or threaten existing dictatorship.[12] In a setting of equal incomes and other political changes, however, a Marxian might maintain, democratic workplace organization would play an important role.

Further, appeals to "material incentives" have dominated Soviet planning since the mid-1930s. A 1937 philosophy textbook described the sense of a common good elicited by this system: "This mutual penetration [of opposites] is manifested in the form of piece-work, the insistence [on] differential wages . . . the bonus system, diplomas . . . and other forms of encouragement designed to enlist all the powers of the individual in the service of society."[13] This justification recalls Adam Smith's "invisible hand." The planners' hand may arrange the market, but the effect on wage and status differentials, individual motivation, and political outlook is broadly similar. As I noted above, not only "primitive socialist accumulation" – a partly misguided term of Preobrazhensky's since the brutality overwhelms the radicalism – but even normal socialist accumulation recapitulates leading features of its capitalist predecessor; for this process tends to crystallize a class of peasants and workers, counterposed to a class of managers and officials distinct in pay and status.[14] The conception of self fostered in this process is the egotistical one familiar in classical and neoclassical economics. "Modernization" theory, extolling industrial hierarchies, not a Marxian account, appears

---

[12] Robert A. Dahl, 1985, pp. 97, 106–8, stresses the domination of councils by managers and a decline in worker participation. As a worker portrayed the glaring status structure of meetings, "You talk about workers' self-management, but during my two years of membership in this body I have noticed that the first rows of this hall are occupied by managers. Then come experts, then clerks, and then us, the workers. The rear left corner of the hall is reserved for us. Evidence is beginning to come in . . . that the State Council has started to exercise greater powers and that the system of shop floor discussion is alive and well. Wouldn't it be normal that we workers have the first row?" (cited in Greenberg, 1986, pp. 103–12, 235).

[13] Shirokov, 1937, p. 167.   [14] E. O. Wright, 1984, pp. 393–4, 395.

– perhaps superficially – to fit such accumulation. The formerly radical aspects of Soviet socialism have faded from the view of its current leaders, not just from Western social science.

Given Bolshevik reliance on material incentives, leftist appeals became hard to sustain. As Mao suggested:

> [The 1950s Soviet textbook on political economy] makes it seem as if the masses' creative activity has to be inspired by material interest. At every opportunity the text discusses individual material interest as if it were an attractive means for luring people into pleasant prospects. This is the reflection of the spiritual state of a good number of economic workers and leading personnel and of the failure to emphasize political-ideological work. Under such circumstances there is no alternative to relying on material incentives. "From each according to his ability, to each according to his labor." The first half of the slogan means that the very greatest effort must be expended in production. Why separate the two halves of the slogan and always speak one-sidedly of material incentive? This kind of propaganda for material interest will make capitalism unbeatable![15]

Liberal views on the coincidence of market incentives and democracy arose against the background of feudalism's coerciveness and denial of personality. That contrast is the source of Hayek's and today's Chinese market socialists' emphasis on collective forms of production as regressive "roads to serfdom." Against feudalism, procapitalist policies served the emergence of individuality; a less politically dominated economy, characterized by self-seeking, was superior in human terms, not just in productivity, to a serf-holding one. In fact, as Montesquieu rightly maintained, a greater stress on individual personality and initiative augmented productivity and helped sustain – restricted – parliamentary forms. But in a communist context, so Marxians contend, that contrast is no longer valid. Even "merit-based" market concessions aid old and new exploitative interests by undercutting an egalitarian social and political structure. Status and class domination can occur whether there is central planning – utilizing material incentives – or a "mix" of market and planning "mechanisms." Thus, a Marxian might insist that the whole liberal problem of plan or market, centralization or decentralization, focuses our attention on the wrong questions. Instead, we should be concerned with the breadth of democratic participation and discussion, to what extent differential status and inegalitarian ideologies persist, and which social classes – or strata – control state power. The reliance on market practices, recommended by liberals, does not mitigate and may often paradoxically strengthen exploitative dictatorship. Given the triumph of reactionary regimes in Russia and China, radicals need

[15] Mao, 1977, p. 79.

to develop a theory of how the tensions between political community and the market, the politics of social individuality and that of status-based ideologies of "individualism," and integrated and defective senses of self may be overcome.

3. How *democratic* is radical democracy?

Against this argument, however, a Weberian critic might insist that modern politics and industrial organization must be heavily bureaucratic. Even if mass organizations such as soviets and village associations flourish during a revolution, a one-party regime will eventually lead to their atrophy. Such a liberal might even grant that a democratic centralist organization, bringing coordinated proposals into the political arena, instigating discussion and action among the oppressed, and respecting the views of others – aside from exploiters and armed counter-revolutionaries – can be a democratic force well into the initial postrevolutionary stage. Yet, he might add, too many tendencies in communist society engender sharp status differentiation and corrupt such a party. Ultimately, that party will hinder, not facilitate, mass democracy. Even where serious radical protest is possible – the "ultraleft" in the cultural revolution – it is still relatively easy to turn a centralized state apparatus into a reactionary dictatorship and use it against the masses. Thus, he suggests, a decent version of party competition, allowing some, perhaps politically tepid – "loyal" – opposition, coupled with a tradition of free, even if nonthreatening, speech is the best one can expect.

Once again, numerous concessions to Marxian theory qualify this minimal defense of capitalist democracy. The liberal may grant, for instance, that electoral party competition has never historically facilitated fundamental social change. Except at its revolutionary and hence quite dictatorial inception in the Puritan, French, and American revolutions and the U.S. Civil War, liberalism is at home on the terrain of moderate, lesser-evil politics; yet only very different policies could have forged that terrain. This defense allows that liberal theory might neither foresee nor deal creatively with major political conflicts.[16]

But this liberal might then turn Marxian justifications of particular policies, based on revolutionary history, against a broader radical argument. He might grant the initial seriousness of Bolshevik attempts to work with other parties. As noted above, however, even the left Socialist-Revolutionaries, infuriated by the concessions to Germany of the Treaty of Brest-Litovsk, launched a campaign of assassination

[16] B. Moore, 1965, chs. 1–3; R. Miller, 1984, chs. 4–5.

against Bolshevik leaders and ultimately joined the counterrevolution. The outlawing of that party, the liberal might stress, just shows how limited the possibility of electoral competition for leadership is under revolutionary circumstances: better to prize even restricted traditions of democratic competition.

A Marxian answer might begin from three broad claims. First, one might initially conceive the freedom of the Commune, on the model of the Greek city, as participation in a small, deliberative assembly. That view interprets political power as a personal power possessed by each citizen. But in a large regime, representation and leadership are necessities. However much a Marxian democratic theory strengthens citizen involvement, that participation, just by itself, is not its primary feature. Instead, as Richard Miller has suggested, a communist revolution makes democratic power comparatively available as a *non-individually owned public good*. A state, dominated by an elite officialdom, with wealth and status interconnections, is unlikely to exhibit empathy for workers and likely to respond to those of similar aspirations. In contrast, a non-status-oriented leadership, such as that of the Commune, creates novel resources to meet the needs and aspirations of ordinary citizens. Institutional possibilities of criticism, recall, and restriction on pay join increased worker composition to further the representatives' concern for the common weal.[17] This regime serves as a medium for and sustainer of local democracy rather than a breeding ground for an exploitative class.[18]

Second, in contrast, even multiparty competition in a setting of extreme social inequality often degenerates into nonradical contention for office among party elites. Historically, mainly electoral radical parties have not overcome these pressures. Aside from the Industrial Workers of the World, the democratic socialist parties of the early twentieth century were, even in their radical phase, notoriously hierarchical. Such parties sometimes used state or elite aid to suppress left-wing opposi-

[17] Soviet and union experience testify that proletarian background combined with differential status and salary do not nurture a leadership concerned to advance the interests of ordinary citizens and workers.

[18] As Miller, 1986, p. 76, puts it, a dictatorship of the proletariat generates gains in democracy for most individuals: "Positive and negative liberties are important. And the democratic values that do not fall in either category are still, in a real sense, individualist. If measures like those taken by the Paris Commune make society more democratic, this is because of changes in the lives of individuals, not just effects on abstract historical trends. But in thinking about democracy, as in other matters, we are apt to reason as if only gains in an individualistic *competitive* framework mattered. The resources that concern us are apt to be means of influence possessed by individuals, by which individuals can triumph over the powers and desires of others. In fact, most people may be missing democratic resources that no one can own."

tion in their midst.[19] In addition, today's decent, conventional liberal theories of democracy – pluralist ones – do not emphasize individual participation, but rather group representation. On this view, at best, a common good arises through negotiation among elites. Its portrayal of politics does not look very democratic; given reasonable factual claims, power appears to be neither neutral nor plurally shared.[20] The hierarchy and antidemocracy of prevailing parties, a radical would argue, suits dominant social interests. These arguments reveal the *public good* of breaking governmental and status inequalities as well as those of class. Further, if parties not geared to revolution and war are often just as hierarchical for antidemocratic purposes, the comparative stigma attached to a notion of democratic centralism is lessened.[21] Though its organization remains a political concession, a revolutionary party that adheres to internal democratic norms and furthers those of the popular associations it works with might be – comparatively – a democratic force. That

[19] Michels, 1966; Przeworski, 1985; Schlesinger, 1984; Schorske, 1972, pp. 108–10. As Schorske reveals, the problem with hierarchy in supposedly democratic parties is not abstract elitism but the gutting of radical policies. German socialist ministers Friedrich Ebert and Gustav Noske recruited the Freikorps to suppress the 1919 Spartacist uprising and were responsible for the police murder of Rosa Luxemberg, Karl Liebknecht, Leo Jogisches, and others (Arendt, 1968, pp. 34–6). The movie "Reds" dramatically reveals the antidemocratic maneuvers of the U.S. socialist party elite against rank-and-file sympathizers of the Russian Revolution (Salvatore, 1982, pp. 319–20). After World War II, liberal and social democratic union leaders, cooperating with a ferocious state attack, expelled radical-led unions from the American CIO. David Caute, 1979, chs. 11–12, 22–7, reviews bizarre, contemporary antiliberal practices – involving a minimal requirement of informing – in U.S. intellectual and cultural institutions. Duberman, 1988. As I saw at the 1969 SDS convention, on a standard American media account, an outvoted leadership could walk out and "expel" a majority of delegates because it feared the triumph of a sharply opposed rank-and-file politics. In capitalist society, even "democratic" opposition politics is often remarkably unconducive to democracy.

[20] In justification of contemporary liberal democracy, pluralists often suggest that the initially oppressive power of private profit seeking – on which they concur with Marxians – can be "countervailed." With organization, perhaps by radical means, each group obtains its share in a common good. Thus, Michael Walzer, 1980b, 1983, is an eloquent pluralist theorist of democratic socialism.

    Originally a doctrine focused solely on power in domestic politics, pluralism's adherents (and many of their critics) rarely consider foreign policy, let alone the issue of democratic internationalism. Yet their failure to envision a mechanism that might check external repression is troubling; for on a pluralist view, General Motors and Chase Manhattan have great leverage to sustain their interests in, say, South Africa or Chile. But who, according to this theory, represents black workers, or the Chilean "disappeared" in *American* politics? The basic implications of pluralism about the oppressiveness of advanced capitalism toward ordinary people in less developed countries are exactly those of Marxian argument; ironically, this theory should expect the evidence marshaled in Chomsky and Hermann, 1979; McCamant, 1984; Saine, 1988.

[21] Dunn, 1984, p. 40.

justification would be more persuasive if the responsiveness of such a party were enhanced by popular review and other checks to its power.

At this point, however, a liberal might rightly insist that balance – and, more aptly, division – of powers mutes the authoritarian and tyrannical possibilities of ordinarily hierarchical parties of notables; such checks would be more necessary and function less easily with a single democratic centralist party. Third, a radical might respond that Bolshevik experience occurred under special historical circumstances. The recent Nicaraguan revolution has not attempted to abolish capitalism; nonetheless, it has self-consciously cultivated a multiparty regime. Probably such competition is not, just by itself, the central feature of a radical view. But as we shall see in Section 5, a Marxian might still recommend it.[22]

A deeper radical response might take two broad directions. For clarity, I will explore them separately, though they may be combined. The first, developed in the next two sections, is that even socialist societies dominated by a single party have relied on significant democratic practices. Perhaps an internal critique and modification could sufficiently strengthen the latter features. This response suggests that given actual political alternatives, radical democracy can achieve admirable results, even though it is not highly democratic.

The second direction, which I will explore in Section 5, responds directly to the liberal criticism that a radical regime requires the substantive undermining of a formal division of powers: It doesn't. Perhaps a variety of ordinary measures to further discussion and limit – potentially tyrannical – willfulness could check the harms of radical politics and reinforce its democratic character. That response suggests that many features of radical democracy need not be very radical.

The initial answer draws upon several important features of Chinese experience. As a first broad innovation, having undermined the old structure of social power, the Communist Party relied on decentralized political experience, mainly that of village associations. It envisioned an importantly democratic strategy: (1) Learn from the experience of the masses (their response to oppression such as the peasant revolts in Hunan in the mid-1920s and later efforts to redistribute existing wealth as a means of abolishing poverty); (2) elaborate the central policies and broad justifications for furthering the revolution (a policy of relying on peasant-based armed struggle; formation of mutual aid teams and cooperatives to generate sufficient wealth to ensure life-sustaining shares); (3) return these ideas for discussion and implementation in nonparty

[22] Parenti, 1986a; Rosset and Vandermeer, 1986, pp. 5, 8. In contrast, Horvat, 1982, pp. 319–22, recommends outlawing of parties.

village associations as well as party organizations; (4) investigate the results and reassess previous policy (learn from extraparty criticism and self-criticism), formulate a modified or new policy, and take it to the masses. Later policy initiatives reiterate the cycle, starting with evaluation of earlier revolutionary activity and self-criticism. According to Mao:

> In . . . the practical work of our Party, all correct leadership is necessarily "from the masses to the masses." This means: take the ideas of the masses (scattered and unsystematic ideas) and concentrate them (through study turn them into concentrated and systematic ideas), then go to the masses and propagate and explain these ideas until *the masses embrace them as their own, hold fast to them, and translate them into action,* and test the correctness of these ideas in such action. Then once again concentrate ideas from the masses and once again go to the masses so that the ideas are persevered in and carried through. And so on, over and over again in an endless spiral, with the ideas becoming more correct, more vital and richer each time.[23]

As William Hinton's *Fanshen* vividly demonstrates, these policies enabled peasants to emancipate themselves from rule by the landlords, create democratic associations that permitted discussion of basic forms of social organization, initiate cooperative production, and criticize village leaders and communists (not coextensive groups). In contrast to liberal democracies, aside from traditional American town meetings, such local democratic forms have been a distinctive feature of revolutionary activity.[24] Unfortunately, the tensions in revolutionary theory and regimes have often led to a radical as well as academic veil of silence about such innovations.[25] As Richard Miller aptly puts it:

[23] Mao, 1965, 3:119.
[24] Historically, despite their participatory successes, town or neighborhood meetings have also had distinctive problems of local elite domination and social pressure (Barber, 1984, pp. 268–9, 272–3; Mansbridge, 1980, pp. 111–14, 117). Radical regimes often undermine the economic basis for elitism. But effective local democracy requires greater commitment to individuality than either the republican or Marxian traditions have sustained.
[25] Hinton, 1966. Hinton's evidence about the achievements and tensions in village democracy is impressive. Similarly, Badeyev, a Bolshevik metal worker, provides insights into maintaining democratic commitments while serving as a representative in the czarist duma (Badeyev, n.d.). The banned American movie "Salt of the Earth," about the tense relations of mainly Chicano women and men in a 1950 radical-led – Mine, Mill, and Smelter Workers Union – strike, is a marvelous depiction of the virtues of radical democracy (Wilson and Rosenfelt, 1978). Worker and peasant participants ordinarily do not write about such events. Yet the limited number of persuasive descriptions and theoretical assessments is, just by itself, a sharp political commentary on previous emphases in revolutionary politics; it reflects insufficient commitment to the democracy that such politics often initiates and furthers (Foucault, 1977, pp. 207–8, 214).

Since Marx, descriptions of post-revolutionary societies have sketched . . . institutions that could be innovations in democracy. I have hedged this claim abundantly because all descriptions of these societies are highly partisan, pro or con. It is all the more frustrating, then, that there are few detailed and concrete accounts of events within these institutions, for example, of what was said in a Soviet factory meeting circa 1930 or of a typical meeting of a Cuban block committee today. I will only offer these further examples as plausible means to make a dictatorship of the proletariat more democratic. (I should confess a source of prejudice, however, concerning the actual existence of democratic innovations that have not been conclusively documented. As an over-aged member of SDS, I saw groups rise to the challenge of combining democracy with effective action. I have seen no record of these events, since. On one memorable occasion, a combined meeting and sit-in at McGovern headquarters at the 1972 Democratic convention, events unfolded before network cameras whose monitors showed that the networks were choosing to broadcast pictures of delegates with funny hats.)[26]

In China, once again, such processes were sustained for a considerable period. They revealed a democratic aspect of radical centralization that is not just a response to the brutality of the old ruling class. Mao's *On Practice* rightly stresses that the formulation, implementation, and criticism of a general line can have aspects of a social scientific experiment: Given previous radical experience and the need for widespread participation, how does one move from a political community marred by residual aspects of economic inequality and status ideology to communism? As his argument shows, serious political experimentation, more than other branches of inquiry, requires *democracy:* Individuals must "embrace these ideas as their own, hold fast to them," act on them, assess the consequences, and help develop them further. Only the self-understanding and self-respect of participants, not the rule of experts, can generate and sustain communism. Yet neither Mao's theory nor, so far, any other refined radical argument has lived up to this central promise.

As a second innovation, the early phase of the Chinese revolution and more strongly the Cultural Revolution sought to democratize all social institutions. Harry Eckstein has spoken of the congruence of authority structures in democracy. Modifying his useful idiom, a Marxian might say, that regime aimed, despite centralized party and governmental organization, to achieve a *downward congruence* of forms of authority that

---

[26] R. Miller, 1986, pp. 67–8.

would secure and radicalize participation.[27] That institutional structure contrasts with the *oligarchic congruence of private institutions in capitalist society*, consonant with hierarchical multiple-, dual-, or single-party politics.[28] After the revolution, however, the Chinese party often adopted hierarchical Soviet organizational forms and economic determinist preconceptions. Aside from the democratic practices of village associations and the prerevolutionary Red Army, a strategy of popular assemblies, gathering all relevant participants, and running factories, schools, and hospitals was implemented only in the Cultural Revolution. Despite the aim of *cooperative modernization*, the revolution not only had an agrarian base; ironically, urban institutions were probably less democratic than rural ones.

Chinese experience suggests two improvements in radical democratic practice. Marxians could stress the ordinarily democratic organization of all *social* institutions. As the threat of war and internal social tension decline, the latter might lead not just to downward congruence, offsetting the hierarchy of centralist decision making, but to thoroughgoing consonance in political procedures.[29]

---

[27] Eckstein recommends democratic political forms checked by comparatively hierarchical social ones: "governmental democracy will tend to be stable only if it is to a significant extent impure – if, in short, the governmental authority pattern contains a balance of disparate elements of which democracy is an important part (but only a part)" (Eckstein, 1968, p. 122). A Marxian might emphasize the harms of oligarchic power permitted in this *upwardly somewhat incongruent* rather than downwardly democratic formulation of his basic insight.

In an Aristotelian and Hegelian vein, John Dewey stresses the creation of democratic consonance: "In a search for the conditions under which the inchoate public now extant may function democratically, we may proceed from a statement of the nature of the democratic idea in its generic social sense. From the standpoint of the individual, it consists in having a responsible share according to capacity in forming and directing the activities of the groups to which one belongs and in participating according to need in the values which the groups sustain. From the standpoint of the groups, it demands liberation of the potentialities of members of a group in harmony with the interests and goods which are common . . . a good citizen finds his conduct as a member of a political group enriching and enriched by his participation in family life, industry, scientific and artistic associations. There is a free give-and-take: fullness of integrated personality is therefore possible of achievement, since the pulls and responses of different groups reinforce one another and their values accord" (Dewey, 1946, pp. 147–8). Foucault, 1977, pp. 209–10.

[28] In China, other nationwide parties existed but were not effective.

[29] Note that a democratic centralist party can have regular conventions about political stands and elections of leaders with internal suffrage. In the interim, it may adopt a referendum policy on crucial decisions. It may emphasize majoritarian decision by nonparty local or regional assemblies and by national representative ones as well. Particularly given antidemocratic Soviet practice, however, most of these parties tend toward hierarchy and centralism, not democracy.

In addition, particular institutions might also adopt a sharply downwardly congruent, though tiered, structure of decision making. All concerned – staff, students and faculty – could determine central features of the running of an academic institution and its relation to the larger society.[30] Some decisions about academic policy could be made in open meetings but with mainly faculty discussion and suffrage. In addition, as Chinese and American experience suggests, students and teachers could do more of the work that sustains the institution.

Contemporary political scientists have often worried that democracy involves "too many meetings" and may revert to a hierarchy of activists. In fact, such a regime requires only regular, well-publicized meetings, not a particular intensity. Except by vote to secure continuity on important, controversial issues, gatherings could occur, for instance, monthly or bimonthly.[31] Further, based on Chinese experience, a wide democratic structure would require decisions about how to signal the importance of neighborhood-based groups – like village associations – in relation to institution-based ones; for such politics are not – or not mainly – those of particular social institutions, even when they take up wider issues.[32] As centrally important common associations, public assemblies could, for example, meet during *generally specified*, released time from work; institution-based democratic committees could meet more flexibly on time off within a socially determined, normal working day.

As a third, broadly democratic concern, the Chinese revolution focused on *some* dangers of radical hierarchy, particularly abuses of power, and elite status. Among other measures, it sought to combine leadership with periods of manual labor, soldiering with contributions to civilian production, coordination in battle with political discussion. That movement tried to facilitate *mass* criticism, not just intraparty criticism, of the policies and lifestyle of leaders. Participatory investigation into the working and living conditions of ordinary people by activists and mass egalitarian campaigns to assess official responsiveness, it was hoped, would sustain a radical, nonbureaucratized leadership. These institutions were all, to some degree, effective and desirable. As Section 5 suggests, ordinary, independent review bodies could probably have reinforced their goals.

---

[30] Amy Gutmann, 1987, pp. 88–94, provides a nuanced discussion of this issue. Today, even middle-class undergraduate and graduate students ordinarily take campus jobs of many descriptions. Professors sometimes do their own grading, research typing, correspondence, and share in administration. In an overall democratic, antistatus design, such features might help erode a hierarchical structure.

[31] Benjamin Barber, 1984, pp. 270–2, suggests a nonmandatory biweekly meeting schedule alternating an evening and a weekend afternoon.

[32] Mill, 1987, pp. 301–5; Dewey, 1946.

As the following four points suggest, broad criticism and intermittent participation of leaders in productive labor, however, will not, just by themselves, curb abuses. First, though stories in revolutionary newspapers emphasized democratic criticisms, the points were often generic. For instance, when a former employee of a Shanghai boiler factory returned for a month's labor, his fellow workers put up a critical wall poster and commented, "It was not because we had anything against you or because there weren't enough workers. But you used to be a worker like us and now that you're on top, we only see you at official assembly meetings! We don't want you to forget the workers here; . . . When someone becomes a cadre, it should not be for honors or so that he will never have to go back to work. If you don't use a hammer anymore, you will change."[33] Such general criticisms – even those focused on differential status – are no substitute for tracing out particular inadequacies of policy and style; they are more likely to dissuade many people from becoming leaders. As *Fanshen* indicates, popular criticisms were not always abstract reminders or, worse, a vehicle for ignorant suspicions, but they quite often were.[34]

Second, outside of the Cultural Revolution, criticisms from below often affected local rather than national leaders. A general emphasis on learning from experience did not ward off the pathetic "cult of Mao," a mirror of the disease of status idealization in revolutionary socialist regimes.[35]

Third, despite concerns about the dangers of authoritarian – "commandist" – and status-oriented leadership, the Chinese Communists oddly adopted wage differentials within the party. Ultimately, egalitarian political practices toward leaders could not offset the impact of these inequalities.

Fourth, criticism, in the absence of mutual respect, friendship, and detailed knowledge of circumstance and personality, may not be strengthening. In fact, following Kohut's argument, it may sometimes

---

[33] Chesneaux, 1979, pp. 221, 169.   [34] Hinton, 1966, chs. 36–9.

[35] Montaigne's last essay portrayed this illness in Alexander the Great: "I find nothing so humble and so mortal in the life of Alexander as his fantasies about his immortalization. Philotas stung him wittily by his answer. He congratulated him by letter on the oracle of Jupiter Ammon which had lodged him among the gods: 'As far as you are concerned, I am very glad of it; but there is reason to pity the men who will have to live with and obey a man who exceeds and is not content with a man's proportions'" (Montaigne, 1923, 3:450).

"Charismatic" cults of personality are hardly restricted to religions and radical regimes – consider the widespread American adulation of Franklin Delano Roosevelt or, more subtly, the claim by a contemporary political scientist that the public interest *is* the interest of the presidency, that good presidents are "strong" presidents (Huntington, 1969, pp. 24–32).

prey on underlying self-hatred and lack of self-confidence rather than aid the development of individuality. Some might develop considerable skill at affecting self-criticism to avoid relevant criticism (in the idiom of the Cultural Revolution, "waving the red flag to hide the red flag"). As a sophisticated politics – one highly dependent on democratic initiative – revolutionary activity has distinctive social and psychological corruptions.

But friendship is not possible on a broad scale; solidarity and citizenship are weaker, more impersonal bonds. Nonetheless, a combination of friendships characterized by considerable psychological insight among activists and conduct with integrity toward a larger number of people – involving conversation and criticism – must play a central role in the lives of radicals. The political and personal quality of such relationships is an important, not well-studied feature of revolutionary change. Yet refining those Chinese innovations that created public space for assessment of policies and leaders is an important way of facilitating democracy.

As a fourth broad democratic innovation, Chinese strategy incorporated Marx's notion of articulating the "future" of the movement – continuing class conflict to realize the "abolition of the wage system" – within the (socialist) "present." For instance, Mao's *Critique of Soviet Political Economy* distinguished a collective interest – the solidarity of workers that produces material benefits for all – from "material" interest in the sense of competitive advance of some at the expense of others. The Soviet view had mistakenly emphasized the latter. In addition, he gave this common interest an Aristotelian or Marxian interpretation as an intrinsic good, valuable in itself, not just as an instrument. These ideas were connected to Mao's subsequent advocacy of the Paris Commune as an ideal (unfortunately, he opposed the Shanghai Commune at the height of the Cultural Revolution): "hard, bitter struggle, expanded . . . production, the future prospects of communism – these are what have to be emphasized, not material interest. The goal to lead people toward is not 'one spouse, one country home, one automobile, one piano, one television.' "

Critics of revolution had advanced a plodding, antipolitical conception: "A ten thousand league journey begins where you are standing." Emphasizing the integrity and energy of political thinking, Mao vividly responded, "but if you look only at the feet without giving thought to the future, then the question is: what is left of revolutionary excitement and ardor? What energy is left for travelling?"[36]

This dialectical stress on the movement's future suggests a qualitative

---

[36] Mao, 1977, p. 112.

point about communist debate in every institution. As in the Paris Commune, the Great Leap Forward, and the Cultural Revolution, popular deliberations must include such issues as the connection between mutual recognition, status differentials, the potential for reactionary dictatorship, and the phases of communism; the threat of war, dependency, and internationalism; and the like. Soviet factory discussions, restricted to proposals for implementing planning objectives do not, by themselves, qualify as genuinely democratic.[37] Instead, these assemblies would sometimes entertain debate and criticism concerning the political dynamic of a communist regime and its relation to their particular activities; these conversations would fit into a broader framework of public discussion and accountability.

Nonetheless, Mao's stress on mass participation, deliberation, and criticism and the eroding of divisions between manual and mental work renders more exact Marx's admiration of the Commune and his strategy for the movement's future, culminating in the abolition of class and status. I will, however, suggest three further internal radical – and liberal – criticisms of this strategy.

The first focuses on the issue of democratic *individuality*. Mao and activists in the Cultural Revolution sometimes employed a misguided contrast between serving the people and serving self, selfless altruism and predatory egotism. That dichotomy neglects the central distinction of the politics of mutual regard and individuality from the "individualist" advancement of some through the diminution of others. The latter "self-seekers," endlessly striving for money and prestige, are, so to speak, never themselves. But a reasonable alternative is hardly not being a self. Now, the Chinese communist emphasis on social and political aspects of an integrated self and deliberative choice of revolutionary participation often pointed in a humane direction. But a publically acknowledged conception of individuality would have strengthened this tendency; for a self-abnegating emphasis on altruism has often, in liberal as well as radical thinking, underpinned a notion of duty. A more profound conception of obligation, however, arises from a desire to be a certain kind

---

[37] Polan, 1984, pp. 93–4. Nor do the sometimes commendable activities of a directly public organization, the Cuban block "Committees for the Defense of the Revolution," which in the 1970s "handle[d] all sorts of community activity: recycling of bottles and newspapers, political education programs, blood drives for Vietnam, vaccination programs, neighborhood cleanup and repair, local guard duty, volunteer labor projects and . . . undert[ook] discussion of and propose[d] amendments to new social legislation." The latter discussions are a potentially important, democratic interaction of citizenry and leadership, but are not sufficiently broad. As MacEwan's sympathetic account indicates, Cuban politics were overwhelming geared to production and did not challenge status hierarchy (MacEwan, 1975, pp. 77, 74).

of self. More emphasis on the interplay of creating a classless society and individuality would facilitate a differentiated public distinction between what a movement or government may appropriately ask individuals to do in extreme circumstances and ordinary cases in which reasonable requests are sharply limited. Failure to uphold individuality and recognize the integrity of mainly nonpolitical intrinsic goods results in an undertow of moral pathology at war with a movement's democratic features.[38]

The other criticisms focus on weaknesses of Leninist political principle. The second stresses that democracy rests on an atmosphere of respect for differences. Exploitation and war undercut reasoned disagreement in conventional politics; revolutionary parties have often been the bearers of real debate more than prevailing "democratic" ones. Unlike the latter, however, radicals seek to change political life from a realm of domination to one of freedom, to realize the promise of democracy foreshadowed in liberal politics. They are plainly obligated to do more than ordinary parties to further, among their followers, a democratic atmosphere. Yet when Leninist parties change position, they often do not recall and respond to the reasons for a previous stand, but simply recommend the new one. The standard justification for this style is the need to fight for stands in a hostile environment, to achieve political advantage. But this approach encourages servile or solely partisan loyalty toward prevailing positions and narrows space, internally and among potential adherents, for reasoned disagreement. That weakness is reinforced by grandiosity about decisions. Though Mao's *On Practice* argues, in principle, for an ordinary attitude about strengths and weaknesses, communist parties, like conventional ones, frequently proclaim themselves to have been right on all important issues.[39] Further, an acerbic tone about disputes, rooted in Marx, has often reinforced that grandiosity. Starting from the insight that seemingly small political divergences can have large consequences, Marx tended not only to disagree

---

[38] Nagel, 1986a, p. 207. Given clear public needs, this undertow has comparatively little force in crises (strikes, revolutions, wars against fascism) but gradually erodes political unity in ordinary times.

[39] Even in exile, Trotsky's "Their Morals and Ours" insisted on this view: "to a Bolshevik the party is everything. . . . To a revolutionary Marxian there can be no contradiction between personal morality and the interests of the party, since the party embodies in his consciousness the very highest tasks and aims of mankind" (Trotsky, 1963, p. 394).

Actually a decision to join a revolutionary party and an adherence to its policies may involve significant conflicts of goods for many of its members. Important decisions in life often do. William Hinton, 1966, pp. 516–17, 268, describes a particularly brutal conflict and displays a rather callous attitude toward it. Such clashes are likely to be destructive of a democratic atmosphere and individuality only if a party has – as radical parties have often had – an undeveloped view of human psychology that makes moral tension and even internal disagreement troubling rather than acknowledged and normal.

with but to mock opponents;[40] later Marxians, often locked in important political battles, have amplified this rhetoric (Lenin on "revisionists" and "renegades").

Five considerations tell against this odd style. First, as Chapter 10 suggests, radical leaderships – including Marxian ones that pursue too few of the elements of a revolutionary strategy – sometimes develop a political, psychological, and social interest in conservative ideas and are likely to fight for them.[41] If Marxian theory is right, however, many of their followers – and perhaps some leaders – have contrary interests. Although Marxians have often drawn this distinction, they have not sufficiently considered the substantive need to preserve mutual respect across differences among ordinary people and, hence, to be cautious in style. Only an atmosphere respectful of disagreement creates the possibility of democratic conversation and response to broad political criticism from below.[42]

Second, as Marx and many others have recognized, nonradicals and noncommunist radicals have many insights from which Marxians can learn. Third, as a liberal might stress, deficient radical practices are comparatively less harmful during the period of opposition to an oppressive regime. Once in power, however, a grandiose, acerbic style of disagreement by former revolutionaries chills self-confident dissent and debate. Idolization of leaders and intimidation – notably illustrated in the Soviet Union in the 1930s – enforces the reactionary rule of "experts."

Fourth, following the epistemological argument of Part I, if a radical outlook involves learning from the experience of previous movements and self-conscious engagement in political experiments, then the statement and analysis of contending points of view are part of its own development. Marx's differences with Proudhon over unions and socialist parties, Lenin's with the German Social Democratic leadership over the need for antipatriotic opposition to one's own "great power" in World War I or with other Bolsheviks over the prospects for a socialist revolution, and Mao's with the leaders of the Third International over reliance on peasants and the possibilities of Chinese radicalism all instigated advance.[43] These historic changes hardly came from acquiescing in prevailing radical theory and expertise.

[40] Alan Gilbert, 1981a, chs. 4–8, maintains that criticisms of Marx's style, which neglect the relevant political issues are misguided; once the point of his critique of other radicals is acknowledged, however, these objections capture an important truth.

[41] Schorske, 1972, pp. 108–10; Miliband, 1969, ch. 6; Gilbert, 1979.

[42] The blunting of radicalism that accompanies acquiescence in the prevailing ideas or, in postrevolutionary times, "technocracy" unfortunately often hinders such respect; "moderates" are often vitriolic about "extremists" and "ultraleftists." Chapter 12 analyzes Weber's influential version of this undemocratic "ethic of responsibility."

[43] Gilbert, 1976b, 1979, 1981a.

Lively debates are part of intelligent policy making in any movement; the more serious the party, one might say, the more thoroughgoing and participatory the conversation. If scientific realism is right, a presentation of major changes of position with a full statement of reasons and straightforward, less hostile treatment of disagreements would be a marked improvement. This epistemological argument strengthens core democratic standards long articulated by liberal and radical critics of absolutism and merely formal democracies. How deeply a revolutionary outlook – given twentieth-century experience – is a war mentality can be seen in the fact that this approach would be an innovation rather than a matter of course.

Fifth, the foregoing considerations underline the lack, among Marxians, of an explicit democratic theory. Here the Rawlsian idea of overlapping consensus on democratic autonomy articulates the basis of radical unity; for given ruling-class-propagated antiradical ideology and the political weaknesses just described, many radicals as well as nonradicals fear that revolutionaries have "other aims" in view, partisan ones opposed to the best interests of their allies.[44] Now, strikes and democratic revolutions against fascism, colonialism, and capitalism all have strong, morally unifying features. So does advocacy of internationalism and a classless society; for the latter positions stress the kind of unity – an inclusive, democratic one – that radicals envision. Yet a new regime must strengthen these commonalities. Rawls's conception of publically articulated democratic autonomy is a *political theory* of unity underlying particular goals. It looks to a social order in which each person is free to elaborate her own comprehensive conception of the good. Democratic commonality rests on the recognition of each participant as a free citizen, capable of self-determination and having an equal say about the political and social conditions under which it will occur. Given the truth of controversial Marxian social theory claims, that common good can be fully realized only, in the *Manifesto's* phrase, in a – classless and statusless – *free association*. On a Rawlsian account, communism realizes the equal regard among persons or democratic autonomy adumbrated in political liberalism.

These five considerations require a nonhierarchical, nondomineering style of radical politics. They raise doubts, to be explored in Section 5, about any single-party system, no matter how much prevailing practice is altered.

As a third, broad, internal criticism, democratic centralist parties, following the Soviet example, have often taken far-ranging positions, extending from central political issues to the arts and personal life. As

---

[44] For an account of antiradical ideology, see Chapter 12, Section 4.

Rawlsian theory suggests, however, these stands often intrude on comprehensive conceptions of good, undercutting individuality; for the political and economic goals of revolution concerning the abolition of classes, democratic autonomy, and internationalism are far clearer, on a radical view, than these other stands. In fact, the latter positions discourage diversity and individuality. Few can acquire subtle knowledge of elaborate positions in disparate areas. Whatever the quality of original debates, such positions are unlikely to be thoughtfully defended by members; they curb spontaneity and particular insight. A few general, legal restrictions, say about advocacy and practice of overt racism, still apply; otherwise, political issues in the arts and personal life can only be reasonably resolved by informed conversation within them.[45] Further, as religious radicals from Thomas Münzer to John Brown to today's liberation theologians and base communities show, Christian ethics can be consistent with Marxian – or even more leftist – social conclusions. Though many radicals are atheists, a revolutionary regime would appropriately adopt a similar policy with regard to freedom of religion.[46]

A Marxian might claim that conceptions of culture and personal life fostered in the public life of liberal (capitalist) democracies are not notably more sophisticated than those propounded by revolutionary parties. But lesser-evil – if, indeed, the evils of radical intervention are *lesser* – extenuations are not telling. Even inadvertent checks to external political involvement – forging space for individuality – are often an improvement.[47] Ideally, radical parties would advance democracy by restricting

---

[45] Demand 13 of Marx's and Engels's March 1848 "Demands of the German Communists" affirms the liberal commitment to separate church and state "completely."

Chapter 9 will emphasize the existence of radical Protestant movements as counterexamples to Weberian claims about the unique social effect of a Reformation ethic.

In a radical regime, despite a decent policy on freedom of conscience, relations with particular religions might be charged with tension and some practices restricted. In so far as organized churches gain wealth from capitalism, or previously from serfdom, revolutions have curtailed their power. One might model an illustration of a difficult conflict of goods on a recent situation in Nicaragua: Although some priests are heavily involved in the Sandinista movement, other elements in the Catholic Church oppose antisexist policies (Rosset and Vandenmeer, 1986, pp. 440–53, 480–1). With regard to basic social and political equality, the latter stand is undemocratic. Let us imagine, hypothetically, the sexism to be intense, to undermine the effectiveness of democracy for most people in circumstances of external attack. If at all possible, radicals should still want to alter such policies through discussion; yet even a sharp legal containment of some practices – if not otherwise counterproductive – would not affect the truth, and need not undercut the plural practice, of religions.

[46] Given the complexity of the human good and the importance of individuality, these realms especially require a varied conversation, not a single voice. The appropriate political unity sustains that diversity. See also R. Miller, 1986a, pp. 69–71.

[47] Since Montesquieu, 1961, bks. 11, 12, this claim has been the central, powerful argument of liberal theories of political institutions and constitutional design (Walzer, 1984).

their common stands to central political issues and encouraging diversity in other spheres.

4. Extreme democracy as a challenge to Chinese status and political hierarchy

Most social scientists and today's "modernizing" Chinese and Soviet regimes ignore positive features of revolutionary history. In this context, it is worthwhile stressing that not only does the Chinese experience provide some grounds for a democratic defense of communism, but millions of workers, peasants, and students sought, against Communist Party leadership, to extend existing democratic practices. For instance, radicals in the Great Leap Forward sought to reinforce an egalitarian pay system and opposed differentials among communists; in Shanghai, in February 1967, at the height of the Cultural Revolution, a demonstration of a million workers demanded a governmental structure modeled on the Paris Commune.[48]

In these cases, an Aristotelian "extreme democracy" dialectically challenged the inadequacies of socialism.[49] On a radical view, this communist egalitarianism is the most consistent rendering of the historic democratic questioning of political and status hierarchy. As I have emphasized, that critique originated in the Greek polis and became a political force in the emergence of communism in the French Revolution, Marx's strategy for Germany in 1848, the Paris Commune, and the Russian and Chinese revolutions. A modern political and ethical way of reading the Marxian claim about the centrality of class struggle in history insists that the recognition of a general capacity for moral personality in particular political, legal, and social forms legitimizes further claims against social inequality. In the *Manifesto*'s phrase, the latter seek "to win the battle of democracy."[50]

---

[48] One needs to distinguish radical aspects of the Cultural Revolution from xenophobic ones.

[49] Popular movements in many countries have generated ideas of "extreme" democracy. As a new democracy without a feudal background and with an illegitimate slaveholding one, the United States has been a laboratory for such ideas. In contrast to many other experiences, American radicalisms have suggested diverse interconnections of egalitarian democracy and individuality. Consider John Brown, Henry David Thoreau, Walt Whitman, Eugene Debs, The IWW, CIO, SNCC, SDS – to mention only a few individuals and movements (Kateb, 1983; 1984, pp. 178–83).

[50] Marx and Engels 1974, p. 52. John Dewey's view of democracy traces a similar working out of an idea whose historical causes are diverse and whose logic goes beyond particular realizations (Dewey, 1946, pp. 144–5, 148–9). The argument of Chapter 1 provides a more objective, Hegelian underpinning for these claims than Dewey's striking but quasi-relativist translation of Hegel into a democratic idiom.

Yet the Chinese Communist leadership repudiated the most radical consequences of a "Maoist" vision, notably the Shanghai Commune, on the basis of singularly "un-Maoist" arguments. For instance, Mao told two Shanghai leaders that this commune would spread and the People's Republic would have to be renamed. Though an advocate of self-reliance in difficult circumstances, he oddly queried, "Would others recognize us? Maybe the Soviet Union would not recognize us whereas Britain and France would." [51] After fierce conflicts, the Communist Party suppressed the radical movement. As subsequent developments have revealed, its comparatively left-wing version of socialism led not toward but away from communism.

Thus, the foregoing argument is a dialectical critique of Chinese leadership including Mao, based on Marxian theory and mass revolutionary activity, not a claim that one or another leadership group "incarnated" radical principle. [52] Ironically, Mao's clearest defense of revolutionary politics occurs in a work that stresses the putative necessity of the "law of value" against the left. Following the Marxian insistence on learning from revolutionary practice, however, one might invoke Chinese experience to criticize the law of value, status hierarchy, and the undercutting of revolutionary democracy.

Marx's *Critique of the Gotha Program* maintained that socialist justice – the principle of equal pay for equal work according to a suitable labor-time standard – would realize the promise of bourgeois justice (overcome the contradiction between this form and its previous exploitative content), yet engender considerable social inequalities. As Chapter 7 shows, he inadequately characterized the predominance of a desert standard over one of need as simply "a defect"; for given previous forms of special oppression – racism, sexism, enforced lack of skill – unchecked by compensatory, internationalist policies, the law of value ("bourgeois right") would perpetuate differences in income and status between men and women, citizens of a (comparatively) advantaged nationality and those of other nationalities, skilled and unskilled workers, and so forth. Further, the larger *historical experience* of such inequalities in socialism – the generalized, corrupting effect of renewed status hierarchy on liberty and political power – is, from a radical point of view, even more troubling. A modern Marxian theoretical argument, refined by eudaemonist psychological insights about the self, illuminates this history: Socialism leads, economically and politically, to the dominion of one-sided, marketable working capacity, driven by status seeking, over the flourishing

---

[51] Meisner, 1977, pp. 327, 321–2; Bettelheim, 1978, pp. 100–107; Mao, 1977, p. 278.
[52] A misguided cult of personality has haunted many Marxian interpretations of the reversal of socialism.

of individuality. It encourages the reemergence of an oppressive regime. This theoretical and historical argument clarifies the basis for Marx's original concern.

Thus, a communist policy of equal incomes becomes a powerful Marxian alternative. Note again that this proposal does not wholly abolish the market: There remains an area in which individual choices strongly affect particular lines of production. What it does transcend, however, is market-based differential incomes and status inequalities. It emphasizes a sphere for the healthy development of individuality and strengthens a modern democratic variant of the Commune.[53] The political consensus surrounding this egalitarian policy would oppose both the despotic consequences of significant inequalities *and* any overly *social* notion of leveling.[54] Paradoxically, if some version of Marxian political theory is true, then, within the idea of "social individuality," it is the element of *individuality,* shared by liberals and radicals, that dialectically motivates egalitarian distributive policies rather than the (mainly) social aspect.

Distinctively political and ethical claims play a fundamental role in the general dialectic of Marxian strategy and historical explanation. Given the broad change from prehistory to fully human history, they do so especially in the achievement and sustaining of communism. A left-wing socialist regime could minimize the use of wage differentials, especially in the party and government. It could also launch more thoroughgoing campaigns to undercut differentials between women and men and between nationalities based on those of earlier socialist regimes and cultivate lively political association more strongly than the Chinese Communists did. Persisting in such policies, that regime might far surpass the democracy of previous socialist practice.

Yet even a left-wing socialism would probably be a now covert, now open war between revolutionary elements and those that breed a strongly inegalitarian, procapitalist mentality. After all, differentials in the party extend normal, extraparty, market practices. If such inequalities are so essential for noncommunists, why should communists "suffer"? An economic determinist emphasis has made cooperation wildly contingent on the level of productivity. But if human insight, accumulated knowledge, political experience, and mutual respect are going to

---

[53] Robert Dahl has defended worker self-management on *democratic grounds:* "The best economic order would help to generate a distribution of political resources favorable to the goals of voting equality, effective participation, enlightened understanding, and final control of the political agenda by all adults subject to the law." These criteria might also justify equal incomes (Dahl, 1985, pp. 84–5, 105–7).

[54] This defense of equal incomes opposes what Marxians have traditionally called "absolute egalitarianism," but not from a status-furthering direction (Hinton, 1966).

play a larger role, why shouldn't cooperation flourish, as a Rawlsian might suggest, in quite moderate economic circumstances?

Radical governments have failed to distinguish (fairly) highly central-ized versions of the dictatorship of the proletariat and emergency exec-utive powers, sometimes justifiable in situations of regime-threatening external attack, and the normal need to guarantee democratic rule. Prima facie, an egalitarian policy of distribution according to need – equal incomes – should provide more leeway for communist democracy and undercut authoritarianism. The next section will sketch further in-novations that radical movements might adopt.

5. How *radical* is radical democracy?

In fact, the earlier criticisms of democratic centralist practice, a liberal might contend, imply that party competition and division of powers – perhaps within the framework of moving toward the abolition of classes – might often further genuine democracy. Now, the most obvious, attrac-tive radical response to this liberal objection, is, *given a revolutionary set-ting*, to grant it; for the greatest paradox of twentieth-century radical politics is that the centralized policy assessment and leadership, useful in the repressive, prerevolutionary period to instigate democratic pro-test, has not been easily democratized. Though liberal measures have often accompanied oligarchy, the radical might say, in a postrevolution-ary phase, these features might work in tandem with others to secure democracy.[55]

But radicals might recommend the adoption of two additional kinds of measures. First, they may insist on strong democratic principles – say, referenda on important issues, publically supported, decentralized ac-cess to media, and perhaps proportional representation of parties in a legislature. These measures are designed to elicit informed citizen par-ticipation on major policies. The point about proportional representa-tion presses toward a counterimage of the revolutionary process to the modified one-party, local and institutional democracy envisioned in the preceding section. It combines the downward congruence of that au-thority structure with a multiparty national system. The vigor of the lo-cal institutions, not the competition of parties, would be the pivotal fea-ture of – and thus a commonality in – an effective democratic regime.

Second, democracy, on this view, is a process of reflection and debate,

---

[55] In the absence of a broad revolutionary movement, Edward Greenberg, 1986, ch. 6, has shown that members of U.S. plywood cooperatives have adopted reactionary political conclusions compared with ordinary factory workers. Contrary to the expectations of some participatory democratic theorists, isolated institutional measures do not have rad-ical consequences.

not reliance on hasty popular decisions or those of prevailing political organizations; for such decisions may not – even when they are right – be politically contested, informed ones. In this regard, radicals may draw upon the resources of liberal and Aristotelian theory to check arbitrary uses of power and produce a stable general will or common good. For example, Marxians have often – at least nominally – acknowledged the importance of an independent judiciary.[56] Their criticisms of judicial bias – say, the longer sentences of blacks than whites, other factors being equal, in the United States – reveal the corrupting influence of class and status inequalities. But such claims sustain the good of fair judicial proceedings, ones reflective, in Railton's idiom, of social rationality or, in Rawls's conception, autonomy. A radical might then endorse a panoply of legal protections: an independent judiciary, the American Miranda ruling, prohibition of "unreasonable searches and seizures," assumption of innocence until proven guilty, habeas corpus, trial by jury, confrontation of witnesses, exclusion of "cruel and unusual punishment," and the like.[57]

This section will explore seven measures that might strengthen both the democracy and the durability of radical policies. Many of these measures are less novel than that of equal incomes; so are, comparatively speaking, the arguments that justify them. What is original in this conception is a detachment of both measures and arguments from liberal or Aristotelian settings and a stress on how they are consistent, once revolution has occurred, with a radical regime. They attend, where Marxians often have not, to political theory and institutional design. To have a democratic effect, however, at least a substantial subset of the following measures would have to be implemented.[58]

First, a general way to balance power is to make sure that constitutional limits on arbitrariness are well formulated and that impartial bod-

---

[56] The USSR has a "Bill of Rights." As Soviet experience attests, without an appropriate background of radical institutions and democratic practices, formal guarantees of impartiality would be corrupted by socialist status, class, and political hierarchy.

[57] On a more thoroughgoing account, a radical would want to limit the character-savaging characteristic of "adversarial" trial proceedings, which is harmful to individuality. She might emphasize mediation by neighborhood or regional association over, say, reliance on expert jurists, let alone psychologically behaviorist Soviet counseling. Nothing in the core claim forbids quite extensive modification of prevailing practice.

[58] The following proposals suppose the existence of an elected legislature – probably on a straight representative by population basis – and an executive, with only a few further specifications (policy review by legislature, proportional representation, and the like). Similar bodies and checks might exist for regional or provincial government. For the purposes of this argument, only measures that point toward greater, more deliberated democracy need emphasis. Branko Horvat, 1982, chs. 10–12 offers other organizational proposals.

ies enforce them. An independent judiciary, as already noted, is needed for the protection of personal liberties.[59] Others might be committees to review policy, oversee freedom of communications and debate, and supervise the fairness of referenda and elections for office. None of these bodies would have legislative or executive powers. Instead, they would have negative powers of investigating and publicizing abuses and sometimes constitutionally specified authority to stop them.

Selection for such bodies has to encourage their independence; it might have four possible origins.[60] Policy-investigating committees are characteristic of parliamentary regimes; in any multiparty setting, committees that reflect that diversity would be a natural check. At least the other committees mentioned, however, need greater isolation from executive and ordinary political influence. Two further vehicles of selection are, again, conventional liberal democratic ones: special elections or long-term appointment without recall (except for crimes).

Selection by lot might serve as another mechanism, particularly for local oversight bodies. As Benjamin Barber has emphasized, lot-generated juries give ordinary citizens experience in judging from a public point of view. Out of qualified individuals, partial selection by

---

[59] Montesquieu, 1961, 11–12, presents an unsurpassed justification of judicial independence. Gilbert, 1986a, b.

Advancing an overly vigorous criticism of Marx, Allen Buchanan, 1986, pp. 142–3, has appropriately pointed to the following values embodied in constitutional protection of rights, "none of which presupposes class conflicts or even egotism": "(1) as constraints on democratic procedures (e.g., for the protection of minorities) or as guarantees of access to participation in democratic procedures, i.e. as safeguards against anti-democratic, elite control; (2) as constraints on paternalism, i.e., as limits on when and how we may interfere with a person's liberty for the sake of benefiting that person (where benefit is understood as welfare or freedom or some combination of these); (3) as constraints on what may be done (and how it may be done) to maximize social welfare, or some other specification of the common good, such as freedom; (4) as safeguards constraining the ways in which coercion or other penalties may be used in the provision of public goods; and, (5) as a way of specifying the scope or limits of our obligations to provide for future generations."

[60] In analyzing the Commune, Marx called for an elected and recallable judiciary rather than an appointed one. He argued against "sham independence" from bourgeois interests but did not specify how genuine impartiality would be obtained. More strikingly, in *Capital*, he styled Leonard Horner, factory inquiry commissioner and inspector, a republican "censor of manufacturers," who relentlessly protested against brutal conditions in the name of a common good: "His services to the working class will never be forgotten." Here Marx appealed to possibilities of public independence, which, though particular and insufficient under capitalism, might be generalized in a more cooperative society. In political theory, however, he failed to draw the appropriate broad distinction between mechanisms that might further a deliberated democratic will and those that secure a transient aggregation of votes (Marx and Engels, 1974, pp. 290–91; Marx, 1977, 1:334, 351, 397, 402, 538–9, 553).

this method, in the context of additional criteria to ensure diversity, might be appropriate for even a regional communications commission or judicial body.[61] Prima facie, such a procedure would be better than political appointment.

In general, the aim of a democratic political life is to ensure a diverse conversation about a common good. Illustrations of that conversation should be present in review bodies; the criteria for their composition should guarantee that if particular procedures, say election and lot, yield too uniform a group, they would be supplemented. Here as elsewhere, skill in constitutional design and wide public discussion would be essential to work out relevant details.

As a second measure to further the democracy but also the durability of opinion on important issues, a radical regime might require an annual series of referenda and/or initiatives. Given the massive threat to life of war and today of nuclear extinction, the main focus of referenda would be international. Radical regimes, like conventional ones, have often treated foreign policy as a state prerogative. In twentieth-century experience, however, ordinary people rarely desire to go to war; their alleged lack of "policy expertise" is compensated by a comparative good sense and decency that can sustain *democratic internationalism.*[62] With modern communications technology, a popular check on major military initiatives would require immediate, preferably preliminary discussion in local political assemblies and verdict by referendum. Fearing swift assessment, some would argue, leaders might be overly hesitant to use force to defend democratic interests. But a radical might respond, given the overwhelming injustice of most wars launched by great powers, and the criminal means, murderous of civilians, of modern war, all the better to curb politicians; better to err on the side of caution. Although unrestricted leadership may have the advantage of surprise attack, democratic interests will not often be sacrificed for want of initial, deceptive strategy.[63]

---

[61] In contrast, the selection of long-term members of comparatively centralized review bodies probably requires election and/or legislative review.

[62] Lifton and Falk, 1982, chs. 6–8, 11; Gilbert, 1978b; Thoreau, 1981, p. 416. Here, Aristotle's historic democratic claim that nothing prevents a collective from being more insightful than an expert deserves to be reinforced (Aristotle, *Politics,* 1281b1–10).

Today's descriptions of liberal democratic politics emphasize how little campaigns deal with issues. On a Marxian view, that is a sign of their alienation, their crippling by elite interests. Even so, in the United States, famous Democrats like Woodrow Wilson and Lyndon Johnson ran as peacekeepers or peacemakers; the public voted intelligently but had no control over what their elected leaders did.

[63] In a democratic internationalist vein, John Rawls, 1971, pp. 381–2, stresses the injustice of most wars waged by such powers to justify civil disobedience, conscientious refusal, and a contingent pacifism in which "the possibility of a just war is conceded but not

But how, a critic might ask, could this democratic organization ever wage war? Surely divided votes on referenda, especially in military units, would undercut a war effort; military authoritarianism is a necessity. Quite the contrary, a radical might insist: A democracy could vote, by majority, for policies that would be carried out legally throughout the relevant institutions. (In this sense, all democratic governments practice "democratic centralism.") Soldiers who had participated in serious discussion, facilitating comparatively precise mutual understanding of the purposes and limits of war, would be more likely to fight, even if, as individuals, they disagreed. If teenagers can die for their country, why can't they – being "all that they can be" – discuss the policies themselves? Such practices would probably rule out characteristic great-power adventures such as U.S. aggression in Vietnam or that of the Soviets in Afghanistan.

In addition, an internationalist might emphasize the danger of belligerent foreign policies short of war, particularly military and police aid and officer training for repressive governments. Most importantly, they harm innocents – civilians – in other countries; further, as Aristotle and Montesquieu stress, such expansionism nurtures antidemocratic forces and practices at home. Referenda on major executive initiatives, with a comparatively short period of debate, might limit these harms.[64]

A radical regime could also use more structured referenda for internal policy issues. The aim of these referenda in Rousseau's idiom would be to ensure a durable *general will* through political discussion, not to elicit a particular *will of all*.[65] Benjamin Barber has suggested an attractive format, based on American experience. Each referendum might have two,

---

under present circumstances." Referenda are especially appropriate in great powers. More leeway for executive action might be constitutionally allowed in small, less industrially developed and potentially domineering regimes because its use would, more likely, be confined to "supreme" emergencies (Walzer, 1977, pp. 251–62). Constitutions in large states could allow some emergency executive powers to respond to *palpably* regime-threatening aggression.

[64] Illicit Reagan administration and congressional aid to the Contras against even a public opinion comparatively uninformed about the historical pattern of U.S. repressive interests and the present brutality of its minions is a classic example (Lafeber, 1984; Chomsky and Hermann, 1979). J. Cohen and Rogers, 1985, nicely links aggression and domestic cutbacks.

Binding referenda on war and military aid, *just by themselves*, would make an enormous difference in contemporary U.S. foreign policy. The interests sustained by U.S. policy, however, though narrow, are powerful; the institution of war referenda could not be effectively adopted just by itself. Even at the height of the anti-Vietnam War movement, the McGovern–Hatfield amendment – which would have left U.S. troops there for eighteen additional months, with possible presidential extension for another nine – had no hope of passing Congress.

[65] Rousseau, 1964, 3:373–4.

possibly even three, readings, at six-month intervals, to permit full debate and reverse hasty decisions. It would be multichoice, with special attention to issues – say abortion – in which competing, though minority, claims could generate considerable social dissension. The alternatives could include qualified "no" votes by people who, in principle, favor a measure but not at current social costs, or call for different phrasing of the suggested law.[66] Reiterated posing, increasingly sensitive to nuance, objection, and revision, would facilitate a more informed, relevant debate. Reinforcing the politics of an original revolutionary movement, a repeated process of this kind would create a vastly more sophisticated democratic public.[67]

The number of referenda per year might ordinarily be limited to, say, three major foreign policy initiatives and three (new) domestic ones. Other issues could be handled in the legislature or by the executive with legislative review. Discussions on referenda would ordinarily occur in neighborhood, rather than work-related, assemblies.

As a third broad measure to further democracy, a referendum policy requires great changes in communication. Rawls, Habermas, Dahl, and Barber among others have emphasized that an ideal, noncoercive democratic setting is one in which deliberators have access to the relevant information. A radical regime might adopt three policies to further this atmosphere. First, Rawls, Cohen, and Rogers have suggested public funding of parties.[68] To ensure access to information, however, the government might also fund diverse groups on particular issues; for focused debate on issues, not party mechanisms to select governmental leaders, is the nub of democratic politics. In fact, as Branko Horvat has sug-

---

[66] Benjamin Barber marshals American evidence to refute standard elitist criticisms. He suggests that "the range of options would include: yes in principle – strongly for the proposal; yes in principle – but not a first priority; no in principle – strongly against the proposal; no with respect to this formulation – but not against the proposal in principle, suggest reformulation and resubmission; and no for the time being – although not necessarily opposed in principle, suggest postponement" (Barber, 1984, pp. 281–9). He also emphasizes democratic uses of an interactive television format for some debates.

[67] Following John Stuart Mill, 1987, pp. 301–19, a democratic citizenry might institute public voting on referenda in place of the privatizing secret ballot. Mill was concerned with a political culture that nurtured a sense of individual responsibility for a common good. As he argued, if voting is about competitive, private advantage, why shouldn't votes be sold? (Teuber, 1986).

Citizens might entertain this practice for candidates as well. It would be more appropriate in a multiparty setting, more dangerous in a single party one.

[68] Rawls, 1971, pp. 225–6. Thomas Ferguson, 1983, pp. 65, 77, offers the interesting suggestion that each adult have a tax-deductible – or government subsidized – equal amount to be used only for political contributions. Such a vote makes *individual* suffrage more effective. But public funding would work only in a more radical setting than these authors envision (J. Cohen and Rogers, 1983, pp. 153–4).

Though socially quite conservative, the Nicaraguan revolutionary government is self-

339

gested, a postrevolutionary decline of social conflict might result in the decay of parties; shifting issue-oriented committees might ultimately become characteristic of a genuinely plural political life.[69]

In repressive, prerevolutionary society, democratic movements do not have "friends in high places" and need to rely on the financial support of ordinary people. Postrevolutionary policy might combine a perhaps quite substantial minimum subsidy – not a "matching fund" – with an expectation that organizations raise money based on popular support.[70]

Second, the regime should ensure diversity of points of view in the communications media themselves.[71] Here, the oversight committee mentioned above would play an important role.

Third, however, noncoercive communication means the elimination of persecution by race, nationality, and sex. Marked organizing against democracy would be checked. Though Cohen and Rogers do not support such limitations, they state the relevant criterion:

> The Principle of Democratic Legitimacy does not specify an initial starting point from which any departures are legitimate if they are made from that point according, for example, to a requirement of majority rule. It specifies a *standing requirement* of an ongoing order, and thus requires that democratic conditions be preserved over time. Insofar as the PDL requires polit-

---

consciously politically innovative. According to Michael Parenti, 1986b, pp. 48–9, seven parties easily qualified for funding and equal media time in the 1984 election; in contrast, the U.S. government sets previous vote qualifications so high that only two parties can qualify. (A party must get, for example, 5 percent of the national vote – millions of votes – to receive the funding that would enable it to make its positions widely known.) See also Rosset and Vandermeer, 1986, pp. 5, 8, 365–6.

[69] Branko Horvat's (1982, pp. 320–2, 508) call for the outlawing of parties would, however, be counterproductive. Some (democratized) overall party leadership and a perhaps lengthy period of transition to a varying plurality of issue-oriented committees would be needed.

[70] This is a minimal feature of what Mill commends as "braving labor and danger" to develop a resilient democratic will (Mill, 1859, 3:238–63; Walzer, 1977, p. 88).

[71] Barber, 1984, pp. 277–81; Parenti, 1986a. In the contemporary American media, no one who holds a radical view – for instance, that American foreign policy is systematically antidemocratic in the less developed countries and that democratic internationalism is desirable, or that given capitalism, ordinary people lose out from both current industrial policy and suggested "corporative," "reindustrializing" modifications – could write a regular column or "host" a talk show. In contrast, a radical regime should encourage systematic advocates of varied versions, of, say, socialism, communism, democracy, less government (anarchy), and the like – as well as proponents of diverse perspectives on particular policies – to make their views public. Such a regime might adopt a democratic qualification based on representation in the population; yet it should also recognize that serious debate involves articulated clashes of opinions, and thus not restrict subsidized communications to leading contemporary options. In a radical democracy, beyond upholding individuality, the future should not be governed by the present (Williams, 1985, pp. 172–73). An analogous approach would ensure diversity in education.

ical liberties, it requires that those liberties by preserved. If they are not preserved, then the order is no longer democratic, and therefore the denial of such liberties is itself undemocratic, since such denial violates the very principles which make the existing procedures of social choice legitimate. Once the principle of individual liberties is violated, then individuals no longer retain their status as participants in an order of equal freedom.[72]

On democratic grounds, this argument constitutionally disqualifies advocacy of and policy based on racism, sexism, slaveholding, brutalization of immigrants, and perhaps large-scale capitalism – practices that deny mutual recognition and the capacity for individuality to large sections of the population. A radical regime requires impartiality *within a democratic framework*; it proscribes explicitly antidemocratic, partial, tyrannical movements.[73] In Rawls's idiom, the realization of equal regard and political autonomy limits permissible conceptions of the good.[74] Yet liberals rightly worry, as we saw in Chapter 7, that such restrictions, though directed against justifiable targets, might impede free discussion. To accommodate this criticism, a Marxian might note, the term "overt" must be specified to mean *very* overt. Public discussion, not rule by communications committee veto or judicial enforcement, should check comparatively subtle, though noxious stereotypes that lead to overt organizing. That political conversation would compare the antidemocratic, intimidating costs of racism and other exclusionary ideologies to those of compromising freedom of speech. Well-specified radical attempts to move swiftly from any emergency restrictions to normal institutional rule might check abuses standard in contemporary revolutionary socialism. Even in the best of circumstances, however, some conflict of goods is probably unavoidable.

As a fourth broad democratic measure, a radical regime should culti-

---

[72] Cohen and Rogers, 1983, p. 160, make the same point about a "requirement of distributional equality," and affirm a Rawlsian difference principle; if the foregoing argument is right, their claim would sustain equal incomes. G. Dworkin, 1975, clarifies the justification of universal but "nonneutral" principles.

[73] Such groups might go the way of advocates of slaveholding but not without difficulty. After all, in the nonfeudal United States, whose "Declaration of Independence," proclaimed each individual's natural right to "life, liberty and the pursuit of happiness," it took a Civil War after nearly a century, and a civil rights movement yet another century later, not to mention international antifascist and anticolonial conflicts, to limit legalized racism.

A century and a quarter ago, Lincoln was keenly aware of the fundamental international harm done to the Declaration and the contemporary novelty of American democratic institutions by the legalization or toleration of such practices: "I hate it [Douglas's indifference to slavery] because of the monstrous injustice of slavery itself. I hate it because it . . . enables the enemies of free institutions, with plausibility, to taunt us as hypocrites" (Oates, 1984, p. 73–4).

[74] Rawls, 1988a.

vate respect for civil disobedience, strikes, and other forms of peaceful or conscientious objection about major public issues. On a Marxian argument, such protests do not – or do not easily – change policies within an oligarchic democracy. But they should have more effect in a radical one. Further, given its emphasis on individuality, a radical regime should expect and tolerate such activities more easily than previous liberal ones.[75] In fact, short of harm to persons, acts of civil disobedience on major issues, especially concerning war, should go unpunished. (A defense of sustaining a greater moral good should be routine.) Such an approach contrasts with the intolerance of protest common on contemporary economic determinist views of socialism. Yet only such a stance might ultimately undercut the necessity of nonelectoral resistance.

Fifth, democracy requires the abolition – or, if not, the dramatic weakening – of centralized police organizations with quasi-secret, interventionary authority. The ideal of civil association is inconsistent with widespread surveillance and harassment; so is that of Marxian social individuality.[76]

Internally, a policy of civilian security run through local organizations – a neighborhood rather than "national" guard – coupled with military training for some and the organized, widespread bearing of arms could lead to democratic law enforcement. This same association could serve as an arena for political discussion – for instance, on referenda – and would have an important share of governing power. In addition, neighborhood associations – or perhaps regional ones – might organize dispute mediation in civil cases.

Given democratic internationalism, the foreign policy activities of "intelligence" agencies should be mainly public and geared to gathering information; outside of rare cases requiring humanitarian intervention or those of "supreme emergency," the regime should bar "covert action." In contrast, following great-power "realist" strategies, the America CIA, as in Guatemala and Chile, often releases "disinformation" and instigates authoritarian movements as do its counterparts.[77] If a statesman wishes to pursue undemocratic policies, then, of course, such an insti-

---

[75] Rawls, 1971, sec. 55–9; Thoreau, 1981, pp. 429–32, 435, 446–7; Kateb, 1984, pp. 141–6.
[76] Oakeshott, 1975, third essay.
[77] "Supreme emergency" includes threat of nuclear war and *might* license *insightful* efforts, based on a genuine nonaggressive policy, to win the population of a menacing nuclear power to oppose aggression.

John McCamant, 1984; Chomsky and Hermann, 1977. Concerned with moral unmasking and truthtelling, contemporary international relations "realists" often reject the "follies" and "excesses" of interventions but do not articulate their harm to democracy. Nearly all realists, for example, opposed the Vietnam War as a "mistake" (Morganthau, 1973, pp. 7–8; Krasner, 1978, pp. 319–26).

tution would be highly useful. But liberal and radical purposes can be accomplished without nefarious, deceptive foreign intervention.[78]

Sixth, within this argument, a sketch of radical institutions must be quite limited. Nonetheless, the organization of the armed forces is clearly a central issue. Military preparedness, for defensive purposes, would also rest on an army drawn from ordinary citizens. Perhaps at the age of eighteen, each person would have to contribute two years of public service, either in military training and some social projects or, if committed to nonviolence, in community activities outside one's own locale. Note that discussion and – at least on many issues – decision making would be an important feature of such institutions; democratic military leadership need not mimic the sordid hierarchy of standing armies. Given the harmful purposes and remarkably authoritarian structure of today's military, notions of "public" service have, justifiably, fallen into popular disrepute. But the idea of such service is an important democratic one. It requires some recognition of the need for basic social cooperation by each citizen.

In the early period of a revolution, as part of its aim to secure a new social and political framework, a radical party would be particularly influential in the military. With equal incomes, much of the status accorded an officer corps would be eliminated. Further, the exploitation of specially oppressed groups, forced through educational discrimination and disproportionate unemployment to be frontline soldiers, would cease. Radical policy should swiftly aim to make the military as democratic and civilian as possible. Today, military leaders by and large see their vocation – and possibilities for upward mobility – in war; perversely from that standpoint, a new regime might focus the role of such leadership on peace, internationalism, and the maintenance of an egalitarian, democratic social structure.

Military organizations would balance the need for some permanent expert leadership with democratic considerations. For instance, units could have technical specialists who conduct particular aspects of training, but temporary (say, for period of service, unless recalled) elected leaders. Elections would presumably occur after "basic training" in which soldiers had some chance to get to know each other.

To the extent nuclear and other massively destructive weapons had not previously been sharply restricted, the selection and leadership of units involved with them would have to be more specialized and long-

---

[78] Herbert Lüthy admirably captures the antidemocratic impact, domestically, of foreign expansion: "The Empire was something with which the French people had nothing whatever to do, and its story was that of machinations of high finance, the Church and the military caste, which tirelessly re-erected overseas the Bastilles which had been overthrown in France" (Lüthy, 1975, p. 205).

lasting, though they could still be democratically organized. Higher leadership could be elected partly by soldiers, partly – for the highest authority, like the American "commander in chief" – by civilians. Terms would be limited. Given the external threat of war involving such weapons, the isolation of radical democracy to one or perhaps a few countries would be a difficult issue. The first such regimes could probably pursue a course of serving as a political example, hoping to make the costs of external attack, both in their own and in domestic resistance within the potential aggressor, too great.[79]

Now, a critic might wonder whether such a regime could influence the adoption of more decent political forms in hostile powers through, as it were, aggressively "democratic" internationalism and minimize this threat. But once again, a radical might emphasize the primacy of resistance movements internal to them. Today, given harsh odds reinforced by external intervention, such movements often debate taking aid from unappealing regimes that urge authoritarian policies. Thus, the greatest recommendation for Soviet aid in South Africa or Nicaragua has been massive U.S. investment in apartheid or sponsorship of authoritarianism from early twentieth-century marine rule to the present "Freedom Fighters."[80] Against U.S. involvement, the argument that reliance on Soviet aid, precisely because of its geographic and social distance, is a lesser evil, becomes persuasive to many participants. If U.S. foreign policy had democratic purposes, it would long ago have canceled (there and elsewhere) nefarious American involvements. Similarly, the greatest recommendation for U.S. aid in Poland or Afghanistan is authoritarian Soviet presence. Except inadvertently, intervention is rarely democratic. If, in contrast to today's great powers, a regime hoped to further serious democratic movements, then the best advice would still be Mill's and Walzer's – except in genocidal emergency, stay out. The force of radical example derives from example, not force. This counsel does not preclude advocacy of a decent regime or provision of nonmilitary aid where it would not be counterproductive.

As a seventh democratic measure, to ensure a broad spectrum of opinion and hinder the emergence of parties of notables, a radical regime

[79] A less important, though very significant, issue is international capital flight and the dominance of oppressive financial institutions, like the IMF (Payer, 1975; Keohane, 1984, pp. 119–20, 253–4; Przeworski, 1985). In a transition period, however much it might try to temporize, a radical regime would confiscate all property of those who tried to shift their capital outward. Given the injustice of international monetary institutions, it would cease to cooperate with them. Though I will not argue the point here, *if* a radical economy can work, then after initial shock, it can work without dependence on such powers.

[80] Barbara Rogers, 1975, chs. 3–4; Lafeber, 1984, pp. 51–4, 64–9.

should probably adopt proportional representation.[81] From a democratic point of view, this policy is less important than that of serial referenda, for the latter ensures public discussion of issues; the former can degenerate, as if often does in European capitalist regimes, into coalitions of elite notables. Yet in a radical setting, the vigorous existence of several parties might create more political space for debate and facilitate the greater internal democracy of each; it would check the dangers of tyranny in a one-party system. Under conditions of equal incomes, public funding, referenda, institutional democracy, and debate on the future of a statusless society, not only would citizen involvement be greater; comparison and criticism would press to undo particular hierarchical practices. But a multiparty system would not, just by itself, substitute for public debate.

6. Democracy as a cluster property

In conclusion, a radical might note, the actual circumstances of revolutionary regimes have been unpropitious. The threat of war has legitimized limitation of possibilities; so has the political underdevelopment of Marxian theory. But modified Chinese practices, coupled with an awareness of democratic autonomy and individuality, the foregoing institutional changes drawn from many experiences, and additional or different measures that would emerge in postrevolutionary public discussion, might go a long way to establishing a genuine democracy. The preceding two chapters have sketched a complex series of proposals to secure such a regime:

1. ending of capitalist and status inequalities, including restriction of overt antidemocratic organizing;
2. public emphasis on furthering democratic autonomy, internationalism, and individuality;
3. equal incomes for all socially recognized work, as well as for children, the handicapped, the aged, and others not able to work;

---

[81] In an interview with Americans, Daniel Ortega provided an interesting, if muted, formulation of radical pluralism: "In Chile, in 1970 under Allende, democracy was put to a test of whether or not it was possible to alter the system with profound changes through the electoral process. The Popular Unity Party of Allende reached power through elections, but because the party presented a challenge to the system itself, the interests of the established system destroyed the Popular Unity. . . . In the case of Nicaragua, where a profound revolution has taken place and where we have not sought the classic alternative of a one party state, we have established a framework, a new system. It is, logically, not similar to that of Chile under Allende, which was unable to defend itself; nor is it similar to that of Cuba or others within the socialist community" (Rosset and Vandermeer, 1986, p. 5).

4. respect for and articulation of differences in public life and within parties;
5. downward democratic congruence of and within ordinary social institutions, including workplace democracy;
6. debate over the history and future of the movement – the nature of a fully radical democracy – in neighborhood assemblies and schools;
7. cultivation of respect for civil disobedience, strikes, and other acts of protest on major public issues;
8. integration of local and national leaders into features of ordinary economic and political life and creation of arenas for criticism;
9. curtailment of almost all direct political intervention in the arts, religion, and personal life;
10. establishment of independent judicial, policy, communication, and electoral review bodies;
11. diversity of perspective in communications and education;
12. use of differential, serial referenda on central issues;
13. public funding of issue-oriented committees as well as parties;
14. takeover of some security and civil judicial functions by neighborhood or regional democratic associations; abolition of centralized, especially secret police powers and units;
15. universal public service, military or community; restructuring of armed forces in a defensive, civilian-oriented direction; removal of authoritarianism of rank and status, and institution of democratic unit organization, allowing serious discussion of policy;
16. proportional representation of parties.

I have made some points about the comparative importance of these measures in securing radical democracy. Such claims are a matter of emphasis within a broad program. Only the adoption of most – those sustaining the integrity of political discussion – and probably all of these measures would give a radical democratic regime a fighting chance.[82] The democratic aspects would strengthen the ones that ensure impartiality and prevent misguided hasty decisions; for these are cluster properties, realized and realized well only when realized together.[83] They undercut wealth, status, and power incentives for tyranny and aggression and create arenas for ordinary people to share power and realize (a feature of) their individuality. These measures consolidate a sophisticated radical political vision in contrast to liberal alternatives.

Given the overemphasis on economics in Marx's theoretical argument and the dictatorial evolution of most revolutionary regimes, many observers have concluded that radicals have a paucity of democratic mea-

---

[82] The measures ensuring political autonomy self-consciously uphold individuality; the tenor of public life would lead, probably quite quickly, to the rejection of residual authoritarianism in other spheres.
[83] George Kateb, 1984, p. 146, makes a similar point in defense of representative democracy.

sures to suggest. On my argument, however, probably something close to the opposite is true. Now, the routine brutality of contemporary capitalist regimes, including formally democratic ones, and the pressure of external attack have been a great check to radical democracy. Caught in an overly economic conception, stultification of Marxian political and social imagination has also been an important limit. In fact, in today's setting, given U.S.-sponsored repression and Soviet and Chinese economic and political power, the latter's strategies of "noncapitalist" – more importantly, noncollective and nondemocratic – development, are influential, to some degree, in many movements.[84] But at current levels of oppression, revolution is a possibility in many countries. Perhaps the greatest need in radical movements is for innovative, thoroughgoing discussion of the institutions and policies that might sustain their purpose and vision.[85] A refined radical theory, more explicit than Marx's in political argument and ethics, can contribute significantly to that debate.

[84] Daniel Ortega offers classical economic determinist justifications for a Nicaraguan economy that is 70 percent privately owned and whose associations do not discuss radical social policies: "We have to start from the premise that Nicaragua is not a country where there are conditions for a class struggle. It is a country with a peasant population and a working population and a small commercial class. The conditions simply do not exist for the 'Marxist' polarization between the working class and the bourgeoisie which takes place in the industrially developed countries" (Rosset and Vandermeer, 1986, p. 8).

A modern radical might wonder whether the condition he cites is not in fact an advantage rather than a drawback, from the standpoint of facilitating a cooperative regime. Furthermore, political innovations in Nicaragua show that external influence – Soviet aid or U.S. threat – need not pervert the development of radical movements.

[85] The political transformations just unfolding in Eastern Europe and the Soviet Union underline this point.

Chapter 9

The Protestant Ethic and Marxian theory

1. Democracy and today's political science

Having sketched the institutions of a radical democracy, I will now pit sophisticated liberal (represented by modified Weberian) arguments against radical social theories. Before I proceed with the main argument of this chapter, this shift needs two brief sections to establish a setting. The first emphasizes the resistance to democratic theory in today's Weberian-inspired political science and the importance of a critique. The second indicates basic issues dividing Weberian and radical social and moral theory.

Political passion and an almost cosmic perspective mark Weber's *Protestant Ethic and the Spirit of Capitalism* and his essays on science and politics as vocations. Many of his successors have foresworn Weber's vision and passion; yet Weber's theories and methodological views survive.[1] In fact, in Anglo-American political science, Weberian conceptions of legitimation, modernization, bureaucracy, parliamentary party competition as democracy, moral relativism, and value neutrality have become dominant alternatives to radical views. Weber defended neither democracy nor individuality for their own sakes. Instead, he originated the operationalist argument, elaborated by Schumpeter, Lipset, Downs, Schlesinger, and others, that democracy exists wherever two or more parties compete for leadership. On that empiricist view, the meaning of a term is reduced to whatever measures it; we cannot have a (radical) democratic *theory* but only a description of current "democratic" practices.

This *leadership competition view* peculiarly makes the antebellum United States and today's South Africa democracies. Often emphasizing great-power "realism," it scorns an alleged popular "stampede" (Schumpeter) or "distemper" (Huntington) and offers a circumscribed, antipolitical vi-

[1] Eckstein, 1989.

348

sion of public life.[2] In the U.S. case, however, any reasonably stated democratic conception would focus, prima facie, on the clash between abstract proclamations of human rights and democracy with unjust war, widespread aid to antidemocratic regimes in less developed countries, unemployment, homelessness amidst affluence, powerlessness of ordinary citizens, on-the-job injury, capitalist hierarchy, and the like. From a commonsense political standpoint, we can see that this reductionist theory closes the field of argument against relevant facts and topics of inquiry.[3] In Rawls's idiom, the party competition view falls outside an *overlapping consensus on democratic autonomy;* it is an implausible ideology posing as science. Further, the easy transfer of bad social scientific arguments from Weber's relativist neo-Kantian to a reductionist empiricist idiom suggests that these epistemologies, despite important contrasts, are subtly linked.

Weber's motivation for proposing the party competition theory was, however, political efficiency. Not bumbling monarchs but policymakers, subjected to parliamentary investigation, would become "heroes" of great-power politics.[4] The juxtaposing of even minimal political competition with tyranny is morally important: Hence, Weber's view appeals to more liberal investigators. It is, nonetheless, startling that so deficient a conception of democracy could feature widely in today's political science. Following another strand of Weberian argument, a major reason, one might suggest, is the "elective affinity" of prevailing political and social powers, characterized by hierarchical class and status interests, for antidemocratic views. That affinity skews, for example, major re-

---

[2] Schumpeter, 1950; Lipset, 1963; Downs, 1957; Schlesinger, 1984.

As Chapter 1 suggested, a denial of any common good is pivotal to this antiliberal view. For instance, Schumpeter contends that since democracy can fairly limit the voting of infants, it may also tolerate the disenfranchisement of a substantial part, even the majority of a "commonwealth": "In no country, however democratic, is the right to vote extended below a certain age . . . fitness is a matter of opinion and of degree. Its presence must be established by some set of rules. *Without absurdity or insincerity* . . . a race-conscious nation may associate fitness with racial considerations" (my emphasis). Writing in 1942, he added, "Thus the United States excludes Orientals and Germany excludes Jews from citizenship; in the Southern part of the United States, Negroes are also often deprived of the vote" (Schumpeter, 1950, p. 244). For affinities of Schumpeter's theory with Weber's, Lipset's, and Huntington's, see Gilbert, 1987. Schumpeter did not recommend genuine democratic leadership, but even if leadership is good, its importance has often been overrated.

[3] As Montesquieu so beautifully and satirically put it in bk. 25 of *Spirit of the Laws,* "When we say things so clear and simple, we are sure never to convince."

[4] In a more peacemaking, less colonialist vein than Weber's, as Chapter 1 emphasized, Montesquieu celebrated the virtues of commerce, Kant and the *Federalist Papers* (no. 4) those of democracy (Gilbert, 1990c).

search awards. Still, within the academic community, this *governance* conception suits only the needs of policy advisors committed to particular leaders rather than a common good. But such advisors are few. Thus, the persistent political science fancy for the "emperor's new clothes" raises deep questions about a theoretical and methodological background that could legitimize it.

Even within the discipline of political science, the prevailing view is anomalous. Many proponents of the once influential post–World War II theory – pluralism – took democracy more seriously. They envisioned a balance of competing interest groups that would sustain an economic common good and "civic culture." Responding to radical criticism, however, creative pluralists such as Robert Dahl and Charles Lindblom now insist that corporate capitalist inequalities undercut political equality. In Lindblom's words, "The large private corporation fits oddly into democratic theory and vision. In fact, it does not fit."[5] As a radical might expect, if power, despite some parliamentary forms, is actually undemocratic, then Dahl's and Lindblom's new theories – seeking to create political and social conditions for democratic plurality – would be, and in fact are, less influential in the discipline and among policymakers than their earlier views.

Dahl and Lindblom share with their adversaries a broadly empiricist methodology. Their argument's evolution was motivated by a moral commitment to democratic theory rather than a methodological concern, characteristic of realism, to contrast leading social theories.[6] Dahl, for example, fails to acknowledge that, in the initial debate with Marxians, his views have moved from liberal to nearly ruling-class arguments; they now contribute to a theory of *radical* democracy. (In contrast, Lindblom stresses the importance of exploring Marxian views.)[7] Their broad methodological self-interpretation cuts short the conversation between clashing *theories* within the discipline and does not sufficiently erode the putative contrast of an "empiricist" or "rational actor" political science

---

[5] Lindblom, 1977, p. 356. Contrary to its self-understanding, empiricism is often aggressively value oriented. Without awareness of inconsistency, Zbigniew Brzezinski introduces Huntington's "Democratic Distemper" (Huntington, 1975, pp. 6–7) by invoking a "value-neutral" policy science to castigate "irresponsible, value-oriented, adversary intellectuals . . . spawned" by the system. On Huntington's operationalist, "might makes right" view, the *public interest* – similar in tyrannies and democracies – is nothing but an interest imputed to the political institution (role) occupied by the leader (Huntington, 1969, p. 25).

[6] Despite references to moral "assumptions" that are, in his case, an artifact of residual empiricist ideology, Dahl, 1985, pp. 53–5, cultivates democratic argument.

[7] See Lindblom's presidential address to the American Political Science Association (1982).

with "normative" views; for an elitist "policy science," drawing upon Weber, has relegated democratic conceptions, including Dahl's, to realms of exile – "theory" or "philosophy."

Like the pluralists, contemporary political theorists widely acknowledge the clash of equal liberty and social inequality. Thus, Rawls, Walzer, Dworkin, Pateman, Barber, Joshua Cohen, Gutmann, and Teuber are social or strong democrats; they stress economic egalitarianism and greater participation in enterprises and politics; in addition, Rawls and Walzer recommend democratic internationalism.[8] Yet the bifurcation of political science and philosophy has also harmed the latter; for following Rawls, many theorists view factual claims, though important, as external, to be settled by standard empiricist or constructivist methods. Neither Walzer nor Rawls, for instance, considers alternative explanations of such morally disturbing phenomena as the level of economic inequality that would still allow peaceful rather than revolutionary transition to full democracy or the character (mainly electoral versus mainly extraparliamentary) of a movement that could transform American foreign policy in a thoroughgoing democratic direction. If, however, as Rawls underlines, public consensus on autonomy has not been translated into policy, then we cannot accept his "intuitive" suggestion that we may, with the moral will, simply work out cooperative arrangements.[9] Reality might be too recalcitrant. Given empirical anomalies in their original views, sophisticated liberals have adopted currently unpopular, redistributive conceptions or proposed democratic justifications of "conscientious refusal" (Rawls) as *inferences to the best (moral) explanation.* Why then do these theorists, paradoxically, stop at just these compelling, yet early points in an argument?[10]

Here also, diverse methodological, ethical, and political reasons contribute to an explanation. For instance, Kantian methodological strategies, emphasizing broad appeals from comparatively uncontroversial premises like equal freedom, play a role. These arguments tend to deemphasize controversial political claims that arise, as it were, only at a

---

[8] Nozick's libertarianism is a significant alternative strain in the United States as is Oakeshott's neo-Hegelianism in England. But Nozick's is more an ideal economic theory than a democratic one, Oakeshott's a legal conception. In fact, neither considers whether a political *regime* of freedom is consistent with their insistence on asocial economic liberty or unbridled capitalist power. See Gilbert, 1989a.

[9] Rawls, 1971, p. 226. At p. 87, Rawls maintains that "presumably" the economic policies of a democratic government could accomplish the necessary reforms. See Gilbert, 1978a.

[10] As the Introduction notes, this book seeks only to establish a radical account's plausibility, to sketch, but not settle, a sophisticated debate between liberals and radicals.

subsequent empirical stage.[11] Among political reasons, even a partial case for nonviolent, let alone violent, revolution involves conflicts of goods; has sometimes been associated with failed radical, now oppressive regimes; presses outside the bounds of currently "respectable" political and intellectual discussion; and lacks a strong constituency. Thus, theorists are, unsurprisingly, cautious. Given the weakness of democratic philosophy in probing social theory, however, other political scientists continue to find Weberian arguments acceptable. This response is encouraged by fashionable postmodernist disdain for democracy (Foucault in some moods) as well as antiliberal Straussian eccentricity. External power considerations aside, substantive reasons join methodological appeals to sustain markedly antidemocratic conceptions within political science.

Part II of this book, emphasizing clashes of worked-out social theories, poses, to differing degrees, an empirical and methodological challenge to each branch of contemporary democratic theory. If successful, its critique of Weberian social science and neo-Kantianism will underline the comparative explanatory, ethical, and democratic attractiveness of radical social theory and of social scientific and moral realism.

2. Does neo-Kantianism cohere with liberal social theory?

The rest of Part II focuses on the social theoretical and ethical differences between Weberians and Marxians – in part as represented by Weber's contemporary, Lenin – on decisive issues of twentieth-century politics. This chapter examines the controversy over the rise of modern civil society instigated by Weber's subtle *Protestant Ethic and the Spirit of Capitalism*. Despite the fame of this debate, I will maintain, his argument poses no serious challenge to a sophisticated Marxian social theory and ethics. This chapter also underlines important, but comparatively fine methodological and moral differences between these accounts. Further, Weber's insistence on the special causal role of Puritanism requires straightforward ethical claims – similar to those invoked in Marxian accounts – and undercuts his metaethical contention about the need for social science to be value free.

The later chapters, however, take up the major theoretical, empirical, and moral clashes between the two positions. Chapter 10 examines imperialism, war, and the choice between patriotism and democratic internationalism; Chapter 11 explores the dialectic of class, status, and racism

---

[11] Rawls, 1981, sec. 12, answers some philosophical challenges on this point. He is so creative and intricate in abstract democratic theory that it seems unreasonable to request comparable achievement in social theory.

under capitalism and its special role in obstructing democracy. Chapter 12 focuses on the ethical and empirical issue of whether a modern state can incorporate a common good, and contrasts Weber's and Lenin's views on the Russian Revolution. It will underline Weber's seemingly un-Weberian stress on the all-compelling powers of industrial organization and bureaucracy that override any significant material impact for revolutionary ideas. Chapter 13 examines the structure of moral disagreement between neo-Kantians and realists; it also explores some of Weber's general arguments on behalf of relativism. In addition, since some of his central claims are not liberal, this chapter traces the impact of a more explicit conception of individuality on Weberian social science.

As I have emphasized, science has progressed by – or undergone revolution through – comparing the few, reasonable, contending theories at a given time and seeking relevant evidence to decide between them. A contrast of radical and Weberian argument will unearth important, surprising differences, ones central to social scientific clarity and advance.

This section will also explore those of Lenin's arguments, which I regard as extensions of Marxian political and social theory. As we have seen, Lenin was a more self-aware moral realist than Marx, at least about the issue of justice. The foregoing criticisms of Marx's economic and political claims, based on a more worked-out notion of social individuality, apply, however, with at least equal force to Lenin's conception of political life and status hierarchy in socialism, to some features of his account of worker acquiescence under capitalism, and to aspects of his endorsement of nationalist movements against imperialism. My subsequent claims that Marx and Lenin produced telling explanations of major phenomena or joined important controversies with a Weberian liberalism should not be confused with a general claim that radical theory on other questions is best realized in their accounts. In fact, if the current Soviet and Chinese regimes develop important features of their theory of socialism, then the central good of communism cannot be actualized by mainly following their postrevolutionary strategies. As Chapters 7 and 8 indicated alternative radical democratic conceptions, this section will concentrate on the relation between Weber's theory and a consistent liberalism; it will, however, also flesh out some distinctive claims of radical social theory and ethical argument.

At the outset, I should also emphasize the significance of theory contrasts for an internal moral critique of Weber's politics and metaethics. Like Marx, Weber stressed the elective affinities of opposed classes for different religious and political views. Both accounts suggest that the thoroughgoing economic and political conflicts of modern society would charge scientific and social scientific disputes with moral implications. In biology, for example, Darwin's materialist theory challenged Christian explanations in general and undercut theodicies of capitalism; it incurred fierce attacks. In social theory, what is true about potentials for human cooperation, freedom, and individuality is even more hotly contested. The vehement political response to Darwin's theory, let alone socialist ones, reveals an important respect in which Weber's rigid epistemological distinction that "causal analysis provides absolutely no value judgment and a value judgment is absolutely not a causal explanation," is mistaken.[12]

Such complicated scientific and moral disputes often seem to fuse empirical clashes in social theory with disagreements of ethical premise, moral theory, and metaethics. Many discussions – Wood's of Marxian argument, for instance – do not even distinguish these elements. Instead, complex moral clashes are taken, without further analysis, to be rooted in underlying normative disputes. Thus, even the issue of what the elements in these debates are, let alone which are central – empirical disagreements, metaethical ones, conflicts about overall moral theories, or underlying ethical standards – is controversial. A closer comparison of Marxian and Weberian theories will isolate their structure and pivotal components.

For Weber, clashes of ultimate ethical standpoint shaped these disputes. He regarded choices of vocation in disparate realms of life, and even of divergent political stands, as based on unarbitrable moral differences, ones about which no science can "pretend" to decide.[13] Such underlying values, he maintained, give historical research its "significance." When the cultural "stars" guiding each epoch shift, so, too, the focus of historical investigation moves.[14] Weber is the most creative, influential social theorist who is also a thoroughgoing metaethical relativist. We may interpret his view as a dramatic, social scientific paradigm for today's neo-Kantian arguments. His controversy with radicals provides a difficult test case for the plausibility of moral realism.

The opposed factual and social theoretical claims of Weberian and Marxian theory, I will argue, generate straightforward ethical differences. According to Weber, science can make a limited moral contribution by examining given normative standpoints and pointing to harmful

---

[12] Weber, *Methodology in the Social Sciences*, hereafter *MSS*, 1949, p. 123. Richard Miller, 1987, notes that much of Weber's fire was directed at vocal German nationalists, who did not attend to the realities of international politics. His separation of causal explanation and value judgments sought to prevent the swallowing up of the former in the latter. But Weber's view of good explanation is, as we shall see, inseparably linked to his own, more sophisticated nationalism. And Marxian causal differences with Weber contribute decisively to their internationalism (Collins, 1986, chs. 6–7; Garfinkel, 1981, ch. 5).

[13] Weber, *MSS*, pp. 6, 8, 14, 17, 18; *Economy and Society* hereafter *ES*, 1968, 3:1381.

[14] Weber, *MSS*, p. 112; Rickert, 1962, p. 145.

consequences of the means used to secure them.[15] Yet in practice, he did not stick to this claim. For instance, based on his theory of nationality conflict and bureaucratization, he denied empirically that humans can realize the goal of more cooperative, less belligerent societies. I will maintain that for at least one outstanding case – Weber's clashes with Marxism – his metaethical thesis about the limitations of scientific evaluation of moral ideals is wrong. In addition, his relativism inhibits him from exploring possible difficulties in and counterarguments to his social theoretical and ethical claims.

Yet Weber's 1917 "The Meaning of 'Ethical Neutrality' in Sociology and Economics" hints at a more objective conception:

> At first, I might make a few remarks against the view that the mere existence of historical and individual variations in evaluations proves the necessarily "subjective" character of ethics. Even propositions about empirical facts are often very much disputed and there might well be a much greater degree of agreement as to whether someone is to be considered a scoundrel than there would be (even among specialists) concerning for instance, the interpretation of a mutilated inscription.[16]

Without further examination, he dropped this line of argument. His comment recalls Engels's recognition of the simplicity of everyday moral standards. Internally developing Weber's insight and invoking some of his criteria for moral judgment, the following chapters will contrast a metaethical realist position to Weberian relativism.

3. Can a Marxian accept *The Protestant Ethic's* basic claim?

Weber was acutely aware of the moral conflicts of modern history and rightly repudiated complacency about human progress. In *The Protestant Ethic*, he offered a complex but negative evaluation of the unfolding of capitalism. Alongside this judgment and inhibiting its clarity, however, Weber seems to have held an overly stringent image of the divinely sanctioned, "all or nothing" character of ethics. But a religious basis for ethics had failed. He stressed the fundamental problem of theodicy: How could a god "who is omnipotent and kind have created an irrational world of undeserved suffering, unpunished injustice, and hopeless stupidity"?[17] From a contrast of an ideal, harmonious human existence with conflict-ridden reality, he insisted on the "ethical irrationality of the world."

---

[15] Weber, *MSS*, pp. 10, 14; *From Max Weber*, hereafter *FMW*, 1958c, pp. 147, 151–2.
[16] Weber, *MSS*, pp. 12–13. Josh Cohen, 1986a, makes the neat parallel point that many empirical claims about slavery are in dispute among today's historians but that its injustice is uncontroversial. See also Habermas, 1984, 1:231.
[17] Weber, *FMW*, p. 122.

On *The Protestant Ethic*'s account, the "ghosts" of Christian vocation haunted many aspects of modern life; in metaethics, however, Weber himself seems pursued by a rigorous Calvinist vision of the cosmic order. For Calvin, the elect and nonelect act in the expectation of God's grace but cannot know their fate. By secret plan, God had determined salvation from eternity. Similarly, Weberian actors in different spheres arbitrarily choose vocations with no objective way of judging their merits or foreseeing their destiny; yet they must conduct themselves with self-discipline as if to please a hidden divinity. But for Weber, as for Nietzsche, God is dead. His ethical injunction "Follow thy demon" retains the Calvinist cosmos but without a maker.[18] Given the failure of religious imperatives, Weber never considered the possibility of any more finely structured moral judgments about a good life for humans.

In surveying ethical progress, as Chapter 5 shows, Marx also emphasized that history has proceeded by the "bad side" of oppression and conflict.[19] A Marxian version of moral realism depicts the conflicting ethical features of such change and offers an alternative interpretation of what Weber called the "ethical irrationality of the world." Where the latter divided different moral aspects of past societies into irreconcilable "perspectives," the former provides a precise, dialectical account of conflicts of intrinsic goods and self-conceptions. Yet like Weber, a Marxian moral realism, before the emergence of a cooperative alternative, resists overall assessment of human advance. Future communist progress, by contrast, is ethically admirable.

But depending on facts – for instance, if Weberian social theory claims about the increasing bureaucratization that must accompany modern civilization are right – a moral realist could characterize the predominant trend as one of decline. Even that concession to Weber's empirical argument would not justify his metaethical assertion that no rational judgment about human progress is possible.[20] I will now examine whether any social theoretical or moral difference with Marxians in *The Protestant Ethic* counters this realist interpretation.

Weber rejected the unsophisticated economic determinist hypothesis that material factors alone governed the rise of modern civilization.[21] Comparing ideal types of the spirit of capitalism and Calvinism, he traced the enormous impact of a religious and cultural outlook on the appearance of a new type of human conduct, the relentless, *innerworldly* asceticism of capitalist accumulation. According to Weber, medieval

---

[18] Weber, *The Protestant Ethic and the Spirit of Capitalism*, hereafter *PE*, 1958d, pp. 182, 109–10; *FMW*, pp. 149, 156; Rickert, 1962, p. 145; Calvin, 1957, 2:ch. 21.
[19] Marx, 1963, p. 121.   [20] Weber, *MSS*, p. 38.
[21] Weber, *PE*, pp. 55–6, 75, 90–2, 183, 217 n. 32, 284 n. 119.

monks led an ordered life, working, praying, and accounting to God, cloistered from the rest of society. Their Catholicism combined methodical rationalization of life with asceticism *for another world*. But Protestantism brought these "stern religious characters" out of the monasteries and attempted to universalize the spirit of calculation and premeditation *in this world*.[22] Its doctrine of salvation sanctified capitalist accumulation and dour abstinence from pleasure seeking. Thus, it redirected vast spiritual energies among capitalists and, to a lesser extent, workers to transform the world.

Once in motion, however, capitalism assumed a machine-like working of its own. With the growth of wealth, so Wesley suggested, "the desire of the eyes and the pride of life" increased; religiosity "decayed."[23] Yet the powerful spirit of Protestant callings still generally haunted middle-class conduct and, as Weber's essays on politics and science as vocations testify, even his own. From the disturbing, ethereal afterlife of these ideas, *The Protestant Ethic* tracked down their once vigorous, causal significance.

Part of this essay's persuasiveness stems from its ethical pathos: its portrait of a cage of modern social life, composed of formally rational, calculated activities that have lost integrity. But Weber's causal argument draws its strength mainly from a telling comparison with a crude economic determinist account. Given his hypothesis about the role of Protestantism in a uniquely Occidental development, he would embark on a monumental sociology of religion, tracing out how the influence of tribal magic or of Buddhist self-cultivation, heedless of this world, or of calculation by Jewish pariah capitalists would have hindered, not spurred, methodical social transformation. Against solely economic analysis, *The Protestant Ethic*, coupled with this broader delineation of religious alternatives, seemed to capture a decisive feature of early capitalism.

Yet Weber astutely limited his antimaterialist claims. Following Marx, he recognized unique economic features of Western development, notably the creation of a large class of formally free laborers and a new "organization of labor."[24] Defending causal pluralism, he cautioned against a misreading of his argument as a religious, cultural determinism:

> We have no intention whatever of maintaining such a foolish and doctrinaire thesis [töricht-doktrinäre These] as that the spirit of capitalism . . .
> could only have arisen as the result of certain effects of the Reformation, or
> even that capitalism as an economic system is a creation of the Reformation. . . . On the contrary, we only wish to ascertain whether and to what

---

[22] Weber, *General Economic History,* hereafter *GEH*, 1961, p. 268.
[23] Weber, *PE*, p. 175. [24] Weber, *PE*, p. 22.

extent religious forces have taken part in the qualitative formation and the quantitative expansion of that spirit over the world.[25]

Weber's 1904 essay entitled " 'Objectivity' in Social Science and Social Policy" spoke of "that ideal-typical construct which is the most important one from our point of view, namely the Marxian theory" and of its "eminent, indeed unique, *heuristic* significance."[26] The turn-of-the-century German government, however, prevented Social Democrats from teaching.[27] The educational status hierarchy and "respectable" media also discouraged fair-minded treatment of Marxian views. Thus, academic sociologists, including Weber, did not pit their theories against a sophisticated Marxian alternative. Instead, *The Protestant Ethic* criticized an unnamed, ideal-typical economic determinist opponent and neglected Marx's nuanced depiction of original accumulation.

In *Capital*, Marx stressed the dialectical role of politics. The English enclosure movement, depriving peasants of the use of common lands, produced a formally free work force. The slave trade, colonialism, and commercial wars, those "hothouse" political methods, created substantial accumulations of wealth. Violence served as the "midwife" of the new order, one of such dialectical impact that Marx described it as "itself an economic power." In comparison with Weber, Marx slighted the role of religion; yet he noticed that the Reformation, an important ideological factor, "hurled" the peasants from lands owned by the Catholic church into urban misery; Protestant ideas contributed to the formation of a new class with only its labor power to sell. He also satirized the Reformation theodicy of capitalist asceticism: "Accumulate, accumulate! That is Moses and the prophets!" As Richard Miller has suggested, Marx's explanation of the rise of capitalism is, in fact, a far more diverse, socially richer, interactive account than *The Protestant Ethic*.[28]

Thus, a Weberian could not properly fault Marx's view for failing to stress the impact of class struggle, force, law, ideology, and even religion in the rise of capitalism. Nonetheless, in contrast to Weber, Marx's explanation gives primacy to certain material processes, such as the forging of a free labor force and shifts in work organization, the emergence of concentrations of capital, new commercial opportunities, and transformations in technology. For Marx, a relatively independent, uneven development of politics and religion furthered the development of capitalism.

---

[25] Weber, *PE*, pp. 91, 183, 284; *Gesammelte Aufsätze zur Religionssoziologie*, hereafter *GAR*, 1947, p. 83; see also Weber, *Critique of Stammler*, hereafter *CS*, 1977, pp. 62–70.
[26] Weber, *MSS*, p. 103.   [27] Ringer, 1969, pp. 141–2.
[28] Karl Marx, 1977, 1:716, 732–6, 751, 595; R. Miller, 1984, p. 238. Randall Collins, 1986, ch. 2, however, stresses the complexity of Weber's later account.

Taking *Capital* as a counterargument, Weber's analysis of religion has far less anti-Marxian theoretical impact than the original controversy with economic determinism promised.[29] Though Weber emphasized ideal factors, a sophisticated Marxism may also account for them. Perhaps he traced a more independent, world-transforming role for ascetic virtuosos than even a sophisticated Marxism can allow. Yet his cautious statement of his argument makes this difference unclear. If he were right, one might conclude that he drew in an important part of the causal picture understated by Marx. In realist epistemological terms, Weber's explanation, combined with Marx's, would produce a more coherent, nuanced approximation of the rise of modern capitalism than the latter alone. In that case, however, the dispute between Weberians and Marxians would not turn on the glaring, substantive point about the kinds of social activity – "ideal" or "material" – that play a decisive historical role, but only on comparatively subtle methodological, social theoretical, and ethical issues.

For instance, as an important methodological concern, Weber's causal pluralism would still contrast with Marx's emphasis on the dialectical primacy of the new mode of production and class struggle. Failing to consider a sophisticated version of Marxism, Weber made no such comparison. Yet ironically, he sometimes suggested a primacy of class conflict. For instance, in *Economy and Society*, he contended that *salvation religions* appealed to oppressed classes. They become the theodicy of the negatively privileged (Theodizee der negative Priviligierten), whereas leading bureaucratic and military strata adopted religions that sanctified their worldly advantages.[30] On this account, Weber stressed the degree to which choice of religion dovetailed with already existing class interests. His analysis clashed with a solely economic, "Marxian" account but resembled sophisticated Marxian claims about dialectical primacy. To make his causal pluralism stick, Weber needed to show that Calvinism played a more decisive, autonomous role, not just furthering or being taken up by an ongoing capitalism, but initiating and shaping it. *The Protestant Ethic's* strategy of argument, unfortunately, diverts attention from this important social theoretical issue.

Weber's nuanced differentiation among types of Protestantism and their diverse social impact accentuates this difficulty. For instance, he contrasted Luther's novel conception of a calling in the world to (as he saw it) "selfish," otherworldly, monastic asceticism and to the comparatively relaxed, "traditional" attitude toward labor of admirable Old Testament "prophets."[31] But Luther's Protestantism was not world trans-

---

[29] Weber, *ES*, 3:1235–62.
[30] Weber, *Sociology of Religion*, hereafter *SR*, 1963, pp. 106–8.   [31] Weber, *PE*, pp. 81, 83.

forming. Worse yet according to Weber, it exemplified, as Marxians would say, an uneven, anticapitalist spiritual development, one more consonant with feudalism. Luther's condemnation of the "sterility of money," Weber insisted, was "backward" even compared with the position of the schoolman Anthony of Florence. He deemed the Lutheran conception of a calling as "of at best of questionable importance for the problems [of innerworldly asceticism] in which we are interested."[32] Following his argument, however, a Marxian critic might emphasize that Florentine Catholicism had nearer "affinities" to early capitalism than this important version of Protestantism. Why didn't that Catholicism, comparatively speaking, stimulate or, more likely, reinforce capitalism? Why did Weber emphasize the socially creative role of the Catholic–Protestant intrareligious controversy?

In contrast to Lutheranism, he insisted, Calvinism had revolutionary implication. Yet even here, he distinguished Calvin's rigorous conception from reformed, mass Calvinism. On Weber's account, Calvin's "magnificently consistent" doctrine emphasized the predestination of the elect. For Calvin, no human could know if he (or she) were damned; each would have to conduct himself in the hope of indecipherable grace. But reformed Calvinism, Weber noted, found this doctrine unlivable. As the idea of predestination came into daily life, it was secularized and made psychologically palatable; success in this world, arraying the outward, monetary signs of inner asceticism, manifested one's possession of grace. Though less abrupt and sarcastic, this claim echoes Marx's "Accumulate! Accumulate! That is Moses and all the prophets!" The reformed conception sanctified glaring inequalities of wealth as a carnal mirror of election and damnation by a capricious God. Weber attributed this causally influential, religiously debased version of Calvinism to human nature. In an age when an afterlife was a preoccupation, each aspirant needed to know if he had been blessed.[33]

---

[32] Weber, *PE*, pp. 82–3, 86. Marx was also well aware of this distinction; *Capital* cited Luther's antiusury sermons (Marx, 1961, 1:592 n. 1, 192). In turn, Jürgen Habermas, 1984, 1:230, notes the secularization of Catholicism among early French capitalists.

[33] Weber, *PE*, pp. 109–11. He was sensitive to a deep theme of Calvin's reasoning about humility: "The subject of predestination, which in itself is attended with considerable difficulty, is rendered very perplexed, and hence perilous by human curiosity, which cannot be restrained from wandering into forbidden paths, and climbing to the clouds, determined if it can that none of the secret things of God shall remain unexplored. When we see many, some of them in other respects not bad men, everywhere rushing into this audacity and wickedness, it is necessary to remind them of the course of duty in this matter. First, then, when they inquire into predestination, let them remember that they are penetrating into the recesses of the divine wisdom, where he who rushes forward securely and confidently instead of satisfying his curiosity will enter an inextricable labyrinth. For it is not right that man should with impunity pry into things which the Lord

But vulgarization for Weber's psychological reason, a Marxian critic might note, could easily be overdetermined by debasement to accord with the status needs of early capitalists. Following Weber's account, this critic might add, capitalists required a theodicy of good fortune to inure themselves against the suffering of the poor and confirm their rejection of a declining, aristocratic order. Yet Weber never considered the possibility of overdetermination. His nuanced portrait of Calvinist influence *undermines* his anti-Marxian claims. To justify causal pluralism, he needed to demonstrate that Calvin's theology was the central element, inspiring, for mainly psychological reasons, capitalist conduct. Any elective social affinities of entrepreneurs for these ideas would have to be secondary – emerging, for example, from patterns of religiously nurtured, this-worldly, nonmonetary conduct that ultimately issued in methodical profit seeking. In contrast, the Marxian can easily combine Weber's religious and psychological claim with a class struggle account. She need merely query, Given uneven development, what else would one expect than that religious theses of an inspired leader would be bent, for mundane reasons, to particular sociological outcomes?[34] She could concur with Weber that prophetic inspiration has its own integrity, yet rightly insist that a Marxian sociology of religion flows naturally from *these* Weberian claims.

4. Can Weber account for Protestant radicalism?

Furthermore, if, as a Marxian might surmise, clashing class forces had influenced the social impact of the original Reformation vision, then Calvinism would have triumphed as the result of an economic and political struggle, stamped by, as well as influencing, the powerful social forces of that era. This conflict would have selected out of Protestantism those doctrines, like predestination, that proved most congruent with prevailing interests. Pursuing this theoretical comparison, a Marxian might then suggest a way of differentiating their arguments. Weber's account requires the unique determination by Calvinism of *procapitalist* conduct among entrepreneurs and workers. In contrast, a Marxian would ex-

---

has been pleased to conceal within himself, and scan that sublime eternal wisdom which it is his pleasure that we should not apprehend but adore, that therein also his perfections may appear. Those secrets of his will, which he has seen it meet to manifest, are revealed in his word" (Calvin, 1957, 2:203–4).

[34] Randall Collins has emphasized the influence of war for Weber on other practical religions: the belligerent role of Jahweh in Judaism and of warrior civic religions in ancient Greece. His reinterpretation makes religion even less centrally causal in Weber's account, "military conditions" more decisive. Referring to Weber's geopolitics, he suggests, amusingly, that Weber is a "more thoroughgoing conflict theorist" than Marx (Collins, 1986, pp. 43–4; Weber, 1952, ch. 4).

pect, clashing class interests might help realize and, in turn, be furthered by conflicting elements within a religious conception. In that case, Protestant influence would parallel that of democratic views. Just as the attempt to realize political equality led to popular demands for social equality and vigorous democratic revolution, as Marx argued in 1848, so did the overthrow of the spiritual hierarchy during the Reformation contribute to Feuerbach's critique of religion and the vision of Christian communist artisans of a republican, cooperative society on earth.[35] Call Weber's the *autonomous, capitalist-impact conception*, and the Marxian a *diverse, class struggle-impact conception*. Contrasted in this way, the issue between the two arguments appears to be, in principle, decidable.

Further, in the light of a relevant causal contrast, Weber's own argument provides evidence for Marxian conclusions. Thus, he insisted, Protestantism stressed simplicity and equality against luxurious court life, individual conscience against Catholic hierarchy. He recognized the early Christian "eschatological hopes," which Protestant readers of the New Testament could revive, and restated Cromwell's hostility to the lavish rich: " 'Be pleased to reform the abuses of all professions: and if there be any one that makes many people poor to make a few rich, that suits not a Commonwealth.' "[36] In highlighting its radical, antiaristocratic features, Weber underlined critical aspects of the Protestant principle that could be turned against the bourgeoisie.[37] Some combination

[35] Gilbert, 1981a, chs. 4, 6; Marx, 1974, p. 63. Though he does not contrast Weberian and Marxian theory and has a quite restrictive conception of what was "structurally possible." Jürgen Habermas, 1984, 1:233–4 (my emphasis) suggests a similar critique: "But if the [procapitalist] Protestant ethic . . . may not be taken simply as the privileged expression of a principled morality, if we take seriously the partial character of this form of ethical rationalization, then those Protestant sects that, like the Anabaptists, wanted to institutionalize the universalistic ethic of brotherliness with fewer reservations – that is, *also* in new forms of social community and of political will-formation – appear in a new light. These social movements, which did not want to divert the potential of ethically rationalized worldviews onto the tracks of disciplined labor *by privatized individuals*, but wanted rather to convert it into social-revolutionary forms of life, failed in this first attempt. For the *radicalized forms of life* did not correspond to the requirements of a capitalist economic ethic."

[36] Weber, *PE*, pp. 84, 82, 157.

[37] Considering the proletarian situation in the light of a philosophical version of the Protestant principle – one that criticizes every practical congealation in the light of prevailing social interests as a (partial) distortion and ideology – Paul Tillich, a creative modern theologian, found communism attractive. While serving as pastor among the Ruhr miners who responded in the 1920s to bitter conditions and repression with armed struggle, he translated the Reformation into radical politics: "The distorted character of the vital existence of millions and millions of proletarians in city and country is too obvious to need much description. . . . It is worse in periods of unemployment and it is intolerable – leading to mass explosions – in times of protracted mass unemployment. In view of

of these elements nurtured radical Christian protest, particularly among artisans and peasants, against the injustices of this world.

A critic could also summon evidence beyond Weber's for a sophisticated Marxian account. For instance, in the Puritan Revolution, the Quakers and Ranters – those "roundheaded rogues" – advanced egalitarian demands. As Joseph Fox put it, "O ye great men and rich men of the earth! Weep and howl for your misery that is coming. . . . The fire is kindled, the day of the Lord is appearing, a day of howling. . . . All the loftiness of men must be laid low."[38] These sects adopted a pacifist outlook only after the revolutionary period had ended. In the nineteenth century, as E. P. Thompson's magisterial *Making of the English Working Class* has shown, radical artisans like Ben Rushton combined Methodism and protest. A Chartist song sounded a different theme than Wesley's:

> Rouse them from their silken slumber
> Trouble them amidst their pride;
> Swell your ranks, augment your numbers,
> Spread the Charter far and wide,
> Truth is with us,
> God himself is on our side.[39]

Similarly, to pursue the example mentioned above, Wilhelm Weitling and many of Marx's and Engels's artisan comrades – Moll, Schapper, Bauer – obtained their initial radical experience in a Christian movement, the Communist Correspondence Societies, which evolved into the Communist League and adopted the *Manifesto* as its program.

Finally, as I note in Chapter 5, Engels's *Anti-Dühring* dialectically captures the element of justice in religious peasant, artisan, and proletarian

these facts, it is dishonest to use the instinctively materialistic reaction of the proletariat to its fate as an excuse for discrediting the proletarian struggle. Much so-called "idealism" has its roots in the social and economic security of the upper classes; and Protestantism has just as little reason to praise this bourgeois idealism as it has to condemn proletarian materialism. . . . No men [or women] in our time, regardless of whether they belong to the bourgeois or the proletarian group, can escape the permanent and essential contradiction of the capitalist system. . . . This does not mean that anyone should or could accept the class struggle as desirable . . . although the proletariat and its leaders urge the fight against the ruling classes, they do not favor the class struggle – which goes on anyway – they try to encourage the fight for the existence of proletarians . . . and to overcome the system as such which by its very structure, produces the class struggle. . . . Protestantism, in the light of its own principle, should be able to understand this situation, to see its demonic implications and its divine promises" (Tillich, 1948, pp. 167–9, 170–4, 180–1).

[38] Hill, 1972, p. 188. For American examples, see Lynd, 1982, pp. 19–20, 24–31, 103–5, 172–3.

[39] Thompson, 1966, p. 399; Gilbert, 1981a, ch. 2.

protest – its indignation at glaring inequalities. Some interpreters suppose that Marxians must place little emphasis on the causal role of religion. Yet ironically, Engels is a striking counterexample. In explaining the sixteenth-century German peasant war, he stressed the relatively independent, dialectical impact of an egalitarian "proletarian-plebeian asceticism." The prevailing form of economic oppression, though horrible, separated the poor and would probably have blocked a peasant war. That religious ideology, he insisted, united them.[40]

Furthermore, Luther may not have been a "this worldly" Protestant, an Engelsian critic might respond to Weber, but Thomas Münzer and the oppressed rural population certainly were. As Engels summarized Münzer's view:

> The source of the evil of usury, thievery and robbery . . . [was] the princes and the masters who had taken all creatures into their private possession – the fishes in the water, the birds in the air, the plants in the soil. And the usurpers, [Münzer] said, still preached to the poor the commandment, "Thou shalt not steal," while they . . . robbed and cursed the peasant and artisan. "When, however, one of the latter commits the slightest transgression," he said, "he has to hang, and Dr. Liar [Luther] says to all this: Amen. . . . Oh, my dear gentlemen, how the Lord will smite with an iron rod all these old pots![41]

Engels also criticized the ascetic aspects of the rebellion's egalitarianism; he admired Münzer's communism for its social, not religious vision. Yet his explanation and moral justification of Münzer's Protestantism show that a sophisticated Marxism may be even more explicitly attentive to the diverse social impact of a complex religious conception than – in this important respect – Weber was. Contrary to Weber's thesis, the Lutheran and Calvinist ideas of a calling could triumph only with the suppression of a protocommunist notion of a kingdom of god on earth.

In *Economy and Society,* Weber recognized the role of radical, in his view, peasant, Protestant sects:

> The taborites, who were partially derived from peasant groups, the German peasant protagonists of "divine right" in the peasant wars, the English radical communist farmers, and above all the Russian peasant sectarians – all these have points of contact with agrarian communism by virtue of their more or less explicit development of institutionalized communal ownership of land.[42]

---

[40] Gilbert, 1981a, ch. 11. [41] Engels, 1966b, p. 68. [42] Weber, *SR*, pp. 81–2.

He also stressed the important social role of artisans in adopting Christianity and giving it a radical bent.[43] But he neither integrated these observations into his overall theory nor brought them to bear on the decisive issue of causal pluralism versus dialectical primacy.[44]

5. Moral explanation in *The Protestant Ethic*

If the *methodological* differences between reasonable statements of Weberian and Marxian argument are relatively fine and difficult to resolve, perhaps striking *ethical* claims divide Weber's account from a Marxian one. Yet paradoxically, as we shall see, *The Protestant Ethic* version of Weber's view seems far closer to Marxism than its reputation as *the* anti-Marxian sociological argument would suggest.

Given Weber's metaethical relativism, however, a critic might even wonder whether we can clearly identify such ethical differences. For example, Weber opened *The Protestant Ethic* on a scholarly note of seeming deprecation about European chauvinism:

> A *product* [*Sohn*] of modern European civilization, studying any problem of universal history, is bound to ask himself to what combination of circumstances the fact should be attributed that in Western civilization, and in Western civilization only, cultural phenomena have appeared which (*at least as we like to think*) lie in a line of development having universal significance and value.[45]

[43] Weber, *SR*, pp. 95–6, 98.
[44] Weber's later analysis of the rise of capitalism is, as Collins has rightly suggested, more complex, emphasizing the role of democratic craft struggles, law, the state, and war: "Weber is somewhat more sympathetic to the importance of revolutions. Perhaps the final conditions for the capitalist takeoff in England were the revolutions of 1640 and 1688. These put the state under the control of political groups favorable to capitalism, thus fulfilling the condition of keeping markets and finances free of 'irrational' and predatory state policies. Of more fundamental institutional consequence were the revolutions within the cities of ancient Greece and of medieval Italy. The latter Weber lists among 'the five great revolutions that decided the destiny of the occident.' For it was the uprising of the plebeians which replaced the charismatic law of the older patrician class with the universalistic and 'rationally instituted' law upon which so much of the institutional development of capitalism was to depend" (Collins, 1986, pp. 40–1, 43). But Collins does not try to specify the decisive theoretical and moral responses that would make a refined view Weberian as opposed to Marxian; greater stress on class struggle and its ironic political and legal consequences renders that theory more Marxian, not less. Collins, 1986, p. 34, also strikingly portrays the particular interrelationship – what Boyd calls homeostatic cluster – of properties that for Weber marks the rise of capitalism.
[45] Max Weber, *PE*, p. 13; *GAR*, p. 1 (my emphasis). As Weber was a passionate German chauvinist, one should not overestimate the note of self-deprecation; relativism can legitimize imperialism since if each argument is as justified as any other, one may as well

365

Despite this self-understanding as a "son" of his civilization and the modest distancing from prevailing evaluation, *"at least as we like to think,"* *The Protestant Ethic* made vivid ethical claims, tracing, for instance, the chilling effect of Puritanism on "spontaneous human relationships" and condemning a modern Western trend toward "specialists without spirit, sensualists without heart" (Fachmenschen ohne Geist, Genussmenschen ohne Herz).[46] In the introduction, Weber also maintained that anyone who looked with clear-sightedness at human destiny must be "shaken"; as one neither artistically "gifted" nor prophetically "called," he suggested, he would refrain from further comment.[47] But despite Weber's disclaimer about *ethics as his vocation,* he was disturbed by that destiny and despised soulless voluptuaries.

As a result of this *ethical* self-restriction, Weber scattered a series of moral observations through *The Protestant Ethic* almost as asides. Yet these observations set the complex underlying tone of his argument, a largely negative one. Curiously, *The Protestant Ethic* understates what Weber admired in European civilization. Thus, only the lines of social causality, not the relevant, multidimensional ethical criteria, receive self-aware examination. The fine hand with which he painted in the nuances of diverse versions of Protestantism is absent in his presentation of "judgments of value and faith." Nonetheless, Weber's insights into the oppressive moral impact of Protestant ascetism on workers also resemble Marxian ones. Foreshadowing E. P. Thompson, for example, Weber brilliantly stressed the role of innerworldly asceticism in training the Protestant laborer to put up with "relentless exploitation" (*Ausbeutung*). He even claimed that "asceticism educated the masses to labour, or, *in Marxian terms, to the production of surplus value,* and thereby for the first time made their employment in the capitalistic labor relation (putting-out industry, weaving, etc.) possible at all."[48] He saw the willingness to be exploited as a rarer, more necessary feature of the labor force required by early capitalism than skill. Perhaps Weber underestimated the role of hunger and of lack of independent control of tools or land in compelling the dispossessed to accede to capitalist terms; nonetheless, his characterization of this central, alienated aspect of religious influence is, in ethical terms, explicitly Marxian.

Weber contrasted these exploited Protestant laborers with the Silesian

opt for ethnocentric superiority and colonialism, based on gut patriotic conviction, as the opposite. A morally objective defense of liberalism is an antidote to chauvinism and captures the important antiethnocentric aims of many anthropologists who endorsed relativism.

[46] Weber, *PE*, p. 182; *GAR*, p. 204.   [47] Weber, *PE*, p. 29; *GAR*, p. 14.
[48] Weber, *PE*, pp. 177–9, 282 n. 107 (my emphasis); *GAR*, p. 200; *GEH*, p. 269; Thompson, 1966.

agricultural worker who chose leisure over harder work and more income. As he would later put it in *General Economic History:*

> At the beginning of all ethics and the economic relations which result, is traditionalism, the sanctity of tradition, the exclusive reliance upon such trade and industry as have come down from the fathers. This traditionalism survives far down into the present; only a human lifetime in the past it was futile to double the wages of an agricultural laborer in Silesia who mowed a certain tract of land on a contract, in the hope of inducing him to increase his exertions. He would simply have reduced by half the work expended because with this half he would have been able to earn [as much as before]. This general incapacity and indisposition to depart from the beaten path is the motive for the maintenance of tradition.[49]

Sociologically speaking, Weber characterized this subsistence laborer as "irrational" and "traditional," making the Silesian's view, as it were, "incommensurable" with that of the "modern," "rational" worker. But he overlooked the role that actual moral claims, not just claims of legitimacy to particular social actors, play in his explanation of the rise of capitalism.

Why, a eudaemonist critic might ask, is the Silesian's choice of leisure ethically and psychologically irrational from the standpoint of individuality? As G. A. Cohen has noted, the worker's conduct is *untraditional* – he works a great deal less than before. Thus, Weber's description is wrong. Further, his account hardly makes the choice of *exploitative* Puritanism "rational"; for given what we know of human psychology, it is hard to understand the willingness of former artisans and peasants to put up with the pain, discipline, boredom, and degradation of the new factory regime. The morally problematic – perplexing from the standpoint of a good life – character of the workers' conduct is what requires a *distinctively sociological* explanation: Weber and Thompson appeal to an *offsetting*, self-punishing religious influence; Thompson also indicates aspects of human psychology susceptible to it.[50]

In contrast, if we imagine a possible world in which humans initially found a cooperative, not all-absorbing work environment, producing goods in accord with a broad consensus and generating increased output – a situation dramatically opposed to actual history – we need no special story about the role of religion and a psychology that permits

---

[49] Weber, *GEH*, pp. 260–1.
[50] For workers to become exploitable, psychologically and sociologically, a version of Protestantism was needed; no utterly malleable human nature – again, a necessity of a minimally plausible, ethical relativist account – made capitalist efficiency possible.

One need not accept Thompson's Freudianism to see that his interpretation of the psychological dynamics of artisan adoption of Methodism deepens Weber's (and Marx's) account. Thompson, 1966, chs. 6–11.

major adaptation to pain. An appropriate psychology would be overdetermining, reinforcing the underlying stability of these arrangements. On Weber's and Thompson's interpretation, however, Puritanism and Methodism stabilize an otherwise discontented capitalist labor force. The latter views are explanations of alienation, the former a transparent account of well-being. Miller's notion of the role of perceptual *truisms* in posing scientific questions – in this case, moral truisms – neatly captures the origin of the *sociological problem* of the creation of a factory proletariat.

Following Weber's analysis internally, we can see that ethical standards of a good life for humans, though uncontroversial, are often ineffective. His argument recalls the emergence of modern sociology in Montesquieu's distinction between what is morally "natural" and the "natural" environmental and social conditions that explain cruelty.[51] But his ostensibly *value-neutral* sociological redescription of the Protestant worker as "rational," the peasant as "traditional," is a misguided external view, reducing the motivations of each actor to the instrumental norms of today's elites. That reductionism undercuts the theoretical interest in Weber's claim about the special role of Protestantism in preparing an exploitable work force precisely because *that sociological explanation is also a moral explanation.*[52]

More deeply, Weber's depiction of the Silesian worker ignores the harsh conflict of goods of capitalism – achievements in science, mechanization, and productivity at the expense of egalitarianism, leisure, and other aspects of proletarian well-being. A careful eudaemonist and realist account would have strengthened his argument. But causal claims about Puritanism and the rise of capitalism are Weber's distinctive sociological contribution. Even if a moral realist critic could advance no similar case about other Weberian explanations, the importance of ethical claims in this one alone defeats Weber's insistence on value freedom as a concomitant of good social science.[53]

Weber stressed other problematic features of Protestant "exploitatibility"; workers who were less enthused thought that Protestant workers' zeal instigated speed up and frequently destroyed their tools.[54] He neglected the extent to which Reformation assertions of individual dignity could become – in such horrendous circumstances – an outlook of arti-

---

[51] Gilbert, 1986a, pt. 2.
[52] Weber, *GEH*, pp. 260–1; G. A. Cohen, 1978, pp. 320–1. Weber's actual argument counts against neo-Kantian claims about ethical incommensurability, suggested by his sociological gloss.
[53] Weber opposed economic determinism. Unlike Marx's account, a narrowly economic explanation does not regard worker adaptation to capitalism as morally and psychologically problematic. For that reason, such explanations are, prima facie, implausible.
[54] Weber, *PE*, p. 63.

san and worker revolt. Considering only *The Protestant Ethic,* his account endorses the Marxian moral conclusions that capitalism misuses workers and that its advance is humanly distorted.

6. Is *The Protestant Ethic* liberal?

Weber also criticized the Protestant hero and his mediocre successors. He characterized the quality of Puritan influence on human conduct as "infinitely burdensome and earnestly enforced" and insisted on its "unexampled tyranny . . . the exact opposite of the joy of living."[55] For Weber, innerworldly asceticism chilled the spontaneity of human relations, play, and the arts: "Asceticism descended like a frost on the life of 'Merrie Old England.' "[56] In eudaemonist terms, play, spontaneous bonding, and the arts are intrinsic goods; pinched, pleasureless money-seeking and status-oriented activities are not. On Weber's account, even the zenith of Puritan world-transforming activism was morally unappealing. But the withering away of divine justification and ritual repetition of activity was worse; he foresaw a desolate bureaucratic "iron cage" of the future, the empty triumph of "specialists without spirit, sensualists without heart," which mocked claims about human progress. He spoke of "a mechanized petrification embellished with a sort of convulsive self-importance [Art von krampfhaften Sich-wichtig-nehmen]." No well-defined movement checked this trend. Only a fantastic rebirth of "old ideals" or charismatic "prophecies" might stay its steady working out.[57] As these powerful images show, Weber's artistic self-deprecation was not called for.

Reminiscent of Nietzsche's "last men" who "invented happiness" and "blink," Weber noted that this "nullity [Nichts] imagines that it has attained a stage of humanity [Stufe des Menschentums] never before reached."[58] Yet he drew a different, ethical implication from this image than Nietzsche's. In a mainly aesthetic vein, Nietzsche scorned the smallness and lack of daring of these "last men," labeling them "flea-beetles." Though Weber shared Nietzsche's contempt for their self-proclaimed "happiness," he stressed an Aristotelian lack of grasp of the appropriate motivations in vocations and relationships.[59] His view

---

[55] Thompson's Marxian account is, ethically, much clearer. It insists on the alternation – sometimes in the same desperate regions, among the same people – of religious withdrawal and Chartist revolt.

[56] Weber, *PE,* pp. 36, 37, 41, 168.   [57] Weber, *PE,* p. 182; *FMW,* p. 156.

[58] Weber, *PE,* p. 182; *GAR,* p. 204.

[59] The most moving passage of his 1918 "Science as a Vocation," written while Weber was "shaken" by German defeat and modern corruption, would also appeal for right conduct in these areas (Weber, *GAW,* p. 555; *FMW,* p. 156; *GAR,* p. 14).

has an undertone of harm to others that, to some extent, humanizes Nietzsche's judgment. A similar compassion for ordinary people spurred Marx's critique of Bentham's "shopkeepers." Opposed to status-seeking emptiness, Weber invokes something close to a notion of individuality, at least an emphasis on the capacity for deliberation. Chapter 10 examines whether his nationalism has any similar basis in eudaemonist standards.

Weber's condemnation of the seemingly overriding modern trend of bureaucratization does not simply reflect the standards and "stars" of his epoch; instead, it invokes transephochal criteria going back at least to the Greeks. Following Walzer, one might broaden Weber's metaethical relativism to include transepochal "Occidental" values. But these broad standards of well-being are independent, that relativism self-refuting. Weber's metaethics prevented him from clarifying the interplay of moral and empirical claims that yields his complex verdict on the modern era.

Though Marxians emphasize capitalist oppression of workers far more strongly than Weber, they also stress, in so doing, criteria of natural justice and individuality. If Weber's broad social theory of Protestantism and bureaucracy were right, they could include his specific moral claims among their own; for they often interpret the corruption that followed the initial, vibrant period of bourgeois activity as cultural and moral *decadence*. The Protestant chilling of some preceding relationships is also a theme for Marxians like Edward Thompson. In contrast to earlier epochs, Marx frequently pointed to retrograde aspects of capitalism – for instance, his juxtaposition of ancient citizenship and modern profit seeking. The critique of reification by Weber's famous student, Georg Lukacs, illustrates this affinity of theme, for his idea of reification unites Marx's commodity fetishism and Weber's formal rationality.[60] The best moral gloss for both conceptions of the formal calculability and substantive – human – irrationality of capitalism is a eudaemonist one. As Weber's direct influence on Lukacs suggests, no admiration for capitalism need have inhibited a person who assumed the moral stance of *The Protestant Ethic* from joining the German – or Hungarian – Communist Party.

Against Marxian claims, a critic might rightly object that Weber meant to include socialist specialists without spirit as part of this negative modern trend. In *The Protestant Ethic*, however, his antisocialist sentiments appear only as an undertone. For instance, though he emphasized "so-

[60] Lukacs, 1971, pp. 95–6, 92. A Hegelian distinction between reason as human freedom (*Vernunft*) and understanding (*Verstand*) interpreted as the – Weberian – rationalization of all spheres of life was central to the development of the Frankfurt school. Following Weber, Adorno, for example, began his subtle interpretation and critique of modernism in music from its increasingly formal character, its rationalization (Weber, 1958a; Jay, 1984, pp. 37, 72, 136, 152).

ber bourgeois," modern accumulation, he attributed the capitalist spirit of greed to all eras: "This kind of entrepreneur, the capitalistic adventurer, has existed everywhere."[61] (As Chapter 12 shows, by ascribing selfishness to human nature, he laid a second basis, distinct from his theory of bureaucratization, for ruling out socialism.) The critic could also elicit from *The Protestant Ethic* a potential parallel between the ironies of Puritanism and – on Weber's view – those of socialism. The bourgeoisie had heroically defended Puritanism; yet contemporary European culture had lost the religious grandeur and moral bizarreness of this spiritual source.[62] Analogously, for Weber, the less picturesque ideals of modern socialism would ironically multiply soulless specialists. Though such a comparison of paradoxical consequences would be strongly Weberian, *The Protestant Ethic* does not make it.[63] Neither his empirical argument on the rise of capitalism nor his evaluation of its spiritual impact need dissuade Marxians from the moral conclusion that *if* an alternative is possible, that system *deserves* to be overthrown. But if Weber's subsequent arguments ruling out communism are right, a radical might be forced to concur with his moral pessimism about modern – capitalist and socialist – decadence.

Yet at this point, a theorist sympathetic to Weber might be troubled by a different question – in what sense was he a liberal? – for as we saw in Chapter 6, Marx admired the alien achievements of capitalism – the wonders forged by "man's productive powers." So far, his endorsement of the formal recognition of democracy, freedom, and individuality contrasts with *The Protestant Ethic's* argument. Perhaps Marx was a liberal, or, more exactly, a radical whose views pass through liberalism, but Weber was not. As we shall see for other aspects of Weber's theory, this question is not easy to answer. Many of his political stands have little in common with genuine liberalism. Furthermore, *The Protestant Ethic* highlights his negative ethical judgments on modern civilization and downplays what he considered its positive features. Yet a eudaemonist interpretation might help us to restore Weber's liberalism and see what differences with sophisticated Marxism remain. That *The Protestant Ethic's* argument is so difficult in this central regard, however, reveals the costs in clarity of Weber's metaethics.

The outset of *The Protestant Ethic* recalls Montesquieu's brilliant insight that "England had progressed farthest in three things: in piety, in commerce and in freedom." Weber then asked, "Is it not possible that their commercial superiority and their adaptation to free political institutions

---

[61] Weber, *PE*, pp. 20, 24; *GEH*, p. 261; *FMW*, p. 309.   [62] Weber, *PE*, pp. 174–6.

[63] Weber, *FMW*, pp. 117, 122–6; *The Religion of China: Confucianism and Taoism*, hereafter *RC*, 1951, p. 238.

are connected in some way with the record of piety which Montesquieu ascribes to them?"[64] Weber's "spirit [*Geist*] of capitalism" echoed Montesquieu's "spirit [*esprit*] of the laws." In the context of modern debates on the rise of capitalism, his sociology of religion extended Montesquieu's empirical argument. In addition, he subscribed to Montesquieu's evaluation that English institutions were free. Yet he failed to comment on Montesquieu's accompanying liberal rejection of Aristotle's justification of "natural" slavery; for as we saw in Chapter 1, by strengthening Aristotle's climatic theory, Montesquieu had offered scientific arguments in defense of modern individuality. He had also insisted that international commerce made customs more gentle and mitigated war.[65] Given Montesquieu's eudaemonist conception of human nature, modern English institutions, despite some loss of the ancient sense of virtue, represented moral progress.[66]

Analyzing the emergence of the Occidental city in *Economy and Society,* Weber vigorously defended Western individuality and freedom. Compared with Indian and Chinese urban settlements, he isolated the termination of slavery or serfdom encapsulated in the famous principle "Stadtluft macht frei" as the West's "great *revolutionary* innovation" (grosse . . . *revolutionäre* Neuerung). Asian cities, ruled by an overlord with a special armed staff, achieved no independence. Its members retained a primary attachment to clans or kinship groups. As we shall see, Weber's sociology adapted republican and Marxian contrasts of alienated armies, quartered on society, and civilian forces.[67] The Occidental burgher, however, joined the communal political association and its Christian community as an individual. Unlike dominated Oriental city dwellers, European citizens were armed.[68] Given Weber's metaethics, he submerges his praise of early Western individuality and urban republicanism in the midst of volume 3 of *Economy and Society.* Yet his political writings also commend the productivity, science, and self-discipline of Occidental civilization.

Furthermore, although Weber was, as Chapters 10 and 11 show, quite ethnocentric, *The Protestant Ethic* had an unspoken opponent aside from Marxians: chauvinists who fantasized "alien" Jewish responsibility for capitalism. The latter would sharply attack Weber's claims. For instance,

[64] Weber, *PE*, p. 45.

[65] As Chapter 10 shows, Weber accepted these last claims.   [66] Gilbert, 1986a,b.

[67] Weber insisted on an analogy with the modern factory: A standing army separates the citizen-soldier from the means of war and concentrates weapons under the control of a professional staff (officer corps). That is also a theme of Lenin's *State and Revolution* (Weber, *ES*, 3:1239; *Wirtschaft und Gesellschaft*, hereafter WG, 1964, 2:913; *GEH*, p. 244).

[68] Weber, *ES*, 3:1239, 1246, 1247, 1261–2.

Werner Sombart maintained that the "baking" Oriental sun had bred a superficial, rootless Jewish character, conducive to usury seeking and inimical to "deep" Germans, nurtured in cool, dark Teutonic forests. In his subsequent *General Economic History*, Weber would explicitly repudiate this racist thesis, pointing out that a special, literally caste group, decried in a larger society, could hardly have brought about its internal transformation. In contrast to "pariah capitalism," he insisted, Protestant innerworldly asceticism could change the world. In context, this argument was strikingly liberal. Yet Weber chose to stress only its social theoretical, not its ethical point.[69]

Although Weber's specific judgments often appealed to objective standards, he interpreted these claims as a relativist endorsement of his culturally inherited "values." His practical, ethical relativism – a vehement adherence to German nationalism – frequently mirrored his metaethical relativism although these other, more clearly moral judgments did not. His relativist distancing from Western values led him to understate the positive achievements of liberal civilization, yet adopt its ethnocentrism. He commended a nationalist pride in that civilization's power at the expense of its virtues. Weber's metaethics and politics prevented a careful formulation of his multidimensional evaluation of modern experience as opposed to *The Protestant Ethic*'s disjointed presentation; it militated against his liberalism. In addition, given the empirical trend toward bureaucratization, he could not simply endorse capitalist civilization.

But if he were right about the lack of an alternative, his overriding of earlier defenses of individuality might be well taken. In that case, rejecting the outcome of modern – capitalist – individuality, he could still have admired the spirit of the common good among ancient Greek citizens, as Montesquieu, Hegel, and Marx did, even though he regarded it as irretrievable.[70] Yet despite their differences, these other writers all condemned slavery or such negative aspects of comparatively "spontaneous human relations" as serfdom more strongly than Weber. On a morally explicit version of his argument, a Weberian might have found it hard to answer a qualified liberal defense of individuality under capitalism.

Recognizing the human suffering accompanying actual historical progress, Marx, like Weber, reached a multidimensional ethical assessment of the rise of capitalism. Unlike some economic determinist and liberal defenders of capitalist progress, he adopted a morally tentative attitude

---

[69] Weber, *GEH*, p. 263; *PE*, pp. 185, 187; Sombart, 1951, pp. 248–51, 334–5. Jeffrey Herf brought this feature of *The Protestant Ethic* to my attention (Herf, 1984, pp. 130 n. 3, 136–51).

[70] Weber, *FMW*, pp. 141, 148.

toward social and ethical advance.[71] As we have seen, original accumulation and the early English raj exemplified industrial progress and might be considered necessities, from the point of view of Marxian theory, in laying the ultimate social and political basis for communism; yet Marx mainly denounced their cruelty. Unlike *The Protestant Ethic*'s scattered remarks, however, Marx presented a connected, microstructural evaluation of these diverse aspects. Precisely because Marxian social theory and moral judgments are dialectical, they offer an ethical handle on complex historical conflicts that a eudaemonist theoretical framework helps to explain. Whether a Weberian or Marxian theory about socialism is true, a Marxian – or Hegelian – version of moral realism furthers sophisticated assessment of modern liberal societies, encompassing the possibility of decline. Weber's relativism – like Marx's occasional metaethical remarks – does not. But these subtle though important distinctions between Weberian and Marxian moral and epistemological claims do not reveal their deepest disagreements. The next chapters will turn to more sharply contested theoretical and practical clashes of imperialism with internationalism, status with democracy, and bureaucratization with cooperative (socialist) revolution.

---

[71] Today's modernization theorists often invoke Weber's rationalism – traditionalism dichotomy with an accentuated emphasis on the putative "irrationality" of tradition.

Chapter 10

Nationalism and the dangers of predatory "liberalism"

1. Patriotism and internationalism

This chapter and the next will explore conflicting Weberian and Marxian explanations and evaluations of two great, interrelated twentieth-century political issues: the conflict of imperialism and predatory nationalism with democratic internationalism, and the domestic interplay of class, status, and racism. Though Weberian and subsequent power-state "realisms" are often invoked by liberals, they are linked to non-liberal political and moral conclusions; their clash with radical claims is glaring.[1] A comparison with Marxism highlights the core features of plausible liberal ethical and empirical claims against Weber's conclusions. Further, these Marxian positions are – at least in an intellectual climate dominated by international politics "realism" – unexpected and, prima facie, implausible. Once we clarify the theoretical contrast, however, we can find considerable evidence for them. In Popperian terms, good philosophy of science justifies exploration of radical claims: As they are surprising, so they are fruitful.[2] Such theories are important, so far undefeated contenders for truth.

At the outset of the twentieth century, the German ruling class sparred with other capitalist powers for worldwide economic and political influence. In this "age of imperialism" and colonialism, European and American elites adopted domineering aims in Africa, Asia, the Middle East, and Latin America. Accompanying industrialization and

[1] Today's international political economy "realists" and neorealists have been unusually concerned with fair theoretical comparison. They acknowledge the force of many Marxian causal claims and view that theory as an important contender for truth (Krasner, 1978, pp. 21–6, 32–3, 152–3, 323–5 n. 98; Gilpin, 1987, pp. 42, 50–1; Keohane, 1984, p. 42; Gilbert, 1990b).
[2] Alan Gilbert, 1984b, sec. 5, contends that Marxian theories of racism meet Lakatos's standards of a progressive research program. For a realist conception of fruitfulness, see McMullin, 1976; 1984, pp. 30–1.

imperialist rivalry in Germany, Russia, France, and to a lesser extent the United States, strong internationalist and socialist working-class movements emerged.[3] At international congresses and in domestic politics, radicals opposed colonial adventures and the prospect of world war on the grounds that they served only capitalists and threatened the lives, dignity, and basic interests of workers. Chauvinism deflected movements for democratic revolution and radical social reorganization. As Lenin summarized a socialist viewpoint, "The international unity of the workers is more important than the national."[4]

Weber, a staunch German patriot, forged his social theory in this conflict-ridden atmosphere. As he found democratic internationalism profoundly disturbing, nationalist themes pervade his argument. Thus, midway through *The Protestant Ethic,* he juxtaposed the still otherworldly Puritan ethic with the "proud" patriotism of Machiavelli's Florentine citizens: "In their struggle against the Pope and his excommunication, the latter had held 'Love of their native city higher than the fear for the salvation of their souls.'" He also conjured Wagner's Siegmund, who, before mortal combat, meditated on Wotan and a warrior's Valhalla.[5] These remarks – though typically made in passing – indicate Weber's own moral stand. "Politics as a Vocation" would recur to these paradigms.[6]

In common with radicals, a concern with international politics dominates his social theory. But as a theoretical "realist," he saw the violent conflict of nations, especially of "power states," as the determining fact of political life. Thus, in a 1906 lecture in Saint Louis, he contrasted relatively tranquil American isolation, which permitted democracy to function, with the German political need, hemmed in by "powerful and warlike neighbors," for an authoritarian "coat of mail."[7] On his view, democratic institutions have no outward-reaching, internationalist character or justification; his great-power "realism" circumscribes his political sociology. Further, he welcomed Germany's "destiny" as a "*Machtstaat*." Meditation upon the future of the Germanic peoples infused his essays with political passion and pathos.

In his 1917 "Deutschland unter den europäishchen Weltmächten" ("Germany among the European World Powers"), Weber embraced his generation's fate (*Schicksal*), its "inescapable responsibility" (unentrinn-

---

[3] Schorske, 1972; Maehl, 1980, p. 488; Haimson, 1964; Badayev, n.d.; Gilbert, 1981.

In Germany despite a period of illegality, the Social Democratic Party (SPD) grew steadily and, by 1912, received over 4 million votes, mainly from workers. As I noted in Chapter 8, the Bolsheviks became the main leaders of unionized workers in Saint Petersburg and Moscow before World War I.

[4] Lenin, *CW*, 35:247; Gilbert, 1978b.   [5] Weber, *PE*, p. 107.

[6] Weber, *FMW*, pp. 123, 126.   [7] Weber, *FMW*, pp. 384–5.

bare Verantwortung vor der Geschichte) to advance German culture, honor, and fame in the "clear hard air of the realm of world history." As we will see, this patriotic meaning molds his famous concept of an "ethic of responsibility" (*Verantwortungsethik*). German destiny would beckon "later travellers to undying remembrance" of his generation's glory.[8] In his 1906 lecture, Weber charged a saying of Carlyle's with patriotic fervor:

> "Thousands of years have passed before thou couldst enter life, and thousands of years to come wait in silence that thou wilt do with this thy life." I do not know if, as Carlyle believed, a single man can or will place himself in his actions upon the sounding-board of this sentiment. But a nation must do so, if its existence in history is to be of lasting value.[9]

Drawing a parallel between politics and scientific clarity, his "Science as a Vocation" also invokes Carlyle's saying.[10]

Anticontextualist readers, drawn to metaethical claims about a value-neutral social science, may misjudge Weber's notions of "clarity" and "responsibility." They are hardly neutral. As his considered view of the "klare harte Luft" of world history centered on the inevitability of great-power competition, he tendentiously restricted "clear" political analysis of means to this end. Consequently, as Chapter 12 shows, he would consign revolutionary politics, even of Lenin's variety, to an irrational "ethic of intention" for failing to recognize putative power-state imperatives. In "Germany among the European World Powers," he stressed the particular international determination of his political and moral stand: "I have always looked at politics solely from a national viewpoint, not only external politics but all politics. By this alone I orient my party allegiance."[11] Power-state concerns should permeate all aspects of a nation's life: "Only he is a *national* politician [*nationaler* Politiker] who looks at internal politics from the standpoint of inevitable adaptation [*Anpassung*] to external political tasks.[12]

2. Weber's four nationalisms

Weber advanced four, sometimes conflicting justifications for his celebration of the German *Volk*: first, a relativist contention that incommensurable demons rule national cultures and that German nationalism is as justifiable as any other; second, an objective claim about the moral achievements of European and, to a lesser extent, German culture in contrast to czarism; third, an objective claim about just, defensive war

---

[8] Weber, *Gesammelte Politische Schriften*, hereafter *GPS*, 1958b, pp. 172, 25.
[9] Wcber, *FMW*, p. 385.   [10] Weber, *FMW*, p. 135.
[11] Weber, *GPS*, pp, 152, 14.   [12] Weber, *GPS*, p. 282.

against Russian aggression; fourth, a reductionist claim that imperialist social structures made all ethical justification mere rationalization, but left German power interests on a par with others. The relativist and reductionist claims cohere with Weber's metaethics and are variants of the neo-Kantianism and empiricism that I considered in Part I. These arguments are self-refuting. But the objective claims – the second and third – conflict with the former epistemological theses. If articulated and defended, they suggest what Weber's analysis might have looked like as a *full-fledged liberal* one in contrast to some of his own practical and epistemological conclusions.

On the first justification, Weber saw different cultures as ruled by belligerent deities: "I do not know how one might wish to decide 'scientifically' the value of French and German culture; for here, too, different gods struggle with one another, now and for all time." [13] To assess this battle, Weber adopted what David Lyons has called an "appraiser's-group relativism": He judged other cultures by the values of his own. [14] His social scientific relativism thus differs markedly from the agent's-group relativism of twentieth-century anthropology, which strives to offer moral judgments from the standpoint of a culture under study and affirms cultural equality; for Weber did not doubt the superiority of German to Russian or Polish culture. In his "Critical Studies in the Logic of the Cultural Sciences," he hailed Eduard Meyer's analysis of the "triumph of the free Hellenic circle of ideas . . . which gave us those cultural values from which we draw our sustenance." He attacked any treatment of other cultures as equal: "The notion of a sort of 'social' justice which would – finally, finally! – take the contemptibly neglected Kafir and Indian tribes at least as seriously as the Athenians . . . is merely childish." [15]

Weber insisted that the victory of the Greeks at Marathon – not comparatively obscure African conflicts – had historically influenced "one's own [i.e., European] values." But is the significance of the Greek polis that it influenced later *European* culture – Weber's relativism – or rather that it revealed something important about *human*, not just Western, potentials for cooperation and freedom? Why, one might ask, is Greek culture – a *non-German* culture, as Weber emphasized – of greater significance, on his view, than the contemporary, widely touted values of the "Teutonic forest"? [16]

Weber's endorsement of Athenian *freedom* pointed to a second possible justification of chauvinism by arguments that Europeans, but only

[13] Weber, *FMW*, 148.   [14] Lyons, 1976.   [15] Weber, *MSS*, p. 172 n. 37.
[16] Mosse, 1964. An objective view also recognizes distinctive non-Greek discoveries about intrinsic goods and realizations of virtues.

Europeans, are capable of civilization and freedom. As Chapter 1 stressed, this position has sometimes – as in Weber's version – sanctioned the oppression of nonwhite peoples. But a defensible, nonchauvinist version of this argument might focus on moral discoveries about human cooperation and freedom; it insists on the great contributions of non-Europeans and European subordinates – consider the slave revolt led by Toussaint L'Ouverture in Haiti, the Chinese revolution, and European and American democratic internationalism.[17] That version also recognizes that European regimes have often violently opposed social and moral advance. The chauvinist lie trades on a truth that it fails to articulate consistently.

Combining chauvinist appeals with ones to ethical and social progress, Weber referred to English culture and to Anglo-Saxon/German culture in the United States as "great" civilizations.[18] Yet the objective component in his argument, for instance about Greek ideas, was often strong. As the preceding chapter notes, he endorsed medieval urban and English freedom because of their political and moral qualities.

In contrast to Weber, a radical might sketch a more finely grained, nonchauvinist and nonrelativist account of French and German culture. Let us suppose, following Weber's view, that one could not arrive at a comparative evaluation of their moral worth as distinct from, say, a contrast of either with that paradigm of barbarism, Nazism. Important features of culture, a moral realist might suggest, are ethically plural or indeterminate.[19] The ethical evaluation of cultures is multidimensional and limited; it distinguishes moral aspects – especially those concerned with the mutual recognition of personality and protection of life – from nonmoral ones.

In this context, we might still analyze the relative contributions of particular cultures to moral progress. Consider the French Revolution's worldwide impact on human freedom from an objective liberal point of view – say, that of Kant or Marx – and the comparative contributions of nineteenth-century French and German communism from a Marxian one.[20] From an international perspective, these important aspects of the two cultures seem mutually reinforcing, more like friends than Weber's belligerents. Once again, as the movements led by Toussaint and Mao testify, these achievements are not merely European. Contrary to Weber, for some important ethical and political theoretical purposes, a finer, objective, microstructural evaluation of cultures seems possible.

---

[17] French revolutionary republicanism, including calls for the abolition of slavery, helped inspire the Haitian movement and was, in terms of antiracism, surpassed by it (Gilbert, 1981a, ch. 2).

[18] Weber, *FMW*, pp. 384–5.   [19] Goldman, 1986, pp. 70–1.   [20] Gilbert, 1981a, ch. 1.

Third, Weber standardly justified German participation in World War I as self-defense. In "Zur Thema der 'Kriegsschuld'" ("On the Theme of 'War Guilt'"), he spoke of czarism's "refined methods of emasculation of peoples [Volksentmannung]."[21] Like many chauvinists, Weber affixed his nationalism to trite masculine metaphors. If his empirical claims were right, however, then the Russian government had launched an unjust war against Germany. Further, in "Germany among the European World Powers," he had contended that this nation of 70 million must act as a *Machtstaat* to protect the independence of "small nations" (Kleinstaaten) – Switzerland, Holland, and Scandinavia – that shared its culture.[22] Thus, he appealed objectively to the theory of aggression and perhaps to other general moral principles such as the right of individuals to security and to a culture of their own as distinct from one imposed by a foreign power.[23] In "War Guilt," Weber claimed that any fair examination of Russian foreign policy – as, for instance, the one by some previously internationalist German Social Democrats – must conclude that "a war against *this* system was a good war [ein guter Krieg]."[24] He substituted the phrase "good war" for just war without altering the substantive moral claims involved. His official, metaethical relativism presents these ethical judgments in their least plausible light.

Fourth, faced with German defeat and the prospect of an onerous Versailles treaty, Weber shifted away from the notion of just war to a reductionist attempt, based on the war's great-power character, to counter claims of special German "guilt." In Germany, intense discussions of wartime responsibility took place both on the left and the right (the standard "stab in the back" theory of how civilian democratic rebellion "sabotaged" the military effort).[25] Conjuring sexist imagery, Weber stigmatized these discussions – "searching like old women for the 'guilty one'" – as unmanly and undignified. Such charges served as mere legitimations since "the structure of society produced the war." Claims of justice must be reduced, in a quasi-empiricist vein, to specific interests.[26] The Versailles settlement should be assessed solely by its likely ultimate offense to German "honor," a cause of renewed war.

This reductionist argument conflicted with his previous extenuation of German self-defense. It undermined alternative, objective claims that

---

[21] Weber, *GPS*, pp. 479–80.   [22] Weber, *GPS*, pp. 171–2.

[23] Given international influence in culture, this idea is clear in some ways (against gross conquest), though obscure, pathetic, malignant in others – say, the intolerant search for purported, primitive Teutonic, Islamic, American (Ku Klux Klan), or other "purity."

[24] Weber, *GPS*, pp. 479–80, 566.

[25] The reactionary image of the Vietnam War suggested in "Rambo" and "Missing in Action" is comparable.

[26] Weber, *FMW*, p. 118; *GPS*, p. 537.

given the responsibility of each great power, a punitive settlement was unjust and thus a cause of German grievance, or, more narrowly, granting the victors' view, that the terms of the Versailles levy would not be proportional to German wrongdoing. Contrary to Weber, a coherent moral argument would have been more dignified. It would have avoided the inconsistency and political shiftiness of moving from a claim of self-defense by the Kaiser to one that no such views can be rationally defended.

On his reductionist account, he maintained that the structures of the contending powers were expansionary or that enduring interests, created by these structures, required war. Though Weber did not spell out this view, his account might be thought to resemble Lenin's, for the latter criticized each regime's claims to fight "justly" in World War I.

Yet the ethical differences are instructive. As we saw in Chapter 1, unlike Weber's, Lenin's social theory overrode claims by these powers to incorporate a common good and, hence, to wage a defensive war: "The proletariat is opposed to defense of the fatherland in this imperialist war because of its predatory, slave-owning reactionary character, because it is possible and necessary to oppose to it (and to strive to convert it into) civil war for socialism."[27]

Lenin considered some wars waged by capitalist powers – for instance, that of the French Revolution against counterrevolutionary invaders – to be just, as well as proletarian civil wars, those of self-defense by socialist regimes, and anticolonial ones.[28] With internationalist and subtle, historical awareness, he offered moral realist arguments about whether the contending powers, given their internal structure and colonial holdings, could fairly advance claims of justice.

In contrast, Weber's "Politics as a Vocation" viewed World War I as a necessity, a force of nature, a nonmoral phenomenon. Yet, following Lenin, one might reformulate his argument in ethical terms. Since the social structure of each power *now* instigates war, perhaps previously appropriate claims about just wars are to be overridden. That statement of a Weberian view still distinguishes defensive wars from mere rationalizations. For reasons that Chapter 12 explores, a Weberian account rules out a more cooperative regime; thus, existing liberal polities should minimize grievances that lead to renewed conflict or increase its magnitude. But the possibility of mitigating grievances belies Weber's original extenuation on grounds of systemic necessity. War's enormous human costs make any sphere of political choice morally important.

To dismiss claims of justice, Weber drew two analogies, the first to a man who abandons one woman for another on the basis of allegations

---

[27] Lenin, *CW*, 22:313, 310.   [28] Lenin, *CW*, 22:309.

about the former's flaws – this attitude "with a profound lack of chivalry, adds a fancied 'legitimacy' to the plain fact that he no longer loves her and that the woman has to bear it"; the second to a war-weary soldier who rationalizes quitting by imagining that he had "to fight for a morally bad cause."[29] Once again, these images of conduct – inadequate soldiering, abandonment of a woman – reflect male gender identity.

But first, a particular *cruel* rationalization does not prove that any such judgment is flawed. Might a woman ever disavow a man who was unfaithful – one of Weber's "scoundrels"? – or vice versa?[30] Or a spouse who beat a child? Love, for Weber, was apparently not a relationship of deep mutual recognition and respect for individuality but a creature of passing fancy.[31]

Weber's second analogy is just as weak; for the Kiel sailors, who risked their lives to revolt, were not simply "war weary." Instead, they opposed a corrupt, belligerent government and initiated the November revolution; from a (liberal) republican standpoint, they were heroic. Given an all-consuming patriotism, Weber, however, inaccurately, needed to maintain that the mutineers had merely rationalized fear. But would Russian soldiers, overturning the czar, have fallen under a similar Weberian stigma? Is Weber's answer "no" during much of the war, "yes" after the Russian Revolution? In contrast, on Lenin's theory, any – antiexpansionary – mutiny against *this* war was just.

3. Weber's social theory and contemporary politics

Before exploring Weber's theory of expansion, I want to emphasize three controversial political stands that arise from the primacy of great-power rivalry: his advocacy of immigration restriction against Poles, his instrumental defense of parliamentary institutions and of a greater role for proletarian leadership, and his recommendation of comparatively moderate aims in World War I. Weber extenuated liberal aspects of his politics and affirmed reactionary positions instrumentally. Since only his unofficial descriptions suggest modern moral achievements, his official political and metaethical argument amounts at best to an *imperialist liberalism* rather than a rational defense of individuality.

Weber's notorious 1895 address entitled "Der Nationalstaat und die Volkswirtschaftspolitik" ("The National State and National Economic

---

[29] Weber, *FMW*, p. 118.
[30] Weber, *MSS*, pp. 12–13.
[31] A critic might grant that in a highly sexist society, many try to live out class, status, and gender roles, and relationships often end for such reasons. In that case, Weber would have overgeneralized a common rationalization at the expense of uncontroversial ethical standards.

Policy") stresses the advancement of the *Volk* as the guiding principle in economics. In a racist vein, he called for preservation of Germanic culture through barring "inferior" Polish agricultural laborers.[32] In this *political economy*, politics overrode the narrow, "unnational" economic interests of Prussian Junkers in securing cheap labor. But the German ruling classes did not follow his counsel. In 1899, Weber resigned from the expansionist Pan German League over its failure to campaign against Polish immigration.

Weber also evaluated institutions in the light of external aims, admiring English parliamentarianism as an efficient vehicle for the pursuit of colonialism:

> The German philistine . . . believes that he can smugly look down on them [parliamentary institutions] from the heights of his own political impotence and . . . fails to consider that the British parliament became, after all, the proving ground for those political leaders who managed to bring a quarter of mankind under the rule of a minute but politically prudent minority.[33]

Weber's 1917 "Parliament and Government in Germany" criticized Bismarck's blunting of parliamentary leadership and the Kaiser's bumbling in foreign affairs.[34] He contended that modern officialdom could not generate competent leaders. Only parliamentary investigation could ensure intelligent policies; this training alone could breed political "heroes" (*Helden*). Such leaders, comparable to the National Liberals of the 1860s and 1870s, might not attain Bismarck's heights – those of a "genius" who comes along every "several centuries" – yet they could translate Weber's sociological category of charisma in pursuit of German imperial aims and "put their hand to the wheel of history."[35]

From his earliest essays, Weber recognized the political "unripeness" of the German bourgeoisie, fearful of proletarian revolution, for overseeing expansionary interests. His argument recalls Marx's analysis of bourgeois "senility" in 1848, its shunning of potentially radicalizing democratic practices.[36] As a self-aware member of that class, Weber concluded that only a nonbourgeois, politically professional elite could sustain capitalist interests. In this context, he might have emphasized as Schumpeter would, the role of aristocrats in English imperial policy. Parliamentar-

---

[32] Weber, *GPS*, p. 10; Bruun, 1972, p. 55 n. 7.   [33] Weber, *ES*, 3:1420.

[34] Weber, *ES*, 3:1387–91, 1404–5, 1419–20, 1431–8.

[35] Weber, *ES*, 3:1387, 1420, 1462; *FMW*, pp. 115, 128. Montesquieu admired English parliamentary investigation for furthering peace, Weber for empire and skilled belligerence (Montesquieu, *EL*, 1:170, 339–40).

[36] Gilbert, 1981a, chs. 2, 10.

ianism, for Weber, enraptured British workers with the "resonance of [a] world power position" (Resonanz der Weltmachtstellung).[37]

Officially, he commended democratic reforms only as a means to expansionary purposes, including deflection of class conflict. During World War I, for instance, he called for the abolition of the antiworker, Prussian three-class suffrage system and its replacement by equal voting. This measure, he contended, might encourage the Social Democratic leadership in its prowar stand, spur its transformation into a "national-social" party, and make it politically "ripe."[38] Weber foresaw a German political vocation as a *"Herrenvolk,"* a term later to become infamous, if its working-class leadership would, like the English, become militantly patriotic.[39] These practical concerns shaped his political theory. Thus, *Economy and Society*'s assessment of the medieval Northern European city stressed that the zenith of expansion accompanied the rise of democratic craft rule (*Zunftherrschaft*): "Wherever 'craft'-rule was installed at all effectively, this coincided with the peak of the city's external power and its greatest internal political independence."[40]

Yet during World War I, Weber opposed the vast aggressive demands of the Vaterlandspartei and most German academics, led by Dietrich Schäfer. The latter sought annexations in Belgium, Poland, western Russia, eastern France, and the English colonies.[41] The chauvinism of these "literati," as Weber contemptuously styled them, would unite the other powers against Germany. It would drive Central European nations to seek protection from the czar. Even temporary successes, he averred, would lead to ultimate failure. Since Thucydides, "realists" have adopted a characteristic, but unavowed moral stance, one of truthtelling and unmasking the (ideological) grandiosity of leaders. "Realism" implicitly relies on appeals to *common* goods of life and economic well-being. Thus, Weber distinguished *realpolitik*, attentive to (what he saw as) fundamental German interests, and self-destructive posturing.[42] Despite the ethical undercurrent, however, injustice was not an overt consideration in his instrumental critique of Prussian aggrandizement.[43]

To underpin his policy recommendations, Weber offered a theory of the dynamics of imperialism and the limits of proletarian victimization.

---

[37] Weber, *GPS*, pp. 20–3, 233; Gilbert, 1981a, chs. 1, 10; 1987; Schumpeter, 1962, p. 298.

[38] Weber, *GPS*, pp. 234–5, 26.   [39] Weber, *GPS*, p. 279.   [40] Weber, *ES*, 3:1282.

[41] Ringer, 1969, p. 190.   [42] Weber, *GPS*, p. 165.

[43] Weber failed to include these "literati" among exemplars of an ethic of intention. Perhaps that decision involves some fine moral derogation – he saw them as conceited belligerents, not potential moralists of integrity; perhaps, restricting "an ethic of responsibility" to great-power politics, he could only view them as irresponsible.

Important facts of German economic and political development, however, are *anomalies* for this argument. They make a radical alternative plausible.

Weber insisted on the "opportunities for profit" of conquered, or, in today's terms, "neocolonially dominated" territories.[44] Like Lenin, Weber had previously maintained that capitalist powers would exhaust internal markets, carve up foreign ones, and clash over that division.[45] But he also looked to additional political and economic dynamics. Thus, his 1917 "War Guilt" contended that England's motive for war (*Kriegsgrund*) stemmed from the naval race and not, as some German politicians had suggested, "envy of trade."[46] Weber had shifted from an economic to a multicausal theory of imperialism.

Economy and Society remarked that political expansion often precedes or accompanies investment and trade. Weber still maintained, however, that "the economic structure in general does codetermine the amount and manner of political expansion." He did not seek a specifically capitalist theory of such aggrandizement, however, but rather a transhistorical one. Studying ancient empires, he noted that the implanting of administration and means of communication were "advantageous for present or future trading needs."[47] Though Weber's argument opposed a mechanical materialism, it could easily cohere with a dialectical one; for, once again, a genuine dispute with Marxians would contrast a multicausal "codetermination" to dialectical primacy: the use of varied political and military strategies to provide for "future trading needs."

Despite his stress on the search for markets, Weber turned his empirical theory in a non-Marxian direction. Flirting with Montesquieu's conception of the peaceful impact of commerce and prefiguring Schumpeter, Weber contrasted a transepochal imperialist role for the state – securing tribute, farming taxes, feeding war industry, and creating "political capitalist" interests – with normal accumulation. As *The Protestant Ethic* recorded, Calvinist entrepreneurs, energetically seeking profits through the market, scorned the charters of "luxurious" court capitalism.[48] In *Economy and Society*, Weber argued, "In general and at all times, imperialist capitalism, especially colonial booty capitalism based on direct force and compulsory labor, has offered by far the greatest opportunities for profit."[49] He now insisted that contemporary European economic expansion had a mainly statist character: "The universal revival of 'imperialist' capitalism, which has always been the normal form in which capitalist interests have influenced politics, and the revival of po-

[44] Weber, *ES*, 2:918–19.   [45] Mommsen, 1959, pp. 86–7.   [46] Weber, *GPS*, pp. 484, 483.
[47] Weber, *ES*, 2:915.   [48] Weber, *PE*, pp. 179–80.   [49] Weber, *ES*, 2:918.

litical drives for expansion are thus not accidental."[50] This claim contradicts his insistence on the specific modern capitalist need for markets.

Yet Weber's argument still has an odd economic determinist ring: Private entrepreneurs who engage in foreign commerce *must* have "pacifist" aims; even their employees will supposedly take up democratic internationalism, based on economic interest. In contrast, state-sponsored enterprises *must* support political expansion and war; their employees will ostensibly embrace patriotism. Weber sometimes recognized overall class conflict, yet he peculiarly identified the dominant interests of workers with the particular interests of their industry.[51] This claim is a remarkably strong, *local, industrial sector reductionism*. As a political view, it is unreflectively elitist, denying to individual workers, a priori, the capacity for complex deliberation that, on a radical account, is central to internationalism. Ironically, though Weber's theory is guided by his political purposes – it is a statist, *national* economy – his sociological conception of others is often remarkably apolitical. Yet no evidence supports his determinism: German socialism neither drew its main strength from workers in private, export-oriented industries nor found itself frustrated in state-nurtured ones.[52]

Weber's general, ideal-typical analysis legitimized private capitalism, restricted the socialist possibilities of a divided working class, and encouraged the Social Democratic leadership to opt for a "realistic," chauvinist course. As a theoretical consequence of his ideal-typical approach, he did not try to explain why specifically late-nineteenth-century European great-power rivalry, in contrast to its commercial predecessors, ransacked all corners of the world. His claims about undifferentiated, universal, state-sponsored capitalism are unhelpful. In contrast, drawing on Weber's earlier thinking, Marxians account for this worldwide expansion by pointing to the emergence of competing modern capitalisms and their economic and political need, in the *Manifesto*'s phrase, to "create a world in their own image."

Note that a radical (broadly Marxian) explanation can be causally flexible. It need not insist on the specific role of monopoly or finance capitalism, but depending on the evidence, might stress, with Robinson,

---

[50] Weber, *ES*, 2:919.   [51] Weber, *ES*, 2:919.

[52] Unlike the Bolsheviks, the SPD did not organize in the military (Schorske, 1972, pp. 72–5). The Kiel revolt proved, however, that sailors and soldiers were open to radical ideas. Their lives were, after all, sacrificed for imperial purposes. Patriotic education and coercive conscription might explain their earlier participation; the inference that their complex "material" interests sustained expansion and belligerence is not obvious.

Comparable to economic determinist versions of Marxism, Weber's industry reductionism recapitulates the lack of empathy of his examples of the Silesian laborer, lover, and rebellious sailor.

Gallagher, and Denny, the competitive character of early English expansion, and with Gerschenkron, the increasing role of the state in latecomers to industrialization and the historical advantages and disadvantages of *particular* powers.[53] It might recognize the divisions of strategy among individuals and interest among strata in the ruling class. Given the brutality of modern history that today's liberals rightly condemn, Marxian theories have resources that make their defeat, by liberal defenses of capitalism, a complex enterprise. A liberal, once again, must claim that intercapitalist competition need not be connected over time to fierce divisions of interest and political clashes, and, better yet, undercuts them.[54] In this debate, Weber's embrace of war as a modern destiny is not a promising liberal alternative.

Further, in historical perspective, even Weber's commendations of private commerce generate two major anomalies. First, during the initial era of laissez-faire trade policy, English capitalism had already organized the empire on which "the sun never sets." Though politically chartered enterprises like the East India Company, colonization, and the slave trade all contributed to accumulation, the "imperialism of free trade," of a burgeoning private capitalism that lacked serious competitors, enabled England to achieve world domination.[55] To counter charges about German war aims, Weber called attention to the already established, "uncontested" British empire.[56]

Second, to become a *Machtstaat*, Germany had to mount a concomitant *political* challenge to England and other emerging great powers. Weber never expected this struggle for a German "place in the sun" to be peaceful; he advocated military strength and the vigorous pursuit of power politics. As Weber's 1895 speech underlined, Friedrich List's demand for state protection of infant industries and opposition to free trade had initiated a theoretical tradition: German economics was a *national, political* discipline.[57] In Weber's historical argument, a dialectical analysis of economic and political components of German and other forms of imperialism seems appropriate, a transepochal, ideal-typical dichotomy be-

---

[53] Robinson, Gallagher, and Denny, 1965, pp. 471–2; Gerschenkron, 1965, ch. 1.

[54] Citing Lenin favorably on the uneven development of great powers, Gilpin's celebrated study of Japan's new economic preeminence over the United States is a startling rebirth of radical argument in the center of contemporary international political economy (Gilpin, 1987). Keohane's game-theoretical study of regimes, replete with criticisms of the negative moral impact of current international cooperation, lays the basis for a distinctively liberal account (Keohane, 1984, chs. 5, 11; Gilbert, 1990b).

[55] Hobsbawn, 1968. Mirroring a common scholarly failure to specify theoretical context, Robinson and Gallagher's causal challenge to a Leninist emphasis on finance capitalism actually sustains radical moral argument.

[56] Weber, *GPS*, p. 169; *ES*, 3:1419–20.

[57] List founded the *Volkswirtschaft* to which Weber self-consciously contributed.

tween commerce and state hard to justify. Emphasizing theoretical "realism," he should have expected such interstate dynamics; his moral and causal claim about the inherent "peaceableness" of private enterprise does not fit his own theory.

4. Can Weber explain internationalism?

In addition, Weber's industry reductionism does not account for a mass German socialist movement. Yet that political fact, coupled with his nationalism, elicited fascination with class struggle. *Economy and Society* depicts a specific modern clash between proletarians and capitalists, based on opposed economic interests.[58] In assessing this conflict, radical and Weberian theory differ over whether workers had strong enough interests, given capitalist oppression, to forge democratic internationalist and socialist movements, and over whether successful revolutionary movements could offset the trend toward bureaucratization and serve a common good. For radicals, democratic internationalism has two components, both of which Weber rejected. First, that outlook requires resistance to every aggressive policy of one's own government, whether or not that regime is formally democratic. (Call this *liberal democratic internationalism*.) Second, that view can sustain support for revolutionary movements abroad and, to check the persecution of internationalism, at home as well. (Call this *radical democratic internationalism*.) A coherent liberal view affirms many of these stands; hence the encompassing term "democratic internationalism" is appropriate. In contrast, Weber hoped that Social Democrats might become leading charismatic nationalists.

Chapter 12 focuses on Weber's denial of the good of socialism. The remainder of this chapter will explore his opposition to internationalism. Given his theoretical stress on the likelihood of a "ripe" nationalist socialism, the existence of a frequently vigorous, internationalist movement is another important anomaly.

In *Economy and Society*, Weber contended that, for workers, democratic internationalist sentiments overrode seeming economic interests in foreign domination:

> Labor in creditor nations is of strongly pacifist mind and on the whole shows no interest whatsoever in the continuation and compulsory collection of such tributes from foreign debtors that are in arrears. Nor does labor show an interest in forcibly participating in the exploitation of foreign colonial territories and public commissions.[59]

---

[58] Weber, *ES*, 2:303–5, 3:931–2; *GPS*, p. 233.   [59] Weber, *ES*, 2:920.

If Weber envisioned a general commitment to nonviolence, then he used the term "pacificism" mistakenly; for as Lenin's argument, cited above, showed, internationalism could support insurrection and revolutionary wars; in 1917, Russian workers overthrew a predatory regime. But Weber vividly acknowledged the broad existence of a socialist, liberal democratic internationalism; his view conflicts with standard procapitalist claims that workers must adopt "national" economic aims. On his account, "certain leading strata" vehemently opposed war. At the outbreak of World War I, the first statement of the Social Democratic Party (SPD) executive (July 25, 1914, reversed August 4) proclaimed:

> The class-conscious proletariat of Germany, in the name of humanity and civilization, raises a flaming protest against this criminal activity of the warmongers. It insistently demands that the German Government exercise its influence on the Austrian government to maintain peace; and, in the event that the shameful war cannot be prevented, that it refrain from belligerent intervention. No drop of blood of a German soldier may be sacrificed to the power lust of the Austrian ruling group [or] to the imperialistic profit-interests.

Between July 26 and July 30, local socialist organizations held antiwar demonstrations throughout Germany.[60] They illustrated Weber's sociological comment: "there are . . . social groups that profess indifference to, and even directly relinquish, any evaluational adherence to a single nation. At the present time, certain leading strata of the class movement of the proletariat consider such indifference and relinquishment to be an accomplishment."[61]

An important nationalist current always existed in German Social Democracy, however, and eventually, accompanied by fierce government pressure, triumphed. Yet the long period of successful democratic internationalist organizing, despite the SPD's internal hesitations, stands out.[62] As a liberal or radical might sadly insist, the socialist international could not stop World War I; as the radical might note, that movement

---

[60] Schorske, 1972, pp. 286–7; Nolan, 1981, pp. 246–7.   [61] Weber, *ES*, 2:924.
[62] Marx and Engels, 1972a, 2:27–8; Schorske, 1972, pp. 75–9.

The SPD had a strong internationalist record. The Kaiser jailed their deputies, Bebel and Liebknecht, for refusing to vote war credits for the Franco-Prussian war; German socialists organized rallies to support the Paris Commune. The later SPD participated in international congresses that made May 1 a day of demonstrations for shorter hours, international solidarity, and socialism in many countries; it advocated common proletarian action against war (Marx and Engels, 1972a, 1:32). In 1907, despite electoral costs, the SPD campaigned against German colonial adventures; the angry Weber condemned its leadership's "posturing" or "heroism of the mouth" (*Maulheldentum*) (Mommsen, 1959, p. 149; Schorske, 1972, ch. 3).

did not revolutionize advanced capitalist societies. But such political goals are enormous and complex. Those failures hardly rule out the importance and potential of massive democratic internationalist movements;[63] for the antiwar stands of the Bolsheviks, Italian Socialists, and American IWW; the outbreak of the Russian Revolution, the German Kiel revolt, and November revolution; and the rapid postwar emergence of communist parties vibrantly reasserted internationalism.

Theoretically, however, Weber mainly offered reasons for the decline of democratic internationalism rather than explanations for its striking, renewed presence. Thus, cessation of imperialist economic advantages would cause a "very palpable decline of purchasing power" and employment.[64] Though modern European proletarians had less compelling interests in aggrandizement than slaveholding Athenians, this *demos*, too, Weber insisted, should support imperialism.

As a psychological impetus, Weber suggested that workers and the petit bourgeoisie yearned for the spoils of victory and would stake their lives upon this gamble:

> Experience shows that the pacifist interests of petty bourgeois and proletarian strata very often and very easily fail. This is partly because of the easier accessibility of all unorganized 'masses' to emotional influences and partly because of the indefinite notion (which they entertain) of some unexpected opportunity somehow arising through war.[65]

Yet he awkwardly contrasted unorganized masses – those mainly influenced by prevailing patriotic ideology – and *organized socialists*. At the conclusion of World War I, "experience" also seemed less favorable to his argument.[66]

In assessing internationalist prospects, Weber noted that "Their [the socialists'] argument meets with varying success, depending upon political and linguistic affiliations and also upon different strata of the proletariat; on the whole, their success is rather diminishing at the present time."[67] He rightly stressed the obstacles posed by divisions of lan-

---

[63] Even G. A. Cohen mistakenly maintains, "It is hard to repel the suggestion that the workers refuted this [a strong trend toward internationalism] when they marched to the trenches of World War I" (G. A. Cohen, 1984, p. 239). Coercion should not be underestimated. Jon Elster seems to think that only local (or perhaps) national attachments are consistent with "personal integrity and strength of character." Actually from a liberal or radical point of view, internationalist resistance to unjust war requires the latter characteristics much more obviously than local "altuisms." Perversely for a self-styled Marxian, Elster, 1985, p. 397, avers, "If *per impossibile* the workers could be brainwashed into thinking of themselves as members of the international proletariat, the cause of international socialism would be lost in advance."

[64] Weber, *ES*, 2:920.   [65] Weber, *ES*, 2:921; *WG*, 2:874.

[66] Ringer, 1969, pp. 444–5.   [67] Weber, *ES*, 2:924.

guage, status, and frequently even political experience. Though his negative argument captures an important limit on internationalism, he did not explain why worker-based internationalist movements played so powerful a role toward the end of World War I. Further, no similar problem of the explanation of antipatriotism arises for modern capitalist classes, for they have played no significant democratic internationalist role in opposition to war. (Those capitalists who oppose a war usually characterize it, in a "realist" vein, as an unsound pursuit of the "national" interest.)[68] Yet following some of Weber's view, a radical would suggest that a political movement, articulating common interests among workers and others, might, under recurring threat of war and the emergence of authoritarian regimes, overcome internal divisions. For radicals, the need to break down intranational – status – divisions mirrors the need for democratic internationalism.

Noting republican internationalism in passing, Weber dismissed proletarian political interests and appealed to the purportedly minor value placed by workers on their lives and those of family and friend:

> [Workers] subjectively risk a small stake in the game. In case of a lost war, the monarch has to fear for his throne; republican power-holders and groups having vested interests in a republican constitution have to fear their own victorious general. Under certain circumstances, should disorganization follow defeat, the ruling stratum of notables has to fear a violent shift in power in favor of the propertyless.[69]

His last point seems prophetic about Russia in 1917 and nearly about Germany itself between 1918 and 1923. But where Marxians asserted that workers, internationally, have nothing to lose but their chains, Weber countered patriotically that they have nothing to lose but their lives. "The 'masses' as such, at least in their subjective conception . . . have nothing concrete to lose but their lives. The valuation and effect of this danger strongly fluctuates in their own minds. On the whole it can easily be reduced to zero through emotional influence."[70] His sociology of modern societies is, in this major respect, inconsistent with democratic individuality and, thus, with coherent liberalism as well as Marxism. Given Weber's political orientation, this psychological claim seems, unfortunately, little more than a call for nationalist manipulation.

Yet his wartime political writings take the rationality of workers more seriously. The change from Prussian claims of defensive war to blatant imperialism would, Weber presciently insisted, reinvigorate Social Democratic internationalism:[71] "The impression that the shameful . . . and

---

[68] In a deep sense, the common good is democratic, democratic internationalism the public or national interest.

[69] Weber, *ES*, 2:921.   [70] Weber, *ES*, 2:921.   [71] Ringer, 1969, pp. 189–90, 192–3.

slanderous agitation of the so-called Fatherland Party has made upon the workers can easily be imagined. After all, every worker *knows* . . . in whose interests these people are working. [They] prepare the most savage protests in the depths of the masses."[72] He denounced the Vaterlandspartei's defense of unequal suffrage and inept monarchy; his fear of radicalism here fairly captured a democratic truth about oppression belied by Schumpeter's "stampede" or Huntington's "distemper." Weber warned of the determining voice that frontline soldiers would have in the "German ideas of 1918."[73] Thus, his "realist" advocacy of moderate expansionary aims rested not only on the calculation of chauvinism's external impact, but, acknowledging and inverting democratic internationalism, on the fear of internal radicalism.

Economy and Society also offered some reasons for the variable intensity among workers of internationalist and patriotic ideas. As noted above, Weber contended that workers not employed in war industry would tend to oppose imperial policies. Further, he cited the class character of conscription and taxes: "Above all, the means of war are raised by way of levies, which the ruling strata, by virtue of their social and political power, usually know how to transfer to the masses."[74] More deeply, German international victories strengthened a ruling class that benefited from proletarian subjugation: "Every successful imperialist policy of coercing the outside normally – or at least at first – also strengthens the domestic prestige and therewith the power and influence of those classes, status groups, and parties, under whose leadership the success has been attained."[75]

Given profound class divisions, Weber recognized special ruling-class interests in propagating nationalism: The ruling classes "will most strongly instill themselves with this idealist fervor of power prestige. They remain the specific and most reliable bearers of the idea of the state as an imperialist power structure demanding unqualified devotion."[76] The rulers would disseminate these ideas among the masses. Thus, he concluded, worker interests in securing power and altering domestic class structure fueled Social Democratic internationalism. He then subtly explained the capitulation of socialist officials. Once they become influential, parliamentary representatives benefit from that "power prestige"; *status seeking* accounts for the conversion of former radicals into chauvinists. But given Weber's underlying view of workers' considerable economic interests in expansion and psychological manipulability, he imagined a "ripe" Social Democratic leadership as a uniquely effective imperialist force.

---

[72] Weber, *GPS*, p. 285.   [73] Weber, *MSS*, p. 47.   [74] Weber, *ES*, 2:920–1.
[75] Weber, *ES*, 2:920.   [76] Weber, *ES*, 2:922; Gilbert, 1978b.

A Marxian might acknowledge Weber's conclusion about the likely patriotism of parliamentary socialist and communist leadership.[77] For the
radical, such capitulations pit leaders against workers. The latter require
cultural, economic, and military pressure – patriotic propaganda, unemployment, and coercion – to risk their lives for alien purposes. As
Chapter 8 notes, the history of twentieth-century soldier and civilian
opposition to war suggests that these forces often fail.[78] Contrary to Weber, a radical would suspect few *boldly* expansionist leaders to emerge
directly out of socialist parties; parliamentary socialists are torn between, on the one hand, their moral and intellectual commitments and
constituents' interests and, on the other, expansionist ones.[79] In addition, as in the Weimar Republic, procapitalist "socialist" leaders often
become dominant during the periods following major revolt. At such
times, strongly expansionist, as opposed to stopgap, policies are especially unlikely to receive mass support. A modern Marxian theory would
expect not parliamentary Social Democracy – pursuing halfheartedly
belligerent policies – but startlingly authoritarian Nazis to guide "social-
national" expansion. The international rise of fascism as a response to
the shock of the Russian revolution, domestic insurrections, internationalism, and economic crisis is evidence in favor of a sophisticated
Marxian account, not a Weberian one.[80]

Where Weber's later views bifurcate peaceful, private capitalism and
war-oriented state capitalism, Marxian theory may trace – depending on
further empirical claims – a complex interplay of economics and politics.
Lenin's account of twentieth-century imperialism focused on the role of
banking control of industry and economic interests in promoting foreign
expansion. It also stressed the triumph, throughout advanced capitalism, of the parasite state, characterized by a privileged officers' corps
and mammoth officialdom. Amplifying Weber's image of the iron cage,
Lenin stigmatized such states as *"monstrous military beasts,* devouring the
lives of millions of people in order to decide whether England or Germany – this or that finance capital – should dominate the world."[81] On a
considered Weberian view, the balance of proletarian interests tips in
favor of imperialism; with prudent policies, nationalists could recruit
them on (quasi)rational grounds. In contrast, radicals contend that the

---

[77] For instance, after World War II, French Communist Party refusal to endorse, let alone
fight for independence for Algeria is an important example.

[78] Gilbert, 1978b.

[79] Mussolini left the Italian socialist movement to become a fascist and later attempted to
crush it.

[80] R. Palme Dutt, 1974, chs. 5–7 captures this point. Scheele, 1946; Waite, 1952; Lyttleton,
1975; Colton, 1964; Gilbert, 1984b, sec. 5.

[81] Lenin, 1971, pp. 100, 39–48 (my emphasis).

complex balance of worker social interests lay in international solidarity.[82]

5. Weberian tensions in Lenin's theory

Nonetheless, some economic aspects of Lenin's analysis resembled Weber's. *Imperialism* emphasized the parasitic "coupon clipping" of advanced capitalist elites, due to the possession of colonies.[83] More importantly, he advanced an argument that, if extended, undercut democratic internationalism. Like Weber, Lenin thought that given imperialist plunder, at least an "aristocracy of labor" would find its economic interests affiliated with those of the capitalists:

> The causes are: 1) exploitation of the whole world by this country [England]; 2) its monopolist position in the world market; 3) its colonial monopoly. The effects are: 1) a section of the British proletariat becomes bourgeois; 2) a section of the proletariat allows itself to be led by men bought by, or at least paid by, the bourgeoisie.[84]

He hoped to explain the weakness of working-class radicalism in late-nineteenth-century England with the suggestion that imperialism had temporarily "bought off" a significant stratum. That economic determinist argument influenced the claim, common among today's dependency theorists, that the working class in advanced capitalist countries has become a labor aristocracy whose interests oppose those of the poor in less developed ones. But these radicals misinterpret the force of their claim, for that view concurs with Weberian social theory; if true, it counts importantly against Marxian argument and democratic internationalism. But even Lenin's original thesis lends plausibility to Weber's account.

That *economic parasitism thesis*, however, fits oddly with the rest of his theory. During World War I, Lenin contended that the previously unheard of slaughter of worker and peasant soldiers – from each major participant, over a million dead – had revealed the political and moral bankruptcy of capitalism. Imperialist war, he maintained, would herald "civil war." This *antiwar, political argument* undermines the claim that any sizable stratum of workers had strong *economic* links to imperialism. Wouldn't war-generated international interests outweigh skilled workers' putative economic interests?

In the 1860s, Marx had similarly stressed the political divisions between English citizens and Irish immigrants as the chief obstacle to a

---

[82] Marx and Engels, 1965, pp. 236–7; Lenin, *CW*, 35:247.
[83] Lenin, *CW*, 22:276–85. Cf. Weber, *GPS*, pp. 237–9.
[84] Lenin *CW*, 22:284, 301. Presumably workers become procapitalist in outlook. Lenin's phrasing is not technically Marxian.

renewed Chartism, not putative proletarian economic gains.[85] In that context, patriotism often meant racist identification with one's own rulers against foreign and immigrant workers. With the subsequent expansion of colonialism and immigration, Lenin's notebooks for *Imperialism* and journalism extended Marx's analysis.[86] Unless revolutionary movements in imperialist countries fought colonialism, he insisted, politically nurtured divisions would maintain proletarian subjugation.

On Lenin's antiwar explanation, a lack of an organized political movement contributed to worker acquiescence in, not enthusiasm for, expansion. As a revolutionary, Lenin considered this victimization and radical possibilities primary, *if* communists made a sustained effort to forge a movement. Yet he also maintained, secondarily, that colonial exploitation enabled capitalists to corrupt an upper stratum, though he offered no estimate of its extent. Granting that better-off workers are *sometimes* less willing to revolt, a Marxian might still consider Lenin's inference a superfluous residue of economic determinism.[87]

Lenin also stressed the status causes of collaboration: the self-conception of union leaders as "labor lieutenants of the capitalist class." More subtly, the SPD leadership had committed itself to an electoral strategy of evolutionary change, focused on neighborhood branches, at the expense of underground organizing in factories and the military. Only the latter would have given a radical movement the extralegal maneuverability to combat war.[88] A radical explanation might join this *political* choice to what Weber rightly saw as external "prestige" successes in influencing the acquiescence of socialist leaders. Thus, within Lenin's theory, the *economic parasitism argument* could fail to account for the conservatism *even* of "responsible" socialist leaders; yet these *strategic and status* causes might generate economic interests of a stratum of union leaders and parliamentarians, who were comparatively well paid, shielded from factory work, and lent "respectability" by the mainstream media, in eschewing democratic internationalism.[89] Lenin's complex theory conflicts with the economic reductionism featured in his own occasional comments, dependency theory, and Weberian "liberalism."[90]

---

[85] Marx and Engels, 1965, pp. 236–7.

[86] Lenin, CW, 21:106, 243, 293–4; 22:283; 39:742.

[87] Lenin, CW, 242–3. Before World War I, the Bolsheviks had their strongest following among comparatively skilled metalworkers. In May 1968, 14 million French 'white collar,' professional and industrial workers and students went on strike; consideration of radical alternatives was not restricted by stratum. See also Szymanski, 1981, ch. 14.

[88] Lenin, CW, 21:250; 22:108–20.

[89] Schorske, 1972, pp. 108–10. Written to get by czarist censors, *Imperialism* does not fill out these political arguments; Lenin's notebooks on imperialism and political circulars do.

[90] An emphasis on workers' economic interests in expansion is doubtfully consistent with liberalism, for its makes great-power aggression inevitable, democratic foreign policy

Table 10.1. *Marxian internationalism versus Weberian chauvinism*

Marxian	Weberian
(a) Capitalism is characterized by victimization of workers and other nonexploiting classes, class conflict, and imperialist expansion	(a) Capitalism is characterized by victimization of workers, class conflict, and imperialist expansion, especially in state-influenced enterprise
(b) Economic rivalry shapes modern national political rivalry and leads to war	(b) Some forms of capitalist expansion extend great-power rivalry and lead to war
(c) Workers have basic interests against capitalist exploitation and its consequences, notably death in imperialist war, though a stratum of workers may be temporarily affected by parasitic gains from imperialism	(c) Proletarians mainly accrue economic advantages from imperialism that offset internal capitalist exploitation, but workers may become internationalist to counter the "prestige" claims of a reactionary capitalist regime or to protect their lives
(d) The ruling class nurtures patriotism and status divisions	(d) The ruling class nurtures patriotism but not status
(e) Divisions among workers and exposure from childhood to the ruling ideas lead to significant acquiescence in or adherence to patriotism	(e) Divisions among workers often block the spread of internationalist ideas
(f) Though mass movements can force some reforms, a capitalist regime serves the interests of exploiters, not workers	(f) A capitalist regime can appeal to the working class by granting equal suffrage and recognizing unions
(g) Given the difficulties in overthrowing capitalism, parliamentary socialist and union leaders will be specially susceptible to nationalist, procapitalist appeals	(g) Leaders of working-class movements, once in power will gain prestige from nationalist policies, which will also benefit their constituents
General conclusion Given a strong revolutionary movement, workers' common interests *can* lead to a democratic internationalist outlook	Intelligent national and social policies can quell internationalism

Table 10.1. *(cont.)*

Marxian	Weberian
Specific conclusion for World War I	
Interimperialist war can be turned into civil war for socialism in Russia, Germany, and throughout Europe	German rulers should adopt a parliamentary democracy comparable to England's and restrict themselves to limited imperial goals

Refining the argument of Chapter 1, we might contrast Weberian and Marxian views on World War I and internationalism shown in Table 10.1. The differences focus on premise (c), how thoroughly and in what ways capitalism victimizes workers, and premise (f), the extent to which a capitalist government can mitigate that victimization by involving workers in expansionary policies. As noted above, both theories suppose that a solely parliamentary radical leadership will tend to conservatism (g), though they disagree about whom this phenomenon serves. As we shall see in Chapters 11 and 12, related controversies grow out of (d) and (a). Marxians affirm but Weberians deny that the ruling class nurtures important status divisions among workers. Weberians affirm but Marxians deny that a revolutionary cooperative regime – what the former calls state socialism – *must* extend bureaucracy and renew imperialism.

6. War and democratic internationalism: the Soviet and Weimar revolutions

Weber's and Lenin's responses to the 1918 German revolution highlight these differences. Given his general argument, Weber expected that, despite German defeat, the nationalist solidarity of the "days of 1914" would hold up. In 1917, he decried the sympathy of the Social Democratic leadership for the post-February Russian Provisional Government as "a stab in the back morally" to frontline German soldiers.[91] The mutiny at Kiel and the November revolution, that "bloody carnival," appalled Weber. In his view, these republican uprisings fatally compromised Germany's power position and allowed its enemies to impose an onerous peace. "Politics as a Vocation" summarized his nationalism:

initiatives ineffective. Even if such claims were well defended, a liberal should go far to resist them.

[91] Weber, *GPS*, pp. 209–10.

"Where there is nothing, not only the Kaiser, but the proletarian has lost his rights."[92]

Yet the February revolution overthrew czarism, and the October revolution removed Germany's greatest enemy, *on Weber's own account*, from the British–French–American coalition that would dominate Versailles. Thus, his hostility to those revolutions conflicted with his insistence on the czar's special domineering role. A critic could ironically frame a patriotic argument against the Russian Revolution parallel to Weber's indictment of the November uprising: Since that revolt undermined the war effort, Prussia could seize part of the Ukraine and force the expansionist Brest-Litovsk Treaty on the new regime. But a liberal Weberian might respond that the cruelty of czarism toward civilians and soldiers produced the revolt. If Weber's moderate war aims, let alone republican internationalism, had been stronger in Germany, this liberal would maintain, then a Russian Revolution would have been justified and *not* led to victimization.

Weber's nationalism internally gives rise to further, striking difficulties. He celebrated the putative necessity of expansionist great-power politics. But his theory of political capitalist booty hunting would make settlements such as Versailles and Brest-Litovsk likely; if true, that theory projects future wars of similar or greater magnitude. Even during World War I, however, power-state adventures wasted millions of lives. Thus, any moderating alternative would have been desirable. In this context, strategies of democratic internationalism from below, however initially difficult or implausible, become potentially attractive alternatives.[93] But Weber's impassioned nationalism cut him off from that possibility.

Thus, in an early-twentieth-century context, radical democratic internationalism captures the force of a coherent liberal view. Lenin traced the corruption, by ordinary moral standards, of prevailing – colonialist – powers and defended antipatriotic solidarity from below. He contended that just demands of workers, peasants, and soldiers impelled the Russian and German revolutions; his October 1917 "Letter to Comrades" supported the Kiel revolt:

> Just think of it: under devilishly difficult conditions, having but one Liebknecht (and he in prison), with no newspapers, with no freedom of assembly, with no Soviets, with all classes of the population, including every well-to-do peasant, incredibly hostile to the idea of internationalism, with the imperialist big, middle and petty bourgeoisie splendidly organized, the Germans, i.e., the German revolutionary internationalists, the Ger-

[92] Weber, *GPS*, pp. 547–8.   [93] Gilbert, 1978b.

man workers dressed in sailors' jackets, started a mutiny in the navy with one chance in a hundred of winning.[94]

Such apparent, negative odds had driven Weber to dismiss democratic internationalism as "irresponsible."

In October 1918, given German revolt, Lenin offered an internationalist justification for the concessionary treaty of Brest-Litovsk:

> If we had not concluded the Brest-Litovsk Peace Treaty, we would at once have surrendered power to the Russian bourgeoisie and thus have done untold damage to the world socialist revolution . . . at the cost of *national* sacrifices we preserved such an international revolutionary influence that today we have Bulgaria directly imitating us, Austria and Germany in a state of ferment, *both* the imperialist systems weakened, while we have grown stronger and *begun* to create a real proletarian army.[95]

The Russian Revolution had ended czarist belligerence, exposed the other powers' predatory character, and shaken their internal hold; a German revolution, foreshadowed at Kiel, Lenin contended, would intensify this process:

> The German workers would do it even more successfully [further the disintegration of the imperialist powers] if they began a revolution disregarding national sacrifices (that alone is internationalism), if they said (and backed their words by *actions*) that they prize the interests of the world workers' revolution *higher* than the integrity, security and peace of any national state, *and of their own in particular*.[96]

The German November *republican* revolution not only toppled the monarchy, but – as Weber failed to remark – abrogated Brest-Litovsk. Lenin's November 20 "The Valuable Admissions of Pitirim Sorokin" noted, "German imperialism which had seemed to be the only enemy [in Russia] collapsed. The German revolution, which had appeared to be a 'dream-farce' (to use Plekhanov's expression), became a fact."[97] Plekhanov's nationalist jibe, mirroring Weber's views, derived from the seeming solidity of great-power rivalry. Yet the Bolsheviks' relatively isolated, persecuted position during the war shockingly altered. Through revolutions in Russia and Germany, democratic internationalism had undermined *both* great-power coalitions. From a liberal point of view, this internationalism strengthened republican regimes and defeated an

---

[94] Lenin, *CW*, 26:204.
[95] Lenin, *CW*, 28:112. He argued that Soviet withdrawal from the war had revealed Anglo-French rapacity.
[96] Lenin, *CW*, 28:113.
[97] Lenin, *CW*, 28:187. The Soviet Union annulled this treaty on November 13, 1918.

unjust treaty. A liberal might have hoped that vibrant internationalist opposition movements – for instance, in the United States, France, and England – could have checked the rapacity of the Versailles settlement. From a Marxian perspective, further socialist – or communist – revolutions might have halted the cycle of imperialist conflagration. Nonetheless, many of today's radicals as well as liberals focus solely on the inability of socialist parties to stop World War I; they have contributed to a current academic international relations consensus on "realism" and quasi-cooperative economic regimes in which the very idea of *democratic* internationalism is foreign.[98] Yet radicals not only predicted the terrible nature and costs of great-power rivalry, but achieved, through popular revolt, humane successes at the war's end.[99] Given the considerable internationalism of resistance movements in the Second World War, such Marxian claims deserve consideration alongside well-stated – democratic internationalist – liberal ones.[100]

Weber's theory recognized widespread, undeserved suffering and the "ineluctable eternal struggle of men against men on the earth."[101] He valued the goods of life, prevention of suffering, and more obliquely, individuality but despaired empirically of protecting them. If liberal or Marxian social theoretical claims about internationalism and radical democracy are right, they provide a complex ethical answer to Weber's argument, based on shared underlying standards. They show that much

[98] Even Robert Keohane, 1984, ch. 11, emphasizes only economic cooperation. His suggestion that current international regimes hurt both the least advantaged in Europe and the least developed countries does not lead him to articulate a *political* conception of democratic internationalism as a basis for change.

Gilpin's unmasking of Reagan's militarism – that administration's blustering about the United States as "number one" coupled with mortgaging its economic future to Japan – also confirms democratic internationalism. He maintains that most citizens are hurt by these policies – "repayment of the immense external debt and the associated interest payments will absorb a large share of America's productive resources for many years to come; these costs will substantially lower the standard of living" – and, thus, have common interests with victims of U.S. intervention in less developed countries (Gilpin, 1987, pp. 335–6; Gilbert, 1990b). As is characteristic of this literature, Gilpin stresses economic losses rather than loss of life and well-being through militarism. Ironically, however, articulating democratic internationalist interests, both of these "mainstream" arguments are far more radical than dependency theory.

[99] Only leftists, notably the Bolsheviks and Spartacists, had remained true to these insights during the war, though the Spartacist uprising was brutally defeated.

[100] Those resistance movements were too tied to Soviet interests. They came into the war only after Germany invaded Russia. Yet participants in antifascist movements, particularly workers, were strongly internationalist. They created mass communist parties in Italy, France, and the Yugoslav, Chinese, and Albanian regimes; even in the United States, the Truman–McCarthy repression checked a strong movement (Caute, 1979; Duberman, 1988).

[101] Weber, *GPS*, p. 29; *FMW*, p. 122.

undeserved suffering can be avoided. Thus, on such major ethical issues as the necessity of imperialism, war, exploitation, and the alleged impossibility of effective international solidarity, Weber's metaethical relativism provides a mistaken gloss on his own empirical and moral argument. Further, great-power "realism" has strongly contributed to the non-democratic climate in today's political science sketched at the outset of Chapter 9. The unexpected plausibility of internationalism strengthens the case for democratic theories and arrangements.

Chapter 11

Democracy and status

1. An unexpected theoretical contrast

Though Marxians have decried status divisions, they have not often articulated a theory about them; economic determinists especially emphasize broad class unity and underplay status stratification. In this context, Weber's social theory appears to provide a more explicit, finely structured analysis of social groupings.[1] This important theoretical and moral conception helps to explain, a Weberian might insist, the blockage of international and internal solidarity.

Weber separated orders of economic class and social status. The former derive from either the possession of property (property classes) or the sale of goods and services (commercial classes) and broadly parallel the Marxian conception of classes emerging from ownership or control of the means of production; the latter stem from the maintenance of lifestyles that accord with customary or religious interpretations of social honor. Yet Weber did not present status hierarchy as independent of class structure. Instead, status frequently depends on class; for example, the "beautiful" and "good" style of the Greek gentlemen required wealth. In turn, status creates intraclass divisions; for instance, ethnic conflict between German citizen and Polish immigrant, on his view, overrode potential common interests.

As with imperialism, however, Weber proposed an abstract, transhistorical, ideal-typical concept of status. As he denied theoretically that economic structures decisively condition other forms of social activity, he never posed the general question What role do diverse status structures play in maintaining particular economic systems? In contrast, even

---

[1] Weber, *ES*, 2:934. Marx provided a theoretical account. See Gilbert, 1984b, sec. 5. Why his analysis took hold mainly among communists – for instance, the Bolsheviks but also the American Communist Party – is an important question in the historical sociology of radical movements.

the first approximation of a Marxian theory of status dynamics investigates whether ruling-class policies sustain status divisions, at least under severe circumstances. As Chapters 7 and 8 stressed, such hierarchies, involving elevation of the few and diminution of many, challenge liberal as well as radical theory; they are inconsistent with the mutual recognition of persons. Looking at Weber's account, a liberal might interpret status differences as an expression not of justified cultural diversity but of a *predatory pluralism*. Thus, a Weberian liberal might also commend the erosion of status divisions to achieve equality.

Furthermore, Weber highlighted only those aspects of status that reinforce a given class structure, not the subversive possibilities of common, transstatus interests.[2] Translated into political theory, his argument stresses only the antidemocratic impact of status, not the strengthened democracy suggested by potentially status-overriding explanations of intra- and interclass commonalities. The unsystematic quality of his analysis does not stem simply from a methodological insistence on clarifying the independent role of status versus a complex Marxian emphasis on its social function; for though status differences are autonomous from class on Weber's account, they are not so independent of – putative – biology. Despite ambivalence, Weber regarded contemporary social Darwinian explanations of status hierarchy as plausible competitors for truth. This substantive theoretical and political claim, not just a contentment with ideal-typical description, characterizes his account. In contrast, a sophisticated Marxian argument exposes both the error and ideological role of eugenic theories as *pseudoscientific* sanctifications of harmful divide-and-rule policies.[3] Contrary to first appearances, Marxian theory offers a novel *political* analysis of such divisions as opposed to Weber's refinement of the prevailing cultural one. (To the extent that he commended "German" status and adopted quasi-eugenic arguments, his account is political though antidemocratic.)[4] Prima facie, to liberals, Weber's insistence about durable status divisions among workers might seem uncontroversial. A contrast of theories not only casts doubt on the implications of Weber's view but suggests unexpected evidence for deciding between them. In context, this theoretical comparison reveals the *political and ethical* cutting edge of diverse claims about stratification.

As the darker side of his patriotism, Weber upheld the honor of *being German*. His 1895 address contended that immigration had reversed a

---

[2] Weber, *ES*, 2:937–8.

[3] Gilbert, 1984b, sec. 5; S. Chorover, 1975, chs. 3–5; Block and Dworkin, 1974. For a discussion of functionalism, see Gilbert, 1987.

[4] Technically, in the Aristotelian idiom of Part I, his account is not fully political because it is not democratic.

historic economic and political tendency. Since the Middle Ages, Germanic culture had colonized Poland: "We first made the Poles into human beings."[5] At the turn of the twentieth century, however, poor Prussian peasants migrated to cities; Polish laborers, willing to work for less, replaced them. This economically based "population trend," on Weber's view, threatened German civilization. In the political dialectic of status and class, he called for closing the border, to "stem the Slavic flood," as well as state purchase and redistribution of land to citizen peasants.[6] In international political economy, Weber's "realism" is ethnic rather than statist.

He saw the "hard struggle" of nationalities for economic "elbow-room," as a basic fact of moral theory, ruling out utilitarianism and neo-Aristotelianism: "Alone: the dark seriousness of the population problem prevents us from being eudaimonists or supposing that peace and human happiness lie hidden in the lap of the future."[7] This putative fact would justify his pessimism but not, as Weber recognized in this context, metaethical skepticism.

Imagine, counterfactually, a more uniform international culture, equipped with adequate though moderate resources and modest population growth. In that case, on his argument, greater human well-being would have been possible. Weber would persistently stigmatize the promise of individual happiness – satisfaction aside from submergence in patriotism – as a "childish revery" and depict an "appalling" human destiny, offset only by the struggle to make one's nationality dominant.[8] These claims overshadowed his occasional, liberal emphasis on democracy and individuality.

Despite his Malthusianism, Weber nonetheless dreamed of awakening from the grave "a thousand years hence" to discover the contemporary German national "type" preserved in its descendants (*Nachfahren*). *Economy and Society*'s later, seemingly detached theoretical observation about stratum-based patriotism might serve as a self-description:

> It [the fervor of national influence] is based upon sentiments of prestige, which extend deep down to the petty bourgeois masses of states rich in the attainment of power-positions. The attachment to all this political prestige may fuse with a specific belief in responsibility towards succeeding generations.[9]

Weber's judgments about culture and status became radically subservient to Prussian power interests. During World War I, as we have seen, he advocated a moderate imperialist policy. His "Germany among the

---

[5] Weber, *GPS*, p. 28.   [6] Weber, *GPS*, p. 10.   [7] Weber, *GPS*, pp. 12, 14.
[8] Weber, *FMW*, p. 143.   [9] Weber, *GPS*, pp. 12–13; *ES*, 2:921.

European World Powers" also mitigated his earlier derogation of that culture.[10] Yet Weber shifted racial targets. To inspire soldiers in "Parliament and Government in Germany," he warned:

> It would be better to keep repeating just one thing: that Germany fights for her life against an army in which Negroes, Gurkhas and all kinds of other barbarians from the most forsaken corners of the world stand poised at the frontiers ready to devastate our country. That happens to be true, that everybody can understand and that would have preserved unity.[11]

In "Russlands Übergang zur Scheindemokratie" ("Russia's Transition to Phony Democracy"), he embellished this description of "savage peoples" and "barbarian trash" with the phrase "half mad with rage, thirst for revenge and greed."[12] Weber was apparently thinking of soldiers of colonial extraction, recruited by the English and French governments. Despite his moderated attitude towards Poles, his stigmatization of the czar's troops still appealed to racism toward Slavs. Such armies, once on German soil, would allegedly commit special "barbarian horrors." Here he grotesquely reduced even European values and civilization to German ones. (In World War II, Nazi propaganda would make a staple of racial analysis of "degenerate" enemy armies.)[13] Weber's wartime writings sustain his earlier empirical claims about the moral impact of population-driven ethnic conflict.

Weber's racism also influenced his view of status rivalries among American workers and "peasants." In his 1906 Saint Louis speech, he remarked on the increasing percentage of farms operated by blacks and "untutored immigrants" – Poles and other Eastern Europeans – compared with Anglo-Saxon, Scandinavian, and German ones. Sounding a eugenic theme, he wondered whether this shift would undermine American "greatness":

> The number of Negro farms is growing as is their migration from the countryside to the cities. If, thereby, the expansive power of the Anglo-Saxon-German settlement of the rural districts, as well as the number of children of the old native-born population are on the wane, and if at the same time, the enormous immigration of untutored elements from Eastern Europe grows, a rural population might soon arise here which could not be assimilated by the historically transmitted culture of this country. This population would decisively change the standard of the United States and would

---

[10] Weber, *GPS*, pp. 168–9, 175.
[11] Weber, *ES*, 3:1382; *GPS*, pp. 295–6.
[12] Weber, *GPS*, p. 210.
[13] Weber would have been appalled by the German role in World War II. Terribly and ironically, Nazi crimes against humanity would become a standard for barbarism.

gradually form a community of a quite different type from the great creation of the Anglo-Saxon spirit.[14]

His theory would repeatedly invoke divisions between Southern whites
and blacks as a paradigm of ostensibly inevitable status hostility.

Many early-twentieth-century European and American scholars
looked to biological distinctions to account for cultural differences. Such
"anthropological" explanations strongly tempted Weber. Despite his
original sociological theorizing, his ambivalence about eugenics reveals
the pivotal role of racism in contemporary academic social science.

2. Eugenic theory and "being German"

Thus, Weber's 1895 lecture flirted with eugenic ideas, referring to the
comparative adaptation capacity (*Anpassungsfähigkeit*) of Poles and Germans, translating the historical process into a breeding or selection process (*Züchtungsprozess, Ausleseprozess*) and attempting to discern racial
qualities (*Rassenqualitäten*).[15] Like many later social scientists, Weber
sought to operationalize a scientific vocabulary concerning "adaptation"
out of an ordinary one, anesthetized from mundane evaluations.[16] His
conception accords with the empiricist and neo-Kantian notion that a
definition of a term is a collection of characteristics as understood by an
ordinary language user. If a scientist changes these characteristics, Weber thought, the meaning fundamentally changes.[17] But racist terms referred to putative properties of different human groups. As realist semantic theories have emphasized, operationalization did not change the
reference. Only a specific antiracist countertheory could show that appropriate social scientific terminology lacks racially restricted referents
and that eugenics has no explanatory interest. Sharing racist values, Weber did not challenge the eugenic connotations of his ideal-typical definitions.

Further, he insisted on the possibility that a eugenic interpretation of
cultural differences was true. Introducing *The Protestant Ethic*, he suggested that the "uniqueness" of Occidental culture – its industrial, scientific, political, and religious accomplishments – might stem from special
biological characteristics. In that case, the new anthropology's "comparative racial neurology and psychology" would explain the "meaningful"
results obtained by the sociology of innerwordly asceticism. Despite his

[14] Weber, *FMW*, p. 384. In the United States today, Richard Lamm, 1985, among others,
sounds this eugenic theme.
[15] Weber, *GPS*, pp. 8–9.
[16] Operationalism, technically speaking, is a subsequent epistemological doctrine.
[17] Weber, *MSS*, pp. 25–6.

recognition of the inadequacy of contemporary anthropological research, "the author admits that he is inclined to think the importance of biological heredity is very great."[18] In "'Objectivity' in Social Science and Social Policy," he likened racial anthropology to historical materialism as a fruitful source of ideal types.[19] *Economy and Society's* highly conceptual argument suggested that Western achievements, described in antiseptic language as "certain types of teleological orientation of action," might correlate with "cephalic index or skin color among other biologically inherited characteristics."[20]

Yet Weber also distanced his position from eugenics. In contrast to prevalent academic racism, his antipathies did not include Jews. Moreover, his theory of the *elective affinities* of specific classes and strata for religious ideas that dovetailed with their interests generates Marxian insights into the social and political role of the eugenics movement.[21] I will examine his class conflict account of religion, legitimation of status, and eugenics; canvass some explanations for his failure to pursue this line of reasoning about turn-of-the-century anthropology; and then contrast Weber's views on status with Marxian ones.

3. Elective affinities and academic racism

Weber sometimes dismissed the dizzying proliferation of biological explanations as a mere product of fashion. As we saw above, *The Protestant Ethic* viewed a "long standing tradition and education in intensive labor" as a necessity in producing an exploitable work force. In a note, Weber remarked sarcastically, "It is congenial to the scientific prejudices of today when such a dependence [as a motivation for capitalist location of industry] is observed, to ascribe it to congenital racial qualities rather than to tradition and education, in my opinion with doubtful validity."[22] He also poked fun at an imaginary eugenicist investigating the Roundheads and Cavaliers of the Puritan revolution who had acted like "radically distinct species of men. . . . It is astonishing enough that it has not yet occurred to anyone to maintain that the plebeian Roundheads were roundheaded in the anthropometric sense."[23]

Despite his neo-Kantianism, Weber's sociology distinguished science and "prejudice," truth and ideology. True views are comparatively uncontroversial; sociological accounts of their origin are secondary. Widespread, bizarre reasoning, however, calls for such explanation. In a note

---

[18] Weber, *PE*, pp. 30–1. [19] Weber, *MSS*, p. 69. [20] Weber, *ES*, 1:8.
[21] Weber, *ES*, 2:934–5. [22] Weber, *PE*, p. 199 n. 17, 61–2.
[23] Weber, *PE*, pp. 216–17 n. 29, 89.

to his 1895 address, he suggested that implausible biological accounts served as an "apology" for a capitalism under radical challenge:

> An error of most natural scientific contributions toward the illumination of questions of our science lies in their failed ambition before all else to "put down" socialism. In their zeal to achieve this goal, these "natural scientific" theories become an unintentional apology [*Apologie*] for the prevailing social order.[24]

This claim suggests a straightforward *class conflict interpretation* of eugenic ideology.

More generally in *Economy and Society,* Weber contended that "every highly privileged group develops the myth of its natural, especially blood, superiority."[25] Fashionable racial anthropology would appear to be a prize candidate for such a myth. In a nearly Marxian vein, he continued that in stable situations, "negatively privileged strata" often accept such demeaning ideas but that

> in times in which the class situation has become unambiguously and openly visible to everyone as the factor determining every man's individual fate, that very myth of the highly privileged about everyone having deserved his particular lot has often become one of the most passionately hated objects of attack; one ought only to think of certain struggles of late Antiquity and of the Middle Ages, and quite particularly of the class struggle of our own time in which such myths and the claims of legitimate domination based upon them have been the target of the most powerful and most effective attacks.[26]

Prima facie evidence to sustain a class conflict interpretation of twentieth-century eugenics was easily at hand. European and American unions and socialist parties had made the misery of the working class, understood as its *exploitation* by capitalists, a political issue. Biological determinists offered precisely the alternative view suggested in *Economy and Society* and Weber's 1895 address: Capitalists did not benefit from a system that preyed upon workers; instead, naturally gifted individuals achieved economic reward through merit, whereas "feeble minded" proletarians, spawned by inferior stock, could only make the best of a

---

[24] Weber, *GPS*, p. 9. Weber's neo-Kantianism cannot sustain this scientific distinction – epistemologically he conceived only of "truth" and "prejudice" within "our" perspective or, in today's idiom, paradigm. But then, his conception of truth begins to wobble – for what differentiates a true view from an ideological one? Nonetheless, Weber's social theory of eugenic error broadly parallels Marx's distinction of truth and ideology traced in Chapter 7.

[25] Weber, *ES*, 3:953.

[26] Max Weber, *ES*, 3:953–4.

sad biological lot. In the United States, the Carnegies, Harrimans, Kel-loggs, and Rockefellers, among other leading industrialists, funded eu-genic research. (In Germany, Krupp sponsored an essay contest on the question "What can we learn from the principles of Darwinism for ap-plication to inner political development and the laws of the state?"; he published the resulting essays in ten influential volumes that recom-mended accelerated upper-class breeding and the curtailing of lower-class births. These views foreshadowed Nazi population policies.)[27]

Through IQ testing of immigrants and soldiers, the American govern-ment fostered virulent racism.[28] Federal and state governments passed discriminatory immigration, miscegenation, and sterilization laws. The impact of the Russian Revolution and widespread strikes led to upper-class hysteria toward "inferior" East European and Jewish radicals, the Palmer raids, and the massive deportations of 1919. Attacking gentle-men socialists in lectures at Princeton in that year, Henry Goddard, ad-ministrator of Ellis Island IQ tests, illustrated the usefulness of eugenics, "the new science of mental levels," as an ideology of the status quo:

> These men in their ultra altruistic and humane attitude, their desire to be fair to the workman, maintain that the great inequalities in social life are wrong and unjust. For example here is a man who says, "I am wearing $12.00 shoes, there is a laborer who is wearing $3.00 shoes; why should I spend $12.00 while he can only afford $3.00? I live in a home that is artisti-cally decorated . . . there is a laborer that lives in a hovel with no carpets, no pictures and the coarsest kind of furniture. It is not right, it is un-just . . ."
>
> Now the fact is, that workmen may have a ten year intelligence while you have a twenty. To demand for him such a home as you enjoy is as absurd as it would be to insist that every laborer should receive a graduate fellowship. How can there be such a thing as social equality with this wide range of mental capacity?[29]

This evidence was available to Weber. In the 1920s, the American eugen-ics movement would nurture the rebirth of a multimillion-member Ku Klux Klan that would dominate the Southern and Rocky Mountain states. Contemporary Nazi psychologists and anthropologists would

[27] Allen, 1975; Mosse, 1964, p. 99; Chorover, 1975. For a contemporary American resusci-tation of Krupp's preoccupations, see Richard Herrnstein's *Atlantic Monthly* articles (1989, 1971) complaining that "high IQ" women produce too few children.

[28] Leon Kamin, 1974, ch. 2.

[29] Cited in Kamin, 1974, p. 8. Taking no account of immigrant unfamiliarity with English, Goddard reported that 83% of the Jews, 80% of the Hungarians, 79% of the Italians, and 87% of the Russians seeking entry into the United States just before World War I were "feebleminded" (Chorover, 1975, pp. 65–6). On the basis of intraregional disparities be-tween whites and blacks, World War I testers alleged genetic differences. They failed to notice that Northern blacks outscored Southern whites.

praise U.S. eugenics legislation as the most advanced in the world, though the Third Reich would surpass it.[30]

Thus, the eugenics movement fit Weber's argument from *Economy and Society;* yet he never moved beyond the 1895 note. Compared to his subtle analysis of the class role and social decline of Puritanism, this failure seems all the more striking. Calvinism not only rewarded capitalists with "an amazingly, even pharisaically clear conscience" but disciplined workers with a theodicy of suffering. Weber's concluding 1919 lecture on *General Economic History* maintained that like other ghosts of Puritanism, the concept of a calling had become, for proletarians, a *"caput mortuum"*:

> Economic ethics arose against the background of the ascetic idea; now it has been stripped of its religious impact. It was possible for the working class to accept its lot as long as the promise of eternal happiness could be held out to it. When this consolation fell away it was inevitable that those strains and stresses should appear in economic society which since then have grown so rapidly. This point had been reached at the end of the early period of capitalism, at least of the age of iron, in the nineteenth century.[31]

Given these "stresses" and the consequent socialist movement, a Weberian might ask, if Puritanism had lost its hold, would some other ideology arise to perform a similar function? Weber's occasional comments and the prominence of European and American eugenics suggest an answer; yet he did not pursue it.

Noting his imperialist and racist views, a critic might be tempted to attribute his curious failure to Weber's ironic self-understanding, announced in his 1895 lecture, as a "class conscious bourgeois." But Weber was too serious, complex a theorist for such an argument alone to be convincing. Four other reasons help to explain his downplaying of a class analysis of eugenics.

First, as Chapters 1 and 3 emphasized, in offering explanations or predictions, every natural and social scientific theory invokes auxiliary statements that include well-confirmed related theories, established facts, and relevant abstractions. During this period, German scientists did not doubt the "inferiority" of Polish culture and other ostensible racist "facts." As most German academics were not democrats, they ignored such evidence of political vigor as the 1846 Cracow uprising or the

---

[30] Baur, Fischer, and Lenz, 1931, pp. 650–6; Günther, 1927, pp. 244–5; Chorover, 1979, chs. 3–5. The existence of the initial eugenics movement and its revival in response to the civil rights movement provides evidence for an important Marxian counter to the liberal claim, discussed in Chapter 8, that democratic forms are a sufficient antidote to the degradation generated by capitalism.

[31] Weber, *GEH*, p. 27.

role of Polish internationalists in nineteenth-century democratic and socialist movements; political and ethnic restrictions on faculty composition maintained this bigoted atmosphere.[32] These putative "facts" served as background information to academic theorizing – biological as well as social – about class, status, and culture. Unlike comparable natural scientific enterprises – for instance, Darwin's theory of evolution – these social scientific accounts – with the exception of Weber's striking claims about Puritanism – were unsuccessful.[33] But until an alternative theory became influential, largely through the emergence of extraacademic antiracist movements, *normal* scientific method could not prevent the reproduction of racist views.[34]

Second, Weber's insistence on the autonomous role of status made him less critical of these "factual" cultural stereotypes. In turn, those stereotypes lent intuitive plausibility to his emphasis on the durability of status divisions. (On his account, it would be appropriate for German workers to scorn Poles.) Third, despite Weber's functional analysis of capitalist and worker affinities for Puritanism, he emphasized the autonomous causal role of religion as the theoretical cutting edge of his critique of Marxism. Even in this case, he failed to resolve the tensions posed internally by his class analysis of religion; in other cases, his functional claims jarred even more strongly with his notions of cultural autonomy. Further, methodologically, Weber highlighted the uniqueness of particular historical sequences.[35] If, on his account, a religion or ideology played a decisive part in one case, he did not routinely look for a comparable sociological pattern in another. Though framed through an important aspect of Weber's analysis, the question about what ideology

---

[32] Ringer, 1969, pp. 128–43.

[33] Based on true arguments about sexual selection in other animals and supposed facts about women and "lower" races obvious to an English gentleman, Darwin's *Descent of Man* criticized Mill's antisexism. In the (male, middle-class) scientific setting of the time, such auxiliary statements seemed to sustain his argument rather than Mill's: "I am aware that some writers doubt whether there is any such inherent difference [between the sexes]; but this is at least probable from the analogy of the lower animals which present other secondary sexual characters. No one disputes that the bull differs in disposition from the cow, the wild-boar from the sow . . . the males of the larger apes from the females. Woman seems to differ from man in mental disposition, chiefly in her greater tenderness and less selfishness. . . . It is generally admitted that with women the powers of intuition, of rapid perception, and perhaps of imitation, are more strongly marked than in man; but some, at least, of these faculties are characteristic of the lower races, and therefore of a past and lower state of civilization" (Darwin, 1874, pp. 575–78). Modern theories of social gender and race stereotyping and human flexibility, coupled with much broader evidence – feminism, anticolonial and antiracist movements, noncolonial societies – have falsified such inferences.

[34] Miller, 1979, pp. 258–60; Gilbert, 1984a, sec. 5.

[35] Weber, *MSS*, pp. 80–1, 101.

411

would replace desiccated Puritanism has a Marxian bent. It implies that given time, continuing class structures will, like hydras, grow new ideological heads if their old ones are cut off. A social mechanism must be identified to make functional analysis work – for instance, the attractiveness to scholars and educators of the new behavioral psychology and intelligence testing, coupled with the reproduction of racist and sexist stereotypes in normal science; capitalist and government funding of eugenics in circumstances of substantial class conflict; and the like.[36] In this important theoretical contrast, the lineaments of such a specification – sufficient to make a Marxian account plausible – are not overly difficult.[37]

Fourth, Weber resonated to the passions elicited by religious conceptions of purity and honor. Given his metaethical views on the unbridgeable gap between ethics and science, he may simply not have entertained the idea that any science – that specifically "irreligious power" as he called it – could play a similar role. Weber also did not conceive of this possibility for social theories and democratic visions that offered an alternative to proletarian suffering.[38] Further, given the success of socialism among organized workers, he may properly have doubted the potential of eugenics as a way of making punishment and exploitation acceptable *to them*.[39] Though Weber was moved by nationalism and thought workers might be too, he did not see eugenics or, for that matter, his own status theory as a politically causal element, legitimizing that passion.

Joined by most contemporary Marxians, he did not foresee the special impact of eugenics in reinforcing Aryan racism and nationalism among professionals, notably doctors and teachers, who would implement Nazi genocide. In this case, more than underlying "Aryan" mysticism, a pseudoscience, linked to political passions, had enormous conse-

---

[36] Today's eugenicists appear less confused and more jaded (Jensen, 1969; Herrnstein, 1971, 1988).

[37] A far more thoroughgoing response to liberal criticisms – one that goes beyond the needs of this argument – would, however, be required to establish the Marxian claim (Gilbert, 1987, sec. 3; 1990a).

[38] Weber, *FMW*, pp. 142–3. In *Economy and Society*, he recorded the antireligious response of workers to a pre–World War I questionnaire: "Their rejection of the God idea was motivated not by scientific arguments, but by their difficulty in reconciling the idea of providence with the injustice and imperfection of the social order" (Weber, *SR*, p. 139). This answer concurred, perhaps too neatly, with Weber's own interpretation of the basic problem of theodicy. It shows that core moral standards underlie socialist positions. But he failed to see that scientific theories that might remedy social *exploitation* could respond to this *ethical* concern.

[39] Ringer, 1969, pp. 445–6. Racial anthropology fit Weber's hopes about the status concerns of workers. The strength of German socialism, not his inclinations, influenced his skepticism about proletarian eugenicism.

quences.[40] Thus, one might conclude, theoretical dispositions, empirical claims, and a methodological weakness on comparing leading theories combined with Weber's politics to prevent him from carrying through his insight into the class conflict functions of eugenics.

4. The American South as test case

Weber's particular conception of status led to central theoretical and moral clashes with Marxism. Yet his view is uncritically embedded in standard sociological and political science, race relations "pluralism," and "consociational democracy" (Lijphart). For these accounts, the American South serves as a test case. Weber's view of Southern white workers as the leading beneficiaries and propagators of racism reflected an influential belief – a Marxian would say, ruling-class-propagated stereotype – and may seem plausible today even to sophisticated liberals.[41] Contrary to prevailing impressions, however, a Marxian critique may unearth striking evidence for its claims.

Weber contended that "the present difficult social problems of the [post-Civil War, American] South . . . are essentially ethnic and not economic."[42] He thus detached the exacerbation of status divisions from any economic and political function in maintaining capitalism. His analysis separated law and custom as sources of ethnic hostility, stressing those of custom: "The [status] barriers imply that marriage is absolutely and legally undesirable quite apart from the fact that such intermarriage would result in a social boycott."[43] Although Weber recognized that the privileged had enacted "Jim Crow" legislation, he contended that status divisions primarily derived from the ardent desire of the less-advantaged members of the dominant status to set themselves apart from the even more "declassed" and "negatively privileged." Note that a sophisticated radical could offer a similar psychological interpretation of a factor sustaining temporary working-class divisions, yet emphasize the long-run impact of common class interests and democratic movements. Probably she would claim that this psychology was less widespread and exacerbated than Weber imagined. Like liberals, this Marxian would consider such a psychology, rooted in status hierarchy, harmful to individuality and unhealthy. In contrast, Weber's uncritical

[40] Mosse, 1964; Chorover, 1979, pp. 98–102; Proctor, 1988.
[41] See Key, 1949, pp. 7–10; Reich, 1981, ch. 6; and the conventional politics of the "New South" and Rainbow Coalition for counterevidence. Though Reich makes a powerful Marxian argument, he ironically adopts the Weberian claim that economically threatened white workers are today the leading source of racist ideology (Reich, 1981, p. 311).
[42] Weber, *FMW*, p. 364.   [43] Weber, *FMW*, p. 406.

nationalism justified status consciousness as, in important cases, a specimen of psychological health.

Weber saw the conflict between capitalists and workers as one between interconnected commercial classes. In contrast, he viewed the relation of white planters and farmers as one of distinct *property* classes that would not lead to a clash: "A classic example of the lack of class conflict was the relationship of the 'poor white trash' to the plantation owners in the Southern States. The 'poor white trash' were far more anti-Negro than the plantation owners, who were often imbued with patriarchal sentiments." [44] He even hypothesized that racial antipathy was "quite foreign to planters." [45] Now a Marxian could adopt his distinction between commercial and property classes and still look, as Marx and Lenin did, to the political unity of diverse oppressed classes – for instance, workers and peasants – against common enemies. [46] Furthermore, Weber's ideal-typical view of rural property classes obscured their interconnection with commercial ones. Southern planters often exploited black and white laborers, leased plots to black and white tenants. They encroached on smallholders through mortgages, debt, and disproportionate political power, manifested in a variety of antidemocratic practices from lynching of organizers to poll taxes. Yet Weber contrasted the putatively separate Southern property classes with the warring creditors and debtors of ancient Rome whom he identified as "urban patricians versus rural peasants." [47] He neglected those common features of the class situation of farmers, tenants, and workers that sometimes drove them to unite – status divisions notwithstanding – against the planters.

Weber contrasted the social role of nationalism, vigorously propagated by the *predominant social classes*, and that of status divisions, furthered mainly by the *less advantaged members of the dominant status* and ignored by the most privileged. But German or "Aryan" nationalism toward Poles and other Slavs as outsiders and inferiors and the attitudes sustaining divisions between citizen and immigrant rural laborers in Germany are identical *on Weber's account*. His radical distinction of the social functions of patriotism from those of status, the order of international from domestic honor, is implausible. Further, the evidence noted above on the class role and funding of eugenics and the passage of racist legislation – resources, social science, biology, and laws hardly stemming from "déclassé" whites – supports a sophisticated radical theory and undermines Weber's insistence on the strict – as opposed to the relative – autonomy of status.

[44] Weber, *ES*, 1:304.   [45] Weber, *ES*, 1:391.   [46] Gilbert, 1981a, chs. 9, 11.
[47] Weber, *ES*, 1:303–4.

5. A Marxian critique of Weber

Marx and Lenin interpreted the perpetuation of major social divisions within oppressed classes as a consequence of the need of the comparatively few beneficiaries of an exploitative system to divide and rule. This argument includes precapitalist *exploitative* systems and allows for the noncapitalist origins of many divisions. Marx also offered an early class conflict account of the influence of Malthus's population arguments, a forerunner of eugenics; the English oligarchy affirmed them as a response to the "hankerings after human development" manifested in popular sympathy for the French Revolution.[48]

Lenin not only generalized Marx's arguments on the need for citizen workers to oppose colonial policies, prejudice toward immigrants, and status divisions; his party acted on this policy. During the resurgence of the working-class movement between 1912 and 1914, for instance, Bolshevik deputies in the czarist duma advanced a "Bill for the Abolition of Disabilities of the Jews and of All Restrictions on the Grounds of Origin or Nationality." According to Lenin, the law would

> deal in particular detail with the restrictions against the Jews. The reason is obvious: no nationality in Russia is so oppressed and persecuted as the Jewish. Anti-Semitism is striking even deeper roots among the propertied classes. The Jewish workers are suffering under a double yoke, both as workers and as Jews. During the past few years, the persecution of the Jews has assumed incredible dimensions. It is sufficient to recall the anti-Jewish pogroms and the Beilis case.[49]

He attacked all Black-Hundred attempts to "sow mutual distrust between the Russian peasant, the Russian petty-bourgeois and the Russian artisan, on the one hand, and the Jewish, Finnish, Polish, Georgian, and Ukrainian peasants, petty bourgeoisie and artisans, on the other."[50]

During the 1905 revolution, Bolshevik activist Osip Piatnitsky described the czarist government as the instigator of Black-Hundred pogroms to deflect the radical movement; in general, Marxians point to evidence of government toleration for and even instigation of violent racist or fascist movements like the Black-Hundreds, the Ku Klux Klan,

---

[48] Marx, 1961, 1:616 n. 2, 301; Gilbert, 1984b.

[49] Lenin, *CW*, 20:172–3. Learning from American experience, the leaders of pogroms advocated *zakon lyncha*, the lynch law practiced in the American South (B. Moore 1965, p. 445). Beilis was accused of ritual sacrifice of a Christian child. The Bolsheviks' antiracist theory and policies make today's Soviet furthering of status divisions all the more glaring.

[50] Lenin, *CW*, 20:237. The Black-Hundreds were a violent, proczarist organization comparable to the KKK.

and the Nazis.[51] Although the Bolsheviks recognized that some workers and peasants adopted Great Russian ideas and breathed new life into czarism, they looked at racism *primarily* as a capitalist device directed against workers of the majority as well as minority nationalities. The success of their organizing among workers showed that racism could be combated. In contrast to Weber's descriptive view, Marxian theory is counterintuitive from the standpoint of the prevailing status structure; it sees major status divisions as the *political outcome of the economic system, harmful to all workers,* rather than as a conflict between mutually isolated ethnic groups.

Like consistent liberals, however, Marxians saw non-status-related cultural differences as an enlivening force; thus the *Manifesto* celebrated the internationalization of cultures, a mutual respect for diversity.[52] Marx and Lenin looked to anticolonial movements – for instance, in Ireland – as a mainly positive development, even though, as subsequent history has demonstrated, nationalism could easily become a new ideology of domination and racism for an indigenous bourgeoisie. In anti-status terms, cultural diversity is an expression of individuality; it illustrates the case for a *nonrelativist* pluralism. As we have seen, an underlying distinction between competitive egotism and individuality is needed to separate the predatory features of nationalism, associated with status hierarchy, from the varied cultures of particular nationalities. In this respect, a refined radical theory of democratic individuality improves on older versions of nationalist anti-imperialism, which frequently confuse these opposed standards.

In summary, we might contrast Weberian and Marxian arguments on status differences within oppressed classes under capitalism as shown in Table 11.1. Weberian and Marxian theory clash strikingly on the analysis of status, eugenics, common interests among workers, and the potentials of democracy. Further, this comparison suggests relevant evidence for deciding which argument is (approximately) true; sophisticated analysis of such issues as the social and political function of status divisions (b–c), whether proletarians of higher status gain or lose from racism (c–e), and the role of the state in furthering chauvinist movements and ideologies (f) would ultimately favor one and rule out the other.

---

[51] Piatnitsky, 1973, pp. 86–8; Neumann, 1944, pp. 202–31; Dutt, 1974, chs. 5–7; Bracher, 1970, pp. 119–20; Dubofsky, 1969, p. 475; Foner, 1976, pp. 33, 229, 230. In times of conflict, a shift tends to occur, as G. A. Cohen suggests, to lucid and cynical defense of the existing order rather than ordinary rationalization (G. A. Cohen, 1978, pp. 290–1). A Marxian explanation, however, need expect no predetermined or general balance between these components.

[52] Marx and Engels, 1974, p. 50.

Table 11.1. *Capitalism and status hierarchy*

Weberian theory	Marxian theory
(a) Economic (commercial) class divisions between capitalists and workers lead to class struggle	(a) Same as Weberian theory
(b) Status or honor hierarchies exist alongside classes and cut across class lines	(b) The persistence of status divisions among workers is explained as a form of divide and rule by their role in maintaining an exploitative class structure
(c) Unlike the case of nationalism, the oppressed members of the predominant status vigorously defend status distinctions and do so increasingly in times of social crisis; they have dominant cultural or "ideal" interests[a] in preserving their comparatively privileged status rather than undoing relative class and status disadvantages	(c) Parallel to the case of nationalism, the ruling class heavily influences such divisions among workers; the exacerbation of these divisions should be regarded in functional terms as the result of more or less conscious ruling-class policies in response to social crises and class conflict; nonetheless, a psychological mechanism exists that facilitates blaming the (more) victim(ized)
(d) Status divisions are sometimes linked to important cultural achievements that should be maintained, i.e., Anglo-Saxon/ German culture vs. that of blacks and immigrants	(d) Though cultural diversity and the internationalization of accomplishments are important goods, status divisions obstruct social, political, cultural, and moral progress
(e) Prestige interests of disadvantaged members of the privileged status accord with their economic interests as competitors with members of the more oppressed status for economic advantages (perhaps regarded as part of a fixed pool)	(e) Though competition among workers is a fact under capitalism and is nurtured by the propagation of egotist, racist, sexist, and nationalist ideas, the overriding interest of "status beneficiaries" among workers is to unite with the more oppressed to make greater economic and democratic gains against the capitalists; that interest is based on realities of

417

Table 11.1. *(cont.)*

Weberian theory	Marxian theory
	psychological health as well as social and political fact
(f) Status divisions may reinforce or provoke governmental actions such as passage of Jim Crow laws	(f) The state serves the ruling class; in differing historical situations, depending on the level of class conflict and unless checked from below, governments will promulgate racist laws and sponsor racist ideologies such as eugenics; they will also tolerate or encourage extralegal, violent racist movements
(g) Multiracial or transstatus movements based on class interests are unlikely (for American blacks and whites and Germans and Poles, Weber never even considered the possibility)	(g) In many circumstances, despite the counterefforts of the ruling class (a–f above), multiracial democratic movements, based on common class interests, can overcome status divisions
Political and moral conclusion National cultural achievements, reflected in status hierarchies, will be and sometimes should be preserved	Determined political efforts can replace status divisions with the democratic unity of the oppressed class, fostering egalitarian social arrangements and cultural and ethical advance

^aStemming from a contrast of bare physical subsistence and nonphysical concerns, the distinction between "ideal" and "material" interests is more Weberian and economic determinist than Marxian, at least on the version of Marxism suggested here. Its quasi-utilitarian justification derives from the importance of minimizing suffering, of maintaining the goods of life and health. But the distinction is confusing; for what is ideal has to do with the self-conceptions of reflective individuals in terms of which they assess – material – resource needs. A communist view of political agency – of being the kind of compassionate, yet militant person who takes initiative in politics – is just as ideal as Weber's view of status. Such choices are part of a person's well-being; they frequently involve the risk of life and hence have strong material consequences.

But the comparative success of these theories has ethical and political consequences. If a Marxian view is right, working-class interests would cut against the victimization of the most oppressed and sometimes generate common revolt. Such interests provide a basis for strong antiracist movements for social reforms, extensions of liberal democracy, and, ultimately, for a nonexploitative society that could respect and benefit from diverse cultural accomplishments.[53] In contrast on Weber's account, antiracist movements are unlikely to become significant, succeed, or retain power, for his theory questions the deep impact of exploitation on workers of the advantaged status; interests in honor might offset potential radicalism. In addition, given Weber's racism about the cultural level of some "negatively privileged" status groups, he would probably deny the Marxian argument about special *victimization* of the least-advantaged workers – they could not "adapt" to better arrangements.

6. Southern multiracial movements

A liberal Weberian could reject Weber's chauvinism and metaethics, yet still consider his theory of status distinctions plausible.[54] As I have

---

[53] As an important qualification to this radical claim, I should note, following Bernard Williams, the modern era irreparably erodes many premodern cultural achievements and ways of life. What can be kept of earlier accomplishments in a liberal or radical society is real but transformed.

[54] A contemporary social scientist might put Weber's argument in game-theoretic terms. Mancur Olson has suggested that individual workers, and by extension, one might claim, especially members of different status groups, will choose not to cooperate even when they have common interests. The latter are even more like the segregated participants in a prisoner's dilemma.

These arguments treat participation as a "cost" to the individual, whose action, on issues of a common benefit to a very large group, can have but a negligible effect on the outcome. Hence, participation for most is "irrational." But these arguments explain too much – they appear to show why it is never rational for workers generally or those of different nationalities to cooperate and thus conflict with routine facts such as the formation of unions, strikes, working-class rebellions, and cases of multiracial unity (Arneson, 1985; Barry, 1982, pp. 54, 63–4; DeNardo, 1985, pp. 52–7; Reich, 1981, ch. 6). Further, radicals tempted by rational-actor explanations have adduced many reasons for occasional working-class cooperation – a common situation that does not leave much choice except to act together, repeated plays of a prisoner's dilemma game that make cooperation rational, the role of dialogue and political organizing in securing common interests (radical internationals, one might say, are a version of Keohane's international regimes, reducing the costs of reliable information), a better psychological description of the motivations for solidarity than those provided by competitive egotism, and the like. If such arguments work, they defeat Olson's argument for the working class as a whole, and thus, for competing statuses within it (Gilbert, 1990b; Keohane, 1984, pp. 100–3, 120–5; Przeworski, 1985, pp. 96–7; Shaw, 1984). So the central theoretical claim is still Weber's insistence on the special tenacity of status differences and their underlying psychological causes, not a game-theoretic formalization of his account.

noted, the historical experience of virulent racism in the American South seems prima facie to support Weber's argument. But a Marxian counter-theory leads to a reconsideration of that history and points, against Weberian claims, to recurrent multiracial movements from below.

In the Civil War, for example, poor whites from Tennessee fought for the North.[55] As Michael Schwartz has shown, the Farmer's Alliance of the 1880s, the largest nonunion protest movement in American history, united hundreds of thousands of poor blacks and whites in parallel and sometimes integrated organizations. In contrast, groups dominated by "paternalist" planters, such as the Democratic Party, excluded blacks.[56] Vigorous multiracial unity, pitted against ruling-class violence and fraud, also characterized the early Populist movement. In organizing to break single-party rule, Tom Watson sounded a democratic theme to which thousands of poor whites and blacks responded:

> Now the People's Party says to these two men [one black, one white], "You are kept apart that you may be separately fleeced of your earnings. You are made to hate each other because upon that hatred is rested the keystone of the arch of financial despotism which enslaves you both. You are deceived and blinded that you may not see how this race antagonism perpetuates a monetary system which beggars both."[57]

Marxian theory did not influence these movements; instead, they provide evidence for a core radical explanatory claim. As the distinguished, non-Marxian historian C. Vann Woodward put it:

> the Southern white masses were beginning to learn to regard the Negro as a political ally bound to them by economic ties and a common destiny, rather than as a slender prop to injured self-esteem in the shape of "White Supremacy." Here was a foundation of political realism upon which some more enduring structure of economic democracy might be constructed.[58]

That economic democracy would have reflected greater political democracy. From a liberal standpoint, the triumph of a regional authoritarianism with profound national influence presented a central obstacle to twentieth-century American democracy.

Other major Southern multiracial movements such as the 1892 Alabama miners' strike and the Industrial Workers of the World organization of lumber workers in the early twentieth century succumbed only under the impact of government and associated Ku Klux Klan vio-

---

[55] Key, 1949, pp. 6–7.   [56] Schwartz, 1976, pp. 95–101.
[57] Cited in Woodward, 1963, pp. 220, 219–22.
[58] Woodward, 1963, p. 222; Key, 1949, pp. 7–8.

lence.[59] These movements preceded Weber's comments on the durability of Southern status antagonism. In the 1930s, further multiracial organizations would arise among industrial workers, the unemployed, and sharecroppers.[60] They won important reforms, yet transformed neither the South nor the United States. A Marxian account underlines their potential, especially if linked to nationwide radical organizing. It stresses the role of the ruling class and federal government in passing racist laws, supporting the Southern one-party system, disseminating the work of racist ideologues, and, at times, stimulating the KKK.

A Marxian theory elicits considerable and, from a Weberian perspective, unexpected evidence. Further, in contrast to Weber's ethnic "realism," liberals are democrats and antiracists. Yet Weber's normative views leave the entire moral terrain of liberalism to radicals. Thus, concurring with (radical) democracy, a sophisticated liberal might accept many Marxian social theory claims about status. To contrast the views, that liberal would insist only on the ultimate plasticity of the state under capitalism, the possible evolution of a nonracist democracy.[61] As a sophisticated radical might respond, that non-Weberian liberalism would still have to contend with the persistence of racism to this day, despite a Civil War and a substantial civil rights movement. Michael Reich's econometric study of the enduring effect of racism on contemporary income inequality among American whites further strengthens a Marxian account: Wherever racism is at its greatest, white workers receive comparatively less pay and social services and the income disparity between most white families and the top 1 percent is at its greatest. A radical view would also expect today's rebirth of eugenics and other blame-the-victim ideologies that arose to counter the civil rights movement. In addition, a Marxian account of racism sharpens the question for social democrats of Chapter 9: Given any significant degree of economic inequality, can a process of mainly peaceful reform create (radical) democracy? Finally, as Chapter 13 underlines, a sophisticated radical theory suggests a distinctive explanation of Nazi genocide, focusing on the political impact of racist ideology in modern class conflict.[62] For purposes of this argument, however, all one need see is that radical democratic claims about common worker – and peasant – interests and potential solidarity are plausible contenders for truth; they deserve thorough comparison to sophisticated liberal accounts.

In a characteristically "realist" vein, Weber's "Science as a Vocation"

---

[59] Reich, 1981; Dubofsky, 1969, pp. 212–20; Foner, 1976, pp. 114–19; Trelease, 1971.
[60] Herndon, 1937; Foner, 1976, ch. 16.   [61] Gilbert, 1987.
[62] Reich, 1981; Chorover, 1975; Gilbert, 1984b, sec. 5.

insists on clarity as the cardinal epistemological virtue. But his method-ological failure to consider contending arguments leads to unclarity about central theoretical issues, relevant evidence, and moral alterna-tives. As the subtle, substantive weaknesses of his theory of class and status illustrate, this philosophical error shapes the overly generalized, misguidedly abstract argument of *Economy and Society.*

Chapter 12

Bureaucracy, socialism, and a common good

1. Intention, responsibility, and sociological reductionism

As opposed to a democratic, eudaemonist conception of the state, Weber's "Politics as a Vocation" and *Economy and Society* defend a sociological, instrumental one. The latter does not countenance a contrast of *rational authority* – one that serves a common good – with *repressive authority* – one instrumental to particular purposes. In sociologically insisting that instruments overshadow aims, Weber promoted a non-Aristotelian, nondemocratic political science. But once again he did not compare his standpoint to any other. Instead, he contended that since political associations have pursued a diversity of particular tasks, they can have no end in common, even, say, to protect their members' lives and capacity for moral personality:

> But what is a "political" association from the sociological point of view? What is a "state"? Sociologically, the state cannot be defined in terms of its ends. There is scarcely any task that some political association has not taken in hand, and there is no task that one could say has always been exclusive and peculiar to those [political] associations.[1]

Thus, Weber sought to analyze all state activity in terms of common means, primarily, the use of physical violence, and secondarily, the need for legitimacy and an administrative staff. His argument weaves together positivist and neo-Kantian features in a way that, as the first section of Chapter 9 emphasizes, has enduringly influenced behavioral sociologists and political scientists. He pursued a reductionist strategy, seeking to reconstruct state activity in terms of a common, observable characteristic. His accompanying relativism about legitimacy allows him to attend to values, yet strive for what would later be called "operationalist value neutrality." His sociological point of view implausibly elides

[1] Weber, *FMW*, p. 77.

423

the fundamental issue of whether any state has ever served a common good or furthered the realization of important human capacities and needs.

Sympathetic to an aspect of Marxian argument, Weber praised Trotsky's Brest-Litovsk comment that "every state is founded on force."[2] Much more strongly than Marxians, however, Weber stressed control of the instruments of violence. To make good on this empiricist reconstruction, he would have needed to show that the notion of control of the means of force is clearer than any goal-oriented insight into the nature of *coercion*. But terms like "coercion" and "domination" point beyond operational discussion. How can one know that the use of force is "coercive," specify against whom – criminals, foreign powers, oppressed classes and nationalities, former oppressor classes – it is to be employed, or assess *which aspects* of citizen conduct are being inhibited without some reflection on the state's complex impact on human well-being? This reductionism denies plain distinctions between tyrannies that murder political dissidents to intimidate the citizenry, states that regularly use less vigorous forms of coercion, and – perhaps rare – ones that mainly enforce a minimal criminal and civil law. It fails to differentiate coercion that defends individuality – say, forcible restrictions on slaveholding – from the enforcement of fugitive slave laws. Even the rhetorical plausibility of Weber's view rests on the anarchist and liberal moral insight that states, whatever their form, are, in general, unjustifiably coercive.

His argument falters *internally* at just his insistence on the central, distinctive role of *domination* in political life. At first, he had maintained that politics is "any kind of independent leadership in action." That view, however, fails to differentiate initiative in a chess club or a friendship from this special leadership involving violence.[3] The state is unique in *dominating* humans, using force to get its way. Further, Weber affirmed that claim as the decisive moral fact about all states – one determining the need for particular legitimations – not just an opinion that some people hold to be just or unjust. His definition of the state requires independent standards of ethical assessment that he inconsistently refused to allow into the analysis of politics itself or into his sociological characterization.

As Weber recognized, rampant coercion is not easy for governments to implement. States generally, a radical might note, seek to avoid too

---

[2] Weber, *FMW*, p. 78.

[3] Weber, *FMW*, pp. 77, 82–3. Do leaders, in a restrictively political vein, "dominate" the led, as "Politics as a Vocation" seems to suggest, or does domination also relate to Weber's separate hierarchies of status and class? The essay never says. Sociological unclarity accompanies moral unclarity.

much naked force; they attempt to divide the population into supporters – reinforced by those who acquiesce – and opponents. In this context, Weber rightly stressed the role of specific forms of legitimacy. His argument is thus sensitive to qualitative differences among regimes but obtuse in its description of those qualities; for he operationalized this notion, envisioning whatever political values a regime encourages people to hold as good, as the sources of legitimacy. In his notion of "legitimate domination," "*Herrschaft*" is the chief motivation of all political life, a form of legitimacy, an ideological ornament that disguises this underlying drive.

Although the term "legitimacy" emerged in postrevolutionary controversies over the blood lineage of French royalty – a discussion that confused pedigree with ethics – the concept of legitimate coercion, like coercion, has moral connotations and leads to reflection about a common good.[4] Semantically, its reference is the configuration of relationships that might embody a common good, even if many opinions about justice – including numerous successful, legitimating ones – represent particular interests, justify harms to most of the population, and distort such a good. Further, Weber's *instrumental* view tends to reduce legitimacy to manipulation. Yet isn't there an important difference between a regime to which citizens may genuinely – upon Rawlsian or Habermasian uncoerced reflection – consent and a regime that "socializes" – "tricks" – them into supporting it?

In contrast to Weber's account, as Chapter 1 shows, the deepening of political science and ethics – its increased internalization and epistemic access – came from discoveries and theory changes broadening the range of those entitled to recognition, ruling out once seemingly "natural" claims of domination and forging and recasting the notion of individuality. A democratic eudaemonist conception stresses the moral aspects of the legitimacy of modern liberalism and radicalism.

Yet Weber was deeply troubled by the suffering imposed or maintained by (most) political life – hence, he insisted on the world's inescapable ethical irrationality. His theory moves toward a depth that later behavioral social science, retaining the form but not the vocation of Weberian sociology, misses; for his stigmatization of all politics as a realm of morally undifferentiated violence makes sense only from a nonpolitical standpoint, one that deprecates ordinary conduct, a divinely oriented ethic of nonviolence. His distinctive sociological approach depends on general, metaethical arguments about the place of politics in the cosmos and the clash of the irreconcilable ethics of saints and warriors. Though analogous to relativist and reductionist versions of Marx-

[4] Holmes, 1982, p. 165.

425

ism, his influential theory of politics and the state uniquely merges neo-Kantian relativism and reductionism.

Weber attempted to justify his empiricist focus on state violence and his relativist account of legitimacy through a famous distinction between an ethic of responsibility (*Verantwortungsethik*) and an ethic of intention (*Gesinnungsethik*).[5] In the context of his social science, this dichotomy is a sophisticated reworking of the fact–value distinction.

2. How radicals become saints

Weber employed the term "*Gesinnungsethik*" in conflicting ways. First, its holders are sometimes moralists who deny the consequences of their actions: "Act rightly and leave the consequences to God," "the world is stupid and base, not I." Yet for Weber, these seekers after spiritual purity often turn out to be secular radicals, syndicalists for example.[6] Sometimes, however, more ideal-typically, proponents of a *Gesinnungsethik* are committed to a specific religious ethic of nonviolence and love. This second sense, however, excludes the violent moralists whom Weber invokes with the first. Imagine an unlikely, stereotypical, bomb-throwing anarchist who does not hope, given her empirical estimate of the consequences, to spur the sluggish masses but cherishes setting off explosions to nurture the "flames of pure intention [die Flamme der reinen Gesinnung] . . . of protest against the injustice of the social order."[7] On Weber's first, broader use of *Gesinnungsethik,* such an anarchist adheres to a *violent* ethic of intention; in the second sense, she fails to exhibit spiritual sensitivity.

Weber could generate the former sense of an "ethic of intention" only by approaching secular radicals through the paradigm of the second sense; prima facie, no one would think that the perspectives of saint and syndicalist have much in common. If we step outside Weber's categorization and examine the syndicalist's position internally, however, we will see that his broader use of an "ethic of intention" is, sociologically and politically, implausible. However oriented toward a purity of stance and – perhaps – misguided in their estimate of consequences, most radicals look toward a secular impact. In fact, even religious pacifists hope that their example will shame corrupt rulers or, more likely, inspire other

---

[5] *Gesinnungsethik* has often been mistranslated as ethic of "ultimate aims." That translation stresses the goals of the actor in a consequentialist-sounding vein in contrast to the seeming emphasis on means of an ethic of responsibility. It thus inverts Weber's actual distinction, for he means a *Gesinnungsethik* to signify *purity of intention* or will heedless of actual outcome, a consequentialist *Verantwortungsethik* to indicate reliable foresight into the likely effects of a course of action.

[6] Weber, *MSS*, p. 16; *FMW*, p. 127.   [7] Weber, *FMW*, p. 121; *GPS*, p. 540.

ordinary people to join in a nonviolent protest movement. Weber's quarrel with radicals is an empirical one – on his account, these means are unlikely to secure *political* ends. His use of *Gesinnungsethik* mistakenly suggests that a great part of political action is – *self-consciously* – action to achieve purity. But the claim that many political actors seek *mainly* to be beautiful souls is an external psychological insight, not these agents' self-description.

Weber backhandedly recognized as much, for he imagined offering a compelling empirical argument to the syndicalist that would isolate the relevant value clash:

> You may demonstrate to a convinced syndicalist, believing in an ethic of intention, that his action will result in increasing the opportunities of reaction, in increasing the oppression of his class, and obstructing its ascent – and you will not make the slightest impression upon him. If an action of good intent leads to bad results, then, in the actor's eyes, not he but the world, or the stupidity of other men, or God's will who made them thus, is responsible for the evil.[8]

But Weber's conditions on this conversation are inconsistent. The typical syndicalist thought that militant example would inspire mass revolt and disagreed with Weber about the empirical consequences; he did not, as Weber claimed, "believ[e] in an ethic of intention." To reshape the syndicalist's argument as a *Gesinnungsethik*, Weber had to impose an *unusual* constraint – empirical accord about the "bad results" between the radical and a nationalist politician. In contrast, one might wonder about the success of Weber's "demonstration": Was he reading his interlocutors accurately or merely projecting his own empirical convictions? In the intense atmosphere following the November revolution, perhaps some radical student, sympathetic to syndicalism, persisted in disagreement and Weber regarded him as empirically hopeless. Shaking his head in exasperation, Weber might have concluded, this syndicalist *must* believe in an ethic of intention. Still, even though it results from an eccentric, hardly insightful reconstruction of a radical view, this conflict does look purely evaluative. Though it seems peculiar to characterize him as striving to be a – violent – saint, *this* syndicalist seems to have some obscure, otherworldly moral vocation. Weber had crafted an unusual example to illustrate his metaethical account.

If we probe this syndicalist's views, however, his stand does not appear to be incommensurable with Weberian responsibility, just incoherent and harmful. The flame of protest against *injustice* arises from a concern for a regime's harms to innocents, not from one for purity of

---

[8] Weber, *FMW*, p. 121. He emphasized the "'generation' of reactionary attitudes" in possible allies as the main harm caused by the syndicalist (Weber, *MSS*, p. 23).

intention. Unless the syndicalist believes in the example set by this militancy – and that is what Weber's condition about empirical agreement excludes – then he takes action that he recognizes, from the start, will result in further harm to innocents. *By core moral standards that are his own, the syndicalist, seeking justice, knowingly acts unjustly.* His view is incoherent. We might fill in a part of the picture that Weber neglected: The syndicalist might still claim – probably rightly – that the oppression visited by the ruling class is more extensive than his own contribution. But that harm does not extenuate the syndicalist's additional harm. Such fundamental incoherence, with terrible consequences, probably reflects a personality disorder.[9] Weber's description of syndicalism as a *Gesinnungsethik* makes neither psychological nor political sense.

Undercutting Weber's attempted assimilation of reconstructed radicals to saints even further, this syndicalist's action is self-consciously malicious. He is a callously self-centered person, who admittedly values others' lives less than his own "feelings." Such radicals are not mainly elitist as Weber suggests – "the world is base and other people stupid, not I" – for elitists may suppose themselves to be noble and intelligent; this agent knowingly hurts the very others that he claims to help and yet maintains that *this* action is the mark of his spiritual purity. We can articulate the incoherence in his viewpoint in another way: This syndicalist starts out with a *social* concern for the good of others – a keen awareness of injustice – but acts only on an *asocial* – probably antisocial – concern for his own purity. His action exhibits not social individuality but a radical antagonism between the individual (or egotistical) and the social.

A contrasting position with a concern for the consequences for others – what Weber calls a "responsible" position – is morally sensitive. In fact, viewing concern for others as a component of individuality is a distinctive feature of moral argument and democratic theory.[10] Thus, Weber's ostensibly descriptive, nonevaluative contrast of his two ethics has an important moral charge. In fact, his reconstructed syndicalist is what is

---

[9] Ideology and personality disorder may be distantly related. As I argued in Chapter 7, inconsistency within a reflective point of view suggests the intrusion of ideology and requires sociological analysis. Cancel the reflectiveness, render the incoherence fundamental and connected to *unusual*, harmful consequences, and a psychological diagnosis is in order. A standard, if implausible, conservative move is to reshape all serious radicalism to fit a paradigm of personality disorder.

[10] Richard Boyd, 1986a, stresses the role of sympathy in the motivation of normal humans for whom awareness of moral facts presents reasons for action. See also Hume, 1948, pp. 4–5, 167–68; Montaigne, 1922, 1:6–7; and Rousseau, 1964, 3:155. A theory that differentiates a comparatively integrated from a radically unhealthy or split-off personality – Kohut's, for example – helps to explain those cases where awareness coexists with inaction or harm.

commonly, derogatorily called a moralist – someone who tries to *impose* inappropriate ethical standards on others and violates their individuality, or even physically harms them in the process.[11]

This Weberian interpretation of an ethic of intention undercuts his metaethical claim about incommensurability in two ways. First, he successfully indicts *this* syndicalist's position. Unfortunately, given his relativism, Weber fails to clarify the straightforward ethical view that informs his interpretation as an undertone. Second, this sense of an ethic of intention is an obtuse reconstruction of syndicalist positions, not a dialectical response to their arguments. An accurate characterization would show that empirical differences, rather than clashes over core standards of life and moral personality, are at the heart of this dispute. This analysis suggests that the concept of *Gesinnungsethik* is not a useful sociological category. The first sense of an ethic of intention, focused on internal purity, is a polemical description of Weber's political opponents but sustains neither his metaethics nor sociological analysis.

These difficulties make Weber's insistence on the concept of *Gesinnungsethik* puzzling. This idea draws its persuasiveness largely from the second sense: saints who act by divine inspiration, heedless of consequence, from an ethic of nonviolence. But saints are rare. Perhaps Jesus and Saint Francis might qualify as exemplars of this ethic. Yet one might wonder, after Weber's time, even about such candidates as Gandhi and Martin Luther King, for both of the latter seemed quite concerned about political impact. Weber stressed the virtue of empathy in sociology. The first, broader use of the term, however, prevents the understanding of non-Weberian political and ethical agents; the second use captures, ideal typically, a genuine mode of political agency – one that refuses on principle to take lives, even to ward off great dangers – but has few proponents. Prima facie, this narrower use of the term has no compelling sociological justification.

Yet for Weber the category has a theoretical usefulness that does not arise from its intrinsic plausibility. The standpoint of an ethic of intention delivers ordinary political life from moral agency and sustains a reductionist account of the state: " 'All they that take the sword shall perish by the sword and fighting is everywhere fighting.' Hence the ethic of the Sermon on the Mount."[12] On this *uniform consequences of violence thesis*, force is equally corrupting whatever the empirical result.

Weber maintains that this ethic is incommensurable with a political,

---

[11] This sense of "moralism" is an aspect of the more general "moralism" that Marx criticized in radical social theory and politics. In Weber's case, as in Marx's, a distinction between morals – the discipline of ethics – and moralism makes sense of why a "moralizing" person is likely to be either obnoxious or harmful.

[12] Weber, *FMW*, p. 119.

warrior ethic. The pure holder of a *Gesinnungsethik* eschews violence; warriors make it a preoccupation.[13] In Weber's mind, this example provides an irrefutable argument for metaethical incommensurability, a case so clear that he barely elaborates it. He thus speaks of clashing demons who rule our lives. Much of his sociology of the state rests on the plausibility of this relativist contrast.

3. Are Weberian politicians responsible?

A critic might offer a telling, general objection to this example, framed within Weber's own account. The saint is not interested in the craft of politics, but she is concerned about its ethical aspects; for nonviolence respects the good of life and, more broadly, human well-being. Yet as Weber recognizes, political agents also justify violence as a means to prevent "evil," to maintain or enhance life and the preconditions for a good life. Thus, the advocate of self-defense and the proponent of nonviolence, however deep their empirical differences and moral conclusions, start from a common moral standard. Contrary to Weber, many religious ethics recognize this initial accord. Thus, Catholic doctrines of just war suggest that regard for life is possible, and possibly concordant, in the ends and means of war: resistance to aggression, abstention from harm to civilians. Sainthood, for the Catholic, is a different, but not wholly other way of life – it shares in a common, cosmic order. Weber's insistence on the incommensurability of religious nonviolence and politics is a controversial, perhaps lapsed Calvinist interpretation of a Christian viewpoint – offered without argument as *the* Christian or even *the* religious understanding – and does not answer the objection that Weber's ostensibly radically sealed-off *ethics* are rendered mutually intelligible as *moral standpoints* through *common* claims about the good of human life.[14]

Weber also responded to this saint: Unless *evil* is resisted by force, it will triumph.[15] This rejoinder defends his own opposition to czarism as well as Catholic, Protestant, and Marxian claims about justice in war. It

---

[13] This Weberian claim might cohere with Bernard Williams's account of morally disparate ways of life.

[14] In his *Institutes*, Calvin insisted on resistance to aggression: "If they [kings] justly punish those robbers whose injuries have been afflicted only on a few, will they allow the whole country to be robbed and devastated with impunity? . . . Natural equity and duty, therefore, demand that princes be armed not only to repress private crimes by judicial inflictions, but to defend the subjects committed to their guardianship whenever they are hostiley assailed. Such even the Holy Spirit, in many passages of Scripture, declares to be lawful" (Calvin, 1957, 2:661–2).

As Weber found syndicalists hard to understand, so he often had trouble passing over into alternative religious stances (Weber, *FMW*, p. 124).

[15] Weber, *FMW*, pp. 119–20.

refutes an *utterly* nonconsequentialist pacifism: Contrary to their intention, its adherents will not save lives; their incoherence will be explained by their fantastic, indulgent, possibly malicious self-conception as beautiful souls. In contrast, the normal pacifist starts from the same premise as Weber about the good of life and the characterization of evil – for instance, aggression. Contrary to Weber's metaethical claims, his answer suggests a *commensurable* ethic of responsibility. On that ethic, whatever one's comprehensive view of the good, one should attend to the impact of one's actions and not wantonly take human life.[16]

Yet, the critic might note, Weber ignores democratic politics. His ethic of warrior pitted against saint again reduces all politics to violence. But on the commensurable, democratic ethic of responsibility just described, responsible political actors would respect the lives of others in pursuing their goals; their actions would be morally decent and intelligent in a way that, as Weber's derogatory use of the term ethic of intention except for saints suggests, adherents to the latter ethic are not. In that case, however, contrary to his account, the integrity of an ethic of responsibility would arise not just from concern about consequences but from a broad, *common* character in permissible aims. Only that diverse range of individual goals would be morally respectable that sustains a minimal cooperative regime, one that secures the good of life and – to make Weber's account fully a *liberal* one – mutual recognition and democracy. For instance, Rawls's theory of overlapping consensus on democratic autonomy captures such a transviewpoint concurrence. Now, given the empirical complexity of elaborated ethical and political positions, many could seek decent aims but achieve harmful results. These positions' social theoretical and factual errors would be revealed in their consequences; more importantly, their own underlying moral premises would condemn this impact. An objective reformulation of Weber's ethic of responsibility dialectically articulates what is true in the notion of an *ethic* of "ultimate aims" and highlights the shared, core moral quality – including the potential to attend to consequences – of a broad range of conflicting viewpoints. As opposed to Weber's sociological reductionism, this democratic conception traces a conversation among such views.

Weber's first version of *Verantwortungsethik* paradoxically emphasizes concern for consequences without moral constraint on ends. That view fails to articulate what "responsibility" means. From that perspective, an eighteenth-century slave trader might be responsible in delivering his

---

[16] Habermas, 1981, pp. 230–1. As John Rawls, 1971, p. 30, rightly stresses, an utterly nonconsequentialist position is "irrational, crazy."

This critique of Weber's position also suggests that the important standard distinction *within moral philosophy* between deontological and consequentialist ethics is, when both are properly stated, not as sharp as many have imagined.

cargo, *if* he took care that unnecessary killing did not occur in the hunting and that comparatively few prisoners died on the voyage. But the example is a satire of "responsibility." A reformulated, transviewpoint ethic of responsibility, insisting on the integrity of a range of potentially ethical aims and ruling out slavery, seems a more promising, coherent sociological, political theoretical, and moral category.

Seeking sociologically to portray an admirable politician, Weber acknowledged the interplay of intention and consequence:

> It is immensely moving when a *mature* man – no matter whether old or young in years – is aware of a responsibility for the consequences of his conduct and really feels such responsibility with heart and soul. He then acts by following an ethic of responsibility and somewhere he reaches the point where he says: "Here I stand: I can do no other." That is something genuinely human and moving. And every one of us who is not spiritually dead must realize the possibility of finding himself at some time in that position. In so far as this is true, an ethic of ultimate ends and an ethic of responsibility are not absolute contrasts but rather supplements, which only in unison constitute a genuine man – a man who *can* have the calling for "politics."[17]

His relativist account provides no useful epistemological and metaethical gloss on this striking claim about "unison." Only a dialectical insight into the common core elements in both positions – one that attends to personal integrity and regard for others – can do that.

Similarly, Weber sometimes formulated his religious critique of politics as a warning about violence, not a ban:

> No ethics in the world can dodge the fact that in numerous instances the attainment of "good" ends is bound to the fact that one must be willing to pay the price of using morally dubious means or at least dangerous ones – and facing the possibility or even the probability of evil ramifications.[18]

But even the violent anarchist might be as alert to this general danger as the responsible Weberian, nationalist hero – yet, given their different empirical estimates of consequences, that awareness would deter neither from action. Weber's phrasing suggests the very distinction that his relativism denies: That the means are "dangerous," "morally dubious," and involve the "possibility . . . of evil ramifications" does not establish that their use inescapably perverts the aims, let alone the "uniform consequences of violence" thesis. He inconsistently puts scare quotes around the "good" of ends but not around what he rightly regards as

---

[17] Weber, *FMW*, p. 127. He mistakenly omitted Rosa Luxemburg among other women from his account of this vocation.
[18] Weber, *FMW*, p. 121.

the generally recognized, transviewpoint evil of the means. As a political person, one sensitive to the ethical problem of "dirty hands," Weber here discerns commonality in what he metaethically insists is incommensurable.

In democratic eudaemonist terms, a liberal Weberian could recognize that in some (perhaps a large number of) cases, defense of life and the capacity for moral personality override the harms of some political violence.[19] As a eudaemonist might insist, a multifaceted political assessment of justified violence partly appeals to intrinsic goods – life, capacity for moral personality, maintenance or extension of democracy – and partly to narrowly consequentialist considerations – tyranny will expend more lives than its overthrow.[20] Weber's metaethical relativism again provides a misleading gloss on his own moral judgments.

He also conflated even his inadequate statement of a cross-viewpoint, broadly consequentionalist *Verantwortungsethik* with another, antidemocratic internationalist sense: Given the struggle of powers, a responsible political outlook must estimate the consequences of an action from the standpoint of one's own state. As Chapter 10 shows, the latter great-power "realist" formulation *is* Weber's political stand. On this usage, he illicitly substituted some relativist version of the value of one's own state – or the lives of members of one's own nationality – for the general good of human life.[21] He then used the allegedly distinctively religious and *moral* justification of an ethic of intention *only* against his political opponents, not to criticize nationalists. Though from a Weberian standpoint, the *"sentimental literati"* of the chauvinist Vaterlandspartei were just as likely candidates for adherence to an ethic of intention as syndicalists, he never included the former among proponents of a *Gesinnungsethik*. In contrast, Weber considered his reconstructed syndicalist would-be saint typical of revolutionaries: "All radical revolutionary political attitudes . . . have their point of departure" in the contention that "the intrinsic value of ethical conduct – the 'pure will' or 'conscience' as it used to be

---

[19] Note that this distinction between a coherent liberal view and Weber's relativist formulations is not distinctively eudaemonist; substitute a preferred *moral theory* – say, sophisticated contractarianism or utilitarianism – and the contrast still holds.

[20] If one can project the consequences of a consolidated tyranny into a substantial future, the radical's case becomes even stronger.

[21] As Steven Krasner's *Defending the National Interest* (1978, pp. 40–5, 53–4) illustrates, today's great-power "realist" arguments substitute an operationalist "might makes right" claim – whatever serves the long-run stability of the leading political institution is the "public" or "national" interest – for ordinary appeals to a common good of freedom (from conquest) and economic well-being. As a moral realist would insist, by denying the integrity of ethics and affirming relativism or reductionism, this move is unattractive and incoherent (Gilbert, 1990b). For a comparatively morally self-aware "realism," see Morganthau, 1973, pp. 10–11.

called – is sufficient for its justification, following the maxim of the Christian moralists."[22] He rhetorically but inconsistently insisted on the *moral lack of distinction of (almost) all violence* – the important exception is nationalist violence – rather than of *all violence*.

Alternatively, one might say, Weber's conflation of a general *Verantwortungsethik* with a nationalist one results in an *unequal empirical treatment of political viewpoints* or *privileged empirical treatment of nationalism*. On his reconstructed account, nonnationalist ethical and political alternatives are, to draw an analogy with a famous phrase of Engels, utopian, not scientific. This usage unofficially recognizes the empirical moral objectivity that Weber metaethically denied.[23]

4. Antiradical ideology and today's social science

Despite their important role in justifying his reductionist sociology of the state, Weber's arguments for the fundamental distinction between *Verantwortungsethik* and *Gesinnungsethik* are thin. Why did Weber – and why do many subsequent Anglo-American social scientists – find these bizarre contentions persuasive, especially about radicals? At least one reason is the long-standing influence of antiradical or anticommunist ideology. That ideology is comparable to, though far less recognized among academics than, racism and sexism.[24] Combined with the impact of a Weberian theoretical idiom and empiricism, it contributes to a normal environment in which scholars experience no obligation – and are unable – to articulate or answer serious radical alternatives.[25] An expla-

---

[22] Weber, *MSS*, pp. 16, 24.

[23] As we saw in Chapter 5, Engels's distinction expressed the confusion in his own and Marx's views on science and ethics.

[24] An important reason for this lack of recognition, is that radicals, including most contemporary communist parties, timid about advocating revolution, have been reluctant to combat it directly.

[25] Michael Reich's analysis of racism, published at a distinguished university press over a decade ago, is ignored in most subsequent social "science" race relations literature. Orthodox scholars do not respond to Chomsky and Hermann, Klare, and McCamant among others who trace patterns of U.S. military and covert aid to repressive regimes.

If there are no merits in radical theories, then a charitable statement and sound response would be no problem. But as the comparatively few genuinely scholarly counterexamples bring out, fairminded alternatives are not so easy to state. Thus, Steven Krasner, 1978, pp. 322–5, rightly stresses the role of anticommunist ideology in explaining often misguided, violent U.S. interventions to secure raw materials. He suggests that statism, not a structural Marxism with which he grapples, better explains this fact. But Krasner confuses Marxism with elite theory – on which the powers that be must always get their way. (If so, how could revolution ever occur?) He mistakenly takes U.S. *defeat* in Vietnam as a purported "realist" counterexample to a view that insists, in the *Manifesto*'s image, that capitalism digs its own grave. Further, he invokes a putatively "exces-

nation that invokes antiradicalism is bound to be controversial, but I hope that readers will find a careful account – for that very reason – worthwhile.

This long-standing ideology may be characterized as antiradical in that it is employed against many opponents of the status quo, including liberals. For instance, leaders of the early-1960s American civil rights and antiwar demonstrations – most of whom were by no stretch of the imagination communists – were stigmatized as "outside agitators," out to stir up otherwise contented people. This ideology may be called anti-communist because its contemporary versions focus on alleged Communists – say, Jesse Helms's opinion of Martin Luther King – as long as one recalls that it has maligned militant unionists, anarchists, and so-cialists and that its contemporary targets are non-Marxian and Marxian, liberal and radical, advocates of nonviolence as well as measured vio-lence, probably just people actively committed to the notion of a human capacity for moral personality. This ideology is thus profoundly anti-democratic.

Antiradical ideology suggests that social movements that challenge previous forms of domination are, like Weber's syndicalists, perverse. For the anticommunist ideologue, most less-privileged people – slaves, peasants, workers – are basically happy though not too bright. They re-volt only because "outside agitators" arouse them. These "ringleaders" have strange characteristics. They are often foreign – in the United States, for example, Molly Maguires, German and Italian anarchists, Russian reds, Chinese "blue ants" – and speak another language, filled with bizarre, unmotivated rhetoric.[26] (For those influenced by this out-look, radical social theory is an offshoot of that rhetoric). Since radicals are profoundly self-seeking, they disguise goals that will harm their fol-lowers. These *anti-internationalist* stereotypes sustain the powers that be, whatever their policies, against democratic "distemper" and resistance.

But as an attempt at explanation, this view is incoherent: Though it starts from a recognition of the existence or danger of a radical move-ment, it fails to show how self-seeking agitators, who don't speak a com-

sive" role of ideology in hegemonic powers to counter (mainly economic) Marxism. But for Marxians, the rulers have some quasi-conscious sense of their oppressiveness and the danger of revolt; they need to project a mirror image on radicals. If there is one ideology that a dialectical Marxian theory can explain, it is that "specter haunting Eu-rope, the specter of communism."

26 Special victims often come from despised races – say, Rosa Luxemburg in Germany and Sacco and Vanzetti, the Rosenbergs, and Paul Robeson in the United States.

Michael Rogin, 1987, chs. 1, 7–8, identifies these international (not to say intergalactic) fears – for instance, in "Invasion of the Body Snatchers" – at the center of Hollywood culture and American political life. See also Gilbert, in press b.

prehensible tongue and whose views are diabolically false, could have the potential to – and sometimes do – attract a large following; for on this argument, followers must act against their interests and undermine their contentment. To force the legion historical participants in radical movements into this mold, antiradicals must deny them their personality and stigmatize them as mere "dupes." This view presents no serious argument against movements for civil rights, unions, or communism – hence the aptness of the term "ideology" – even though good arguments may be offered on behalf of the status quo. Those arguments would, however, be well defended by sophisticated liberals who rejected this ideology; for the core insight of democratic liberalism as the politics of mutual regard rules out the practice and ideology of repression and exclusion that are embodied in antiradicalism.[27]

Antiradical ideology explains Weber's odd reconstruction of the syndicalist. On that view, radicals are self-seeking would-be manipulators, just as his syndicalist is. Their views are incoherent, but as they are damaged, evil people, they don't care. If this fit between the syndicalist's views and antiradicalism were a special case, Weber's appeal to this ide-

---

[27] Perhaps the purest form is the standard American anticommunism of the early 1900s, the 1950s, and of contemporary groups like Accuracy in Academia. It is especially striking and ironic in institutions that formally uphold the open pursuit of truth. Proponents start from the allegation that the views – whatever they may be – of communists are false. Yet they suggest that the presence of even one communist professor will corrupt large numbers of students and faculty who supposedly will easily believe unconventional lies. Hence, otherwise well-trained communists, they insist, are not qualified to teach and should be discharged. But there are notoriously few communists, or even Marxians, on such faculties. One – or a few radicals – on a faculty of hundreds or thousands speaking to even more thousands of students, would have trouble making her voice specially heard, even if her views were true. In fact, the recommended repression would make sense only if radical claims are at least in some important respects accurate; for if the Marxian's views are false and perverse as alleged, then the exertion of outside political pressure to fire her seems unnecessary. Perhaps others could learn to state and refute such viewpoints precisely because they are openly aired. Presumably, it is the sometimes implicit, often explicit antiradical contention that most students, faculty, and campus workers are stupid that explains the imagined "Pied Piper of Hamlin effect" and "requires" the firing of radicals. If *in fact* many have adopted oppositional views under such punitive conditions, a plausible alternative inference would be that such beliefs contain some important democratic insights.

Faced with major political issues, university leaders often bring antiradical ideology to the fore. In response to the Harvard antiwar strike of 1969, President Pusey said that he could not imagine how "anyone" could systematically disagree with U.S. government policies toward less developed countries and stigmatized strike leaders as "evil" (*Harvard Crimson*, April 7, 1989). Such extreme cases reveal an ideological continuum that generally makes avowal of radical or serious democratic arguments more difficult than others. Just by itself, the widespread influence of antiradical ideology in social science and university life is an important measure of the antiliberalism of contemporary liberal democracy.

ology might not undermine his sociology. But much of his use of the two ethics as well as his empirical claims about the logic of modern bureaucracy and international politics are designed to render *all radical views, without internal consideration*, empirically mistaken. In a positivist vein, Weber set up many a priori filters against radical claims. Antiradical ideology lends plausibility to this counterintuitive approach.

Weber's hostile use of *Gesinnungsethik* focused on radicals: "The Bolshevik and Spartacist ideologists bring about exactly the *same* results as any militaristic dictators just because they use this political means [violence]."[28] For this claim to be right, Spartacist-instigated antiwar revolt could have achieved only the equivalent of the Prussian conduct of the war. But Weber criticized the expansionary irresponsibility of the monarch's war aims;[29] he acknowledged a range of different consequences of diverse goals. Further, the republican internationalist canceling of the Brest-Litovsk Treaty was hardly the same as the imposing of it.

Similarly, despite important concessions to the old order, which I traced in Chapter 8, the Bolsheviks withdrew Russia from World War I, recognized oppressed nationalities, brought large numbers of workers into official positions, sanctioned peasant land division, and the like. But they used revolutionary violence. If all violence were morally similar, then despite these very *different, unusual* empirical results, Weber's judgment might make some sense. Precisely because violence is sometimes justified, however, as the next section will show, he had to distort these consequences.

He also misconstrued radical antiwar aims. In "Politics as a Vocation," he translated Bolshevik and Spartacist indictments of intercapitalist war into warmongering: "As is generally known, even during the war, the revolutionary socialists [Zimmerwald faction] professed a principle that one might strikingly formulate: 'If we face the choice either of some more years of war and then revolution, or peace now and no revolution, we choose some more years of war.' "[30] Once again, on Weber's reformulation, the radical argument becomes incoherent: Bolsheviks and Spartacists started out from hatred of war; yet they putatively worked to prolong (imperialist) war, hoping that even more massive suffering would bring on revolution. Following the stereotype, such radicals seem bent on imposing that suffering. Further, their antiwar supporters would hardly have approved efforts to extend suffering – in virtue of

---

[28] Weber, *FMW*, p. 119; *GPS*, p. 538.   [29] Weber, *GPS*, p. 165.

[30] Weber, *FMW*, p. 121. The Bolsheviks and Spartacists both participated in the internationalist conference at Zimmerwald during World War I.

Even if Weber's "translation" were accurate, he would accuse radicals of doing no more than ordinary nationalists who would not accept "peace now" at any price – for instance, that of being conquered.

seeking this external aim, they presumably would have had to be dishonest as well. In effect, Weber attempted to shift the blame for the continuing conflict from the great powers and their nationalist defenders to radical workers, at least in making the latter complicitors.[31] But these democratic internationalists actually argued that despite peaceful appeals to end war, imperial powers would *unjustly* continue to waste workers' lives. They thus advocated *militant opposition to their own warmaking governments to halt the belligerence more rapidly* through transnational solidarity from below; they sought to instigate the antimonarchical, antiwar soldier and sailor mutiny that ultimately undermined both regimes and infuriated patriots like Plekhanov and Weber.

In addition, where Weber recognized popular antiwar revolt, he depicted it as a caricature of an ethic of intention. Thus, he asserted, rebellious sailors and workers failed to "turn the other cheek" toward the Prussian government, but did so toward the victors of Versailles:

> Take the example "Turn the other cheek": this command is unconditional and does not question the source of the other's authority to strike. Except for the saint it is an ethic of indignity. This is it: one must be saintly in everything at least in intention. . . . *Then* this ethic makes sense and expresses a kind of dignity; *otherwise it does not.*[32]

By the strictures of his second notion of *Gesinnungsethik*, radicals lacked dignity; since they were not nonviolent on all fronts, they were "dilettantes" in Christian spirituality. And on his second sense of *Verantwortungsethik*, they were irresponsible; they did not answer foreseeable *foreign* blows. In line with antiradical stereotypes, they hurt their followers through allowing the imposition of the Versailles levy.[33]

But revolutionary German sailors and workers were neither candidate saints nor neophyte patriots. Instead, they struck a blow against what they regarded as a mortal enemy, Prussian autocracy. They brought into being the new Weimar democracy, which was opposed even by the promonarchical Social Democratic leaders whom they forced into power. From a liberal democratic standpoint, they arguably achieved a major political and moral victory, one hardly canceled even by an onerous treaty.[34] (Since the foreign policy of oligarchies is especially reactionary, liberal variants of democratic internationalism are often stigmatized as radical.) Furthermore, they not only eliminated an important form of domestic oppression, but as internationalists, abrogating the expansion-

---

[31] The last clause is a generous interpretation of Weber. He does not mention the warmakers.

[32] Weber, *FMW,* p. 119; *GPS,* p. 538.   [33] Weber, *FMW,* p. 128.

[34] Unfortunately, it does not go without saying, given Weber's account, that although radical, they were hardly all Spartacists.

ary Brest-Litovsk Treaty, mitigated harms to others. Theirs was a plausible attempt at an ethic of responsibility that a liberal or radical democrat might prefer to Weber's nationalism. Now, Weber could still have claimed that the damage to German national interests – *arguing* that they were *common* interests – and the threat of renewed belligerence outweighed these empirical claims; he could fairly have tried to show that the radicals held a mistaken *Verantwortungsethik*. Instead, he utilized the less plausible versions of each ethic to fulminate against them.

I will emphasize two general theoretical implications of Weber's critique of radicalism and then turn to the interplay of this animus with his theory of the Russian Revolution and socialist regimes. First, Weber's minimizing of contemporary empirical alternatives, mischaracterization of his opponents' political stands, conflation of other viewpoints with religious pacifism, and adoption of an illicit, great-power "realist" standard for "responsibility" combine with his relativism – the allegedly incommensurable demons of love and war – to reinforce his sociological reductionism. But none of these arguments is sound. His sociology initially seems a promising paradigm for an empiricist or neo-Kantian epistemology and metaethics. But a reasonably stated, democratic ethic of responsibility – one that Weber's account suggests – acknowledges the core moral standards of life and capacity for moral personality. That view underpins a *liberal* political science. Internally examined, Weber's argument sustains neither a reductionist nor a relativist sociology.

Second, on a methodological level, Weber's use of his twin ethics is an important specimen of ideal-type analysis; it reveals further sociological and democratic weaknesses. Thus, the attempt to shape such types out of – what seem to the social scientist – plausible reasoning about a situation and the alleged motivations of *a category* of social actors can become an excuse for an absence of empathy with varied agents, notably political opponents.[35] Weber's reconstructions of disagreement are, unfortunately, sometimes just as obtuse as those of economic determinist Marxians. More importantly, his neo-Kantian, ideal-typical analysis molded particular views and the facts they selected as explanatory tools in isolation from sharp theoretical criticism. That methodology has legitimized today's misguided social scientific practice of failing to compare proposed theories carefully with leading alternatives. In contrast, a Hegelian, internally critical analysis, starting from common moral standards and exhibiting the empirical differences central to complex disputes, facilitates a fair political, ethical, and scientific conversation between liberals and radicals.

---

[35] Weber, *MSS*, pp. 90–1.

5. Weber's rejection of the Russian Revolution

Weber's argument with radicals focused on the putative harmful effects of their actions on prospects for revolution and the current well-being of workers. Such claims, however, do not work directly against victorious socialist regimes. So he advanced four empirical criticisms of the October revolution: a claim about the impact of the unsavory motivations of ordinary revolutionaries, a related claim about popular imperialism as the basis for state expansion, a contention about immediate, postrevolutionary adoption of the old regime's hierarchy, and a general claim that the technical necessities of modern life would extend this bureaucracy. In contrast to most of his critique of prerevolutionary radicalism, the first and second claims causally stress the motives of ordinary participants rather than those of leaders. These two antidemocratic claims attempt to explain the *popular imperialism* that Weber supposed to be characteristic of socialism. His third claim about postrevolutionary hierarchy lends plausibility to the fourth one about the necessity of bureaucracy; yet the latter contention is a distinct, long-term argument about the social dynamic of revolution. Curiously, Weber's two most general antisocialist claims – those about imperialism and bureaucratization – have little obvious relationship to one another. Perhaps the threat of great-power rivalry necessitates a strong bureaucracy, though it is unclear why the latter should undertake predatory expansion. If popular pressure were the root of imperialism as he suggested, then the causation would be separate (or perhaps the former would be the cause of bureaucracy). Further, aside from a broad claim about the importance of calculable administration in a modern economy, he did not show why they are each so difficult to alter. The remainder of this chapter will examine these objections and a refined version of Weber's view.

His first claim about the deficiencies of radical regimes concentrated on the motivations of supporters that would putatively drive leaders to corrupt policies. Since ordinary people did not aspire to sainthood, he alleged that the Russian Revolution of 1917, the German democratic revolution of 1918, and the Berlin workers' uprising of January 1919 were engendered by the aims of looting and destruction. We might call his view the *human selfishness, rebellion as resentment objection*. On his reductionist sociology, all contemporary political associations and parties require a "machine" characterized by similar, unflattering motives:

> Under the conditions of the modern class struggle, the internal premiums consist of the satisfying of hatred and the craving for revenge [Rachsucht], above all, resentment. . . . The external rewards are adventure, victory, booty, power, and spoils. The leader and his success are completely depen-

dent upon the functioning of his machine and hence not on his own motives.[36]

Here Weber adopted a hard-line, empirical view of human nature, which riveted the competitive strivings of particular socially created status hierarchies into unchangeable human psychology and undercut cooperative possibilities. In describing radical movements, he asserted that the cause "never on earth [inspires] even the majority" of the rank and file. This claim recalls his account of the degeneration of Protestantism from Calvin's austere version to his followers' secular, procapitalist interpretation. But a critic might find communism and internationalism psychologically less alienated goals compared either with striving to accord one's actions with the will of a hidden, inscrutable god or with accumulating capital. Further, Weber provided no evidence for this controversial empirical description. Instead, linking class conflict to Nietzsche's analysis of slave morality, he reduced radical beliefs to a putative psychological urge – resentment at the better situation of others.

Weber also advanced the standard bourgeois claim, when faced with massive class struggle, that rebels are criminals.[37] He again superimposed a Christian idiom, redolent of his second ethic of intention, on a "materialist" point of view in order to characterize proletarian motives as "predominantly base": "We shall not be deceived about this by verbiage; the materialist interpretation of history is not a cab to be taken at will; it does not stop short at the promoters of revolutions."[38] A Marxian standpoint, however, is not mainly a debunking account of individual motives. As a grain of truth in Weber's conception, this theory suggests that oppressive systems encourage selfish conduct and associated ideologies especially in the privileged classes; if applied too uniformly even in this case, the debunking aspect can mistakenly seem to rest on restrictive psychological theses about selfishness.[39] But on a Marxian account

[36] Weber, *FMW*, p. 125; *GPS*, p. 544.   [37] Gilbert, 1981a, ch. 9.

[38] Weber, *FMW*, p. 125. Like the Marxian critique of democratic revolution, Weber rightly thinks that social upheavals often lead to paradoxical, unintended consequences. But his claim here is one about motivation.

[39] In the introduction to *Capital*, Marx separates his explanatory account of economic and sociological tendencies from any psychological claim about the inflexibility of *human* motivation or denial, on the basis of selfishness, of a moral psychology of individuality, even for capitalists: "To prevent possible misunderstanding, a word . . . here individuals are dealt with only insofar as they are the personifications of economic categories, embodiments of particular class-relations and class-interests. My standpoint . . . can less than any other make the individual responsible for relations whose creature he socially remains, however much he may subjectively raise himself above them" (Marx, 1961, 1:10). He claims only that as a broad social trend, to remain capitalists, owners of the means of production must, by and large, act in ways that harm workers and cultivate a corrupt, ideological viewpoint.

441

as we saw in Chapter 5, claims asserting the interests of the oppressed, even where they appear in "ideological form" in peasant or worker demands for fairness, do not involve selfishness, capture important aspects of truth, and justify cooperation. Once again, Marxian theory is a *moral sociology*, which draws complex distinctions between true and ideological aspects of popular viewpoints; Weber's reductionism denies such distinctions.

In moving from an indictment of opposition radicalism to that of newly triumphant socialism, antiradical ideology changes its focus and transvalues ethical assessments. The informed, if "manipulative," leaders and follower "dupes" now become the active, selfish masses and the constrained, originally morally naive leaders. This view examines the actual positions of radicals in neither case. Weber's view of the Russian Revolution unfortunately shares this ideology. He denied prerevolutionary mass radicalism and accused the Bolsheviks of warmongering to instigate revolution; afterwards he saw popular participation as a spur to reactionary policies. But his psychological reduction of proletarian claims to envy is reasonable only if the capitalists came by their wealth and power without misusing workers. Otherwise, as a Marxian might suggest, invidious resentment turns out to be *justified* anger at oppressors.

Thus, we might compare with Weber's account an observant, though hostile, report of the widespread multiracial "riots" in Britain in 1981: "The perception of injustices and of lack of opportunity seems just as great as was the case in America, and many *who participated in the looting profess to feel that they are merely evening the score.*"[40] Weber's reductionism contradicts his acknowledgment in *The Protestant Ethic* and *General Economic History* that workers are exploited. It prevents him from considering moral motivations beyond justice – for instance, the Marxian claim that cooperation in revolutionary activity inspired Communards, or recognizing that English abolitionist workers and Kiel mutineers could engage in democratic deliberation about internationalist alternatives to great-power policies. Weber's psychology permits only competitive selfishness and the altruism of sainthood, not genuine interest in being a self.[41] But although altruism is rare, solidarity is not. This reductionism rules out any empathetic appraisal of proletarian motivations even from the perspective of his own theory – for instance, a claim that though such rebellions express justified anger, revolution is an ultimately coun-

---

[40] *New York Times*, July 15, 1981, p. 4 (my emphasis).
[41] If one draws a distinction between status-oriented selfishness and self-reflection, even the surprising actions of saints might realize their individuality (Arendt, 1968, pp. 57–69).

terproductive response. A Weberian liberal could, however, drop this Nietzschean psychology without detriment to the core of Weber's theory of socialism.

As a second empirical claim, he insisted that the new Soviet regime *must* harbor imperialist aims. As Chapter 10 shows, Weber regarded czarism, that "castrating power," as Germany's main enemy. Confronted with the insurrections of February and October, he insisted that Russian aims had not changed. Whether the regime bore "a tsarist, Cadet or Bolshevik label [*Etiquette*]," it remained emphatically imperialist.[42] In effect, he extended his broader *necessity of great-power imperialism argument* into a supposed *necessity of socialist imperialism*.

During the February revolution, Weber claimed that an "expansionary tendency" (*Expansionstendenz*), a "people's imperialism" (*Volksimperialismus*), resulted from the "land hunger of the Russian peasants." In a different, quasi-radical vein, he also pointed to the Provisional Government's financial dependence on domestic and foreign capitalism, criticized its suppression of peasant demands and harassment of radicals, and indicted it as a "phony democracy" (*Scheindemokratie*).[43] He even suggested that artisans, workers not employed in war industry, and peasants might initiate a genuine Russian democratic movement and, in principle, recognized a social basis for radical political change.[44] Whether empirically plausible or not, these sociological distinctions weaken his psychological insistence on selfishness; "selfish" pacifism and solidarity seem much more promising for the success of radicalism than selfish warmongering. Ignoring these implications of his arguments, however, he aimed to discourage the burgeoning republican and socialist *German* solidarity for the February revolution and to sustain the monarchy's belligerence.

The Bolsheviks similarly criticized the Provisional Government, but from the left. Yet when they took power, Weber insisted that their policies must replicate those of their predecessors. He dismissed as "pure nonsense" the claim that a "proletariat of a West European stamp" – one that presumably, on Weber's mechanical argument, would be mainly oriented toward peace – backed this revolution. Instead, he averred, an expansionist "*soldier* proletariat stands behind [the regime]," seeking spoils (Soldatenproletariat steht hinter ihm).[45] From peasant land hunger to a spoils-oriented soldier proletariat, Weber stressed the sociological and psychological quality of supporters, not the manipulativeness of

---

[42] Weber, *GPS*, p. 159.
[43] Weber, *GPS*, pp. 205–9. He claimed that a cultural conservatism, nurturing expansion, still prevailed in peasant politics (Weber, *GPS*, p. 159).
[44] Weber, *GPS*, pp. 250–6.   [45] Weber, *GPS*, pp. 280–1.

leaders, as the source of radical policies. He did not offer a *sociological*, structural account of the particular dynamics of a socialist imperialism, comparable to a theory of the interplay of intercapitalist competition for markets and resources with political expansion; rather, he affirmed a basically *psychological* view, claiming to derive transgovernmental policies from individual motivations.[46]

One might ask, Why should selfishness, by itself, lead to expansion? Perhaps in normal conditions, most citizens, whatever their branch of work, would "selfishly" resist sacrificing their lives for the sake of conquest. To fill out the argument, Weber might have contended, socialism is not and could not be a dynamically productive system. Increases in wealth would have to emerge from foreign plunder. Further, most disadvantaged citizens, not just at times of starvation but generally, would have to regard such increases as essential. But Weber never defended these claims. Instead, to justify German power politics, he utilized both his psychological and industrial-sector reductionisms to translate mass worker opposition to czarist war aims into putative imperialism.

As Chapter 10 shows, Weber erred about Bolshevik composition, which was concentrated among industrial workers.[47] So even if his reductionist sociology were right, one might expect the Bolsheviks to adopt internationalist policies of a "Western" stamp, just as they did, and reject his conclusion about expansion. Actually the Bolsheviks were more radical in wartime than most "Western" socialist parties and endured concomitant persecution.[48]

But a critic might also question Weber's reductionism: Why stigmatize conscripted soldiers, mainly workers and peasants, as "greedy looters" and "imperialists"? The rebellion of Russian soldiers halted the war and overturned the czar; even Weber, inconsistently, acknowledged their "warweariness." And as we saw in Chapter 10, this critic might turn his

[46] The causal mediation of employment of individuals in war industry, the army, or on the land does not make this picture distinctively sociological.

[47] Haimson, 1964; Rainbowitch, 1976; Gilbert, 1981a. In 1917, based on its prewar activity, this party was able to expand to a quarter of a million members among workers and soldiers. It had thus become a large organization, compared with contemporary Russian parties, with a distinct, political program and influence.

[48] Weber's 1919 "Zur Thema der 'Kriegsschuld' " mistakenly asserted that "no [Russian] stratum with any positive influence did *not* want war in 1914" (Weber, *GPS*, p. 479; my emphasis). By positive influence, perhaps he meant a pronationalist one, influential with the czar; prima facie, it seems peculiar by 1914 to call the Bolsheviks a group that did not have to be taken – warily – into account in government policy making. During the war, the czarist government prosecuted and jailed the Bolshevik duma representatives – all workers – for their advocacy of transforming imperialist war into civil insurrection (Badayev, n.d.). In 1917, the Mensheviks, Cadets, and Socialist-Revolutionaries failed to share Weber's conviction; they hunted Lenin as a "traitor."

analysis around: Were not many internationalist "Western" workers employed in war-related industries and the military (for instance, at Kiel)?

Weber advances a general claim about the necessity of a state imperialism that is not simply driven by popular pressure from below. As Chapter 10 recounts, he maintained that state ("booty") capitalism, unlike private capitalism, is the source of expansion; presumably the emergence of a modern bureaucracy, with increased – a Marxian would say, parasitic – needs for resources, compounds it. That claim applies equally to capitalist and socialist governments. But if Schumpeter's subsequent Weberian claims about the meekness of corporate executives have any validity, they probably characterize government bureaucrats as well; modern officials may carry out brutal policies – consider Arendt's description of Eichmann – but they are hardly swashbucklers.[49] Thus, a *sociological* theory of contemporary imperialism cannot consist of bare, transepochal abstractions about state power – did the Vikings have a government in the modern sense? – and greed. Some argument about the dynamics of specific social systems – internal, or resulting from a particular international regime, or an interplay of the two – is needed to explain twentieth-century expansion.

Weber's most likely claim is international: a "realist" insistence that all states must participate in great-power politics. But except in terms of geographic advantages, that argument does not differentiate comparatively predatory from peaceful powers, for both are subject to the same international pressures;[50] it implausibly likens England, the United States, Switzerland, and czarist Russia. (As Chapter 10 argues, it also provides no insight into when and why particular powers acquire novel worldwide concerns and interests while others do not.) That theory includes no sociological claims. Although powerful oppressive, expansionary trends have emerged in subsequent socialism, Weber offered no plausible account of this dynamic.

6. Is bureaucratic domination necessary?

As a third, hostile empirical claim, Weber maintained that the Russian Revolution had extended *all* the most vicious aspects of capitalist and dictatorial domination:

---

[49] Schumpeter, 1951, pp. 26–30, 31, 33–4.
[50] Comparatively isolated, oceanic powers like the United States, Weber suggested, can afford to be less militarized.

Randall Collins, 1986, pp. 161–2, pursues an argument about the geopolitical determination of internal legitimacy as an instigator of expansion, but recognizes Weber's inadequate formulation.

The Soviets have preserved, or rather reintroduced, the highly paid enter-
priser, the group wage, the Taylor system, military and workshop discipline, and a search for foreign capital. Hence in a word, the Soviets have
had to accept absolutely all the things that Bolshevism had been fighting
as bourgeois class institutions. They have had to do that in order to keep
the state and economy going at all. Moreover the Soviets have reinstituted
the agents of the former Ochrana [the czarist secret police] as the main
instrument of state power.[51]

Given these empirical claims, he rendered a striking ethical verdict on
Soviet innovations: To harmful features of the old regime, the Bolsheviks
added looting. Weber extended his views on the *normal* domination of
all modern regimes to a special *socialism as vandalism objection.* In part, he
might claim to criticize socialist arguments internally – such governments retain *what socialists see* as objectionable features of capitalism and
worsen them through plunder. But he also criticized oppression and
stealing from *his own point of view* – that of an ethic of responsibility.

His critique works, however, only if, *empirically,* the Russian Revolution had no justifiable radical features and merely extended hierarchy.
Further, he needed to show that the Bolsheviks made concessions not as
contingent responses to imperialist attack and the horrendous difficulties of the postrevolutionary period but as necessities of socialist development; for if they successfully challenged the old order in significant
ways and strengthened some revolutionary features over time, then Weber's objection collapses.[52] As we saw in Chapter 8, this regime in a backward country, ravaged by war and civil war, adopted even more war-
and economic-determinism-justified concessions than Marx's theory
envisioned.[53] Such policies confirm some important aspects of Weber's

---

[51] Weber, *FMW,* p. 100.
[52] Weber idiosyncratically translated Spartacist as well as Soviet revolutionary aims: "Upon
the further question: 'What can this revolution bring about?' Every scientifically trained
socialist would have had the answer: one cannot speak of a transition to an economy
that in our sense could be called socialist; a bourgeois economy will reemerge merely
stripped of feudal elements and dynastic vestiges" (Weber, *FMW,* p. 121). That argument
would have applied even more strongly to the victory of Bolshevism in backward Russia.
Given initial concern for injustice, this interpretation again makes the revolutionary
view incoherent: On their own account, their goals will replicate at least the major objectionable features of the warmaking, oppressive system whose consequences they decry.
  But the version of Marxian theory – "science" – that the Spartacists held envisioned
socialism in Germany; the Bolsheviks, as internationalists, supported proletarian revolution in Western Europe and democracy and – after 1917 – socialism in Russia as well.
Perhaps "every scientifically trained socialist" is another ideal type based on some conversation between Weber and a radical student. Once again, he fails to reach the empirical claims of actual revolutionary opponents.
[53] Lenin, *CW,* 32:289.

claim. But in his *socialism as vandalism objection*, the revolution vanishes under the weight of the concessions.

As Chapter 8 also contends, the Bolsheviks initiated a strong, revolutionary countercurrent. Further, subsequent Chinese experience and an internal critique of Marxian theory suggest that even many Bolshevik concessions were unnecessary. Thus, despite the ultimate emergence of a hierarchical, expansionary regime, Weber's account is not powerful. In addition, the preceding criticism of Marx's conception of the initial phase of communism provides some indications for an interpretation of that socialist imperialism: An exploitative apparatus might seek to carve out an international sphere of influence to secure additional wealth for economic growth, for its own prestige and consumption, and perhaps for modest benefits to the populace; to nurture nationalism in order to justify its position and compete with more obviously capitalist rivals; and to undercut radical movements – potentially threatening counter-examples – abroad. In fact, as in ordinary capitalist cases, given the many-faceted oppressiveness of working-class experience, the regime's *political* need to further an ideology of a common good probably outweighs any economic benefits to ordinary citizens.[54] The account of Chapter 8 criticizes Marxian theory internally and underlines the need for a nuanced, historical depiction of revolutionary experience. It contrasts with overly easy, a priori dismissals of the Russian and Chinese revolutions based on economic determinist – "too low a level of produc-

---

[54] This argument partly concurs with Weber's claim about the legitimizing effects of (reactionary) foreign successes, except that he denies what it would emphasize: Internationalist policies and successes that cut against prevailing great-power arrangements – despite its clouded diplomacy and internal repression, even Soviet efforts in World War II – are much more deeply and genuinely legitimizing.

Recent Soviet ideas of a division of labor in the world socialist camp and a "noncapitalist road of development" throughout the less industrialized countries illustrate a fundamental change in outlook. The notion of a noncapitalist road – neither capitalist nor socialist – is puzzling from a Marxian point of view, for which class controls the state? If it is not workers or workers and peasants, the state broadly continues to serve exploiters; perhaps privileged managers in the bureaucracy and officers rather than private capitalists. More generally, many of the charges of dependency theory about advanced capitalist powers work for the Soviet Union and its trading and aid relationships with less developed countries. Through economic and military aid, it sustains dictatorial (except the Sandinistas) and inegalitarian regimes. Further its economic aid is "doubly tied" to the purchase of Soviet equipment; thus it both sustains its own growth and secures profit. In addition, the ideology of the division of labor in the socialist camp sanctifies the lesser development of many of the USSR's Third World trading partners who specialize in raw materials. It would take a far more complex, historical argument than I can offer here to account for these developments, but these changes pose a fundamental challenge to standard economic determinist claims that a socialist system cannot be imperialist in roughly the same sense as a capitalist one.

tive forces" – or Weberian – "the necessity of bureaucratization" – preconceptions, which ignore their cooperative, democratic features. That theory suggests a radical response to a more worked-out version of Weber's argument.

A Weberian could abandon Weber's one-sided empirical account and raise a fourth *omnipotence of bureaucracy objection*. On his view, no modern administrative, military, or industrial enterprise can function without a substantial cohort of officials. To be efficient, that bureaucracy must exhibit a hierarchical division of labor and accompanying status differentials. In the case of socialism, a Weberian might insist, even with an admixture of workers, a standard bureaucracy would quickly reemerge and become all-powerful. This Weberian might cite Lenin's worries about bureaucracy in his 1923 circular "Better Fewer but Better." As Weber, perhaps not presciently, formulated this objection in summer 1917:

> The majority of the Russian soldiers did not want to continue the war. But they had no choice, for both the means of destruction and of maintenance were controlled by persons who used them to force the soldiers into the trenches, just as the capitalist owner of the means of production forces the workers into the factories and mines.[55]

The role of soldiers, sailors, and workers in overthrowing the old regime underlines the limitations of Weber's argument. So do many subsequent examples such as the jarring impact of 14 million striking French workers and students in May 1968; recent strikes in Poland; and the lengthy defiance of martial law, given considerable political support in the military, by the Chinese democracy movement. As he rightly notes, state bureaucracies control a centralized violence, alienated from ordinary soldiers and citizens, whereas private capitalists do not; otherwise, Weber overrated officialdom's power.

But a refined version of his theory might contend that workers, soldiers, and other oppressed groups cannot shape government policy *except* through the shock of periodic revolt; an *omnipotence of bureaucracy except in crisis criticism*. Ordinarily on most issues, the bureaucracy will influence policy conservatively in its particular interest(s). This reformulation abandons one of Weber's most passionately held empirical convictions – that great-power rivalry ineluctably motivates a substantial military and war production officialdom – for while his ideal-typical formulations about the necessity of modern bureaucracy are independent of this sociological and political preoccupation, his claims about power-state rivalry help to make his account plausible.

---

[55] Weber, *ES*, 3:1394.

7. Radical democratic rejoinders

This *omnipotence of bureaucracy except in crisis objection* is a genuinely troubling one, for which, given socialist experience, Marxians have no easy answer. Yet a radical might foresee four causes for declining bureaucratic impact in ordinary political life. First, given the dramatic role of workers in the Russian Revolution and other radical movements, one might wonder with Lenin whether Weber's conception of strict specialization and long training is necessary; many tasks involved in running the post office, file keeping, and the like do not require an elevated level of skill and would be naturally done with a down-to-earth, unmysterious style.[56] Second, as we saw in Chapter 8, if a regime pursues democratic internationalist policies, it needs a diminished "intelligence" and military apparatus. In addition, the foregoing argument against specialist domination applies to a democratized military.

Third, Bolshevik and Chinese revolutionaries often worked without special material and status privileges. Neither a division of manual and mental labor required at the outset of communism, nor the selection of political leaders for substantial periods, a radical might maintain, need result in *major status divisions* and the emergence of an exploitative regime. Further, in less civilized circumstances, productive activity absorbs a great part of human energy. To most people, the aspect of hierarchy that contributes to that productivity seems especially significant and lends legitimacy to the aspect of control. A communist regime, however, emerges from separating these aspects and diminishing the latter. Even at the outset, communist emphasis on nonnecessary activity as the primary arena for realizing individuality would erode the *social* significance of remaining differences in necessary work. Individuality would be self-consciously disconnected from distinctions of productive and social status; stratification would decline.[57]

Fourth, a *general* economic determinist analysis of socialism, ultimately adopted by contemporary Communist regimes, undercuts revolutionary politics. On that view, a socialist regime is sustained by state ownership of the means of production plus some development of productivity. Except during the early postrevolutionary period and war, such regimes have often insisted, politics is administration; unity through behind-the-scenes elite negotiation replaces democratic dia-

---

[56] Lenin, 1971, pp. 43–4, 83–4.
[57] If such a communist regime adopts income egalitarianism, social status would arise purely from distinctions of leadership and honor. Note, however, that this broad radical response to Weber does not *require* specific arguments about equal incomes.

logue.[58] Now, even an economic determinist argument does not require this technocratic misconception; a reasonable level of productivity might permit a liberal socialism that encouraged open divergence of views and interests. A reactionary ideology, however, mutes even the democratic possibilities of an economic determinist view and legitimizes the choice of narrowly administrative alternatives. On this account, what the Weberian interprets as a technical necessity of bureaucratization is really the result of a misguided implementation of economic determinist theory; for even though its causal focus is productivity, not organization, that antipolitical view is closely related to Weber's. Like their capitalist counterparts, such socialist regimes have sometimes achieved efficient administrative handling of problems and sometimes, as in contemporary China and Eastern Europe, generated significant discontent and revolt. Chapter 8 emphasizes the possibilities of democratic innovations in initial revolutionary politics. Contrary to Weber, the triumph of technocracy is contingent.

In a broad intellectual perspective, Weber's controversy with Marxians over socialism is ironic. In the scholarly debate initiated by *The Protestant Ethic,* he is reputed to be the leading proponent of the role of ideas in history; his argument contrasts with mechanical, determinist accounts. But the internal, Hegelian examination of a social theory often leads to unexpected results. In his less cautious moments, Weber implied that a religious conception inspired the rise of capitalism; yet he thought that communist ideas would have no comparable material impact. At most, they would legitimize the trend to bureaucratization and imperialism. Instead of the fine divergence between Weberian multicausality and Marxian dialectical primacy, the theory of socialism ironically pits radical multicausality and the *primacy of politics* against Weberian organizational monocausality. His view of revolutionary regimes is a paradigmatic case of a position changing into its opposite. There, radical democratic theory inherits the dialectical emphasis on ideology, ethics, and politics of *The Protestant Ethic,* and Weber, in seemingly un-Weberian fashion, avows the crude technological determinism and sociological reductionism that he had so skillfully, though inaccurately, attacked as Marxism.

---

[58] The Chinese Communist Party and the Sandinistas, though not socialist, have sometimes advanced broader views of postrevolutionary politics.

Chapter 13

Levels of ethical disagreement and the controversy between neo-Kantianism and realism

The foregoing account of objectivity has marked an intricate interplay between core moral standards, social theoretical disputes, complex ethical judgments, overall moral theories, and metaethics. As they became relevant, I have pointed to these five levels; more conceptual apparatus was not needed. But the interplay of these levels is complex and has itself generated metaethical confusion.

This chapter will show that the conflict between neo-Kantians and realists does not pivot on just one level – say, controversies over the role of empirical disagreements in broader moral disputes – but that each metaethical view selects different subsections within the structure of moral argument for emphasis. Broadly speaking, for Weber, starting points in disparate realms of life determine clashes of fact and social theory, and more complex ethical assessment; thus, quite high level judgments about moral epistemology and vocational standpoint shape the argument all the way down. He occasionally noticed core standards – those involved in claims about "being a scoundrel"; yet in his reflection on the structure of broader ethical clashes, these criteria vanish. For the realist, moving in the opposite direction, underlying ethical standards and discoveries determine what it is for an argument to be *moral* at all. These standards provide *broad* parameters for evaluating conflicting moral theories; they justify some important inferences in moral epistemology. This chapter will treat Weber's relativism as a paradigm in a contrast of neo-Kantian and realist visions of the tapestry of ethical argument; it will invoke his moral judgments as a counterexample to his metaethics. In addition, it will suggest that the latter hinders Weber's formulation of a liberal conception of democratic individuality.

Before further specifying these five levels, however, a caveat is in order. Because moral argument is interwoven, levels frequently overlap; complex judgments arise from the interplay among them. Thus, verdicts in metaethics and moral theory often include judgments at the other levels. Some contrasts of level are easy – say, the distinctions among the ordinary standard involved in a murder trial, the complex theory dispute over whether a uniform measure of happiness or pleasure exists, and the metaethical controversy over whether moral judgments may be true in the same sense as scientific judgments. Nonetheless, boundaries between levels are often imprecise. Further, the status of particular judgments sometimes changes historically. The clash over the ostensible justification of slavery was once an example of a complex moral dispute, depending on social theoretical – economic and biological – claims; the recognition of a universal capacity for moral personality is today a core standard. As Part I showed, that standard has proved to be far more central than others in distinguishing modern liberalism and radicalism from ancient views. Thus, some of the following sorting of judgments and controversies depends on the particular purposes of this argument and would shift for others.

For these purposes, however, the intricate interplay of levels of moral judgment and the diverse subsets on which relativist and realist metaethics focus lend some credence to arguments for incommensurability. Theorists have often been hard pressed to see just where moral disagreements come from. A delineation of this web of judgments, showing why many-leveled controversies give only apparent comfort but no confirmation to relativism, will deepen the case for realism.

1. The complexity of core standards

On the first level, as we have seen, long-standing human practice and ethical discovery give rise to broad reflection on and considered judgments about human potentials for a good life, moral character, and the integrity of relationships and activities. I have called these relatively uncontroversial underlying verdicts *core moral standards*. Simplicity is not their distinguishing feature; for although standards involving murder are not complex, Aristotle's account of the distinctive human capacity for freedom in the polis is quite intricate.[1] In Shapere's apt terminology, core standards are ones relevant to the questions and aims of ethics as a

---

[1] Once one gets beyond prototypical premeditated murder, however, refined notions of intentionality and responsibility give rise to more intricate judgments. Similarly, even where an uncontroversial standard of deliberation, exemplified in the debates in Athenian assemblies, exists, any attempt to elucidate this idea becomes quite complicated – for example, specifying what it means to reason about competing moral considerations. Aristotle's account of deliberation theorizes the core standard in a complex, potentially controversial way that is part of what I will call the third and fourth levels: elaborated ethical judgment and theory.

For a useful analogous discussion of how a core notion of epistemological justifiedness underlies the "close knit family" of accounts of justification, see Goldman, 1986, pp. 58–9 and ch. 5.

domain of inquiry; investigators treat as core those standards about which *there are no specific, compelling reasons for doubt*. As the argument concerning moral discovery indicates, even these standards are subject to possible revision; so is the terrain of this domain. Thus, a modern theory of a good life, in contrast to Aristotle's, stresses individuality. Given contemporary recognitions of human diversity and choice, the fundamental question – how am I to live? – has less definite answers than Aristotle conceived or, alternatively, goes far beyond ethics.[2] But the idea of democratic individuality is a core standard, a defining feature *internalized* in moral reflection. Thus, comparatively central standards – say, those about life and capacity for moral personality – are quite secure. In Miller's idiom, such claims are "ethical truisms," though, given their a posteriori character, that term may suggest too great a simplicity.[3] On Boyd's conception, such standards are part of the background knowledge that contributes to the reliability of complex moral theories.

For particular deliberators, however, the multidimensionality of core standards sanctions a great range of reflective decisions about a good life in specific circumstances. In fact, the variability of appropriate choices illustrates individuality and the *nonrelativist plurality* of ways of moral learning.[4] Although such standards set some broad limits on appropriate reasoning, they do not give rise to uniform decisions except in extreme cases. As many modern theorists have surmised, they do not often sharply constrain particular deliberations. Furthermore, serious clashes of goods as well as subtle differences in individual choices concerning goods or virtuous actions in specific circumstances are important features of moral argument even on this initial level.

2. Empirical conflicts

On a second level, however, conflicts occur over the facts of a specific case or over the causal theory invoked to explain them. In the former instance, those who share core standards about just war might clash over which power committed aggression; in the latter, Hegel shared Aristotle's admiration for Greek freedom but denied his social theoretical claims about a disparateness of human capacities that would render slavery "natural." Now, first-level standards also involve some straightforward factual and social theoretical claims – for instance, about the *human* lives harmed by aggression. The demarcation between first and

---

[2] Williams, 1985, ch. 1.
[3] Given an important epistemological caveat about historical revisability, this point correctly restates the insight in Aristotle's claim that universally agreed-upon ethical standards are true.
[4] Goldman, 1986, pp. 69–71; R. Miller, 1985.

second levels of argument grows out of the *lack of controversy* over the general factual claims in core standards contrasted with the sometimes complex empirical disputes – instances in which the relevant facts cannot be easily ascertained or cases in which agreement is blocked by ideology and conflicting interests – of level two.[5] Given underlying, shared first-level standards, we can choose to look at second-level disagreements in a comparatively nonmoral, empirical way.

3. Moral controversies

Yet on a third level, we can also interpret these empirical disputes as clashes of complex ethical judgment. This level *combines* the core standards and empirical claims of the previous two levels into what are sometimes intricate objects of analysis and practical deliberation. The distinction of two kinds of empirical disagreement helps to isolate these debates. The least complicated second-level clashes focus on factual claims; litigants may disagree over whether a particular person is a murderer, but they know what they mean by murder and what factual claims would serve to convict, extenuate, or exonerate the accused. One might be inclined to say that these controversies are *second-level moral judgments* – our interest in the facts is pretty narrowly guided by core standards. In contrast, distinctive third-level disagreements often take up important social theoretical (and factual) differences between quite disparate kinds of argument involving multiple underlying criteria. In these theoretical efforts to understand cluster properties, the moral contrasts are complex and less easily resolvable if a relevant set of facts falls a certain way.

For instance, Hegel's clash with Aristotle over the role of subjective particularity in the modern state is a mainly ethical dispute in that it focuses on distinctively moral concepts – a version of individuality versus, say, functional contribution to society or an infinite, reflective will versus a gentleman's deliberative character.[6] Yet as we saw in Chapter 1,

---

[5] This claim recalls the arguments on clashing interests and ideology of Chapters 4 and 7. Notions of interest may also sometimes be relevant in explaining internal contradictions within arguments at higher levels of ethical disagreement.

[6] In contrast to the ancients, a coherent modern functional account can only explain the emergence of individuality, not substitute for it or purport that it is an illusion. Montesquieu's views on the role of a moderate climate in Northern freedom and Protestantism are, once again, a prototype of such an account (Montesquieu, *EL*, 1:342; Gilbert, 1986b). Insofar as Weber was less committed to objective claims about individuality, the functional strand in his account is deficient.

that dispute centered on psychological claims about sufficient, universal human capacities versus bifurcated ones; it was linked to other theoretical clashes about the nature of historical change and how to assess political association. These moral and empirical disputes were, in turn, rooted in changes in society.[7] As Shapere has put it, however, complex *chains of reasoning* link the two conceptions, in Hegel's case, very self-consciously.[8]

Given the contemporary prevalence of relativist metaethics, the significance of this complex disagreement between Aristotle and Hegel has been obscured. Further, unlike most of today's first-level judgments, the theoretical history of abolitionism helps to justify the important epistemological – what I will call fifth-level – inference that given new human potentials manifested historically, even seemingly core ethical standards are *revisable*, and discoveries are to be expected (the second distinction in the history of political thought traced in Chapter 2).[9] Because this moral debate plays a controversial role in today's *metaethical* disputes, I have chosen to regard it as a paradigm of third-level disagreements. But I could also have focused on, say, the clash between Kant's or Marx's democratic internationalism and Hegel's ethically coherent, "realist" view of war.

A distinctive feature of third-level judgments is that they require(d) intricate theoretical argument and moral analysis. They involve dramatic, sometimes epochal theoretical change: *Diverse modern notions of individuality in, say, Hegel or Kohut, are not a quantitative extension of Aristotelian conceptions of freedom and deliberation but a transformation of them;*[10] democratic internationalist arguments envision possibilities unimagined by Thucydides. Given deep theoretical differences, these ethical arguments might not – semantically speaking – refer to the same phenomena; hence relativist *epistemological* – fifth-level – inferences often derive from an external consideration of such disputes. Yet an internal, dialectical account reveals important continuities. The third level includes unresolved ethical clashes, pivoting on social theoretical debates – for instance, radical claims about the possibilities of democracy, internation-

---

[7] In addition, on my categorization, disputes about who committed aggression are usually second-level empirical controversies; the broad disagreement over the justice of wars of enslavement or to advance (modern) free regimes are third-level arguments.

[8] Shapere, 1984, intro.

[9] Aristotle's distinction between emergent Greek freedom and despotism also justifies this epistemological inference.

[10] More exactly, we can view the modern recognition of the human capacities of slaves or women as quantitative; yet the core notion of individuality and varied elaborations are qualitative. See also Michael Oakeshott, 1975.

alism, and individuality that, if true in contrast to liberal Weberian alternatives, would advance moral theory and promise progress.[11]

4. Hard cases and ethical theory

On a fourth level, conflicts of intrinsic goods suggest a need for moral theory. Disputes often occur about which broad theory – for instance, one focused on rights, happiness, or intrinsically valuable activities and relationships – best explains our ethical judgments and provides the most reasonable guidance in hard cases. The starting points of such theories are controversial; they stress some core standards as opposed to others – consider the attribution of rights to individuals compared to claims about well-being or about virtues, or, within rights-based theory, between basic rights (liberty, individuality) and derivative rights (subsistence, the difference principle, equal incomes). Such theories invoke quite complex factual and theoretical claims – for instance, the utilitarian psychological contention that there exists some uniform mental entity, say, pleasure, which we can quantify across diverse individuals. Through comparison of arguments about human cooperation, freedom, and individuality, ethical theory aims to specify – and perhaps decrease – the range of moral plurality and indeterminacy. Distinctive fourth-level controversies often focus on the internal consistency and explanatory fruitfulness of overall conceptions. In Weber's somewhat unusual version, however, a wider range of stances are candidate moral outlooks – thus, the saint and the warrior are thought to move in mutually sealed-off realms of life, to employ incommensurable standards. In contrast, on an objective account, his ethics is not sufficiently constrained by a recognition of the general capacity for moral personality.

5. Naturalistic moral epistemology

The fifth level of potential debate is moral epistemology – for instance, denials of ethical continuity versus affirmations of advance. As Chapters 1 and 3 suggest, such epistemological judgments are inferences to the best explanation about competing moral verdicts and social and ethical theories. Debates on this plane are inductive, arising from conclusions

---

[11] The first two kinds of controversies over a decent communism and capitalism, described in analyzing Miller's argument in Chapter 7, are also useful illustrations of third-level disputes. In contrast, the last controversy, supposing factual agreement and comparatively subtle differences in evaluation of a liberal capitalism and moderate communism, is a first-level debate.

and surviving disputes on other levels. Realist inferences defend the integrity of ethics and block self-refuting relativist ones. In addition, the adoption of a sophisticated realist *metaethical* program often has important intellectual and moral consequences.

Instead of external contrasts of viewpoints sealed by epoch, realism leads to nuanced comparisons. In place of the putative utter reshaping of social universes, it discerns continuities in democratic and ethical theory and practice, and highlights moral discoveries. Further, relativism often coexists with and justifies an empirical and epistemological failure to examine leading contending theories and, thus, an acceptance of a prevailing moral and political framework. As in Weber, lack of comparison leads to a failure to state liberal or, alternatively, radical positions sharply. In addition, when relativists downplay the debates about slavery and democratic individuality through which modern theory emerged, their stand weakens resistance to the political undermining of any moral point of view whatever.[12] Finally, a realist metaethics contributes to openness about future research and moral advance. Based on past experience, we might expect to discover novel, focused, comparatively admirable possibilities of human cooperation – for instance, in a way of raising children that furthers individuality. Similarly, on a liberal or Marxian view, the experiences of modern democracies, however problematic, have been important, naturally occuring social experiments in individuality. Through the very limited history of socialist societies, a radical might suggest, we have just begun to learn about the potential contribution of egalitarian arrangements to the concordant flourishing of goods, democracy, and internationalism.

In assessing fifth-level judgments, much of today's metaethical debate is framed in a naturalized, a posteriori idiom, tied to the internal examination of moral judgments and the history of ethics. These trends accord with realism. Alternatively, however, one might conceive moral theory as an a priori enterprise, which would deductively shape the other levels. Kant's theory is one kind of example; a relativism that starts from clashes of incommensurable life spheres is another. In such cases, conceptions of moral epistemology would decisively influence the interpretation of conflicts at other levels.

---

[12] This claim is only about a range of clustered effects of relativism, amplified in certain cases, diminished in others. Stephen Holmes's *Benjamin Constant and the Making of Modern Liberalism* is a counterexample on important dimensions. It endorses metaethical relativism and relativism about human nature; yet it advances well-argued claims about moral progress, focused on the abolition of slavery and hierarchy. The metaethical component in his argument is self-refuting; the comparison with radical views is weak, yet his liberalism is eloquent (Holmes, 1984, pp. 200–4).

6. Diverse subsets of ethical argument

We can now return, with more precision, to the Weberian and radical characterization of such differences. If we scrutinize these five levels through the lens of Weber's metaethical relativism, fourth-level clashes of overall standpoints become primary. Thus, he metaethically stressed the conflict of international violence with religious love as the key to internally coherent, irreconcilable outlooks.[13] On this account, he interpreted third-level conflicts of complex judgment – say, eudaemonist versus Weberian views about population growth and happiness – as derivative from incommensurable fourth-level decisions about ultimate moral positions. The latter stands would shape the opponents' view of facts and social theory (second level). Given clashing life spheres, he inferred, fourth- (and fifth-) level viewpoints remain immune from factual and theoretical criticism, though he acknowledged, as we have seen, a limited moral role for science: Social theory may criticize the means invoked by a particular position (second-level).

Weber's metaethics is inconsistent with many of his moral and political judgments and even his theoretical claims. The plausibility of a hostile use of ethic of responsibility against radicals depends, as Chapter 12 contends, on the objectivity of social theory debates and their ethical ramifications; yet his official metaethical account minimizes the role of such disputes. In moral theory, Weber scorned eudaemonist conceptions of happiness, based on his second-level empirical conclusions about population clashes. Yet that theoretical verdict is an anomaly on his metaethical account; for he not only dismissed the eudaemonist's means, given the facts, but also ruled out the hope of happiness – the central moral claim of eudaemonism – as an illusion. Metaethically, however, Weber ignored this interplay of empirical argument and moral theory. Like many modern skeptics, he mistakenly sought to *insulate* metaethical judgments from the rest of his moral viewpoint.[14]

Thus, his relativist fifth-level position selects out disputes at the fourth and third levels for special emphasis. Like most neo-Kantians, his metaethical account ignores first-level standards, ones he often invoked, such as the goods of life and medieval urban freedom. For Weber, ethics has no transtheoretical integrity, no *internalization*.

Moral realism, by contrast, stresses the historical experience that gives rise, through human reflection on a good life, to first-level standards. The realist notes the multidimensionality of intrinsic goods and complex ethical differences even at the first level; further, she points out, intricate third-level debates rarely center on underlying moral differences but

[13] Weber, *FMW*, p. 143.   [14] Annas, 1986, pp. 27–9.

rather on complicated social theoretical clashes (second level). A realist account recognizes approximate truth in some complex moral judgments, and the possibility of progress. Stressing the first three levels, realism works from the bottom up. Where, for Weber, conflicts of ultimate, fourth-level worldviews determine complex moral clashes, for the realist second-level social theoretical and factual differences govern these third-level disagreements. In fact, the developed theories of the fourth level secure their *moral* coherence as elaborations of discoveries at the first and second levels. Once again, on a realist view, ethical theories help us to make fine discriminations in hard cases – that is a truth in Rawls's important notion of reflective equilibrium. Contrary to neo-Kantians, however, such theories do not reshape first-level core standards, that is, reorder the moral universe. Instead, as Part II contends, the underlying commonalities of Marxian ethical judgments, contractarian notions of political autonomy, and eudaemonist theories of democratic individuality are illuminated by a metaethical realist account.

7. Core standards and "Science as a Vocation"

Every reader of Weber recognizes the moral pathos of many of his essays. Although his 1919 "Science as a Vocation" argues for his metaethical perspective, its basic argument is better interpreted by moral realism.

The essay suggests, for example, that we cannot rationally assess whether modern medicine – "a practical technology which is highly developed scientifically" – is worthwhile. Through this hard case, Weber questioned the core standard that "medical science has the task of maintaining life as such and of diminishing suffering as such to the greatest possible degree":

> The medical man [or woman] preserves the life of the mortally ill man [sic], even if the patient implores us to relieve him of life, even if his relatives, to whom his life is worthless [*wertlos*] and to whom the costs of maintaining this worthless life grow unbearable, grant his redemption from suffering. Perhaps a poor lunatic is involved, whose relatives whether they admit it or not, wish and must wish for his death.[15]

As we saw in Gutmann's controversy with Williams, difficult medical cases, cutting so near the good of life itself, are often telling for a moral theory. Such examples appeal to the influential idea, which we have examined in a number of theorists, that hard cases are frequent. Yet we may separate common, morally plural cases – difficult for an individual to decide but not involving injury – from a rarer kind of hard case in which either course of action entails a contending harm. Philosophers

[15] Weber, *FMW*, p. 144; Weber, *GAW*, p. 541.

have sometimes misguidedly taken the latter to justify a metaethical inference that core standards are problematic.[16] Yet ironically, we can only clarify the moral issues involved in Weber's example by appeal to such standards.

To Weber, contemporary law that requires keeping *even* this patient alive seems overly rigid. From this relevant worry, he infers that the standards underlying medical practice have no justification. But the moral intelligibility of his query flows from the goods that he tacitly acknowledges as coincident in ordinary health care – preserving life and diminishing suffering. This *special* case pits those normally concordant goods against one another to suggest the plausibility of allowing the patient to die or, perhaps, of carrying out euthanasia. Properly understood, Weber's argument singles out a subset of instances of conflict of goods within a much larger array of uncontroversial cases in which both life and health can be preserved. If he were right to imagine that the maintenance of life is not ordinarily a good, we would need no *special* conditions about extreme suffering to override it. One could bizarrely recommend – as Weber did not – the cessation of treatment for illness, the random extinction of patients to provide unused beds, and other atrocities.

In conflict with his factual repudiation of the possibility of human happiness, Weber implies a quasi-utilitarian standpoint: If the suffering is great enough, the good of relieving pain may outweigh that of life. But the latter is so basic that he has to depict great suffering to make the case difficult: The patient is irrevocably lost – "mortally ill" – and perhaps a (permanent) lunatic; she consents to die – even implores it – and the relatives yearn to be released from financial and spiritual burdens.[17] Though Weber's combination of conditions seems to elevate abstract, total suffering, his failure to focus on appropriate core standards undercuts his argument. The only relevant features are mortal illness and consent. The pain must seem so great to the patient that life, for her, loses its savor. As a response to suffering including concern for others, the patient *might* be justified in committing suicide or mandating euthana-

[16] For instance, Rawls and Brandt treat basic judgments as intuitive or vague. Rawls invokes the comparatively purified verdicts of a thoughtful, experienced person as a starting point, which can sometimes be overridden in reflective equilibrium. My claim that intuitions are judgments about a good life subject to no specific doubt is a reinterpretation of his view, removing an element of self-refuting relativism but permitting overriding in particular cases; in contrast, however, Brandt maintains that basic moral terminology is vague and needs reinterpretation.

[17] As the good of life is a prerequisite for a pleasant life, this good is also hard to override on utilitarian grounds. Given ordinary empirical claims, a utilitarian argument strongly justifies the medical practice that Weber questions.

sia.[18] But she bears the burden of this decision. Otherwise, the case decays into uncontroversial medical murder.

The negative feelings of the relatives hardly justify euthanasia. Precisely because the domain of ethics has integrity, crude contentions of utilitarian form – "I have never liked you and especially not now that you are ill, cranky, loony; further, your emotional capacity is reduced and can't weigh in the scales with the intensity of my annoyance" – are not serious. As argument, they reflect illness; if acted on, they are evil.[19] Furthermore, Weber's condition of lunacy nullifies the worth of the patient's consent.

Examining euthanasic proposals in historical context, a critic might also focus on Weber's problematic second-level social theoretical claims about eugenics and status. Highly stratified, capitalist societies, including Weimar Germany and the Third Reich, have offered eugenic justifications for the sacrifice of "useless eaters." Thus, in 1920, Karl Binding, director of the psychiatric clinic at Freiburg, and Alfred Hoche, professor of jurisprudence at Leipzig, published *The Release and Destruction of Lives Devoid of Value* [*wertlos*], advocating the intentional killing of mental patients. The chilling antiliberal notion that some lives are *wertlos* to society unfortunately echoes Weber's claim that the patient's life was *wertlos* to relatives. The subsequent controversy instigated extensive Weimar government research into American eugenic laws. Though Weber could not have foreseen such consequences, prestigious doctors and psychiatrists, with Nazi sanction, would organize the murder of some 275,000 mental patients between 1939 and 1945.[20] They also murdered "defective" Aryan children and many others. Marxian or Weberian class analyses of

---

[18] Since extreme suffering clouds reflection on alternative possibilities in a sustained life, suicide is problematic. There are, I think, circumstances in which an individual can reasonably decide that suicide is the best alternative. But nothing in this argument depends on that claim.

[19] Weber appeals to extraneous considerations. Payment for care may be a hardship for the relatives. But this economic concern suggests the need not for euthanasia, but for *social* provision of adequate care. With a moderate development of knowledge and civilization, no decent society would allow patients to be sacrificed because their lives are "a bother" to relatives.

[20] As Chorover reports, "The [German] Foreign Office immediately [in 1923] contacted its embassy in Washington, and requests for information were sent from there to German consulates throughout the United States. Inquiries were duly made of American mental institutions, state governments, and prisons. . . . Proposals for sterilization laws began to rely more and more heavily on data from the U.S. for their justification. One of these proposals devoted six full pages of text to praise for American work in biological reform, and another employed quotations from the writing of several prominent American eugenists. . . . The issue of eugenic control by the state was now seriously considered by those in the upper echelons of government and medicine. . . .

"In July of 1939, [a] fateful conference took place in Berlin. A number of the most

eugenics are plausible explanations of these policies. If these empirical claims are right, they reinforce, in such inegalitarian societies, the medical concern to preserve life.[21]

Weber's questioning of core judgments seems to arise out of inordinately high standards for moral argument, a view that ethics must provide uniform guidance for action in each circumstance (the *objectivity as absolutism criticism*). That stricture is probably a survival from the image of ethics as external, divine injunction rather than as reflection on human well-being. From such cases, he also mistakenly inferred the undecidability of all conflicts of complex, third-level moral assessments. As internal examination of this example reveals, however, the real controversy centers on third-level factual – and perhaps social theoretical – claims. His hard case sustains moral realism.

Contrary to Weber's metaethics, the pathos of "Science as a Vocation" derives from a straightforward claim about the relevant reasons for scientific activity. He began the essay by referring to a "pedantic habit" of "national economists" who investigate "external conditions" for the pursuit of knowledge. He abruptly used these conditions – for Germany and the United States – to expose advancement of mediocrity (*Mittelmässigkeit*) at the expense of those with scientific merit.[22] As in Aristotle, olympic prizes should go to the swiftest; so in Weber, academic positions should be awarded to the knowledgeable and diligent. He never entertained the thought that the able and ignorant equally deserved advancement. As a professional, he had to advise talented young men – here he reflected contemporary academic sexism – about whether to pursue an academic career. In prevailing circumstances, he found this task unbearable. Core moral standards – the good of knowledge and the virtue of ordinary compassion – explain and justify his emotion. Given these standards, he criticized common political and racial restrictions on university employment, observing that he would have to counsel able Jews: "Lasciate ogni speranza [toil without hope]."[23] As in Montesquieu and perhaps in good social theory generally, the distance of reality from

illustrious members of the psychiatric profession in Germany, including the leading professors and department heads from the universities of Berlin, Heidelberg, Bonn, and Wurzburg gathered to discuss a momentous project: the mass killing of German mental patients. Although no official order has been found, and no law mandating the extermination of mental patients had been passed, there is ample documentation to show that from its very inception the project was guided in all important matters by physicians" (Chorover, 1975, pp. 97–101, 79). Wertham, 1969, p. 155; Proctor, 1988.

21 The only important exception, in either divided or egalitarian societies, would be those who are "brain dead," sustained only by machine. But it may often be hard, practically, to draw the line of demarcation.
22 Weber, *FMW*, pp. 132, 134.   23 Weber, *FMW*, p. 134.

what is ethically natural gives rise to satire; Weber's "pedantic" sociological examination issues in pointed indictment.

He interpreted this pathos in a relativist vein, insisting on the changed character of social life and intellectual pursuits. Sympathetic to Tolstoy, he contrasted a peasant who dies full of years, sated with life (*lebensgesättigt*), with a specialist, a soon to be surpassed cipher in the advance of knowledge who dies merely "tired of life" (*lebensmüde*).[24] Perhaps a Renaissance scholar, on Weber's account, or a philosopher might also have achieved an integrity denied the scientist. The latter does not lead a good life.

Probing Weber's argument internally, we can see that based on core standards, only his social theoretical claims about the "ethical irrationality" of academia are controversial. Thus, a radical, sharing part of Weber's complex ethical evaluation, might suggest that political pressures, stemming from capitalist interests, shaped the German university environment. Those pressures excluded Social Democrats as well as those deemed sexually and racially inferior.[25] Furthermore, as the discussion of *The Protestant Ethic* in Chapter 9 shows, this atmosphere prevented a fair comparison of Marxian theories with prevailing ones. It distorted the quality of theory, not just academic composition. A radical might even suggest that the political intervention of communist revolution, if it altered these conditions in an egalitarian direction, *might* stimulate research based on scientific merit.[26]

To establish his explanation of academic corruption, Weber would have needed to show that general sociological "laws of human cooperation," not those of a specific mode of production and its "theodicy of good fortune," resulted in the frequent elevation of mediocrities. Yet he never specified such laws. These interpretations – as well as a non-Weberian defense of German university life on grounds that among those allowed to compete, faculties often hired and promoted able candidates – rest on second-level social scientific differences.

Finally, the power of the conclusion to "Science as a Vocation" also derives from core standards. There, Weber remarked that he was "shaken" by the national destiny of Jews. He set their two millennium tarrying in the diaspora as a warning to the defeated Germans.[27] Yet he could see no easy political solution. Recalling *The Protestant Ethic*'s vivid imagery, he eschewed professorial prophecy – "furnishing" one's soul with "genuine religious antiques" to make a hit on the lecture circuit – as well as vain specialists and sensualists. Instead, he called for integrity in one's vocation and personal relations to meet (literally, do justice to –

---

[24] Weber, *FMW*, pp. 139–40; *GAW*, pp. 536–7.   [25] Weber, *FMW*, p. 132; *GAW*, p. 527.

[26] Weber, *FMW*, pp. 132–3.   [27] Weber, *FMW*, p. 156; *PE*, p. 29; *GAR*, p. 14.

gerecht werden) the "demands of the day."[28] His concluding metaethical remark about obedience to fates, the putatively incommensurable, warring "demons who hold the threads of our lives," does not cancel out his straightforward moral appeal.

8. Individuality and Weberian liberalism

An awareness and experience of suffering mark his writings. Given the overall paradoxes and complexities of modern history, Weber fell back on uncontroversial standards of private and public action. Yet these standards of natural justice are not, just by themselves, sufficient to articulate a liberal view. They do not, as it were, cohere in diverse personalities. In Weber's lapsed Protestant idiom, the discovery and enactment of *vocations* are not just activities and relationships governed externally by the structure and history of human goods (or divine sanction); they are, more importantly, the particular choices of individuals. Weber often praised individual freedom; yet he offered no worked-out account of individuality.

As Chapters 7 and 8 show for Marxian theory, an internal critique that insists more strongly on democratic individuality can have dramatic *empirical*, not just moral, consequences. On that argument, the project of modern ethics is intimately tied to and, in central respects, a part of modern political science – the study of the possibilities of democratic associations that facilitate the flourishing of individuality – sociology, and psychology.[29] Similarly, a liberal defense of individuality would recast Weber's distinction between an ethic of responsibility and one of intention; it would undercut his radical separation of what is legitimate from what is just. It would thus alter his view of what public life is about, making it less narrowly violence oriented, more sustaining of mutual recognition and political discussion. In any case, it would rule out his – and later political science – justification of democracy as an instrument of power politics and his chauvinist defense of nationalism and status; it would qualify his one-sided depictions of the spiritual sources of modern liberalism and its decline. Such changes would focus the social scientific and political conversation between (a Weberian) liberalism and radicalism.

Yet the refinements in his view, brought about by an internal ethical

---

[28] Weber, *FMW*, pp. 154, 156; *GAW*, pp. 553,555. In personal life, judgments about caring – perhaps misguided ones about chivalry or manly companionship – underlie his argument. A eudaemonist contrast of concern for a friend's well-being with deficient, inegalitarian relationships would refine Weber's account of the core standard.

[29] See Gilbert, 1986a, c, for a further account of the centrality of this good in modern political philosophy.

critique, are not as dramatic as those wrought by a similar examination of Marxian theory: Marx was far more aware of both the conflicts and possible concordances of goods; his conception of the first phase of communism already articulates the political importance of clashing moral commitments and a hope, over time, to resolve them through the deliberations of a commune-like association. In the Marxian case, a radical democratic critique led to a far greater emphasis on the role of egalitarian relationships in individuality, a further departure from an economic determinist account of socialism. But the dialectical interplay of nuanced moral assessment and social theory in Weberian argument is still very important.

The conflicts of Weberian and radical theory pivot neither on the paradoxes of ancient and capitalist moral progress nor on fine methodological points, but on great contemporary political issues: imperialism, war, and democratic internationalism; class conflict, status, and multiracial alliances; the prospects of a common good, revolution, and radical democracy. These issues bear on the ethical project, initiated by Aristotle, of acquiring knowledge about human potentials for cooperation, freedom, and individuality. In this perspective, liberal and radical conceptions and movements are better interpreted by moral realism than by metaethical relativism.

Conclusion: the project of democratic individuality

If we imagine the disciplines of scientific and moral epistemology, ethics, social theory, and political theory as a series of steep hills, only partly visible to one another, then you and I, dear reader, have traversed a long, sometimes tortuous trail of arguments across them. Having reached a stopping place, we should now survey the terrain we have covered.

Older scientific epistemologies placed moral knowledge in doubt. So did cultural relativism. Leading figures in contemporary moral and political philosophy – Rawls, Walzer, Williams, Berlin, Taylor, Wiggins, Miller, Popper, and many others – have glimpsed, and then lost sight of, *the integrity of ethics*. The ascent from moral judgment to ethical epistemology has somehow made even such elementary points as the injustice of slavery, serfdom, sexism, tyranny, colonialism, fascism, rape, and murder obscure.

Yet several philosophers of science – Richard Boyd, Peter Railton, Nicholas Sturgeon, David Brink, Dudley Shapere, and Hilary Putnam – have undermined the older contrasts of scientific and ethical epistemology. Their arguments suggest the possibility of moral objectivity. As its central vista, my conception offers a substantive account of moral realism and progress, worked through leading arguments in political and social theory and the history of democratic institutions.[1] It employs recent insights in scientific epistemology – especially claims about inference to the best explanation – to highlight certain general facts about persons that no contemporary *political* theory can ignore. A universal human capacity for moral personality – for sufficient reason, empathy,

---

[1] In contemporary philosophy, moral realism is a just emerging theory. Thus, based on the new philosophy of science and practical moral considerations, the essays in Geoffrey Sayre-McCord's excellent edited collection (1988) make preliminary arguments for realist intuitions about ethics. Yet this view has, so far, been a promising possibility in search of worked-out versions. Only Boyd gives even a sample sketch of a realist account of the good.

and compassion to participate as free and equal citizens – is one such fact. Its existence is not just a modern "assumption," but a historic ethical and social scientific discovery, captured in an interrelated series of major political theories – those, for example, of Aristotle, Montesquieu, Hegel, Marx, and Mill. The historically deepening public recognition of this capacity is the natural focus of a progress, required by an argument for moral realism, which is comparable to the advance stressed by scientific realists in other branches of knowledge.

John Rawls has reflected for several years on a metaethical constructivism that is an alternative to moral realism. In conversation, however, he suggested that some view such as mine about slavery must be right; for our arguments pivot on similar – historic – examples of the *integrity of ethics*, of the "very great values" of mutual regard embodied in democracy.[2] His view provides an attractive counterpoint to epistemologically motivated moral skepticisms; moral realism applies recent naturalistic claims to the same purpose, uniting objectivity about the capacity for moral personality and as much constructivism about the comprehensive good for individuals – or in Walzer's idiom, leeway about complex cultural constructions – as Rawls means to defend. In addition, moral realism seeks to convey what it is for a modern political and ethical theory to be, in Shapere's idiom, internalized and metaethically coherent. In contrast, Rawls's publically motivated epistemological caution – his starting point in agreement on the underlying standards of American public life – runs the danger of being self-refuting. The further argument in Part I that *moral explanation* is a component of the best historical accounts of the decline of slavery shows only that no formal, philosophy of science-based ethical conventionalism such as Harman's is a reasonable alternative.

Moral realism includes a developed, historical account of modern democratic and social theory. Thus, I argue that sophisticated liberalism and radicalism are not two incompatible perspectives, distinguished primarily by clashing underlying value commitments, but are, more fruitfully, seen to grow out of a similar tradition, to elaborate a theoretical ethical project initiated centuries ago in Aristotle's *eudaemonism*. Moral realism stresses the complexity of ethics, of the diversity of intrinsically good relationships, activities, and traits of character. It also highlights the intricate structure of debates between modern liberals and radicals. As Part II suggests, previous antirealist views capture neither the substance nor the complexity of these disagreements. Even subtle moral relativisms still have a nationalist – by this, I do not mean chauvinist – and an antidialectical slant, attempting a clear account of only one concep-

---

[2] Rawls, 1988c, p. 1.

tion – "our" view, whether based on particular Western, democratic standards, those of a class, or those of a postmodernist, solipsistic author (and by invitation an ironically less solipsistic reader who "shares the same discourse").[3] To my mind, the comparative explanatory fit of moral realism to intricate political theoretical, social scientific, and moral controversies is a great epistemological attraction.

This moral realism fleshes out a claim about the coherence of debates, in connected disciplines suggested, but not elaborated, by contractarian theorists.[4] Knowledge of social and political theory and institutional history is vital, as Rawls notes, to a worked-out ethics. Despite its comparative emphasis on clarity, much Anglo-American philosophy, like contemporary social science, has lost the interplay of theory and history in overspecialization. Arcane technical issues, suggested by a misguided scientific epistemology and semantics, have misshapen the idiom of metaethical debate, substituting artificiality, the illusion of an "analytic" starting point, for clarity. Comparatively few theorists – John Rawls, Richard Miller, and Alasdair MacIntyre aside – have wandered into the relevant, philosophically unmapped, argumentatively thicketed, if not positively treacherous, regions. Yet as Rawls's and Miller's work illustrate, today's best moral and political theories have strong elements of coherence, uniting claims across diverse fields. So my version of realism traces the connection of debates in political and social theory, international relations, history, psychoanalysis, ethics, scientific and moral epistemology, and semantics. Its scope was needed not only to promise a shift in these fields' terrain – a new account of their interplay – but to effect it.

Moral realism seeks to make contemporary ethics and social theory into self-aware democratic theories. It maintains that refinements of Aristotle – for instance, those of Hegel, Mill, Marx, Whitman, Kohut, Gilligan, Levine, and Taylor – offer qualitative, varied insights into the human capacity for individuality and uses these arguments to overcome political deficiencies in modern social theories. Now, many have thought that modern social and psychoanalytic theory must compromise ethical objectivity; for some of Marx's, Weber's and Freud's true substantive claims undercut moralisms, those powerful ethical ideologies internalized by agents who have not worked out their individuality. But as Part II shows, the rich political implications of these theories depend on the affirmation of individuality. Merely implicit democratic and

---

[3] The latter reductionisms make opposite errors. Class perspectives, where decent, banish individuality in impersonal moral concern; deconstructionisms, where critical, ignore the capacity for moral personality and confuse individuality with subjectivity.

[4] *A Theory of Justice* is, however, comparatively worked out along these lines.

469

moral arguments in – for instance, Marx's economic theory or Weber's *Protestant Ethic* – lead not to empirical accuracy, but to misguided, non-democratic or antidemocratic claims. Thus, I had to search for Weber's liberalism, buried in remarks about Montesquieu, or separate apt eudae-monist judgments about relationship and vocation from chauvinist de-lusions about nationality and status. Similarly, my argument had to ar-ticulate the continuity of Marx's theory of Commune-like democracy with liberal claims about an independent judiciary, to discredit economic determinist emphases on planning expertise as a basis for antipolitical unity by stressing the decisive role, in radical democracy, of conversa-tion, controversy, referenda, strikes, and civil disobedience.

Both *Democratic Individuality* and my previous *Marx's Politics: Commu-nists and Citizens* maintain that basic disputes in political and social theory arise out of the historic project of creating democratic institu-tions. Athenian politics, the Christian movement, Spartacus's revolt against Rome, the American Revolution, the French Revolution, Tous-saint L'Ouverture and the Haitian freedom movement, Chartism, American abolitionism, feminism, the Russian and Chinese revolutions, anticolonialism, and antifascism are parts of a complex, not always pro-gressive movement, gaining insight and territory, losing ground previ-ously attained, articulating the limited actuality and magnificent prom-ise of decent regimes. Radical and liberal social theories are made possible by, interpret, and seek to extend these movements. In this per-spective, an internal critique of the clashes between Weber and Marx is not of antiquarian scholarly interest – however important it may be in politics to recapture lost insights – but articulates central substantive dis-agreements about the vision, theory, and strategy of democratic move-ments. Thus, we looked at the surprising importance of democratic in-ternationalism in reasonable assessments of imperialism and patriotism; critical explanations of ideologies – racism, status, and antiradicalism – that suggest unexpected possibilities of democratic alliance; the role of a common good in a modern state's legitimacy and the promise of com-munism; and the like. The epistemological justification of abolitionism in Part I served as prelude to the theory of radical democracy, individu-ality and internationalism of Part II.

In this book, Rawlsian contractarianism has attractively completed eu-daemonist individuality. I would like to conclude on a moral commonal-ity and difference between these conceptions. Since *A Theory of Justice*, Rawls has taken the lead among philosophers and political theorists in elaborating a theory of deliberative democracy. Sharing his conception of autonomy, Chapters 7 and 8 on radical democracy supplement his innovations. Yet relying too heavily on Rousseau and Kant, Rawls's ar-gument also has a significant defect. It captures mainly *impersonal* features of modern individuality, not the *reasoned disagreements* that characterize debates in an ideal regime, let alone the sharp political conflicts of nearly just ones.[5] A eudaemonist theory of democratic individuality must flesh out the basic Rawlsian claim. Stressing common, mutually respectful politics and not "society," stemming from the diversity and unfreneticness of individuality rather than the driven creativity of all-talented, universal individuals,[6] that theory would also make good on the Marxian project of a communism in which the "free development of each is the condition for the free development of all." A moral realist view explains and recasts what I regard as the leading political and social theories, a democratic contractarianism and a radical conception of free association. This book's journey has brought the project of this transformation, and some of its substance, into view. But a full account must await another occasion.

[5] Bernard Manin, 1987, subtly emphasizes this point against the misguided communitarian criticism that Rawls has too thin a notion of the self. Rawls's abstraction is appropriate to a leading feature of ethical and political theory, that of reasoning as one free person among others. His conception is not inconsistent with greater political and psychological thickness; in fact, the often unread moral psychology of pt. 3 of *A Theory of Justice* provides a richer account. Nonetheless, as the argument of Chapter 7 on the clash between, say, the justifications of a difference principle and equal incomes indicates, a full democratic view requires a more worked-out theory of individuality.

Rawls, 1988c, pp. 4–5 has recently suggested some important sources of reasonable disagreement.

[6] I have benefited on this point from discussions with David Blaney and from ch. 2 of his insightful dissertation.

Bibliography

In the text I have cited the most frequently used works in political theory by title or abbreviation. Otherwise, items are cited by date of publication.

Ackerman, Bruce A. (1980). *Social Justice in the Liberal State*. New Haven, Conn.: Yale University Press.

(1988). "Why Dialogue?" Unpublished.

Adelman, Jonathan. (1978). "The Formative Influence of the Civil Wars." *Armed Forces and Society*, 5(no. 1):93–116.

(1980). *The Russian Civil War: The Formative Years*. Unpublished.

Ali, A. Yusif, trans. (1973). *The Quran*. Lahore: Sheikh Mohammed Ashraf.

Allen, Garland E. (1975). "Genetics, Eugenics and Class Struggle," *Genetics*, 79:29–45.

Althusser, Louis. (1965). *Lire le capital*, 2 vols. Paris: Maspero.

Annas, Julia. (1986). "Doing Without Objective Values: Ancient and Modern Strategies." In Malcolm Schofield and Gisela Striker, eds., *The Norms of Nature: Studies in Hellenistic Ethics*, pp. 3–29. Cambridge University Press.

Arendt, Hannah. (1968). *Men in Dark Times*. New York: Harcourt Brace & World.

(1977). *On Revolution*. Harmondsworth: Penguin.

Aristotle. (1975). *The Nicomachean Ethics*. Loeb Classical Library. Cambridge, Mass.: Harvard University Press (cited in notes as *Nicomachean Ethics*).

(1977). *Politics*. Loeb Classical Library. Cambridge, Mass.: Harvard University Press (cited in text as *Politics*).

Arneson, Richard J. (1985). "Marxism and Secular Faith." *American Political Science Review*, 79(no. 3):627–39.

Avineri, Shlomo, ed. (1968). *Karl Marx on Colonialism and Modernization*. New York: Doubleday.

(1970). *The Social and Political Thought of Karl Marx*. Cambridge University Press.

(1972). *Hegel's Theory of the Modern State*. Cambridge University Press.

Badayev, A. (N.D.). *The Bolsheviks in the Tsarist Duma*. San Francisco: Proletarian.

Baier, Annette. (1985). *Postures of the Mind*. Minneapolis: University of Minnesota Press.

Ball, Terence, and Farr, James, eds. (1984). *After Marx*. Cambridge University Press.

Barber, Benjamin R. (1984). *Strong Democracy: Participatory Politics for a New Age.* Berkeley and Los Angeles: University of California Press.

Barker, Ernest, trans. (1977). *The Politics of Aristotle.* Oxford: Oxford University Press.

Barry, Brian. (1982). "Political Participation as Rational Action." In Brian Barry and Russell Hardin, eds., *Rational Man and Irrational Society.* Beverly Hills: Sage.

Basseches, Nicholaus. (1952). *Stalin.* New York: Dutton.

Baur, Erwin; Fischer, Eugen; and Lenz, Fritz. (1931). *Human Heredity.* New York: Macmillan.

Beiner, Ronald. (1983). *Political Judgment.* Chicago: University of Chicago Press.

(1984). "Walter Benjamin's Philosophy of History." *Political Theory,* 12(no. 3):423–34.

Beitz, Charles R. (1975). "Justice and International Relations." *Philosophy and Public Affairs,* 4(no. 4):360–89.

(1980). "Nonintervention and Communal Integrity." *Philosophy and Public Affairs,* 9(no. 3): pp. 385–91.

Berki, R. N. (1979). "On the Nature and Origin of Marx's Concept of Labor." *Political Theory,* 7(no. 1):35–56.

Berlin, Isaiah. (1969). *Four Essays on Liberty.* New York: Oxford University Press.

(1988). "On the Pursuit of the Ideal," *New York Review of Books,* March 17:1–18.

Bettelheim, Charles. (1978). "The Great Leap Backward." In Charles Bettelheim and Neil Burton, *China Since Mao.* New York: Monthly Review Press, 37–130.

Blackburn, Simon. (1971). "Moral Realism," In John Casey, ed., *Morality and Moral Reasoning: Five Essays in Ethics,* pp. 101–24. London: Methuen & Co.

(1981). "Rule-Following and Moral Reasoning." In Stephen H. Holtzman and Christopher M. Leich, eds., *Wittgenstein: To Follow a Rule,* 163–87. London: Routledge & Kegan Paul.

(1984). *Spreading the Word.* New York: Oxford University Press.

Blaney, David. (1990). *Self, Class and Communism.* Unpublished.

Bloch, N. J., and Dworkin, Gerald. (1974). "I.Q., Heritability and Inequality," Parts 1 and 2. *Philosophy and Public Affairs,* 3:331–409; 4:40–99.

Blum, Lawrence A. (1980). *Friendship, Altruism and Morality.* London: Routledge & Kegan Paul.

Bosanquet, Bernard. (1965). *The Philosophical Theory of the State.* London: Macmillan Press.

Bottomore, T. B., ed. (1964). *Karl Marx's Early Writings.* New York: McGraw-Hill.

Boyd, Richard N. (1979). "Metaphor and Theory Change: What Is 'Metaphor' a Metaphor for?" In Andrew Ortony, ed., *Metaphor and Thought,* pp. 356–408. Cambridge University Press.

(1980a). "Scientific Realism and Naturalistic Epistemology." In P. D. Asquith and R. N. Giere, eds., *PSA,* 2:613–62.

(1980b). "Materialism without Reductionism: What Physicalism Does Not Entail." In Ned Block, ed., *Readings in the Philosophy of Psychology,* 1:67–106. Cambridge, Mass.: Harvard University Press.

(1984). "The Current Status of Scientific Realism." In Jarrett Leplin, ed., *Scien-*

tific Realism, pp. 41–82. Berkeley and Los Angeles: University of California Press.

(1985). "Lex Orandi est Lex Credendi." In Paul M. Churchland and Clifford A. Hooker, eds., *Images of Science: Essays on Realism and Empiricism,* pp. 3–34. Chicago: University of Chicago Press.

(1986). "How to Be a Moral Realist." Unpublished.

(1989). "Realism, Conventionality and 'Realism About.'" Unpublished.

Bracher, Karl Deitrich. (1970). *The German Dictatorship.* New York: Praeger.

Brandt, Richard B. (1979). *A Theory of the Right and the Good.* Oxford: Clarendon.

Brecht, Bertolt. (1966). *The Caucasian Chalk Circle.* Trans. Edward Bentley. New York: Grove.

Brink, David O. (1984). "Moral Realism and the Skeptical Arguments from Disagreement and Queerness." *The Australasian Journal of Philosophy,* 62(no. 2):111–25.

(1986). "Externalist Moral Realism." In Norman Gillespie, ed., *Moral Realism, The Southern Journal of Philosophy,* 24, supplement:23–41.

Bruun, H. H. (1972). *Science, Values and Politics in Max Weber's Methodology.* Copenhagen: Munksgaard.

Buchanan, Allen E. (1980). "Revolutionary Motivation and Rationality." In Marshall Cohen, Thomas Nagel, and Thomas Scanlon, eds., *Marx, Justice and History,* pp. 264–87. Princeton, N.J.: Princeton University Press.

(1986). "The Conceptual Roots of Totalitarian Socialism." *Social Philosophy and Policy.* 3(no. 2):127–44.

Calvin, John. (1957). *Institutes of the Christian Religion,* 2 vols. Grand Rapids, Mich.: Eerdmans.

Carnap, Rudolf. (1969). *The Logical Structure of the World: Pseudoproblems in Philosophy.* Berkeley and Los Angeles: University of California.

Carr, E. H. (1975). *Socialism in One Country,* 3 vols. Baltimore, Md.: Penguin.

Castells, Manuel. (1975). "Immigrant Workers and Class Struggles in Advanced Capitalism: The Western European Experience." *Politics and Society,* 5:33–66.

Caute, David. (1978). *The Great Fear: The Anti-Communist Purge Under Truman and Eisenhower.* New York: Simon and Schuster.

Chesneaux, Jean. (1979). *China: The People's Republic 1949–76.* New York: Pantheon.

Chodorow, Nancy Julia. (1986). "Toward a Relational Individualism: the Mediation of the Self through Psychoanalysis." In Thomas Heller, Martin Sosna, and David Wellberry, eds., *Reconstructing Individualism,* pp. 197–207. Palo Alto, Calif.: Stanford University Press.

Chomsky, Noam, and Herman, Edward. (1979). *The Political Economy of Human Rights: The Washington Connection and Third World Fascism.* Boston: South End Press.

Chorover, Stephan. (1975). *From Genesis to Genocide.* Cambridge, Mass.: MIT Press.

Churchland, Paul M., and Hooker, Clifford A., eds. (1985a). *Images of Science: Essays on Realism and Empiricism.* Chicago: University of Chicago Press.

(1985b). "The Ontological Status of Observables: In Praise of the Superempirical Virtues." In Paul M. Churchland and Clifford A. Hooker, eds., *Images of Science*, pp. 35–47. Chicago: University of Chicago Press.

Cohen, G. A. (1978). *Karl Marx's Theory of History: A Defense*. Princeton, N.J.: Princeton University Press.

(1980). "The Labor Theory of Value and the Concept of Exploitation." In Marshall Cohen, Thomas Nagel, and Thomas Scanlon, eds., *Marx, Justice and History*, pp. 135–57. Princeton, N.J.: Princeton University Press.

(1984). "Reconsidering Historical Materialism." In J. Roland Pennock, ed., *Marxism. Nomos*, 26:227–52. New York: New York University Press.

Cohen, Joshua. (1986a). "Do Values Explain Facts? – The Case of Slavery." In *American Political Science Association Proceedings*. Ann Arbor: University of Michigan Press.

(1986b). "Structure, Choice and Legitimacy: Locke's Theory of the State." *Philosophy of Public Affairs*, 15(no. 4):301–24.

(in press a). "The Economic Basis of Deliberative Democracy." *Social Philosophy and Policy*.

(in press b). "Democratic Equality." *Ethics*.

Cohen, Joshua, and Rogers, Joel. (1983). *On Democracy: Toward a Transformation of American Society*. Harmondsworth: Penguin Books.

(1985). *Inequity and Intervention*. Boston: South End Press.

Collins, Randall. (1986). *Weberian Sociological Theory*. Cambridge University Press.

Colton, Joel R. (1964). *Leon Blum: Humanist in Politics*. New York: Knopf.

Connolly, William E. (1983). *The Terms of Political Discourse*. Princeton, N.J.: Princeton University Press.

Crawford, S. Cromwell. (1982). *The Evolution of Hindu Ethical Ideals*. Honolulu: University of Hawaii Press.

Cusack, David. (1977). *Revolution and Counterrevolution in Chile*. Denver, Colo.: Graduate School of International Studies, University of Denver.

Dahl, Robert A. (1985). *A Preface to Economic Democracy*. Berkeley and Los Angeles: University of California Press.

Daniels, Norman. (1975). "Equal Liberty and Unequal Worth of Liberty." In Norman Daniels, ed., *Reading Rawls*, pp. 753–81. New York: Basic.

Darwin, Charles. (1874). *The Descent of Man and Selection in Relation to Sex*. London: Wheeler.

(1974). *The Origin of Species*. Harmondsworth: Penguin.

DeNardo, James. (1985). *Power in Numbers: the Political Strategy of Protest and Rebellion*. Princeton, N.J.: Princeton University Press.

Devitt, Michael. (1981). *Designation*. New York: Columbia University Press.

Dewey, John. (1946). *The Public and Its Problems*. Chicago: Gateway Books.

(1984). *Realism and Truth*. Princeton: Princeton University Press.

Dobb, Maurice. (1948). *Soviet Economic Development Since 1917*. New York: International Publishers.

(1973). *Theories of Value and Distribution Since Adam Smith*. Cambridge University Press.

Doppelt, Gerald. (1980). "Statism without Foundations." *Philosophy and Public Affairs*, 9(no. 4):398–403.

Downs, Anthony. (1957). *An Economic Theory of Democracy.* New York: Harper.

Doyle, Michael W. (1983). "Kant, Liberal Legacies, and Foreign Affairs," pts. 1 and 2. *Philosophy and Public Affairs,* 12(nos. 3–4):205–35, 323–53.

Draper, Hal, ed. (1971). *Marx and Engels: Writings on the Paris Commune.* New York: Monthly Review Press.

Drier, Jamie. (1987). "Speaker Relativism." Unpublished.

Duberman, Martin Bauml. (1988). *Paul Robeson.* New York: Knopf.

Dubofsky, Melvin. (1969). *We Shall Be All.* Chicago: Quadrangle.

Duhem, Pierre. (1954). *The Aim and Structure of Physical Theory.* Princeton, N.J.: Princeton University Press.

Dummett, Michael. (1978). *Truth and Other Enigmas.* Cambridge, Mass.: Harvard University Press.

Duncan, Graeme. (1982). "The Marxist Theory of the State." In G. H. R. Parkinson, ed., *Marx and Marxisms,* pp. 129–43. Cambridge University Press.

Dunn, John. (1984). *The Politics of Socialism: An Essay in Political Theory.* New York: Cambridge University Press.

Dutt, R. Palme. (1974). *Fascism and Social Revolution.* San Francisco: Proletarian.

Dworkin, Gerald. (1975). "Nonneutral Principles." In Norman Daniels, ed., *Reading Rawls,* pp. 124–40. New York: Basic.

Dworkin, Ronald. (1975). "The Original Position." In Norman Daniels, ed., *Reading Rawls,* pp. 16–53. New York: Basic.

(1977). *Taking Rights Seriously.* Cambridge, Mass.: Harvard University Press.

(1981). "What Is Equality?" 1: "Equality of Welfare" and "What Is Equality?" 2: "Equality of Resources." *Philosophy and Public Affairs,* 10(no. 3):185–246; 10(no. 4):283–345.

(1985). *Matters of Principle.* Cambridge, Mass.: Harvard University Press.

Easton, Loyd and Guddat, Kurt, eds. (1967). *Writings of the Young Marx on Philosophy and Society.* New York: Doubleday.

Eckstein, Harry. (1965). *Division and Cohesion in Democracy.* Princeton, N.J.: Princeton University Press.

(1968). "A Theory of Stable Democracy." In Frank Lindenfeld, ed., *A Reader in Political Sociology,* pp. 115–28. New York: Funk & Wagnalls.

(1989). "A Comment on Positive Theory." *PS,* 22(no. 1):77.

Elster, Jon. (1979). *Ulysses and the Sirens.* Cambridge University Press.

(1984). "Exploitation, Freedom and Justice." In J. Roland Pennock, ed., *Marxism, Nomos,* 26:277–304. New York: New York University Press.

(1985). *Making Sense of Marx.* Cambridge University Press.

(1986). "Self-Realization in Work and Politics: the Marxist Conception of the Good Life." *Social Philosophy and Policy,* 3(no. 2):97–126.

Engels, Friedrich. (1962a). "Preface to the Second Volume of *Capital.*" In Marx and Engels. *Selected Works.* Moscow: Foreign Languages Publishing.

(1962b). *The Housing Question.* In Karl Marx and Friedrich Engels. *Selected Works,* Vol. 2. Moscow: Foreign Languages Publishing.

(1966a). *Herr Eugen Dühring's Revolution in Science.* New York: International Publishers.

(1966b). *The Peasant War in Germany.* New York: International Publishers.

Feigl, Herbert. (1956). "Some Major Issues and Developments in the Philosophy of Science of Logical Empiricism." In Herbert Feigl and Michael Scriven, eds., *Minnesota Studies in the Philosophy of Science*, 1:3–37. Minneapolis: University of Minnesota Press.

Ferguson, Thomas. (1983). "Party Alignment and American Industrial Structure: the Investment Theory of Political Parties in Historical Perspective." *Research in Political Economy*, 6:1–82.

Feyerabend, Paul A. (1975). *Against Method*. London: New Left Books.

Field, Hartry. (1973). "Theory and Change and the Indeterminacy of Reference." *Journal of Philosophy*, (no. 74) 462–81.

——— (1974). "Quine and the Correspondance Theory." *The Philosophical Review*, 83:200–28.

Fine, Arthur. (1984)."The Natural Ontological Attitude." In Jarrett Leplin, ed., *Scientific Realism*, pp. 83–107. Berkeley and Los Angeles: University of California Press.

Finnis, John. (1980). *Natural Law and Natural Rights*. Oxford: Clarendon.

Fishkin, James S. (1984). *Beyond Subjective Morality: Ethical Reasoning and Political Philosophy*. New Haven, Conn.: Yale University Press.

Fisk, Milton. (1975). "History and Reason in Rawls' Moral Theory." In Norman Daniels, ed., *Reading Rawls*, pp. 53–80. New York: Basic.

——— (1980). *Ethics and Society: A Marxist Interpretation of Value*. New York: New York University Press.

Foner, Phillip. (1976). *The Black Worker and Organized Labor 1819–1973*. New York: International Publishers.

Förder, Herwig, Hundt, Martin, Kandel, Jefim, and Lewiowa, Sofia, eds. (1970). *Der Bund der Kommunisten: Dokumente und Materalien*. Berlin: Dietz.

Foucault, Michel. (1975). *Surveiller et punir: Naissance de la prison*. Paris: Editions Gallimard.

——— (1977). *Language, Counter-Memory, Practice: Selected Essays and Interviews*. Ed. Donald Bouchard. Ithaca, N.Y.: Cornell University Press.

Fox-Keller, Evelyn. (1985). *Reflections on Gender and Science*. New Haven, Conn.: Yale University Press.

Frankel, Henry. (1979). "The Career of Continental Drift Theory." *Studies in the History and Philosophy of Science*, 10:21–66.

Gallie, W. B. (1962). "Essentially Contested Concepts." In Max Black, ed., *The Importance of Language*, pp. 121–45. Englewood Cliffs, N.J.: Prenctice-Hall.

Galtung, Johan. (1976). "Conflict on a Global Scale: Social Imperialism and Subimperialism." *World Development*, 4(no. 3):153–65.

Garfinkel, Alan. (1981). *Forms of Explanation*. New Haven: Yale University Press.

Gerschenkron, Alexander. (1943). *Bread and Democracy in Germany*. Berkeley: University of California Press.

——— (1965). *Economic Backwardness in Historical Perspective*. New York: Praegar.

Gilbert, Alan. (1976a). "Salvaging Marx from Avineri." *Political Theory*, 4(no. 1):9–34.

——— (1976b). "Changing the World: The Revolutionary Strategies of Marx and Lenin." *American Political Science Association Proceedings*. Ann Arbor: University of Michigan Press.

(1978a). "Equality and Social Theory in Rawls' *A Theory of Justice.*" *The Occasional Review,* 7:95–117.

(1978b). "Marx on Internationalism and War." *Philosophy and Public Affairs,* 7(no. 4):346–69.

(1979). "Social Theory and Revolutionary Activity in Marx." *The American Political Science Review,* 73(no. 2):521–38.

(1981a). *Marx's Politics: Communists and Citizens.* New Brunswick, N.J.: Rutgers University Press; Oxford: Martin Robertson. (1988 paperback. Boulder: Rienner).

(1981b) "Historical Theory and the Structure of Moral Argument in Marx." *Political Theory,* 9 (no. 2): 173–206.

(1982). "An Ambiguity in Marx's and Engels's Account of Justice and Equality." *The American Political Science Review,* 76(no. 2):328–46.

(1984a). "Marx's Moral Realism: Eudaimonism and Moral Progress." In James Farr and Terence Ball, eds., *After Marx,* pp. 15–83. Cambridge University Press.

(1984b). "The Storming of Heaven: *Capital* and Marx's Politics." In J. Roland Pennock, ed., *Marxism, Nomos,* 26:119–68. New York: New York University Press.

(1986a). "*The Spirit of the Laws* and the Spirit of Liberalism: Individuality and Political Association in Montesquieu." Unpublished.

(1986b). "Moral Realism, Individuality and Justice in War." *Political Theory,* 14(no. 1):105–35.

(1986c). "Democracy and Individuality." *Social Philosophy and Policy,* 3(no. 2):19–58.

(1987). "Democracy and the Recognition of Persons." Unpublished.

(1989a). "Rights and Resources." *The Journal of Value Inquiry,* 23:227–47.

(1989). "Neutrality and Democratic Autonomy." Unpublished.

(1990a). "On a Theory of Radical Democracy." In Lyman Legters and John Burke, eds., *Normative Theories of Democracy.* Unpublished.

(1990b). "Must International Politics Constrain Democracy? Realism, Regimes and Democratic Internationalism." Unpublished.

(in press a). "Political Philosophy: Radical Democracy." In Terrell Carver, ed., *Cambridge Companions to Philosophy: Marx.* Cambridge University Press.

(in press b). "Does the American Experiment Realize Democracy?" In Robert Utley, ed., *Modern Critiques of the Federalists.* Cranbury, N.J: University Presses of America.

Gilligan, Carol. (1982). *In a Different Voice.* Cambridge, Mass.: Harvard University Press.

(1986). "Remapping the Moral Domain: New Images of the Self in Relationship." In Thomas Heller, Martin Sosna, and David Wellberry, eds., *Reconstructing Individualism,* pp. 237–65. Palo Alto, Calif.: Stanford University Press.

Gilpin, Robert. (1987). *The Political Economy of International Relations.* Princeton, N.J.: Princeton University Press.

Goldman, Alvin H. (1986). *Epistemology and Cognition.* Cambridge, Mass.: Harvard University Press.

Goodman, Nelson. (1973). *Fact, Fiction and Forecast,* 3d ed. Indianapolis, Ind.: Bobbs-Merrill.

(1978). *Ways of Worldmaking.* Indianapolis, Ind.: Hackett.

Greenberg, Edward S. (1986). *Workplace Democracy: the Political Effects of Participation.* Ithaca, N.Y.: Cornell University Press.

Günther, Hans F. K. (1927). *The Racial Elements of European History.* London: Methuen & Co.

Guntrip, Harry. (1973). *Psychoanalytic Theory, Therapy, and the Self.* New York: Basic.

Gutmann, Amy. (1980). *Liberal Equality.* Cambridge University Press.

(1987). *Democratic Education.* Princeton, N.J.: Princeton University Press.

Habermas, Jürgen. (1979). *Communication and the Evolution of Society.* Trans. Thomas McCarthy. Boston: Beacon.

(1984). *The Theory of Communicative Action,* Vol. 1: *Reason and the Rationalization of Society.* Trans. Thomas McCarthy. Boston: Beacon.

Hacking, Ian. (1983). *Representing and Intervening.* Cambridge University Press.

(1984). "Experimentation and Scientific Realism." In Jarrett Leplin, ed., *Scientific Realism,* pp. 154–72. Berkeley and Los Angeles: University of California Press.

(1985). "Do We See Through a Microscope?" In Paul M. Churchland and Clifford A. Hooker, eds., *Images of Science,* pp. 132–52. Chicago: University of Chicago Press.

Haimson, Leopold. (1964). "The Problem of Social Stability in Urban Russia, 1905–17." *The Slavic Review,* 23:619–42.

Hammen, Oscar. (1969). *The Red '48ers: Karl Marx and Friedrich Engels.* New York: Scribner's.

Hampshire, Stuart. (1983). *Morality and Conflict.* Cambridge, Mass.: Harvard University Press.

Harman, Gilbert. (1965). "The Inference to the Best Explanation." *Philosophical Review,* 74:88–95.

(1973). *Thought.* Princeton, N.J.: Princeton University Press.

(1975). "Moral Relativism Defended." *The Philosophical Review,* 84:3–22.

(1977). *The Nature of Morality.* New York: Oxford University Press.

(1983). "Human Flourishing, Ethics and Liberty." *Philosophy and Public Affairs,* 12:307–22.

(1986a). "Moral Explanations of Natural Facts – Can Moral Claims Be Tested Against Moral Reality?" In Norman Gillespie, ed. *Moral Realism. The Southern Journal of Philosophy,* 24, supplement:57–68.

(1986b). *Change in View: Principles of Reasoning.* Cambridge, Mass.: MIT Press.

Harrison, Royden. (1965). *Before the Socialists.* London: Routledge & Kegan Paul.

Hayek, F. A. (1945). "The Use of Knowledge in Society." *American Economic Review,* 35(no. 4):519–30.

Hegel, G. W. F. (1952). *Phänomenologie des Geistes.* Hamburg: Meiner (cited in notes as *PG*).

(1955a). *Die Vernunft in der Geschichte*. Hamburg: Meiner (cited in notes as *VG*).

(1955b). *Lectures on the History of Philosophy*. 3 vols. London: Routledge & Kegan Paul.

(1966). *Politische Schriften*. Frankfurt: Suhrkamp.

(1970). *Grundlinien der Philosophie des Rechts*. Stuttgart: Reclam (cited in notes as *GPR*).

(1975). *Lectures on the Philosophy of World History: Introduction*. Trans. H. B. Nisbet. Cambridge University Press.

(1977a). *The Philosophy of Right*. Trans. T. M. Knox. Oxford: Oxford University Press.

(1977b). *The Phenomenology of Spirit*. Trans. A. V. Miller. Oxford: Oxford University Press.

Herf, Jeffrey. (1984). *Reactionary Modernism: Technology, Culture and Politics in Weimar and the Third Reich*. Cambridge University Press.

Herndon, Angelo. (1937). *Let Me Live*. New York: Random House.

Herrnstein, Richard J. (1971). "IQ." *The Atlantic Monthly*, 228(no. 3):43–64.

(1989). "IQ and Falling Birth Rates." *The Atlantic Monthly*, 283(no. 5):72–9.

Hill, Christopher. (1972). *The World Turned Upside Down*. New York: Viking.

Hinton, William. (1966). *Fanshen*. New York: Vintage.

Hobsbawn, Eric J. (1968). *Industry and Empire: The Making of Modern English Society*. New York: Pantheon.

Holmes, Stephen T. (1982). "Two Concepts of Legitimacy." *Political Theory*, 10(no. 2):165–83.

(1984). *Benjamin Constant and the Making of Modern Liberalism*. New Haven, Conn.: Yale University Press.

Hook, Sidney. (1965). *Political Power and Personal Freedom*. New York: Collier.

Horvat, Branko. (1982). *The Political Economy of Socialism: A Marxist Social Theory*. New York: Sharpe.

Hume, David. (1948). *Moral and Political Philosophy*. New York: Hafner.

Huntington, Samuel P. (1969). *Political Order in Changing Societies*. New Haven, Conn.: Yale University Press.

(1975). "The Democratic Distemper." In Huntington, Michel Crozier, and Joji Watanuki, eds., *The Crisis of Democracy*, pp. 59–118. New York: New York University Press.

Husami, Ziyad I. (1978). "Marx on Distributive Justice." In Marshall Cohen, Thomas Nagel, and Thomas Scanlon, eds., *Marx, Justice and History*, pp. 42–79. Princeton, N.J.: Princeton University Press, 1980.

Irwin, Terence. (1977). *Plato's Moral Theory*. Oxford: Oxford University Press (Clarendon Press).

Jay, John, Hamilton, Alexander, and Madison, James. (1961). *The Federalist Papers*. New York: Mentor.

Jay, Martin. (1984). *Adorno*. Cambridge, Mass.: Harvard University Press.

Jensen, Arthur. (1969). "How Much Can We Boost Scholastic Achievement?" *Harvard Educational Review*, 39(no. 1):1–123.

Kamin, Leon J. (1974). *The Science and Politics of I.Q.* New York: Wiley.

Kant, Immanuel. (1795). *Zum Ewigen Frieden*. Bern: Scherz.

(1963). *On History.* Indianapolis, Ind.: Bobbs-Merrill.

(1975). *Was Ist Aufklärung?* Göttingen: Vandenhoeck & Ruprecht.

Kateb, George. (1983). *Hannah Arendt: Politics, Conscience, Evil.* Totowa, N.J.: Rowman & Allanheld.

(1984). "Democratic Individuality and the Claims of Politics." *Political Theory,* 12 (no. 3): 331–60.

Keohane, Robert O. (1984). *After Hegemony: Cooperation and Discord in the World Political Economy.* Princeton, N.J.: Princeton University Press.

Key, V. O. (1949). *Southern Politics.* New York: Knopf.

Klare, Michael T. (1972). *War Without End.* New York: Vintage.

(1977). "Pointing Fingers." *New York Times* (Aug. 10).

Klosko, George. (1986). *The Development of Plato's Political Theory.* New York: Methuen.

Kohut, Heinz. (1977). *The Restoration of the Self.* New York: International Universities Press.

(1984). *How does Analysis Cure?* Chicago: University of Chicago Press.

Kolakowski, Leszek. (1978). *Main Currents of Marxism.* 3 vols. Oxford: Oxford University Press (Clarendon Press).

Krasner, Stephan D. (1978). *Defending the National Interest: Raw Materials Investments and U.S. Foreign Policy.* Princeton, N.J.: Princeton University Press.

Kratochwil, Friedrich V. (1983). "Thrasymachos Revisited: On the Relevance of Norms and the Study of Law for International Relations." *Journal of International Affairs,* 37(no. 2):343–56.

(1989). *Rules, Norms and Decisions: On the Conditions of Practical and Legal Reasoning in International Relations and Domestic Societies.* Cambridge University Press.

Kripke, Saul. (1980). *Naming and Necessity.* Cambridge, Mass.: Harvard University Press.

Krupskaya, Nadesdha. (1930). *Memories of Lenin.* 2 vols. London: Lawrence & Wishart.

Kuhn, Thomas S. (1957). *The Copernican Revolution.* Cambridge, Mass.: Harvard University Press.

(1970). *The Structure of Scientific Revolutions.* Chicago: Phoenix.

(1977). *The Essential Tension.* Chicago: University of Chicago Press.

Kymlicka, Will. (1987). "Liberalism and Native Rights." Unpublished.

(1988). "Rawls on Teleology and Deontology." *Philosophy and Public Affairs,* 17(no. 3):173–90.

Lafeber, Walter. (1984). *Inevitable Revolutions: The United States in Central America.* New York: Norton.

Lakatos, Imré. (1970). "Falsification and the Methodology of Scientific Research Programs." In Imré Lakatos and Alan Musgrave, eds., *Criticism and the Growth of Knowledge,* pp. 91–195. Cambridge University Press.

Lamm, Richard. (1985). *Megatraumas.* Boston: Houghton Mifflin.

Lane, David. (1971). *An End of Inequality? Stratification Under State Socialism.* Harmondsworth: Penguin.

Larmore, Charles E. (1987). *Patterns of Moral Complexity*. Cambridge University Press.

Laudan, Larry. (1977). *Progress and Its Problems*. Berkeley and Los Angeles: University of California Press.

(1984). "A Confutation of Convergent Realism." In Jarrett Leplin, ed., *Scientific Realism*, pp. 218–49. Berkeley and Los Angeles: University of California Press.

Laudan, Rachel. (1980). "The Recent Revolution in Geology and Kuhn's Theory of Scientific Change." In Gary Gutting, ed. (1980), *Paradigms and Revolutions*. South Bend, Ind.: University of Notre Dame Press.

Leeds, Stephen. (1973). "How to Think about Reference." *Journal of Philosophy*, 70(no. 15):485–503.

(1978). "Theories of Reference and Truth." *Erkenntnis*, 13:111–29.

Lenin, V. I. (1960). *Selected Works*. 3 vols. Moscow: Foreign Languages Publishing.

(1969). *What Is to Be Done?* New York: International Publishers.

(1971). *State and Revolution*. New York: International Publishers.

(1974). *Collected Works*. 45 vols. Moscow: Progress (cited in notes as CW).

Leplin, Jarrett. (1982). "The Assessment of Auxiliary Hypotheses." *British Journal for the Philosophy of Science*, 33(no. 3):235–49.

(ed.) (1984a). *Scientific Realism*. Berkeley and Los Angeles: University of California Press.

(1984b). "Truth and Scientific Progress." In Leplin, ed., (1984):193–217.

Levine, David P. (1988). *Needs, Rights and the Market*. Boulder, Colo.: Lynne Rienner.

Lewis, David A. (1983a). *Philosophical Papers*. 2 vols. Oxford University Press.

(1983b). "New Work for a Theory of Universals." *Australasian Journal of Philosophy*, 61 (Dec.):343–77.

(1984). "Putnam's Paradox." *The Australasian Journal of Philosophy*, 62:221–36.

Lifton, Robert Jay, and Falk, Richard. (1982). *Indefensible Weapons: The Political and Psychological Case Against Nuclearism*. New York: Basic.

Lindblom, Charles. (1977). *Politics and Markets*. New York: Basic.

(1982). "Another State of Mind." *American Political Science Review*, 76(no. 1):9–21.

Lipset, Seymour M. (1963). *Political Man*. New York: Doubleday.

Locke, John. (1965). *Two Treatises on Government*. Ed. Peter Laslett. New York: Mentor.

(1979). *An Essay Concerning Human Understanding*. Ed. Peter Nidditch. Oxford University Press (Clarendon Press).

Luban, David. (1980). "The Romance of the Nation-State." *Philosophy and Public Affairs*, 9(no. 3):392–7. Reprinted in Charles Beitz, ed. (1985). *International Ethics*, 238–93. Princeton, N.J.: Princeton University Press.

Lukacs, Georg. (1971). *History and Class Consciousness: Studies in Marxian Dialectics*. Trans. Rodney Livingstone. Cambridge, Mass.: MIT Press.

Lukes, Steven. (1982). "Marxism, Morality and Justice." In G. H. R. Parkinson, ed., *Marx and Marxisms*, 137–205. Cambridge University Press.

Lüthy, Herbert. (1957). *France Against Herself.* New York: Meridian.

Lycan, William G. (1986). "Moral Facts and Moral Knowledge." In Norman Gillespie, ed., *Moral Realism. Southern Journal of Philosophy,* 24, supplement:79–94.

Lynd, Staughton. (1982). *Intellectual Origins of American Radicalism.* Cambridge, Mass.: Harvard University Press.

Lyons, David. (1976). "Ethical Relativism and the Problem of Incoherence," *Ethics,* 86(no. 2):107–21.

——— (1977). "Human Rights and the General Welfare." *Philosophy and Public Affairs,* 6(no. 2):113–29.

——— (1978). "Mill's Theory of Justice." In A. I. Goldman and J. Kim, eds., *Values and Morals,* 1–20. Dordrecht: Reidel.

——— (1984). *Ethics and the Rule of Law.* Cambridge University Press.

——— (1979). "Liberty and Harm to Others." *The Canadian Journal of Philosophy,* 5, supplement:1–19.

Lyttleton, Adrian. (1975). *The Seizure of Power.* London: Weidenfeld & Nicolson.

MacEwan, Arthur. (1975). "Ideology, Social Development and Power in Cuba." *Politics and Society,* 5:67–82.

MacIntyre, Alasdair. (1981). *After Virtue.* South Bend, Ind.: Notre Dame University Press.

Mackie, J. L. (1977). *Ethics: Inventing Right and Wrong.* Harmondsworth: Penguin.

Maehl, William Henry. (1980). *August Bebel.* Philadelphia: American Philosophical Society.

Manin, Bernard. (1987). "On Legitimacy and Political Deliberation." *Political Theory,* 15(no. 3):338–68.

Mansbridge, Jane. (1980). *Beyond Adversary Democracy.* New York: Basic.

Mao Tse-tung. (1965). "Investigation of the Peasant Movement in Hunan." *Selected Works.* Peking: Foreign Language Press.

——— (1977). *Critique of Soviet Political Economy.* Trans. Moss Roberts. New York: Monthly Review Press.

Marx, Karl. (1952). *Theories of Surplus Value.* New York: International Publishers.

——— (1960). *Politische Schriften.* Ed. Hans-Joachim Lieber, 2 vols. Stuttgart: Lotta.

——— (1961). *Capital.* Trans. Edward Moore and Samuel Aveling. New York: International Publishers.

——— (1963). *The Poverty of Philosophy.* New York: International Publishers.

——— (1967). *Writings of the Young Marx on Philosophy and Society.* Eds. Loyd D. Easton and Kurt H. Guddat. New York: Doubleday.

——— (1969). *The Civil War in the United States.* New York: International Publishers.

——— (1970). *Okonomisch-Philosophische Manuskripte.* In Herwig Forder, ed., *Der Bund der Kommunisten.* Berlin: Dietz.

——— (1972a). *Das Kapital: Kritik der Politischen Okonomie.* 3 vols. Frankfurt: Marxistische Blätter.

——— (1972b). *On America and the Civil War.* Ed. Saul K. Padover. New York: McGraw-Hill.

——— (1973). *Grundrisse.* Trans. Martin Nicolaus. New York: Random House.

(1974). *Theses on Feuerbach*. In Karl Marx and Friedrich Engels, *Selected Writings in One Volume*. New York: International Publishers.

(1977). *Capital*. Vol. 1. Trans. Ben Fowkes. New York: Random House.

Marx, Karl, and Engels, Friedrich. (1959). *Werke*. 39 vols. Berlin: Dietz.

(1962). *Selected Works*. 2 vols. Moscow: Foreign Languages Publishing (cited in notes as *SW*).

(1964). *The German Ideology*. Ed. S. Ryazanskaya. Moscow: Progress Publishers.

(1965). *Selected Correspondence*. Trans. I. Lasker, ed. S. Ryazanskaya. Moscow: Progress Publishers.

(1971). *Writings on the Paris Commune*. Ed. Hal Draper. New York: Monthly Review.

(1972a). *Ireland and the Irish Question*. Ed. R. Dixon. New York: International Publishers.

(1972b). *The Revolution of 1848–49: Articles from the Neue Rheinische Zeitung*. Trans. S. Ryanzanskaya, ed. Bernard Isaacs. New York: International Publishers.

(1974). *Selected Works in One Volume*. New York: International Publishers.

Massey, Steven. (1983). "Is Self-Respect a Moral or a Psychological Concept?" *Ethics*, 93(no. 2):246–61.

Maxwell, Grover. (1963). "The Ontological Status of Theoretical Entities." In Herbert Feigl and Grover Maxwell, eds., *Scientific Explanation, Space and Time*, pp. 3–27. Minneapolis: University of Minnesota Press.

McCamant, John F. (1984). "Intervention in Guatemala: Implications for the Study of Third World Politics." *Comparative Political Studies*, 17:373–407.

McMullin, Ernan. (1976). "The Fertility of Theory and the Unit for Appraisal in Science." In Robert S. Cohen and Marx Wartofsky, eds., *Boston Studies in the Philosophy of Science*, 39:395–432.

(1984). "A Case for Scientific Realism." In Jarrett Leplin, ed., (1984), *Scientific Realism*, pp. 8–40. Berkeley and Los Angeles: University of California Press.

McNamara, Robert S. (1973). *One Hundred Countries, Two Billion People*. New York: Praeger.

Meisner, Maurice. (1977). *Mao's China*. New York: Macmillan.

Merrill, G. H. (1980). "The Model-Theoretic Argument Against Realism." *Philosophy of Science*, 47:69–81.

Michels, Robert. (1966). *Political Parties*. Trans. Ellen and Cedar Paul. New York: Free Press.

Miliband, Ralph. (1969). *The State in Capitalist Society*. New York: Basic.

Mill, John Stuart. (1859). *Dissertations and Discussions*, Vols. 1, 3. London: Parker.

(1948, 1987). *On Liberty, Representative Government, the Subjection of Women*. Oxford University Press.

(1961). *Essential Works*. Ed. Max Lerner. New York: Bantam.

(1977). *Collected Works:* Vol. 5, *Essays on Economics and Society;* Vol. 19, *Essays on Politics and Society*. Toronto: Toronto University Press.

Miller, Alice. (1981). *The Drama of the Gifted Child*. New York: Basic.

Miller, Jean Baker. (1966). *Toward a New Psychology of Women*. Boston: Beacon.

Miller, Richard W. (1975). "Rawls and Marxism." In Norman Daniels, ed., *Reading Rawls*, 206–30. New York: Basic.

——— (1979). "Reason and Commitment in the Social Sciences." *Philosophy and Public Affairs*, 8 (no. 4): 241–66.

——— (1981a). "Marx and Morality." Reprinted in J. Roland Pennock, ed., *Marxism, Nomos*, 26:3–32. New York: New York University Press.

——— (1981b). "Marx and Aristotle: A Kind of Consequentialism." *Canadian Journal of Philosophy*, 7, supplement:323–52.

——— (1981c). "Rights and Reality." *Philosophical Review*, 10(no. 3):383–407.

——— (1984). *Analyzing Marx*. Princeton, N.J.: Princeton University Press.

——— (1985). "Ways of Moral Learning." *Philosophical Review*, 94(no. 4):507–56.

——— (1986). "Democracy and Class Dictatorship." *Social Philosophy and Policy*, 3(no. 2):59–76.

——— (1987). *Fact and Method*. Princeton, N.J.: Princeton University Press.

Mommsen, Wolfgang J. (1959). *Max Weber und die Deutsche Politik, 1890–1920*. Tübingen: Mohr.

——— (1974). *The Age of Bureaucracy*. New York: Oxford University Press.

Monod, Jacques. (1975). "On the Molecular Theory of Evolution." In Rom Harré, ed., *Problems of Scientific Revolution: Progress and Obstacles to Progress in the Sciences*, pp. 11–24. Oxford University Press.

Montaigne, Michel de. (1922). *Les essais*. Paris: Libraire Félix Alcan.

Montesquieu, Charles Louis de Secondat, baron de la Brède et de. (1951). *Oeuvres complètes*. 2 vols. Paris: Gallimard (cited in notes as *OC*).

——— (1960). *Lettres persanes*. Paris: Garnier (cited in notes as *LP*).

——— (1961). *De l'esprit des lois*. 2 vols. Paris: Garnier (cited in notes as *EL*).

——— (1964). *The Persian Letters*. Trans. George R. Healy. Indianapolis, Ind.: Bobbs-Merrill.

——— (1965a). *Considerations on the Greatness of the Romans and Their Decline*. Trans. David Lowenthal. New York: Free Press.

——— (1965b). *The Spirit of the Laws*. Trans. Thomas Nugent. New York: Hafner.

Moore, Barrington, Jr., (1965). *Social Origins of Dictatorshp and Democracy*. Boston: Beacon.

Moore, George Edward. (1951). *Principia Ethica*. Cambridge University Press.

——— (1963). *Ethics*. Oxford University Press.

Morganthau, Hans J. (1973). *Politics among Nations*. New York: Knopf.

Mosse, George L. (1964). *The Crisis of German Ideology*. New York: Grosset.

Musgrave, Alan. (1985). "Realism versus Constructive Empiricism." In Paul A. Churchland and Clifford A. Hooker, eds., *Images of Science*, 197–221. Chicago: University of Chicago Press.

Myrdal, Gunnar. (1970). *The Challenge of World Poverty*. New York: Pantheon.

Nagel, Thomas. (1978). *The Possibility of Altruism*. Princeton, N.J.: Princeton University Press.

——— (1986a). *The View from Nowhere*. New York: Oxford University Press.

——— (1986b). "Moral Conflict and Political Legitimacy." *Philosophy and Public Affairs*, 16(no. 3):215–40.

Nardin, Terry. (1983). *Law, Morality and the Relation of States*. Princeton, N.J.: Princeton University Press.

Nee, Victor. (1973). "Revolution and Bureaucracy: Shanghai in the Cultural Revolution." In James Peck and Victor Nee, eds., *China's Uninterrupted Revolution*, pp. 322–414. New York: Random House.

Neumann, Franz. (1944). *Behemoth*. New York: Oxford University Press.

Nolan, Mary. (1981). *Social Democracy and Society: Working-class Radicalism in Dusseldorf, 1890–1920*. Cambridge University Press.

Norton, David. (1976). *Personal Destinies*. Princeton, N.J.: Princeton University Press.

Oakeshott, Michael. (1975). *On Human Conduct*. Oxford University Press.

Oates, Stephen B. (1984). *Abraham Lincoln: The Man Behind the Myths*. New York: New American Library.

Ollman, Bertell. (1975). *Alienation: Marx's Conception of Man in Capitalist Society*. Cambridge University Press.

O'Neill, Onora. (1985). "Lifeboat Earth." In Charles Beitz, Marshall Cohen, Thomas Scanlon, and A. John Simmons, eds., *International Justice*, pp. 262–81. Princeton, N.J.: Princeton University Press.

Parenti, Michael. (1986a). *Inventing Reality: The Politics of the Mass Media*. New York: St. Martin's.

(1986b). "Is Nicaragua More Democratic than the United States?" *Covert Action Information Bulletin* (no. 26):48–52.

Payer, Cheryl. (1975). *The Debt Trap*. New York: Monthly Review.

Peacocke, Christopher. (1979). *Holistic Explanation: Action, Space, Interpretation*. Oxford University Press.

Piatnitsky, Osip. (1973). *Memoirs of a Bolshevik*. Westport, Conn.: Hyperion.

Piven, Francis Fox, and Cloward, Richard. (1977). *Poor People's Movements*. New York: Pantheon.

Plato. (1982). *Republic*. Loeb Classical Library. Cambridge, Mass.: Harvard University Press (cited in notes as *Republic*).

Plekhanov, G. V. (1961). *Selected Philosophical Works*. London: Lawrence & Wishart.

Polan, A. J. (1984). *Lenin and the End of Politics*. Berkeley and Los Angeles: University of California Press.

Popper, Karl. (1963). *The Open Society and Its Enemies*. 2 vols. Princeton, N.J.: Princeton University Press.

(1968). *Conjectures and Refutations*. New York: Harper.

Proctor, Robert. (1988). *Racial Hygiene: Medicine under the Nazis*. Cambridge, Mass.: Harvard University Press.

Proudhon, Pierre-Joseph. (1924). *De la capacité politique des classes ouvrières*. Paris: Rivière.

(1932). *Système des contradictions économiques ou philosophie de la misère*. Paris: Rivière.

Przeworski, Adam. (1980). "Material Interests, Class Compromise and Socialism." *Politics and Society*, 10:125–53.

(1985). *Capitalism and Social Democracy*. Cambridge University Press.

Putnam, Hilary. (1975). *Collected Philosophical Papers.* 2 vols. Cambridge University Press.

(1978). *Meaning and the Moral Sciences.* London: Routledge & Kegan Paul.

(1981). *Reason, Truth and History.* Cambridge University Press.

(1983a). *Collected Papers,* Vol. 3. Cambridge University Press.

(1983b). "Vagueness and Alternative Logics." *Erkenntnis,* 19:297–314.

(1988). *Reality and Representation.* Cambridge, Mass.: MIT Press.

Quine, Willard Van Orman. (1969). *Ontological Relativity and Other Essays.* New York: Columbia University Press.

(1980). *From a Logical Point of View.* Cambridge, Mass.: Harvard University Press.

Rabinowitch, Alexander. (1976). *The Bolsheviks Come to Power.* New York: Norton.

Railton, Peter. (1986). "Moral Realism." *Philosophical Review,* 95(no. 2):163–207.

Rawls, John. (1971). *A Theory of Justice.* Cambridge, Mass.: Harvard University Press.

(1975). "Fairness to Goodness." *Philosophical Review,* 84(no. 4):53–54.

(1980). "Kantian Constructivism in Moral Theory." *Journal of Philosophy,* 77:515–72.

(1981). "The Basic Liberties and their Priority." *The Tanner Lectures.* Salt Lake City: University of Utah Press.

(1982). "Social Unity and the Primary Goods." In Amartya Sen and Bernard Williams, eds., *Utilitarianism and Beyond,* pp. 159–85. Cambridge University Press.

(1985). "Justice as Fairness: Political not Metaphysical." *Philosophy and Public Affairs,* 14(no. 3):223–51.

(1987). "The Idea of an Overlapping Consensus." *Oxford Journal of Legal Studies,* 7(no. 1):1–25.

(1988a). "The Priority of Right and Ideas of the Good." *Philosophy and Public Affairs,* 17(no. 4):251–76.

(1988b). "On the Idea of Free Public Reason." Unpublished.

(1988c). "The Domain of the Political and Overlapping Consensus." Unpublished (in press, *New York University Law Review*).

(1988d). "Political Constructivism and Objectivity." Unpublished.

Raz, Joseph. (1986). *The Morality of Freedom.* Oxford University Press.

Reich, Michael L. (1981). *Racial Inequality: A Political-Economic Analysis.* Princeton, N.J.: Princeton University Press.

Ricardo, David. (1948). *The Principles of Political Economy and Taxation.* London: Dent.

Rickert, Heinrich. (1962). *Science and History: A Critique of Positivist Epistemology.* Trans. George Reisman. Princeton, N.J.: Nostrand.

Rigby, T. H. (1969). *Communist Party Membership in the USSR 1917–1967.* Princeton, N.J.: Princeton University Press.

Ringer, Fritz K. (1969). *The Decline of the German Mandarins.* Cambridge, Mass.: Harvard University Press.

Riskin, Carl. (1973). "Maoism and Motivations: Work and Incentives in China."

In James Peck and Victor Nee, eds., *China's Uninterrupted Revolution*, pp. 415–61. New York: Random House.

Robinson, Ronald, Gallagher, John, and Denny, Alice. (1965). *Africa and the Victorians: the Official Mind of Imperialism*. London: Macmillan.

Roemer, John. (1982). *A General Theory of Exploitation and Class*. Cambridge, Mass.: Harvard University Press.

(1985). "Should Marxists Be Interested in Exploitation?" *Philosophy and Public Affairs*, 14(no. 1):30–65.

Rogers, Barbara. (1975). *White Wealth and Black Poverty*. Westport, Conn.: Greenwood Press.

Rogin, Michael Paul. (1987). *Ronald Reagan the Movie and Other Episodes in American Political Demonology*. Berkeley and Los Angeles: University of California Press.

Rorty, Amelie O. (1980). *Essays on Aristotle's Ethics*. Berkeley and Los Angeles: University of California Press.

Rorty, Richard. (1979). *Philosophy and the Mirror of Nature*. Princeton, N.J.: Princeton University Press.

(1982). *Consequences of Pragmatism*. Minneapolis: University of Minnesota Press.

Rose, Hilary. (1983). "Hand, Brain and Heart: A Feminist Epistemology for the Natural Sciences." *Signs*, 9:73–90.

Rosenblum, Nancy. (1987). *Another Liberalism*. Cambridge, Mass.: Harvard University Press.

Rosset, Peter, and Vandermeer, John. (1986). *Nicaragua: The Unfinished Revolution*. New York: Grove Press.

Rousseau, Jean-Jacques. (1964). *Oeuvres complètes*. 3 vols. Paris: Gallimard (cited in notes as *OC*).

Rubin, Lillian Breslow. (1976). *Worlds of Pain*. New York: Basic.

Saine, Abdoulaye S. M. (1988). *The Political Economy of Internal and External Military Interventions in Africa*. Unpublished.

Salvatore, Nick. (1982). *Eugene V. Debs: Citizen and Socialist*. Urbana: University of Illinois Press.

Sayre-McCord, Geoffrey. (1988). *Essays on Moral Realism*. Ithaca, N.Y.: Cornell University Press.

Scanlon, Thomas. (1982). "Contractualism and Utilitarianism." In Amartya Sen and Bernard Williams, eds., *Utilitarianism and Beyond*, pp. 103–28. Cambridge University Press.

Scheele, Godfrey. (1946). *Ouverture to Nazism*. London: Faber & Faber.

Schlesinger, Joseph. (1984). "On the Theory of Party Organization." *Journal of Politics*, 46(no. 2):369–400.

Schlick, Moritz. (1959). "Positivism and Realism." In A. J. Ayer, ed., *Logical Positivism*, pp. 82–107. Glen Cove, Ill.: Free Press.

Schofield, Malcolm, and Striker, Gisela. (1986). *The Norms of Nature: Studies in Hellenistic Ethics*. Cambridge University Press.

Schorske, Carl E. (1972). *German Social Democracy, 1905–1917*. New York: Harper.

Schram, Stuart, ed. (1979). *Chairman Mao Talks to the People*. New York: Random House.

Schumpeter, Joseph. (1950). *Capitalism, Socialism, and Democracy*. New York: Harper & Row.

—— (1951). *Imperialism and Social Classes*. New York: Kelley.

Schwartz, Michael L. (1976). *Radical Protest and Social Structure: The Southern Farmers' Alliance and Cotton Tenancy*. New York: Academic Press.

Scott, James C. (1976). *The Moral Economy of the Peasant: Rebellion and Subsistence in Southeast Asia*. New Haven, Conn.: Yale University Press.

Sen, Amartya. (1982). "Rights and Agency." *Philosophy and Public Affairs*, 11(no. 1):3–39.

Sennett, Richard, and Jonathan Cobb. (1972). *The Hidden Injuries of Class*. New York: Knopf.

Shapere, Dudley. (1982). "The Concept of Observation in Philosophy and Science." *Philosophy of Science*, 49:485–526.

—— (1984). *Reason and the Search for Knowledge*. Dordrecht: Reidel.

—— (1988). "External and Internal Factors in the Development of Science." *Science and Technology Studies*, 4(no. 1):1–9.

Shaw, William. (1984). "Marxism, Revolution and Rationality." In Terence Ball and James Farr, eds., *After Marx*, 12–35. Cambridge University Press.

Shirokov, M., ed. (1973). *Textbook of Marxist Philosophy*. Moscow: Leningrad Institute of Philosophy.

Shklar, Judith N. (1979). "Let Us Not Be Hypocritical. *Daedalus*, 108:1–25.

—— (1984). *Ordinary Vices*. Cambridge, Mass.: Harvard University Press.

Shue, Henry. (1980). *Basic Rights: Subsistence, Affluence and U.S. Foreign Policy*. Princeton, N.J.: Princeton University Press.

Singer, Peter. (1972)."Famine, Affluence, and Morality." *Philosophy and Public Affairs*, 1(no. 3):229–43.

—— (1975). *Animal Liberation*. New York: Avon Books.

Smart, J. J. C. (1963). *Philosophy and Scientific Realism*. London: Routledge & Kegan Paul.

Smith, Adam. (1979). *The Wealth of Nations*. Harmondsworth: Penguin.

Sombart, Werner. (1951). *The Jews and Modern Capitalism*. New York: Free Press.

Stevenson, Charles L. (1959). "The Emotive Meaning of Ethical Terms." In A. J. Ayer, ed., *Logical Positivism*, pp. 264–81. New York: Free Press.

—— (1963). *Facts and Values: Studies in Ethical Analysis*. New Haven, Conn.: Yale University Press.

Strauss, Leo. (1959). *What is Political Philosophy and Other Essays*. Illinois: Free Press of Glencoe.

—— (1965). *Natural Right and History*. Chicago: University of Chicago Press.

Sturgeon, Nicholas L. (1982). "Brandt's Moral Empiricism." *Philosophical Review*, 91(no. 3):389–422.

—— (1984). "Moral Explanations." In David Copp and David Zimmerman, eds., *Morality, Reason and Truth: New Essays on the Foundations of Ethics*, 49–78. Totowa, N.J.: Rowman & Allanheld.

(1985). "Gibbard on Moral Judgments and Norms." *Ethics*, 96(no. 1):22–33.

(1986a). "What Difference Does It Make Whether Moral Realism Is True?" In Norman Gillespie, ed., *Moral Realism. Southern Journal of Philosophy*, 24, supplement:115–91.

(1986b). "Harman on Moral Explanations of Natural Facts." In Norman Gillespie, ed., *Moral Realism. Southern Journal of Philosophy*, 24, supplement:69–78.

Sweezy, Paul, and Bettelheim, Charles. (1971). *On the Transition to Socialism*. New York: Monthly Review.

Szymanski, Albert. (1981). *The Logic of Imperialism*. New York: Praeger.

Taylor, Charles. (1973). "Neutrality in Political Science." In Alan Ryan, ed., *The Philosophy of Social Explanation*, pp. 139–70. Oxford University Press.

(1977). "What is Human Agency." In Theodore Mischel, ed., *The Self*, pp. 103–35. Totowa: Rowman & Littlefield.

(1982). "The Diversity of Goods." In Amartya Sen and Bernard Williams, eds., *Utilitarianism and Beyond*, pp. 129–44. Cambridge University Press.

Teuber, Andreas. (1986). "Mill's Opposition to the Secret Ballot," Unpublished.

Thompson, Edward P. (1966). *The Making of the English Working Class*. New York: Random House.

(1971). "The Moral Economy of the English Crowd in the Eighteenth Century." *Past and Present*. 50:76–136.

Thoreau, Henry David. (1981). *Works*. New York: Avenel.

Tillich, Paul. (1948). *The Protestant Era*. Chicago: University of Chicago Press.

Trelease, Allen W. (1971). *White Terror*. New York: Harper and Row.

Trotsky, Leon. (1963). *Basic Writings*. Ed. Irving Howe. New York: Harper & Row.

Tucker, Robert W. (1977). *The Inequality of Nations*. New York: Basic.

Van Fraassen, Bas C. (1980). *The Scientific Image*. Oxford: Clarendon.

(1984). "To Save the Phenomena." In Jarrett Leplin, ed., *Scientific Realism*, pp. 250–9. Berkeley and Los Angeles: University of California Press.

(1985). "Empiricism in the Philosophy of Science." In Paul M. Churchland and Clifford A. Hooker, eds., *Images of Science*, pp. 245–300. Chicago: University of Chicago Press.

Vernant, Jean-Pierre. (1981). *Les origines sociales de la pensée grecque*. Paris: Quadrige.

Waite, Robert G. L. (1952). *Vanguard of Nazism: The Free-Corps in the Weimar Republic, 1918–23*. Cambridge, Mass.: Harvard University Press.

Walzer, Michael. (1973). "In Defense of Equality." *Dissent*, (Fall):399–408.

(1977). *Just and Unjust Wars*. New York: Basic.

(1980a). "The Moral Standing of States." *Philosophy and Public Affairs*, 9(no. 3):209–29.

(1980b). *Radical Principles: Reflections of an Unreconstructed Democrat*. New York: Basic.

(1983). *Spheres of Justice*. New York: Basic.

(1984). "Liberalism and the Art of Separation." *Political Theory*. 12(no. 3):315–330.

(1985). *Exodus and Revolution*. New York: Basic.

(1987). *Interpretation and Social Criticism*. Cambridge, Mass.: Harvard University Press.

(1988a). "Objectivity and Social Meaning." Unpublished.

(1988b). *The Company of Critics: Social Criticism and Political Commitment in the Twentieth Century*. New York: Basic.

Weber, Max. (1922). *Gesammelte Aufsätze zur Wissenchaftslehre*. Tübingen: Mohr (cited in notes as *GAW*).

(1947). *Gesammelte Aufsätze zur Religionssoziologie*. Tübingen: Mohr (cited in notes as *GAR*).

(1949). *The Methodology of the Social Sciences*. Trans. Edward A. Shils and Henry A. Finch. New York: Free Press (cited in notes as *MSS*).

(1951). *The Religion of China: Confucianism and Taoism*. Trans. H. H. Gerth. New York: Macmillan (cited in notes as *RC*).

(1952). *Ancient Judaism*. Trans. Hans H. Gerth and Don Martindale. Glencoe: Free Press.

(1958a). *The Rational and Social Foundations of Music*. Trans. Don Martindale, Johannes Riedel, and Gertrude Neuwirth. Carbondale: Southern Illinois Press.

(1958b). *Gesammelte Politische Schriften*. Tübingen: Mohr (cited in notes as *GPS*).

(1958c). *From Max Weber: Essays in Sociology*. Ed. H. H. Gerth and C. Wright Mills. New York: Oxford University Press (cited in notes as *FMW*).

(1958d). *The Protestant Ethic and the Spirit of Capitalism*. Trans. Talcott Parsons. New York: Scribner's (cited in notes as *PE*).

(1961). *General Economic History*. Trans. Frank H. Knight. New York: Collier Books.

(1963). *The Sociology of Religion*. Trans. Ephraim Fischoff. Boston: Beacon (cited in notes as *SR*).

(1964). *Wirtschaft und Gesellschaft*. Köln: Kiepenheuer & Witsch (cited in notes as *WG*).

(1968). *Economy and Society*. 3 vols. Ed. Guenther Roth and Claus Wittich. New York: Bedminster Press (cited in notes as *ES*).

(1977). *Critique of Stammler*. Trans. Guy Oakes. New York: Free Press (cited in notes as *CS*).

Wertham, Frederick. (1969). *A Sign for Cain*. New York: Macmillan.

Wiggins, David. (1980). "Deliberation and Practical Reason." In Amelie Oksenberg Rorty, ed., *Essays on Aristotle's Ethics*, Berkeley and Los Angeles: University of California Press.

(1980a). *Sameness and Substance*. Cambridge, Mass.: Harvard University Press.

Williams, Bernard. (1972). *Morality*. New York: Harper & Row.

(1973). *Problems of the Self*. Cambridge University Press.

(1982). *Moral Luck*. Cambridge University Press.

(1985). *Ethics and the Limits of Philosophy*. Cambridge, Mass.: Harvard University Press.

Wilson, Michael, and Rosenfelt, Deborah S. (1978). *Salt of the Earth*. Old Westbury, N.Y.: Feminist Press.

Wittgenstein, Ludwig. (1958). *Philosophical Investigations*. Trans. G. E. M. Anscombe. New York: Macmillan.

Wittke, Carl. (1950). *The Utopian Communist: a Biography of Wilhelm Weitling*. Baton Rouge: Louisiana State University Press.

Wollheim, Richard. (1984). *The Thread of Life*. Cambridge, Mass.: Harvard University Press.

Wong, David B. (1984). *Moral Relativity*. Berkeley and Los Angeles: University of California Press.

Wood, Allen W. (1972). "The Marxian Critique of Justice." *Philosophy and Public Affairs*, 1(no. 3):244–82. Reprinted in Marshall Cohen, Thomas Nagel, and Thomas Scanlon, eds., *Marx, Justice, and History*, pp. 5–41. Princeton, N.J.: Princeton University Press.

(1979). "Marx on Right and Justice: A Reply to Husami." *Philosphy and Public Affairs*, 8(no. 3):267–95. Reprinted in Marshall Cohen, Thomas Nagel, and Thomas Scanlon, eds. (1980). *Marx, Justice, and History*, pp. 106–34. Princeton, N.J.: Princeton University Press.

(1986). "Marx and Equality." In G. A. Cohen, Jon Elster and John Roemer, ed., *Analytical Marxism*. Cambridge University Press.

Woodward, C. Vann. (1963). *Tom Watson*. New York: Oxford University Press.

Wright, Crispin. (1985). "Review of Simon Blackburn, *Spreading the Word*." *Mind*, 94(no. 374):310–19.

Wright, Erik Olin. (1984). "A General Framework for the Analysis of Class Structure." *Politics and Society*, 13:383–423.

Zerilli, Linda. (1986). "Harriet Taylor Mill and the Higher Natures." Unpublished.

Index

Index

Ball, Terence, xiv
Barber, Benjamin, xiv, 8, 14, 71, 79, 98,
	172, 173
	and "absence of an independent
		ground," 77–8
	and democratic institutions, 76–8, 320,
		323, 336, 339
Barlas, Asma, xiv
Barry, Brian, 419
Basseches, Nicolaus, 312
Bauer, Heinrich, 363
Baur, Erwin, 410
Bebel, August, 63, 389
Beilis case, 415
Beitz, Charles, xiv, 64, 66–7, 207
Beiner, Ronald, 247
Benjamin, Amy, xiv
Benjamin, Walter, 247
Bennacerraf, Paul, xiv
Bentham, Jeremy, 190, 240–1, 370
Berlin, Isaiah, 14, 71–4, 78, 79, 85, 88–9,
	96, 467
	on positive and negative freedom, 73–4
Bettelheim, Charles, 313
Binding, Karl, 461
biology, 42, 57, 68, 228–9, 406–7; see also
	Darwin, Charles
Bismarck, 62, 63, 383
Blackburn, Simon, 153, 155
	and fallibilism, 9, 151
	and quasi-realism, 9, 167–72
Black-Hundreds, 415–16
Blaney, David, xiv, 471
Blanqui, Louis-Auguste, 227
Block, Ned, 403
Blum, Lawrence, 191
Boas, Franz, 302
Bolsheviks, 311, 328, 390, 395, 398–401,
	402, 415–16, 437–8, 443–5, 447–8, 449
borderline cases, 169, 185–8, 299–301, 460;
	see also goods, conflicts of
	and bivalence criticism of realism, 185–6
	in ethics, 456
Bosanquet, Bernard, 74
Bottomore, Thomas, 243
Bovingdon, Gardner, xiv
Boyd, Richard, xiv, 12, 96, 107, 127, 173,
	184–5, 197, 222, 247, 428, 453, 467
	and epistemic access, 114, 142–3, 146–7,
		187
	and homeostatic properties, 28 , 144,
		147, 185–6, 260–1, 262
	and metaphor, 143, 146
	and scientific realism, 111, 112, 113, 115,
		185–6
	and take-off in science, 27, 186

Boyle, Robert, 114
Bracher, Karl, 416
Brandon, Mark, xiv
Brandt, Richard, 115, 203, 460
Bray, John, 227
Brecht, Bertolt, 212
Brest-Litovsk, Treaty of, 316, 398–99, 424,
	437, 438–9
Brink, David, 41, 104–5, 107, 115, 191, 255,
	467
Brown, John, 330, 331
Buchanan, Allen, 336
Buddhism, 357

Caesar, 60
Caligula, 303
Calvin, John, 356, 360–1, 364, 385, 430, 441
cannibalism, 46, 99–100, 166
capacity for moral personality, 2, 18, 21,
	49, 56, 87, 259; see also moral theories
	as abolitionist, 84, 240–1, 331
	abstract, 9, 29, 81, 157, 172, 471
	and ambiguities of liberalism, 72, 75–6,
		77–8, 79–82, 166–7, 193–4
	and democracy, 77, 98, 471
	and eudaemonism, 30
capitalism, 62–7, 204–5, 206–10, 235–8,
	248, 366, 371, 381, 441
	and democracy, 11, 61–2, 74, 83, 97–8,
		255, 277–8, 348–52
	and eugenic theories, 408–9
	rise of, 355–61
Caporaso, James, xiv
Carlyle, Thomas, 377
Carnap, Rudolf, 115, 118–19
Carnegie, Andrew, 409
Carthage, 38, 50
caste system, 97, 171
Catholicism, 51, 127, 164, 330, 357, 360,
	362, 376; see also Finnis, John
causal pluralism, 357
	and dialectical primacy, 358–69, 385
causal powers (non-Humean), 132, 175,
	183–5
	and depth of explanation, 230, 303–4
	and interest relativity, 183–4
Caute, David, 10, 318, 400
charity (epistemological), 137–8
Chartism, 246, 290, 303, 363, 470
Charvet, John, xiv
Chesneaux, Jean, 324
Chilean socialism, 66, 207–8, 310, 318, 342,
	345
Chinese communism, 246–7, 278, 305–7,
	400, 449, 470

Index

democracy *(cont.)*
and congruence of social institutions, 308, 321–2
and equality, 8, 43, 264, 348–52
and individuality, xiii, 5, 9, 10, 77, 95, 146–7, 181, 272–5, 283–88, 301, 345, 346, 456
and justification of majority rule, 95, 301
and leadership competition view, 348–51, 383–4
and liberalism, 8, 78, 79
and participation, 253–6
and policy-making elites, 207–10, 348–52
and rational vs. repressive authority, 423–4
and status hierarchy, 402–22
and today's nondemocratic political science, 348–52, 423–6, 431
democratic autonomy, 5, 11, 82–4, 140, 147, 152, 173, 254, 277, 282–3, 295, 346–7, 428, 431, 470, 471; *see also* democratic education; political science; political theory; radical democracy
and capitalism, 83, 348–52
and difference principle, 255
justification of economic equality driven by, 83, 255, 349, 351–2
and moral explanations, 232–3
democratic education, 321–4, 346
democratic internationalism, 9, 18, 41, 62–7, 152, 173, 207–8, 285, 337–8, 342–4, 351, 376, 388–401, 455, 457, 470; *see also* great-power "realism"; nationalism; racism; radical democracy; status hierarchy
and abrogation of Brest-Litovsk Treaty, 399–400
and American anti-imperialism, xiii, 243, 337–8
as anomaly in today's international relations theory, 318, 349–52, 400
and antiradical ideology, 435–6
Aristotle on, 35, 263, 283–8, 338
and English abolitionism, 285–6, 442
and *Federalist Papers*, 349
and German Social Democracy, 389–90, 398–400
Kant on, 59–60, 61, 349
Lenin on, 63–5, 394–401, 437–8
liberal and radical, 388
Marx on, 62–3, 160, 206, 245, 249, 263, 272, 283–8
Montesquieu on, 50, 61, 338
and a public interest, 391
Rawls on, 337

Weber on, 388–94, 397–401
and Zimmerwald faction, 437–8
democratic military organization, 337–9, 346
Denardo, James, 419
Denny, Alice, 387
deontology, 431
dependency theory, 66–7, 207–9, 395, 400, 447
desert, 277, 311, 315
Desimone, Joseph, xiv
Devitt, Michael, 110–11, 112, 173, 175, 178
Dewey, John, 78, 79, 173, 193, 322, 323, 331
dictatorship of the proletariat, 297–301, 308–9
divide-and-rule policies, 403, 415–21
Dobb, Maurice, 225
Donald, David, 231
Doppelt, Gerald, 64
Douglas, Stephen, 341
Downs, Anthony, 348
Downs, George, xiv
Doyle, Michael, xiv, 59 n.88
Draper, Hal, 250
Drier, Jamie, xiv, 155
Duberman, Martin, 102, 318, 400
Dubofsky, Melvin, 421
Duhem, Pierre, 120
Dühring, Eugen, 216
Dunn, John, xiv, 318
Dutt, R. Palme, 393, 416
duty, 261, 272
Dworkin, Gerald, 341, 403
Dworkin, Ronald, 7, 31, 82, 83, 277–8, 295, 351

East European democracy movements, 450
East India Company, 58
Easton, Loyd, 243
Ebert, Friedrich, 318
Eckstein, Harry, 308, 312, 348
Eden, Robert, xiv
education, 56–7
egotism, 41
Eichmann, Adolf, 445
Einstein, Albert, 13, 72, 78, 121, 142, 225, 299, 301
eligible properties, 181
Elster, Jon, 234–5, 242, 245, 250, 272, 276, 278, 390
emotivism, 87, 92, 104, 123, 151, 168, 203
empathy, 2, 76, 78
empiricism, 12, 14, 109, 114–25; *see also* positivism
characteristic claims of, 115–18